Cyber Defense

Cyber Defense

Best Practices for Digital Safety

Jason Edwards

San Antonio,
TX, USA

Registered Office
John Wiley & Sons, Inc., 111 River Street, Hoboken, NJ 07030, USA
John Wiley & Sons Ltd, New Era House, 8 Oldlands Way, Bognor Regis, West Sussex, PO22 9NQ, UK

For details of our global editorial offices, customer services, and more information about Wiley products visit us at www.wiley.com.

The manufacturer's authorized representative according to the EU General Product Safety Regulation is Wiley-VCH GmbH, Boschstr. 12, 69469 Weinheim, Germany, e-mail: Product_Safety@wiley.com.

Wiley also publishes its books in a variety of electronic formats and by print-on-demand. Some content that appears in standard print versions of this book may not be available in other formats.

Library of Congress Cataloging-in-Publication Data has been applied for:

Hardback ISBN: 9781394337019
ePDF ISBN: 9781394337033
epub ISBN: 9781394337026

Cover Design: Wiley
Cover Image: © 3alexd/Getty Images

Set in 9.5/12.5pt STIXTwoText by Lumina Datamatics

Printed and bound by CPI Group (UK) Ltd, Croydon, CR0 4YY

C9781394337019_110625

*To my incredible family—my wife, Selda, and my children, Michelle, Chris, Ceylin, and
Mayra—thank you for your unwavering love, patience, and support. You are my foundation
and my inspiration.*

*To my readers and followers, both on social media and BareMetalCyber.com, your engagement and
passion fuel my drive to share and teach.*

*To the kids who carry Darwin's legacy forward through the Darwin the Cyber Beagle books and at
CyberBeagle.kids—thank you for keeping his memory alive and for embracing the lessons of digital
safety.*

*To my coworkers, who graciously endure my quirks and humor every day. You make the grind
worthwhile and always entertaining.*

*To my students at the universities and programs I've been privileged to teach, and to all those who
are now proud members of CtrlAltAlumni.com. You are a testament to the boundless potential of
this field. It has been an honor to be part of your journey.*

*And finally, to you, the reader, taking this step to learn how to protect yourself and others—you are
the reason this book exists. Thank you for joining me in making the digital world safer for everyone.*

Be safe and be happy.

—Jason

Contents

About the Author

Jason Edwards is a distinguished cybersecurity leader, educator, and author with over two decades of experience in safeguarding critical infrastructure and advising global organizations. A veteran of the U.S. Army and a recipient of the Bronze Star, Jason's career has spanned roles in cybersecurity strategy, risk management, and compliance for Fortune 100 companies. Holding a Doctorate in Information Systems and Cybersecurity, he combines technical expertise with a passion for education, serving as an adjunct professor and publishing extensively on cybersecurity and digital safety topics. His commitment to empowering individuals and organizations drives his work, including this latest contribution to digital safety awareness. Find him at Baremetalcyber.com.

Introduction

As a cybersecurity professional with over two decades of experience, I've witnessed the digital revolution and its profound impact on every aspect of our lives. From protecting global enterprises to educating students in classrooms and mentoring communities on digital safety, I've always been driven by a singular mission: empowering individuals to navigate the digital world securely.

Throughout my career, I've noticed a recurring pattern—while many people recognize the importance of cybersecurity, there remains a significant gap in understanding the practical steps needed to protect oneself online. Even professionals in the field sometimes overlook the foundational principles of cyber hygiene, leaving them vulnerable to threats that could have been easily mitigated.

This book was born out of my desire to bridge that gap. It is designed to demystify cybersecurity and make digital safety accessible to everyone, regardless of their technical background. Whether you're a parent teaching your child about online threats, a business owner safeguarding sensitive information, or someone trying to avoid phishing scams, this book is for you.

I've packed this guide with actionable advice, real-world examples, and recovery strategies because prevention is powerful, but knowing what to do when things go wrong is equally essential. I hope this book will equip you with the tools to protect your digital life and empower you to help others create a safer online environment.

Cybersecurity challenges are evolving rapidly, fueled by technological advancements like artificial intelligence and the Internet of Things. Yet, amidst this complexity, one truth remains constant: good cyber hygiene practices are the cornerstone of digital safety. My goal is to provide you with a comprehensive resource that simplifies these practices and helps you build habits that will protect you today and in the future.

Thank you for embarking on this journey with me. Together, we can make the digital world safer—one secure habit at a time.

Sincerely,
Dr. Jason Edwards
www.baremetalcyber.com
www.cyberbeagle.kids

1

Why Cyber Safety Matters Today

The rapid expansion of digital technologies, coupled with an increasing reliance on the internet for personal, professional, and commercial activities, has made us more vulnerable to cyber threats than ever. Every digital interaction—shopping online, conducting business transactions, or simply browsing social media—presents a potential entry point for cybercriminals. As our digital presence grows, so does the complexity and scale of the threats we face, making it crucial to understand the risks and take proactive measures to protect ourselves.

The digital transformation of our world has led to an unprecedented increase in connectivity. Smartphones, the Internet of Things (IoT), and social media platforms now play a central role in our daily lives. While offering unparalleled convenience, this connectivity also opens the door to a wide range of cyberattacks, from simple phishing scams to highly sophisticated ransomware campaigns. These attacks are not limited to large corporations or government institutions—they target individuals, small businesses, and organizations of all sizes, with devastating consequences.

As we continue to embrace new technologies, we also witness a shift in the tactics employed by cybercriminals. Today's cyber threats are increasingly advanced and multifaceted, making traditional security measures insufficient. The emergence of complex attack vectors like advanced persistent threats (APTs), state-sponsored cyberattacks, and malware designed to exploit specific vulnerabilities requires a more nuanced and proactive approach to cybersecurity. Cybercriminals have evolved alongside technology, often leveraging artificial intelligence and machine learning to enhance the effectiveness of their attacks, making it more critical than ever to stay ahead of these threats.

The implications of cyber insecurity are profound and far-reaching. Financial losses due to fraud and identity theft, privacy violations, emotional stress, and damage to one's professional reputation can result from a single breach. Yet, the consequences extend beyond the personal—cyberattacks can disrupt entire industries, cause national security threats, and undermine trust in the digital ecosystem. Whether you are an individual or part of an organization, understanding the potential risks and adopting a proactive approach to cybersecurity is essential to safeguarding your personal information, assets, and privacy in this interconnected world.

Cyber safety is not just about the tools and technologies used to defend against attacks but also about cultivating a mindset of vigilance and awareness. By learning about the evolving threat landscape and understanding the importance of secure practices, you empower yourself to recognize potential threats before they can cause harm. This chapter will cover the various aspects of cyber safety, outlining the most common threats and their potential impact and providing practical strategies to mitigate risks and enhance your digital security. The goal is to equip you with the knowledge and tools necessary to defend your digital life and help create a safer online

Cyber Defense: Best Practices for Digital Safety, First Edition. Jason Edwards.
© 2025 John Wiley & Sons Ltd. Published 2025 by John Wiley & Sons Ltd.

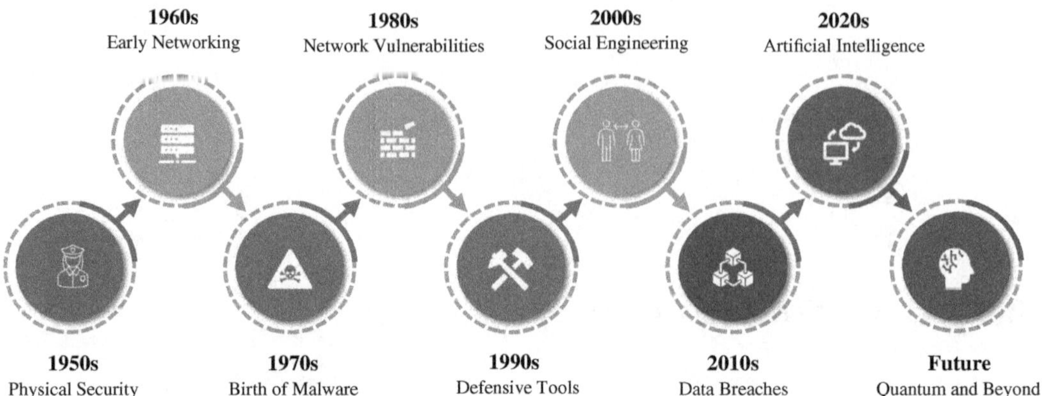

Figure 1.1 The growth of digital connectivity over time.

environment for yourself and those around you. The history of digital connectivity and grown exponentially as shown in Figure 1.1.

The Rise of Digital Connectivity

The internet has evolved profoundly since its early days of dial-up connections and rudimentary websites. What was once a niche technology reserved for academics and government agencies has blossomed into an omnipresent force that powers nearly every aspect of modern life. The development of broadband internet, high-speed connections, and cloud computing has allowed vast amounts of data to be transferred and processed in real time. This has led to a world where information flows effortlessly across borders, enabling unprecedented connectivity and resource access. As more and more devices are linked to the internet, we find ourselves in an era where digital connectivity is no longer just a convenience but a necessity.

One of the most significant shifts in recent years has been the ubiquity of smartphones and mobile devices. The rise of these devices has revolutionized not only how we communicate but also how we live, work, and play. Smartphones have become our personal assistants, entertainment hubs, and gateways to the world. With apps for everything from banking and shopping to transportation and health tracking, mobile devices have become an extension of ourselves. However, this convenience comes at a cost. The more we rely on these devices, the more we expose ourselves to cyber threats. Every app we download, every service we use, and every piece of data we share add to the digital footprint we leave behind. As mobile devices become more powerful and feature-rich, they become more attractive targets for cybercriminals seeking to exploit their vulnerabilities.

The IoT has further compounded the complexity of our digital landscape. IoT refers to the network of everyday objects—refrigerators to security cameras, fitness trackers to thermostats—connected

---

Ask the AI

"What are the most common social engineering tactics cybercriminals use?"

"How has the Internet of Things (IoT) expanded the attack surface for cybersecurity?"

"How does the shift toward remote work impact cybersecurity risks, and what are common mitigations?"

to the internet and capable of sharing data. These devices have enhanced the functionality of our homes, businesses, and personal lives, offering automation, efficiency, and convenience. However, many IoT devices were not originally designed with security in mind, and their proliferation has created a vast surface area for potential cyberattacks. From unsecured smart home devices to compromised industrial sensors, the IoT presents unique challenges for maintaining digital safety. As the number of connected devices grows, securing this expanding ecosystem becomes increasingly difficult for manufacturers and consumers alike.

Social media platforms and online communities have become central to daily personal and professional interactions. Platforms like Facebook, Twitter, LinkedIn, and Instagram have fundamentally changed how we communicate, share information, and perceive the world. Social media has allowed individuals to broadcast their thoughts, ideas, and experiences to a global audience. It has enabled businesses to reach their customers in new and innovative ways, and it has created virtual communities that transcend geographic boundaries. However, the rapid rise of social media has also raised significant concerns about privacy, data security, and the spread of misinformation. The very platforms that connect us also expose us to a range of cyber risks, from identity theft and phishing to cyberbullying and online harassment.

The shift toward remote work and virtual collaboration has further transformed the digital landscape, particularly during the COVID-19 pandemic. With businesses and organizations embracing flexible work arrangements, the reliance on digital tools and platforms has surged. Video conferencing apps like Zoom, cloud storage solutions like Google Drive, and project management software like Slack have become integral to daily operations. This transition to a more digitally interconnected workforce has highlighted the vulnerabilities inherent in remote work. Organizations face new challenges in protecting their digital assets, from unsecured home networks to inadequate employee cybersecurity training. Recognizing these gaps, cybercriminals have increasingly targeted remote workers with sophisticated phishing attacks, malware, and other forms of exploitation.

Globalization has also played a critical role in the rise of digital connectivity. The interconnectedness of the world's economies, industries, and cultures has been made possible by the internet, enabling instant communication and information access. Businesses operate globally, with teams and clients across continents, time zones, and cultures. This global reach has opened up new economic growth and innovation opportunities and introduced new cybersecurity challenges. Cyberattacks no longer have to come from a local source; they can originate anywhere. The ability for cybercriminals to operate anonymously and easily cross international borders has made it more difficult for law enforcement and cybersecurity professionals to track and neutralize threats.

The Expanding Threat Landscape

The digital landscape and the threat landscape accompanying it have evolved quickly. Modern cyber threats have grown in sophistication and frequency, affecting individuals, businesses, and even entire governments. Malware, once a simple annoyance, has become a highly effective weapon used by cybercriminals to steal data, disrupt operations, or hold systems hostage. The days when viruses and Trojans were the main concerns have passed; today's malware can be far more stealthy and targeted. Often, it operates in the background without the user's knowledge, quietly infiltrating systems to steal sensitive information or gain control of an environment. Table 1.1 shows an overview of the key risks and vulnerabilities shaping our digital landscape.

Table 1.1 Cybersecurity threats.

Cyber threat	Description	Common targets	Typical impact	Mitigation
Phishing	Fraudulent attempts to obtain sensitive information through deceptive emails.	Individuals	Organizations	Data theft
Ransomware	Malicious software that locks files and demands payment for decryption.	Businesses	Government agencies	Loss of data access
Malware	Software designed to damage or gain unauthorized access to systems.	Individuals	Organizations	System compromise
Advanced persistent threats (APTs)	Long-term targeted cyberattacks, usually by state-sponsored hackers.	Governments	Critical infrastructure	Data theft
Denial-of-service (DoS)	An attack is designed to disrupt the normal traffic of a server or network.	Web servers	E-commerce sites	Website downtime
Insider threats	Security threats posed by individuals within an organization.	Businesses	Organizations	Data leaks
Man-in-the-middle (MitM)	Interception of communication between two parties to steal data.	Individuals	Organizations	Data theft
Social engineering	Manipulating individuals into divulging confidential information.	Individuals	Organizations	Identity theft
SQL injection	Exploiting vulnerabilities in web applications to execute arbitrary SQL code.	Websites	Web applications	Data loss
Zero-day exploit	Exploit of an unknown vulnerability in software.	Software vendors	IT systems	Unauthorized access

Phishing attacks are one of the most common and effective cyber intrusion methods. These attacks deceive users into divulging personal information, often by impersonating legitimate organizations or individuals. Phishing emails can be incredibly convincing, with attackers using official logos, branding, and personalized messages to trick victims. More advanced phishing tactics, such as spear phishing, target specific individuals or organizations, increasing the chances of success. Cybercriminals rely on the gullibility of users and the speed at which information spreads online, making phishing a persistent and dangerous threat to personal and organizational security.

Ransomware has become another prevalent and highly damaging form of cybercrime. This type of malware locks users out of their files or systems, demanding a ransom payment in exchange for restoring access. Ransomware attacks have become increasingly sophisticated, with cybercriminals often exploiting vulnerabilities in software to gain access to sensitive systems. Businesses of all sizes, government agencies, and even critical infrastructure systems have fallen victim to ransomware. The financial toll can be staggering, with some companies paying millions to regain control of their systems. However, paying the ransom does not always guarantee that the attacker will release the files or refrain from further attacks, making ransomware a particularly insidious form of cybercrime.

The increase in cybercrime rates has profoundly impacted both individuals and businesses. According to recent reports, cybercrime is expected to cost the global economy trillions of dollars annually. This is not just a matter of lost revenue or direct financial theft. The long-term repercussions of cybercrime are felt in the form of reputational damage, legal liabilities, and lost trust. Small businesses are at high risk because they often lack the resources to implement strong cybersecurity measures. Many small businesses fail to recover from a major cyberattack; some even go out of business.

Cybercriminals are becoming more organized, operating in large, sophisticated networks that span the globe. These networks often function like traditional criminal organizations, with clearly defined roles and hierarchies. Some cybercriminal groups specialize in specific attacks, such as malware development or distributing phishing emails, while others may be involved in money laundering or identity theft. These networks often operate in the shadows of the dark web, where stolen data and illicit services are traded freely. This dark web economy has enabled cybercriminals to flourish, as they can operate anonymously without fear of immediate law enforcement intervention. This means that the threat landscape is no longer just a matter of random, opportunistic attacks for businesses and individuals but is increasingly driven by organized groups with significant resources and expertise.

The rise of APTs and state-sponsored attacks has added another layer of complexity to the threat landscape. APTs are highly targeted, prolonged cyberattacks designed to infiltrate and remain within a network for extended periods. These attacks are often carried out by well-funded and highly skilled actors, such as nation-states or sophisticated hacker groups. The objective of an APT is usually not immediate financial gain but rather to gather intelligence, disrupt operations, or sabotage critical infrastructure. State-sponsored cyberattacks have become a prominent feature of geopolitical conflicts, with countries using cyberattacks as part of their broader strategy. These attacks target anything from government agencies and military networks to private sector companies with sensitive data or critical infrastructure.

One of the biggest challenges organizations face in defending against APTs and state-sponsored attacks is that these threats are often very difficult to detect. APTs are designed to remain undetected for as long as possible, allowing attackers to exfiltrate data or cause disruption without raising alarms. Once attackers have gained access to a system, they may move laterally within the network, gathering intelligence and compromising additional systems. Detecting and mitigating such attacks requires highly advanced cybersecurity measures, including continuous monitoring, threat intelligence, and incident response capabilities. Unfortunately, many organizations still rely on insufficient, outdated defenses to thwart these sophisticated threats.

Another significant issue contributing to the expanding threat landscape is the prevalence of vulnerabilities in outdated systems and unpatched software. While modern operating systems and applications often have built-in security features, many organizations still rely on legacy systems that lack proper security controls. These older systems may no longer receive vendor updates or

---

Ask the AI

"What are the main differences between traditional cyber threats and advanced persistent threats (APTs)?"

"How do cybercriminal networks operate, and what makes them difficult to disrupt?"

"How can organizations reduce their exposure to zero-day vulnerabilities?"

patches, making them susceptible to cyberattacks. Cybercriminals are keenly aware of these vulnerabilities and often exploit them to access sensitive networks or systems. Unpatched software, particularly in web browsers, email clients, and content management systems, can give attackers an easy entry point into a system.

Sometimes, organizations delay or neglect to apply patches due to the perceived disruption that an update may cause. However, this complacency can lead to disastrous consequences, as cybercriminals can exploit unpatched vulnerabilities to launch attacks. For example, the infamous WannaCry ransomware attack exploited a vulnerability in Microsoft Windows that had been publicly disclosed months before the attack occurred. The delay in applying the patch allowed the malware to spread rapidly across the globe, causing significant damage to organizations, including hospitals, government agencies, and businesses.

Personal Implications of Cyber Insecurity

Cyber insecurity is not a faceless threat but only affects faceless corporations or distant governments. For individuals, the implications of cyberattacks are real, personal, and often devastating. Financial losses due to fraud and identity theft are among the most immediate consequences when individuals' digital security is compromised. Cybercriminals use sophisticated methods to steal personal and financial information, from credit card numbers to social security details, and exploit them for profit. The financial impact can be significant, whether through unauthorized transactions draining bank accounts or fraudulent charges piling up on credit cards. In some cases, the effects linger long after the money is stolen, as victims spend months or even years working to repair their financial records, disputing fraudulent charges, and rebuilding their credit scores. Table 1.2 presents best practices for enhancing your cyber safety, essential for navigating today's digital threats effectively.

The consequences of a cyberattack don't stop at financial losses. Privacy invasion is another major concern that many people fail to consider until it happens to them. In an era where nearly everything about an individual's life is stored online—banking records, health information, personal conversations, and even intimate photos—the stakes are high. Unauthorized access to personal data by hackers or malicious insiders can result in severe privacy violations. Once sensitive data such as passwords, emails, and personal photos is compromised, it can be used for further exploitation or even public humiliation. This breach of privacy can extend beyond the digital world, with cybercriminals using personal information for blackmail, harassment, or impersonation. In some instances, individuals may never fully understand the extent of the information exposed, adding a layer of uncertainty and fear to their daily lives.

The emotional and psychological effects of cyber insecurity can be just as profound as the financial or privacy-related impacts. Victims of cyberattacks often experience significant stress and anxiety, worrying about what information has been exposed, who has accessed it, and how it might be used. The violation of one's personal space—especially in cases of identity theft or cyberstalking—can feel like an ongoing invasion, with the victim constantly wondering when the next shoe will drop.

Ask the AI

"What are the psychological effects of a data breach on individuals and organizations?"
"How can individuals protect their data from identity theft?"
"What are the legal consequences of a company failing to secure customer data?"

Table 1.2 Best practices for cyber safety.

Best practice	Description	Why it's important	Implementation tips
Strong passwords	Use unique, complex passwords for each account.	Prevents unauthorized access to sensitive accounts.	Use password managers to generate and store complex passwords.
Two-factor authentication (2FA)	Enable an additional layer of security by requiring two forms of identification.	Adds another barrier to prevent unauthorized account access.	Enable 2FA on all supported accounts and services.
Regular software updates	Keep your operating system and applications up to date.	Patches vulnerabilities and ensures the latest security features.	Enable automatic updates and review manual updates periodically.
Backup your data	Regularly back up critical data to an external location.	Protects data from loss due to malware, hardware failure, or cyberattacks.	Use cloud backups and offline storage solutions like external hard drives.
Secure your Wi-Fi	Ensure your home or business Wi-Fi network is protected with strong encryption.	Prevents unauthorized access to your local network and sensitive data.	Use WPA3 encryption and a strong, unique password for Wi-Fi.
Secure mobile devices	Protect your smartphone or tablet with PINs, passwords, or biometrics.	Prevents unauthorized access to sensitive mobile data.	Install device encryption, enable biometric security features, and avoid jailbreaking or rooting your device.
Beware of phishing	Recognize and avoid phishing attempts in emails, text messages, or websites.	Prevents falling victim to identity theft or credential theft.	Learn common phishing tactics and always verify the sender before clicking links.
Monitor your accounts	Regularly review financial and personal accounts for suspicious activity.	Helps identify and stop fraud or theft early.	Set up account activity alerts and review statements regularly.
Use antivirus software	Install and maintain up-to-date antivirus software on all devices.	Protects against malware, ransomware, and other malicious software.	Choose reputable antivirus software and run regular scans.
Limit personal information	Be cautious about sharing personal details on social media or websites.	Reduces the risk of identity theft and targeted cyberattacks.	Review privacy settings on social media and limit sharing of sensitive details.

For many, the psychological toll of being targeted by cybercriminals extends beyond the immediate aftermath of an attack. There is often a deep sense of betrayal, especially if the attack came through an avenue they trusted, like a work network, an online retailer, or a social media platform. As trust erodes, individuals become more wary of every email, text, and website, making them feel constantly on edge. The emotional strain, coupled with the logistical and financial hurdles of recovering from a cyberattack, can result in lasting trauma that affects one's mental health.

The damage to personal and professional reputation can be another lasting effect of cyber insecurity. A breach in personal data, particularly if it involves sensitive or embarrassing information, can have far-reaching consequences for an individual's reputation. For example, if personal emails or social media accounts are hacked and shared publicly, it may affect how others view the individual—friends, family, colleagues, and even potential employers. In a professional context, a data breach or cyberattack could result in a loss of client trust, harm to partnerships, or a tarnished career trajectory. Online reputation, becoming increasingly important in personal and professional spheres, can be severely damaged. For many, repairing this damage involves more than just recovering stolen data; it requires rebuilding trust, which can be time-consuming and difficult. In the modern digital age, reputation often precedes an individual, and once it is compromised, it can take years to recover fully.

In addition to damaging reputation, cyber insecurity can pose serious risks to personal safety and well-being. While this might seem like an exaggerated concern, the reality is that cyberattacks can have very real consequences for an individual's physical security. Stalkers, for example, can use information gleaned from online activity to track their victims, monitor their movements, and create situations where physical harm becomes a real risk. Similarly, personal information exposed during a data breach may be used by criminals to steal not only money but also a person's identity, further putting them at risk of fraud or even physical harm. In cases of doxxing—where personal details such as home addresses or phone numbers are published online—victims have faced harassment, threats, and even direct physical assaults. As our physical and digital lives become increasingly intertwined, ensuring digital safety becomes essential to personal safety.

Legal consequences of cyber negligence are often overlooked, but they are becoming more and more relevant in today's interconnected world. For individuals, failing to take the necessary steps to secure their data can lead to severe legal repercussions. For instance, victims may be held legally responsible for not safeguarding that information if sensitive financial information is stolen due to negligence—such as failing to update passwords or install necessary security patches. While it's true that the burden of responsibility lies primarily with cybercriminals, some jurisdictions now impose legal requirements on individuals to protect their data, especially when it comes to preventing identity theft. For businesses, the legal implications of a cyberattack can be even more severe. In addition to the risk of lawsuits from affected customers, companies may face regulatory fines for failing to comply with data protection laws such as GDPR or the CCPA. As the digital world becomes more regulated, individuals and businesses must be aware that neglecting cybersecurity practices can open them to legal consequences beyond an attack's immediate financial costs.

The Importance of Proactive Cyber Safety

In today's rapidly evolving digital landscape, adopting safe online practices is no longer optional but essential. The benefits of proactively securing one's digital life extend beyond the immediate sense of protection to a more resilient and robust defense against cyber threats. When individuals adopt safe practices—such as using strong, unique passwords, enabling multi-factor authentication (MFA), and exercising caution when clicking on links—they drastically reduce the likelihood of falling victim to cyberattacks. These measures may seem simple, but their impact is profound. By fortifying the most vulnerable entry points into a system, individuals can create layers of defense that make it much harder for cybercriminals to breach their digital lives. Proactive cyber safety doesn't just prevent immediate threats; it fosters a mindset of vigilance and precaution that keeps digital environments secure over the long term.

One of the most effective ways to reduce exposure to cyber risks is through awareness and education. Most cyberattacks, such as phishing scams or malware infections, rely on human error as a point of vulnerability. A lack of understanding about common threats or the latest tactics used by cybercriminals can make individuals and organizations easy targets. Individuals can make informed decisions about their online behavior by educating themselves and others about the various risks—recognizing phishing emails, understanding the importance of regular software updates, or knowing the signs of a compromised account. When people are aware of potential dangers, they are far more likely to take the necessary steps to protect themselves, such as avoiding suspicious downloads or verifying the authenticity of unsolicited communications. A culture of awareness instilled through continuous education is the first defense against the ever-expanding array of cyber threats.

The role of individuals in a collective security ecosystem cannot be overstated. Cybersecurity is a technical concern and a shared responsibility involving everyone interacting with digital systems. The security of one device or account can have ripple effects throughout a network, especially in today's interconnected world. When individuals neglect basic cybersecurity practices, such as using weak passwords or failing to secure personal data, they jeopardize their safety and potentially expose others to risk. In a workplace setting, for example, one employee's lapse in security can serve as a gateway for an attack that compromises an entire organization's network. Similarly, individuals who fail to take care of their personal devices—whether by neglecting software updates or using encryption—can inadvertently contribute to the success of cybercriminals who target the weakest links in the chain. By adopting secure practices and holding themselves accountable, individuals contribute to a collective security ecosystem that benefits everyone.

The long-term consequences of ignoring cyber threats can be severe, often felt long after an attack. Cybercriminals do not limit their attacks to the present; they plan for the future. When individuals or organizations neglect their cybersecurity, they expose themselves to the possibility of long-term damage. The financial costs of a data breach or ransomware attack can be staggering, not to mention the potential legal liabilities or regulatory fines that may follow. However, the damage often extends beyond the immediate financial implications. Victims of cyberattacks may also face lasting reputational harm as trust in the compromised individual or organization diminishes. Recovery from a cyberattack is rarely swift, and the consequences can reverberate across years of financial reports, customer relationships, and even personal security. For this reason, the cost of ignoring cyber threats is often much greater than the investment required to prevent them in the first place.

Encouraging a culture of security mindfulness is essential in both personal and professional contexts. A security-conscious mindset is more than just knowing how to configure your privacy settings or install antivirus software; it involves adopting a holistic approach to every aspect of online activity. Whether checking the URL before entering sensitive information, being wary of unsolicited calls or emails, or regularly backing up important data, cultivating mindfulness around cybersecurity can drastically reduce the likelihood of falling victim to an attack. In professional

Ask the AI

"What are the most effective ways to raise cybersecurity awareness in the workplace?"
"How can organizations build a comprehensive cybersecurity awareness program?"
"What are the emerging trends in cyber threats that individuals and businesses should be aware of?"

environments, organizations can foster this culture by offering ongoing cybersecurity training to employees, encouraging transparent communication about potential threats, and creating clear security policies that everyone follows. When individuals are consistently reminded of the importance of cyber safety and are empowered with the tools to protect themselves, the collective security of the organization or community is vastly improved. Security is not a one-off event; it's a continuous, proactive practice that must be woven into daily life's fabric.

Staying ahead of emerging threats requires continuous learning and adaptability. Cybercriminals are nothing if not creative; they evolve their tactics to exploit new vulnerabilities and bypass traditional security measures. This means that cybersecurity is not a set-it-and-forget-it endeavor—it's an ongoing process that demands constant vigilance. As new technologies and digital trends emerge, so too do new vulnerabilities. For instance, the rise of the IoT and the increasing use of artificial intelligence have introduced new potential attack vectors that must be accounted for. By staying informed about the latest developments in cybersecurity—whether through attending industry conferences, reading up on the latest research, or taking part in online forums—individuals and organizations can be proactive rather than reactive. The key to maintaining robust digital safety is to keep learning, adapting, and evolving with the changing threat landscape. Cybercriminals are always looking for new opportunities; those who stay ahead of them are in a much better position to defend their digital lives.

Adopting safe online practices offers a wealth of benefits that go far beyond just avoiding cyberattacks. At its core, proactive cyber safety is about minimizing vulnerabilities before they can be exploited. Simple actions, such as regularly updating passwords, using encryption, and enabling MFA, can dramatically reduce the likelihood of an attack. These measures protect sensitive data and create a defense-in-depth strategy that makes it harder for cybercriminals to succeed. Each added layer of protection increases the complexity for potential attackers, making the target far less attractive. By incorporating these practices into daily life, individuals and organizations can safeguard against current and future threats.

Risk exposure is not just a product of what we do but, more importantly, what we know. Reducing that exposure requires ongoing awareness and education, which are key components of any solid cybersecurity strategy. Many cyberattacks succeed because users are unaware of the risks or lack the knowledge to recognize phishing attempts, malware, or even basic signs of an intrusion. Educating users about these threats, from the common to the more sophisticated, is essential for creating a more secure environment. The more informed individuals are, the better equipped they become to make safe decisions online. Awareness also includes understanding the consequences of seemingly small mistakes, like clicking on a link in a suspicious email, which could lead to disastrous outcomes if not handled with caution. Table 1.3 outlines cybersecurity best practices tailored for different user roles, ensuring tailored protection across various positions.

Cybersecurity is not solely the responsibility of security experts or IT departments; it's a collective effort, and every individual plays a crucial part. The role of individuals in a collective security ecosystem is vital because one person's negligence can compromise an entire network. For example, a weak password or a failure to install critical security updates can provide the gateway for attackers to exploit. When everyone adopts best practices for online security, the entire ecosystem becomes

---

Ask the AI

"Explain the key differences between multi-factor and single-factor authentication."

Table 1.3 Cybersecurity best practices by user role.

User role	Best practices	Why it's important	Implementation tips
End users	Use strong, unique passwords, enable 2FA, and avoid clicking suspicious links.	Protects personal and organizational data from breaches.	Set password complexity rules and educate on phishing risks.
IT administrators	Regularly update software, monitor network traffic, and apply patches.	Ensures systems are protected from known vulnerabilities.	Automate software updates, deploy regular scans, and patch management.
Security officers	Implement security policies and conduct security awareness training.	Ensures the organization follows security best practices.	Create regular security training and testing schedules.
HR department	Secure employee records, use encryption for sensitive data, and implement access controls.	Safeguards employee privacy and sensitive personal data.	Use secure HR systems with encryption and limited access.
Finance department	Monitor financial transactions, implement secure payment systems, and use MFA.	Prevents fraud financial data theft and unauthorized transfers.	Train staff on recognizing phishing attempts and secure financial practices.
Developers	Secure coding practices, conduct vulnerability assessments, use secure development environments.	Prevents application vulnerabilities and exploits.	Adopt secure coding standards and use automated vulnerability scanning tools.
Legal and compliance	Ensure compliance with data privacy regulations (e.g., GDPR) and monitor contracts.	Reduces legal and regulatory risks associated with data breaches.	Implement legal review processes and ensure staff understand privacy laws.
C-suite/executives	Support and allocate resources for cybersecurity initiatives, and implement a security-first culture.	Demonstrates commitment to security and ensures resource allocation.	Encourage cybersecurity initiatives, and provide budget for training.
Contractors/ freelancers	Adhere to company security protocols and use secure communication channels.	Protects company data and systems from external threats.	Ensure contractors use secure devices and access protocols.
Customers	Use strong passwords, and be cautious about sharing personal information online.	Protects individual identity and ensures secure transactions.	Educate customers about safe online practices and phishing attacks.

stronger and more resilient to threats. This collective approach is particularly important in organizational settings, where employees, contractors, and partners must all be aligned on cybersecurity protocols. Just as physical security is reinforced by everyone locking doors and windows, cybersecurity thrives when all parties are mindful and vigilant.

Ignoring cyber threats has serious long-term consequences, many of which only become apparent long after an attack. The financial repercussions of a cyberattack can extend well beyond the immediate costs of data recovery or ransom payments. For businesses, a data breach or ransomware attack can result in lost customers, diminished brand trust, and the possibility of legal action. Similarly, individuals who fail to secure their online presence may find their data sold on the dark web or used to facilitate identity theft. The damage to one's personal or professional reputation can linger long after any financial losses are recouped. Additionally, individuals or organizations that ignore cyber threats risk falling behind in their security practices, making them prime targets for future attacks. In the long run, neglecting cybersecurity often ends up costing far more than the price of preventive measures.

Creating a culture of security mindfulness is not just about implementing the right tools but fostering a mindset that prioritizes safety at every level. Cybersecurity should be treated as an ongoing, integral part of daily activities rather than an afterthought or managed only when an incident occurs. Cybersecurity becomes embedded in the culture when individuals are routinely reminded to stay vigilant—whether through regular training, reminders to update passwords, or company-wide phishing exercises. A mindful approach involves actively considering the risks of each digital action, from clicking on an email link to accessing sensitive work systems. It's not enough to have security measures in place; they must be adopted as part of the daily routine, ensuring that security becomes second nature rather than an occasional concern.

To stay ahead of emerging threats, continuous learning is a necessity. Cybersecurity is a dynamic field where threats evolve rapidly, often outpacing traditional defense mechanisms' ability to adapt. New attack methods, like APTs or zero-day vulnerabilities, emerge regularly, requiring a different defense strategy. In addition to technological solutions, keeping up with the latest research, threat intelligence, and industry news is crucial for understanding where the next attack might come from. Continuous learning involves not only updating technical knowledge but also understanding broader trends in cybersecurity, such as the rise of artificial intelligence in cyberattacks or the vulnerabilities introduced by new technologies like the IoT. By staying informed and adaptable, individuals and organizations can maintain a proactive stance against even the most advanced threats.

Recommendations

1. **Adopt Strong Password Practices:** Make it a habit to use strong, unique passwords for every online account. Avoid reusing passwords across different platforms, and ensure each contains a mix of uppercase and lowercase letters, numbers, and special characters. Utilize a password manager to store these complex passwords securely and change them regularly to minimize the risk of breaches.
2. **Implement MFA:** Enable MFA on all accounts that support it. This added layer of security ensures that even if an attacker compromises your password, they will still need a second form of authentication to access your account. Start by applying MFA to critical accounts, such as email, banking, and social media, and gradually expand it to other services as you go.
3. **Regularly Update and Patch Systems:** Stay proactive about updating your operating systems, applications, and software. Most cyberattacks exploit known vulnerabilities in outdated software, so it's crucial to install patches and updates as soon as they are released. Set your devices to update automatically whenever possible to ensure you're always running the latest, most secure versions.
4. **Educate Yourself and Others About Cyber Threats:** Continuously learn about the latest threats in cybersecurity. Follow reliable sources, such as industry blogs or trusted cybersecurity organizations, to stay informed about emerging risks like phishing, ransomware, and malware. Share this knowledge with friends, family, and colleagues to ensure everyone knows common threats and how to recognize them.

5. **Foster a Security-conscious Environment:** If you work in an organization, help create a culture where cybersecurity is a shared responsibility. Encourage colleagues to adopt safe practices, such as verifying email senders and avoiding clicking on suspicious links. Organize or participate in regular cybersecurity training sessions to reinforce the importance of proactive security measures.

6. **Be Mindful of Your Digital Footprint:** Regularly review the personal information you share online, especially on social media platforms. Limit the sensitive data you make publicly available, such as your full birthdate or home address. Adjust privacy settings to control who can view your posts, and be cautious about accepting friend requests or connections from strangers.

7. **Monitor Your Financial Accounts Frequently:** Set up alerts for your bank and credit card accounts to track unusual activity. Regularly review account statements for any unauthorized transactions. Early detection of fraudulent activity can prevent further damage, so stay vigilant about your financial health and report any suspicious transactions immediately.

8. **Use Encryption for Sensitive Data:** Use encryption to protect sensitive data, whether stored on your device or transmitted online. Encryption ensures that even if someone intercepts your data, they won't be able to access it without the decryption key. Encrypting emails, files, and even your hard drive can safeguard your privacy in a breach.

9. **Implement a Backup Strategy:** Regularly back up important files and data to an external drive or cloud service. Backups ensure you won't lose critical information in a ransomware attack or hardware failure. Automate the backup process so that it happens regularly and without the need for constant oversight.

10. **Stay Informed About Emerging Technologies and Their Risks:** As new technologies, such as IoT devices or artificial intelligence, become more integrated into daily life, stay informed about the potential security risks they pose. Research the vulnerabilities of your devices and apply the same proactive security measures to these emerging technologies as you would for your computer or smartphone. By avoiding potential threats, you can mitigate risks before they impact your security.

Conclusion

As we navigate an increasingly digital world, the need for robust cybersecurity practices becomes increasingly apparent. Today's threats are diverse and constantly evolving, targeting everything from personal data to global infrastructures. In this chapter, we've explored the expanding threat landscape, examined the personal implications of cyber insecurity, and underscored the importance of taking a proactive approach to protecting our digital lives. Cyber threats are not only a concern for IT professionals and businesses but for everyone who interacts with digital technology—making digital safety a shared responsibility.

While the rise of new technologies has brought unprecedented convenience and connectivity, it has also opened up numerous avenues for exploitation. The consequences of cyber insecurity can be severe, from the pervasive risks of phishing to the devastating impact of ransomware attacks. However, by understanding cybercriminals' risks and tactics, we can better prepare ourselves to defend against them. Education and awareness play a key role in mitigating these risks, as the more we understand the methods used to breach our security, the better equipped we are to prevent them.

Taking proactive steps to protect your digital presence can significantly reduce the chances of falling victim to an attack. Simple actions, such as using strong, unique passwords, keeping software up to date, and practicing caution when interacting with unfamiliar links or emails, can go a long way in securing your personal information. But cybersecurity is not just about technology; it's also about mindset. Adopting a security-first mentality that prioritizes vigilance and encourages regular security checks can make a significant difference in staying ahead of emerging threats.

The importance of cybersecurity extends beyond individual protection. Everyone creates a safer online environment as part of a broader, collective digital ecosystem. By cultivating a culture of security mindfulness, we contribute to a stronger, more resilient internet where personal and organizational data is better protected. The more individuals and businesses prioritize cybersecurity, the more difficult it becomes for cybercriminals to succeed in their malicious activities.

Looking ahead, the field of cybersecurity will continue to evolve, and so will our approaches to digital safety. As cyber threats grow in complexity, so will the tools and practices we use to combat them. It is crucial to keep learning, stay informed, and continually update our security measures to stay ahead of cybercriminals. This chapter has provided foundational knowledge, but the journey toward complete digital safety is ongoing. The threat landscape may change, but we can build a more secure digital future for ourselves and others with vigilance, education, and a proactive mindset.

Chapter Questions

1 What is the primary benefit of adopting strong online password practices?
   A. To make accounts easier to remember
   B. To protect accounts from unauthorized access
   C. To reduce the need for software updates
   D. To improve internet connection speeds

2 Which of the following is an effective method to reduce the likelihood of an account being compromised?
   A. Using the same password across all accounts
   B. Using multi-factor authentication (MFA)
   C. Avoiding software updates
   D. Disabling firewalls on devices

3 Why is it crucial to regularly update and patch software systems?
   A. To keep your system up to date with the latest features
   B. To prevent vulnerabilities from being exploited by cybercriminals
   C. To increase internet bandwidth
   D. To reduce power consumption

4 What is the primary purpose of educating yourself and others about cybersecurity threats?
   A. To make the internet more entertaining
   B. To ensure people know the latest internet slang
   C. To make informed decisions and recognize potential cyber threats
   D. To enable the sharing of passwords across platforms

5 What role do individuals play in a collective cybersecurity ecosystem?
   A. They have no responsibility for cybersecurity
   B. They are responsible only for securing their own devices
   C. They contribute to the security of the entire network by adopting safe practices
   D. They are responsible only for updating software

6 What is a major long-term consequence of ignoring cybersecurity threats?
   A. Increased digital storage capacity
   B. Financial and reputational damage
   C. Improved system performance
   D. Increased network speed

7 What is the significance of fostering a culture of security mindfulness?
   A. To make people more paranoid about online activity
   B. To ensure cybersecurity becomes part of daily routines and decision-making
   C. To increase the number of passwords used
   D. To encourage the use of outdated software

8 Why is continuous learning crucial for staying ahead of emerging cyber threats?
   A. Cybersecurity experts are always wrong
   B. Cyber threats are static and rarely change
   C. New attack methods and vulnerabilities are constantly emerging
   D. It makes your computer run faster

9 What is a proactive measure to safeguard sensitive data online?
   A. Ignoring all security warnings
   B. Using encryption for sensitive communications and files
   C. Never updating passwords
   D. Disabling firewalls on devices

10 How can individuals contribute to a stronger collective cybersecurity ecosystem?
   A. By keeping their own security practices private
   B. By sharing their passwords with others in the network
   C. By adopting secure online practices and encouraging others to do the same
   D. By ignoring updates and security patches

11 Why should multi-factor authentication (MFA) be enabled on critical accounts?
   A. To make logging in faster
   B. To provide an additional layer of protection beyond just passwords
   C. To reduce the number of accounts
   D. To lower the cost of cybersecurity tools

12 What is the primary reason to implement a backup strategy for important data?
   A. To save space on your device
   B. To ensure data recovery in the event of a cyberattack or system failure
   C. To make accessing data faster
   D. To enable real-time data sharing

13 What can happen if individuals neglect their cybersecurity practices over time?
   A. Their devices will become more secure
   B. Their risk of a cyberattack increases, leading to financial and reputational loss
   C. They will have faster internet speeds
   D. Their accounts will become more difficult to hack

14 Why should individuals monitor their financial accounts regularly?
- **A.** To detect unusual activity and prevent fraud
- **D.** To improve online shopping experiences
- **C.** To accumulate loyalty points
- **D.** To track spending habits for tax purposes

15 Why is it important to limit the personal information shared on social media?
- **A.** To improve social media interactions
- **B.** To reduce the risk of privacy invasion and identity theft
- **C.** To get more followers
- **D.** To increase online engagement

2

Understanding Cyber Safety in the Digital Age

With the rapid pace of technological advancement, digital threats are evolving faster than ever, targeting everything from personal data to critical infrastructure. Whether accessing social media, shopping online, or simply using email, we are all exposed to potential risks in the digital space. This chapter provides the foundational knowledge to securely navigate the complex digital landscape, ensuring you can protect yourself and your information from cyber threats.

Cyber safety and cybersecurity are often used interchangeably, representing two distinct but complementary fields. Cybersecurity typically focuses on defending systems, networks, and digital infrastructure against attacks, emphasizing technical solutions like firewalls, encryption, and secure protocols. On the other hand, cyber safety encompasses the practices that individuals adopt to protect their personal information and online behaviors. It involves understanding how human actions—intentional or unintentional—can expose vulnerabilities and how to mitigate these risks through informed decision-making.

Moving through this chapter, you'll encounter key concepts crucial for personal and organizational security. We will explore the core principles of digital safety, including recognizing common threats, understanding the importance of digital literacy, and learning how your behaviors can significantly impact your security. The chapter covers practical steps to improve cyber hygiene, from understanding phishing attacks to setting up strong passwords. It will also touch on more advanced concepts like encryption, two-factor authentication (2FA), and recognizing malicious activity, providing you with a comprehensive toolkit for safer digital engagement.

However, it is not just the technology and tools that shape the cybersecurity landscape; human behavior also plays a pivotal role in determining outcomes. No matter how sophisticated a security system may be, it can still be bypassed through human error, such as clicking on a malicious link or using weak passwords. Throughout this chapter, you will learn how human behavior interacts with technology to strengthen or weaken digital defenses. Recognizing the psychological and social factors that contribute to risky online behavior will help you understand why certain security measures work—and why others may fail. Figure 2.1 contrasts cyber safety and cybersecurity, delineating their unique roles and intersections in digital protection.

Defining Cyber Safety and Security

Cybersecurity and cyber safety are often used interchangeably, but they represent distinct aspects of the digital landscape. Cybersecurity focuses on the technical defenses to protect systems, networks, and data from malicious attacks, breaches, and unauthorized access. It encompasses everything

Figure 2.1 Cyber safety and cybersecurity.

from firewalls to encryption, intrusion detection systems, and endpoint protection. Conversely, cyber safety is broader and centers on individuals' behaviors and actions to protect their personal data, privacy, and digital well-being. While cybersecurity addresses the technical infrastructure, cyber safety empowers users with the knowledge and habits to avoid threats and minimize vulnerabilities in their everyday digital interactions. Table 2.1 defines essential cybersecurity terms and concepts, providing a foundational glossary for understanding the field.

Personal cyber safety is rooted in several key principles that can help individuals safeguard themselves in an increasingly connected world. The first is awareness—understanding the risks associated with online activity and staying informed about the latest threats. Being cautious about sharing personal information, using strong and unique passwords, and applying regular updates to software are fundamental steps in maintaining safety. Another core principle is vigilance: staying alert to potential threats, such as phishing emails or suspicious links, and recognizing the signs of a compromised account or device. Finally, proactive engagement in regular backups and secure online practices forms the backbone of personal cyber safety, ensuring that users are prepared to recover from any potential breach.

A common misconception about online security is that only large organizations or government entities are targeted by cybercriminals. Individual users are prime targets for various reasons, including the relative ease of exploiting their vulnerabilities. Many people mistakenly believe that cyberattacks are sophisticated and require advanced knowledge to perpetrate. However, many attacks—such as phishing and social engineering—rely on exploiting basic human behavior, such as curiosity or carelessness. This misconception leads to a false sense of security, where users may assume that they are immune simply because they do not fit the profile of a "high-value" target when, in fact, they are often the low-hanging fruit of cybercriminal activity.

The relationship between technology and human behavior is at the heart of many cyber safety challenges. Technology can be a powerful tool for protection, but it is only effective if used correctly. Human error remains one of the largest vulnerabilities in cybersecurity. Users may inadvertently expose themselves to threats by reusing passwords, failing to enable 2FA, or clicking on malicious links without thinking. Cybercriminals are keenly aware of this fact and often tailor their attacks to exploit common human behaviors, which is why fostering good digital hygiene habits is critical to personal cyber safety. Recognizing that the effectiveness of technology is directly tied to human behavior is essential for building a more secure digital environment.

In the digital age, risk management is not just a concept for large enterprises but a crucial part of everyday online activity. Risk management involves identifying potential threats, assessing

Table 2.1 Cybersecurity terms and concepts (see Appendix for more).

Term	Definition	Category	Example
Cybersecurity	Practices designed to protect systems networks and data from cyber threats	Security	Using firewalls to protect network traffic
Cyber safety	Protecting personal data behaviors and online interactions to minimize risks and vulnerabilities	Personal safety	Using strong passwords on websites
Phishing	A type of social engineering attack where attackers impersonate legitimate sources to steal info	Attack method	Fake emails asking for account login
Malware	Malicious software designed to harm or exploit digital devices	Attack method	Virus ransomware or spyware
Social engineering	Manipulating people into divulging confidential information	Attack technique	Impersonating a colleague to steal credentials
Encryption	The process of converting data into a code to prevent unauthorized access	Protection mechanism	Using HTTPS for secure website connections
Two-factor authentication (2FA)	A security measure requiring two forms of identity verification	Authentication	Entering a code sent to your phone along with a password
Phishing email	An email designed to trick recipients into revealing personal information or downloading malware	Threat type	Fake Amazon order confirmation
Ransomware	A type of malware that encrypts data and demands payment for its release	Attack type	WannaCry ransomware attack
Botnet	A network of infected computers controlled remotely to launch cyberattacks	Cyber weapon	Using infected devices to send spam emails

their likelihood, and implementing mitigating measures. For individuals, this means understanding the risks associated with online activities, from browsing the web to interacting with social media platforms. A personal risk management strategy may involve balancing convenience with security, such as deciding whether to use a password manager or relying on built-in browser autofill features. It is also about being aware of emerging threats and adapting one's digital habits accordingly, whether it's avoiding risky apps, keeping software up to date, or learning about the latest scams.

Understanding the concept of risk management also involves acknowledging that not all risks can be entirely avoided. Some threats, such as zero-day vulnerabilities, are out of the user's control, but many can be mitigated by practicing good cyber safety habits. For example, regularly updating

---

Ask the AI

"What are the main differences between cybersecurity and cyber safety?"
"What are the key principles of personal cyber safety?"
"What is the role of risk management in cyber safety?"

software ensures that known vulnerabilities are patched, reducing the chances of exploitation. Similarly, making informed decisions about the data shared online—whether through social media, online shopping, or personal communications—can minimize the risk of exposure. The key to successful risk management in a digital context is recognizing that while no system is foolproof, well-placed actions can significantly reduce the likelihood and impact of a breach.

The concept of personal responsibility in cyber safety cannot be overstated. It is not enough to rely on technical solutions or external security measures to protect oneself in the digital space; individuals must actively safeguard their information. This includes adhering to best practices such as setting strong, unique passwords, enabling 2FA where available, and regularly monitoring accounts for unauthorized activity. Personal responsibility also extends to individuals' choices about the technologies they use. For example, users should be cautious about the permissions they grant to apps and services, always questioning whether the app needs to access certain data or features.

Moreover, personal responsibility involves recognizing the interconnectedness of one's digital presence. Each piece of personal data, whether an email address, a phone number, or a home address, can be a potential target. Taking steps to limit the exposure of such data—such as using disposable email addresses or adjusting privacy settings on social media—can help protect against identity theft and other forms of cybercrime. Remembering that cyber safety is not a one-time task but an ongoing responsibility is also critical. Just as physical security requires regular maintenance—like checking locks or replacing security batteries—digital security also demands vigilance and proactive care.

Fundamentals of Digital Literacy

Navigating the Internet securely and efficiently is essential in the digital age. The Internet offers a wealth of information, communication tools, and services but presents various risks. Understanding how to use the Internet safely requires more than knowing how to search for information or access websites. It involves understanding the underlying technologies, recognizing potential threats, and taking steps to protect personal data. Users must become adept at identifying safe websites, using secure connections, and avoiding dangerous behaviors such as clicking on unfamiliar links or downloading unverified software. Simple actions like ensuring that a website's URL begins with "https://" or using trusted search engines can reduce exposure to cyber threats.

Basic technological literacy is foundational to digital safety. Individuals need to understand key terms and concepts like "firewall," "encryption," "malware," and "phishing," as well as how these technologies work to protect users. For example, understanding the concept of secure sockets layer (SSL) encryption allows users to recognize when a website is safe enough to enter sensitive information, such as passwords or credit card numbers. Similarly, being aware of the risks of "malware" and how it can be delivered (e.g. through email attachments, malicious links, or compromised websites) can help users stay one step ahead of cybercriminals. Technological literacy also extends to knowing how to download apps and software safely, the importance of using strong passwords, and the value of enabling 2FA.

One of the most important skills in digital literacy is the ability to evaluate the credibility of online information. The Internet is a vast knowledge repository, but not all information is reliable or accurate. In an age of misinformation and fake news, users must be equipped with the skills to assess the trustworthiness of the sources they encounter. This includes checking the credentials of the website or author, looking for corroborating evidence from other reputable sources, and being cautious of sensationalist headlines designed to provoke emotional responses. Additionally, distinguishing between genuine online reviews, paid promotions, or biased opinions is vital for making informed decisions. A critical approach to digital information can protect users from falling victim to scams, conspiracies, and misleading narratives.

Recognizing safe versus unsafe online behavior is a core component of digital literacy. Online security revolves around common sense and recognizing when something feels off. For example, unsolicited emails or messages offering too-good-to-be-true deals are often signs of phishing attempts. Clicking on these messages or interacting with unknown senders can compromise personal information or install malware on a device. Similarly, sharing personal information on social media or unsecured websites can expose users to identity theft or financial fraud. Users must develop the instinct to question unfamiliar requests for personal details and be cautious when interacting with unknown individuals or organizations online. Understanding that not every link, offer, or request is legitimate is crucial to staying safe in the digital environment.

Software updates and security patches play a critical role in maintaining digital safety. It may seem inconvenient to regularly update your devices. Still, these updates are not simply about adding new features—they often contain important security patches that protect against newly discovered vulnerabilities. Cybercriminals are constantly looking for system weaknesses; once a vulnerability is identified, attackers will frequently move quickly to exploit it. Software companies are aware of these threats and work to release updates that address these vulnerabilities. Delaying or ignoring these updates creates opportunities for malicious actors to infiltrate a device, system, or network, putting personal data and information at risk. Staying on top of updates for your operating system, browsers, apps, and antivirus software is one of the simplest but most effective ways to secure your digital life.

Utilizing digital tools and resources responsibly is another pillar of digital literacy. The sheer variety of digital tools available today—from social media platforms to productivity applications and online services—requires users to exercise responsibility in engaging with them. For instance, while it may be tempting to download a new app or use an online service that promises to make life easier, it's important to consider the potential risks. Does the app require excessive permissions? Is the website or service reputable? Does it use encryption to protect your data? By thinking critically about the tools and platforms you engage with, you can avoid exposing yourself to unnecessary risk. Additionally, responsible use extends to respecting the privacy of others, not sharing sensitive information without consent, and using tools like virtual private networks (VPNs) to safeguard your online activity.

An essential aspect of responsible digital tool usage is the management of personal data. Many digital services require users to provide personal information, from names and addresses to credit card details and even biometric data. It's important to ask whether the service truly needs this information and whether it's protected. For example, many people unknowingly share large amounts of personal data on social media platforms, including location, travel plans, or life events. This can create opportunities for identity theft or stalking. Users should consider implementing privacy settings, limiting who can see their posts, and refraining from oversharing details that

Ask the AI

"What basic technological terms and concepts should I know for online safety?"
"How do I evaluate the credibility of online information?"
"Why are software updates and security patches important for digital safety?"

could make them vulnerable. The "less is more" principle applies to personal data—minimizing exposure is key to protecting one's privacy online.

The importance of digital literacy extends beyond individual users to the larger community. As more aspects of daily life move online—from banking and shopping to education and healthcare—understanding the fundamentals of digital literacy is vital to ensure that society remains safe and secure. Schools, businesses, and governments must work together to promote digital literacy, teaching people of all ages about the importance of online security, critical thinking, and ethical digital behavior. Digital literacy also means advocating for better online safety practices in the workplace, including training employees on how to spot phishing attempts or safely store sensitive information. Ultimately, fostering a digitally literate society helps create a safer online environment for everyone, reducing the risks posed by cyber threats and increasing the overall resilience of the digital ecosystem.

Developing Critical Thinking Skills Online

In today's digital landscape, distinguishing between misinformation and disinformation has become crucial for every internet user. Misinformation refers to incorrect or misleading information shared without malicious intent, while disinformation is intentionally false or manipulated content designed to deceive or manipulate others. Both can spread quickly online, especially on social media platforms, where information is often shared without verification. Critical thinking is essential in identifying these harmful narratives, which may appear as sensational headlines, altered images, or fabricated quotes. Users need to develop the habit of cross-checking facts, looking for credible sources, and questioning the motivations behind shared content. Recognizing the difference between legitimate and misleading information helps prevent the spread of falsehoods and protects individuals from being misled by digital content.

Assessing the reliability of websites and digital content is foundational to navigating the Internet safely. A website's appearance, URL, and overall credibility play a significant role in determining whether the information provided is trustworthy. Reliable websites typically have professional designs, clear ownership, and verifiable sources. Users should be cautious when visiting sites that lack these markers or appear cluttered with intrusive pop-ups or unrelated advertisements. Tools like website reputation checkers or browser extensions can help assess a site's credibility before trusting its content. Additionally, it's important to be wary of content that appeals primarily to emotions or uses sensational language to drive traffic. A critical thinker recognizes that well-researched, balanced content is more likely to come from reputable sources than those trying to sell a product or manipulate a viewpoint.

Understanding social engineering and manipulation tactics is another key element of developing critical thinking skills online. Social engineering refers to the psychological manipulation of individuals into divulging confidential information, often by impersonating a trusted entity. Cybercriminals and fraudsters use various methods to exploit human vulnerabilities, such as creating a sense of urgency or playing on emotions like fear or greed. Common tactics include phishing emails, phone calls, and fake technical support messages encouraging users to provide passwords, credit card numbers, or other sensitive details. Critical thinkers can recognize these tactics by noting inconsistencies in communication, such as odd language, mismatched logos, or requests for information that would normally not be shared via email or phone. By questioning the authenticity of such communications and verifying requests through official channels, users can protect themselves from falling victim to manipulation.

Analyzing online offers, ads, and promotions critically is essential for avoiding scams and fraudulent schemes. The digital space is flooded with advertisements, from limited-time offers to "too-good-to-be-true" discounts, many designed to deceive. Some ads may redirect users to fake websites that collect personal information or spread malware. A critical approach involves considering the source of the offer, the platform on which it appears, and whether the promotion seems excessively urgent or unrealistic. For example, an ad that promises an enormous discount on an item without clear details or official affiliation should raise immediate red flags. Users must develop the ability to assess whether offers are consistent with market prices and whether the retailer or service provider is known and trusted. Moreover, users should be cautious about entering personal information or financial details on unfamiliar sites, even if the promotion seems attractive.

Questioning unexpected communications and requests is another crucial component of digital safety. Cybercriminals often target individuals through unsolicited messages, pretending to be from reputable organizations such as banks, government agencies, or popular retailers. These messages usually ask the recipient to take immediate action—confirming account details, downloading an attachment, or clicking on a suspicious link. A critical thinker doesn't simply react to such requests but takes a step back to evaluate them. Verifying the legitimacy of unexpected communications by checking official channels, contacting the organization through known contact methods, or researching the request online is essential. If something feels off, it's often a sign that further scrutiny is required, and the user should avoid clicking on links or providing personal information until their concerns are addressed.

Strategies for making informed decisions in the digital space are deeply tied to developing a skeptical mindset. In the digital age, users are constantly bombarded with information, decisions, and offers; not all are in their best interest. To make informed choices, individuals should employ strategies such as breaking down the information into its core components, researching multiple sources, and considering the long-term impact of any decision. Whether to share personal information, make an online purchase, or engage with content, assessing the risks involved is crucial. Tools like privacy settings, encryption, and trusted reviews can help make safer decisions when engaging with digital platforms. Critical thinkers don't just take things at face value; they ask questions, seek evidence, and are willing to look beyond the surface before taking action.

In addition to questioning the information they encounter, individuals must develop a deeper understanding of the algorithms and technologies that influence the content they see. Search engines, social media platforms, and news outlets often use algorithms to determine which content is shown, and these algorithms are not neutral. They are designed to prioritize content that generates engagement, usually sensational or controversial content. Understanding this helps individuals recognize that online information is often curated to fit specific patterns rather than provide an objective view of reality. By critically analyzing the algorithms that shape online content, users can make more informed decisions about consuming and engaging with digital media. They can also use these insights to adjust their digital habits, ensuring they're not unduly influenced by content designed to manipulate their emotions or opinions.

Ask the AI

"What psychological tactics are used in social engineering attacks?"
"How can I analyze online ads and promotions critically to avoid scams?"
"What are common signs of phishing emails or fraudulent online communications?"

As part of a broader critical thinking approach, individuals should also be mindful of their digital footprints and the data they generate online. Every search query, purchase, or social media post contributes to a digital profile that can be used by companies, advertisers, or even malicious actors. Critical thinkers don't take their online privacy for granted and actively manage what data they share. This includes using privacy-focused search engines, reviewing the privacy policies of websites, and adjusting settings to limit data collection. In addition, individuals should consider the long-term consequences of their online actions, as data shared today may be used in ways that weren't anticipated when it was first shared. Informed decision-making in this context involves not just protecting one's data but understanding how it may be exploited or used by third parties down the line.

The Human Element in Cybersecurity

Human behavior plays a pivotal role in determining the effectiveness of cybersecurity measures and the overall security of digital environments. While technical defenses such as firewalls, encryption, and antivirus software are critical to protecting systems and data, they are not infallible without user cooperation. The reality is that many cyber threats result from human error, negligence, or ignorance. For example, users who recycle weak passwords across multiple accounts or fail to enable 2FA expose themselves and their organizations to significant risk. Even sophisticated security tools can be undermined by individuals bypassing safeguards, falling for phishing scams, or inadvertently disclosing sensitive information. As such, cybersecurity outcomes are deeply influenced by the behavior of individuals, both within organizations and in personal online interactions.

The psychological aspects of cyber threats and attacks further complicate the human element in cybersecurity. Cybercriminals are increasingly aware of the psychological factors that drive human behavior and use these to exploit vulnerabilities. Social engineering tactics, for instance, leverage emotions like fear, urgency, and curiosity to manipulate individuals into revealing sensitive information. Phishing emails often create a false sense of urgency by claiming that an account has been compromised or that immediate action is required to avoid consequences. Similarly, scammers may prey on people's desire to "win" something, offering fake rewards or prizes to lure them into providing personal details. Understanding these psychological tactics is crucial for both users and cybersecurity professionals. By recognizing the emotional triggers that cybercriminals exploit, individuals can better resist manipulation and make more informed decisions online.

Social factors play an important role in online risk-taking behavior, often influencing individuals to engage in risky activities without fully understanding the potential consequences. One common social factor is the pressure to conform or fit in, particularly on social media platforms. Many users, especially young adults, and teens, may engage in risky online behaviors—such as oversharing personal information or participating in dubious online challenges—because they feel it is expected or because their peers are doing it. In the workplace, social influences can also lead to poor cybersecurity practices, such as using easily guessable passwords or neglecting to update software simply because "everyone else does it" or because the risks seem abstract. This peer-driven behavior can be dangerous, as it amplifies the impact of individual vulnerabilities. Understanding the social dynamics that shape online behavior helps cybersecurity professionals design more effective awareness programs and encourages individuals to think critically about the risks of their online actions.

Case studies of human error leading to security breaches offer valuable insights into how lapses in judgment can result in significant data losses, financial consequences, or reputational damage.

For example, one high-profile case involved an employee clicking on a malicious email attachment that unleashed ransomware, encrypting an entire company's network and demanding a large ransom to restore access. In another case, a password manager with insufficient encryption protections led to the mass exposure of users' passwords, as the company failed to communicate the risks associated with the tool. In both scenarios, human error—whether in the form of a lack of caution or insufficient training—was the catalyst for the breach. These examples highlight the importance of addressing human factors in cybersecurity by implementing training programs, creating clear protocols, and fostering a culture of security awareness. Cybersecurity is about technology and equipping people with the knowledge and mindset to make safer choices.

Promoting responsible digital citizenship is crucial to mitigating human error in cybersecurity. Digital citizenship encompasses the rights and responsibilities of individuals in the online world, emphasizing respectful, ethical, and safe behavior. As more activities shift to digital platforms—such as education, work, and social interaction—individuals must take responsibility for their actions and consider the broader impact of their online behavior. This includes understanding how personal actions can affect others, such as sharing misinformation, engaging in cyberbullying, or neglecting to protect one's data, which can harm individuals or communities. Cybersecurity is closely tied to responsible digital citizenship, as individuals must protect their information and respect the security and privacy of others. Promoting digital citizenship in schools, workplaces, and communities helps cultivate a culture of accountability and responsibility, where individuals are more aware of the consequences of their online behavior. Table 2.2 outlines effective cyber safety practices, offering practical strategies to safeguard digital environments.

The importance of ethics and integrity in the digital realm cannot be overstated. As online environments become more complex and interconnected, ethical behavior in cyberspace is essential to maintaining trust and security. From respecting intellectual property to ensuring that personal data is handled responsibly, ethical conduct is the foundation of a secure digital society. Ethical dilemmas can arise in numerous scenarios, such as data-sharing practices, the collection of user information, or how algorithms are designed to influence user behavior. Individuals, businesses, and governments must strive to act with integrity when making decisions that impact digital security. For example, organizations must disclose security breaches promptly and transparently, allowing affected users to take necessary precautions. Similarly, users should be cautious when sharing personal data or engaging with online content, considering the ethical implications of their actions and decisions. Promoting a culture of ethical behavior in cybersecurity helps foster trust and ensures that the Internet remains a safe and secure space for all.

The role of education and awareness in addressing the human element of cybersecurity cannot be ignored. While many users may have a basic understanding of digital tools and platforms, they often lack the knowledge to effectively protect themselves from cyber threats. Educational initiatives to increase cybersecurity awareness are essential in teaching individuals how to recognize risks and make better online decisions. These programs should focus on secure password management, the dangers of clicking on suspicious links, and the importance of privacy settings on social media. In addition to formal training, ongoing awareness campaigns—public service announcements,

---

Ask the AI

"How does human behavior influence cybersecurity outcomes?"
"What are the psychological factors that lead to risky online behavior?"
"What are examples of human error leading to security breaches in real-life case studies?"

Table 2.2 Effective cyber safety practices.

Practice	Description	Why it's important	Example
Use strong passwords	Create complex passwords with a combination of letters numbers and symbols	Weak passwords are easily cracked making accounts vulnerable to attacks	A strong password might be G!8Rk2z$4zW
Enable 2FA	Use a secondary form of verification such as a code sent to your phone	It adds an extra layer of protection even if your password is compromised	Using Google Authenticator for added security on accounts
Regular software updates	Keep all your software including apps and browsers up to date	Outdated software can have vulnerabilities that hackers can exploit	Enable automatic updates for apps like Google Chrome and Windows
Avoid public Wi-Fi for sensitive transactions	Refrain from accessing personal accounts or conducting financial transactions over public Wi-Fi	Public Wi-Fi networks are not secure and can be a target for cybercriminals	Use a VPN when accessing sensitive data over public Wi-Fi
Back up your data regularly	Store copies of important files on a secure cloud or external drive	Regular backups ensure data can be recovered in case of ransomware or system failure	Use Google Drive or an external hard drive for regular backups
Monitor your bank and credit card statements	Check your statements regularly for unusual activity	Early detection of fraud can help prevent more significant financial losses	Set up transaction alerts with your bank to spot unauthorized charges quickly
Be skeptical of unsolicited emails or messages	Always verify the legitimacy of any unsolicited communication before taking action	Cybercriminals often use unsolicited communication to scam or steal information	Call the company directly to verify suspicious emails requesting sensitive data
Use a firewall	Enable your device's firewall to filter incoming and outgoing traffic	Firewalls help prevent unauthorized access to your device or network	Ensure your computer's built-in firewall is enabled or use third-party firewall software
Protect your personal information on social media	Limit what you share online and adjust privacy settings	Over-sharing can make you a target for identity theft and social engineering	Set social media profiles to private and avoid posting personal details
Educate yourself and others about cyber threats	Stay informed about the latest cyber threats and share your knowledge with others	Awareness is the first step in preventing cyber threats from impacting you and your loved ones	Attend cybersecurity webinars and share best practices with friends and family

workplace training, or social media outreach—can reinforce best practices and help individuals stay informed about the latest cyber threats. By equipping individuals with the right knowledge and skills, we can reduce the impact of human error and create a safer digital environment for all.

Creating a strong cybersecurity culture within organizations and communities requires ongoing effort and commitment. This involves implementing technical safeguards and fostering a mindset where security is everyone's responsibility. In the workplace, for example, it is important to encourage employees to think critically about their online behavior, report suspicious activities, and be proactive in securing company data. Similarly, families and communities can benefit from shared knowledge and collective action to ensure the safety of personal and sensitive information. A robust cybersecurity culture hinges on individuals being aware of the risks and empowered to act ethically and responsibly online. When cybersecurity becomes a shared value rather than a set of technical rules, the entire digital ecosystem becomes more resilient to attacks and more secure for its users.

Recommendations

1. **Understand the Impact of Human Behavior on Cybersecurity:** Recognize that human actions in professional and personal settings largely shape cybersecurity outcomes. Avoid complacency and make cybersecurity a personal responsibility by consistently following best practices, such as using strong, unique passwords and avoiding risky behaviors like clicking on suspicious links. Regularly reassess your digital habits to ensure they align with secure online practices.

2. **Develop a Psychological Awareness of Cyber Threats:** Learn to recognize psychological manipulation techniques cybercriminals use, such as fear, urgency, and greed. Understand that phishing attacks often rely on triggering an emotional response to deceive individuals into revealing sensitive information. Stay vigilant and resist pressure to act impulsively when confronted with unexpected or unsolicited digital communications.

3. **Be Aware of Social Engineering Tactics:** Train yourself to identify social engineering attacks that manipulate human trust to gain access to sensitive information. Be especially cautious with unsolicited phone calls, emails, or messages that ask for personal information, even if they seem to come from reputable sources. Always verify requests through official channels and never share personal details unless you know the request's legitimacy.

4. **Evaluate Online Content Critically:** Before acting on information found online, assess its credibility and accuracy. Check the source, verify facts through multiple reputable outlets, and avoid making decisions based on sensational headlines or emotionally charged content. Question everything from online offers to news articles, and never accept information at face value without proper verification.

5. **Promote Responsible Digital Citizenship:** Take responsibility for your online actions and consider how your behavior may affect others. This includes not sharing misinformation, respecting privacy, and protecting sensitive information. Encourage others in your community or workplace to follow ethical digital practices and foster a culture of cybersecurity awareness by leading by example.

6. **Commit to Ongoing Cybersecurity Education:** Stay informed about emerging cyber threats and cybersecurity best practices. Make a habit of reading up on the latest trends in cybersecurity, whether through news sources, educational blogs, or formal training courses. The more knowledgeable you are, the better equipped you'll be to recognize and mitigate potential risks.

7. **Exercise Caution with Online Offers and Promotions:** Be critical of online offers that seem too good to be true. Before clicking on ads or entering personal information for promotions, assess the offer's legitimacy by researching the business or website behind it. Use ad-blockers and avoid engaging with suspicious content that may lead to phishing sites or malware.

8. **Review and Strengthen Your Digital Privacy Settings:** Take the time to review and adjust the privacy settings on your social media accounts, search engines, and other online platforms. Limit the personal information you share publicly and ensure that only trusted individuals can access your sensitive data. Regularly update your settings to reflect changes in privacy policies and platform features.

9. **Question Unexpected Digital Communications:** If you receive an unsolicited email, message, or phone call requesting personal information, always verify the source before responding. Use official contact methods—such as calling a known company number or visiting a company's verified website—to confirm whether the request is legitimate. Avoid clicking links or downloading attachments from unfamiliar or suspicious sources.
10. **Foster Ethical Behavior Online:** Develop a strong sense of ethics when navigating digital environments, and always consider the implications of your actions online. From respecting others' privacy to avoiding illegal downloading or using copyrighted materials without permission, acting with integrity online protects your security and helps maintain trust and safety within the digital community.

Conclusion

As we conclude this chapter, it is important to recognize that digital safety is an ongoing journey, not a one-time fix. The tools, techniques, and best practices we've discussed provide a solid foundation, but the landscape of cyber threats constantly evolves. Staying secure in the digital age requires continuous learning, adaptation, and vigilance. With cyber threats becoming more sophisticated and widespread, relying on security software is no longer enough; individuals must take personal responsibility for their digital safety.

Throughout this chapter, we've explored key concepts such as the distinction between cyber safety and cybersecurity, the importance of digital literacy, and how human behavior can impact the security of both individuals and organizations. Understanding the nuances of these concepts empowers you to recognize potential risks and take proactive steps to protect yourself. Whether it's learning to spot phishing emails, using stronger passwords, or regularly updating software, these practices can significantly reduce your exposure to common digital threats. The more knowledgeable and prepared you are, the better equipped you'll be to mitigate risks before they become problems.

While the technical aspects of cybersecurity are crucial, this chapter has also emphasized the human element—how your behaviors, decisions, and habits play a critical role in securing your digital life. From practicing good password hygiene to being cautious of unsolicited emails, how we engage with technology directly affects our security. It's easy to fall into a false sense of security, thinking that sophisticated tools or systems will protect us. However, even the best defenses can be circumvented without a mindful and educated approach to technology use.

Looking ahead, your role in maintaining digital safety is not just about following guidelines—it's about fostering a mindset of ongoing vigilance and education. As cyber threats grow more complex, the need for proactive, informed individuals will continue to rise. The skills and knowledge you've gained from this chapter will be a stepping stone to more advanced cybersecurity concepts, helping you stay ahead of emerging threats. Remember, digital safety is not a static achievement but an evolving responsibility that demands your attention and commitment every time you interact with technology.

By embracing these practices, being mindful of the risks, and adopting a proactive stance, you will protect your information and contribute to a more secure digital environment for others. This chapter has provided you with essential tools for navigating the digital world securely, but the journey doesn't end here. The digital landscape will continue to shift, but with the right mindset and knowledge, you can stay one step ahead. Your commitment to learning, adapting, and remaining aware of cyber threats will be the key to safeguarding your digital life and the broader online community.

Chapter Questions

1 What is the main factor that influences cybersecurity outcomes?
   A. Technological tools and firewalls
   B. Human behavior
   C. Software updates
   D. Data storage capacity

2 Which of the following is a psychological tactic used in social engineering attacks?
   A. Providing technical documentation
   B. Creating a sense of urgency
   C. Offering free software downloads
   D. Asking for complex authentication

3 What does "social engineering" primarily involve?
   A. Exploiting software vulnerabilities
   B. Manipulating human behavior to gain access to information
   C. Attacking computer hardware directly
   D. Cracking encryption codes

4 What type of attack relies on exploiting emotions like fear or greed?
   A. Phishing
   B. Man-in-the-middle
   C. Malware
   D. Denial of Service

5 Which of the following is an important step in assessing online content?
   A. Checking the website's design
   B. Clicking on every link in the article
   C. Accepting the content without verifying its source
   D. Ignoring the website's URL

6 What is a key reason for individuals to practice responsible digital citizenship?
   A. To protect their privacy and others' privacy
   B. To collect more data for advertisers
   C. To reduce online costs
   D. To generate traffic for their websites

7 How can you best protect yourself from phishing attacks?
   A. By ignoring all emails from unknown senders
   B. By using strong passwords
   C. By verifying requests through official channels
   D. By avoiding online shopping

8 What is one of the best ways to evaluate the credibility of a website?
   A. Check if the website has many advertisements
   B. Look for a professional design and known branding

    C. Analyze the website's color scheme
    D. Visit the site only during the night

9 Why is it important to avoid online offers that seem too good to be true?
    A. They could contain viruses
    B. They often come from unverified sources or are scams
    C. They might offer free educational materials
    D. They may slow down your internet speed

10 What is the most effective method to avoid social engineering attacks?
    A. Responding quickly to all online requests
    B. Using complex passwords for all accounts
    C. Always verifying requests through official, trusted channels
    D. Disabling all email accounts

11 What does "critical thinking" in the digital space primarily involve?
    A. Ignoring the emotional appeal of online content
    B. Accepting all content shared on social media
    C. Questioning the validity and sources of online information
    D. Relying only on expert opinions

12 Which of the following is an example of ethical behavior online?
    A. Sharing personal login details with a colleague
    B. Downloading movies without permission
    C. Protecting privacy and avoiding identity theft
    D. Ignoring the privacy settings on social media

13 How can digital privacy settings help protect personal information?
    A. By limiting who can see your posts and data
    B. By providing free storage for your files
    C. By improving internet speed
    D. By collecting more data for advertisements

14 What is a common mistake that leads to cybersecurity breaches?
    A. Using multi-factor authentication
    B. Failing to verify the legitimacy of digital communications
    C. Updating software regularly
    D. Using encryption for sensitive data

15 What should be done when receiving unexpected digital communications requesting personal information?
    A. Ignore the message entirely
    B. Verify the request through official contact methods
    C. Click on any links to resolve the issue quickly
    D. Provide the information immediately

3

Understanding and Preventing Identity Theft

With an increasing number of individuals relying on online services for everything from banking to socializing, the opportunities for cybercriminals to exploit personal information have grown exponentially. Identity theft is not just about credit card fraud or stolen bank details; it encompasses various malicious activities, including tax fraud, medical identity theft, and criminal identity theft. As cybercriminals become more sophisticated, protecting one's digital identity becomes increasingly complex, requiring vigilance, education, and effective cybersecurity measures.

Understanding how identity theft occurs and how to prevent it is crucial for safeguarding personal and financial information. The theft of sensitive data, such as Social Security numbers, credit card details, and login credentials, can have devastating consequences for individuals and families. While some forms of identity theft are obvious, such as unauthorized charges or credit card fraud, others may go unnoticed for years. This chapter explores the various forms of identity theft, how they occur, and, most importantly, what steps you can take to prevent them. By understanding the methods employed by cybercriminals, you can better protect yourself from becoming a victim.

Prevention is the first line of defense in the battle against identity theft. Simple steps, such as using strong, unique passwords, regularly monitoring credit reports, and encrypting personal documents can reduce the risk of data breaches and unauthorized access to sensitive information. However, no system is foolproof, and even the most cautious individuals can fall victim to identity theft. This chapter will explore the steps to take if your identity is compromised, including how to report the theft, freeze your credit, and restore your identity.

Finally, it's essential to recognize the role of companies, institutions, and government agencies in preventing and responding to identity theft. Businesses must protect customer data under laws such as the General Data Protection Regulation (GDPR) and the California Consumer Privacy Act (CCPA), yet breaches still occur. This chapter will highlight the importance of data security measures and the legal implications of identity theft for individuals, organizations, and businesses. By taking a comprehensive approach to understanding and preventing identity theft, we can better protect ourselves and our digital futures. Figure 3.1 depicts the lifecycle of stolen personal data, illustrating the stages from theft to misuse in the cybercrime ecosystem.

What Is Identity Theft?

Identity theft involves obtaining and using someone else's personal information without permission, typically to commit fraud or other crimes. In its simplest form, identity theft involves the unauthorized use of information such as Social Security numbers, credit card details, or bank

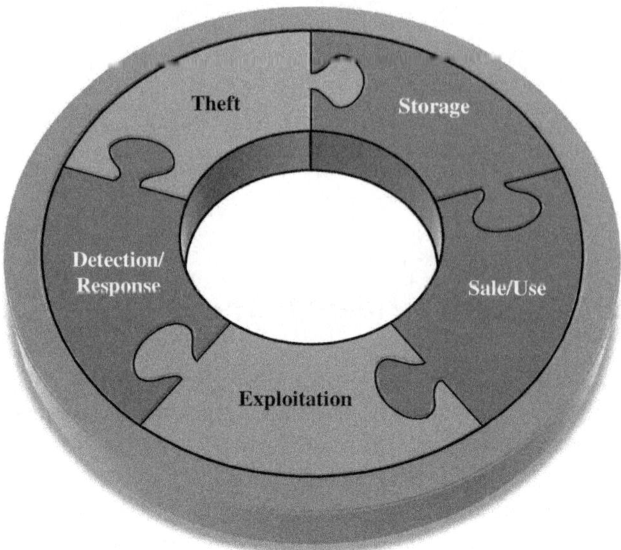

Figure 3.1 The lifecycle of stolen personal data.

account credentials. However, it can also extend to more complex forms, such as synthetic identity theft, where perpetrators combine real and fabricated information to create a fictitious identity. The range of potential thefts is vast, and with the rapid rise of digital platforms, identity theft has evolved into new and sophisticated ways. It is no longer just about stealing credit card numbers—cybercriminals now target every facet of an individual's online presence, from social media profiles to digital wallets. Table 3.1 categorizes common forms of identity theft, detailing the various methods and their impacts on individuals.

The digital age has made identity theft more prevalent and dangerous. With the rise of online banking, shopping, social media, and even work-from-home arrangements, personal data is stored, transmitted, and shared across many digital platforms. The very conveniences that modern technology offers, such as instant access to services and digital payments, have inadvertently opened new vulnerabilities. Hackers use phishing, data breaches, and social engineering techniques to gather personal information. Once in possession of a victim's data, criminals can perform various malicious acts, from draining bank accounts to opening lines of credit in the victim's name.

The motivations behind identity theft are varied but can typically be categorized into two broad groups: financial gain and espionage. Financial gain is by far the most common reason behind identity theft. Perpetrators use stolen identities to access funds, commit fraudulent transactions, or leverage credit in the victim's name. The rise of organized cybercrime syndicates has also led to a surge in identity theft for laundering money, selling stolen data on the dark web, or using a victim's information for black-market transactions. In some cases, identity theft may even be used for espionage or to infiltrate sensitive systems, particularly when individuals with high-security clearance or access to valuable information are targeted. These actions not only threaten financial stability but can have far-reaching consequences in terms of national security.

The consequences of identity theft on individuals and families can be devastating. Victims often find themselves in a constant battle to regain control of their personal information and restore their financial well-being. Resolving identity theft typically involves reporting the crime to law

Table 3.1 Common forms of identity theft.

Type of identity theft	How it happens	Commonly targeted data	Typical impact on victims
Financial identity theft	Using stolen credit card information or bank account numbers	Credit card numbers, bank account details	Unauthorized purchases, debt accumulation
Medical identity theft	Using personal information to gain medical services	Insurance numbers, medical records	Fraudulent claims to insurance companies, fake prescriptions
Criminal identity theft	Using someone else's identity when arrested or involved in crimes	Social Security numbers, driver's license	Criminal charges in victim's name, wrongful arrest
Tax identity theft	Using stolen personal information to file false tax returns	Social Security numbers	Tax refund fraud, financial loss, delayed refunds
Child identity theft	Using a child's personal information for fraudulent activities	Social Security number, school records	Loans or credit cards taken out in the child's name
Synthetic identity theft	Combining real and fake information to create a new identity	Made-up or partial personal details	Fake Social Security numbers, new accounts opened in fake identities
Employment identity theft	Using stolen personal data to get a job or benefits	Social Security number, employment records	Fake employment history, tax-related fraud
Social security identity theft	Using a person's Social Security number to commit fraud	Social Security number	Unauthorized tax returns, benefit fraud
Credit card identity theft	Stealing and using a person's credit card details for purchases	Credit card number	Credit card fraud, unauthorized transactions
Account takeover	Stealing personal banking or social media account information	Banking login credentials, email passwords	Access to financial resources, unauthorized transfers

enforcement, contacting credit agencies, and potentially seeking legal counsel. During this period, the victim may face difficulties obtaining loans, renting homes, or even securing employment, as their credit history may be tarnished by fraudulent activity. On top of financial hardships, victims also endure emotional stress, anxiety, and a loss of trust in digital systems that many of us take for granted.

Common myths and misconceptions surrounding identity theft often add to confusion and a sense of vulnerability. A widespread belief is that identity theft only happens to those who are careless with their personal information or who fail to take precautions. While neglecting digital security can certainly increase the risk of identity theft, even the most cautious individuals can fall victim to sophisticated attacks, such as data breaches at major corporations or social engineering scams. Another misconception is that identity theft only occurs in cases of large-scale financial fraud. In reality, even seemingly small acts of impersonation or the theft of a single piece of personal information can lead to severe consequences, such as unauthorized medical procedures or unlawful access to government services.

The legal implications for perpetrators of identity theft are significant. In many jurisdictions, identity theft is a felony with severe penalties, including imprisonment, substantial fines, and restitution to victims. The law has evolved to keep pace with the increasing sophistication of cybercriminals, with new statutes specifically targeting digital identity theft and cyber fraud. Beyond the penalties for the perpetrators themselves, individuals found guilty of identity theft may also be subject to civil lawsuits filed by the victims. These lawsuits can result in additional financial burdens, tarnishing the perpetrator's life and reputation. While the legal consequences are designed to act as a deterrent, they have also spurred greater attention to victim support and the development of proactive prevention measures.

Legal frameworks are continuously updated to deal with identity theft, with laws such as the Identity Theft and Assumption Deterrence Act (ITADA) in the United States criminalizing the use of stolen personal information for fraud. Additionally, victims of identity theft are protected under various consumer protection laws, allowing them to dispute fraudulent charges and clear their credit records. However, these laws are not foolproof, and enforcement can be challenging, especially when perpetrators operate from overseas. This reality has highlighted the need for greater international cooperation in tackling identity theft and ensuring that perpetrators are held accountable regardless of location.

Despite legal protections and increased awareness, identity theft continues to rise as criminals become more sophisticated in their methods. One of the key factors contributing to the rise of identity theft is the widespread collection and storage of personal data by businesses and governments. While data collection can offer benefits, such as personalized services and targeted advertising, it also poses a significant risk if not adequately secured. Organizations that store sensitive customer information are prime targets for cybercriminals, making it critical for companies to implement strong data protection practices and educate consumers on the importance of safeguarding their personal information.

Moreover, many individuals remain unaware of the potential threats lurking in their digital lives. Simple actions, such as clicking on suspicious links in emails or using easily guessable passwords, can unknowingly open the door to identity thieves. While technological safeguards such as multi-factor authentication (MFA) and encryption can offer added layers of protection, education remains the most powerful weapon in the fight against identity theft. This book aims to empower readers with the knowledge and tools to recognize and mitigate these threats, ensuring they are aware of the risks and prepared to take the necessary steps to defend their digital identities.

Recognizing Signs of Identity Theft

One of the first and most alarming signs of identity theft is the appearance of unexplained charges or withdrawals from your accounts. If you notice transactions you don't recognize, it's critical to investigate them immediately. These unauthorized charges could range from small, seemingly insignificant amounts (which thieves often test to see if the account is active) to large withdrawals

---

Ask the AI

"What are the different forms of identity theft, and how do they occur?"
"How has the rise of digital technologies affected the frequency and types of identity theft?"
"What are the primary motivations behind identity theft?"

that drain your funds. Identity thieves frequently use stolen credit or debit card information to make purchases or access your accounts online transfer funds to an untraceable location. Keeping a close eye on your account activity and regularly reviewing statements can help you spot these fraudulent transactions early, minimizing the potential damage.

Many financial institutions now offer account alerts, which can notify you in real-time when a transaction occurs. These notifications can be a useful tool for catching suspicious activity quickly. However, not all financial institutions send alerts for smaller transactions, and criminals know this, often making several small charges before a larger, more noticeable one. If you notice anything unfamiliar, don't wait for your monthly statement; contact your bank or card issuer immediately to freeze the account and begin the process of disputing and investigation. Prompt action can sometimes prevent unauthorized withdrawals and help you regain control over your finances.

Unexpected bills or credit card statements can also indicate that something is amiss with your finances. If you receive a bill for a credit card or service you didn't sign up for, this could be a red flag for identity theft. Criminals often open credit accounts in the victim's name and start making charges, sometimes without triggering the victim's immediate suspicion. These bills may not always reach the victim's primary address if the thief has changed the billing information, but when they arrive, they signal that something has gone wrong. Additionally, if you begin receiving credit card statements that don't match your spending patterns—whether due to unfamiliar charges or unanticipated increases in your credit balance—this could also be a sign of fraudulent activity.

It's important to regularly review your credit card statements and watch for any unfamiliar charges, particularly those that seem out of character for your typical spending. Many people, unfortunately, ignore their credit card statements until payment time arrives, but this lapse in attention can lead to serious financial consequences. When dealing with unexplained charges on new credit accounts, contacting the card company to inquire about the application details is also wise. In many cases, the application for the card can be traced back to a fraudster's actions, and reporting it can help prevent further damage.

Another common sign of identity theft is the denial of credit applications without clear or justifiable reasons. This can occur when a thief has already used your identity to open credit accounts or loans in your name, causing your credit report to reflect higher debt levels or missed payments. When you apply for a loan, mortgage, or credit card, the lender will check your credit report to assess your financial standing. If your credit report has been compromised—perhaps due to fraud or identity theft—the lender may see information that negatively affects your creditworthiness, leading them to deny your application. You might wonder why your credit score has suddenly dropped, even if you've always paid bills on time.

Denial of credit can often be a wake-up call that something isn't right. If this happens, you should obtain a copy of your credit report from one or more major credit bureaus to check for unfamiliar accounts or activity. The Fair Credit Reporting Act (FCRA) mandates that consumers are entitled to a free credit report once every 12 months from each of the three major credit bureaus (Equifax, Experian, and TransUnion). By regularly monitoring your credit report, you can catch identity theft early and begin the process of disputing fraudulent accounts and transactions. Moreover,

<table>
<tr><td>

Ask the AI

"What are the most common warning signs of identity theft on a credit report?"
"How can I differentiate between legitimate and fraudulent financial transactions?"
"What steps should be taken if I notice an unfamiliar account on my credit report?"

</td></tr>
</table>

some credit monitoring services offer real-time alerts to notify you of new accounts or changes to your credit report, further enhancing your ability to catch discrepancies quickly.

Financial institutions have increasingly sophisticated systems designed to detect and flag suspicious activity on accounts, and their alerts can often serve as a red flag for identity theft. These alerts may come in emails, phone calls, or text messages, informing you of unusual activity, such as login attempts from an unfamiliar device or significant transactions that differ from your usual spending habits. While such alerts are intended to protect you, they can also indicate that a thief is in the process of accessing your account or has already gained control of it. If you receive a notification like this, verifying the message's authenticity is crucial, as phishing attempts often masquerade as legitimate communications from your bank or credit card provider.

When you receive such alerts, take immediate action. Contact your financial institution directly through their official contact methods, such as their customer service number on the back of your card or via their secure website, rather than responding directly to the message or link in the email or text. The quicker you respond to these alerts, the more likely you are to prevent further unauthorized access. In some cases, financial institutions may even be able to freeze your accounts or initiate an investigation to secure your finances, preventing a thief from making further moves under your name.

Errors on your credit report or unfamiliar accounts listed can be another clear sign that you are a victim of identity theft. Your credit report provides a snapshot of your financial activities, including open credit accounts, payment history, and recent inquiries made by lenders or service providers. If you spot accounts you didn't open or information that doesn't seem to belong to you, it could indicate that someone has used your personal information to open new accounts, take out loans, or make purchases in your name. Errors can also appear if a fraudster changes your personal information—like your name, address, or employment details—to cover their tracks. Table 3.2 lists the signs of identity theft, providing key indicators to help recognize when personal information may be compromised.

The FCRA gives you the right to dispute any inaccuracies in your credit report. If unfamiliar accounts appear, it's essential to dispute them directly with the credit bureau and the company responsible for the fraudulent account. This process might take time, but it is necessary for restoring your credit history and ensuring no fraudulent activity remains on your record. In addition to disputing fraudulent accounts, consider placing a fraud alert or credit freeze on your credit report to help protect yourself from further harm.

One of the more unsettling signs of identity theft is receiving communications from debt collectors for debts you don't recognize. When a thief opens a line of credit in your name and fails to make payments, the account is often passed to collections. Initially, you may not notice the impact, but over time, collectors may begin to contact you regarding unpaid bills, often with aggressive tactics and threats of legal action. These communications can arrive via mail, phone, or email, and they can be especially disorienting when you've never opened the account or incurred the debt.

If you receive calls or letters from debt collectors regarding debts you don't recognize, it's important to remain calm and take immediate action. Do not provide personal information over the phone or email without verifying the debt collector's identity. Instead, ask for written verification of the debt and request details about the account in question. Once you have the information, you can dispute the debt with the collection agency and the original creditor. Ignoring such communications will only lead to further complications, including damage to your credit score, so addressing these issues promptly is key to mitigating long-term damage.

Table 3.2   Signs of identity theft.

Sign of identity theft	Example	What it means	What action to take
Unexplained charges	Charges on your credit card statement that you don't recognize	Someone may have used your card information fraudulently	Review statements, dispute charges with the bank, consider freezing your credit
New accounts you didn't open	An account you never applied for shows up on your credit report	A fraudulent account may have been opened in your name	Contact the creditor to dispute the account and report it to the credit bureaus
Misspelled name	Your name appears with a different spelling on certain accounts	A sign that someone may have intentionally altered your personal information to open accounts	Contact the credit bureaus to correct the information
Denied credit	You are denied credit or loans unexpectedly	Even though your credit history is strong, something could be wrong	Contact the lender to review your credit report for errors or fraud
Unfamiliar inquiries	There are inquiries from companies you don't recognize on your credit report	It could indicate someone trying to get credit in your name	Contact the company that made the inquiry and dispute it if unauthorized
Address change	You find an unfamiliar address listed on your credit report	It may indicate someone has redirected your mail to steal your personal information	File a fraud alert and contact your bank and the credit bureaus
Late payments for accounts you didn't open	Seeing late payments on accounts you didn't open indicates misuse of your credit	Someone may be making purchases and missing payments on your behalf	Dispute the late payments with the creditor and credit bureaus
Collections on unknown accounts	Receiving collection notices for accounts you never opened	Someone may have opened accounts in your name and not paid	Contact the collection agency to dispute the debt and contact the credit bureaus
Incorrect personal information	Errors in your personal data like your date of birth or Social Security number	It could suggest your information was altered to perpetrate fraud	Request corrections from the credit bureaus and review your report for suspicious activity
Credit limit changes	Noticing a sudden drop in your credit limit	It may be due to fraudulent activity on your account	Contact the creditor and review your credit history to identify the cause

Understanding Data Breaches

Data breaches occur when unauthorized individuals gain access to sensitive or confidential information. These breaches can happen in several ways, each presenting unique challenges to individuals and organizations. One of the most common methods is hacking, where cybercriminals exploit vulnerabilities in a company's digital infrastructure, often by leveraging sophisticated attack techniques such as phishing, ransomware, or software flaws. Hackers may breach a system by infiltrating unsecured networks, exploiting weak passwords, or bypassing outdated security protocols. Once inside, they can exfiltrate large amounts of data, often to be sold or used for malicious purposes.

Insider threats also contribute to data breaches, though this type of breach is typically less publicized. Employees, contractors, or business partners with legitimate access to company systems may intentionally or unintentionally leak data in these cases. Insider breaches can be particularly difficult to detect, as they often involve authorized users who exploit their access to cause harm. Negligence is another significant contributor to data breaches. Companies that fail to implement proper security controls or adhere to best practices, such as using outdated software, neglecting to encrypt sensitive data, or failing to secure backup systems, are more likely to experience breaches. In many cases, the cause of a breach is a combination of hacking, negligence, and insufficient internal controls, creating a perfect storm for data theft.

The data types most commonly targeted in breaches are personal, financial, and medical. Personal data, including names, addresses, email addresses, and Social Security numbers, is highly valuable to criminals because it can be used to commit identity theft, open new accounts, or carry out fraudulent activities. Financial data, such as credit card numbers, bank account details, and transaction histories, is sought after by hackers because it can be used to steal money or engage in fraudulent purchases. The consequences of financial data theft can be immediate and devastating, ranging from drained bank accounts to months of fighting fraudulent charges.

On the other hand, medical data has become an increasingly attractive target for cybercriminals in recent years. This information includes health records, insurance details, and other personal health information (PHI). Medical identity theft can have long-term consequences for individuals, as thieves can use stolen medical data to access healthcare services or obtain prescriptions. Moreover, medical data is often considered more valuable than financial data on the black market because it is harder to change or invalidate. For organizations that store sensitive medical data, such as hospitals or insurance companies, the breach of patient information can lead to significant reputational damage, regulatory fines, and legal consequences.

High-profile data breaches have garnered significant attention over the years, with some of the most notable examples including the breaches of Equifax, Target, and Marriott Hotels. The Equifax breach, for instance, exposed the personal data of over 147 million people, including Social Security numbers, birth dates, and addresses. The impact of this breach was far-reaching, as individuals affected by the breach faced the potential for identity theft and fraud. Similarly, the 2013 Target breach compromised the credit card information of more than 40 million customers, leading to widespread concerns about the security of retail transactions. The breach caused Target to lose millions of dollars in revenue and deal with costly legal settlements.

Marriott Hotels' breach, which exposed the personal and financial information of over 500 million customers, highlighted the vulnerabilities in the hospitality industry. In this case, hackers accessed the company's reservation database, which contained sensitive guest details such as passport numbers, dates of birth, and payment information. These high-profile breaches have shown consumers

---

Ask the AI

"How do hackers typically breach sensitive data in organizations?"
"What types of data are most commonly targeted in data breaches?"
"How does stolen data end up on the dark web?"

that even large, well-established companies are not immune to cyberattacks. The impact on consumers in the aftermath of such breaches can be profound, as affected individuals often must deal with the anxiety of potential identity theft, the inconvenience of credit freezes, and the costly process of restoring their financial security. These events also highlight the importance of individuals and businesses proactively safeguarding personal data.

Once data is stolen in a breach, it often ends up on the dark web, a hidden portion of the internet where illegal activities such as buying and selling stolen data occur. The lifecycle of stolen data typically begins with the hacker or malicious actor obtaining the data and packaging it for sale. Personal information, financial records, login credentials, and medical data are sold in bulk or piecemeal to the highest bidder on the dark web. These marketplaces operate much like any other online store, with sellers offering stolen data for specific prices, depending on the type of information and its perceived value.

Once the data is sold, it can be used for various malicious activities, including identity theft, financial fraud, and phishing scams. For example, stolen credit card numbers can be used to make unauthorized purchases, while social security numbers may be used to open new lines of credit. Additionally, cybercriminals may use the data to create synthetic identities by combining stolen personal information with fictitious data. The dark web is a thriving marketplace where the stolen data circulates, often for years, as criminals profit from it. For individuals whose data has been compromised, this is a sobering reality—stolen data can live on long after the breach, leading to ongoing risks of fraud and misuse.

Companies and organizations play a crucial role in protecting customer data from breaches. This responsibility goes beyond simply securing networks or installing firewalls; it involves creating a comprehensive security culture and implementing best practices across all levels of the organization. Data protection must be a priority in every department, from IT to human resources, and should be built into the infrastructure from the ground up. Companies must implement encryption technologies to protect data in transit and at rest, enforce secure authentication measures, and require MFA for sensitive transactions.

Regular employee training on data protection policies and security protocols is also essential. Insider threats, intentional or accidental, can be mitigated with proper training and clear guidelines for handling sensitive information. Additionally, companies should regularly perform vulnerability assessments, penetration testing, and audits to identify and proactively address weaknesses in their security posture. Ultimately, the responsibility for data protection lies with the company, and failing to invest in security measures can lead to severe consequences, including financial losses, legal action, and reputational damage. Organizations must view cybersecurity as a fundamental aspect of their business operations, not an afterthought.

Businesses have legal obligations to protect customer data and respond swiftly if a breach occurs. In many countries, laws and regulations require businesses to implement specific measures to secure personal data and provide consumers with clear notice in case of a breach. For example, the GDPR in the European Union mandates that companies notify affected individuals within 72 hours of discovering a data breach. In the United States, the CCPA and various state-level regulations require similar actions, including reporting breaches and offering identity theft protection services to affected individuals.

In addition to the requirement for notification, businesses may also be liable for the financial damage caused by a breach. If a company fails to comply with data protection regulations, it could face hefty fines and penalties, which can be particularly damaging for small and mid-sized businesses. Beyond the financial implications, the breach of consumer trust is often the most harmful consequence. Customers who believe their data is not properly protected may take their business elsewhere, losing revenue and market share. Thus, compliance with legal standards and the proactive protection of customer data are not just legal obligations—they are essential for maintaining customer loyalty and the organization's long-term success.

Preventing Identity Theft

Securing personal information is the cornerstone of preventing identity theft. The first step in protecting your data is understanding where it resides and who has access to it. Personal information exists in various formats, from physical paperwork to digital records, and each must be safeguarded accordingly. Always store sensitive documents, such as Social Security cards, passports, and financial records, in a secure location, like a locked drawer or a safe. Digitally, sensitive information should be encrypted whenever possible, whether stored on a personal device or in the cloud.

Another critical practice is minimizing the number of places where your personal information is stored. While storing your passwords, addresses, or credit card details across various accounts or apps might seem convenient, creating multiple data breach opportunities. Use services that allow for encrypted storage, such as a reputable cloud service with strong encryption protocols. Consider scanning important records into encrypted files for physical documents so they're only accessible to you. Regularly review who has access to your personal information, especially in shared digital spaces or with third-party services, and limit that access wherever possible.

The importance of using strong, unique passwords cannot be overstated when preventing identity theft. Weak or reused passwords are an open invitation to cybercriminals, who can easily exploit them using brute force attacks or credential stuffing. A strong password should be at least 12–16 characters long and include a mix of upper and lowercase letters, numbers, and special characters. More importantly, never reuse the same password across multiple sites, especially for sensitive accounts like banking, healthcare, or social media. Using the same password for various accounts creates a domino effect: once one account is compromised, all others with the same password are at risk.

To manage multiple strong passwords, consider using a password manager. A password manager securely stores your passwords and can generate complex, unique passwords for every account you create. Using a password manager eliminates the temptation to use easily guessed passwords or to write them down, which could be exposed to others. Many password managers also offer additional features, like two-factor authentication (2FA) or biometric login, which further enhance the security of your accounts. Choosing a password manager with a strong reputation and robust encryption standards is important, ensuring your data remains secure even if cybercriminals target the password manager itself.

Protecting sensitive documents is a multi-layered process that includes physical and digital safeguards. Physical documents, such as tax returns, insurance information, and bank statements, should be stored in a secure location, such as a locked drawer, filing cabinet, or safe. These physical storage solutions ensure that unauthorized individuals cannot easily access your sensitive information. Limiting the number of people accessing these documents is equally important,

Ask the AI

"What are the best practices for creating strong and secure passwords?"
"What are some effective ways to digitally and physically protect sensitive documents?"
"How can I regularly monitor my credit and financial accounts for signs of fraud?"

particularly in shared living or office environments. Furthermore, any physical documents no longer needed should be securely shredded to prevent them from falling into the wrong hands.

On the digital side, sensitive documents should be stored in encrypted files or folders on local devices and cloud storage platforms. Without encryption, even if hackers access your devices, they can easily read and misuse these files. For cloud storage, always choose a service that uses end-to-end encryption, ensuring your documents are unreadable even to the service provider. Backup copies of sensitive documents should also be encrypted and stored separately on an external hard drive or another secure cloud service. It's critical to regularly update the passwords protecting these accounts to ensure continued security.

Disposing of personal data and old devices securely is just as important as protecting your data while in use. When it comes to old devices—whether smartphones, computers, or external drives—simply deleting files or performing a factory reset is insufficient. Data can often be recovered from old devices through specialized software, even after deleted files. Instead, use data-wiping software to securely erase sensitive information on the device, ensuring it is completely unrecoverable. Many professional services also offer secure disposal options for electronics, where they physically destroy the storage devices to prevent any possibility of data recovery.

For documents, shredding is the safest option for disposal. Regular trash bins are easily accessible to identity thieves who might dig through discarded materials to find valuable personal information. Always shred paper documents containing personal data before disposal, including old tax returns, medical records, and financial statements. If digital documents are no longer needed, use file deletion programs that overwrite the file data several times to ensure it is unrecoverable. By taking the time to dispose of sensitive information securely, you eliminate a common vulnerability in the fight against identity theft. Table 3.3 details preventative measures against identity theft, offering strategies to protect personal information from being stolen.

In the digital age, sharing personal information has become routine through social media, online shopping, or business transactions. However, the convenience of sharing information online comes with a hidden cost: the potential for identity theft. To minimize this risk, be cautious about how much personal information you share and with whom. Avoid oversharing on social media platforms, as cybercriminals can use seemingly harmless information—like your birthdate, pet's name, or location—to crack passwords or answer security questions.

Always verify the legitimacy of websites or services before providing any personal information. Look for signs that a website is secure, such as a URL beginning with "https" and a padlock symbol in the address bar. If you must share sensitive data, ensure that it is necessary for the transaction and that the website is reputable. Additionally, avoid sharing personal information through unsecured channels, such as public Wi-Fi networks or over email. If unsure whether an email is legitimate, verify its source through official contact before responding or clicking any links.

Regularly monitoring your personal and financial accounts is one of the most effective ways to detect potential identity theft early. Set up alerts for unusual transactions or account activities, such as withdrawals or purchases exceeding a certain threshold. Many financial institutions offer free alerts, which can notify you via email or SMS when something unusual happens. Regularly review your bank and credit card statements and reports to ensure no unfamiliar charges or new accounts you did not authorize. If you notice anything suspicious, immediately contact your bank or credit card provider to freeze the account and begin the investigation process.

In addition to financial accounts, monitoring your online accounts for any signs of unauthorized access is essential. This includes checking social media accounts, email accounts, and other platforms where you store personal information. If you notice strange activity—such as posts you didn't make, messages you didn't send, or login attempts from unfamiliar locations—it could

Table 3.3 Preventative measures against identity theft.

Preventative measure	Description	Tools/resources	Action to take
Use strong unique passwords	Passwords should be long, complex, and different for each account	Password managers like LastPass and 1Password	Set up passwords of at least 12 characters with a mix of letters, numbers, and symbols
Enable multi-factor authentication (MFA)	MFA adds an extra layer of security beyond just a password	Authenticator apps like Google Authenticator and Duo security	Enable MFA on all accounts that support it, including banking, email, etc.
Monitor your credit	Regularly checking your credit report helps detect early signs of fraud	Credit monitoring services like Experian and TransUnion	Set up credit monitoring or regularly check your credit reports for any unauthorized activity
Use encryption for sensitive documents	Encrypting files ensures that they are protected from unauthorized access	Encryption tools like VeraCrypt and BitLocker	Encrypt sensitive personal data both digitally and physically on devices
Shred sensitive documents	Shredding documents with personal information reduces the risk of it being stolen	Paper shredders or shredding services	Shred old bills, tax documents, and papers containing sensitive data
Secure your devices	Ensuring your phone computer and tablets are safe from hackers	Antivirus software like Norton and McAfee	Use strong passwords to keep antivirus software up to date and install updates regularly
Dispose of old devices securely	Old devices may still contain personal information that could be stolen	Software tools for wiping devices like DBAN	Always wipe data or physically destroy old devices before discarding
Be cautious sharing personal information	Be mindful of sharing personal details over the phone online or in person	Data privacy guidelines	Don't share your Social Security number or account info unless absolutely necessary
Use firewalls and VPNs	Firewalls and VPNs help protect your internet connection from unauthorized access	VPN services like NordVPN and ExpressVPN	Use a VPN when connecting to public Wi-Fi and ensure your firewall is enabled
Secure your social media	Limit what you share on social media platforms to avoid oversharing	Social media privacy settings	Review privacy settings and avoid posting sensitive personal details like your full name, address, or phone number

indicate that someone has gained access to your account. Many social media platforms and email providers offer account security logs that let you track logins and activity. Make it a habit to regularly change your passwords and enable MFA whenever possible to add a layer of security.

Taking these proactive steps to prevent identity theft is crucial in today's interconnected world. Each measure—from using strong passwords to monitoring financial accounts—adds another layer of defense against those who seek to exploit your personal information for malicious gain.

By securing physical and digital data, being mindful of what you share online, and actively monitoring your accounts, you can significantly reduce the chances of falling victim to identity theft. While no approach can offer complete protection, a comprehensive strategy combining vigilance and strong security practices can make all the difference in safeguarding your digital life.

Responding to Identity Theft and Data Breaches

When you first discover that your identity has been compromised, acting quickly is crucial to minimize the damage. Your immediate steps can significantly impact how effectively you recover your identity and prevent further financial loss. Start by gathering all relevant information about the breach. This includes details about suspicious activities, such as unfamiliar transactions or accounts opened in your name. Document everything you know about the breach to help you identify patterns and provide proof when working with authorities or institutions.

Once you've gathered the necessary information, begin by securing your accounts. This typically involves changing passwords for any accounts that may have been compromised, especially financial accounts. If possible, enable MFA to add an extra layer of security. For accounts where you are unsure of the level of compromise, it's a good idea to lock or suspend them temporarily. Immediately contact your bank, credit card companies, and other financial institutions to alert them of the breach and ensure no further unauthorized transactions are processed. They will typically assist you in securing your accounts and may also issue temporary holds or new account numbers to protect your finances.

The next step is to assess whether any of your data has been exposed to a data breach. This might include checking if your Social Security number, bank account information, or other sensitive data has been exposed in high-profile breaches. Many organizations will notify you directly if your data has been compromised, but it's still important to check third-party breach notification services. Equifax, for instance, offers a tool that can show if your data has been affected by known breaches. The more proactive you are in gathering information, the better equipped you'll be to respond swiftly.

Once you've initiated securing your accounts, it's time to report the incident. The first report should be made to the Federal Trade Commission (FTC) if you are in the United States. The FTC operates the Identity Theft Report system, which helps victims track their recovery efforts and provides official documentation for dealing with creditors and institutions. For international victims, local consumer protection agencies can provide similar services. The FTC also works with other agencies, such as the FBI and law enforcement, to track identity theft and investigate large-scale criminal activity.

In addition to reporting to the FTC, you should notify the credit bureaus—Equifax, Experian, and TransUnion. These agencies can help place a fraud alert or even a credit freeze on your accounts, which prevents creditors from accessing your credit report without your consent. A fraud alert is free and informs creditors that they should take extra steps to verify their identity before extending credit. If you're concerned about ongoing threats to your financial well-being, you may want to place a credit freeze on your reports. This ensures that no one can access your credit report, even to open new lines of credit in your name.

Reporting to the credit bureaus also enables you to receive a free copy of your credit report. Under U.S. law, you are entitled to one annual free credit report from each major credit bureau. In the event of identity theft, however, the bureaus must provide additional reports and updates, allowing you to monitor fraudulent activity more closely. This information will be invaluable as you recover from identity theft, providing a snapshot of any unauthorized accounts or inquiries made in your name.

Freezing your credit is one of the most effective ways to protect your financial identity after a data breach or identity theft incident. A credit freeze restricts access to your credit report, making it impossible for potential creditors to open new accounts in your name. This means that if a thief attempts to open a credit account or take out a loan using your personal information, they will be unable to do so without your authorization. While it's a powerful tool, a credit freeze can only be applied to your credit reports. It does not stop thieves from using your existing accounts, so taking steps to secure your current accounts is essential.

Once your credit is frozen, you must unfreeze it to apply for new credit. Fortunately, credit freezes are temporary and can be lifted for a specific period if you need to access your credit reports for any reason. Freezing and unfreezing your credit is free and available to anyone affected by identity theft. In addition to freezing your credit, consider subscribing to a credit monitoring service, which can alert you to any changes or suspicious activity on your credit report. Credit monitoring services can track activity in real time, providing additional protection as you recover from identity theft.

Credit monitoring is often offered as a complimentary service by financial institutions or credit bureaus when a breach occurs. Many companies also offer enhanced services for a fee, providing more detailed reports and faster alerts. These services monitor your credit for new accounts, address changes, or significant financial transactions. If fraud is detected, the service will notify you and allow you to take immediate action to address the situation.

Working closely with your financial institutions is crucial when responding to identity theft. These institutions can help you immediately secure your accounts and minimize further damage. Start by reporting the fraudulent activity to your bank, credit card provider, and other financial institutions where accounts may have been opened or compromised. Banks and credit card companies can freeze or close affected accounts, issue new account numbers, and initiate investigations into unauthorized transactions.

Your financial institutions may also offer fraud protection services, including temporary holds on your accounts, automatic reversals of fraudulent transactions, and assistance recovering stolen funds. They may even reimburse you for unauthorized purchases from your credit or debit cards. However, it's essential to read and understand the terms and conditions of these protections, as they can vary significantly between institutions. You should also ask about setting up additional security measures for your accounts, such as stronger authentication methods or alerts for unusual activity.

Many financial institutions also offer identity theft protection services, which may include assistance with filing claims, monitoring your credit reports, and providing resources for recovery. Even if the institution does not offer these services directly, they can direct you to third-party services specializing in identity theft recovery. These services can be particularly valuable if you don't feel confident handling the recovery process on your own or if the scope of the breach is extensive.

In the aftermath of identity theft, many victims turn to identity theft protection and recovery services for help. These services are designed to assist with everything from monitoring your credit to guiding you through the complex recovery process. Identity theft protection services often include

---

Ask the AI

"What are the immediate steps to take if I discover my identity has been stolen?"
"What legal protections are available to victims of identity theft?"
"How do identity theft protection services work, and what should I look for when choosing one?"

credit monitoring, fraud alerts, and identity restoration assistance. Some services go a step further, offering insurance that can reimburse you for the costs associated with identity theft recovery, including legal fees, lost wages, and other expenses.

While identity theft protection services can be a helpful resource, it's important to understand that no service can prevent identity theft from happening. They can, however, make the recovery process easier by alerting you to suspicious activity and providing the support needed to resolve issues quickly. Some services even offer a dedicated case manager who will work with you to restore your identity, handle disputes, and provide step-by-step instructions on actions to take next. Suppose you're dealing with a significant breach, such as one involving your Social Security number or medical information. In that case, utilizing a professional service can help you manage the situation's complexity.

Review the offerings before subscribing to an identity theft protection service and ensure they meet your specific needs. Some services may offer more comprehensive monitoring, while others focus primarily on credit protection. The best service for you will depend on your level of exposure and the extent of the breach. In addition to identity theft protection, you may consider legal assistance, especially if the breach results in fraudulent charges or identity misrepresentation.

As a victim of identity theft, you have legal rights designed to help you recover from the damage. Under the FCRA, you can request free credit report copies and dispute any fraudulent charges or information. In addition, the ITADA allows victims to report identity theft to the FTC and take legal action against those who steal their personal information.

Many states also have consumer protection laws that provide further safeguards for victims of identity theft. These laws may include provisions for protecting personal data, the right to place fraud alerts or freezes on credit reports and assistance with restoring your credit and identity. You may also be entitled to compensation for financial losses from identity theft, although this typically requires legal action. In some cases, the perpetrator may be prosecuted under criminal law, though recovery of stolen funds can often be a lengthy and complicated process.

Victims of identity theft can also take advantage of various support resources, including advocacy organizations and government programs. The FTC offers resources for filing complaints and reporting identity theft, and many nonprofit organizations provide free counseling, legal advice, and other forms of assistance. Credit bureaus and banks must also provide resources for victims, including steps to take and points of contact for resolving issues. Although recovering from identity theft can be overwhelming, these resources can guide you through it and ensure you know your rights at every step.

Recommendations

1. **Act Quickly When Identity Theft Is Suspected:** If you believe your identity has been compromised, immediately secure your accounts. Change passwords, enable MFA, and contact financial institutions to freeze or secure accounts. Document the breach, including any unauthorized transactions or new accounts, to help authorities and institutions track the damage and begin their recovery processes.
2. **Report to the Appropriate Authorities:** Immediately report any identity theft incidents to the FTC or equivalent in your country. This creates an official record of the theft and allows you to start the recovery process. Follow up with credit bureaus to place fraud alerts or credit freezes, and report the incident to law enforcement if necessary, especially if the theft involves larger-scale financial crimes.

3. **Monitor Your Credit Reports Regularly:** Regularly check your credit reports with the three major credit bureaus: Equifax, Experian, and TransUnion. Take advantage of your right to free annual credit reports, and consider signing up for additional credit monitoring services to catch fraudulent activity early. Set up alerts with the credit bureaus for any changes or new accounts opened in your name.

4. **Freeze Your Credit to Prevent New Fraudulent Accounts:** Protect your financial identity by freezing your credit with all three major bureaus. A credit freeze makes it impossible for unauthorized individuals to open accounts or apply for loans using your information. Remember, you can temporarily unfreeze your credit if you need to access it for legitimate purposes, but the freeze will provide a strong layer of security for your identity.

5. **Work with Your Financial Institutions to Secure Your Accounts:** Contact your bank, credit card companies, and other financial institutions to alert them of the breach. Request new account numbers, change PINs, and implement additional security measures, such as stronger authentication processes. Review recent transactions closely and work with the institution to reverse unauthorized charges.

6. **Utilize Identity Theft Protection Services:** Consider subscribing to a reputable identity theft protection service that includes credit monitoring, fraud alerts, and identity recovery support. These services can help track suspicious activity and guide you through recovery, offering tools to restore your identity and even covering costs incurred from the theft.

7. **Secure Sensitive Personal Data in Both Digital and Physical Formats:** Ensure that personal information, both physical and digital, is kept in secure locations. Use a locked drawer or safe for physical documents; for digital files, use strong encryption. Regularly audit your digital devices and cloud accounts to ensure that sensitive data is not exposed to unauthorized access.

8. **Shred and Properly Dispose of Unneeded Documents:** Safeguard yourself from identity theft by properly disposing of old or unneeded personal documents. Use a paper shredder to destroy sensitive documents, including tax returns, medical records, and financial statements. Similarly, wipe hard drives or use data destruction software before discarding old devices or external storage media.

9. **Be Cautious When Sharing Personal Information Online:** Limit the personal information you share on social media and other online platforms. Avoid posting sensitive details, such as your full birthdate, home address, or financial information, which can be used to answer security questions or impersonate you. Use privacy settings to control who can see your posts, and be mindful of phishing scams designed to steal your personal information.

10. **Know Your Legal Rights and Resources:** Familiarize yourself with your legal rights as a victim of identity theft. Understand the laws that protect you, including the FCRA and the ITADA. Take advantage of free resources and support, such as credit bureaus' fraud assistance programs and government resources, to help you recover and ensure that your personal information is restored and protected.

Conclusion

As we navigate an increasingly digital world, the need for robust identity protection has never been more critical. Identity theft can strike anyone, regardless of how vigilant or tech-savvy they are. Every action, from online shopping to social media, leaves a digital footprint that malicious actors can exploit. While it's impossible to eliminate all risks, the steps outlined in this chapter provide a comprehensive framework for minimizing exposure and protecting your personal information. Understanding the mechanisms of identity theft and its warning signs gives you the tools to defend against this pervasive threat.

As emphasized throughout this chapter, prevention remains the most effective strategy for protecting your digital identity. Adopting best practices such as using strong passwords, encrypting sensitive data, and regularly monitoring your accounts reduces the chances of becoming a target. Additionally, vigilance is key—recognizing the early signs of identity theft, such as unfamiliar accounts or unexplained charges, allows you to take swift action before significant damage occurs. The more proactive you are, the harder it becomes for cybercriminals to succeed in stealing your identity.

However, even the most prepared individuals can find themselves victims of identity theft, and when it happens, a clear and swift response is crucial. Knowing the steps to take immediately—such as reporting the incident to authorities, freezing your credit, and using identity theft protection services—can significantly mitigate the consequences. Recovery from identity theft can be a lengthy and complicated process, but with the right actions, it is possible to regain control over your personal and financial security. This chapter has provided a roadmap for responding effectively to these crises, ensuring you can bounce back with minimal damage.

As the digital landscape continues to evolve, so will cybercriminals' tactics. The fight against identity theft is ongoing, and staying informed about emerging threats and evolving best practices is essential. Both individuals and organizations are responsible for safeguarding sensitive information, making cybersecurity an ever-important issue. By continuously refining your data protection strategies, you defend against identity theft and contribute to a safer, more secure digital environment for everyone.

Chapter Questions

1   What is the first step after discovering your identity has been stolen?
    A. Ignore the issue and wait for it to resolve
    B. Change your passwords and secure your accounts
    C. Wait for authorities to contact you
    D. Contact a lawyer immediately

2   Who should you report identity theft to immediately?
    A. Your local bank only
    B. The Federal Trade Commission (FTC)
    C. Your friends and family
    D. Your employer

3   What action should you take with the credit bureaus if your identity has been stolen?
    A. Request to close your credit accounts
    B. Place a fraud alert or freeze on your credit report
    C. Request to delete your credit history
    D. Ignore your credit report

4   What is the benefit of freezing your credit after identity theft?
    A. It prevents access to your credit report by unauthorized parties
    B. It improves your credit score

    C. It clears any fraudulent transactions from your history
    D. It allows creditors to process your loan faster

5 What should you do when you notice unfamiliar transactions on your financial accounts?
    A. Wait and see if the transactions are reversed automatically
    B. Contact your financial institutions immediately
    C. Ignore them until the next billing cycle
    D. Only report them to the police

6 How can multi-factor authentication help protect your accounts after identity theft?
    A. By making it harder for attackers to access your accounts
    B. By enabling automatic account recovery
    C. By providing access to all of your accounts simultaneously
    D. By increasing the time it takes to hack into accounts

7 What should you do with physical documents containing personal information?
    A. Store them in an unlocked drawer
    B. Shred or store them in a secure location
    C. Throw them away in the trash
    D. Leave them on your desk for easy access

8 Which of the following is a common consequence of identity theft?
    A. Immediate financial gain for the victim
    B. Fraudulent charges made in the victim's name
    C. Increased credit score
    D. Faster processing of loan applications

9 What is the purpose of credit monitoring services after identity theft?
    A. To report fraudulent activity to the police
    B. To alert you to any changes or suspicious activity on your credit report
    C. To help you improve your credit score
    D. To delete all your previous credit history

10 What is a fraud alert?
    A. A service that helps you dispute all charges
    B. A notification to creditors that they should take extra steps to verify your identity
    C. A feature that increases your credit score
    D. A program to monitor social media activity

11 What is a potential risk if you don't securely dispose of old devices?
    A. They might be recycled properly
    B. Hackers may retrieve personal information stored on them
    C. They may increase the value of your home
    D. They could become more useful to you over time

12 What can be included in an identity theft protection service?
   A. A new credit score
   B. A credit monitoring system and fraud alerts
   C. A lawyer to sue the thief
   D. Access to free loans

13 What should you do if you receive a suspicious email or phone call asking for personal information?
   A. Ignore the message and continue as usual
   B. Respond with the requested information immediately
   C. Report it to the appropriate authorities
   D. Click on any links provided to verify the request

14 How can a credit freeze help protect you?
   A. It prevents anyone from accessing your credit report to open new accounts
   B. It makes all of your previous loans disappear
   C. It removes any negative items from your credit report
   D. It improves your credit score

15 What legal action can be taken after identity theft has occurred?
   A. You can request to remove the incident from your credit report
   B. You can file a complaint with the FTC and report to law enforcement
   C. You can prevent the authorities from investigating
   D. You can erase the identity theft incident from public records

4

Protecting Your Accounts with Strong Passwords and MFA

Cybercriminals constantly evolve their methods, looking for weaknesses in account security to exploit. While still the most widely used form of authentication, passwords are often the weakest link in the security chain. Simple passwords or the reuse of credentials across multiple platforms make it all too easy for attackers to gain unauthorized access to sensitive accounts and data. As a result, robust password management and multi-factor authentication (MFA) have become essential components of any comprehensive cybersecurity strategy.

Passwords are no longer enough on their own. Even the most complex password can be compromised by cybercriminals using tools that exploit predictable patterns or known vulnerabilities. To combat this, many services now offer MFA, which adds an extra layer of protection by requiring users to provide something in addition to their password. This second form of authentication—whether a one-time code sent via SMS, an app-generated token, or biometric verification—dramatically reduces the chances of unauthorized access, even if a password is compromised. As such, implementing MFA alongside strong, unique passwords is one of the most effective ways to safeguard your digital accounts from cyber threats.

This chapter will guide you through the process of strengthening your account security, starting with the basics of password creation and management. You will learn what makes a password strong, why reusing passwords across multiple accounts poses a significant risk, and how to employ strategies to protect your credentials from being easily cracked by attackers. We will also explore the critical role of MFA, examining its different methods and explaining how to integrate them into your accounts to provide an additional, crucial layer of defense. By the end of this chapter, you will have the knowledge and tools necessary to protect your accounts with confidence. Figure 4.1 illustrates password security statistics, highlighting key data points and trends in password management practices.

The Importance of Strong Passwords

Weak passwords are a prime target for cybercriminals, serving as low-hanging fruit for attackers looking to exploit vulnerable systems. The simplest passwords are often the first to fall to brute-force or dictionary attacks, where hackers use automated tools to try combinations of common words, numbers, and phrases. For example, passwords like "password123" or "qwerty" are easily guessed and often fall within the first few attempts. These weak passwords allow attackers to quickly gain access to personal accounts, email systems, and corporate networks, where they can cause significant damage, steal sensitive data, or perform malicious actions. When we talk about password strength, we're not just referring to its length but also its complexity and unpredictability of the combinations.

Figure 4.1 Password security statistics.

Statistics on password-related breaches are staggering, underlining the widespread danger of weak credentials. According to recent reports, over 80% of data breaches are attributed to compromised passwords, making them a leading entry point for attackers. A study by Verizon highlighted that more than 60% of hacking-related incidents involve stolen or weak passwords. Furthermore, in 2023 alone, there were over 1 billion exposed password records from high-profile breaches. These numbers should send a clear message: password security is often the first defense in protecting your digital identity. Failure to maintain strong passwords can have cascading effects, from compromised social media accounts to financial theft.

One of the most common mistakes users make when creating passwords is relying on simple or easily guessable patterns. People tend to default to simple combinations like "123456," "qwerty," or their pet's name, making it easy for attackers to break into their accounts with little effort. Another mistake is using obvious substitutions, such as replacing the letter "o" with a zero, thinking this will provide additional security. In reality, these modifications are well-known to password-cracking tools, which use massive wordlists to test variations of popular phrases systematically. Using simple, predictable passwords is a security risk and a psychological bias: people often prioritize convenience over complexity, which hackers are quick to exploit (Table 4.1).

The issue of password reuse is another critical vulnerability that many individuals and organizations overlook. When a password is reused across multiple accounts, a breach of one system can give hackers access to others. For example, the damage is immediate and far-reaching if an attacker compromises a user's email password, which is used for banking, social media, and work accounts. Cybercriminals know that most users recycle their passwords for convenience, and they exploit this behavior by testing known passwords from one breach against a wide range of other sites and services. The risk of password reuse is compounded by the fact that many people use the same password across multiple accounts without realizing that the exposure of one system can have ripple effects across others.

Hackers employ various techniques to crack passwords, and as technology advances, so do their methods. Brute-force attacks are among the most straightforward approaches, where attackers try every possible combination of characters until they find a match. However, more sophisticated attacks like dictionary attacks and rainbow table attacks, have emerged. These methods leverage precomputed lists of common passwords or previously leaked datasets to guess passwords more efficiently. One increasingly common method is credential stuffing, where attackers use large volumes of stolen login credentials (often obtained from previous breaches) to attempt unauthorized access to unrelated services. This technique is effective because many people use the same or

Table 4.1 Common password mistakes and best practices.

Common mistake	Best practice	Why it's a risk	Suggested action
Using password123	Use a passphrase with at least 12 characters	Easily guessable by attackers	Create complex random passphrases
Reusing passwords across accounts	Use unique passwords for each account	One breach compromises all accounts	Use a password manager to store passwords
Using personal information	Avoid using names, birthdays, or pets names	Easy to guess or find through social media	Use random, unique combinations of letters
Not updating passwords regularly	Change passwords at least every 3–6 months	Attackers can exploit old credentials	Set up calendar reminders for regular updates
Writing down passwords on paper	Use password managers with encryption	Passwords can be lost or stolen	Invest in a reliable password manager
Sharing passwords insecurely	Use encrypted password sharing methods	Unprotected sharing can lead to leaks	Share passwords securely using password managers
Using simple patterns (e.g., qwerty)	Use a mix of uppercase, lowercase, numbers, and symbols	Simple patterns are vulnerable to brute-force attacks	Choose a diverse combination of characters
Ignoring password strength checker	Use a password strength checker to evaluate passwords	Weak passwords are often missed	Test passwords using strength checkers
Avoiding two-factor authentication (2FA)	Enable 2FA for critical accounts	Provides an additional layer of security	Implement 2FA on all sensitive accounts
Forgetting to log out from shared devices	Log out of accounts after use especially on public computers	Unauthorized access if session is left open	Use session timeouts or manual log out

similar passwords across multiple sites, making credential stuffing a highly efficient and damaging approach for attackers.

The evolution of password policies has seen significant changes as the understanding of digital security has grown. In the past, simple requirements like a minimum length or using at least one number were considered sufficient to protect users' accounts. However, in light of the rising sophistication of cyberattacks, password policies have become more stringent. Modern password guidelines recommend longer passphrases—typically 12 characters or more—incorporating a mix of upper- and lowercase letters, numbers, and special characters. These requirements make passwords harder to guess or crack using common techniques. In addition, security experts now advise against using personal information (e.g. names, birthdays) in passwords, as such details can be easily uncovered through social engineering or data mining.

Ask the AI

"What are the most common password mistakes that make accounts vulnerable?"
"Can you explain why password reuse is a major security risk?"
"How do brute-force attacks work, and how can I protect my passwords?"

A growing trend in password security is the shift towards MFA as a complementary security layer. While strong passwords remain essential, MFA significantly reduces the likelihood of unauthorized access even if a password is compromised. MFA requires users to verify their identity using something they know (a password), something they have (a smartphone app or hardware token), or something they are (biometric data like fingerprints or facial recognition). This two-step (or more) verification process makes it exponentially harder for attackers to breach an account, even with access to the password. As more organizations and platforms implement MFA, it's becoming an industry standard, and its adoption is strongly recommended for anyone concerned about digital safety.

Despite these advancements in password security, many users still resist implementing stronger password practices, either due to convenience or a lack of understanding. It's common to hear people express frustration at the complexity of modern password requirements. However, the reality is that these safeguards are necessary to mitigate risk in an increasingly hostile digital environment. To help manage the complexity, many users turn to password managers, which securely store and encrypt passwords for easy retrieval. By using a password manager, individuals can generate strong, unique passwords for each account without the burden of remembering them all. This enables users to follow best practices without sacrificing convenience, helping to close the gap between security needs and user behavior.

Creating and Managing Strong Passwords

A strong password is both a string of random characters and a carefully constructed combination that resists human guessing and machine-based cracking methods. The most important characteristics of a strong password are length and complexity. Experts recommend that passwords be at least 12 characters long, though longer ones are better. Passwords should incorporate a mix of upper- and lowercase letters, numbers, and special characters, making them more difficult for attackers to predict or crack using brute-force or dictionary attacks. The key is to create something that balances strength with memorability so that it's both secure and manageable in daily use.

Creating a memorable yet secure passphrase can be a challenge, but with the right approach, it's entirely possible. One effective strategy is to think of a phrase or sentence that's both meaningful and obscure. For example, instead of using a simple word like "apple," you might choose a more complex passphrase like "MightyEagleFliesHigh9!" This passphrase is long, complex, and unique, making it difficult to guess while still being something you can remember. You can also use random word combinations or a sentence from a favorite book or movie modified with numbers or symbols. The idea is to create something personal yet unpredictable, avoiding common patterns or phrases that hackers could easily guess.

Another essential guideline when crafting passwords is to avoid using personal information that can be easily discovered or guessed. While it may seem convenient to use a favorite pet's name, birthdate, or a family member's name, these are details that hackers can gather through social media or public databases. Social engineering tactics often exploit these data points to breach accounts. For instance, if your password is your child's name combined with a birth year, an attacker might already know that information from your social profiles, making your password vulnerable. The more abstract and unrelated your password is to personal information, the harder it will be for someone to crack it.

Using password generators and strength checkers can greatly improve the quality of your passwords. Password generators, which can create long, complex strings of random characters, are invaluable tools for ensuring that your passwords meet modern security standards. While these passwords are often difficult to remember, combining them with a password manager allows you to store and retrieve them securely. Many password managers also include built-in password strength checkers that evaluate the robustness of your passwords and suggest improvements. For example, they may flag weak passwords or advise you to add more complexity, such as by including a mix of special characters or avoiding dictionary words.

Regularly updating and changing passwords is a crucial habit for maintaining account security. Even the strongest passwords can be compromised over time, especially if they are exposed to a data breach. Changing your passwords periodically reduces the chances of a compromised password remaining in use for too long. While some organizations recommend changing passwords every 60 to 90 days, the most important factor is to update them whenever there is a known security risk or breach. Additionally, if you suspect an account has been compromised, changing the password immediately is the best way to mitigate potential damage.

Password storage and retrieval are often overlooked aspects of good password hygiene. If you're relying on a system of scribbling passwords on sticky notes or keeping them in an easily accessible file on your computer, you're making your accounts vulnerable. Instead, consider using a reputable password manager to store your passwords securely. These tools encrypt your password database, ensuring only you can access your stored credentials. For those who prefer an analog approach, storing passwords in a locked, secure location (such as a safe) is another viable option. However, digital solutions provide far more convenience and security. When using password managers, always remember to use a strong master password to protect access to the vault of credentials.

A key practice to consider is using MFA in combination with strong passwords. While a robust password is an excellent line of defense, MFA provides an added layer of protection that is much more difficult to bypass. With MFA, even if a password is compromised, an attacker still needs a second form of verification, such as a code sent to your phone or an authentication app. Many services now offer MFA by default, and it's highly recommended that this feature be enabled whenever possible. This added layer of security significantly reduces the risk of unauthorized access, making it much harder for hackers to penetrate your accounts, even if they manage to crack your password.

The management of strong passwords also involves practicing vigilance against common threats like phishing. Even the best password can become ineffective if handed over to an attacker through a well-crafted phishing email. Always be cautious about clicking links or downloading attachments from unknown sources, and avoid entering your passwords on websites unless you are certain they are legitimate. Using password managers with browser integration can help automatically fill in login credentials on trusted websites to reduce the risk of phishing. These tools can often detect fraudulent sites and prevent you from inadvertently providing your credentials to malicious actors.

Understanding MFA

MFA is an essential security measure that adds a critical layer of protection to your online accounts. Unlike traditional password-only authentication, which relies on something you know, MFA requires two or more verification factors before granting access. These factors typically fall into three categories: something you know (a password or PIN), something you have (a smartphone or security token), and something you are (biometric information like fingerprints or facial

---

Ask the AI

"What are some strong passphrases that combine letters, numbers, and symbols?"
"What are the risks of using personal information, like birthdates or names, in passwords?"
"Can password length make a password more secure? How does length impact security?"

recognition). The importance of MFA cannot be overstated, as it dramatically reduces the chances of unauthorized access. Even if an attacker compromises your password, they would still need the second (or third) factor to breach your account, making MFA an incredibly effective defense against many common attack methods, such as phishing and credential stuffing.

MFA comes in several forms, each providing a different level of security based on what is being used for verification. The most common type is SMS codes, where a user receives a one-time passcode via text message that must be entered alongside their password. While convenient, SMS-based MFA has some vulnerabilities, such as SIM swapping, where an attacker tricks a mobile carrier into transferring a victim's phone number to their device, allowing them to intercept the authentication code. A more secure alternative is using authenticator apps like Google Authenticator, Authy, or Microsoft Authenticator. These apps generate time-sensitive codes tied to the specific device and user account, making them more resistant to interception. Another option is hardware tokens, such as YubiKey or RSA SecurID, which generate or store cryptographic keys for authentication. These physical devices provide one of the most secure methods of MFA, as they require physical access to the token itself, making them harder to compromise remotely (Table 4.2).

The main strength of MFA is that it adds an extra layer of protection to an otherwise vulnerable system. A password, while necessary, is often insufficient on its own because it can be stolen, guessed, or exposed in a data breach. By requiring a second form of authentication, MFA ensures that even if an attacker has gained access to your password, they still cannot access your account without the second factor. For example, if an attacker successfully steals your password through a phishing attack, they would still need access to your phone (for an SMS code or authenticator app) or a physical token (like a USB security key). This greatly reduces the chances of a successful attack, especially on accounts with valuable or sensitive information. Adding biometric factors, such as fingerprint scans or facial recognition, further strengthens MFA by requiring something unique to the user, making it difficult for attackers to spoof.

Setting up MFA is relatively straightforward on most popular platforms and services, though the process can vary slightly depending on the provider. For example, Google and Facebook offer easy-to-follow instructions for enabling MFA on their accounts. To set up MFA on Google, users must log in to their Google account, navigate to the security settings, and enable two-factor authentication. After that, you can receive codes via the Google Authenticator app or a linked phone number. Similarly, on Facebook, users can enable two-factor authentication through their account

Table 4.2 Types of multi-factor authentication (MFA) and their security levels.

MFA method	Description	Security level	Pros	Cons
SMS-based authentication	Sends a one-time code to the user's mobile device via text message	Medium	Easy to implement	Susceptible to SIM swapping or interception
Authenticator apps	Generates time-based one-time passcodes on the user's device	High	More secure than SMS	Can be inconvenient if the phone is lost or not accessible
Hardware tokens	Physical device that generates or transmits a one-time passcode	Very high	Highly secure, requires no internet connection	Can be lost or stolen; may require extra hardware for every user
Biometric authentication	Uses unique biological features to verify identity	Very high	Convenient and difficult to replicate	Can be bypassed with advanced spoofing techniques

settings, with options to use an authenticator app or SMS. Many other services, including online banking and corporate platforms, have made setting up MFA even easier, offering step-by-step guides and in-app instructions. Once MFA is enabled, these platforms will typically prompt you for the second factor whenever you log in from a new device or after a period of inactivity, ensuring your account is protected against unauthorized access.

Despite its clear advantages, adopting MFA can sometimes present challenges for users. One common issue is the inconvenience of providing multiple forms of authentication each time you log in. For example, users may find it frustrating to enter an SMS code or use an authenticator app each time they access their account, especially if they are in a hurry. Another challenge is the loss or theft of the second factor, such as a lost phone or hardware token, which can lock users out of their accounts. However, most platforms offer recovery options, such as backup codes or alternate contact methods, to help users regain access. Additionally, some users may be hesitant to adopt MFA due to concerns about privacy or the complexity of managing multiple authentication methods. While these challenges are real, they are typically outweighed by the added security benefits of MFA, and the inconvenience can be minimized through good planning and the use of recovery options.

Balancing security with convenience is often delicate, and MFA is no exception. While MFA provides significantly enhanced security, it can also slow down the authentication process, which may feel burdensome for users who value speed and simplicity. However, many services have reduced this friction, offering options like "remember this device" to avoid repeated MFA prompts on trusted devices. Additionally, biometric factors such as fingerprint or facial recognition can speed up the process, offering convenience and security. For businesses, there is often a tradeoff between providing strong authentication and maintaining a user-friendly experience for employees or customers. However, with the increasing sophistication of cyberattacks, it's becoming clear that the security benefits of MFA far outweigh the minor inconvenience it may cause. In most cases, the added peace of mind from knowing your accounts are more secure is well worth the extra steps.

For organizations, MFA is a non-negotiable measure in the fight against cybercrime, especially when dealing with sensitive or proprietary information. Many industries have regulatory requirements mandating MFA, such as financial services and healthcare, where protecting customer data is paramount. MFA is a critical component of compliance with data protection standards like Health Insurance Portability and Accountability Act (HIPAA) and Payment Card Industry Data Security Standard (PCI-DSS) in such cases. Furthermore, MFA is not just for personal accounts; it is increasingly required to access corporate networks, internal systems, and cloud-based resources. For companies, rolling out MFA across all user accounts is essential to improving cybersecurity posture and reducing the risk of costly data breaches.

Advanced Account Security Measures

Biometric authentication methods, such as fingerprints and facial recognition, have become increasingly popular in recent years as they offer an additional layer of security while maintaining convenience. Unlike traditional passwords, which can be guessed, stolen, or cracked, biometric

Ask the AI

"How does multi-factor authentication add an extra layer of security to my accounts?"
"What are the different types of MFA, and how do they compare in terms of security?"
"Why is SMS-based MFA considered less secure than authenticator apps or hardware tokens?"

data is unique to the individual, making it significantly harder for attackers to replicate. Fingerprint recognition, which is commonly used in mobile devices, scans the unique patterns of ridges and valleys on a user's fingertip. Facial recognition, on the other hand, uses specialized algorithms to analyze facial features and match them against a pre-registered image. While no security system is completely foolproof, biometrics provide assurance that is difficult for hackers to bypass, especially when used with other forms of authentication like PINs or passwords. However, users should remain aware of potential vulnerabilities, such as spoofing or deepfake technology, and make sure that biometric data is stored securely within the device rather than uploaded to cloud servers, where it may be vulnerable to breaches (Table 4.3).

Security questions, often used as a fallback mechanism when users forget their passwords, are increasingly criticized for their lack of effectiveness in securing accounts. The problem with security questions is that social engineering can easily guess or find many answers. Questions like "What is your mother's maiden name?" or "What was your first pet?" often have readily available answers through social media profiles or public records. Hackers know this and can leverage this information to gain access to sensitive accounts. To mitigate this risk, it's recommended to use obscure answers that are not easily discoverable or, if the service allows, to treat the answers as additional passwords using a random string of characters. Some platforms have started offering MFA as a backup to security questions, significantly reducing the risks posed by relying on them.

Phishing attacks remain one of the most effective tactics for stealing account credentials, including MFA tokens. Attackers often target users by sending fake messages that appear to be from legitimate sources, such as banks, email providers, or social media platforms, to steal login credentials or trick users into revealing their authentication codes. Phishing attempts targeting MFA can be especially dangerous, as attackers may attempt to spoof the MFA code delivery method by posing as your phone carrier or a service provider. For example, an attacker might send a text message or email claiming they need to "verify your account" or "reset your MFA settings" and prompt you to enter your authentication code. Once they have your code, they can access your accounts. To avoid such scams, it's important to remain skeptical of unsolicited messages that ask

Table 4.3 Advanced account security measures.

Security measure	Description	Security level	Pros	Cons
Biometric authentication	Uses physical characteristics to authenticate	Very high	Difficult to replicate or steal	Can be bypassed with spoofing or advanced methods
Account recovery options	Methods to regain access to accounts if login credentials are lost	Medium to high	Allows users to recover accounts easily	Can be vulnerable to social engineering or hijacking
Session timeouts	Logs out inactive users after a certain period	Medium	Prevents unauthorized access on unattended devices	Can be inconvenient for users who need to stay logged in
Account activity monitoring	Monitoring and alerting for suspicious login attempts or changes	High	Helps detect unauthorized access early	Can generate false positives if not configured correctly
Deactivation of unused accounts	Disabling accounts that are no longer needed or are inactive	High	Reduces the attack surface and potential entry points	Requires regular review and maintenance

you to take immediate action. Always verify the message's legitimacy by contacting the organization directly through trusted channels, and never share your MFA code with anyone.

Account recovery options are vital to account security but can also serve as an attack vector if not properly secured. These recovery mechanisms, such as backup email addresses, phone numbers, or security questions, help users regain access to their accounts if they forget their passwords or lose their MFA device. However, if an attacker gains access to your recovery email or phone number, they could bypass traditional security measures. Therefore, securing recovery options is as important as securing the primary account. One step is to ensure that recovery methods, like email or phone numbers, are protected with strong, unique passwords and MFA. Additionally, consider using a recovery email address separate from your main account, with its strong security practices in place. Regularly review and update your recovery options to ensure they remain secure and up to date.

Monitoring account activity and setting up alerts is essential for identifying potential unauthorized access or suspicious behavior early. Many services offer account activity logs and alert systems that notify you of login attempts, password changes, or access from unfamiliar devices or locations. For example, Google and Facebook allow you to view recent sign-ins and set up email or SMS alerts when suspicious activity is detected. By enabling these features, you can quickly react to unusual behavior, such as logins from an unfamiliar geographic region or attempts to change your account settings. Reviewing your account activity periodically and proactively responding to alerts is a good idea. Even small discrepancies, like a password reset request you did not initiate, should prompt you to change your password immediately and investigate further. These proactive measures can help mitigate the damage from a potential account compromise before it escalates.

Deactivating or deleting unused or compromised accounts is another key step in minimizing your digital footprint and protecting your overall security. Many users forget about old accounts they no longer use, leaving them vulnerable to attacks. Hackers often exploit unused or abandoned accounts, knowing they are less likely to be actively monitored by the account owner. If you have accounts that you no longer need or use, take the time to deactivate or permanently delete them. This may include old email addresses, social media profiles, or accounts on third-party services. For accounts that are compromised, the risk is even higher, and you should take immediate action to secure them by changing passwords, enabling MFA, and contacting the service provider for assistance. Remember, any account you don't actively use still represents an entry point for attackers, so regular account audits should be part of your ongoing cybersecurity routine.

Protecting Business and Shared Accounts

Securing work-related accounts is critical for protecting sensitive organizational data and maintaining the integrity of business operations. In a business environment, compromised accounts can lead to a cascade of security breaches, including data theft, intellectual property loss, or exposure to confidential client information. Cybercriminals often target employees with access to

Ask the AI

"What are some advanced methods for securing an account beyond using strong passwords and MFA?"

"How does biometric authentication, like fingerprint scanning, work in securing accounts?"

"Why is monitoring account activity critical in identifying potential unauthorized access?"

high-value accounts, such as those holding financial records or proprietary software, knowing that their credentials can provide access to valuable resources. Beyond individual accounts, a breach in shared business accounts—whether for cloud storage, project management tools, or financial platforms—can disrupt entire teams and cause widespread damage. Ensuring that work-related accounts are properly secured with strong passwords, MFA, and other protective measures is essential to minimizing risk and safeguarding business assets and reputation.

Implementing MFA in professional settings is one of the most effective ways to bolster account security. Many businesses now require MFA for employees accessing internal systems or cloud-based services, particularly for high-risk or sensitive activities. MFA adds an extra layer of protection by requiring users to provide more than just a password to access their accounts. In professional settings, this often involves something the user knows (a password), something the user has (a smartphone or hardware token), or something the user is (a fingerprint or facial recognition). With MFA, even if an attacker successfully acquires an employee's password through phishing or other means, they would still be unable to access the account without the second factor. It's also worth noting that MFA solutions should be selected based on the needs of the business and the specific risks it faces. For example, businesses handling sensitive financial data may prefer hardware tokens or biometric verification for their highest-level accounts. In contrast, others may opt for more convenient methods like app-based authentication.

Role-based access control (RBAC) and permissions management are key in minimizing the potential impact of a compromised account within a business. RBAC restricts system access to authorized users based on their organizational role, ensuring that employees can only access the necessary resources. This principle of least privilege is foundational to account security in business settings, as it reduces the attack surface and limits the potential damage an attacker can cause. For example, a marketing employee may need access to customer-facing systems but should not be granted access to sensitive financial records or proprietary development tools. Businesses can ensure that only the right people can access critical systems by managing permissions carefully and regularly reviewing who has access to what. When an employee's role changes or they leave the company, their access rights should be updated or revoked to prevent unauthorized access to business resources.

When credentials must be shared within an organization, secure practices are necessary to protect them from falling into the wrong hands. It is common for businesses to require the sharing of credentials for accessing shared accounts, such as project management tools, cloud storage services, or databases. However, sharing credentials via insecure channels like email or text messages can expose sensitive information to interception. Instead, organizations should adopt secure methods for credential sharing, such as using a password manager with encrypted storage and sharing features. This way, employees can securely share access without exposing passwords in plain text. Additionally, businesses should discourage writing down or storing passwords in unsecured locations, such as sticky notes or spreadsheets. When credentials are shared, it's essential to limit the number of people accessing them and monitor usage to detect suspicious activity promptly.

Ask the AI

"What steps should I take to secure work-related accounts and ensure they aren't vulnerable to attacks?"
"How can businesses use MFA to strengthen security for team members working remotely?"
"How do employee training programs on account security reduce organizational risk?"

Establishing clear and robust account creation, usage, and termination policies is critical to business cybersecurity. These policies should define who is authorized to create accounts, under what conditions accounts should be provisioned or revoked, and how credentials should be managed throughout the employee lifecycle. For instance, when an employee joins the company, they should be assigned an account with the appropriate level of access based on their role, and their credentials should be configured according to company security standards. Similarly, when employees leave the organization or change roles, their access rights should be promptly revoked to prevent them from retaining access to business systems. Account termination should also involve securely archiving any data they may have worked on and ensuring no sensitive information is exposed. Regular audits of user accounts and access rights are necessary to ensure compliance with these policies and to detect any anomalies. This proactive approach to account lifecycle management helps prevent security gaps that malicious actors could exploit.

Training and educating team members on account security is one of the most effective ways to mitigate the risk of human error leading to security breaches. Employees should be well-versed in the principles of secure account management, including how to create strong passwords, recognize phishing attempts, and why MFA is essential. Regular cybersecurity awareness training is vital, particularly in industries that deal with sensitive or regulated data, where the consequences of a breach can be significant. Additionally, businesses should educate employees on the importance of account hygiene, such as not reusing passwords across multiple platforms and not sharing credentials without using secure methods. Encouraging a security culture within the organization ensures that all team members are aligned to protect company resources and sensitive data. Security awareness training should be continuous, with employees revisiting best practices periodically to stay updated on emerging threats and technologies.

In shared business accounts, security best practices extend to internal communication and collaboration tools. For example, platforms like Slack, Microsoft Teams, and Zoom are commonly used for team communication; securing these tools is essential. Businesses should enable MFA for these services and ensure employees use strong, unique passwords for each platform. Additionally, organizations should restrict access to sensitive information by using appropriate encryption settings and sharing permissions within these platforms. Any file sharing, document collaboration, or discussion involving confidential information should be carried out to ensure the information is only accessible to those who need it. By securing communication and collaboration tools alongside traditional accounts, businesses can reduce the risk of data leakage or unauthorized access.

Recommendations

1. **Prioritize MFA:** Implement MFA across all business accounts to ensure that even if an attacker obtains a password, they cannot gain access without the second factor. Start by enabling MFA on critical accounts such as email, cloud storage, and banking systems. Gradually expand this requirement to all accounts with sensitive data or privileged access.
2. **Adopt RBAC:** Implement RBAC to ensure employees can only access the resources necessary for their job functions. Regularly review and update roles to ensure that users do not retain unnecessary permissions. This minimizes the risk of an insider threat or accidental data exposure.
3. **Use Secure Credential Sharing Methods:** Avoid sharing passwords via unsecured channels like email or messaging apps. Instead, password managers should be implemented to share credentials between team members securely. These tools provide encryption and ensure passwords are only accessible to authorized personnel.

4. **Develop and Enforce Account Lifecycle Policies:** Create clear account creation, usage, and termination policies. Ensure that accounts are provisioned with the correct permissions at onboarding and promptly deactivated when employees leave or change roles. Regular audits should be conducted to ensure compliance with these policies.

5. **Train Employees on Cybersecurity Best Practices:** Regularly train employees on secure account practices, such as recognizing phishing attempts and creating strong passwords. Emphasize the importance of MFA and secure credential management. Create a culture of security awareness so that every team member contributes to safeguarding company resources.

6. **Monitor Account Activity Proactively:** Enable activity monitoring for all critical accounts to detect suspicious or unauthorized behavior. Set up alerts for activities like login attempts from unfamiliar devices, password changes, or access from unusual locations. Regularly review logs to identify potential threats early.

7. **Secure Account Recovery Options:** Secure recovery options include backup emails, phone numbers, and security questions with strong passwords and MFA. Avoid using common or easily guessed answers to security questions, and ensure recovery processes are managed through secure channels.

8. **Regularly Review and Update Permissions:** Perform user permissions reviews to ensure access rights align with employees' current roles. When employees change departments or roles, their access should be adjusted accordingly. Remove access to any resources no longer needed to prevent unnecessary exposure.

9. **Establish a Clear Account Deactivation Process:** Set up a standardized procedure for deactivating or deleting unused or compromised accounts. Ensure that access to business-critical systems is revoked immediately when an employee leaves the organization or an account is no longer needed. This helps to reduce the potential for unauthorized access.

10. **Secure Communication and Collaboration Tools:** Ensure that communication platforms such as Slack, Microsoft Teams, and Zoom are secured with MFA and that sensitive information is only shared with the right people. Use encryption and carefully manage user access to protect confidential business data during digital collaboration.

Conclusion

As we conclude this chapter on protecting your accounts, it's important to remember that securing your digital life is not a one-time effort but an ongoing commitment. Cyber threats are constantly evolving, and so should your approach to account security. While strong passwords and MFA significantly reduce the chances of unauthorized access, they are part of a broader security strategy that should be continuously reviewed and updated. Regularly updating your passwords, enabling MFA on every critical account, and being vigilant for signs of suspicious activity are essential practices in today's interconnected world.

The key takeaway from this chapter is that security is about layers. Combining a strong password policy with MFA adds multiple barriers that cybercriminals must overcome to access your accounts. Each layer, whether using a password manager, adopting biometrics for authentication, or monitoring your accounts for unusual activity, contributes to a defense-in-depth strategy that strengthens your overall security posture. While no system can be 100% secure, the more layers you implement, the harder it becomes for attackers to succeed.

For businesses, securing shared and role-based accounts is just as critical as protecting individual accounts. Access control policies, secure credential management, and continuous staff training are all key factors in reducing organizational risk. This chapter has provided actionable guidance to implement these security measures effectively, ensuring that personal and business accounts are shielded from unauthorized access. By incorporating these practices into your daily routine and organizational protocols, you are taking a proactive stance toward safeguarding your sensitive information.

Finally, it's crucial to recognize that cybersecurity is an evolving field, and staying informed about new threats and defensive techniques is vital to maintaining strong security. Technologies such as MFA and biometric authentication are only the beginning of what's possible to protect digital identities. As we move forward, continue to educate yourself on the latest security practices, embrace new technologies as they emerge, and always remain cautious of the risks posed by cybercriminals. By implementing and regularly reviewing strong passwords and MFA, you lay the foundation for a secure digital future, no matter how the landscape changes.

Chapter Questions

1   What is the most effective method for improving the security of business accounts?
    A. Use weak passwords to simplify login
    B. Implement multi-factor authentication (MFA)
    C. Limit the number of accounts used
    D. Disable all account recovery options

2   What does role-based access control (RBAC) help ensure in a business setting?
    A. Only the IT department has access to critical systems
    B. Employees can only access resources necessary for their job
    C. All users have the same level of access to all systems
    D. Employees do not need to sign into systems

3   Which of the following is the most secure method for sharing credentials within a business?
    A. Sending passwords via email
    B. Sharing passwords on sticky notes
    C. Using a password manager with encrypted sharing
    D. Asking employees to memorize passwords

4   What should businesses do when an employee leaves or changes roles?
    A. Leave their accounts as is
    B. Revoke their access and update permissions immediately
    C. Continue to allow them access for a month
    D. Set up a new account for them in their new role

5   Why is monitoring account activity essential for business security?
    A. It allows businesses to track employee productivity
    B. It helps detect unauthorized or suspicious behavior early
    C. It reduces the need for password changes
    D. It improves system performance

6 How should businesses handle recovery options like backup emails and phone numbers?
   A. Allow users to use any easy-to-guess information
   B. Protect them with strong passwords and MFA
   C. Avoid setting up any recovery options
   D. Disable them entirely for security reasons

7 What is the main purpose of having clear policies for account creation, usage, and termination?
   A. To ensure employees know when they need to log in
   B. To protect the company from unauthorized access and ensure consistent security practices
   C. To speed up the account creation process
   D. To make it easier to share passwords

8 Why is training employees on cybersecurity best practices important?
   A. It makes employees aware of the latest software updates
   B. It reduces the chances of human error leading to security breaches
   C. It helps employees use more social media
   D. It increases employee productivity

9 What is the risk of leaving unused or compromised accounts active in a business?
   A. It reduces the total number of accounts to manage
   B. It exposes the business to potential unauthorized access
   C. It improves business continuity
   D. It simplifies password management

10 How can businesses ensure secure communication and collaboration on digital platforms?
   A. Avoid using any form of encryption
   B. Restrict the use of these platforms altogether
   C. Implement MFA and control who can access sensitive information
   D. Allow employees to share information freely

11 What should businesses do if they notice suspicious behavior in account activity?
   A. Ignore it, as it may be a false alarm
   B. Investigate it immediately and take action to secure the account
   C. Allow the employee to continue using the account
   D. Increase the password length

12 What is the benefit of using a password manager for businesses?
   A. It helps employees remember passwords without any other security measures
   B. It securely stores and shares passwords with encryption, reducing the risk of exposure
   C. It eliminates the need for any password policies
   D. It tracks the time employees spend on passwords

13 What is the purpose of regularly reviewing and updating permissions in a business?
   A. To ensure that employees can access all systems at all times
   B. To maintain the principle of least privilege, ensuring employees only have the necessary access
   C. To make the login process quicker
   D. To allow for more flexible security policies

14 How can businesses handle account deactivation for employees who leave?
  A. Wait until the employee requests deactivation
  B. Immediately revoke all access and properly archive data
  C. Deactivate their account after 30 days
  D. Let the employee manage their account until it is no longer needed

15 What is the primary purpose of setting up account alerts for unusual activity?
  A. To track employee work hours
  B. To identify potential security threats as soon as they occur
  C. To increase system performance
  D. To monitor software bugs

5

Email Security Best Practices

Email has become one of the most ubiquitous forms of personal and professional communication. However, its convenience has also made it a prime target for cybercriminals looking to exploit unsuspecting users. Cybersecurity experts agree that email is one of the most common attack vectors for various threats, including phishing, malware, and business email compromise (BEC). Given the sensitive nature of many communications conducted over email, it is crucial to understand the potential risks and how to mitigate them effectively.

As an essential tool for business, education, and personal communication, email is often the first defense against identity theft, financial fraud, and data breaches. Attackers use various techniques to compromise email security, from impersonation and phishing attacks to malware distribution and credential theft. It's important to realize that securing your email account isn't just about using a strong password—there are multiple layers of protection you must consider. Understanding these risks and taking proactive measures can significantly reduce your vulnerability and safeguard your digital life.

This chapter will explore the best practices for securing your email accounts and recognizing common threats. We will dive into the different types of email-based attacks that cybercriminals use, including phishing, spear phishing, and whaling. Additionally, you will learn how to spot suspicious links, attachments, and other red flags that indicate a potential security breach. By becoming familiar with the tactics used by attackers and implementing simple but effective security measures, you will be better equipped to prevent email-related attacks from affecting you or your organization.

Email security isn't just about avoiding malware or phishing emails; it is also about adopting safe habits, understanding security features like multi-factor authentication (MFA), and recognizing the human element in security. Often, employees and users unknowingly open the door to threats through their behavior—clicking on suspicious links, sharing sensitive information, or falling for social engineering tactics. This chapter aims to empower you with the knowledge and tools to recognize threats, adopt secure practices, and effectively manage your email security. Whether securing a personal inbox or implementing organizational email security policies, this guide will provide you with the foundational practices needed to defend against the evolving landscape of email-based threats.

By the end of this chapter, you will have a solid understanding of how to protect your email accounts, identify potential attacks, and foster a culture of security awareness. Through careful planning, consistent vigilance, and using available security tools, you can significantly reduce the chances of becoming a victim of email-based cybercrime. Email security is a critical skill for all digital users, and mastering it will enhance your overall digital safety. With these best practices, you can confidently navigate your email inbox and communicate securely in today's digital landscape.

Understanding Email Threats

Email is an essential communication tool in both personal and professional settings, but it also serves as a prime target for malicious actors looking to exploit unsuspecting users. Understanding the various threats associated with email is critical to building a solid defense against cyberattacks. One of the most common email-based threats is phishing, which involves deceptive messages that trick recipients into divulging sensitive information such as usernames, passwords, or financial details. These phishing emails often appear legitimate, mimicking trusted entities such as banks, online retailers, or colleagues, leading recipients to click on malicious links or open dangerous attachments. Spear phishing and whaling are more targeted variations of this tactic, where attackers customize their messages to specific individuals or high-level executives, increasing the likelihood of success. In these cases, attackers often research their targets to create highly convincing emails, leveraging personal details or corporate knowledge to establish trust. Table 5.1 lists common email-based attacks and their characteristics, providing insights into the tactics used by cybercriminals.

Another prevalent risk associated with email is malicious attachments and links. Once an unsuspecting user opens an attachment or clicks on a link, malware can be downloaded onto the system, resulting in various potential security breaches. These attachments often appear harmless, such as PDF documents, Word files, or invoices, but they are laced with harmful code that, when executed, can compromise the user's machine. The links in phishing emails can lead to fake websites that resemble legitimate sites, capturing sensitive information like login credentials or triggering the automatic download of harmful software onto the device. In more sophisticated attacks, these links may even redirect the victim to an encrypted site, making it difficult for traditional security systems to detect the threat until it's too late.

Email spoofing and impersonation are also tactics commonly used in email attacks. Spoofing refers to the technique of forging the sender's address to appear as though the email is coming from a trusted source, such as a colleague or well-known brand. This increases the likelihood that the recipient will open the email and act on its contents without suspicion. Conversely, impersonation may involve copying the style, tone, and formatting of legitimate emails from reputable sources to convince the recipient that the message is authentic. These methods exploit trust and the assumption that email communication is generally reliable, making it even more challenging for users to discern legitimate emails from fraudulent ones. While these attacks may not necessarily involve malware, they can manipulate the recipient into transferring funds, sharing personal data, or engaging in risky behaviors compromising security.

While often viewed as a nuisance, spam emails can also play a significant role in spreading malware. These unsolicited messages may contain malicious links or attachments that lead to security compromises if clicked or downloaded. Often, spam messages are part of larger botnet operations where massive volumes of email are sent out to catch a small percentage of recipients. In addition to spreading malware, spam emails can serve as a vehicle for launching other attacks, including distributed denial of service (DDoS) attacks, by utilizing infected devices to flood systems with traffic. While spam filters effectively reduce the volume of unwanted emails, relying solely on them is insufficient for comprehensive email security. Users must be vigilant about the contents of any unsolicited message and avoid clicking on links or opening attachments unless the source is confirmed.

Table 5.1 Common email-based attacks and their characteristics.

Attack type	Description	Target	Common tactics	Indicators
Phishing	Mass phishing attacks designed to trick individuals into giving up personal information or clicking malicious links	General public	Generic emails, urgent tone, links to fake websites	Unsolicited emails, suspicious URLs
Spear phishing	Highly targeted attack aimed at specific individuals often using personalized information	High-value individuals	Personalized emails, fake website URLs, requests for sensitive info	Personalized subject lines, relevant to victim's life
Whaling	A type of spear phishing aimed at high-level executives or decision-makers	Executives and decision-makers	Impersonation of trusted sources, requests for wire transfers	Urgent financial requests, CEO impersonation
Business email compromise	A scam where attackers impersonate a business executive to request wire transfers or sensitive data	Businesses, especially finance departments	Impersonation of CEO, email addresses slightly altered, urgent wire transfer requests	Emails from suspicious addresses, slight misspellings
Malware delivery	Emails designed to deliver malware when attachments are opened or links are clicked	General public and businesses	Email with infected attachments or links to malicious websites	Unexpected attachments or links, suspicious sender's address
Ransomware phishing	Phishing emails that deliver ransomware once an attachment is opened	General public and businesses	Infected attachments such as Word documents or PDFs, fake invoices	Unexpected attachments, misleading subject lines
Impersonation or spoofing	Emails that appear to come from a legitimate source but are actually from an attacker	General public and businesses	Email addresses that closely resemble legitimate ones	Minor discrepancies in the sender's email address
Spam	Unsolicited bulk emails often used for marketing or spreading malware	General public	Large volume of unsolicited email often advertising or suspicious links	Emails with excessive ads or irrelevant content
Clone phishing	A legitimate email that has been copied and altered to include a malicious link or attachment	Targeted individuals	Copy of a previous legitimate email with an altered link or attachment	Email looks familiar but has a suspicious link
Social engineering via email	Emails designed to manipulate the recipient into taking action such as clicking a link or giving sensitive information	General public and businesses	Requests for sensitive info, fake customer service emails	Requests for urgent action or personal info

Business email compromise (BEC) is another serious email-related threat that targets organizations of all sizes but is particularly dangerous for larger companies. BEC scams typically involve attackers impersonating executives or employees to deceive other staff members into transferring money or sensitive information. In these schemes, attackers may spend weeks or months monitoring email communications to learn the usual patterns of interaction and then craft emails that appear to be from an authorized figure within the company. These emails often urge the recipient to act quickly, creating a sense of urgency that leads to poor decision-making. BEC attacks can be incredibly costly, with losses often amounting to millions of dollars, and they require a concerted effort to prevent and recover from once they occur.

The human factor plays a critical role in email vulnerabilities. Despite the growing sophistication of email security technologies, human error remains among the most common reasons for successful email attacks. Users may fail to recognize phishing attempts or may be overly trusting of emails that appear to come from familiar sources. Employees may also use weak passwords or reuse credentials across multiple sites, making it easier for attackers to access corporate systems if they successfully infiltrate an email account. Furthermore, social engineering techniques often exploit psychological factors, such as fear, urgency, or greed, to manipulate individuals into rash decisions. This underscores the importance of user education and awareness as a cornerstone of any effective email security strategy.

Organizations and individuals must adopt a multi-layered defense approach to mitigate the risks associated with email threats. This includes utilizing advanced email filtering systems to block known malicious content and training users to recognize the signs of phishing and other email-based threats. Strong authentication methods, such as MFA, should be employed to protect sensitive accounts, and regular security updates must be applied to all email-related software. Organizations should also implement email encryption to safeguard the confidentiality of sensitive information transmitted via email. By fostering a culture of vigilance and regularly updating security protocols, it is possible to significantly reduce the risk of falling victim to email-based cyber threats.

Recognizing and Avoiding Phishing Attempts

Phishing remains one of the most common and effective tactics cybercriminals use to deceive individuals into providing sensitive information, often with dire consequences. Recognizing the signs of phishing emails is the first line of defense in avoiding these attacks. Phishing emails typically contain a sense of urgency or pressure, urging the recipient to act quickly to avoid a penalty, secure a limited offer, or respond to a "critical" issue. These emails may ask the user to click on a link, open an attachment, or provide personal details such as passwords or credit card numbers. The language often plays on fear, greed, or curiosity—triggers that attackers rely on to prompt quick, unthinking actions. The urgency conveyed in the message is a common tactic, so if the request feels

---

Ask the AI

"What are some examples of phishing email subject lines designed to create a sense of urgency?"

"What is the difference between phishing, spear phishing, and whaling, and how can they be detected?"

"How do email spoofing and impersonation work, and what are the best ways to protect against them?"

Table 5.2 Recognizing phishing email indicators.

Phishing indicator	Description	Example
Suspicious sender email	The sender's email address may look suspicious or slightly altered from the legitimate one	name@paypa1.com instead of name@paypal.com
Generic greeting	Phishing emails often use a generic greeting such as Dear Customer instead of using your name	Dear Customer, Your account has been compromised
Urgency and threats	Phishing emails create a sense of urgency or threaten negative consequences to compel action	Your account will be locked if you do not respond within 24 hours
Suspicious links	Links that direct you to unknown or fraudulent websites often disguised to look legitimate	Click here to reset your password www paypa1.com
Unexpected attachments	Phishing emails often include attachments that you did not expect or that seem irrelevant to the conversation	Attached Invoice 12345 pdf
Spelling and grammar errors	Phishing emails often contain noticeable spelling or grammatical mistakes	Your account is locked, please verify your email address
Too good to be true offers	Phishing emails may offer something too good to be true such as large sums of money or prizes	You have won a 1000 gift card. Click here to claim it
Unusual language or requests	Phishing emails often ask for sensitive information that would not normally be requested via email	Please send us your full SSN to verify your account
Uncommon domains	Phishing emails may come from domains that do not belong to legitimate organizations or are slightly altered	info@micr0soft.com instead of info@microsoft.com
Poor email formatting	Phishing emails may have poor formatting inconsistent fonts or images that do not load properly	The email may be messy with multiple font styles or broken images

too pressing or unusual, it is always worth scrutinizing further before acting. Table 5.2 identifies key indicators of phishing emails, equipping users with the knowledge to detect and avoid deceptive communications.

Attackers utilize various techniques to deceive recipients and bypass traditional email security systems. One of the most sophisticated methods is social engineering, where attackers gather personal information about a victim through various means, such as social media profiles, and craft highly personalized phishing emails. These emails may appear to come from a trusted colleague, friend, or even a family member. In some cases, attackers may even exploit a recent event, like a natural disaster or a political crisis, to create a sense of urgency that drives recipients to click on malicious links. Another common tactic is embedding hyperlinks within an email masquerading as legitimate URLs. The displayed link text may seem harmless—such as a link to a bank or well-known retailer—but when hovered over or clicked, the URL may reveal itself as a fake website designed to harvest login credentials or infect the device with malware.

Verifying the authenticity of the sender is critical when dealing with suspicious emails. One method for confirming the sender's identity is by inspecting the email headers, which contain detailed information about the email's origin, including the sender's IP address and routing information. Often, phishing emails have telltale signs such as mismatched or altered sender addresses that may resemble legitimate domains at first glance, but a closer inspection will reveal inconsistencies. For example, an email from a financial institution might look like it's from "support@bank-secure.com." However, a deeper investigation could show that the sender uses a domain such as "@bank-secure.co," which may belong to a completely different entity. Additionally, the body of the email should be carefully examined for spelling errors, unusual formatting, or generic greetings like "Dear Customer" instead of addressing the recipient by name. These are common red flags signaling a phishing attempt, as legitimate companies and services rarely, if ever, send out messages with such errors.

When an email arrives unexpectedly, especially if it involves requests for sensitive information or urgent actions, it's best to proceed cautiously. A safe practice when handling such emails is never clicking links or downloading attachments without verifying the source. If the email purports to be from a legitimate organization, contact the organization directly using known contact methods, such as their official website or customer service number. Avoid using any contact information in the suspicious email, as this could redirect you to an attacker's phone line or website. For example, if you receive an email that claims to be from your bank asking you to reset your password, instead of clicking the link in the email, manually type the bank's website address into your browser to check for any security notices or verify the request. Taking a few extra moments to verify the email can save you from potentially devastating consequences.

Reporting phishing attempts is a crucial step in mitigating the wider impact of these attacks. When phishing emails are reported, it helps both service providers and security systems recognize and block these attempts from reaching other users. Most email providers, such as Gmail, Yahoo, and Outlook, have built-in tools that allow users to report phishing emails with just a few clicks. These reports enable email service providers to take quick action, including filtering future emails from the same malicious sender and updating their systems to detect similar phishing attempts in the future. In the event of a successful phishing attack, it is also important to report the incident to the affected organization, whether it is a bank, government agency, or workplace. By sharing information about the attack, victims help to bolster the collective defense against these threats and prevent future attacks from affecting others.

Phishing attacks are not just a theoretical threat—they happen every day, and many high-profile cases serve as cautionary tales. For example, in the 2016 attack on the Democratic National Committee (DNC), hackers used a well-crafted phishing email to gain access to sensitive email accounts and gain a foothold in the network. The attackers sent an email to a DNC staffer who appeared to be from Google's security team, warning the user to reset their password. The email included a link to a fake Google login page that captured the staffer's credentials. Once the attackers had access, they could steal thousands of emails, which were later leaked to the public. This breach underscores how a single, well-executed phishing attempt can lead to widespread damage in terms of lost data and reputational harm.

Another notable example is the 2011 attack on RSA, the security firm known for its SecurID two-factor authentication products. In this case, attackers used a phishing email to deliver a malicious Excel file that, when opened, exploited a vulnerability in the software to install malware on RSA's network. Once inside, the attackers were able to steal information about RSA's SecurID product, which numerous organizations use to secure their systems. This breach had far-reaching consequences, as it compromised the security of thousands of organizations worldwide, highlighting how

---

Ask the AI

"What are some red flags in email headers that suggest an email might be a phishing attempt?"
"How can I identify a phishing email when the sender's email address looks legitimate?"
"What are the most common social engineering tactics used in phishing attacks, and how can I defend against them?"

even trusted entities are vulnerable to phishing attacks. These real-world examples demonstrate the importance of vigilance and caution when dealing with unexpected emails, especially those that require immediate action or offer too-good-to-be-true deals.

Securing Your Email Accounts

One of the foundational elements of securing your email account is strong, unique passwords. It might seem like a no-brainer, but many individuals continue to use weak passwords or reuse passwords across multiple accounts, which increases the risk of a breach. A strong password should be long, complex, and contain a mix of uppercase letters, lowercase letters, numbers, and special characters. Avoid using easily guessable information, such as your name, birthdate, or the word "password" itself. In addition, employing a password manager can make it easier to generate and store complex, unique passwords for each of your email accounts. This reduces the temptation to use the same password for multiple sites, one of the most common mistakes people make regarding account security. Figure 5.1 illustrates the MFA workflow, demonstrating the steps and processes involved in securing access.

Enabling MFA is another vital step in securing your email account. MFA adds an extra layer of protection beyond just your password by requiring a second form of verification, typically something you possess (like your phone or an authentication app). For example, when logging into your email, you might be required to enter a one-time code sent to your phone or generated by an app like Google Authenticator or Authy. Even if a malicious actor manages to steal your password, they would still need access to this second factor to complete the login process, significantly reducing the likelihood of unauthorized access. Many email services, such as Gmail, Outlook, and Yahoo, offer MFA as a standard feature, and enabling it should be considered a critical step in your overall email security strategy.

Regularly updating your recovery information is an often overlooked but essential part of securing your email account. Recovery options, such as alternate email addresses or phone numbers, are used by service providers to verify your identity if you ever forget your password or if there are suspicious login attempts. Ensure that your recovery information is current and accessible, as this could be the difference between quickly regaining access to your account and being locked out for days. Many people make the mistake of neglecting to update their recovery options,

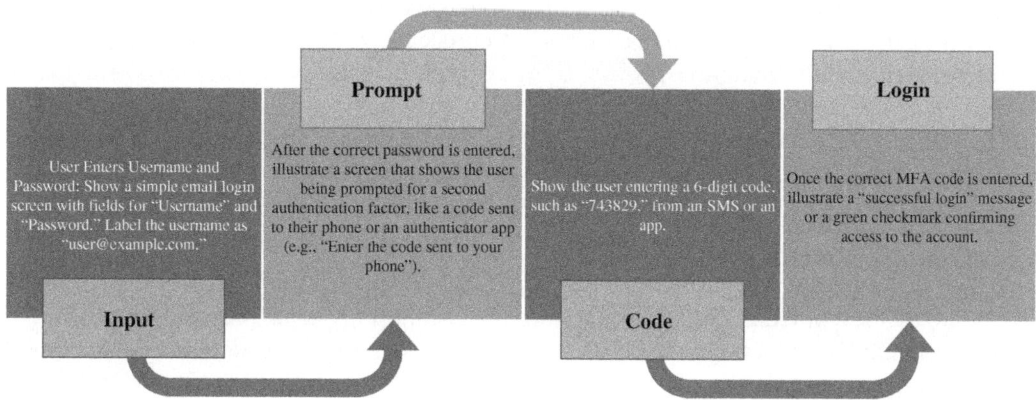

Figure 5.1 The MFA workflow.

leaving outdated phone numbers or inactive email addresses that attackers could exploit. It's also a good idea to periodically review the security questions used for account recovery, as many of the answers to common security questions (like your mother's maiden name) are often readily available through social media or public records.

Setting up email filters and spam protection is a straightforward but highly effective way to improve the security of your email account. Spam filters can help to screen and sort incoming emails automatically, filtering out those that may be potentially harmful or irrelevant. Most email services provide built-in spam filters, but reviewing these settings is essential to ensure they are properly configured regularly. By customizing your spam filters, you can ensure that emails containing links to malicious websites or suspicious attachments are flagged and sent to your spam folder before you can open them. Additionally, consider creating custom filters to block specific keywords, email addresses, or domain names that you know to be associated with phishing attacks or other malicious activities. This small action can prevent most low-level threats from ever reaching your inbox, allowing you to focus on legitimate communications.

Monitoring account activity and setting up login alerts is another effective means of securing your email account. Many email providers allow you to track recent login activity, including the IP addresses and locations from which your account has been accessed. If you notice any suspicious activity, such as logins from unfamiliar locations or devices, you should take immediate action to secure your account by changing your password and enabling MFA. Some services also allow you to receive alerts whenever your account is accessed from a new device or location, giving you real-time visibility into unauthorized attempts to access your email. The sooner you spot unusual activity, the quicker you can respond, potentially minimizing the damage caused by a security breach. Table 5.3 outlines email security best practices for personal and professional use, offering guidelines to protect against malicious threats.

Understanding email encryption options is also essential for securing sensitive communications. While most email services provide basic security, such as transport layer security, to encrypt emails in transit, this doesn't necessarily protect the content of the email from being accessed by anyone with unauthorized access to your email account. To enhance the privacy of your messages, consider using end-to-end encryption tools, which encrypt the email content itself, making it unreadable to anyone except the intended recipient. ProtonMail and Tutanota offer built-in end-to-end encryption, while third-party tools like Pretty Good Privacy (PGP) or Secure/Multipurpose Internet Mail Extensions (S/MIME) can encrypt emails in other systems. Encryption should be a nonnegotiable step in your digital safety practices if you are exchanging sensitive information via email.

Regularly reviewing and updating your email account's security settings is not just about adopting new measures; it's about remaining vigilant and proactive. Cyber threats evolve rapidly, and attackers are constantly finding new ways to bypass traditional security measures. Periodically checking your account for any vulnerabilities or signs of compromise can help you stay one step ahead. For example, email providers often update their security protocols, and it's important to be aware of these changes so that you can take full advantage of any new protective features.

Ask the AI

"What are the best practices for creating a strong password for email accounts?"
"How does multi-factor authentication (MFA) work to protect email accounts, and what types of MFA are most effective?"
"What should I do if I suspect my email account has been compromised?"

Table 5.3 Email security best practices for personal and professional use.

Best practice	Description	Why it is important
Use strong unique passwords	Create passwords that are long, complex, and unique for each account	Weak or reused passwords make accounts easier to hack. Unique passwords ensure that one breach does not affect multiple accounts
Enable MFA	Activate MFA for email services to require an additional authentication step such as a code sent to your phone	MFA provides an added layer of security, reducing the chances of unauthorized access even if a password is compromised
Regularly update recovery information	Keep your recovery email and phone number up-to-date to help with account recovery in case of compromise	If an attacker gains access to your email, having updated recovery info helps you regain control faster
Use Email Filters and Spam Protection	Set up filters to segregate spam and phishing emails from legitimate messages	Filters help keep your inbox organized and protect you from malicious emails entering your main inbox
Monitor account activity and login alerts	Regularly check for unusual login activity and enable alerts for sign-in attempts from new locations or devices	Monitoring ensures that you can quickly spot unauthorized access and take action to secure your account
Understand email encryption options	Use encryption when sending sensitive or confidential information through email	Encryption ensures that even if an email is intercepted, its contents remain secure and unreadable
Be cautious with auto-reply and out-of-office messages	Avoid sharing too much personal information in auto-replies or out-of-office emails	Auto-replies are public and could reveal information about your absence or sensitive data that attackers could exploit
Separate personal and professional emails	Use different email accounts for personal and work-related communication	Separation helps mitigate the risk of attacks that target one account and spill over into the other
Educate colleagues on email security	Ensure everyone in your organization understands the importance of email security and how to recognize phishing and other threats	Employee awareness reduces the likelihood of a successful phishing or social engineering attack
Report suspicious emails	Use the report phishing function in your email service provider to flag potentially harmful emails	Reporting helps improve spam and phishing detection for everyone and prevents further attacks

Taking the time to review your settings, change passwords, and update recovery options at least every six months ensures that you continually enhance your email accounts' security.

In addition to the technical steps, educating yourself about the latest threats is equally important. Many email-based attacks, such as phishing and spear phishing, rely on social engineering tactics to exploit human vulnerabilities. Awareness of attackers' latest trends and techniques can help you recognize suspicious emails and avoid falling victim to a scam. Many email service providers also offer security tips and updates to their users, which can be invaluable in helping you stay informed. Additionally, attending cybersecurity webinars, reading up on emerging threats, and participating in online forums can give you the knowledge you need to maintain strong email security.

Safe Email Practices

One of the simplest yet most effective ways to protect your email account is by avoiding clicking on unknown links or downloading attachments from unfamiliar sources. Cybercriminals often use these tactics to spread malware, steal sensitive data, or trick users into giving away personal information. When you receive an email that asks you to click a link, especially if it's from an unrecognized sender or seems out of place, it's important to scrutinize it. Instead of clicking the link directly, hover your mouse over it to see if the URL matches the text or if it redirects to an unexpected or suspicious website. If you have any doubts, avoiding the link entirely is safer, as well as verifying the email's legitimacy through other means, such as contacting the organization directly. Similarly, attachments—especially unsolicited or unexpected—can carry harmful payloads and should never be opened unless you know the sender's identity and the file's content.

Whenever you receive a request for sensitive information via email, it's essential to confirm the request's legitimacy before acting. Cybercriminals often impersonate trusted entities, such as your bank, employer, or a colleague, to obtain private information under the guise of urgency or necessity. If the email asks you for personal data, financial details, or login credentials, stop and double-check the request. The safest approach is to reach out to the requester using a known and trusted communication channel, such as calling a verified customer service number or replying to the official email address. This simple extra step helps avoid phishing schemes or BEC attacks. Remember, legitimate organizations will never ask for sensitive information via email unless you've initiated the communication.

Another area of concern involves the handling of auto-reply and out-of-office messages. While these messages are generally harmless, they can inadvertently provide valuable information to attackers. For instance, an out-of-office message that includes specific dates might reveal that cybercriminals could use your absence to target your inbox when you might be less likely to respond. Similarly, auto-reply messages could inadvertently confirm that your email address is valid, allowing attackers to target you with more personalized or frequent phishing attempts. If possible, limit the personal information shared in these automated responses and avoid revealing your absence or the precise vacation dates. Additionally, consider enabling an auto-reply only when necessary and be mindful of the security implications of the information you disclose.

Managing your subscription and mailing list preferences is another effective way to minimize unwanted and potentially malicious emails. Over time, people often forget about the subscriptions they've signed up for or the lists they've joined, leading to an overflowing inbox filled with unnecessary messages. These emails can sometimes contain malicious links or attachments, increasing the likelihood of accidentally clicking on a phishing attempt. Many email providers allow you to unsubscribe from mailing lists directly through a link provided at the bottom of the message, which can reduce the volume of spam you receive. Additionally, consider using an email alias or secondary email account for newsletters, promotions, and other non-essential communications to keep your primary inbox focused on important matters. Regularly reviewing and cleaning up your subscriptions can keep your inbox manageable and reduce exposure to email threats.

Ask the AI

"What are the risks of clicking on unknown links or downloading attachments in email messages?"
"How can I securely handle sensitive information requested through email?"
"What tools can help me filter spam and prevent malicious emails from reaching my inbox?"

Protecting your contacts and preventing the spread of malicious emails is essential for personal security and those within your network. Malicious actors often attempt to leverage the trust inherent in your relationships by sending out emails that appear to come from you but are attempting to spread malware or phishing links. To avoid infecting your contacts, ensure your email account is secure by using strong passwords, enabling MFA, and regularly reviewing your account activity. If you suspect that your account has been compromised and is being used to send malicious emails, notify your contacts immediately, take swift action to reset your credentials, and review your security settings. Additionally, avoid sending sensitive information via email whenever possible, as email is often not fully secure, and always consider encrypting messages that contain personal data or confidential information.

Cleaning and organizing your inbox is an often overlooked but important part of maintaining email security. Over time, emails accumulate, making it easier for malicious messages to slip through unnoticed. Regularly deleting old, unnecessary emails, particularly those containing attachments or links, reduces the risk of interacting with dangerous content accidentally. Furthermore, keeping your inbox organized allows you to more easily spot unusual or suspicious messages that may require further scrutiny. Email folders or labels can help sort communications by topic or importance, ensuring that important messages are kept separate from less critical ones. Implementing a regular inbox management routine, such as setting aside weekly time to clean up and organize, can be an excellent way to maintain a well-secured email environment.

Additionally, consider setting up and maintaining email filters to automate sorting or blocking known threats. Email providers often offer customizable filters that allow you to block certain types of content, such as attachments with specific extensions (e.g., .exe files) or emails containing common spam keywords. By fine-tuning these filters, you can prevent malicious or unwanted emails from reaching your inbox. Suppose you often receive promotional or irrelevant emails. In that case, it's a good idea to create rules that automatically sort these messages into a separate folder, keeping your main inbox free of distractions. Filters can also help automatically detect and mark potential phishing attempts, ensuring that any suspicious messages are flagged for review before they have a chance to cause harm.

Using the "report phishing" feature available in many email services is another useful method for ensuring that malicious emails are identified and prevented from reaching others. When you encounter a phishing email or any suspicious communication, reporting it to your email service provider helps them improve their security filters and prevent similar emails from reaching other users. Providers like Gmail and Outlook allow users to report phishing directly from the email interface, which helps identify harmful patterns and enhances their ability to filter future threats. Reporting phishing attempts also contributes to a broader community effort to combat cybercrime, and many organizations track these reports to improve their overall security defenses. By actively reporting phishing emails, you help make the internet a safer place for everyone.

Professional Email Etiquette and Security

One of the first steps in maintaining professional email security is to separate personal and professional email use. Many people make the mistake of using their work email for personal matters, such as online shopping or subscribing to newsletters. This increases the likelihood of exposure to phishing attacks and spam and creates a situation where your professional email account becomes a potential target for cybercriminals. Keeping personal emails and professional communications separate can minimize the risk of inadvertently compromising your work-related information. Additionally, using different email accounts for work and personal use allows you to implement security measures specific to each context more easily, such as setting up stronger spam filters or using more robust encryption for sensitive professional correspondence.

Understanding your employer's policies on email communication is another essential aspect of professional email security. Most organizations have strict guidelines regarding using company email accounts, and failing to follow these policies can expose the individual and the company to serious security risks. Employers often set specific rules regarding what can and cannot be communicated via email, including handling sensitive or confidential information. For example, many businesses prohibit employees from using work email accounts for non-business-related communications, as this increases the likelihood of the email account being compromised. Familiarizing yourself with your company's email security policies and ensuring you adhere to them will not only help protect you from potential security threats but also ensure that you're compliant with the organization's security practices.

Security should be at the forefront of everyone's mind when handling confidential information in professional emails. Sending sensitive data through email, whether personal identifying information, financial records, or proprietary business information, always carries some risk. While encryption can significantly improve the confidentiality of email communications, it's important to follow best practices for secure transmission. For example, always use end-to-end encryption when sending sensitive attachments or email content that could be used maliciously if intercepted. Additionally, be cautious about how you share confidential information—avoid including sensitive details directly in the body of an email unless absolutely necessary, and instead use secure file-sharing services that offer encryption and authentication. Before sending any confidential data, please verify that the recipient is the correct individual and that they have the appropriate clearance to receive such information.

Recognizing social engineering attacks in professional contexts is critical for maintaining email security. Social engineering manipulates individuals into revealing confidential information or performing actions that compromise their security, often by impersonating a trusted entity. In a professional setting, attackers might pose as a coworker, a superior, or an external partner to gain access to sensitive company data. These attacks can take many forms, including phishing emails that request urgent action, such as transferring funds or providing login credentials. They might also involve impersonating IT support, asking employees to reset their passwords, or providing false links that direct users to fraudulent login pages. By being aware of these tactics and questioning unexpected requests, even if they seem to come from trusted colleagues or partners, you can avoid falling victim to social engineering schemes.

Educating colleagues about email security is an often underestimated but highly effective strategy for reducing the risks associated with email-based attacks. No matter how strong your email security practices are, an organization's overall security is only as strong as its weakest link. The organization becomes more vulnerable to cyber threats if one employee is unaware of best practices for recognizing phishing emails or securing their email account. Regular training sessions, email security awareness programs, and simulated phishing exercises can help employees learn how to identify and

---

Ask the AI

"What common email security policies should organizations implement for employees?"
"How can employees spot and report suspicious emails professionally?"
"What legal considerations should be kept in mind when handling confidential information via email?"

avoid common email-based threats. It's also helpful to foster an environment where team members feel comfortable reporting suspicious emails, creating a security culture where email-related threats can be swiftly addressed. The more informed your colleagues are, the more resilient your organization will be against email-based cyberattacks.

Legal considerations in email correspondence play a significant role in email security and professional communication. Emails are often considered legal documents, and the content of a professional email can be used as evidence in legal proceedings, both for and against an individual or company. For this reason, it is essential to understand the legal implications of what is written in emails, particularly when dealing with confidential or sensitive information. Certain types of communication, such as contracts, agreements, and terms of service, may need to be encrypted or signed digitally to ensure their legal integrity. Moreover, employees must be aware of the potential for their emails to be subpoenaed or used as part of an investigation, and they should always be cautious of the language and content they include. Using company-approved email accounts for professional communication helps to ensure that emails are subject to the organization's oversight, which may include retaining copies for legal compliance or regulatory purposes.

In addition to understanding the legal considerations, it's also critical to implement proper data retention and disposal policies for professional email correspondence. Many industries have strict guidelines for how long certain emails should be retained, particularly those involving financial transactions or contracts. For example, in sectors such as healthcare or finance, email communications may need to be archived for several years to comply with industry regulations. Once an email has outlived its useful purpose, it should be securely deleted to prevent unauthorized access or exposure. Using automated email retention tools or implementing manual processes for archiving and purging old emails can help ensure that your organization complies with legal and regulatory requirements while reducing the risk of unnecessary exposure to sensitive data.

Email security also extends beyond the technical measures implemented to safeguard email accounts; it involves building a culture of awareness and vigilance within your organization. Encouraging employees to question suspicious emails, report phishing attempts, and adhere to security protocols ensures that your organization is collectively invested in protecting its digital communication channels. For example, employees should be trained to recognize the signs of a phishing attempt, such as misspelled domain names, strange attachments, or urgent, unsolicited requests for sensitive information. Regularly reminding staff about the dangers of opening suspicious emails or clicking on unknown links can reinforce the importance of email security and minimize the chances of successful attacks. Furthermore, implementing a company-wide incident response plan for email breaches ensures that the organization can respond swiftly and reduce the impact if a security issue arises.

Recommendations

1. **Separate Personal and Professional Email Accounts:** Create distinct email accounts for personal and work-related communications. This practice helps minimize the risk of exposure to malicious emails in your professional inbox and ensures that individual accounts are not mixed with sensitive work-related matters. Keeping these accounts separate also allows you to implement tailored security measures, such as stronger spam filters for work accounts and more vigilant monitoring of personal accounts for phishing attempts.
2. **Please Review and Follow Employer Email Policies:** Familiarize yourself with your organization's email security policies and consistently follow them. These policies often include

guidelines for handling sensitive information, restrictions on email use for personal purposes, and procedures for responding to potential security breaches. Adhering to these guidelines will help protect your data and reduce the risk of compromising your company's security framework.

3. **Encrypt Sensitive Information:** When emailing sensitive data, always use encryption to protect its confidentiality. Many email services offer built-in encryption tools, but you can also use third-party software for enhanced security. For particularly sensitive communications, consider end-to-end encryption, which ensures that only the intended recipient can access the message's content, even if it is intercepted during transmission.

4. **Educate Your Colleagues on Email Security Best Practices:** Organize regular email security training for yourself and your coworkers to help identify common threats like phishing, social engineering, and malware. Encourage your organization to run simulated phishing campaigns and offer constructive feedback. By building awareness and improving your team's ability to recognize suspicious activity, you can strengthen your organization's collective defense against email-based attacks.

5. **Confirm Suspicious Requests via Alternate Channels:** If you receive an unexpected email asking for sensitive information or urgent action, verify the request by contacting the person through a known and trusted communication channel. Never reply directly to suspicious emails. A phone call or a direct message through an internal chat system can ensure that the request is legitimate, helping you avoid falling victim to phishing or social engineering attacks.

6. **Implement Strong Passwords and MFA:** Use strong, unique passwords for your email accounts and enable multi-factor authentication (MFA) whenever possible. MFA adds an extra layer of security by requiring a second form of verification, such as a code sent to your phone, in addition to your password. This significantly reduces the likelihood that your email account will be compromised by attackers, even if your password is leaked.

7. **Be Cautious with Auto-reply and Out-of-office Messages:** Avoid revealing too much personal or professional information in your auto-reply or out-of-office emails. If you need to use these features, ensure that they don't disclose your absence dates or sensitive project details, as this can provide valuable information for attackers seeking to exploit gaps in your availability or targeting specific times for phishing.

8. **Regularly Clean and Organize Your Inbox:** Regularly clean your inbox by deleting unnecessary or outdated emails, especially those containing attachments or links. Sorting your inbox into folders can also help you manage important communications more efficiently and make spotting unusual or suspicious messages easier. An organized inbox reduces the risk of overlooking a malicious email, which might be buried among legitimate messages.

9. **Enable and Customize Email Filters:** Use your email provider's filter settings to block spam, unwanted newsletters, and malicious attachments. Customize your spam filters to automatically flag or route suspicious emails into a separate folder for review. Email providers typically allow you to block known phishing sources or filter out specific keywords, reducing the number of malicious emails that land in your inbox.

10. **Report Suspicious Emails to Your Email Provider:** Use your email provider's built-in "report phishing" or "mark as spam" feature whenever you encounter a phishing attempt or a suspicious email. By reporting these emails, you help protect your account and contribute to the provider's efforts to improve security for all users. Over time, reporting helps strengthen the system's ability to filter out similar threats before they reach your inbox.

Conclusion

In conclusion, securing your email accounts is not just a one-time task but an ongoing process that requires vigilance and proactive management. As we've seen throughout this chapter, the risks associated with email communication are real and diverse, ranging from phishing attacks and malware to BEC and identity theft. However, you can significantly reduce your exposure to these threats by adopting best practices such as using strong, unique passwords, enabling MFA, and being cautious with email attachments and links. Email security is the first defense in protecting personal and organizational digital assets from malicious actors.

Implementing effective email security practices also involves recognizing the role of human behavior in cybersecurity. Even with advanced technical defenses in place, the success of cyber-attacks often hinges on user actions—such as clicking on a suspicious link or opening an unexpected attachment. By educating yourself and others about email security and fostering a culture of awareness, you can strengthen your overall security posture. Security is only as strong as the weakest link, and often, that link is human error, which is why user education is essential in mitigating risks.

The tools and strategies discussed in this chapter are critical for defending against email-based threats, but they must be part of a broader, holistic cybersecurity approach. Strong email security practices contribute to the overall integrity of your digital environment, complementing other layers of security, such as firewalls, encryption, and secure networks. It's also important to stay informed about emerging threats, as cybercriminals constantly evolve tactics to exploit new vulnerabilities. By remaining vigilant and adaptable, you can keep up with these changes and ensure your email practices align with the latest security standards.

As email is integral to our personal and professional lives, we must prioritize its security. The good news is that securing your email doesn't have to be an overwhelming task. With the right tools, habits, and a commitment to best practices, you can protect yourself and your organization from most email-based threats. By implementing the strategies outlined in this chapter and staying proactive about email security, you can confidently navigate the digital world, knowing that your communication is safe, secure, and resilient to attack.

Chapter Questions

1 What is the primary purpose of separating personal and professional email accounts?
   A. To reduce the risk of malicious emails affecting personal accounts
   B. To make it easier to track personal communications
   C. To prevent cross-contamination between personal and work-related information
   D. To save time by using one account for everything

2 Which of the following is a best practice for handling sensitive email communications?
   A. Sending all emails unencrypted
   B. Using encryption for sensitive email content
   C. Writing confidential information directly in the subject line
   D. Sharing passwords through email for easy access

3 What is the main benefit of implementing multi-factor authentication (MFA) for your email account?
   A. It simplifies the login process
   B. It adds an extra layer of security, reducing the risk of account compromise
   C. It eliminates the need for strong passwords
   D. It prevents spam from entering your inbox

4 When should you confirm requests for sensitive information via alternate communication channels?
   A. Only when the email is from a known colleague
   B. Only when the request is unsolicited
   C. Always, especially when the email requests urgent action
   D. Never, since email is secure enough for all types of communication

5 What is the primary reason for regularly cleaning and organizing your inbox?
   A. To make it easier to find important emails
   B. To ensure you don't miss a phishing email hidden among legitimate ones
   C. To improve the speed of your email provider
   D. To reduce storage space

6 How can you protect yourself from phishing emails?
   A. By clicking on all links to verify their authenticity
   B. By opening all attachments from known contacts
   C. By confirming any unusual or urgent requests through another communication method
   D. By ignoring the sender's email address

7 What is the purpose of using email filters and spam protection tools?
   A. To automatically delete all incoming emails
   B. To block and segregate suspicious emails from your inbox
   C. To make emails appear more attractive
   D. To allow all emails to reach your inbox without filtering

8 Why is educating colleagues about email security practices important?
   A. It reduces the need for IT support
   B. It minimizes the chances of falling victim to phishing or other email-based threats
   C. It ensures that everyone uses email more frequently
   D. It helps employees find emails faster

9 What type of information should not be included in auto-reply or out-of-office emails?
   A. Availability dates
   B. Personal contact information
   C. Sensitive project details or confidential information
   D. None of the above

10 What should you do when you receive a suspicious email asking for sensitive information?
   A. Open all attachments and verify the authenticity of the request
   B. Reply to the email asking for more details
   C. Contact the sender through a trusted method, like phone or company messaging systems
   D. Ignore the email and delete it

11 Why should you verify the sender's email address in suspicious emails?
   A. To ensure the email is legitimate and not an attempt to impersonate a trusted sender
   B. To verify that the email came from a known colleague
   C. To confirm the message is from a reputable company
   D. To improve the chances of the email reaching your inbox

12 What is a recommended action to take if you encounter a phishing email in your inbox?
   A. Delete the email immediately without reporting it
   B. Report the phishing email to your email provider
   C. Reply to the email to confirm the sender's identity
   D. Open the links in the email to see where they lead

13 What should you do to ensure your email account is secure?
   A. Use the same password across all accounts for convenience
   B. Enable multi-factor authentication (MFA) for added security
   C. Use weak passwords to make it easier to remember
   D. Regularly change your password to an easily guessed one

14 How does email encryption improve email security?
   A. By preventing unauthorized access to email contents during transmission
   B. By making it easier to read email attachments
   C. By ensuring emails are automatically deleted after sending
   D. By verifying the sender's identity

15 Why is it important to understand legal considerations in email correspondence?
   A. Because emails can be used as evidence in legal proceedings
   B. Because email correspondence is not subject to privacy laws
   C. Because email communication cannot be subpoenaed
   D. Because emails are less likely to be used in business negotiations

6

Managing Your Digital Footprint and Online Reputation

Every action we take online—whether posting a social media update, making an online purchase, or simply browsing the web—contributes to the vast and ever-expanding trail of digital data we leave behind. This data, collectively called your "digital footprint," reflects your online activities, preferences, interactions, and even personal information. Understanding the scope and implications of your digital footprint is crucial in a world where personal data is frequently exploited for good and evil.

Managing your digital footprint is not just about maintaining privacy—it's also about shaping your online reputation. What others find when they search for you online can significantly impact your personal and professional life. Employers, clients, friends, and even strangers can form opinions based on what they encounter in search results, social media profiles, or public databases. As a result, carefully curating and monitoring your online presence is key to maintaining control over how others perceive you.

This chapter will provide you with the knowledge and tools necessary to take charge of your digital footprint and online reputation. We will explore how digital footprints are created, tracked, and potentially exploited, as well as their long-term implications on your privacy and security. From understanding the difference between active and passive footprints to how data is gathered and stored, you will learn the critical components of your digital identity. Through a series of best practices and actionable recommendations, you will discover how to monitor your online presence, manage privacy settings, and cultivate a positive reputation in the digital space.

As the digital landscape evolves, staying informed about new technologies and trends affecting your online footprint is important. The rise of AI, facial recognition software, and advanced data collection techniques makes it more important to be proactive in protecting your personal information. This chapter will also discuss emerging challenges, such as the implications of deepfake technology and the complexities of the "right to be forgotten." By the end of this chapter, you will understand the importance of managing your digital footprint and have the tools at your disposal to protect and enhance your online reputation for years to come. Figure 6.1 depicts the digital footprint lifecycle diagram, illustrating the stages from creation to management of digital traces online.

Understanding Your Digital Footprint

Understanding your digital footprint is crucial to maintaining control over your online presence. Your digital footprint consists of the traces you leave behind as you interact with the internet, ranging from social media posts to search history. Every action you take online—liking a post, making a purchase, or commenting on a forum—contributes to this footprint. Even seemingly

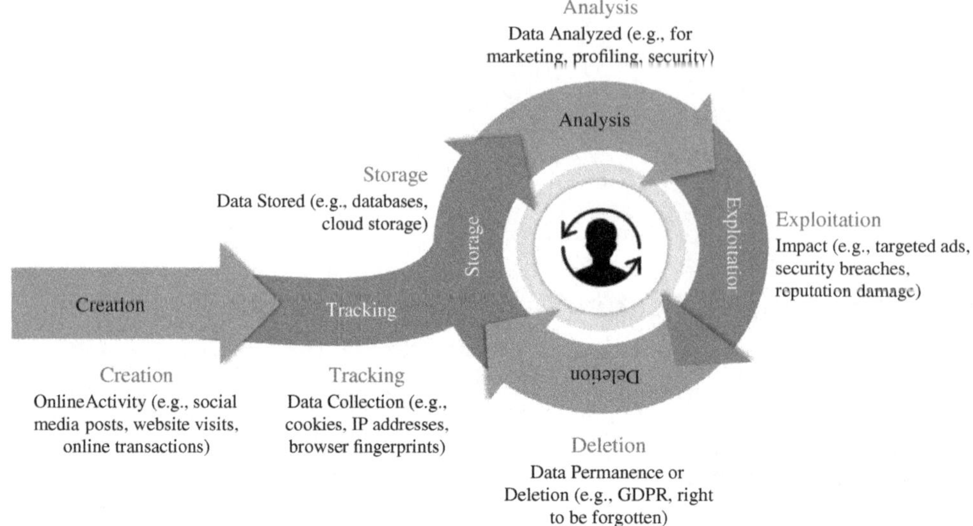

Figure 6.1 Digital footprint lifecycle diagram.

benign activities, such as browsing websites or mobile apps, can leave a lasting imprint. The data generated through these interactions paints a detailed picture of who you are, where you've been, and what you've done, even if you're not consciously sharing that information. For example, geo-location data embedded in photos or apps can reveal your movements, habits, and preferences without you even realizing it.

There are two primary types of digital footprints: active and passive. Active footprints are the data you intentionally share, such as creating social media profiles, posting content, or commenting on blogs. You're consciously contributing to your digital identity whenever you publish something online. Passive footprints, however, are the traces left without your explicit action, such as your IP address or the cookies that track your browsing behavior. While active footprints are directly tied to your choices, passive footprints accumulate from routine online interactions, often without your awareness. Together, these two footprints form a comprehensive record of your online existence, and understanding their distinction helps you better manage the flow of personal information you expose. Table 6.1 categorizes types of digital footprints and tracking methods, detailing how online activities are monitored and recorded.

Online activities are tracked and recorded in many ways, from the simple cookies used by websites to sophisticated algorithms employed by advertisers. Cookies are small files stored on your computer that help websites remember your preferences and login information. However, they also track your browsing history and behaviors across multiple sites, enabling advertisers to tailor ads to your interests. Beyond cookies, websites and apps also use tracking pixels and beacons—small, invisible elements that gather data about your interactions. Search engines, social media platforms, and even e-commerce sites collect vast amounts of data about your searches, purchases, and browsing habits. This tracking can sometimes be done without transparency, making it difficult to fully grasp how much of your activity is being observed and recorded.

One of the most concerning aspects of a digital footprint is the permanence of online information. Unlike physical interactions, which fade with time, digital data tends to stick around. Once something is uploaded to the internet, whether a social media post, a comment on a forum, or even a photo shared with a friend, it can be difficult or impossible to erase. The data may be archived by search engines, stored on servers, or backed up in ways you may never even see. While some platforms allow

Table 6.1 Types of digital footprints and tracking methods.

Type of digital footprint	Description	Examples	Tracking methods
Active digital footprint	Information you intentionally share online	Social media posts, blog comments, online purchases	Cookies, account tracking, IP addresses
Passive digital footprint	Data collected from your online actions without your direct input	Web browsing history, location data, online purchases	Browser fingerprinting, cookies, third-party tracking
Social media footprint	Data shared on social media platforms	Profile information, photos, status updates	Platform algorithms, data analytics, cookies
Browsing footprint	Online activities while surfing the web	Websites visited, time spent on pages, interactions	Browser cookies, IP tracking, website analytics
Email footprint	Information from email interactions	Subscriptions, promotional emails, communication history	Email trackers, metadata analysis
Location footprint	Data related to your geographic location	Geotagged photos, GPS data, location-sharing apps	GPS tracking, mobile apps, IP address geolocation
Search footprint	Data generated from search engine queries	Search history, saved search preferences	Search engine data collection, cookies
Device footprint	Data related to the device you use online	Device specifications, operating system, IP address	Device fingerprinting, network analysis
Financial footprint	Data collected from financial transactions	Banking records, payment methods, shopping preferences	Transaction tracking, financial institution data
Health footprint	Health data collected through digital health platforms	Fitness app data, medical records, symptom tracking	Health apps, wearable devices, medical databases

you to delete posts or accounts, traces of that information may still linger in the digital ecosystem. Understanding this permanence is essential for anyone hoping to maintain a positive online reputation, as it highlights the long-term consequences of every digital action.

To help you navigate the complexities of managing your digital footprint, various tools and methods are available to analyze your digital presence. Search engines like Google allow you to perform a self-audit by searching for your name or other identifying information. This can reveal what publicly available information about you is indexed and easily discoverable. More advanced tools, such as privacy-focused search engines or dedicated reputation management services, can provide deeper insights into your online presence, identifying obvious and obscure data points.

Ask the AI

"What is the difference between an active and passive digital footprint, and how are they created?"
"How do companies track and record users' online activities through cookies and IP addresses?"
"What are the long-term implications of a permanent digital footprint, and how does it affect privacy?"

These tools may also help you track how your digital footprint changes over time, allowing you to adjust your privacy settings, remove outdated content, or take corrective action when necessary.

The implications of your digital footprint on privacy and security are significant and often underestimated. Every piece of data you leave behind can be used to build a profile that may be exploited for malicious purposes. Cybercriminals can harvest your online behaviors to craft convincing phishing scams, impersonate you online, or even steal your identity. In the case of data breaches, hackers can sell or use the personal information they've stolen, causing damage to your finances and reputation. Even legitimate companies often share or sell your data to third parties, potentially exposing you to unwanted solicitations or fraud. As your digital footprint grows, so does the risk of privacy violations, so it's essential to remain vigilant and proactive about what you share and with whom.

Many individuals fail to realize how much their digital footprints can impact their professional lives. Employers, colleagues, and business partners often search online for information about candidates, employees, or collaborators. Inappropriate content, negative reviews, or poorly handled social media accounts can tarnish a person's professional reputation. In some industries, the consequences can be dire, with a damaged digital reputation potentially leading to job loss or missed career opportunities. Even if you maintain a private account, the sheer volume of publicly available information can reveal more than you think, leading to judgments based on incomplete or outdated perceptions. This highlights the need for careful management and the understanding that what's shared in private spaces may eventually become public, intentionally or not.

Monitoring and Controlling Your Online Presence

Conducting regular self-audits is one of the most effective ways to stay on top of your digital presence. By searching your name online, you can uncover readily available information to the public and identify anything that might need attention. This process involves more than just Googling yourself; you should also check for mentions of your name on social media platforms, review images and posts associated with you, and see what other people say about you. Remember that this exercise is about monitoring negative content and understanding how much of your personal information is floating around the digital ecosystem. Doing so regularly, at least every few months, helps you stay informed about the digital trail you're leaving behind so you can take action when necessary.

Setting up alerts for mentions of your name, brand, or specific keywords related to your online identity can significantly improve your real-time ability to monitor your digital footprint. Platforms like Google Alerts or services like Talkwalker allow you to create notifications that notify you whenever your name, brand, or other pertinent terms are mentioned in news stories, blogs, or social media. These alerts help you track positive and negative mentions, allowing you to respond quickly if anything damaging or inaccurate appears. This proactive approach can help you manage your online reputation before a small issue snowballs into something larger. Alerts can also remind you to watch over the ongoing changes in your digital identity, ensuring you don't miss anything important. Table 6.2 details privacy settings by platform, offering a comprehensive guide to configuring security options across various digital services.

Reviewing and adjusting privacy settings on social media platforms is an essential aspect of managing your online presence. Every social network, whether it's Facebook, Instagram, LinkedIn, or Twitter, offers a range of privacy settings that determine who can see your posts, who can contact you, and what information about you is visible. However, many users neglect these settings, exposing their accounts more than they realize. For instance, on Facebook, you can limit who can see your

Table 6.2 Privacy settings by platform.

Platform	Privacy setting	Action to take	Effect of setting
Facebook	Profile Visibility	Adjust audience settings for posts and profile	Limits who can see your posts and personal details
Twitter	Tweet Privacy	Set tweets to Protected	Only approved followers can view and interact with tweets
Instagram	Story Privacy	Enable Close Friends list for stories	Only selected friends can view your stories
LinkedIn	Profile Visibility	Limit profile visibility to connections only	Restricts public access to your professional information
Google	Search History	Turn off Web and App Activity tracking	Prevents Google from saving your search queries and activity
Snapchat	Location Sharing	Turn off Share My Location	Prevents others from tracking your physical location on the map
YouTube	Video Privacy	Set videos to Private or Unlisted	Prevents others from seeing your uploaded videos unless you share the link
Reddit	Comment Privacy	Use anonymous commenting or private subreddits	Protects your identity when engaging in discussions
WhatsApp	Last Seen Privacy	Set Last Seen visibility to Nobody or Contacts Only	Hides your last activity time from strangers
TikTok	Direct Message Privacy	Limit who can send you direct messages	Reduces unsolicited communication from strangers

posts or even look up your profile using your email or phone number. Similarly, platforms like Instagram and Twitter allow you to control who can comment on your posts or tag you in photos. Regularly reviewing these settings, especially after platform updates or changes to terms of service, is essential to ensure that you aren't inadvertently sharing more than you intend to.

Removing unwanted or outdated information from the internet is crucial for maintaining a positive digital footprint. Over time, you may accumulate posts, photos, or videos that no longer align with your current values or identity. The first step is to critically examine what's publicly available about you, including on your own social media accounts and those of others. Sometimes, removing content is as simple as deleting a post or untagging yourself from a photo. However, it can be more complicated when the information is hosted by third parties or archived by search engines. In such cases, you may need to contact website administrators directly, request the removal of certain data, or employ a reputation management service to help erase or suppress unwanted content. While you can't always erase everything, staying proactive in your digital hygiene enables you to keep your online presence in line with your current identity.

Managing online profiles and personal websites is another important aspect of controlling your online reputation. A personal website or blog can be a great way to showcase your expertise or hobbies. However, managing these spaces actively is essential to ensure they reflect your most current interests and career trajectory. Consider updating your site regularly with relevant content, such as blog posts, professional achievements, or portfolio work, so it represents your identity. Similarly, professional platforms like LinkedIn need regular attention to keep your work history, skills, and certifications current. A stale or outdated profile can create confusion for potential employers, clients, or colleagues who may be searching for you online. Even a well-maintained profile on platforms like LinkedIn should be checked for accuracy periodically to ensure that it reflects your latest accomplishments and aspirations.

Understanding data brokers and opting out of data collection is essential for reducing your digital footprint. Data brokers collect and sell personal information to marketers, advertisers, and other brokers. These organizations gather data from public records, online purchases, social media activity, and more to build detailed profiles of individuals. Although legal frameworks in place, such as GDPR in Europe, aim to regulate data collection, many people remain unaware of how much of their personal information is being sold. By opting out of these services, you can reduce the amount of personal data available to third parties. Some data brokers provide online forms to request that your data be removed from their databases, while others may require more extensive efforts to contact them directly. Taking the time to identify and manage the data brokers with access to your personal information can be a valuable step in limiting your exposure.

The importance of regularly updating and refining your privacy settings extends beyond social media platforms and personal websites. Many third-party services you use daily—such as apps, online stores, and cloud services—store data about you, ranging from your purchasing habits to your search history. These platforms often provide privacy controls that can help you manage what information you share, but they may not always make those settings easy to find or understand. For instance, some services offer data downloads that let you see what information they have on file about you, while others allow you to control ad targeting preferences. Understanding how these services use your data is crucial for managing your online footprint. If you're uncomfortable with a particular service's data collection practices, consider alternatives that prioritize privacy or adjust your settings to minimize the information shared.

Building a Positive Online Reputation

Curating content that reflects well on you is essential in building a positive online reputation. Every post, comment, or image shared online contributes to the digital persona you present to the world. Whether you are sharing your thoughts on current events, promoting a personal project, or commenting on others' work, ensuring that your content aligns with the values and image you want to project is important. When curating content, consider the long-term impact of your posts. What might seem harmless today could be viewed differently in the future, and it's difficult to predict how an offhand comment or an outdated post may influence your reputation later. Ensuring that the content you share reflects professionalism, thoughtfulness, and authenticity will help you build a reputation that aligns with your personal and professional goals.

Engaging positively in online communities is another key component of building a positive online reputation. The internet offers countless forums, discussion boards, and social networks where people exchange ideas, seek advice, or share knowledge. By participating in these communities constructively and respectfully, you can contribute to the conversation and establish yourself as a

---

Ask the AI

"How can I set up alerts to monitor mentions of my name or brand online?"
"What are the best tools for self-audit my digital presence?"
"How can I manage privacy settings on popular social media platforms like Facebook, Instagram, and LinkedIn?"

reliable, thoughtful individual. It's important to approach every interaction with an open mind, offer support to others when possible, and avoid engaging in negative or controversial exchanges that can undermine your reputation. In communities such as Reddit, Quora, or even industry-specific forums, establishing yourself as a helpful, knowledgeable participant can open doors to new opportunities and create lasting positive impressions. Table 6.3 lists tools for monitoring and managing your online reputation, providing resources to oversee and protect your digital presence.

Networking professionally through platforms like LinkedIn is a powerful way to strengthen your online reputation. LinkedIn, in particular, offers a space for professionals to connect, collaborate, and showcase their expertise. Regularly updating your profile with current achievements, skills, and projects ensures that your digital resume truly reflects your professional abilities. LinkedIn's endorsement and recommendation features also allow colleagues and peers to vouch for your skills and character, adding credibility to your profile. However, it's important to approach networking with a genuine interest in building relationships rather than simply using the platform for self-promotion. A well-crafted LinkedIn profile and meaningful engagement with your network can boost your credibility and make you a respected presence in your professional field.

Showcasing skills and achievements responsibly involves more than just listing accomplishments; it requires a thoughtful presentation of your abilities and successes. Consider how your achievements are framed when promoting yourself online, whether through a personal website, a LinkedIn profile, or other professional platforms. It's crucial to strike a balance between confidence and humility. You want to convey your expertise and accomplishments without appearing boastful or self-serving. For example, instead of simply listing awards or certifications, provide context on how those achievements contributed to your growth or the success of a project. This approach

Table 6.3 Tools for monitoring and managing your online reputation.

Tool name	Purpose	Features	Platform
Google Alerts	Monitor mentions of your name or keywords online	Set up alerts for specific keywords or phrases; receive email notifications	Web
BrandYourself	Reputation management and online profile improvement	Build a personal brand; remove negative content; improve search rankings	Web
DeleteMe	Help remove personal data from public databases	Delete personal information from data brokers and public records sites	Web
Reputation Defender	Reputation management and online privacy tools	Monitor reputation; remove negative search results; control personal information	Web
Social Search	Search for your social media profiles and mentions	Find social media profiles; review mentions; and assess privacy settings	Web
Pipl	Search for personal data and online profiles	Find data leaks, social media presence, and online history	Web
PrivacyDuck	Privacy-focused service to remove personal data	Opt-out of data brokers; remove personal info from people-search sites	Web
Webmii	Search engine for online presence management	Monitor your online presence; see public information about yourself	Web
Whois	Monitor domain registration data	Check Whois data for domains related to your name or business	Web
DuckDuckGo	Privacy-focused search engine	Search anonymously; track no user data; limit digital footprint	Web and mobile

highlights your qualifications and demonstrates your ability to reflect on and learn from your experiences, adding depth to your professional image.

Balancing transparency with privacy is an ongoing challenge in today's interconnected world. On one hand, being open about your experiences, values, and interests can help build a strong connection with your audience. On the other hand, oversharing or being too candid can expose you to risks, such as identity theft or personal attacks. Finding a middle ground where you can maintain your authenticity without compromising your personal security or well-being is important. This could mean sharing professional accomplishments or personal insights relevant to your audience while keeping sensitive details—like your home address, financial information, or private life—out of the public domain. The key is to stay true to yourself while maintaining control over the information you make available to others.

Addressing negative content or reviews appropriately is crucial to maintaining a positive online reputation. At some point, nearly everyone will face criticism or encounter negative feedback online, whether it's on a professional platform, a social media post, or a review site. How you respond to such content can significantly impact how others perceive you. The best approach is to remain calm, professional, and constructive. If the criticism is valid, acknowledge it, apologize if necessary, and take steps to address the issue. If the feedback is unfounded or malicious, respond politely and, if possible, offer to resolve the situation offline. Ignoring negative content entirely can sometimes exacerbate the issue, while an overreaction can escalate it unnecessarily. By addressing negative content with grace and maturity, you can often turn a potentially harmful situation into an opportunity to demonstrate professionalism and a commitment to growth.

In addition to managing direct criticism, it's important to keep an eye on indirect mentions and to be proactive about addressing potentially damaging content before it becomes a bigger issue. This can be particularly challenging in the case of rumors, misinformation, or incomplete stories that can spread quickly across social media or review sites. Tools like Google Alerts or reputation management services can help you track mentions of your name or brand, allowing you to respond swiftly if any negative content arises. Maintaining emotional detachment when responding to online criticisms or negative reviews is also important. Your digital reputation can be easily influenced by how you engage with these challenges, so answering with a composed, measured approach will reflect more positively on you in the eyes of your audience and potential employers or clients.

Privacy Considerations

Understanding terms of service and privacy policies is an essential yet often overlooked aspect of maintaining control over your digital footprint. These documents, which are frequently long and filled with legal jargon, outline how a company collects, uses, and shares your data. While it's tempting to click "I Agree" without reading through the fine print, doing so can expose you to unexpected privacy risks. Terms of service and privacy policies often include provisions that allow companies to collect and sell your data, track your online behavior, or share your information with

---

Ask the AI

"How can I build a professional online profile that enhances my career prospects?"
"What are the key differences between professional networking platforms like LinkedIn and social platforms like Facebook?"
"How can I handle negative reviews or comments online without damaging my reputation?"

third parties. By reading these documents—at least the sections pertaining to data collection and user privacy—you can make more informed decisions about which services and platforms are worth your time and trust. Without a clear privacy policy, it's wise to reconsider using a service that doesn't respect transparency regarding your data.

Managing cookies and tracking technologies is another critical part of protecting online privacy. Cookies are small data stored on your device by websites to remember your preferences, login details, or browsing history. While they can enhance your online experience by making websites faster and more personalized, they also allow companies to track your behavior across the internet, building detailed profiles that can be used for targeted advertising or sold to third parties. Many websites will prompt you to accept or reject cookies when you visit them, but some cookies can be set even before you make a choice. You can block or limit tracking technologies that collect unnecessary information by using tools like cookie managers or privacy-focused browsers (e.g., Brave or Firefox with enhanced tracking protection). Additionally, regularly clearing your cookies or adjusting your browser's privacy settings ensures that you're not leaving behind a trail of data that could be exploited.

The impact of facial recognition and tagging features on privacy is growing more significant as social media platforms and other services increasingly use these technologies. Facial recognition allows companies to identify individuals based on their facial features by comparing photos in a database or tracking individuals in real time using camera networks. While it has legitimate uses in security, such as unlocking phones or verifying identities, the widespread application of facial recognition can pose serious risks to privacy. For instance, social media platforms often offer tagging features that automatically suggest people in photos, even without their consent. These systems can create detailed digital profiles, sometimes without a person's knowledge, and can be used to track individuals' movements or behaviors across various locations. To protect your privacy, it's wise to disable automatic tagging features on social media platforms, review who has access to your photos, and be cautious about the facial recognition technology you interact with.

Risks associated with sharing personal information online are substantial and often underestimated. Every time you share personal details—whether it's your home address, phone number, or even seemingly innocuous information like your birthday—you are increasing your exposure to potential privacy violations. Cybercriminals and identity thieves thrive on the data people willingly post, using it to craft social engineering attacks or build a comprehensive profile that can be exploited for fraud. Even seemingly innocent personal details can give attackers the foothold they need to manipulate you. To mitigate these risks, limiting what personal information you share is crucial, especially on platforms not specifically designed for secure communication. The less you share publicly, the harder it is for malicious actors to exploit your information.

Online anonymity and pseudonymity offer additional protection for individuals who want to maintain privacy. Using a pseudonym or a fake name allows you to engage in online activities without revealing your identity. This can be particularly valuable in online forums, review sites, or even social media settings where you might not want your personal life connected to your online interactions. However, anonymity and pseudonymity are not foolproof. Even if you use a pseudonym, the data you generate can still be tracked through other means, such as IP addresses or digital fingerprints from your device. To maintain true anonymity, you may need to use additional

---

Ask the AI

"What are the most common terms in privacy policies that users should watch out for?"
"How can I control or limit website cookies and tracking technologies?"
"What are the risks of facial recognition and tagging features on social media?"

privacy tools, such as a VPN or the Tor network, which can help mask your identity and location online. While anonymity can provide a sense of freedom, it also requires a thorough understanding of how your digital actions are tracked and the tools available to protect your true identity.

Future Implications of Your Digital Footprint

How employers and institutions use online information has become increasingly important in the modern digital landscape. Today, not just what's on your resume matters—it's what can be found about you with a simple online search. Employers frequently look at candidates' social media profiles, professional blogs, and even personal websites to assess their character, professionalism, and suitability for a role. Sometimes, an applicant's digital presence can weigh as heavily as their qualifications. For instance, a well-maintained LinkedIn profile may showcase your skills and achievements, but a careless or controversial social media post could lead to disqualification from a job. Understanding that potential employers have access to your entire digital footprint helps reinforce the importance of managing your online reputation with intention, both during the hiring process and throughout your career.

The impact of your digital footprint extends far beyond the professional sphere—it can also influence personal relationships and social interactions. In a world where everything from birthday parties to political opinions can be shared online, your digital presence is often the first place that friends, family, and acquaintances will go to learn about you. Social media platforms like Facebook, Instagram, and Twitter shape how people perceive you, often before they've even met you in person. Negative or overly personal content can lead to misunderstandings, strained relationships, or even the loss of friendships. Conversely, a positive and authentic online presence can foster stronger connections and open doors to new social opportunities. Striking a balance between sharing meaningful aspects of your life and protecting your privacy is crucial to maintaining healthy personal interactions and a positive digital reputation.

Data permanence and the right to be forgotten are increasingly important as more people become aware of the long-lasting nature of online information. Once something is shared on the internet, it's extremely difficult to erase, even if you delete the original post or image. Search engines, websites, and archives may retain copies of your data, making it accessible to anyone who knows where to look. While some countries have enacted legislation, like the European Union's General Data Protection Regulation (GDPR), which includes a "right to be forgotten," not all jurisdictions offer the same protections. The concept behind this law is to allow individuals to request the removal of personal data that is no longer necessary for the purpose for which it was collected. However, enforcing this right can be challenging, especially globally, where local laws may not be compatible. As you manage your digital footprint, it's important to recognize the permanence of online information and take proactive steps to minimize potentially damaging data, even if complete erasure is not always possible.

Preparing for technological advancements, such as deepfakes, is critical to safeguarding your digital identity in the future. Deepfakes, which use artificial intelligence to create highly convincing

---

Ask the AI

"How are employers using social media and online data to assess potential candidates?"
"What are deepfakes, and how do they impact privacy and online reputation?"
"What legal protections are available for the digital privacy of individuals in different countries?"

but fake audio and video content, present a unique threat to personal and professional reputations. Imagine a scenario where a video surfaces online showing you saying or doing something you never did—it could cause irreparable damage, especially if it's shared widely. As technology improves, deepfakes will become more sophisticated, making distinguishing between real and fabricated content harder. While current tools can sometimes detect deepfakes, the technology is evolving at a pace that makes it difficult to stay ahead. Preparing for these threats involves staying informed about emerging technologies, monitoring your digital presence, and being cautious about the information you share. Additionally, having a plan in place for how to address the creation or distribution of false content about you—such as legal action or engaging with reputation management services—can help mitigate potential damage.

Strategies for long-term management of your digital presence require ongoing vigilance and adaptability. As your career, interests, and personal life evolve, so should your online presence. Regularly updating your social media profiles, personal websites, and other online platforms is important for ensuring they reflect your current identity. Over time, you may want to reframe certain posts or remove content that no longer aligns with your values or professional goals. Additionally, it's helpful to periodically audit your digital footprint to ensure that no outdated or irrelevant information is lingering. Implementing a digital housekeeping routine—reviewing privacy settings, removing old accounts, or deleting outdated content—will help you maintain control over your online reputation and ensure that it evolves with you. Long-term digital footprint management requires a balance of consistency, caution, and intentionality.

Educating others about digital footprint awareness is important in fostering a culture of responsible online behavior. While many individuals are becoming more aware of the risks associated with oversharing online, there is still a lack of understanding, especially among younger generations, about how their digital actions can affect them in the future. By educating friends, family, and colleagues about the implications of their online behavior, you can help them avoid common pitfalls, such as oversharing personal information or engaging in inappropriate conduct on social media. Promoting digital literacy—teaching others how to curate their online presence, review privacy settings, and understand the long-term impact of their digital actions—will contribute to a safer, more secure online community. For businesses, this type of education should also extend to employees, as they are often the first line of defense in preventing reputational damage. Encouraging responsible online behavior in personal and professional contexts will help create a more informed and privacy-conscious society.

Recommendations

1. **Review Terms of Service and Privacy Policies:** Make it a habit to read the terms of service and privacy policies of every platform or service you use. Pay close attention to how your data is collected, shared, and stored. If a policy seems overly permissive or unclear, consider opting out or seeking alternatives that offer more transparent data handling practices. This will help you decide which platforms are trustworthy and which may pose privacy risks.

2. **Audit Your Digital Presence Regularly:** Set a schedule to periodically search for your name online and review its associated content. This self-audit will help you identify outdated or potentially harmful information affecting your reputation. Use privacy tools like Google Alerts to track new mentions of your name or brand, and take proactive steps to manage any negative content that arises.

3. **Limit Personal Information Shared Online:** Be mindful of the personal details you share on social media and other online platforms. Avoid sharing sensitive information like your

home address, phone number, and travel plans. This will help you protect yourself from identity theft, phishing attacks, and other privacy violations from oversharing online.

4. **Update Privacy Settings Across Platforms:** Review and adjust the privacy settings on your social media accounts, professional profiles, and any other online platforms you use. Ensure that your data is shared only with trusted individuals or organizations and that third-party advertisers are not tracking your online activities without your consent. Regularly revisiting these settings will help you maintain control over your digital footprint.

5. **Use Pseudonyms and Anonymity Where Appropriate:** When engaging in online activities where your real name and identity aren't necessary, consider using pseudonyms or anonymous accounts. This can help protect your privacy while allowing you to participate in online communities without risking the Exposure of your personal information. Just follow the platform's terms of service and avoid violating any rules about identity misrepresentation.

6. **Respond Professionally to Negative Content:** If you come across negative reviews, comments, or misinformation about yourself online, handle the situation calmly and professionally. Engage politely with those involved, correct any false information, and, when appropriate, take the conversation offline to resolve issues privately. A measured response can turn a potentially damaging situation into an opportunity to demonstrate professionalism and commitment to transparency.

7. **Monitor Emerging Technologies Like Deepfakes:** Stay informed about the development of emerging technologies such as deepfakes, which could impact your online reputation. Be proactive in educating yourself about how these technologies work and the potential risks they pose. This awareness will help you recognize fake content about you and take immediate action to mitigate damage if necessary, such as reporting deepfakes to platforms or engaging legal assistance.

8. **Develop a Long-term Digital Strategy:** Create a long-term plan for managing your digital presence, considering how your online reputation will evolve. Regularly update your profiles, remove outdated content, and ensure your digital identity aligns with your personal or professional goals. A consistent approach to managing your digital footprint will ensure that you remain in control of your online image as your life and career progress.

9. **Educate Friends and Family About Digital Footprint Risks:** Share the importance of digital footprint management with friends, family, and colleagues. Encourage them to be mindful of the information they post online and help them understand how their digital actions can have long-term consequences. Educating those around you will create a more privacy-conscious environment and help protect everyone's reputation in the digital world.

10. **Understand Your Legal Rights Over Data and Images:** Familiarize yourself with the legal protections surrounding your data and image. Research the privacy laws in your country or region, such as the GDPR, which may grant you the right to request the deletion or correction of personal data. Understanding these rights will help you protect your digital identity and take action if others use your data inappropriately.

Conclusion

In conclusion, understanding and managing your digital footprint and online reputation has never been more critical. Every interaction you have online—intentional or passive—creates a permanent record that can influence how others perceive you, impact your professional opportunities, and even affect your relationships. The digital world does not operate in isolation; the data you leave behind can be aggregated, analyzed, and used in ways that may not always be in your best interest.

As a result, it is essential to take proactive steps to monitor and control your online presence, ensuring that your digital footprint reflects your values, professionalism, and privacy needs.

Throughout this chapter, we've examined how your digital footprint is formed and tracked, highlighting active and passive data collection methods. By understanding these processes, you are better equipped to protect your privacy and secure your personal information against misuse. The tools and strategies shared here—from setting up alerts to reviewing privacy settings across platforms—empower you to avoid potential threats to your digital reputation. It's not just about mitigating risks but also about actively managing the narrative of your online presence in a way that aligns with your goals and values.

As you move forward, remember that managing your digital footprint is an ongoing process that requires vigilance and adaptability. Technology continues to evolve, and new challenges will inevitably arise, such as the increasing use of AI-driven data analysis and the spread of digital misinformation. However, you can maintain control over your online identity by remaining informed, adjusting your strategies when necessary, and embracing privacy best practices. Your digital reputation reflects how you engage with the online world. With the right tools and knowledge, you can shape that reputation into one that enhances your personal and professional life.

Chapter Questions

1 How can employers use the information found online about potential employees?
   A. To judge their academic qualifications
   B. To assess their character and professionalism
   C. To determine their salary expectations
   D. To decide if they qualify for employee benefits

2 What is one risk of oversharing personal details on social media?
   A. Losing followers
   B. Exposure to identity theft
   C. Decreasing internet speed
   D. Becoming less visible to friends and family

3 What should you do when you come across negative content about yourself online?
   A. Ignore it completely
   B. Respond in a hostile manner
   C. Address it calmly and professionally
   D. Delete your online profiles

4 What is the right to be forgotten?
   A. The ability to delete all online content automatically
   B. The right to have certain personal data removed from search results
   C. The power to erase your social media accounts with one click
   D. A law that deletes all public records upon request

5 How can deepfakes impact your online reputation?
   A. They can help improve your public image
   B. They can create misleading or harmful fake content

    C. They can increase your social media followers
    D. They are only used in entertainment

6 What is one strategy for managing your long-term digital presence?
    A. Delete all personal content regularly
    B. Update and remove outdated profiles and content
    C. Use only one social media platform
    D. Share everything you do online

7 Why is it important to review privacy settings on social media?
    A. To keep the platform's algorithms running smoothly
    B. To control who can see and use your personal data
    C. To increase your follower count
    D. To keep your profile visible to everyone

8 What is a potential risk of facial recognition technology?
    A. It can automatically tag your friends in photos
    B. It can be used to track and identify individuals without consent
    C. It helps identify lost pets
    D. It enhances user experience on social media

9 What should you do to limit the data tracking on websites?
    A. Disable cookies and tracking technologies
    B. Share all your data with websites
    C. Use the same password across multiple sites
    D. Allow all cookies to improve website functionality

10 What is one benefit of using a pseudonym online?
    A. It ensures all your posts are completely anonymous
    B. It protects your true identity in non-professional contexts
    C. It increases your social media following
    D. It ensures complete legal protection

11 What is a common problem with online content once it is posted?
    A. It can be completely erased immediately
    B. It remains accessible even after it is deleted
    C. It will automatically disappear after a set period
    D. It can be shared only by the original poster

12 How can data brokers affect your online privacy?
    A. They may collect and sell your personal information
    B. They help increase your online visibility
    C. They secure your data from being accessed by third parties
    D. They manage your social media accounts

13 Why is it important to understand the legal rights regarding personal data?
  A. To ensure that companies are using your data for marketing purposes
  B. To help you protect your personal data from misuse
  C. To make sure you receive personalized ads
  D. To guarantee your data is shared with third parties

14 What is a good practice for educating others about digital footprint awareness?
  A. Encourage them to share more personal information online
  B. Advise them to avoid using privacy settings
  C. Teach them about managing their online presence and privacy
  D. Suggest they never delete anything from their social media

15 What is a potential consequence of not managing your digital footprint effectively?
  A. Increased job opportunities
  B. A stronger online reputation
  C. Damage to your personal and professional reputation
  D. More followers on social media

7

Safe and Professional Use of Social Media

In today's digitally connected world, social media has become an integral part of our daily lives, offering vast opportunities for communication, networking, and professional development. However, this convenience has significant risks that can compromise personal and professional security. Whether for work or leisure, social media platforms expose users to potential threats, ranging from cyberattacks to social engineering tactics. As a result, understanding how to use these platforms safely and professionally is essential to protecting your digital identity and maintaining a secure online presence.

The primary challenge of using social media lies in balancing engagement and security. While social media platforms offer unparalleled convenience for connecting with friends, colleagues, and potential clients, they also serve as prime targets for cybercriminals looking to exploit user behavior. Attackers use phishing, fake profiles, and social engineering tactics to extract personal information or gain unauthorized access to accounts. This chapter explores the strategies and best practices for mitigating these threats and guiding you in navigating social media securely and professionally.

Protecting personal information is at the core of safe social media use. The more details that are shared online—intentionally or not—the greater the risk of exposure to malicious actors. The importance of maintaining robust privacy settings, being cautious about which personal information is shared, and managing connections carefully cannot be overstated. This chapter provides detailed guidance on recognizing and addressing potential privacy risks, including the risks associated with oversharing, third-party apps, and location-based data.

In a professional context, social media serves as both a powerful tool for networking and a potential liability if not used correctly. Many professionals now use platforms like LinkedIn, Twitter, and even Facebook to build their brands and engage with industry peers. However, the platforms that facilitate professional growth can also pose risks to one's reputation, career, and security if not used carefully. We will delve into the importance of separating personal and professional accounts, adhering to ethical online behavior, and the impact of professional conduct on digital platforms.

Navigating Social Media Platforms Securely

Social media platforms are ubiquitous in daily life, enabling us to stay connected with friends, family, colleagues, and businesses. The most popular platforms, such as Facebook, Instagram, Twitter (now X), LinkedIn, and TikTok, each offer unique functionalities that cater to different forms of interaction. While these platforms provide incredible convenience, they also introduce distinct security challenges. Understanding the security features of each platform is critical for safeguarding your data and privacy. The more familiar you become with the inner workings of these platforms, the better equipped you will be to navigate them securely and avoid potential pitfalls. Table 7.1 outlines common social media threats and how to recognize them, equipping users with the knowledge to identify and avoid potential risks.

Each social media platform has security tools and features to protect users from unauthorized access and potential threats. For instance, Facebook offers two-factor authentication (2FA), which adds an extra layer of security by requiring users to enter a code and password sent to their mobile devices. Similarly, Instagram provides privacy settings that allow users to make their profiles private, limiting access to their posts to only approved followers. Understanding these platform-specific security features is crucial, as they can significantly reduce your risk of being hacked or falling victim to scams. However, these features are only effective if they are used properly, and users must proactively ensure that they are enabled and correctly configured.

Table 7.1 Common social media threats and how to recognize them.

Threat	Description	How to recognize	Recommended action
Phishing attempts	Attempts to trick users into revealing personal information	Suspicious messages or links requesting personal data	Verify the source before clicking any link, and avoid entering sensitive information
Fake profiles	Accounts created with the intent to impersonate someone or scam users	Limited activity, lack of personal information, suspicious friend requests	Ignore or report fake accounts, and block the user
Bots	Automated accounts that often spam or manipulate interactions	Excessive, irrelevant posts, follows/unfollows large numbers of users	Report the account, and block it if necessary
Harassment	Aggressive or unwanted behavior directed toward a user	Frequent negative comments, insults, or threats	Block the user, report the behavior, and take screenshots for evidence
Malicious links	Links shared by unknown users that direct to harmful websites	Links that look unfamiliar or have unusual URLs	Do not click on suspicious links. Verify through other channels
Impersonation	Accounts pretending to be someone else to manipulate or scam others	Use of another person's profile picture and name	Report the account and inform the impersonated individual
Social engineering	Manipulative tactics used to gather personal information	Messages or requests that seem unusually personal or urgent	Be cautious with unsolicited requests. Verify through another method
Location spoofing	Attempts to trick users into revealing their location information	Unexpected or fabricated location-based posts	Disable location sharing, double-check geotagging settings
Phishing via ads	Ads that lead to malicious sites or ask for personal information	Unsolicited pop-up ads or requests for personal data	Avoid clicking on unsolicited ads, and report suspicious ads
Data harvesting	Scammers use fake contests or quizzes to gather information	Requests for personal details in exchange for prizes or offers	Avoid participating in unfamiliar contests or quizzes

While security features are essential for using social media safely, it is equally important to recognize the platform-specific threats that users may face. Phishing scams are a common threat on platforms like LinkedIn, where attackers may impersonate colleagues or business partners to steal login credentials or financial information. On Instagram and Facebook, malicious third-party apps or fake giveaways can trick users into providing sensitive information. Even popular apps like TikTok have experienced an increase in scams targeting users through malicious links in video descriptions or direct messages. It is important to remain vigilant for signs of suspicious activity and avoid engaging with unsolicited messages or links, no matter how convincing they may appear.

Safe account creation and management are foundational to maintaining a secure social media presence. When creating a new social media account, using a strong, unique password that combines letters, numbers, and special characters is vital. Reusing passwords across multiple platforms significantly increases your exposure to attacks, as a breach on one site can lead to unauthorized access on others. Additionally, enabling 2FA is essential. This extra security layer, though often an extra step, ensures that your account remains protected even if your password is compromised. Never rely on default or weak passwords; change them regularly to mitigate the risk of long-term exposure.

In the age of smartphones, it's easy to forget that location sharing and geotagging can unwittingly expose your movements and activities. Many social media platforms allow users to share their location when posting photos or status updates, and malicious actors can easily exploit this feature. While showing off your location may be tempting, it's important to be mindful of who can see that information and understand its implications. For example, geotagging could inadvertently disclose your home address or vacation whereabouts, making you vulnerable to burglaries or other risks. It's essential to review and control your location-sharing settings on each platform, and whenever possible, avoid tagging your location in real-time.

The risk of oversharing is also prevalent when it comes to location data. Many users may not realize that the photos they share online, particularly on Instagram or Facebook, can contain embedded metadata, including GPS coordinates, which pinpoint the exact location where a photo was taken. This creates an easy target for cybercriminals to exploit, especially when combined with information from other social media interactions. To mitigate these risks, you should disable location services for social media apps or remove geotagging features from your photos before uploading them. This extra step helps protect your privacy and prevents your movements from being tracked without your knowledge.

One often overlooked aspect of social media security is the importance of regularly reviewing and updating privacy settings. Social media platforms frequently update their privacy policies, and what was once considered a safe setting could become a security risk over time. For instance, changing Facebook's privacy settings could mean your posts are no longer private to your intended audience, exposing personal details to strangers. Regularly checking your privacy settings ensures that only the information you want to share remains visible to others. As a rule of thumb, make it a habit to review your settings every few months or after major updates to the platform. Figure 7.1 depicts the social media account security workflow, illustrating the steps to secure accounts against unauthorized access and threats.

Ask the AI

"What are some strong passphrases that combine letters, numbers, and symbols?"
"What are the risks of using personal information, like birthdates or names, in passwords?"
"Can password length make a password more secure? How does length impact security?"

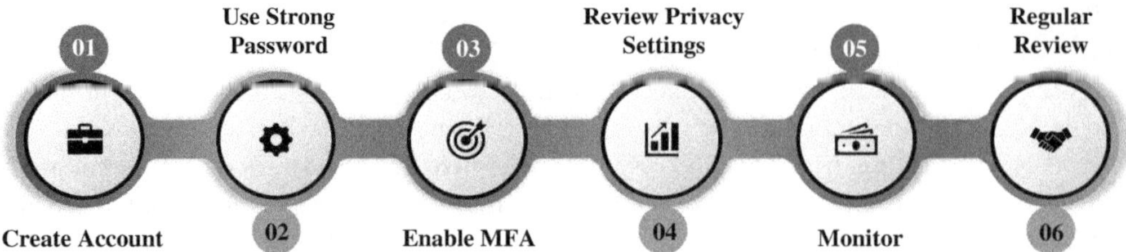

Figure 7.1 Social media account security workflow.

Protecting Personal Information

In the digital age, the information we share online is incredibly valuable, not just to marketers but also to cybercriminals. Limiting the amount of personal data shared on social media platforms is one of the first steps to protecting yourself online. While it may seem harmless to share your birthday, relationship status, or the names of your family members, this information can be used to build a profile of you that cybercriminals can exploit. This is especially true when such details are combined with other publicly available data, like your location or workplace, to gain access to more sensitive accounts. By thinking critically about what data you share, you can reduce the chances of falling victim to identity theft, phishing attacks, or social engineering schemes.

Oversharing on social media is one of the most common ways personal information gets unintentionally exposed. It's easy to get caught up in the moment and share everything from your current location to intimate details about your personal life, but this can create vulnerabilities that cybercriminals eagerly exploit. For example, oversharing can provide attackers with clues to answer security questions for your online accounts or reveal sensitive personal information that they can use for malicious purposes. In particular, information about your schedule or plans—like your vacation dates—can be a signal for burglars to target your home. It's important to take a step back and assess what is necessary to share and what can remain private. When in doubt, consider whether the benefit of sharing that information outweighs the potential risk.

The distinction between public and private profiles is critical for protecting personal information. Many social media platforms allow users to set their accounts to "private," meaning only approved followers can see your posts and interactions. While this may seem like a simple way to protect your information, it's not a catch-all solution. Even with private profiles, data can still be leaked if others share your posts, screenshots are taken, or your privacy settings are misconfigured. Public profiles, conversely, make all your information visible to anyone, including people you don't know. Understanding the risks of these different settings and adjusting them according to your comfort level with privacy is essential for managing what personal information is accessible to others. Table 7.2 details social media privacy settings and best practices, guiding users on how to safeguard their personal information online.

Managing your friend and follower lists carefully is another important strategy for safeguarding your personal information. Social media platforms often encourage users to accumulate as many followers or friends as possible, which can inadvertently expose them to unnecessary risks. Accepting friend requests or followers without scrutinizing who they are or their intentions can open the door to malicious actors, who might be attempting to gather information for fraudulent purposes. Be cautious about who you interact with online, especially if you don't know them personally. A sudden surge in friend requests from strangers, especially with no mutual connections,

Table 7.2 Social media privacy settings and best practices.

Platform	Privacy setting	Description	Best practice
Facebook	Profile visibility	Controls who can see your profile, posts, and personal information	Set your profile to private, and customize who can see your posts
Instagram	Story privacy	Controls who can view your stories	Use the "Close Friends" list to limit who sees your stories
Twitter	Tweet privacy	Controls who can see your tweets	Set tweets to private and only allow approved followers to view your content
LinkedIn	Profile Visibility	Controls who can view your profile and network connections	Set profile to private or visible only to your network
Snapchat	Location sharing	Controls whether your location is visible to others	Disable location sharing and only share with trusted contacts
TikTok	Account privacy	Controls whether your account is public or private	Set account to private to limit exposure to strangers
YouTube	Video privacy	Controls who can view your videos	Use "Unlisted" or "Private" settings for sensitive content
WhatsApp	Last seen	Controls who can see when you were last online	Limit visibility of "Last Seen" to contacts or set to "Nobody"
Messenger	Message requests	Controls who can send you messages	Only accept messages from people you know or have interacted with
Pinterest	Profile visibility	Controls who can see your pins and boards	Set boards to "Secret" for privacy or restrict who can follow you

should raise red flags. The more carefully you manage your lists, the better you'll be able to control who has access to your data.

Third-party apps and quizzes that require access to your social media profiles are another area where caution is necessary. While it may seem harmless to take a quiz or try out a new app, many of these tools request access to sensitive information, such as your contacts, photos, or even direct messages. Some apps may misuse this information or share it with other parties without your explicit consent. Others might not be secure and can introduce vulnerabilities, allowing cybercriminals to access your data. Before authorizing any third-party application, carefully review the permissions it requests and ensure that it comes from a trusted source. Whenever possible, limit the amount of data these apps can access, and if an app isn't essential to your experience, it's safer to avoid it altogether.

Personal photos and media fall into another sensitive information category that requiring special handling. Pictures may seem innocuous, but they can contain valuable metadata, such as geo-tags, that can inadvertently reveal your location or other details about your environment. A seemingly innocent vacation photo might disclose your current whereabouts, which could be a security risk if shared publicly. Even photos that don't contain geotags can be used to extract personal information, especially if they depict details of your home, your workplace, or your daily routines. It is critical to understand how to remove metadata from your photos before posting them online. Additionally, be mindful of the context in which you share media and the potential for images to be misused or distributed without your consent.

Even when sharing photos in private settings, be cautious about how much personal information they reveal. A family photo, for example, might give away details about your living situation, such as your children's names or the neighborhood you live in. Similarly, an image posted at a specific event or location can provide cybercriminals with enough information to mount a targeted attack. The more personal details that can be extracted from an image, the higher the risk that they will be used maliciously. This doesn't mean you must give up sharing photos altogether, but it requires a more thoughtful approach to what you share and where.

Professional Conduct on Social Media

Maintaining a professional image online is crucial in today's interconnected world, where the lines between personal and professional lives often blur. What you post on social media can significantly influence how potential employers, colleagues, and clients perceive you. A single offhand comment or controversial post can stay online indefinitely, affecting your reputation for years. Employers often review candidates' social media profiles as part of the hiring process, so ensuring that your online presence aligns with the professional image you wish to project is essential. Carefully consider the content you share, the tone you use in discussions, and how others could interpret your posts. Maintaining this professional standard online is just as important as in-person conduct, if not more so, due to social media's public and permanent nature.

Understanding and adhering to your employer's social media policies is another critical aspect of professional conduct. Many organizations have strict guidelines regarding what employees can and cannot post online, especially when it comes to work-related content or the use of company branding. These policies are designed to protect the organization's reputation and ensure that employees do not inadvertently share confidential information or create conflicts of interest. For instance, discussing work projects in a public forum without proper clearance can breach confidentiality agreements, while sharing negative opinions about a colleague could lead to a toxic work environment. It's important to familiarize yourself with your employer's policies and ensure your social media activity complies with them. This means understanding the written guidelines as well as the unspoken expectations around professional behavior in online spaces.

Separating personal and professional accounts is a best practice that helps maintain clear boundaries between work and private life. While combining your personal and professional online identities might be tempting, doing so can create risks. For example, a single post about a controversial political opinion or an informal chat in a group could inadvertently reflect poorly on you professionally. Additionally, work-related information shared in private social groups may not remain confidential, especially if those groups are not adequately secured. Having separate accounts for personal and professional use allows you to control what is visible to each audience and ensures that you present yourself appropriately in each context. This separation also makes it easier to focus on building a professional network without the distractions or complications of personal posts.

Ethical considerations in online interactions are at the core of professional conduct on social media. When engaging with others online, especially in professional forums or networking events,

---

Ask the AI

"What are the most common types of personal data that users should avoid sharing on social media?"

"How can oversharing on social media lead to security risks like identity theft or phishing?"

"What steps can you take to ensure your location is not accidentally shared on social media?"

it's essential to treat others with respect and uphold ethical standards. This includes avoiding defamatory language, respecting others' privacy, and adhering to honesty and integrity. Disparaging comments about competitors, coworkers, or customers can damage your reputation and your trust in your professionalism. Additionally, spreading misinformation, even inadvertently, can undermine your credibility. Always strive for positive, constructive interactions that reflect your ethical standards in face-to-face meetings. A well-managed online presence demonstrates professionalism and fosters trust with others in your field.

Networking effectively on social media is one of the most powerful ways to advance your career, but it must be done securely. Social media platforms like LinkedIn offer a unique opportunity to connect with colleagues, potential clients, and industry leaders. However, these platforms are also targets for cybercriminals looking to exploit personal or professional connections for malicious purposes. To ensure that your networking efforts do not compromise your security, it's crucial to verify the identities of those you connect with, particularly if they reach out to you unsolicited. Be cautious of messages that ask for personal information, even if they appear to come from trusted connections. Setting clear privacy settings for your networking accounts, such as limiting who can view your profile details, helps safeguard against unauthorized access while allowing you to engage with your network effectively.

Addressing inappropriate content or interactions online requires a proactive and measured approach. If you encounter inappropriate content, whether directed at you or others, it's important to address the situation in a way that reflects your professional values. In some cases, it may be appropriate to report the content to the platform's moderators or to remove it yourself, especially if it involves harassment, discrimination, or hate speech. Always approach the situation professionally for interactions that happen in a professional context. If an online discussion becomes heated or inappropriate, it's often best to disengage or redirect the conversation to a more appropriate venue, such as private messaging or a formal meeting. This approach helps to maintain your professional demeanor while minimizing the potential for conflict.

Dealing with Social Media Threats

Using social media for positive engagement can have a powerful impact, both personally and professionally. Platforms like LinkedIn, Twitter, and Facebook provide unique opportunities to foster connections, share knowledge, and support causes that align with your values. When leveraged responsibly, social media can be a force for good, allowing you to advocate for important issues, engage in meaningful discussions, and build relationships beyond virtual boundaries. Positive engagement means sharing content that adds value to conversations, whether that's through insightful commentary, helpful resources, or uplifting messages. By remaining mindful of the impact of your words and actions, you can contribute to a healthier and more productive online environment.

Educating others about security and privacy is a key aspect of responsible social media use, particularly given the increasing frequency of cyber threats. Many people remain unaware of the risks

---

Ask the AI

"What are some best practices for separating personal and professional social media accounts?"
"How can I create a professional image on social media while maintaining my privacy?"
"What are the ethical considerations when interacting with others on professional networks like LinkedIn?"

of oversharing or failing to secure their social media accounts. As a cybersecurity expert, you are uniquely positioned to help raise awareness about safe practices and the importance of maintaining privacy. This can be as simple as sharing tips about creating strong passwords, enabling 2FA, or understanding the dangers of clicking on unfamiliar links. By actively educating your network and promoting best practices, you contribute to your safety and the collective security of the online community. You help create a ripple effect beyond your immediate circle whenever you educate someone about protecting their personal data.

Promoting awareness campaigns responsibly requires a strategic and ethical approach. Social media is an incredibly effective tool for raising awareness about important social, environmental, or security issues, but it's essential to approach this task with care. Misinformation can spread just as quickly as legitimate content, so it's crucial to verify the accuracy of the information before sharing it. When promoting a campaign or cause, provide context, cite reputable sources, and encourage critical thinking among your audience. This way, you ensure that the message you're spreading is both accurate and impactful. Whether you're advocating for digital safety, mental health, or climate change, handling sensitive topics with respect and consideration for your audience's needs and understanding is important.

Staying updated on platform changes and updates is another key element of leveraging social media safely. Social media platforms are constantly evolving, introducing new features, privacy settings, and, unfortunately, new security vulnerabilities. These changes can affect how your data is shared, how your privacy is protected, or even the tools you use to navigate these spaces. As a responsible user, it's important to stay informed about these updates through official announcements from the platform or security blogs and newsletters. Taking the time to familiarize yourself with these changes allows you to adapt your behavior accordingly, ensuring that your security settings remain up-to-date and that you're aware of any new risks or features that might affect your digital safety.

Contributing to safe online communities is another crucial aspect of using social media responsibly. Online communities—whether centered around professional interests, hobbies, or social causes—can be great resources for support and connection. However, these spaces are prime targets for malicious activity, ranging from spam and scams to harassment and cyberbullying. You can help set the tone for respectful and secure interactions by actively participating in creating a safe environment. This includes reporting inappropriate behavior, encouraging positive discussions, and supporting those whom malicious actors may target. The more individuals contribute to creating safe online communities, the less room for bad actors to thrive.

Leveraging Social Media Safely

Recognizing fake profiles and bots is crucial in today's online environment, where malicious actors constantly seek to exploit unsuspecting users. Fake profiles are often created to impersonate real individuals or organizations in order to deceive others. These profiles may be used to gather personal information, spread misinformation, or scam individuals out of money. On the other hand, bots are automated accounts designed to manipulate social media interactions on a large

---

Ask the AI

"What are the signs of a fake profile or bot on social media?"
"How can I identify phishing attempts or malicious links shared on social media?"
"What steps should I take if I experience harassment or cyberbullying online?"

scale, often through activities like spamming, posting fake reviews, or attempting to sway public opinion. One of the first signs that an account might be fake is a lack of meaningful content, with many posts appearing generic or copied from other sources. Another indicator is the absence of a personal connection, such as mutual friends or followers. Carefully inspecting an account's activity and comparing it with legitimate profiles can help you identify potential fake accounts before engaging with them. Table 7.3 outlines steps to take if your account is hacked or compromised, providing a clear action plan to mitigate damage and regain control.

Avoiding phishing and malicious links shared via social media is essential for maintaining a secure online experience. Phishing attacks often involve deceptive messages or links that appear to come from trusted sources, such as friends, colleagues, or even well-known companies. These links frequently redirect you to fake websites that steal sensitive information, such as login credentials, financial details, or personal identification. The trick with phishing is that the messages can appear very legitimate—sometimes even mimicking the style and branding of a company you trust. However, a closer look will usually reveal telltale signs, such as an unrecognized URL, strange wording, or inconsistencies in the sender's email address or social media profile. Always

---

Ask the AI

"How can I use social media to promote a cause or awareness campaign while keeping my personal information secure?"

"What are some best practices for balancing social media engagement with real-world activities?"

"How can I contribute to online communities positively and securely?"

Table 7.3 Steps to take if your account is hacked or compromised.

Step	Action	Why it's important
1	Change your password immediately	Prevents further unauthorized access to your account
2	Enable two-factor authentication (2FA)	Adds an extra layer of security by requiring a second form of verification
3	Check recent account activity for suspicious actions	Identifies any actions that were made without your consent
4	Revoke access to any third party apps that might have been connected	Ensures malicious apps no longer have access to your account
5	Report the incident to the platform's support team	Helps the platform take action against the hacker and track the breach
6	Alert your contacts about the hack	Warns others that your account might be used to send spam or malicious content
7	Run a security scan on your device	Detects malware or viruses that may have facilitated the hack
8	Update all passwords for other accounts linked to the same login credentials	Prevents the hacker from gaining access to other accounts using the same password
9	Review your privacy settings and adjust as necessary	Ensures that your account is secure and your information is properly protected
10	Consider using a password manager for future account management	A password manager stores complex passwords securely, preventing future breaches from weak passwords

be wary of unsolicited messages containing links, particularly if they ask for personal information or redirect you to unfamiliar websites. If in doubt, verify the request through other means before clicking on any link or providing sensitive information.

Reporting and blocking abusive users are among the most effective ways to protect yourself from further harm and minimize the reach of malicious behavior. Nearly every social media platform offers mechanisms for reporting inappropriate content or abusive users. These reports are typically reviewed by platform moderators who can remove harmful content or suspend accounts that violate the platform's terms of service. Additionally, blocking users prevents them from seeing your posts, sending messages, or engaging with you online. While reporting and blocking may not eliminate harassment, they can avoid further engagement with toxic individuals and provide a sense of security. It's important to understand how to use these tools effectively and to take advantage of privacy settings that allow you to control who can contact you and who can view your posts. Regarding online threats, taking a proactive approach to reporting and blocking helps mitigate potential damage.

Protecting against social engineering attacks is critical in defending yourself from threats designed to manipulate your behavior into revealing sensitive information. Social engineering attacks typically involve tactics that exploit psychological manipulation, often through emotional appeals, trust-building, or exploiting social norms. For instance, a scammer may pose as a friend or colleague needing help, asking for money or access to personal details. These attacks can be highly convincing because they are tailored to the victim's emotional triggers, making it crucial always to question unsolicited requests, even if they appear to come from trusted contacts. Social engineering can also occur in more subtle forms, such as when attackers use public social media information to craft personalized messages to gain access to your accounts or networks. Always be skeptical of requests for personal information, and verify suspicious interactions through another communication channel if necessary. By recognizing the psychological techniques used in these attacks, you can avoid falling victim to them.

Recovering hacked or compromised accounts requires prompt action and careful attention to detail. Social media accounts are often targeted because they contain a wealth of personal information, including contact details, photos, and even access to financial accounts. If you suspect that your account has been compromised, the first step is to change your password immediately, using a strong and unique one. Most social media platforms also offer 2FA as an added layer of security, which helps prevent unauthorized access even if someone obtains your password. In addition to changing your login credentials, review your account's recent activity to identify any suspicious actions or changes. If the attacker has made unauthorized changes to your account settings or content, report the issue to the platform's support team, providing them with all relevant details. Most platforms have dedicated recovery procedures for hacked accounts, and the faster you act, the better your chances of regaining control. Always enable additional security measures to monitor future threats, such as email alerts for account activity.

Recommendations

1. **Recognize Fake Profiles and Bots:** Pay close attention to profiles that lack personal content or meaningful engagement. Fake accounts often have minimal posts or are solely used to broadcast generic information. Before accepting a connection, review the account's activity and check for any red flags like unusual language or a lack of mutual connections. Trust your instincts and avoid engaging with suspicious profiles if something feels off.

2. **Stay Wary of Phishing Links:** Always be cautious when receiving unsolicited messages with links, especially if they ask for personal information. Verify the sender by checking their profile for legitimacy and look out for small details, such as misspelled URLs or unusual email addresses. Never click on links that seem out of place, and instead, visit the website directly through your browser to ensure its authenticity. Confirm with them directly using another communication method if the message is from a friend or colleague.

3. **Document and Report Harassment:** If you experience harassment or come across abusive content, document the interaction by taking screenshots or saving messages as evidence. Reporting the incident to the platform administrators is important in stopping harassment and ensuring accountability. Most platforms provide tools to report abusive content; many have dedicated teams to address these concerns. By reporting harassment, you help protect yourself and others from similar experiences.

4. **Utilize Blocking and Privacy Features:** Take advantage of blocking and privacy settings to protect yourself from unwanted interactions. Blocking abusive users immediately limits their ability to contact or view your content. Review your privacy settings regularly to ensure only trusted individuals can access your posts and personal information. Customizing these settings can help create a safer online environment tailored to your comfort level.

5. **Be Cautious with Social Engineering Requests:** Always question unsolicited requests for personal information, especially from unfamiliar or unexpected sources. Social engineers often impersonate trusted contacts or create emotional appeals to manipulate you into revealing sensitive details. If you receive a suspicious request, stop and verify the details through a different communication channel before acting on it. Cybercriminals thrive on exploiting trust, so healthy skepticism is crucial for security.

6. **Enable 2FA:** Strengthen your social media accounts by enabling 2FA wherever possible. This adds an extra layer of protection by requiring your password and a code sent to your phone or email. 2FA greatly reduces the risk of unauthorized access, even if someone gains access to your password. It's an essential practice for safeguarding your accounts against hacks.

7. **Stay Informed About Platform Changes:** Regularly check for updates to the social media platforms you use, as they often introduce new features, security settings, or policy changes that could affect your privacy. Proactively learning about these updates helps you adapt your security practices accordingly. Many platforms offer security tips or blog posts regarding new changes, which can help you avoid emerging threats.

8. **Be Mindful of What You Share Online:** Limit the personal or sensitive information you share on social media platforms. Oversharing can make you vulnerable to identity theft, phishing attacks, and social engineering. Consider the long-term impact of the information you post, as it may be used against you or exploited later. Always think before posting anything that could compromise your safety or privacy.

9. **Recover Accounts Quickly if Compromised:** If your account is hacked, act swiftly by changing your password and securing your account with 2FA. Most social media platforms offer account recovery tools that allow you to regain control, but the faster you respond, the better your chances of minimizing the damage. After regaining access, review recent activity for signs of tampering and report any suspicious actions to the platform's support team.

10. **Promote Safe Online Communities:** Contribute positively to online communities by showing respectful and responsible behavior. Engage in constructive discussions and report any harmful content you encounter. Being active in fostering safe spaces online helps make platforms more secure for everyone. Encourage others to adopt safe practices and support those cyberbullies or scammers may target.

Conclusion

As we've explored throughout this chapter, the benefits of social media are undeniable, but so are the risks associated with its use. In an increasingly connected world, the line between personal and professional online activity is often blurred, making it essential to take proactive steps to protect oneself from the ever-evolving threats lurking in the digital landscape. Social media can be a powerful tool for personal engagement and professional networking when used safely and thoughtfully. However, the platforms that connect us can expose us to serious security risks without the proper precautions.

The key to managing these risks lies in understanding the potential threats and taking deliberate action to secure your accounts and information. From recognizing phishing attempts and fake profiles to configuring privacy settings and monitoring your digital footprint, every step you take toward strengthening your security posture reduces your exposure to cybercrime. Being vigilant about privacy settings and mindful of what you share can significantly lower the likelihood of falling victim to common social media threats. Regularly reviewing your online presence and understanding the implications of oversharing are fundamental to maintaining control over your digital life.

In a professional context, how you engage with others on social media can impact your reputation and career trajectory. You can foster a positive and secure digital presence by establishing clear boundaries between personal and professional profiles, adhering to ethical online behavior, and managing your network cautiously. Social media should be seen as a tool for professional advancement, but only when used in alignment with your values and security principles. Safeguarding your professional image online not only protects your career but also enhances your credibility in your field.

It's important to stay informed about the evolving risks and the continuous updates social media platforms make to enhance security. Cyber threats are always changing, so the tools and practices we use to defend against them must evolve. The recommendations provided in this chapter are just the beginning of your journey toward safe social media use. By continuously educating yourself on emerging threats and adapting your strategies, you can ensure that your digital presence remains secure and professional for years to come.

In summary, social media is a powerful tool that demands responsibility. By following the best practices outlined here and staying vigilant, you can mitigate the risks and fully benefit from these platforms' opportunities. The goal is not just to avoid threats but to use social media confidently, securely, and in a way that supports your well-being and professional success. Take the time to implement the strategies discussed in this chapter and enjoy the advantages of a safe and secure social media experience.

Chapter Questions

1 What is a key sign that a social media profile may be fake?
   A. Frequent posting of original content
   B. Lack of mutual connections
   C. High engagement with followers
   D. Detailed personal information

2 What should you do if you receive a suspicious link from an unknown source on social media?
   A. Click on the link to see where it leads
   B. Ignore the link and continue browsing
   C. Verify the source and URL before clicking
   D. Share the link with friends for their opinion

3 What is the best course of action if you encounter online harassment?
  A. Ignore the messages and do nothing
  B. Respond with a similar level of aggression
  C. Take screenshots and report the behavior to the platform
  D. Leave the platform entirely

4 What is the purpose of enabling two-factor authentication (2FA) on social media accounts?
  A. To receive notifications for every activity on your account
  B. To prevent unauthorized access by requiring a second form of identification
  C. To simplify the login process
  D. To share your activity history with others

5 How can you protect yourself from social engineering attacks on social media?
  A. Always trust direct messages from people you know
  B. Question unsolicited requests for personal information and verify them through other channels
  C. Share personal details only with trusted contacts
  D. Accept friend requests from anyone, as it's harmless

6 What is an effective way to stop unwanted interactions on social media?
  A. Respond to all messages politely
  B. Block or report abusive users
  C. Ignore abusive content and move on
  D. Engage in arguments with the user to resolve the situation

7 What should you do if you suspect that your social media account has been hacked?
  A. Change your password immediately and enable 2FA
  B. Ignore the issue and hope it resolves itself
  C. Post about the incident on your feed to inform others
  D. Continue using the account without making changes

8 How can you identify phishing attempts in social media messages?
  A. They often include a request to share personal information
  B. They come only from unknown senders
  C. They are written in perfect, formal language
  D. They provide extensive information about your social media activities

9 What should you do if you encounter a suspicious account impersonating someone you know?
  A. Ignore the account and continue browsing
  B. Report the account and warn the person being impersonated
  C. Engage with the account to verify its authenticity
  D. Block the account and do nothing else

10 Why is it important to regularly check and update your social media privacy settings?
  A. To ensure your posts are visible to as many people as possible
  B. To protect your information by keeping privacy settings current
  C. To increase your follower count
  D. To make your profile more appealing to advertisers

11 What is the role of bots in social media security threats?
  A. They help increase user engagement by automatically liking posts
  B. They can automate malicious actions like spamming or manipulating interactions
  C. They are used for providing customer service on platforms
  D. They generate content that promotes the platform

12 What is a sign that an account may be a bot?
  A. The account frequently posts original and engaging content
  B. The account follows and interacts with hundreds or thousands of random users
  C. The account has a profile picture and bio
  D. The account responds to messages immediately and personally

13 When should you report a post or user on a social media platform?
  A. Only when it violates the platform's terms of service
  B. When you find the post to be inappropriate or harmful
  C. Only when the post is made by someone you don't like
  D. When the post appears to be an advertisement

14 What is the benefit of using blocking features on social media?
  A. It stops the user from commenting on your posts only
  B. It prevents the user from sending you messages or interacting with your posts
  C. It increases your follower count by removing unwanted users
  D. It sends the blocked user a notification

15 Why should you be cautious about sharing personal information on social media?
  A. It could be used against you in a social engineering attack or identity theft
  B. It may increase your social media following
  C. It allows your friends to see more of your personal life
  D. It helps you maintain a more engaging profile

8

Dealing with Cyberbullying and Online Harassment

In our increasingly interconnected world, digital communication is central to how we interact, socialize, and conduct business. However, as our dependence on digital platforms grows, so does the potential for harm, particularly in the form of cyberbullying. Cyberbullying, a form of harassment or bullying that takes place over digital platforms such as social media, messaging apps, and online forums, can have a significant impact on individuals, particularly vulnerable groups such as children, teenagers, and even adults in professional settings. Unlike traditional bullying, which typically occurs in person, cyberbullying can be relentless, pervasive, and sometimes anonymous, making it more difficult to escape and address.

The nature of cyberbullying has changed with the advent of social media, smartphones, and instant messaging platforms. These technologies have made it easier for bullies to reach their targets at any time, from virtually anywhere, with a much wider audience. As a result, victims can experience harassment and humiliation in public spaces—both online and offline—and often feel as if they have nowhere to turn. The anonymity provided by the internet can embolden perpetrators, who may act with a sense of detachment from the harm they are causing, making it even harder to intervene effectively.

This chapter delves into the complex issue of cyberbullying, exploring its various forms, the psychological dynamics behind it, and the profound impact it can have on its victims. It also provides practical strategies for identifying signs of cyberbullying, protecting oneself from digital harassment, and advocating for stronger measures to prevent it. By understanding both the causes and consequences of cyberbullying, we can begin to foster a safer and more supportive digital environment for everyone. Whether you're a parent, educator, or professional or have experienced cyberbullying firsthand, this chapter will equip you with the knowledge and tools to effectively address and prevent this pervasive issue.

Cyberbullying can affect individuals in many different ways, from causing emotional distress and psychological trauma to impacting physical health and academic or work performance. Victims may experience feelings of isolation, anxiety, and depression, and in severe cases, the effects of cyberbullying can even lead to self-harm or suicide. Recognizing the signs of cyberbullying early is crucial for mitigating these impacts and providing the necessary support. While the responsibility to combat cyberbullying lies with multiple stakeholders—individuals, communities, educational institutions, and technology platforms—each of us has a role in creating a safer online space.

Ultimately, addressing cyberbullying requires a combination of prevention, intervention, and advocacy. From setting clear guidelines for online behavior to educating users on the impact of their words and actions, everyone has the power to contribute to the solution. By fostering a culture of respect, empathy, and accountability, we can reduce the prevalence of cyberbullying and make digital spaces more inclusive and supportive. In the following sections, we'll explore actionable strategies for victims and advocates, helping you better navigate and respond to this increasingly prevalent issue.

Understanding Cyberbullying and Harassment

Cyberbullying refers to the use of digital platforms and technologies to harass, intimidate, or harm others. It encompasses a range of behaviors, including spreading false information, sending threatening messages, and deliberately excluding someone from online groups or social media circles. This form of bullying typically involves repeated actions where the perpetrator seeks to cause distress, harm, or emotional pain to the victim. Unlike traditional bullying, cyberbullying can occur 24/7, and victims may feel trapped in an inescapable cycle of harassment, as the digital world offers few safe spaces. Social media, online gaming platforms, and messaging services provide easy access for bullies to target individuals anonymously, which significantly alters the nature and scope of this behavior. Figure 8.1 illustrates common signs of cyberbullying in victims, highlighting key indicators to help identify those affected by online harassment.

The main difference between cyberbullying and traditional bullying lies in the attack and its reach. Traditional bullying often occurs face-to-face, typically within schools or local communities, where the perpetrator and the victim are both physically present. In contrast, cyberbullying transcends physical boundaries, taking place in the digital world where victims may not always know their harassers personally. It also allows the bullying to continue even when the victim is away from school or other physical locations. This persistent nature, coupled with the ability to reach a wider audience, can make cyberbullying more damaging. The anonymity of online interactions also removes the immediate feedback of seeing someone's emotional reaction in real time, which can embolden bullies.

The psychology behind online harassment is complex and often rooted in a desire for power, control, or retaliation. Cyberbullies may target individuals who are perceived as different, vulnerable, or unable to defend themselves effectively in an online space. The relative anonymity of digital interactions can lower a perpetrator's inhibitions, leading them to behave in ways they might not in face-to-face encounters. There is often a sense of detachment when bullying online, as the consequences of one's actions are not always immediately visible. This detachment can create a false sense of security for the bully, who may feel less accountable for their behavior.

The impact of cyberbullying on victims can be severe and long-lasting. Victims may experience emotional distress, including feelings of anxiety, depression, and isolation. In some cases, the constant barrage of harassment can lead to more serious psychological issues such as post-traumatic

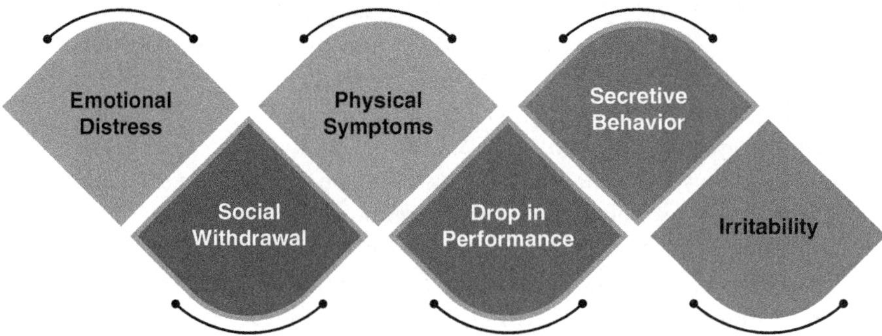

Figure 8.1   Common signs of cyberbullying in victims.

stress disorder (PTSD), self-harm, and suicidal ideation. The emotional toll of being targeted online can also affect a person's self-esteem, leading them to withdraw from social activities or avoid engaging with others. Beyond emotional scars, the consequences of cyberbullying can manifest physically, as victims may experience sleep disturbances, appetite changes, or physical symptoms of stress such as headaches and stomach aches. In severe cases, the effects of cyberbullying may lead to irreversible psychological damage, making it a pervasive concern for mental health professionals.

From a legal perspective, cyberbullying is not only a harmful behavior but also a punishable crime in many jurisdictions. Laws surrounding cyberbullying vary by country and region, but in general, they seek to provide legal recourse for victims and hold perpetrators accountable. In some places, cyberbullying falls under harassment laws, while others have specific legislation designed to address the unique nature of online harm. These laws may result in criminal charges, civil suits, or orders of protection against cyberbullies. However, the legal landscape is still developing in many parts of the world, and the difficulty of prosecuting online harassment—due to issues like anonymity and jurisdictional challenges—means that many perpetrators evade legal consequences.

Anonymity plays a significant role in enabling online harassment. The ability to hide behind a screen allows individuals to avoid immediate consequences for their actions. This sense of invisibility can embolden bullies to escalate their behavior, as they do not have to face their victim directly. Anonymity also makes it difficult for victims to identify their harassers, leaving them feeling powerless and unsure of how to stop the abuse. While anonymity may protect the bully's identity, it also prevents the victim from gaining closure or understanding the reasons behind the attack. This lack of transparency further compounds the emotional distress experienced by the victims, as they are left in the dark about who is behind the harassment and why they are being targeted.

The role of digital platforms in facilitating cyberbullying cannot be understated. Social media websites, messaging apps, and gaming platforms have become central to our daily lives, offering positive and negative experiences. These platforms often lack sufficient safeguards to protect users from harassment, leaving individuals vulnerable to abuse. While many platforms have implemented reporting systems and harassment policies, the sheer volume of content and users makes monitoring and intervening effectively in all cases difficult. As a result, many victims find themselves facing ongoing abuse without adequate support from the platforms themselves. The very design of some social media platforms—encouraging constant interaction, validation through likes, and the sharing of personal details—can inadvertently fuel a culture of bullying where aggressive behavior is normalized or, worse, celebrated.

Recognizing Signs of Cyberbullying

Cyberbullying can be difficult to identify because it often occurs in private or online spaces where others may not witness the harassment. However, several behavioral and emotional changes in victims can be warning signs. One of the most noticeable indicators is a sudden change in behavior or mood. Victims of cyberbullying may become more withdrawn, anxious, or irritable, and they may seem unusually preoccupied or upset after spending time online. The emotional toll of ongoing

---

Ask the AI

"What are the different types of cyberbullying, and how do they differ from traditional bullying?"
"What are the psychological effects of cyberbullying on both victims and perpetrators?"
"How does anonymity online contribute to the rise of cyberbullying and harassment?"

harassment can lead to a marked shift in personality, often resulting in a visible decline in overall well-being. If someone who was once outgoing becomes unusually quiet or displays mood swings without clear reason, it may be worth investigating whether online bullying contributes (Table 8.1).

Another common sign of cyberbullying is a marked social withdrawal or reluctance to engage with digital devices. Victims may avoid using their phones, computers, or other digital platforms that were once integral to their daily lives. They may stop participating in social media conversations or become hesitant to join online communities or groups they once frequented. This reluctance to engage with digital technology is often a direct result of the emotional distress caused by the harassment. The sense of safety that social media and other online platforms once offered may quickly turn into a source of anxiety, making victims reluctant to interact with their devices, which they now associate with the bullying.

A more subtle but significant sign of cyberbullying is a sudden and unexplained decline in academic or work performance. Individuals who are being bullied online may become distracted, unable to focus, or less motivated to complete tasks. In school, a victim may start skipping classes or turning in assignments late due to a lack of concentration or a desire to avoid the harassment. Similarly, a person might show up late, miss deadlines, or lack engagement with their colleagues in the workplace. These changes in behavior may be a result of the emotional strain caused by the constant pressure of online abuse. The stress and anxiety of being targeted can overshadow the individual's ability to focus on work or academic responsibilities, leading to a significant drop in performance.

Changes in online activity patterns can also be indicative of someone experiencing cyberbullying. Victims may reduce or alter their online presence by cutting back on the time spent on digital platforms or changing the types of sites they visit. For example, someone might start avoiding certain social media platforms or stop sharing personal information, fearing it could be used against them by the bully. The shift in activity may not always be immediately obvious, but it can serve as a red flag for someone withdrawing from the digital world to avoid further harassment. In extreme cases, victims might delete their social media accounts or change their usernames to escape ongoing attacks.

Table 8.1 Signs of cyberbullying in victims.

Sign	Possible indicator
Social withdrawal	Victims may avoid social media or decrease communication with others
Changes in online activity patterns	Sudden decrease in time spent online or increased secrecy about online activity
Emotional distress	Frequent mood swings, anxiety, or depression related to online interactions
Physical symptoms	Complaints of headaches, stomachaches, or other stress-related issues
Decline in academic/work performance	Drop in grades or reduced productivity due to emotional distress
Increased irritability	Victim may become more easily frustrated or upset
Reluctance to use devices	Avoidance of technology or devices that are associated with bullying
Unexplained absences	Skipping school or work due to fear or emotional distress from online interactions
Sleep disturbances	Difficulty sleeping due to stress, anxiety, or nightmares related to cyberbullying
Secretive behavior	Increased privacy regarding online activities and reluctance to share information

Physical symptoms, though often overlooked, are another critical sign of cyberbullying. Victims may begin to experience headaches, stomachaches, or other stress-related physical ailments. These symptoms often stem from the constant emotional and psychological strain caused by online harassment. The toll of cyberbullying can manifest physically as the body reacts to the heightened stress levels caused by the anxiety and fear associated with being harassed. Headaches, dizziness, or gastrointestinal problems can all be linked to the mental and emotional distress that bullying creates. These physical symptoms may not seem related to online harassment at first, but they can be an important clue when considering the broader impact of cyberbullying on an individual's health.

In addition to the direct signs of cyberbullying, friends, and peers of the victim may unintentionally provide indirect cues that something is wrong. Concerned friends may notice the victim appearing agitated, sad, or distracted more frequently. In some cases, peers may report worrying behavior, such as reluctance to participate in group activities or a noticeable change in how the individual interacts with others. Friends might also observe that the victim has started to act secretively or avoid talking about their online experiences. These indirect signs are especially important because they come from individuals who may have witnessed the victim's behavior before the bullying began. Often, close friends can spot subtle changes in someone's demeanor, even before the victim realizes the full extent of the impact cyberbullying has on them.

In some instances, victims of cyberbullying may exhibit a heightened sense of fear or anxiety when it comes to interacting with online content, even outside of the harassment. This includes an aversion to checking messages, emails, or social media notifications, as the victim anticipates receiving negative or threatening messages. A once enthusiastic person about digital communication might now hesitate to engage with even neutral online content. This behavior change often signals that the victim is living in a constant state of alert, expecting the next attack. The desire to avoid online spaces altogether may result in them becoming more isolated, further exacerbating the emotional toll of the bullying.

Victims may also display signs of emotional distress that can be difficult for outsiders to interpret. They might experience emotional outbursts, such as crying or sudden fits of anger, which are often tied to the frustration of being unable to escape or stop the harassment. In some cases, individuals may turn to unhealthy coping mechanisms, such as substance abuse or self-harm, as a means of dealing with the overwhelming emotions caused by bullying. The mental and emotional consequences of being bullied online can be profound, and the victim may not always know how to express the pain they are feeling. These signs of emotional distress should never be dismissed, as they can be clear indicators of deeper issues rooted in the experience of cyberbullying.

Strategies for Victims

For individuals experiencing cyberbullying or online harassment, the first and most important step is to document the incidents. Victims should take screenshots or save copies of threatening messages, inappropriate content, or any interactions that illustrate the bullying behavior. This documentation serves as evidence, which may be crucial if the situation escalates or requires intervention from

---

Ask the AI

"What are the early warning signs that someone might be a victim of cyberbullying?"
"How can you differentiate between normal behavioral changes and those triggered by online harassment?"

platform administrators, law enforcement, or legal counsel. It is important to capture not only the content of the messages but also the dates and times they were received, as this can help establish patterns of harassment. If the bully changes usernames or deletes messages, the saved documentation may be the only proof available, underscoring the importance of keeping accurate records (Table 8.2).

Once the documentation is in place, the next critical step is to avoid engaging directly with the bully or harasser. It might be tempting to retaliate or try to reason with the perpetrator, but this usually exacerbates the situation. Engaging in arguments online can escalate the bullying, making it even more intense or prolonged. Bullies thrive on attention, and responding to their taunts can provide them with the reaction they seek, feeding the cycle of abuse. Additionally, responding may give the bully more ammunition, as they may twist the victim's words or manipulate the interaction to further harm them. The best action is to ignore the bully and focus on taking the steps needed to protect oneself.

Adjusting privacy settings on social media platforms and blocking users from engaging in harassment are other important strategies for victims. Many social platforms offer robust privacy controls that allow users to limit who can contact them, view their profiles, or comment on their posts. Victims should use these tools to restrict access to their personal information, ensuring that only trusted friends or contacts can interact with them. Blocking users who are harassing or bullying will prevent further contact, although it's worth noting that this may not prevent the bully from creating new accounts to continue their attacks. Despite this, blocking can still develop a sense of safety and reduce the victim's exposure to harmful interactions. Victims should also regularly review their online presence for greater protection, ensuring that no sensitive information is publicly available or easily discoverable.

Reporting incidents to platform administrators is an essential step in addressing online harassment. Social media networks, online forums, and other digital platforms typically have mechanisms for users to report abusive behavior. These platforms often employ moderation teams or automated systems to review reported content and take action against violators. Depending on the

Table 8.2 Strategies for victims of cyberbullying.

Strategy	Description
Document incidents	Take screenshots, save messages, and keep a record of the bullying for reporting purposes
Do not engage with the bully	Avoid responding or retaliating, as it may escalate the situation
Adjust privacy settings	Make social media profiles private and block or mute the bully
Report to platform administrators	Report the harassment to the platform or service provider for action
Seek support from trusted individuals	Talk to family members, friends, or counselors for emotional support
Use digital tools for protection	Install security tools, such as anti-virus or monitoring apps, to protect your privacy
Reach out to school/workplace officials	If the bullying is affecting school or work, inform relevant authorities or HR
File legal complaints when necessary	In severe cases, consider involving law enforcement or legal advisors
Take a break from social media	Temporarily disconnect from social media to regain control over your mental health
Engage in self-care activities	Practice mindfulness, relaxation, or hobbies to reduce stress and build resilience

platform, this may result in removing offensive posts, warnings to the harasser, or even permanent bans. By reporting the bullying, victims protect themselves and help reduce the likelihood of the bully targeting others in the future. While it can feel like a daunting process, especially when facing an anonymous bully, reporting incidents sends a clear message that online harassment is not acceptable and should not be tolerated.

In addition to reporting online harassment to administrators, victims should seek support from trusted individuals. This can include family members, friends, or professional counselors who can provide emotional support and practical advice. The social and emotional impact of cyberbullying can be isolating, and having a support network can help victims feel less alone in their struggle. Trusted individuals may also offer a fresh perspective, helping the victim to assess the situation more rationally and avoid escalating emotions. Support groups, either online or in person, can also be invaluable for sharing experiences and coping strategies. These groups often provide a sense of solidarity and comfort, knowing that others have faced similar challenges and successfully navigated them.

There are also legal options available for victims of cyberbullying, especially if the harassment escalates to threats, stalking, or other criminal behavior. Many countries have laws that address online harassment, cyberstalking, and defamation. If the bullying is severe, victims may consider consulting an attorney specializing in Internet law or digital privacy to explore their legal options. In some cases, it may be necessary to file a police report, particularly if the bullying includes threats of violence, extortion, or actions that could lead to physical harm. Legal intervention can sometimes lead to restraining orders or criminal charges, depending on the severity of the harassment. Victims should remember that while the law provides avenues for recourse, it's crucial to understand when it is necessary to involve authorities. If at any point the harassment feels threatening or unsafe, contacting the police should be considered a priority.

When deciding when to involve authorities, victims must trust their instincts and assess the gravity of the situation. While not every instance of cyberbullying requires legal intervention, certain signs—such as persistent threats, physical harm, or a marked decline in the victim's mental health—can signal that the involvement of law enforcement is warranted. For example, if a bully's behavior crosses into illegal activities such as doxxing (publicly revealing private information), identity theft, or extortion, it may require legal action. Authorities can investigate the matter, subpoena data from online platforms, and potentially bring criminal charges against the perpetrator. In these cases, the victim must continue documenting incidents and record all interactions to assist in the legal process.

Preventing Cyberbullying

Promoting respectful online communication is one of the most effective strategies for preventing cyberbullying. In the digital age, communication is often quick, impersonal, and lacks the social cues that govern face-to-face interactions. The absence of nonverbal signals, such as body language or tone of voice, can make it easier for individuals to misunderstand one another or, worse, to

---

Ask the AI

"What are the best ways to document evidence of cyberbullying, including screenshots and messages?"
"How can adjusting privacy settings on social media help prevent further harassment?"
"What are the legal options available to victims of cyberbullying, and when should they involve authorities?"

misinterpret messages in a harmful way deliberately. We can help reduce the likelihood of conflict and bullying by emphasizing the importance of clear, respectful communication. Encouraging users to think before they type and to consider how others might perceive their words fosters a more positive online environment, where respect is valued over anonymous negativity (Table 8.3).

Educating individuals, particularly young users, about the impact of their words and actions online is another critical step in preventing cyberbullying. Many individuals, especially those new to digital spaces, may not fully comprehend the consequences of their actions. A single unkind message can impact a person's emotional well-being, even if not intended to cause harm. By fostering awareness of the potential consequences of online behavior, we can encourage individuals to choose their words more carefully and avoid engaging in harmful conduct. Education should focus not only on the immediate emotional effects on the victim but also on the long-term psychological damage that can result from cyberbullying, which may extend well beyond the moment of the harassment.

Encouraging empathy and understanding is foundational to preventing cyberbullying. One of the reasons cyberbullying thrives is because it often occurs in spaces where the bully and victim are disconnected, both physically and emotionally. Empathy helps individuals understand how their actions affect others, cultivating a sense of responsibility for their digital space. When individuals understand the emotional weight their words and actions can carry, they are less likely to engage in harmful behavior. Teaching young users about the power of kindness and encouraging them to place themselves in others' shoes can foster a more compassionate digital culture where understanding outweighs judgment.

Setting clear rules and guidelines for online behavior is essential for creating a safe digital environment. Just as rules govern behavior in physical spaces like schools or workplaces, clear online rules help to ensure that individuals know what is acceptable and what is not. These rules should

Table 8.3 Prevention and advocacy strategies.

Strategy	Description
Promote respectful online communication	Encourage kindness, empathy, and thoughtfulness in online interactions
Set clear online behavior guidelines	Establish clear rules for acceptable behavior within online communities or households
Educate about the impact of cyberbullying	Host workshops, seminars, or discussions to raise awareness about the harm caused by cyberbullying
Monitor online activity	Parents and guardians should regularly check children's social media activity and online interactions
Provide support systems	Offer counseling services, hotlines, and support groups for victims of cyberbullying
Advocate for stronger policies	Push for laws and regulations that make digital harassment punishable and provide legal protections
Foster community involvement	Encourage schools, workplaces, and communities to take collective action against cyberbullying
Encourage digital citizenship education	Implement programs that teach responsible, respectful, and safe online behavior
Engage in online advocacy campaigns	Support or create digital campaigns to raise awareness and push for change
Create safe online spaces	Design online environments that are monitored for harmful behaviors and promote positive interactions

cover harassment, cyberbullying, and sharing personal information. Establishing a framework for inappropriate behavior can guide users in making responsible decisions online. Schools, workplaces, and social platforms should work to develop and enforce these guidelines, offering clear consequences for those who fail to adhere to them. By providing structure and accountability, we can create environments where digital spaces are respected as much as physical ones.

Parental involvement and monitoring are key elements in preventing cyberbullying, particularly when it comes to younger users. Parents should actively engage with their children about the digital platforms they are using, ensuring that they understand both the benefits and risks of these spaces. In addition to having open conversations about appropriate online behavior, parents should use available monitoring tools to track their children's online activity. This includes reviewing social media profiles, checking privacy settings, and discussing what to do if they encounter bullying or inappropriate content. While respecting a child's privacy is important, active monitoring ensures that parents can intervene early if necessary, providing guidance and support before any harm is done.

Schools and community organizations also have a crucial role in preventing cyberbullying by implementing educational programs and awareness campaigns. These initiatives should focus on the risks associated with online behavior, the importance of digital citizenship, and how to recognize the signs of cyberbullying. Schools, in particular, are uniquely positioned to reach large groups of students and offer training on interacting respectfully online. Community outreach programs can further extend these lessons to parents and guardians, ensuring that the education around cyberbullying extends beyond the classroom. By creating a culture of awareness and providing resources for intervention, these programs help communities to collectively combat online harassment and protect individuals from its damaging effects.

It is important to recognize that prevention efforts must begin early, with digital safety education integrated into the curriculum from a young age. Children should be taught the importance of online respect, responsible behavior, and handling conflicts or negative interactions online. As the internet continues to be a central part of everyday life, this education will help to equip the next generation with the tools they need to navigate it safely and with empathy. These lessons should focus on preventing cyberbullying, building positive digital relationships, encouraging collaboration, and fostering healthy online communication. A proactive approach to online behavior will create a generation of users who understand the power and responsibility of participating in the digital world.

Supporting Others and Advocacy

Recognizing when someone else is being bullied online can be challenging, especially since the signs are not always immediately visible. Unlike traditional bullying, where a victim may show clear physical signs of distress, the effects of cyberbullying are often hidden behind screens. However, some telltale signs exist that someone may be enduring online harassment. A person who suddenly

---

Ask the AI

"How can schools and parents collaborate to prevent cyberbullying and promote positive online behavior?"
"What are some effective community programs designed to educate and raise awareness about cyberbullying?"
"What online communication strategies can help foster respectful and empathetic interactions among digital users?"

becomes withdrawn avoids certain digital platforms, or exhibits emotional distress after using their devices may be experiencing cyberbullying. In some cases, a victim may also show signs of anxiety or fear when discussing their online experiences, or they may be hesitant to share personal details about their digital interactions. As a friend, colleague, or bystander, it is crucial to remain observant and ready to offer support if you suspect someone is being targeted by cyberbullying.

When you recognize that someone is being bullied online, knowing how to be an effective bystander or upstander is important. Simply observing the situation without taking action can inadvertently contribute to the perpetuation of the bullying. Bystanders have a unique opportunity to step in and disrupt the cycle of harassment by supporting the victim and holding the bully accountable. An upstander actively intervenes to support the victim, whether by offering emotional support, reporting the bullying to authorities or platform administrators, or encouraging others to join in standing up against the harassment. The key to being an effective upstander is to remain calm, respectful, and empathetic in your response and take action that will empower the victim and discourage the bully. By supporting the victim, you help them feel less isolated and send a strong message that bullying will not be tolerated in your community.

Providing resources for counseling and support is a critical part of supporting those who are being bullied. Victims of cyberbullying often experience emotional and psychological trauma that can have lasting effects on their mental health. Having access to mental health resources, including counseling services, is crucial for helping individuals navigate the emotional aftermath of being targeted. Many online platforms and organizations offer confidential support services, such as helplines or chat-based therapy, which can provide immediate assistance for victims who may feel overwhelmed or unsure where to turn. Encouraging those who are being bullied to reach out to mental health professionals can be a lifeline for recovery, offering them strategies to cope with the stress, anxiety, and feelings of isolation that often accompany cyberbullying. Moreover, providing these resources empowers victims to take control of their mental well-being and begin the healing process.

Advocacy for stronger policies and protections is another essential component of combating cyberbullying. While many platforms have policies to address harassment, these policies are often inconsistent, difficult to enforce, or lack clarity. Advocating for stronger and more comprehensive policies, both within organizations and at a broader legislative level, can help ensure that victims have better protection from online abuse. This includes pushing for clearer guidelines about cyberbullying, establishing more robust reporting mechanisms, and ensuring perpetrators face meaningful consequences. In addition to corporate policies, there is also a need for legal protections that hold online harassers accountable. Advocating for laws that address cyberbullying at the local, state, or national level can help create a safer digital environment where individuals are more likely to report harassment without fear of retaliation.

Engaging in community initiatives is another powerful way to support victims of cyberbullying and advocate for positive change. Community programs focused on digital literacy, online safety, and bullying prevention can help raise awareness of the issue and provide resources for those who

Ask the AI

"What are the most effective ways for bystanders to intervene when they witness cyberbullying?"
"What resources are available for counseling and emotional support for victims of online harassment?"
"How can I advocate for stronger policies and protections against cyberbullying within my community or workplace?"

need help. By joining or starting a community initiative, individuals can foster an environment of support where people collectively come together to address the problem of cyberbullying. These initiatives might include workshops on recognizing and responding to cyberbullying, awareness campaigns highlighting the importance of empathy and respect online, or collaborations with local schools and businesses to promote digital safety. In communities where cyberbullying is prevalent, these initiatives can serve as a beacon of hope, offering education and support to those in need.

Spreading awareness through education and outreach is a critical tool in the fight against cyberbullying. Many individuals, particularly young people, may not fully understand the impact of their online actions or realize the serious consequences of bullying others. Educating communities—whether through schools, workplaces, or online platforms—about the dangers of cyberbullying and the importance of fostering a respectful digital environment can make a significant difference. This education should focus not only on the emotional and psychological effects of cyberbullying on victims but also on promoting responsible and positive behavior in digital spaces. Public awareness campaigns, school presentations, and online outreach can help shift the culture from tolerance toward bullying to active prevention and support. By creating a culture of understanding and empathy, we reduce the chances that cyberbullying will occur in the first place.

In addition to community-level education, outreach programs should equip individuals with the necessary tools to take action. Whether this involves teaching students how to report harassment, explaining how to protect personal information online, or providing guidance on how to intervene as a bystander safely, outreach efforts should empower individuals to make a difference. This includes encouraging people to speak out if they witness cyberbullying, to offer support to victims, and to be vocal advocates for safer online spaces. It also means providing victims with information about where they can seek help, whether through professional counseling, legal recourse, or digital safety organizations. Empowering individuals to act, whether as upstanders or as advocates for change, is crucial for creating lasting change in the fight against cyberbullying.

Recommendations

1. **Recognize the Signs of Cyberbullying:** Stay vigilant in observing changes in behavior that may indicate someone is being bullied online, such as sudden withdrawal, emotional distress, or reluctance to use devices. If you notice these signs in friends, colleagues, or family members, approach them with empathy and support. Offering a safe space for conversation can help the victim feel understood and encourage them to seek help.
2. **Act as an Upstander:** If you witness cyberbullying online, don't remain passive. Step up as an upstander by offering emotional support to the victim, reporting the harassment to platform administrators, or directly confronting the bully calmly and respectfully. Your intervention can disrupt the cycle of bullying and empower others to take similar action.
3. **Encourage Respectful Online Communication:** Promote the importance of respectful, clear, and empathetic communication in digital spaces. Encourage friends, family, and colleagues to pause before they post, considering how their words might affect others. Lead by example in your online interactions to foster a more positive and respectful digital environment.
4. **Provide Counseling and Support Resources:** If you or someone you know is affected by cyberbullying, don't hesitate to seek professional help. Encourage the use of counseling services, both online and in-person, to support victims in managing the emotional and psychological effects of bullying. Having a trusted counselor to talk to can provide crucial coping strategies and help individuals heal from the trauma of harassment.

5. **Advocate for Stronger Digital Policies:** Take an active role in advocating for stronger anti-cyberbullying policies at schools, workplaces, and online platforms. Work with decision makers to ensure clear guidelines exist to address harassment and push for consistent enforcement of these policies. Your advocacy can help create a safer environment for everyone in the digital space.

6. **Get Involved in Community Initiatives:** Participate in or support local community initiatives to raise awareness about cyberbullying. Whether through volunteering for digital literacy programs or organizing workshops on online safety, your involvement can help educate others about the risks of online harassment and the importance of a respectful digital culture.

7. **Promote Digital Citizenship Education:** Encourage schools, community groups, and organizations to incorporate digital citizenship education into curricula. Teaching children and adults how to navigate digital spaces responsibly, recognize harmful behavior, and stand up against bullying can prevent online harassment before it starts.

8. **Monitor Digital Activities (for Parents and Guardians):** If you are a parent or guardian, take an active interest in your child's digital life. Use available parental control tools to monitor social media activity and online interactions and establish an open line of communication about digital safety. Regular conversations about online behavior can help children understand the importance of responsible internet use and provide early detection of potential issues.

9. **Utilize Reporting Mechanisms:** Familiarize yourself with the reporting tools available on social media platforms, websites, and online games. If you encounter cyberbullying, report them promptly to the platform administrators. These reporting mechanisms help ensure that harmful behavior is addressed and that platforms maintain a safe space for all users.

10. **Spread Awareness and Educate Others:** Take the initiative to spread awareness about cyberbullying prevention within your circle. Share information about the psychological impacts of cyberbullying, the resources available for victims, and the importance of empathy in online interactions. Hosting informational sessions or distributing educational materials can empower others to take action and create a ripple effect of positive change in your community.

Conclusion

As we've seen throughout this chapter, cyberbullying is a complex and multifaceted issue that requires a concerted effort from all corners of society to address effectively. From the role of technology companies in creating safer platforms to the responsibility of individuals in promoting positive online behavior, everyone has a part to play in combating digital harassment. The anonymity and constant connectivity afforded by the internet make it all too easy for bullying behavior to flourish, but they also provide unique opportunities for intervention and support. By understanding the dynamics of cyberbullying, recognizing its signs, and taking proactive measures, we can begin to mitigate its harmful effects and create safer online spaces for all.

One of the most important takeaways from this chapter is education's critical role in preventing cyberbullying. Whether it's educating children and teenagers about the potential consequences of their online actions or teaching adults about the impact of digital harassment on their colleagues or peers, awareness is key. Promoting respectful communication, empathy, and responsible online behavior can go a long way in fostering a culture of digital citizenship. By instilling these values early and consistently, we can reduce the likelihood of cyberbullying and ensure that future generations are equipped with the tools to thrive in a digital world.

At the same time, we must recognize that preventing and addressing cyberbullying requires collaboration across various stakeholders, including parents, schools, employers, and social media platforms. Keeping individuals safe online does not rest solely on the shoulders of one group or another; it is a shared responsibility that requires a collective, sustained effort. Communities and organizations can implement programs and policies that create safe spaces for open discussions, support victims, and hold perpetrators accountable. In doing so, we can foster environments where digital interactions are both positive and constructive.

Finally, while we cannot eliminate the risks of cyberbullying entirely, we can take meaningful steps to reduce its prevalence and impact. We can collectively make the digital world safer by empowering victims to take action, equipping bystanders to intervene effectively, and advocating for stronger policies and protections. The strategies outlined in this chapter—from documenting incidents and adjusting privacy settings to seeking legal recourse—provide practical tools for anyone facing online harassment. As we continue to evolve our understanding of cyberbullying and its effects, we must remain committed to creating a culture of respect, responsibility, and support in both our online and offline lives.

Chapter Questions

1   What is the primary role of an upstander in addressing cyberbullying?
    A. To avoid intervening in the situation
    B. To offer emotional support and report the bullying
    C. To encourage the victim to ignore the bully
    D. To support the bully in their actions

2   Which of the following is a common sign that someone may be experiencing cyberbullying?
    A. Increased online activity
    B. Sudden withdrawal and emotional distress
    C. Excessive use of social media
    D. Improved academic performance

3   What is the first step a victim of cyberbullying should take to protect themselves?
    A. Respond to the bully to stand up for themselves
    B. Document the incidents through screenshots and messages
    C. Change all their social media passwords
    D. Immediately block the bully without any further actions

4   Which of the following is the best way to encourage respectful online communication?
    A. Ignoring any negative comments
    B. Promoting empathetic responses and thinking before posting
    C. Arguing with the person who posted the negative comment
    D. Deleting negative posts without responding

5   What should parents do to help prevent cyberbullying in their children?
    A. Allow unlimited screen time for their children
    B. Regularly monitor their children's online activity and set clear guidelines

   C. Prevent their children from using the internet entirely

   D. Encourage children to avoid speaking to strangers online

6 How can community initiatives help prevent cyberbullying?

   A. By enforcing strict digital laws on all citizens

   B. By educating people about online safety and encouraging positive online behavior

   C. By limiting access to social media

   D. By shutting down online platforms that promote bullying

7 What is one of the best ways to address the psychological effects of cyberbullying on victims?

   A. Encouraging them to ignore the problem

   B. Directly confronting the bully

   C. Providing access to counseling and mental health resources

   D. Reporting the bully to law enforcement immediately

8 What is the role of digital citizenship education in preventing cyberbullying?

   A. To teach children how to block others online

   B. To help individuals navigate online spaces responsibly and recognize harmful behavior

   C. To encourage people to avoid using social media altogether

   D. To promote a competitive attitude in digital spaces

9 What should someone do if they witness cyberbullying happening online?

   A. Ignore the situation and continue with their own activities

   B. Share the post to increase awareness

   C. Step in as an upstander by offering support and reporting the incident

   D. Laugh it off and move on

10 What is the role of advocacy in combating cyberbullying?

   A. To support bullies and enable their behavior

   B. To ensure victims are ignored and left to handle the situation alone

   C. To push for stronger anti-bullying policies and better enforcement

   D. To encourage a more aggressive approach to online conflicts

11 Which action can parents take to ensure their children are safe online?

   A. Use parental control tools to monitor online activity

   B. Give their children free access to all websites

   C. Prevent their children from interacting with others online

   D. Encourage children to accept all friend requests

12 How can spreading awareness through education help prevent cyberbullying?

   A. By teaching people to retaliate against online harassers

   B. By informing others about the emotional impact of cyberbullying and how to respond appropriately

   C. By encouraging children to avoid using digital devices

   D. By limiting the number of online interactions children have

13 What is an important factor in setting effective guidelines for online behavior?
   A. Allowing unrestricted freedom online
   B. Clearly defining what constitutes harassment and setting consequences for it
   C. Promoting anonymity online
   D. Avoiding any form of intervention in digital spaces

14 What is a recommended approach when dealing with someone who is being cyberbullied?
   A. Discourage them from reporting the bullying
   B. Suggest that they handle it on their own
   C. Offer emotional support and guide them to professional help if needed
   D. Ignore their situation and focus on your own concerns

15 What can schools and community programs do to raise awareness about cyberbullying?
   A. Ignore the issue as it doesn't affect everyone
   B. Offer digital literacy workshops and promote responsible online behavior
   C. Encourage students to engage in online arguments
   D. Promote the use of unfiltered social media for students

9

Children's Online Safety and Parental Controls

As technology continues to evolve, it is essential to equip the younger generation with the tools, knowledge, and guidance to navigate the online world safely. The digital environment not only offers incredible educational resources, social interaction platforms, and entertainment but also exposes young users to various risks. Cyber threats such as cyberbullying, online predators, inappropriate content, and identity theft are just a few examples of the dangers that children may encounter if they are not properly educated or monitored.

This chapter provides parents, educators, and caregivers with practical strategies to protect children and teens while helping them develop responsible digital habits. Understanding the risks is only part of the equation; creating a supportive framework for children to explore and enjoy their digital experiences safely is equally important. From implementing parental controls and monitoring tools to engaging in open conversations about online safety, every step can contribute to building a safer digital environment for young users. The goal is not to restrict access to technology but to empower children to use it in productive and secure ways.

One of the most important aspects of digital safety is education. By teaching children how to identify online risks, use privacy settings, and understand the permanence of the content they share, we are giving them the tools they need to protect themselves. Encouraging critical thinking and skepticism when navigating online spaces is equally important, as it helps children make informed decisions about the information they encounter and share. While many dangers exist, an informed and empowered user is far less likely to fall victim to cyber threats.

In addition to education, effective monitoring and oversight are vital components of any digital safety strategy. Parental control tools can provide an added layer of security by restricting access to harmful content, limiting screen time, and ensuring that children interact with age-appropriate material. However, these tools must be used with open, ongoing conversations about the risks and responsibilities of online activity. Creating a partnership between parents, schools, and communities can further reinforce the importance of digital safety, ensuring that children receive consistent, clear messages about how to behave online and report uncomfortable or harmful experiences.

As we move through this chapter, we will explore practical methods for communicating with children about cybersecurity, discuss how to implement protective tools, and highlight key strategies for managing screen time. Whether you are a parent, guardian, or educator, the insights provided here are designed to equip you with the knowledge and strategies to guide the younger generation toward safer online behaviors. With a proactive, informed approach, we can help ensure that the digital world remains a space for growth, learning, and connection rather than a breeding ground for potential harm.

Darwin, the Cyber Beagle is an excellent resource for teaching children about cybersecurity and digital safety. Written by the author of this guide, *Darwin the Cyber Beagle* uses an engaging and approachable format to introduce young readers to the world of online safety. Through the adventures of Darwin, a clever beagle with a knack for sniffing out cyber threats, children learn about the dangers of the internet, such as phishing, identity theft, and the importance of creating strong passwords. The book is designed to spark curiosity while imparting essential lessons on digital security in a fun and memorable way.

What sets *Darwin the Cyber Beagle* apart is its ability to make complex topics accessible to younger audiences. The story is crafted with a sense of adventure, featuring Darwin as he embarks on various missions to help his human friends navigate the tricky waters of online life. Each chapter tackles a different aspect of cyber safety, such as safe browsing practices, the dangers of oversharing, and the importance of privacy. The book engages children with colorful illustrations and a lighthearted narrative while reinforcing key lessons about protecting their digital selves. This makes it an ideal tool for parents, educators, or anyone looking to introduce children to the critical concepts of cybersecurity in an approachable and effective way. Find Darwin at **cyberbeagle.kids**.

The Digital World of Children and Teens

The digital world presents a vast and increasingly complex landscape for children and teens, offering opportunities for growth and significant risks. From social media platforms to online gaming and educational tools, young users are navigating spaces not designed with their cognitive or emotional maturity in mind. Many children and teens today interact with digital devices from a very young age, making it essential for parents, educators, and caregivers to understand the platforms and services children frequent. These platforms include everything from TikTok and Instagram to the multiplayer environments of Fortnite and Roblox, each presenting its challenges and opportunities. Digital safety is paramount in this environment, as children and teens are often exposed to situations and individuals they are ill-prepared to handle.

One of the most pressing concerns for younger users is the exposure to inappropriate content. While the internet provides boundless opportunities for learning and entertainment, it is also rife with material unsuitable for developing minds. This can include explicit imagery, violent content, or even cyberbullying. Younger users may lack the critical thinking skills required to filter out harmful information, putting them at risk of being inadvertently exposed to distressing or age-inappropriate content. Even seemingly benign platforms like YouTube can have algorithm-driven recommendations that lead children down a dangerous path. To protect young users, digital safety protocols must include robust parental controls, content filters, and open lines of communication about the dangers lurking in digital spaces.

Social media is another major influence on the lives of children and teens, shaping their self-image, peer relationships, and overall mental health. From TikTok trends to Instagram likes,

Ask the AI

"What do children and teens use the most popular platforms in 2024?"
"What features make online gaming communities engaging yet risky for younger users?"
"How can parents balance screen time effectively while encouraging offline activities?"

these platforms often measure self-worth by external validation, which can profoundly affect a young person's development. Teens are especially vulnerable to the pressure of curating a perfect online persona, leading to anxiety, depression, and even risky behavior as they try to fit in or gain attention. While social media can provide a sense of community and belonging, it can also facilitate harmful behaviors, such as cyberbullying, body shaming, or the spread of dangerous misinformation. Parents and educators must help guide children through these platforms, teaching them to recognize both the benefits and dangers of social media and how to interact with it responsibly.

In addition to social media, online gaming communities present a unique set of risks. While gaming can offer positive experiences, such as improving cognitive skills and fostering teamwork, it also exposes children to unregulated environments where they can be harassed or manipulated by other players. Many online games include chat functions allowing players to communicate in real-time, opening the door to inappropriate language, bullying, or predatory behavior. Moreover, in-game purchases and microtransactions can lead to financial concerns, especially if children are unaware of the real-world value of virtual items. Parents must set boundaries around gaming time, educate their children about the potential dangers, and use parental controls to ensure a safer experience in these virtual worlds.

The rise of educational technology tools has brought advantages and challenges to the digital landscape. Platforms like Google Classroom, Khan Academy, and educational apps have revolutionized how children learn, making education more accessible and interactive. However, as these tools move online, they also bring concerns about data privacy and security. Children may not fully understand the implications of sharing personal information through these platforms, making them vulnerable to data breaches or targeted advertisements. Furthermore, while online learning can offer flexibility and engaging content, it can also contribute to over-reliance on screens and the erosion of traditional face-to-face social skills. As educational technology becomes more prevalent, parents and educators must balance leveraging its benefits and protecting children's personal information.

Balancing screen time with offline activities is one of the most crucial aspects of fostering a healthy relationship with technology. While digital devices are essential to modern life, especially for learning and socialization, they should not replace outdoor play, family time, or other offline activities. Excessive screen time can lead to physical health problems such as eye strain, poor posture, and sleep disruptions. Additionally, it can contribute to mental health issues, including decreased attention span and social isolation. Encouraging a balance between screen time and offline activities allows children to develop a well-rounded sense of self and healthier habits. This can include setting daily limits on screen time, promoting hobbies that don't involve screens, and making space for family interactions without digital distractions.

The risks associated with children's digital lives are not just limited to online activities but also how those activities influence real-world behaviors. The sense of anonymity that comes with digital platforms often leads to a disconnect between the virtual and the real world, making it easier for young people to engage in risky or inappropriate behaviors. Without proper guidance, children and teens can easily fall prey to the dangers of sexting, online predators, or dangerous social media challenges. Moreover, the digital world often exacerbates peer pressure, as children may feel compelled to engage in behaviors they wouldn't otherwise consider to gain acceptance or avoid exclusion. This underscores the importance of teaching children about the consequences of their online actions, the permanence of their digital footprints, and how to handle peer pressure in both virtual and physical spaces.

The growing complexity of the digital landscape means that keeping children safe online requires constant vigilance and proactive effort from parents, caregivers, and educators. Digital safety is not a one-time lesson but an ongoing conversation. Children must be taught to recognize risks, report inappropriate behavior, and protect their personal information from online predators. Parents must be informed about the latest online trends and potential dangers to guide their children through the evolving digital world. It's also important to foster a sense of responsibility in children, encouraging them to treat others with respect online and to be mindful of the information they share. Ultimately, adults can help young people navigate the digital world safely and responsibly by working together.

Communicating with Children About Cyber Safety

Starting age-appropriate conversations about cyber safety is essential for responsibly helping children navigate the digital world. It's important to recognize that children's understanding of technology evolves as they grow, so how we approach discussions about online risks must be tailored to their developmental stages. For younger children, conversations should focus on simple concepts such as the difference between a stranger online and someone they know in real life. As children grow older and begin using more advanced platforms, the conversations can shift toward issues like cyberbullying, online predators, and the permanence of digital footprints. The key is to introduce these topics understandably, without overwhelming them with complex or scary details, and to ensure that the discussion remains ongoing, not a one-time event. Table 9.1 provides age-appropriate guidelines for online activity, offering tailored advice to ensure safe internet use across different age groups. Table 9.2 provides a list of online cyber dangers for children and recommendations to combat them.

Building trust and open communication channels is one of the cornerstones of a successful digital safety strategy for children. Children must feel comfortable talking to their parents or guardians about any concerns they have regarding their online activities. If children believe they will be punished for making mistakes or asking questions about something they encountered online, they are less likely to reach out when they are in trouble. Open communication starts with a non-judgmental, supportive attitude, where children understand they can ask questions without

Table 9.1 Age-appropriate guidelines for online activity.

Age range (years)	Recommended online activities	Guidelines	Supervision level
5–7	Educational games, basic video chatting, watching child-friendly videos	Limit screen time to 30–60 minutes per day	High
8–10	Educational games, social media for kids, video streaming	Talk about online privacy and appropriate behavior, and monitor content actively	Moderate
11–13	Social media use with restrictions, online learning, and gaming with parental controls	Talk about online relationships, peer pressure	Moderate
14–16	Social media, gaming, messaging, and streaming	Teach critical thinking and safe sharing, and allow supervised use of platforms.	Moderate–low
17–18	Social media, gaming, and independent browsing	Discuss online reputation, privacy settings, and responsible content sharing	Low

Table 9.2 Common online dangers and safety tips.

Danger	Description	Safety tip	Recommended action
Cyberbullying	Online harassment or bullying through social media, email, or messaging apps	Encourage children to report bullying	Monitor online conversations and intervene when necessary
Stranger danger	Communicating with unknown people online who may not have good intentions	Teach children not to share personal information online	Set strict privacy settings on social media
Inappropriate content	Exposure to violent, explicit, or disturbing content online	Use content filters and monitor browsing activity	Use parental controls to block adult content
Phishing scams	Attempts to trick users into providing sensitive information through fraudulent messages	Educate children to avoid clicking on suspicious links	Regularly discuss the importance of verifying the sender before clicking links
Sexting	Sending sexually explicit messages or images	Teach the importance of consent and the consequences of sexting	Set clear rules and monitor phone activity
Addiction to screens	Excessive use of screens leading to physical and mental health problems	Encourage breaks and time offline	Set time limits for screen usage and encourage offline activities
Exposure to misinformation	Falling for fake news or misleading online content	Encourage critical thinking and fact-checking	Help children verify sources before believing and sharing information
Gaming addiction	Spending too much time on video games	Teach the importance of balance and moderation	Set limits on gaming time and encourage other activities
Malware	Malicious software that can damage devices or steal data	Educate children about safe downloading practices	Ensure antivirus software is installed and up-to-date
Online scams	Fraudulent online offers that trick users into giving money or information	Teach children to avoid offers that sound too good to be true	Discuss common scams and ensure children understand red flags

fear of reprimand. By fostering a relationship of trust, parents and caregivers create a safe space for children to share concerns, which is crucial for spotting potential dangers before they escalate.

Teaching critical thinking and skepticism is perhaps one of the most effective ways to equip children with the tools they need to stay safe online. The internet is a breeding ground for misinformation, scams, and deceptive practices, and children are often particularly susceptible to these pitfalls. By encouraging children to think critically about the content they see online, parents can help them discern between trustworthy information and misleading or harmful material. This means discussing with children how to evaluate sources of information, question unsolicited messages, and recognize when something feels "off" or too good to be true. Critical thinking should also extend to understanding the difference between public and private information, helping children become more discerning about what they share and with whom. Figure 9.1 presents an online safety checklist for children, outlining essential steps to protect young users in the digital world.

Discussing the importance of privacy and personal information is essential to cyber safety education. Children often fail to realize the long-term implications of sharing personal details online, whether through social media profiles, gaming platforms, or even seemingly harmless chats with

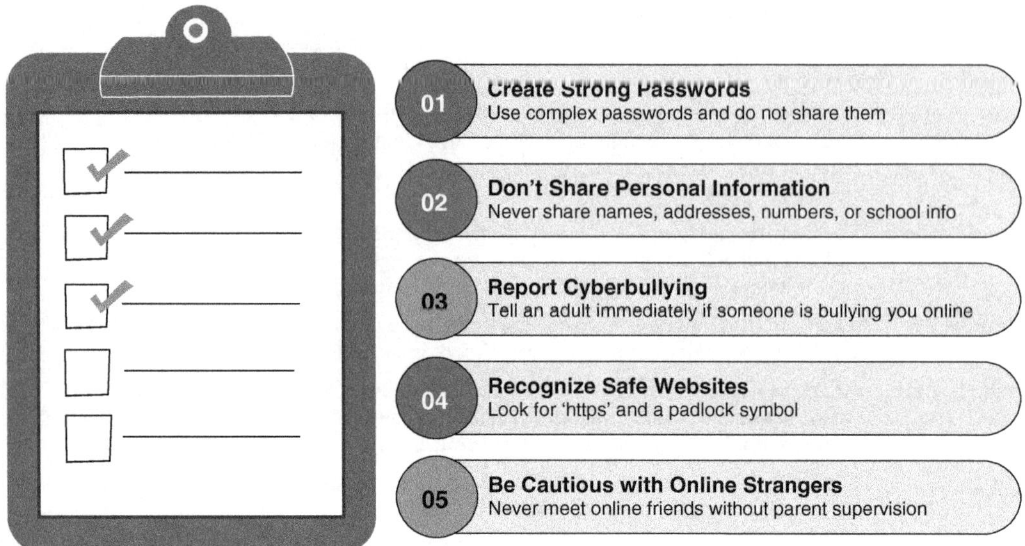

Figure 9.1 Online safety checklist for children.

friends. In today's world, where data is currency, it's vital to explain to children how their personal information can be used or misused if it falls into the wrong hands. By teaching them to safeguard details like their full name, address, phone number, and even their daily activities, parents help create a strong foundation for their online safety. This education should also explain privacy settings on social media platforms, showing children how to manage who sees their posts and how to control their digital footprint.

Role-playing scenarios to practice safe responses can be a highly effective way to reinforce lessons about cyber safety. While theoretical knowledge is important, children need the opportunity to practice responding to online threats in a safe and controlled environment. Role-playing can simulate situations such as receiving a suspicious email or being contacted by someone they don't know in a game. Through these exercises, children can practice saying "no," blocking someone, or reporting suspicious activity, which can help them feel more confident in handling similar situations when they arise. It's also an opportunity for parents to correct misconceptions, model appropriate behavior, and reinforce the importance of reacting quickly to potential threats.

Encouraging children to report uncomfortable experiences is crucial in maintaining a safe digital environment. Children may encounter situations online that make them feel uneasy, such as a friend asking them for personal information or an inappropriate comment in a chat. If they do not feel empowered to report these experiences, they may try to deal with them independently, potentially escalating the situation. Parents create a proactive culture of safety by making it clear

---

Ask the AI

"What are some age-appropriate ways to explain privacy and data sharing to children?"
"How can parents encourage children to report uncomfortable online experiences without fear of judgment?"
"What strategies can help children practice critical thinking when evaluating online content?"

that reporting is not only okay but encouraged. It's important to emphasize that children should not feel embarrassed or ashamed when they report something uncomfortable and that their safety should always come first.

As children's online experiences expand, their understanding of digital risks must also grow. It's essential to continue to engage in age-appropriate conversations about new dangers that may arise as technology changes. Regular check-ins can help parents gauge their children's understanding of online risks and ensure that children still practice the safe habits taught earlier. Being vigilant and proactive can prevent serious incidents and allow parents to guide their children through challenges. This ongoing communication ensures that children have the tools to make informed, safe decisions as they explore the digital world.

Another critical aspect of these discussions is instilling a sense of responsibility in children regarding their online actions. As children mature and gain more independence in the digital world, they must understand that their online actions have consequences. This includes respecting the privacy of others, being cautious when interacting with people they don't know, and thinking before posting anything that could have lasting effects. Parents can reinforce this sense of responsibility by discussing cyberbullying, digital etiquette, and respecting others' boundaries in the virtual space. Teaching children to act with integrity online prepares them to be safe and responsible digital citizens.

Implementing Parental Controls and Monitoring

Parental control tools and software are critical components of any digital safety strategy for families. These tools allow parents to actively protect their children from inappropriate content, online predators, and excessive screen time. The range of parental control options available today includes everything from basic content filtering software to more advanced tools that provide detailed reports on internet usage, app downloads, and online interactions. Many devices, including smartphones, tablets, and computers, come with built-in parental control features that can be easily activated to restrict access to certain types of content, manage screen time, and monitor activity. While these tools are not foolproof, they are a useful first defense in ensuring children explore the internet safely and responsibly.

Setting up filters and content restrictions is one of the most fundamental aspects of using parental control tools. These filters allow parents to block access to websites and content that may be inappropriate for their child's age, such as adult websites, violent video games, or social media platforms that may not be age-appropriate. Most modern parental control tools offer customizable settings, so parents can choose the level of restriction they want for each family member. For example, filters can be set to allow only educational content or certain types of entertainment while blocking more harmful or distracting material. Additionally, many tools include categories for filtering content based on types—such as news, shopping, or social media—so parents can

<table>
<tr><td>

Ask the AI

"What are the top-rated parental control tools for smartphones and tablets in 2024?"
"How can I ethically monitor my child's online activity without breaching their trust?"
"What features should I prioritize when setting up content filters and app restrictions?"

</td></tr>
</table>

fine-tune what their children are exposed to online. This level of control provides peace of mind, knowing that children are browsing in a safer digital environment.

Ethical monitoring of online activity is another important aspect of digital safety. While parents need to keep track of their children's online behavior, it's equally important to approach monitoring in a way that respects the child's privacy and fosters trust. Monitoring should not be about spying but about creating an open dialogue and demonstrating the importance of online safety. Some parents install software that allows them to see the websites their children visit, the apps they download, or the messages they exchange in chat rooms or social media. However, instead of relying solely on surveillance, it is critical to combine monitoring with education. Explaining the reasons behind monitoring and reinforcing the importance of online safety helps children understand that the goal is not to invade their privacy but to keep them safe while developing responsible digital habits.

Establishing usage time limits is another key element in maintaining a healthy balance between online and offline activities. Excessive screen time can negatively impact children's physical health, contributing to poor posture, eye strain, sleep disturbances, and mental well-being, leading to social isolation or attention problems. Many parental control tools allow parents to set daily or weekly usage limits for certain apps or devices, automatically locking the screen when the limit is reached. These limits help children develop a balanced relationship with technology, encouraging them to spend time away from screens to engage in physical activities, hobbies, and socializing. It's also an opportunity to teach children about self-regulation and time management, skills that will serve them well as they grow older and encounter more digital responsibilities.

Managing app and game downloads is another crucial responsibility for safeguarding children's digital lives. Many apps and games that appear harmless at first glance may contain in-app purchases, hidden advertising, or inappropriate content. Some apps may access children's personal information, making them a potential risk for data privacy breaches. Parental control software allows parents to manage and restrict which apps and games can be downloaded to children's devices. Parents can ensure their children are not exposed to potentially harmful content or spending money on unwanted in-app purchases by requiring approval for new app downloads. This step is particularly important for children learning to differentiate between safe and risky content.

Adjusting settings as children age is a dynamic aspect of implementing parental controls. As children mature, their needs and behaviors online change, and so should the way parents monitor and regulate their activities. When children are very young, strict filters and time limits may be necessary to protect them from exposure to harmful material. However, as children grow into teenagers, allowing more autonomy while maintaining oversight is important. This means gradually relaxing certain restrictions, such as time limits or content filters while introducing new tools to help teens make informed decisions about their online presence. For example, parents might give older children the ability to manage their own social media privacy settings or allow them to make decisions about app downloads but still monitor their activity through periodic check-ins or reports. This approach fosters a sense of responsibility and trust, empowering children to take control of their digital lives while benefiting from parental guidance.

Additionally, parental control tools can help create a healthy digital environment by encouraging positive behavior online. For instance, some apps and software allow parents to reward children for adhering to usage limits or using technology in educational ways. These positive reinforcements can motivate children to respect the boundaries set by their parents and encourage them to engage with the internet productively and safely. Conversely, if rules are not followed, these tools can impose consequences, such as temporarily disabling access to apps or limiting screen time, reinforcing the idea that responsible digital behavior is a privilege. This proactive approach helps children understand that digital safety is about avoiding danger and cultivating positive online habits that will benefit them in the long run.

When implementing parental controls, parents need to stay informed and adaptable. Digital safety is not a one-size-fits-all solution, and the tools available should evolve alongside a child's growing understanding of the digital world. Parents should take time to research and test different parental control options to find what works best for their family's unique needs. Furthermore, while tools and software are important, they should never replace the essential role of communication and trust in maintaining a safe online environment. Parents must continue to engage in open conversations with their children about the risks of the digital world, the importance of privacy, and the responsibilities of being online. A combination of effective tools and open dialogue is the best approach to ensuring that children are safe and empowered in their digital lives.

Educating Children on Safe Online Practices

Creating strong passwords and keeping them confidential is one of the fundamental skills children need to develop to protect their digital lives. In today's world, passwords are the keys to nearly everything online—from social media accounts to school portals and gaming platforms. Teaching children how to create strong and memorable passwords is critical to preventing unauthorized access. This means using a combination of uppercase and lowercase letters, numbers, and symbols while avoiding easily guessable information like their name or birthdate. Moreover, children must understand the importance of not sharing their passwords with anyone, even with close friends or family. In addition to creating strong passwords, children should be taught to update them regularly and to use different passwords for different accounts to minimize the risk of a security breach.

Recognizing and avoiding strangers online is an important aspect of online safety that is sometimes overlooked. While it may be easy for adults to spot suspicious or unknown individuals online, children often lack the experience to recognize potentially harmful interactions. Online predators, cyberbullies, and scammers frequently present themselves as friendly or trustworthy, and children may not immediately understand when they are being targeted. It's essential to educate children about the risks of interacting with strangers online, teaching them to avoid engaging with people they don't know. This includes social media, chat rooms, gaming platforms, and any online community where communication with unknown individuals occurs. Children should also understand that even if someone appears to be a friend or acquaintance, they should never share personal information or engage in private conversations without parental approval.

Understanding the permanence of digital content is a key concept in helping children navigate the online world safely. Unlike spoken words, which fade into memory, anything posted online can live forever, accessible to anyone with an internet connection. This permanence can have significant consequences, especially as children transition into adolescence and adulthood. Children must understand that even if they delete something they've posted or shared, it can still be stored on other servers or archived elsewhere. The idea that "once it's online, it's always online" should be a guiding principle in their digital behavior. Educating children about the long-term implications of their online actions, such as the potential impact on their future academic or job prospects, helps them make more informed decisions about what to post and share. This lesson promotes safer online behavior and cultivates a sense of responsibility in managing their digital footprints.

Being cautious when sharing photos and videos is another important practice that children need to internalize. The ease with which pictures can be taken and shared through smartphones and social media platforms can lead children to post images without considering the consequences. What might seem like an innocent selfie or a fun video can quickly spread to unintended audiences, including strangers or malicious individuals. It's important to educate children about the risks of sharing photos, particularly those that reveal sensitive information, such as their location or personal activities. Children should also be taught to respect the privacy of others and to think twice before sharing images or videos of friends, family, or classmates. In addition, parents should set clear guidelines about what types of content are appropriate to post and encourage their children to always ask for permission before posting images of others.

Handling cyberbullying and peer pressure is one of the more challenging aspects of online safety for children. Cyberbullying can take many forms, from hurtful comments and rumors spread on social media to more severe cases of harassment or exclusion in online games. The anonymity of the internet can embolden bullies, and children may struggle to identify when they are being bullied or how to respond. Equally concerning is the pressure children face to conform to online trends or engage in harmful activities to gain peer acceptance. It is essential to educate children on recognizing signs of cyberbullying, whether it's being targeted with hurtful messages or witnessing a friend being bullied online. Children should be encouraged to report these incidents immediately to an adult or through platform reporting tools. In addition, teaching children to respond with kindness and empathy toward others online can help reduce the prevalence of cyberbullying and promote a more positive online environment.

Encouraging positive online interactions is crucial to fostering a healthy digital experience for children. Just as children learn to interact respectfully with others physically, they should also be taught to engage in positive, supportive ways in digital spaces. This includes treating others with kindness and respect and being mindful of their tone and words in online conversations. Children should be aware that behind every screen is a real person with feelings, and their online words and actions can significantly impact others. Positive interactions also extend to how children represent themselves in digital spaces—teaching them to constructively create authentic, positive online identities and engage in online communities. This can be encouraged through open conversations about digital etiquette, the importance of empathy, and how online actions can both build and damage relationships.

As children become more involved in online activities, fostering a sense of self-awareness and accountability in their digital behavior is important. This means helping them recognize when they spend too much time online or engage in negative online behaviors. For example, suppose they notice they're becoming upset or frustrated after interacting on social media. In that case, they should be encouraged to take a break and reflect on managing those feelings. Similarly, children should be taught to recognize when they might be influenced by peer pressure to engage in activities that don't align with their values or best interests. By helping children cultivate a strong sense of digital self-awareness, parents can empower them to make better online decisions and recognize when it's time to step back and reset.

Ask the AI

"How can I teach children to create strong, secure passwords they can remember?"
"What are effective ways to explain the concept of a digital footprint to a child or teen?"
"What steps should children take if they experience cyberbullying or peer pressure online?"

Collaborating with Schools and Communities

Understanding school policies on technology use is crucial in ensuring that your child's digital safety is supported at home and in the classroom. Many schools now incorporate technology into their curricula, so children regularly use digital devices for research, assignments, and communication. Parents must know the school's policies regarding acceptable use, privacy, and security measures. These policies often outline the school's approach to monitoring students' online activity, the types of websites or apps permitted, and how personal information is handled. Schools may also have rules to prevent cyberbullying or other online misconduct. By reviewing these policies, parents can ensure that the school is aligned with best practices for cyber safety and work with educators to address any concerns.

Participating in cyber safety education programs is one of the most effective ways to reinforce the messages of digital safety at home. Many schools and community organizations offer programs that teach children to stay safe online through in-person workshops, modules, or interactive learning activities. Parents should take advantage of these programs and attend any available sessions that provide insight into what children are learning about cyber safety. By participating, parents can gain a deeper understanding of the digital risks children face and learn more about how they can reinforce those lessons at home. These programs often cover many important topics, such as creating strong passwords, recognizing online predators, avoiding cyberbullying, and understanding digital footprints. Additionally, schools may offer resources for parents, including guides or webinars that help them stay informed about the latest developments in online safety.

Engaging with other parents and caregivers is an often-overlooked strategy for improving children's digital safety. Parents must collaborate to share insights, strategies, and experiences in managing their children's online activity. Whether through informal gatherings or more organized parent groups, connecting with others facing similar challenges can provide knowledge and support. Parents can discuss best practices for setting up parental controls, managing screen time, and addressing children's social pressures in the digital world. When parents are united in safeguarding their children's online experiences, they can create a stronger protection network. Moreover, these discussions can help reduce feelings of isolation, as parents can realize they are not navigating the complexities of digital safety alone.

Staying informed about emerging trends and risks in the digital world is vital for parents and educators. As technology evolves, new threats and online behaviors emerge that may not have been anticipated even a few years ago. This is especially true as new platforms, apps, and social media networks continuously gain popularity among children and teens. Parents must stay current on these trends to proactively anticipate and address potential risks. For instance, the rise of new messaging apps or online gaming platforms may introduce new ways for children to be exposed to cyberbullying or online predators. Following reputable sources, such as cybersecurity blogs, government websites, or online safety organizations, can help parents remain informed about these emerging issues. Regularly attending digital safety workshops or webinars is another way to ensure parents are equipped with the latest knowledge to protect their children.

Ask the AI

"What are effective ways to advocate for updated cybersecurity policies in schools?"
"How can parents and schools collaborate to offer better digital safety education programs?"
"What are some community-based initiatives for promoting online safety among children?"

Advocating for child-friendly online environments is essential in shaping a safer digital landscape for children. While parents can take steps to protect their children, the broader online ecosystem must also evolve to prioritize safety for young users. Parents can advocate for policies and regulations protecting children's privacy, limiting harmful content, and promoting positive online interactions. This could include supporting initiatives requiring websites and apps to adhere to stricter age verification processes or better protections against cyberbullying and online harassment. Parents can help drive change that creates safer spaces for children to learn, play, and communicate by engaging with policymakers, school administrators, and digital platforms. This advocacy can also extend to pushing for greater transparency in how data is collected and used by online platforms, ensuring that children's personal information is better protected from exploitation.

Sharing resources and support networks with other families is another powerful way to foster a community of digital safety. Many parents are unsure where to find reliable resources or how to approach the complexities of online safety for their children. By sharing helpful resources—such as digital safety guides, parental control tools, or links to online safety programs—parents can empower one another to take meaningful steps toward protecting their children. Additionally, support networks can provide a space for parents to discuss challenges they face, such as handling cyberbullying incidents or addressing peer pressure related to social media use. These networks can be formal, like school-organized parent groups, or informal, like social media groups where parents can exchange advice. The key is to create a supportive environment where parents can share information, learn from each other, and feel encouraged in their efforts to safeguard their children's digital lives.

In addition to sharing resources, parents should also work together to hold digital platforms accountable for keeping children safe. This includes advocating for stronger age restrictions on social media platforms and gaming sites and pressuring tech companies to provide more robust tools for parents to monitor and control their children's online interactions. Platforms like Instagram, TikTok, and YouTube may have age restrictions, but enforcing those rules can be challenging, and platforms are often slow to respond to concerns about safety. By joining forces with other concerned parents and community members, the collective voice can be more impactful in pushing for policy changes or safer features. This collaboration also extends to educational institutions, where parents and caregivers can work together to ensure that school digital policies and safety practices evolve with the changing digital landscape.

Recommendations

1. **Review School Policies:** Familiarize yourself with your child's school technology policies. Take the time to read through the school's guidelines regarding digital device use, online privacy, and internet safety protocols. This will help ensure that you understand how the school addresses cybersecurity and how you can complement their efforts at home. If policies seem outdated or unclear, consider discussing them with school administrators to advocate for improvements.

2. **Participate in Cyber Safety Education Programs:** Enroll your child in cyber safety education programs offered by their school or community organizations. These programs are often designed to equip children with the knowledge they need to stay safe online. Attend parent workshops or webinars whenever possible to stay informed about the latest cyber threats and digital safety tools. By engaging in these programs, you can reinforce safe online behaviors at school and home.

3. **Collaborate with Other Parents and Caregivers:** Build a support network with other parents to exchange ideas and strategies for managing your child's online safety. Join parent groups, both online and in-person, to discuss best practices for digital safety, including screen time limits, monitoring tools, and setting expectations. Sharing experiences can help you identify new risks and solutions and ensure you provide a consistent message about online behavior.

4. **Stay Informed About Emerging Risks:** Stay current on new digital platforms, apps, and risks children may encounter online. Follow cybersecurity blogs, educational newsletters, and trusted online safety organizations to keep track of emerging threats. By understanding new trends and how they impact children's online safety, you'll be better equipped to discuss potential dangers with your child.

5. **Advocate for Safer Digital Spaces:** Become an advocate for child-friendly online environments. Support policies and initiatives prioritizing children's privacy, limiting harmful content, and promoting positive online behavior. Work with other parents, educators, and community members to push for regulations and features that make digital platforms safer for young users.

6. **Share Resources for Digital Safety:** Share useful digital safety resources with other parents, such as guides, articles, or apps designed to help monitor online activity. Ensure the resources you share are reliable and easy to understand, empowering other caregivers to act. Additionally, consider forming a group or community network where parents can access updated information on digital safety tools and resources.

7. **Promote Ongoing Communication About Digital Safety:** Keep the lines of communication open with your child about their online experiences. Encourage regular conversations about what they do online, who they interact with, and any concerns they may have. Regular check-ins help build trust and ensure digital safety issues are addressed promptly.

8. **Foster Community-wide Digital Safety Education:** Work with local schools, libraries, and community organizations to offer digital safety workshops or seminars for children and adults. These programs can help build awareness of cyber risks and teach families how to protect their digital lives. By organizing or participating in these educational initiatives, you contribute to a broader effort to improve digital safety in your community.

9. **Encourage Reporting of Online Incidents:** Teach your child the importance of reporting any suspicious online behavior, cyberbullying, or negative experiences they may encounter. Reinforce that it is safe to speak up and that they should never feel ashamed or embarrassed to talk about online issues. Establish a trusting environment where they feel comfortable discussing their digital experiences without fear of punishment.

10. **Collaborate with Schools to Update Policies:** If you notice gaps or outdated policies regarding digital safety at your child's school, consider discussing improvements with school administrators. Work with other concerned parents to push for more comprehensive guidelines around technology use, online privacy, and cyberbullying prevention. By advocating for change at the school level, you help ensure the entire community benefits from updated practices that protect children online.

Conclusion

As we conclude this chapter on cyber defense best practices, it is clear that the digital safety of children and teens requires a multifaceted approach. With all its benefits, the internet also presents various risks that can compromise young users' safety, well-being, and privacy. By implementing a combination of practical tools, fostering open communication, and educating children on the principles of digital safety, we can significantly reduce their exposure to these dangers. Creating a safe online environment is the responsibility of parents and guardians, educators, policymakers, and the broader community.

Effective digital safety practices begin with proactive education. Teaching children how to recognize the signs of potential risks, like phishing attempts or cyberbullying, empowers them to make safer online decisions. Just as importantly, helping children understand the consequences of their online actions—oversharing personal information or engaging in inappropriate conversations—will foster a sense of responsibility. Children must know they are not alone in the digital world; they should feel comfortable turning to trusted adults whenever they feel uncertain or threatened online.

In addition to education, robust monitoring and control systems are essential in safeguarding children from harmful content. When used thoughtfully, parental controls can offer extra protection, blocking inappropriate material, limiting screen time, and tracking online activity. However, these tools should never replace direct conversations with children about the importance of safe online behavior. Rather, they should complement ongoing discussions and provide tangible safeguards that align with a family's values and goals for digital engagement.

As children grow older and become more adept at navigating the digital world, their ability to make independent, safe decisions will increase. It is important to adjust safety practices and controls as they mature, gradually shifting from more active monitoring to fostering trust and responsible self-management. The balance between supervision and independence is delicate but necessary for helping children develop the critical thinking skills required to protect themselves. Encouraging positive online interactions, promoting healthy screen time habits, and addressing signs of trouble early on are all vital components of a long-term digital safety strategy.

Ultimately, digital safety education aims not to isolate children from the online world but to prepare them to engage with it responsibly. By creating a partnership between parents, schools, and communities, we can ensure that children receive consistent and clear guidance on navigating the digital landscape. As the online world evolves, staying informed about emerging trends, risks, and tools will be key to maintaining a safe environment. With the right education, tools, and mindset, we can help our children thrive in the digital age while minimizing the risks they face.

Chapter Questions

1 What first step should parents take to ensure their child's digital safety at school?
    A. Review their child's social media accounts
    B. Familiarize themselves with the school's technology policies
    C. Set parental controls on school-issued devices
    D. Monitor their child's homework assignments

2 What should parents do to reinforce the cyber safety lessons children learn at school?
    A. Encourage children to avoid technology at home
    B. Participate in cyber safety education programs
    C. Let children manage their online activity independently
    D. Limit screen time to one hour a day

3 How can parents engage with other parents to improve children's digital safety?
   A. Ignore the use of technology and let kids figure it out
   B. Build a support network to exchange ideas and strategies
   C. Discourage children from using digital devices
   D. Let children interact with online strangers freely

4 Why is it important for parents to stay informed about emerging risks in the digital world?
   A. To keep up with new trends in online shopping
   B. To better monitor their child's grades
   C. To anticipate potential online dangers and address them proactively
   D. To help their child select new video games

5 What is one way parents can contribute to safer digital spaces for children?
   A. Advocate for child-friendly online environments
   B. Allow children to use devices without restrictions
   C. Limit their child's interaction with teachers and other students
   D. Encourage children to share personal details online

6 How can parents share digital safety resources with others in their community?
   A. By ignoring online safety and focusing on other topics
   B. By sharing only their own personal experiences
   C. By offering trusted guides, articles, or apps to other parents
   D. By restricting access to all online content

7 What should parents regularly do to ensure they're on top of their child's online behavior?
   A. Limit screen time to weekends only
   B. Promote ongoing communication about digital safety
   C. Let their children handle all technology decisions
   D. Use technology only for educational purposes

8 How can parents promote digital safety beyond their household?
   A. By working with local schools and libraries to offer workshops
   B. By ignoring online safety concerns from other families
   C. By preventing all technology use in the community
   D. By not allowing their children to interact with peers online

9 What is one of the key actions parents should take to address cyberbullying?
   A. Ignore the issue and hope it resolves itself
   B. Encourage their children to report any negative online experiences
   C. Block their child's internet access
   D. Tell their children to fight back against cyberbullies

10 How can parents ensure that their child's school keeps up-to-date with digital safety?
   A. Organize a group of parents to meet with school administrators
   B. Ignore school policies and deal with issues on their own
   C. Avoid discussing online safety with teachers
   D. Let the school handle everything without parental involvement

11 What is one potential danger parents should know when new apps or platforms become popular?

A. New apps may introduce new ways for children to be exposed to online risks

B. New apps are always safer than old ones

C. New platforms offer no privacy concerns

D. Older platforms are always more dangerous

12 How can parents ensure that they are properly addressing their child's digital safety needs?

A. By attending digital safety workshops or webinars

B. By limiting their child's access to technology

C. By checking homework only, not online activity

D. By avoiding any discussions about online behavior

13 How can parents advocate for policy changes that promote child safety in the digital world?

A. By demanding that children be allowed to use any platform they choose

B. By supporting initiatives that require platforms to enforce age verification and privacy protections

C. By promoting unrestricted access to online platforms

D. By refusing to engage with digital platforms

14 What is an effective way for parents to keep up with the latest digital safety tools?

A. By relying solely on outdated resources

B. By sharing resources with other parents and caregivers

C. By avoiding digital safety resources altogether

D. By restricting children's access to all technology

15 What is a key component of fostering a community-wide approach to digital safety?

A. Ignoring digital safety and focusing on other issues

B. Hosting open discussions about online risks and safety

C. Letting children decide the rules for their own online activity

D. Avoiding any public discussions about online safety

10

Avoiding Online Scams and Social Engineering Tricks

Scams have become increasingly sophisticated, targeting individuals at an alarming rate. From phishing emails to fake job offers, the tactics used by cybercriminals are constantly evolving, making it essential for everyone to understand how to recognize and avoid these threats. As we continue integrating digital platforms into nearly every aspect of our daily lives, the need for effective cybersecurity practices grows more urgent. This chapter will provide a comprehensive guide on identifying common scams, recognizing red flags, and taking proactive steps to protect yourself from falling victim to fraud.

Social engineering lies at the core of most scams, where cybercriminals manipulate human psychology rather than relying solely on technical vulnerabilities. These attackers prey on trust, fear, curiosity, and urgency, leveraging these emotions to trick people into making hasty decisions. Understanding the psychology behind scams can be the first step in preventing them. By being aware of how scammers manipulate victims, we can train ourselves to become more skeptical and vigilant when interacting with unfamiliar sources online.

As scammers adapt their methods to the digital world, they exploit various communication channels such as email, social media, and even phone calls. While some scams are easy to spot, others are highly sophisticated and can easily deceive the unprepared. Recognizing these scams requires a mix of awareness, attention to detail, and an understanding of common patterns used by fraudsters. Identifying these red flags is crucial in protecting yourself from financial loss, identity theft, and other forms of cybercrime.

One of the most effective ways to safeguard yourself is by implementing a set of best practices that reduce your exposure to online threats. Simple habits, like verifying requests for information and avoiding suspicious links, can go a long way in preventing attacks. Staying informed about new scam tactics, reporting suspicious activity, and educating those around you are critical elements of a strong defense. The more proactive and aware you are, the better equipped you will be to recognize scams and avoid becoming a target.

This chapter aims to empower you with the knowledge and tools to protect your digital life from scams. By the end, you'll have a deeper understanding of the common types of scams, how to recognize the warning signs, and what actions you can take to defend yourself. Armed with this knowledge, you'll be better prepared to navigate the complex world of online interactions, ensuring you can enjoy the benefits of the digital age without falling prey to its risks. Figure 10.1 depicts the ripple effect of cybersecurity education, illustrating how spreading knowledge can enhance protection across communities and organizations.

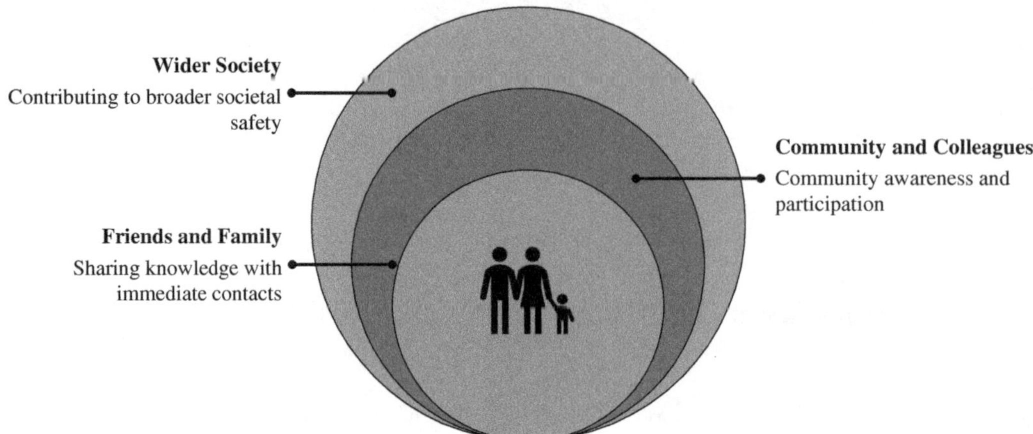

Figure 10.1 The ripple effect of cybersecurity education.

Understanding Social Engineering

Social engineering manipulates individuals into divulging confidential information or performing actions that compromise security. Unlike traditional hacking, which involves exploiting technical vulnerabilities, social engineering primarily targets the human element. It exploits our psychological tendencies, such as trust, fear, and urgency, to bypass security measures. Attackers use these psychological triggers to convince victims to act in ways they would not ordinarily do, such as clicking on a malicious link, disclosing sensitive information, or granting unauthorized access to a system. It is a form of exploitation that operates on the premise that people are often the weakest link in any security protocol.

The psychology behind social engineering is rooted in manipulation and control. Scammers often leverage cognitive biases such as reciprocity, authority, and scarcity to influence their targets. For example, a scammer may pose as a figure of authority—such as a manager or IT specialist—to coerce an employee into sharing passwords or performing actions that undermine security. The "urgency" tactic is also commonly employed, where an attacker creates a false sense of time pressure, making the victim believe that immediate action is required. By manipulating emotional responses, social engineers exploit human behavior to bypass the technical layers of cybersecurity, making their approach effective even when systems are otherwise secure.

Scammers use several common tactics that target the natural human instinct to trust or be helpful. Phishing, one of the most widely known social engineering attacks, involves sending fraudulent emails or messages that appear to come from reputable sources. These messages often contain links or attachments that, when clicked, install malicious software or redirect the victim to a fake login page designed to steal their credentials. Vishing, or voice phishing, is another prevalent tactic where attackers impersonate trustworthy figures over the phone to extract personal information or credentials. Smishing, an extension of phishing, involves text messages that lure individuals into clicking on malicious links or downloading harmful software. These methods are effective because they exploit basic human behavior, making it easier for attackers to trick individuals into compliance.

Manipulation and deception are the driving forces behind social engineering attacks. Attackers use a range of psychological tricks to manipulate their victims into making decisions that are not in their best interest. To influence their choices, a scammer might appeal to the victim's emotions, such as sympathy or fear. For example, a scammer may claim to be from a well-known charity, ask for a donation, or create a fabricated sense of urgency by stating that the victim's bank account has been compromised and immediate action is required. In each case, the victim is manipulated into responding without considering the request's legitimacy or the potential risks. The goal is to sidestep the victim's usual skepticism by bypassing their rational thought process and appealing directly to their emotions.

One of the reasons social engineering is so effective is that it exploits people's inherent trust in others, especially when they believe they are interacting with legitimate entities. This trust is often misplaced in the digital age, where many people interact with strangers online or receive communication from unfamiliar sources. Even the most technically aware individuals can be tricked by well-crafted social engineering attacks, as the scammer often uses legitimate or personal information to make the interaction more convincing. Furthermore, social engineers rely on people to underestimate the risks posed by seemingly innocuous requests or communications. This makes it easier for attackers to access information or systems that robust security protocols might heavily protect.

Social engineering attacks come in many forms, each with its methods and targets. Phishing attacks, for instance, may target individuals or groups within an organization, while spear-phishing focuses on a specific person or department. The attacker may gather information from public sources, such as social media profiles, to craft a highly personalized and credible message. Impersonation is another common tactic, where the attacker pretends to be a trusted person or institution, such as a company's IT department or a colleague. Pretexting is a technique in which the attacker invents a scenario to gain information or access, such as posing as a surveyor or investigator to gather sensitive details. Baiting, meanwhile, involves enticing the target with something desirable, like a free download or a prize, to trick them into downloading malware or disclosing personal information.

Real-world examples of social engineering scams demonstrate how attackers use these tactics to exploit their targets successfully. One well-known example is the 2016 attack on the Democratic National Committee (DNC), where hackers used spear-phishing emails to gain access to confidential emails and documents. The emails were crafted to appear as though they were from Google, asking recipients to reset their passwords by clicking on a link that led to a fraudulent website. In another high-profile case, a bank employee received a phone call from someone claiming to be from the company's IT department. The attacker requested the employee's password to perform system maintenance, which the employee unknowingly provided, giving the attacker access to sensitive banking data. These attacks show how social engineering can bypass even the most advanced security measures by manipulating individuals into taking actions they would not otherwise take.

The risks associated with social engineering are not confined to individuals. Organizations are also frequently targeted, with attackers using a combination of psychological manipulation and technical tactics to breach corporate security. A notable example occurred in 2019 when a major

---

Ask the AI

"What psychological tactics are commonly used in social engineering attacks?"
"How can businesses train employees to recognize social engineering attempts?"
"What are the long-term effects of successful social engineering attacks on individuals or organizations?"

cybersecurity company was compromised by an attacker who used social engineering to manipulate an employee into granting access to the company's network. The attacker posed as a trusted vendor and convinced the employee to download a malicious file, subsequently allowing the attacker to infiltrate the company's systems. This example highlights how social engineering can target individuals and entire organizations, exploiting trust and human behavior to gain unauthorized access to critical systems.

Common Online Scams

Phishing is one of the most prevalent and damaging online scams, and it comes in many forms. Phishing involves an attacker impersonating a trusted entity—such as a bank, government agency, or popular service provider—to steal sensitive information. These phishing attempts can appear as emails, text messages, or even social media posts that direct victims to fake websites designed to harvest login credentials, credit card numbers, or other personal data. Phishing emails often appear legitimate, using well-known company logos and even familiar language to trick the recipient into believing the communication is real. One of the most effective ways to spot a phishing attempt is to scrutinize the sender's email address, which may look similar to a trusted source but usually has subtle discrepancies. If you're unsure, don't click on links in unsolicited messages—go directly to the organization's website by typing the URL into your browser to check for alerts or notifications (Table 10.1).

Tech support scams are another widespread form of online fraud. In these scams, cybercriminals often use pop-up windows or unsolicited phone calls to convince victims that their computer is infected with malware or has some other serious technical problem. The scammer pretends to be a representative from a reputable tech support company like Microsoft or Apple, offering to fix the issue for a fee. In many cases, the attacker may request remote access to the victim's computer to install unnecessary software, which may be malware that allows the scammer to take control of the system. These scams are dangerous because they prey on people's fears and confusion about their devices. If you ever receive a call or pop-up claiming your system is compromised, remember that legitimate tech companies will never ask for remote access or payment upfront. Always hang up or close the pop-up and contact the company directly through official channels for assistance.

Lottery and prize scams exploit a victim's hopes of winning something for nothing. In these schemes, individuals receive notifications—often via email or social media—telling them they've won a large sum of money, a car, or some other extravagant prize. However, they must pay taxes, and fees, or provide personal information to claim their winnings. These scams often involve convincing messages that appear legitimate, citing official-looking logos and documentation, which can make the victim believe the offer is real. The scammer disappears once the victim provides the requested payment or information, and no prize is ever delivered. It's important to remember that if you don't enter a contest or lottery, you cannot win it, no matter how official the message looks. Any unsolicited communication claiming you've won a prize is almost certainly a scam.

Romance and relationship scams prey on emotions, particularly loneliness or the desire for companionship. Scammers create fake profiles on dating websites or social media platforms, portraying themselves as someone seeking love or friendship. They develop online relationships with victims, gaining their trust over time. Once a connection is established, the scammer will fabricate a crisis—such as a medical emergency or financial hardship—and ask the victim for money or personal assistance. These scams can be particularly damaging because they exploit personal emotions and relationships. Victims may not only lose money but also experience emotional distress.

Table 10.1 Common scams and their characteristics.

Scam type	Description	Common signs to look out for	Example of scam
Phishing emails	Deceptive emails or messages are designed to steal personal information	Suspicious email addresses, urgent language request for personal info	A fake email from "your bank" asking for your account number
Tech support scams	Scammers pretending to be tech support to gain access to your system or install malware	Unsolicited phone calls or pop-up alerts claiming system issues	A pop-up saying "Your computer is infected" asking you to call tech support
Lottery and prize scams	Fraudulent notifications claiming you've won a prize to steal money or personal info	Claiming you've won a large sum of money, asking for payment or banking details	An email stating you've won a lottery and need to pay taxes to claim it
Romance scams	Scammers using fake identities to exploit emotional connections and gain money	Online relationships that quickly move to financial requests, emotional manipulation	A person you've met online requests money for an "emergency"
Investment scams	Fake investment opportunities promising high returns with little risk	Unrealistic high returns, pressure to act quickly	A message offering a "limited-time" opportunity to invest in cryptocurrency with guaranteed returns
Fake charity scams	Scammers pretending to represent a charity to steal donations	Urgency, emotional appeals	A phone call asking for donations for "victims of a disaster"
Job offer scams	Fraudulent job offers that require upfront fees or personal info	Request for payment to secure a job, too-good-to-be-true salary	An email offering a high-paying job that requires a deposit for "training"
Fake E-commerce sites	Websites set up to steal credit card information under the guise of selling products	Unusual product prices, poor website design, lack of contact info	A website selling branded goods at unrealistically low prices
IRS/Tax scams	Fraudulent communications pretending to be from tax authorities requesting payment or personal information	Threatening language, demand for immediate payment, often via gift cards	A call from "the IRS" saying you owe back taxes and must pay now
Fake subscription services	Scams that offer fake subscriptions or services to steal payment info	Monthly charges without service, difficulty in contacting customer support	A subscription to a magazine or service you never signed up for

A good rule of thumb is to avoid sending money to someone you've never met in person, especially if you've only interacted online. True relationships are built on trust, not financial transactions.

Investment and financial fraud scams are designed to lure victims into making high-risk investments, promising huge returns that are often too good to be true. Scammers pitch these deals through unsolicited emails, social media ads, or even cold calls, selling fake opportunities in cryptocurrency, real estate, or stocks. These scams often mimic legitimate investment platforms and offer persuasive arguments about the supposed profitability of the investment. Once the victim has invested, the scammer either disappears with the money or continues to ask for more. These scams are dangerous because they appeal to the victim's desire for quick financial gain. The best defense against investment fraud is to conduct thorough research on any financial opportunity before committing any funds and be especially wary of any investment promising guaranteed returns with little risk involved.

Job offers and employment scams are particularly common in today's job market, where many individuals search for work online. In these scams, attackers create legitimate job postings, offering attractive salaries or work-from-home opportunities. After the victim applies, the scammer may ask for personal information such as a Social Security number, banking details for direct deposit, or even an upfront payment for training materials. These scams may also involve fraudulent interview processes, often conducted via email or messaging apps, making it difficult for the victim to detect their authenticity. Once the scammer has the victim's information or money, they vanish, and the supposed job never materializes. It's essential to be cautious of any job offer that requires payment upfront or asks for sensitive information before a formal contract or job offer is made. Always verify the company and the offer through independent channels before applying.

One of the reasons why these online scams are so effective is that they play on fundamental human psychology. They create a sense of urgency, playing into fears or desires to get the victim to act without thinking. Phishing and tech support scams often work because they develop a sense of alarm—telling you that your bank account has been compromised or your computer is infected with malware. Similarly, romance scams prey on emotional vulnerabilities, convincing individuals to believe in a relationship that isn't real. Lottery and prize scams exploit the victim's desire for an easy financial windfall, while investment scams appeal to the hope of getting rich quickly. Understanding the psychological tactics in these scams can make you more vigilant and help you avoid falling victim to them.

As technology continues to evolve, so do the tactics used by scammers. New scams are constantly being developed and often take advantage of emerging technologies or trends. For instance, cryptocurrency-related scams have surged in recent years as digital currencies become more mainstream. Fake investment opportunities in NFTs, blockchain technology, and digital assets have gained traction, often with misleading claims of guaranteed profits. Cybercriminals also use increasingly sophisticated methods to create counterfeit websites and fraudulent social media accounts nearly indistinguishable from legitimate ones. As such, staying informed about current scams and adopting a skeptical mindset when interacting online is crucial for protecting oneself from fraud.

Recognizing Red Flags

One of the first signs that an online communication may be a scam is when you receive unsolicited messages requesting some form of action. These may come via email, text, or even direct messages on social media, asking you to click on a link, download an attachment, or provide sensitive

---

Ask the AI

"What makes phishing emails the most common type of online scam?"
"How do romance scams evolve to gain a victim's trust?"
"What are some methods to spot fake e-commerce websites used in scams?"

information. Often, these messages will appear to come from trusted sources, such as your bank, a well-known retailer, or a government agency. However, there will be no prior communication to establish the request's legitimacy. Scammers rely on the assumption that people are likely to act quickly when they're not expecting a message and believe it's urgent. It's critical to be suspicious of any unsolicited request, no matter how official it looks. The rule of thumb is simple: Don't take the bait if you didn't initiate the communication. Always independently verify the request through official channels before taking any action (Table 10.2).

Another common red flag is when an offer seems too good to be true. Scammers often use this tactic to lure victims by offering products, services, or opportunities at prices that are too appealing to resist. For example, you might receive an email offering a high-end product for a fraction of its value or an investment opportunity that promises unrealistically high returns with minimal risk. These offers are designed to prey on your desires, whether saving money, getting rich quickly, or acquiring something exclusive. In reality, these deals rarely, if ever, live up to their promises. It almost certainly is if an offer is too good to be true. Always ask yourself: "Why is this being offered at such an incredible price?" If the answer is unclear or doesn't make sense, proceed with extreme caution.

Table 10.2   Red flags of scams.

Red flag	What it means	Why it's a red flag
Urgent or threatening language	Messages demanding immediate action or claiming dire consequences	Scammers use urgency to pressure victims into acting without thinking
Too-good-to-be-true offers	Offers that promise unrealistically high returns or prizes	Legitimate offers rarely seem too good to be true; scammers prey on greed and impatience
Requests for personal or financial information	Unsolicited requests for sensitive data like bank details or Social Security numbers	Legitimate organizations will never ask for sensitive information through email or phone without proper verification
Unsolicited communications	Unexpected emails, calls, or messages asking for action or money	Scammers often contact you out of the blue to exploit your trust
Poor grammar or spelling	Messages with noticeable spelling and grammatical errors	Professional organizations maintain high standards in communication, while scams often show signs of hastily written messages
Suspicious email addresses	Email addresses that don't match the company or organization they claim to represent	Scammers often use email addresses similar to legitimate ones but with subtle differences
Generic greetings	Emails or messages that use vague greetings like "Dear Customer" instead of your name	Legitimate companies usually address you by name in emails; scammers use generic terms to send mass messages
Links to unfamiliar websites	Hyperlinks that lead to websites you have never seen before or don't trust	These could lead to fake websites that steal your data or infect your computer with malware
Inconsistencies in contact details	Phone numbers or addresses that don't match official records	A legitimate business or organization will have consistent, verifiable contact details across its communications
Demands for immediate payment	Requests for payment via non-traditional methods like gift cards or cryptocurrency	Legitimate businesses usually don't demand immediate payments in untraceable forms

Urgent or threatening language is a powerful psychological tactic often used in scams to push victims into making hasty decisions without considering the consequences. Messages that create a sense of panic, such as warnings about a compromised account or a supposed legal issue, are meant to manipulate the recipient into acting immediately. Scammers may claim you must act "now" to prevent a financial loss, avoid penalties, or secure your account. These communications often play on common fears—such as the fear of identity theft or financial ruin—prompting a rash response. It's essential to remain calm when you receive urgent requests. If the message pressures you to act quickly, take a step back and evaluate the situation. Legitimate businesses or organizations will never demand immediate action under threat of consequences, especially not in unsolicited communication.

Requests for personal or financial information should always raise a red flag, particularly when they come from an unknown source. This can include asking for your Social Security number, bank account details, passwords, or credit card numbers. Fraudulent messages may ask for this information under the guise of verifying your identity, confirming your account, or updating your records. A legitimate company will never request sensitive information via email, text, or social media, particularly unsolicited. Even if the request appears to come from a trusted source, the best practice is to ignore it and reach out to the company or organization directly using known contact details. Never enter personal information through links provided in messages unless you are certain of the authenticity of the request.

Poor grammar and spelling errors are often overlooked but should never be dismissed when evaluating the legitimacy of a message. Many scam emails or texts are hastily put together, and one of the easiest ways to spot them is by looking for spelling, grammar, and punctuation inconsistencies. Common signs of these errors include strange wording, awkward phrasing, and missing or misplaced punctuation marks. For instance, a scam email from a supposed bank might contain the phrase "Dear Customer, your accout is suspended," where the misspelled word "accout" clearly indicates that the communication is not legitimate. Trusted companies, especially large organizations, maintain high standards for their communications and will not send out messages with glaring mistakes. If you encounter this kind of sloppy writing, it's best to treat the message with suspicion.

Inconsistencies in sender details or URLs are a significant clue that an email or message might not be legitimate. Cybercriminals often disguise their email addresses to appear as coming from a trusted source, but a closer look will reveal subtle inconsistencies. For instance, the sender's email address might look like it's from your bank—e.g. "support@bank-usa.com"—but a small discrepancy like an additional letter or domain change can be the giveaway, such as "support@bank-usa1.com." Similarly, phishing websites often use URLs that closely resemble legitimate ones but with slight variations, such as an extra hyphen or a misspelled word. Before clicking on any link or entering sensitive information, please hover your mouse over the URL to ensure it leads to the official website. If uncertain, type the URL directly into your browser rather than clicking the link in the message.

Even if a message looks official and there are no obvious errors, there may still be hidden red flags that indicate it's a scam. A lack of personalization is one of these subtle clues. Legitimate

---

Ask the AI

"What are the top signs that an email or message is a phishing attempt?"
"Why do scammers often use poor grammar and spelling errors in their communications?"
"How can inconsistencies in sender details, such as email domains, indicate a scam?"

communications from companies you deal with often include your name or other identifying details. On the other hand, scammers often use generic greetings like "Dear Customer" or "Dear User" instead of addressing you directly. This lack of personal connection can be a sign that the message was sent in bulk to many targets, with the hope that a few will fall for the scam. If a company knows your name, but the message uses a generic greeting, it's worth investigating further before responding or clicking any links.

Scammers may also use social engineering tactics to lower your defenses by seeming overly familiar or even polite. For example, they might try to build rapport by offering compliments or showing excessive empathy—such as telling you they're there to "help" or "understand your concerns." These attempts to create false trust are part of the manipulation process. They may sound reassuring, but this behavior should raise a red flag. True representatives of legitimate companies typically stick to professional and straightforward language. The use of overly friendly or sympathetic language can be a sign that the communicator is trying to exploit your emotions and gain your trust.

Lastly, being aware of the timing of the communication can also offer insights into its legitimacy. Scammers often exploit moments of vulnerability, such as during a crisis, during holiday shopping seasons, or after a high-profile data breach. For example, a scam might arrive during tax season, offering fake tax refunds or following a major retailer's sale, claiming that your order is being processed and asking for payment details. Scammers are adept at capitalizing on these periods when you're preoccupied or distracted. If a message seems to take advantage of a specific event or timing, approach it cautiously and check the facts before taking action.

Protecting Yourself from Scams

One of the most effective ways to protect yourself from scams is to verify the legitimacy of any unsolicited request before taking action. If you receive a message, phone call, or email asking for personal information, financial details, or access to your accounts, always take a moment to verify the request independently. Don't use any contact information provided in the suspicious communication. Instead, reach out to the company or organization directly through their official website, customer service number, or email address. By doing so, you can ensure that the request is genuine and avoid falling victim to a phishing or impersonation scam. A few extra minutes of caution can save you from significant financial or personal harm (Table 10.3).

Avoiding unknown links or attachments is one of the simplest yet most effective defenses against many online scams. Cybercriminals often use email, text, or social media messages to trick victims into clicking on malicious links or downloading dangerous attachments. These links may lead to fake websites that steal your personal information or install malware on your device. On the other hand, attachments may contain viruses or ransomware that can encrypt your files or steal sensitive data. It's crucial to avoid clicking on links or opening attachments from unknown or suspicious sources. If you ever find yourself uncertain about the legitimacy of a link or attachment, it's safer to err on caution and delete the message altogether.

When making transactions online, always use secure payment methods that offer protection against fraud. Avoid wire transfers, prepaid gift cards, or other untraceable payment methods, as scammers commonly use these to make tracing or recovering funds difficult. Credit cards, PayPal, and other trusted payment processors typically offer consumer protection, allowing you to dispute fraudulent charges or request a refund if something goes wrong. Additionally, these payment systems often have fraud detection mechanisms to flag suspicious activity. When purchasing items from

Table 10.3 Best practices for protecting yourself from scams.

Best practice	Description	Why it's important	Example
Verify requests independently	Always verify unsolicited personal or financial information requests by contacting the source directly	It helps ensure you deal with a legitimate entity, not a scammer	Calling your bank directly instead of using the phone number in a suspicious email
Avoid clicking on unknown links	Don't click on links or download attachments from unknown sources	Scammers often use links and attachments to spread malware or steal your data	Do not click on a suspicious link that claims to be from your bank
Use secure payment methods	Use trusted payment methods like credit cards or reputable online payment services	These methods offer fraud protection and can help resolve disputes	Paying for online purchases with a credit card instead of a prepaid card
Keep personal information private	Share sensitive information only with trusted entities and only when necessary	Keeping personal data secure reduces the risk of identity theft and fraud	Do not post sensitive details like your Social Security number on social media
Stay informed about common scams	Regularly check cybersecurity blogs or official sources for the latest scam tactics and trends	Staying informed helps you spot new scams before they impact you	Following a trusted cybersecurity blog to stay up-to-date with new scam alerts
Report scams to authorities	If you encounter a scam report it to the relevant authorities like the Federal Trade Commission (FTC) or local law enforcement	Reporting scams helps authorities track fraudulent activities and protect others from falling victim	Reporting a phishing email to your email provider or the FTC
Use Multi-factor authentication (MFA)	Enable MFA for online accounts whenever possible to add a layer of security	MFA helps protect your accounts even if your password is compromised	Setting up MFA on your email account to prevent unauthorized access
Monitor your accounts regularly	Regularly review your bank and credit card statements to detect unauthorized transactions	Early detection can help minimize damage and prevent further fraud	Checking your bank statement for unfamiliar charges at least once a month
Be skeptical of unsolicited communications	Always question unsolicited calls, emails, or messages asking for personal information	Skepticism helps protect against scams that rely on emotional manipulation or urgency	Rejecting unsolicited calls asking for payment or account details
Use strong unique passwords	Create strong, unique passwords for each online account and avoid reusing them	Strong passwords reduce the likelihood of unauthorized access to your accounts	Using a password manager to create and store complex, unique passwords for each site

unknown websites, always check for secure payment options and look for indicators such as "https" in the website's URL or a padlock icon in the browser's address bar, signaling a secure connection.

Keeping your personal information private is another critical step in protecting yourself from scams. Many scammers rely on social engineering tactics to gather personal details about you, which they then use to craft convincing fraudulent messages. Scammers often gather information from social media profiles, data breaches, or public records to make their approach appear more legitimate. Avoid oversharing personal details online, especially on social media platforms. While it's tempting to share every detail of your life with friends and followers, remember that even seemingly harmless information can be used by cybercriminals to manipulate you. Be mindful of what you post and who can access it, and always review your privacy settings to ensure you're not inadvertently making yourself an easy target.

Staying updated on common scam tactics is essential for maintaining a strong defense against fraud. Cybercriminals constantly evolve their methods to exploit new technologies, social trends, and global events. For example, during tax season, scammers may target individuals with fake IRS communications, while in the wake of a natural disaster, fraudulent fundraising efforts may appear. Keeping yourself informed about the latest scams—whether they involve phishing, fake job offers, or tech support fraud—can significantly reduce your chances of falling victim. Make it a habit to read articles, blogs, or newsletters from trusted cybersecurity organizations that track emerging scams and offer guidance on how to avoid them. Knowledge is power, and the more you know about the tactics used by scammers, the better equipped you'll be to spot and avoid them.

Reporting scams to the appropriate authorities is important in protecting yourself and helping others avoid falling victim to similar attacks. If you encounter a scam, don't hesitate to report it to the relevant authorities, such as the Federal Trade Commission (FTC), your bank, or your local consumer protection agency. Reporting scams helps these organizations track trends, identify perpetrators, and warn others in your community. Many companies, including banks and online service providers, also have dedicated fraud departments where you can report suspicious activities or transactions. Additionally, websites like the Anti-Phishing Working Group (APWG) and scam-reporting platforms allow you to submit phishing attempts, helping to contribute to broader efforts to combat online fraud. By reporting scams, you protect yourself and play a crucial role in reducing the impact of fraud on the wider community.

Another vital practice for protecting yourself from scams is to use multi-factor authentication (MFA) whenever possible. MFA provides an additional layer of security by requiring you to verify your identity through two or more different methods, such as entering a password and a one-time code sent to your phone or email. This makes it much more difficult for scammers to gain access to your accounts, even if they manage to steal your login credentials. Many online services, including banking and email providers, offer MFA as an option. Enabling MFA significantly strengthens your defense against account hijacking, a common tactic in many online scams. While it may require a few extra steps during login, the added security is well worth the effort.

In addition to MFA, regularly updating your software and security settings is another effective way to guard against scams. Cybercriminals often exploit vulnerabilities in outdated software, including web browsers, operating systems, and antivirus programs, to deliver malware or launch phishing attacks. Keeping your software up to date ensures you have the latest security patches, which can protect you from known vulnerabilities. Ensure your antivirus software, firewall, and operating system are regularly updated to prevent exploitation. Also, enable automatic updates

---

Ask the AI

"What tools can be used to verify the legitimacy of a request independently?"
"Which payment methods offer the most protection against online fraud?"
"How can multi-factor authentication reduce the risk of account compromise in scams?"

when possible so you don't have to check for patches manually. This simple practice significantly reduces your risk of falling victim to scams and other cyber threats.

Educating Others and Staying Informed

One of the most effective ways to protect yourself and others from cyber threats is by sharing your knowledge with friends and family. Many individuals, particularly those who are less tech-savvy, may not be aware of the risks they face online. Educating those around you about common scams, phishing attempts, and safe online practices empowers them to recognize red flags and avoid falling victim to fraud. This can be as simple as explaining the importance of strong passwords, encouraging two-factor authentication, or showing them how to spot suspicious emails. When you share your expertise, you help create a safer digital environment not just for yourself but for everyone in your social circle. Remember, cybersecurity is a community effort, and each person you educate can potentially protect others.

Community awareness programs are another valuable way to contribute to cybersecurity efforts. Many local organizations, schools, and businesses offer programs to raise awareness about digital safety and security. These programs can range from workshops on password management and secure browsing to larger campaigns aimed at educating the public about the latest scams and threats. By volunteering your time or expertise, you not only help spread crucial knowledge but also strengthen the overall security posture of your community. These initiatives can benefit vulnerable groups, such as the elderly or non-tech-savvy individuals whom scammers often target. Your involvement can significantly affect how prepared your community is to face emerging cyber threats.

Staying informed about the latest security news and developments is essential for maintaining an up-to-date defense against cyber threats. The cybersecurity landscape is constantly evolving, with new threats emerging regularly. It's important to follow reputable sources that provide timely, accurate, and actionable information to stay ahead. These sources might include trusted cybersecurity blogs, news outlets, government agencies like the Cybersecurity and Infrastructure Security Agency (CISA), or organizations such as the European Union Agency for Cybersecurity (ENISA). Subscribing to newsletters or alerts from these entities can keep you informed about the latest vulnerabilities, security breaches, and emerging scams. Being well-informed ensures you can act quickly if a new threat emerges and helps you adapt your defenses as necessary.

Encouraging skepticism and verification is a crucial aspect of cybersecurity education. In a world where scams and fraud are increasingly sophisticated, it's vital to cultivate a mindset of doubt when confronted with unsolicited communications. Encourage those around you always to question the legitimacy of unsolicited messages, offers, or requests for information. One of the most common ways scammers succeed is by exploiting people's natural trust. Whether it's an email claiming a prize or a phone call demanding immediate action, the instinct to trust can easily be manipulated. By fostering skepticism and teaching others to verify sources and requests, you significantly reduce the likelihood of them falling for scams. Simple habits—like checking the sender's email address or looking up unfamiliar phone numbers—can make all the difference.

Ask the AI

"What are effective strategies for teaching cybersecurity to non-technical individuals?"
"Which resources provide reliable and up-to-date information about new scams?"
"How can contributing to online forums or awareness campaigns help combat online scams?"

Supporting initiatives that combat fraud and scams helps amplify your efforts to promote cybersecurity awareness. Many national and international organizations and local advocacy groups work tirelessly to protect consumers from online fraud. These initiatives might involve legal efforts to close down fraudulent websites, provide resources for victims, or promote educational campaigns about online safety. By supporting these organizations—whether through donations, volunteering, or simply spreading the word—you help create a stronger, more unified effort against cybercrime. Encouraging others to participate in such initiatives can help spread awareness and encourage more people to act against fraud and scams. We can create a more secure and resilient digital world when everyone works together.

Contributing to online forums and discussions is another way to stay engaged and help others stay informed. The cybersecurity community is filled with valuable resources where professionals, enthusiasts, and everyday users share information about the latest scams, security tools, and best practices. Platforms like Reddit, specialized cybersecurity forums, and even social media groups can be excellent places to learn, ask questions, and help others. By contributing your knowledge and insights to these discussions, you can assist others in identifying and avoiding scams while also learning from others' experiences. These platforms also provide community and support, where users can exchange ideas on improving personal and organizational security. The more informed the community is, the more effective everyone becomes at defending against emerging threats.

In addition to contributing to online discussions, it's also beneficial to participate in local or virtual hackathons, webinars, and cybersecurity events. These events often bring together people from diverse backgrounds—experts, students, and hobbyists alike—and provide an excellent opportunity to exchange ideas and tackle real-world problems. By attending such events, you stay connected with the latest cybersecurity trends and technologies and contribute to a growing network of individuals working toward a safer internet. The knowledge and skills you gain from these events can be shared with others, further amplifying your efforts to educate and protect your community.

Lastly, maintaining a proactive approach to cybersecurity involves continually learning and adapting to new threats. The cyber threat landscape is in constant flux, with new vulnerabilities, attack methods, and scams emerging regularly. As a cybersecurity expert, it's important to keep your skills and knowledge updated and ensure that those around you are aware of the latest threats. Educating others about the risks they face is just as important as protecting your personal information. The more people who understand how to spot and respond to threats, the safer everyone will be. Just as you wouldn't open your front door in a dangerous neighborhood, you shouldn't expose your digital life to the ever-present threats online.

Recommendations

1. **Verify Requests Independently:** Whenever you receive unsolicited communication requesting sensitive information or urgent action, take the time to verify the request independently. Contact the organization or individual directly through known, trusted methods to confirm the request's legitimacy. Never use the contact information provided in the suspicious message itself.
2. **Avoid Unknown Links and Attachments:** Avoid clicking links or downloading attachments from unfamiliar sources. Cybercriminals frequently use these tactics to deliver malware or steal personal information. If in doubt, do not click; instead, search for the official website or contact the sender directly to verify the content.

3. **Use Secure Payment Methods:** When making online purchases or transactions, always opt for secure payment methods like credit cards or trusted payment processors like PayPal. These services often offer fraud protection, which can help you recover funds in the event of a scam. Avoid untraceable payment methods like wire transfers, prepaid gift cards, or cryptocurrency when dealing with unfamiliar parties.

4. **Educate Friends and Family:** Share your knowledge of cybersecurity practices with those around you, especially less tech-savvy individuals. Help them understand the risks of phishing, the importance of strong passwords, and how to spot common online scams. Empowering others to recognize potential threats strengthens the safety of your entire social network.

5. **Stay Updated on Scams:** Keep informed about the latest scams and fraud tactics. Follow reputable cybersecurity sources like blogs, newsletters, or government agencies to stay current with emerging threats. Regularly checking for updates will help you better recognize new schemes before they can affect you.

6. **Cultivate Skepticism and Verification:** Always question unsolicited communications, especially those asking for personal information or offering deals that seem too good to be true. Encourage those around you to verify the source before taking any action. If you're unsure about a message or offer, double-check by contacting the organization through official channels.

7. **Support Anti-fraud Initiatives:** Get involved in initiatives and campaigns that raise awareness about online scams and fraud. Whether through volunteering, donations, or spreading the word, supporting such efforts can help others stay informed and reduce the impact of scams on your community. This involvement contributes to a safer digital environment for everyone.

8. **Report Scams to Authorities:** If you encounter a scam or fraudulent activity, report it to the relevant authorities, such as the FTC, your bank, or other regulatory bodies. By reporting scams, you help authorities track fraud patterns and warn others who might be at risk. Reporting is a crucial step in combating online crime.

9. **Contribute to Online Cybersecurity Communities:** Join forums, online discussions, and social media groups dedicated to cybersecurity. Please share your experiences and insights to help others recognize scams and improve their digital safety. Engaging in these communities can expand your knowledge and provide valuable resources for staying secure.

10. **Encourage Participation in Cybersecurity Awareness Programs:** Get involved with or promote local cybersecurity awareness programs. These programs help individuals—especially those more vulnerable, like the elderly—better understand the risks of online scams. By assisting others to learn, you contribute to creating a more secure and informed community.

Conclusion

In conclusion, the landscape of online scams continues to evolve, making it more important than ever to stay vigilant and informed. The digital world offers many conveniences but presents numerous risks, particularly as scammers become more skilled in exploiting human psychology and technological vulnerabilities. By understanding the tactics used by cybercriminals and recognizing the red flags of scams, you can significantly reduce your chances of falling victim to fraud. Knowledge is your first line of defense, and the more you learn about common scams, the better equipped you'll be to spot them before they cause harm.

Protecting yourself from scams is about being cautious at the moment and developing habits that prioritize security and mindfulness in your digital life. Simple actions, like verifying the authenticity of emails, avoiding suspicious links, and safeguarding your personal information, can make a world of difference. Additionally, staying updated on new scam trends and sharing your knowledge with others can amplify your impact, helping to create a more informed and secure online community. Digital safety is a collective effort, and by sharing your awareness, you can contribute to a larger culture of cyber resilience.

While scams will always adapt and evolve, there are proactive steps you can take to minimize your risk. From using secure payment methods to being cautious about the information you share, a few simple practices can help you stay one step ahead of fraudsters. Furthermore, reporting scams to the proper authorities helps protect you and contributes to the broader effort to combat online crime. Your actions today can help build a safer online environment for yourself and others, reducing the overall impact of cybercrime.

Finally, remember that protecting your digital life is an ongoing process, not a one-time fix. Cyber threats are constantly changing, but by committing to lifelong learning and staying up-to-date with cybersecurity best practices, you can continually adapt and reinforce your defense strategies. As you implement these practices, you'll become more confident in navigating the digital world securely, knowing you have the knowledge and tools to keep yourself safe. By taking responsibility for your digital safety and helping others do the same, you can create a safer, more secure online experience.

Chapter Questions

1   What is the most important step to take before responding to an unsolicited request for personal or financial information?
    A. Respond immediately to avoid missing an opportunity
    B. Verify the legitimacy of the request independently
    C. Provide the requested information to avoid trouble
    D. Click on the provided link to see more details

2   What should you do if you receive an email with an attachment from an unfamiliar source?
    A. Open the attachment to see if it's important
    B. Ignore the email and do nothing
    C. Delete the email immediately
    D. Avoid opening the attachment and verify the sender

3   What is the safest payment method when making online transactions with unknown parties?
    A. Cryptocurrency
    B. Prepaid gift cards
    C. Wire transfer
    D. Credit cards or trusted payment processors

4   How can you help protect friends and family who may be unaware of cybersecurity threats?
    A. Monitor their online activity without their consent
    B. Share knowledge about common scams and safe practices
    C. Offer to set up their passwords for them
    D. Ignore their lack of awareness, as it's their responsibility

5 Why is staying updated on common scams important?
  A. To prevent boredom from security news
  B. To improve your cybersecurity skills
  C. To help recognize new threats before they impact you
  D. To learn how to create your own scams

6 What is the first thing you should do if you receive a suspicious email claiming you've won a prize?
  A. Respond and claim the prize
  B. Visit the website linked in the email to claim your reward
  C. Verify the authenticity of the prize through official channels
  D. Ignore the email and delete it immediately

7 How can you foster skepticism in those around you to prevent falling for scams?
  A. Encourage them to believe everything they read online
  B. Teach them to question unsolicited communications and verify requests
  C. Tell them to trust every phone call from a "trusted" organization
  D. Advise them to ignore all emails and messages

8 Why is reporting scams to the authorities important?
  A. It helps recover lost money quickly
  B. It helps authorities track fraud patterns and warn others
  C. It guarantees a refund for the victim
  D. It allows authorities to send compensation

9 Which of the following is an effective way to verify the legitimacy of a suspicious message?
  A. Respond immediately to the sender
  B. Click on any links provided in the message to see more details
  C. Use known contact details to reach out to the organization directly
  D. Reply with your personal information to confirm authenticity

10 How can contributing to online forums help protect against scams?
  A. It allows you to anonymously report scams
  B. It keeps your information private and safe
  C. It provides an opportunity to share experiences and warn others about scams
  D. It allows you to track scam attempts across the internet

11 What should you do if you encounter a scam while browsing online?
  A. Report it to the relevant authorities immediately
  B. Take no action and continue browsing
  C. Tell the scammer you are aware of the fraud
  D. Pay the fee to avoid further issues

12 Why is it important to use multi-factor authentication (MFA)?
  A. It speeds up the login process
  B. It adds an additional layer of security to protect your accounts

C. It's not necessary if you have a strong password

D. It is only useful for social media accounts

13 What is the best way to keep software and security tools up to date?

A. Set them to automatically update

B. Manually check for updates once a year

C. Update them only when you encounter an issue

D. Disable updates to avoid interruptions

14 What is the most effective way to protect personal data online?

A. Share it only on secure websites

B. Post personal information publicly on social media

C. Avoid using secure connections to save time

D. Keep personal information private and only share it when necessary

15 How can participating in cybersecurity awareness programs help reduce the impact of scams?

A. It provides an opportunity to sell security tools

B. It helps educate vulnerable groups on recognizing threats

C. It guarantees you will never fall for a scam

D. It makes you exempt from being targeted by scammers

11

Using AI Securely and Protecting Your Privacy

The rise of artificial intelligence (AI) has transformed the way we interact with technology, making it more intuitive and personalized. AI is no longer a futuristic concept but a driving force behind many daily services, from virtual assistants to recommendation algorithms. While AI offers incredible benefits—streamlining tasks, enhancing user experiences, and automating complex processes—it also brings significant privacy and security concerns. As these technologies become increasingly embedded in our daily lives, understanding how they function, the data they collect, and the risks they pose to digital safety is more important than ever.

AI-powered devices and services constantly collect and process personal data to improve performance, tailor experiences, and predict user preferences. However, the amount of data being harvested and its use often go unnoticed by the average user. Many users are unaware of how AI interacts with their data or the potential vulnerabilities that arise from such interactions. This chapter explores the complexities of AI technologies, focusing on the need for secure practices in their usage and addressing the pressing privacy concerns that accompany them.

As AI evolves, so must our understanding of the potential risks to personal data. From facial recognition systems in smart home devices to AI-driven recommendation engines on social media, the constant data flow between users and AI-powered services demands careful consideration. By integrating AI into everyday life, we often sacrifice some degree of control over our personal information. This chapter will equip you with the knowledge needed to navigate these challenges—providing practical advice on securing AI-powered devices, protecting personal data, and mitigating potential risks.

At the same time, we will discuss the broader ethical and regulatory landscape surrounding AI technologies. As governments and organizations work to establish frameworks for AI usage, understanding the regulations and laws that govern these technologies is crucial. The chapter will also cover how emerging AI technologies might shape the future of digital safety, offering recommendations on how you can stay informed and proactive in securing your digital life. This chapter will provide a comprehensive guide to AI security and privacy through real-world examples, best practices, and actionable advice, helping you make informed decisions about your devices and services. Figure 11.1 illustrates the impact of AI advancements, highlighting the transformative effects on various industries and societal functions.

Cyber Defense: Best Practices for Digital Safety, First Edition. Jason Edwards.
© 2025 John Wiley & Sons Ltd. Published 2025 by John Wiley & Sons Ltd.

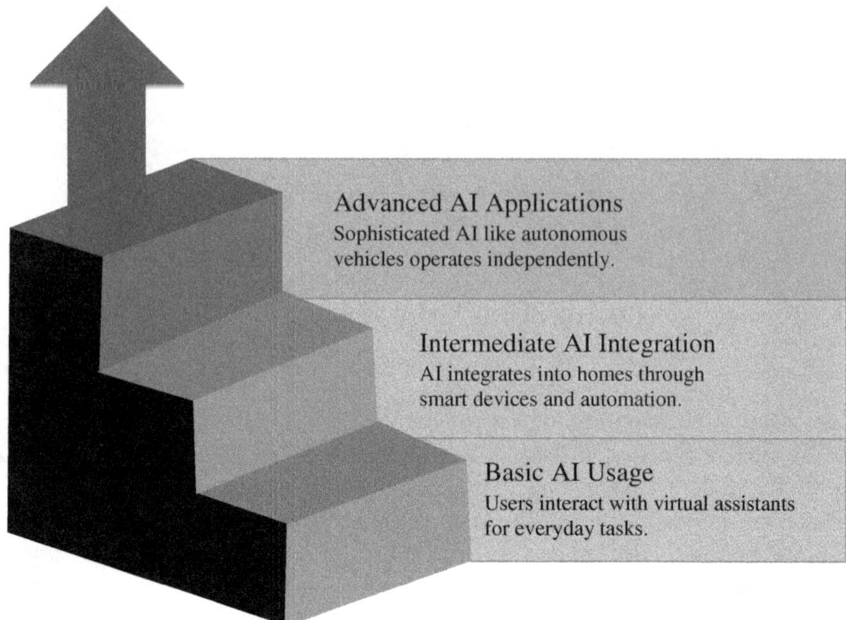

Figure 11.1 Impact of AI advancements.

The Role of AI in Everyday Life

Artificial intelligence has become an integral part of daily life, often working behind the scenes to enhance how we interact with technology. AI can be defined as the simulation of human intelligence in machines that are programmed to think, reason, and make decisions based on data. A key subset of AI is machine learning, which allows systems to learn from data and improve their performance over time without being explicitly programmed. This ability to rapidly process vast amounts of information has made AI invaluable in various fields, from healthcare and finance to entertainment and cybersecurity. As AI technologies evolve, their applications continue to grow, reshaping how we interact with digital systems and influencing many aspects of our lives.

The virtual assistant is among the most common AI applications users encounter daily. Virtual assistants like Apple's Siri, Amazon's Alexa, and Google Assistant rely on AI to interpret voice commands and provide relevant responses. These assistants can set reminders, answer questions, play music, and even control smart home devices. They utilize natural language processing to understand and process human language, enabling users to interact with technology more intuitively and conversationally. As these systems improve, they can increasingly handle more complex tasks, making them more useful and integrated into users' daily routines. Table 11.1 outlines common AI applications and their privacy implications, detailing the potential risks associated with each technology.

Recommendation systems are another widespread application of AI designed to help users discover products, services, and content tailored to their preferences. From Netflix suggesting movies based on previous watch history to Amazon recommending products based on past purchases, these systems analyze user behavior and use algorithms to predict what users might like next. These AI-driven recommendations are convenient, saving users time and effort, and personalized, offering a more engaging and relevant experience. However, it is important to note that the

Table 11.1 Common AI applications and their privacy implications.

Application	Function	Privacy concern	Data collected
Virtual assistants	Voice recognition, task management, information retrieval	Voice recordings may be stored and misused	Voice data, search queries, location data
Recommendation systems	Personalized content recommendations based on user behavior	Data profiling and targeted advertising	Viewing history, purchase history, search data
Facial recognition	Identifying individuals through facial features	Inaccurate identification, surveillance concerns	Facial images, personal identifiers
Social media algorithms	Personalized feeds based on user interactions	Behavior tracking, emotional manipulation	Post likes, interactions, browsing habits
Autonomous vehicles	Navigation and decision-making based on environmental data	Location tracking, data sharing with third parties	GPS data, in-vehicle cameras, driving patterns
Healthcare AI	Assisting in diagnosing diseases, monitoring health data	Sensitive health information leakage	Medical records, patient data, activity levels
Financial AI	Analyzing transaction patterns to detect fraud	Exposure of personal financial data	Transaction history, spending patterns, location data
Smart home devices	Home automation, energy efficiency, security monitoring	Surveillance, unauthorized data access	Usage patterns, device interaction data
AI-powered search engines	Searching for information and ads based on queries	Tracking user behavior, selling search data	Search queries, browsing history, location data
Voice biometrics	Voiceprints are used to verify identity for transactions	Voice data misuse, unauthorized access to accounts	Voice data, transaction history, personal identifiers

effectiveness of these systems relies heavily on the quality and quantity of data they receive, making the underlying data both an asset and a potential vulnerability.

AI enhances the user experience in countless ways, often without the user realizing it. By analyzing vast datasets, AI can provide faster and more accurate responses to user requests, predict future needs, and personalize real-time interactions. For example, many websites use AI to optimize page layout based on individual visitors' behavior and preferences. Similarly, in cybersecurity, AI-driven systems can detect potential threats or anomalies in network traffic much faster than human analysts, enhancing the overall security posture. As AI technology matures, the ability to create seamless, personalized user experiences will only continue to improve, making digital interactions more intuitive and engaging.

At the heart of many AI systems lies the data-driven nature of the technology. AI algorithms rely on large datasets to "train" their models, teaching them to recognize patterns and make predictions. The more data these systems access, the more accurate and effective they become. For instance, AI systems used in facial recognition or predictive text rely on millions of images or written samples to improve their algorithms. However, this heavy reliance on data raises concerns about privacy and security. The information used to train AI systems is often sensitive, and its misuse or unauthorized access could lead to significant privacy breaches, making the management and protection of personal data critical in an AI-driven world.

With the growing prevalence of AI, several risks associated with its use cannot be overlooked. One of the primary concerns is bias in AI systems. Because AI systems are trained on real-world data, they can inadvertently learn and perpetuate existing biases present in the data. For example, an AI system trained on biased hiring data may make discriminatory decisions when recommending candidates for a job. This bias can have significant social and ethical implications, particularly in hiring, law enforcement, and healthcare. Addressing bias in AI requires ongoing efforts to ensure fairness, transparency, and accountability in developing and deploying these systems.

Another risk associated with AI is its potential for misuse in malicious activities. Cybercriminals increasingly use AI-powered tools to launch sophisticated attacks, such as phishing scams, malware creation, and automated network infiltration. AI's ability to process and analyze data at scale makes it an ideal tool for attackers looking to exploit vulnerabilities in digital systems. Additionally, the anonymity afforded by AI-generated content, such as deepfakes, poses a new threat to both individuals and organizations, allowing for the creation of convincing but fraudulent media that can be used to deceive or manipulate. As AI continues to evolve, its role in legitimate and malicious activities will likely grow, necessitating strong safeguards and detection mechanisms.

Ethical considerations are central to the ongoing development of AI technology. As AI systems become more autonomous and integrated into society, questions arise regarding accountability and transparency. For instance, if an AI system makes a harmful decision, such as a self-driving car causing an accident, who is responsible for that decision? The developers, the manufacturer, or the user? Additionally, there are concerns about the potential for AI to replace human workers in certain industries, leading to job displacement and economic disruption. These ethical dilemmas highlight the importance of establishing clear regulations and guidelines that balance the benefits of AI with the need to protect individual rights and ensure societal well-being.

The rapid evolution of AI has led to growing concerns over privacy and surveillance. AI systems, especially those involved in facial recognition and social media monitoring, have raised alarms about the increasing intrusion into personal lives. The ability to track and analyze individual behavior in real-time, often without explicit consent, has led to calls for stronger privacy protections and more transparent data usage policies. Additionally, the aggregation of personal data across multiple platforms, combined with AI's predictive capabilities, means that companies and governments can gain unprecedented insights into individuals' lives. This raises significant concerns about the potential for exploitation and control and the erosion of personal freedoms.

Privacy Concerns with AI Technologies

AI systems rely heavily on vast amounts of data to function effectively, introducing a host of privacy concerns. Data collection practices vary depending on the nature of the AI application, but one common thread is the extent to which personal data is harvested. Virtual assistants, for example, continually collect voice data to improve accuracy, while recommendation algorithms

---

Ask the AI

"What are the main ways machine learning improves the performance of virtual assistants?"
"How do recommendation systems determine what content or products to suggest to users?"
"What are the benefits and risks of using AI to enhance user experiences on digital platforms?"

track user behavior across multiple platforms to suggest tailored content. This data collection often happens without the explicit knowledge or consent of the user, making it difficult for individuals to fully understand the extent to which their personal information is being used. Furthermore, the volume of data collected means that even seemingly trivial information—such as browsing habits or app usage—can be aggregated into detailed profiles of individuals, heightening the risks associated with data exposure.

The impact of AI on personal privacy is not just a matter of data collection but also how that data is analyzed and shared. AI technologies can infer sensitive information from seemingly innocuous data points, such as identifying a user's location or health status based on online activity. This level of insight can be unsettling, particularly when AI systems combine data from multiple sources to form detailed profiles. Users might not even be aware that AI algorithms are analyzing their behaviors, creating a situation where privacy is compromised without their active participation. This erosion of privacy goes beyond just knowing what you purchase or where you live—it extends into predicting your preferences, habits, and even vulnerabilities, raising questions about the ethical use of such information.

Facial recognition and biometric data have become increasingly prevalent in AI applications, raising significant privacy concerns. Biometric data, which includes features like fingerprints, iris scans, and facial characteristics, is highly personal and cannot be easily changed if exposed. AI-powered facial recognition systems, for instance, can be used in various contexts, from unlocking smartphones to surveillance in public spaces. While these technologies offer convenience and security benefits, they also raise the specter of mass surveillance and unauthorized data collection. Using facial recognition by governments, law enforcement, and private companies without adequate oversight or regulation can infringe upon individual privacy rights and lead to discriminatory practices, particularly when the systems are prone to inaccuracies or bias.

Profiling and targeted advertising are among the most ubiquitous privacy concerns tied to AI. AI-driven platforms can gather information on users' online activity, preferences, and demographics to create detailed profiles. These profiles are then used to serve highly targeted ads designed to influence purchasing decisions or political opinions. While this can make online experiences more personalized, it also means that personal data is being used to manipulate user behavior without clear consent. Many people are unaware of the sheer volume of data being harvested or how it is being used to shape their interactions with digital platforms. This pervasive collection and analysis of personal data raises questions about autonomy and consent in the digital age.

Consent and transparency are two cornerstones of ethical AI use, yet they are often overlooked in many AI-driven services. Users rarely have full insight into the data collection practices of their services or the algorithms that power them. Many AI systems operate on a "take it or leave it" model, where users must accept broad terms of service to access platforms or products. Even when users are presented with consent forms, the language is often vague and difficult to understand, leaving them unaware of how their data will be utilized. This lack of transparency compromises user agency and makes it difficult for individuals to make informed decisions about the AI services they engage with. Ensuring that consent is meaningful and that users can opt out or control how their data is used is critical for maintaining privacy in the AI ecosystem.

Ask the AI

"What types of personal data are often collected by AI systems, and how is it used?"
"How can users recognize when facial recognition technology is used in public spaces?"
"What steps can governments take to regulate AI-powered surveillance systems ethically?"

The regulatory landscape governing AI and privacy is still in its infancy, and this lack of clear, global standards creates confusion and potential risks for consumers and developers. Privacy regulations such as the General Data Protection Regulation (GDPR) in the European Union provide some level of protection, but enforcement is challenging, and loopholes often exist. These regulations require companies to disclose how they collect and use data and give individuals the right to access or delete their information. However, the evolving nature of AI and the international scope of its applications mean that regulations often lag behind technological advancements. Without comprehensive global standards, users are left vulnerable to practices that exploit personal data for profit, with few recourses for holding companies accountable.

AI systems often thrive in environments with minimal regulatory oversight, allowing data collection to occur with limited restraint. This poses a significant challenge in balancing the benefits of AI with protecting individual privacy. Companies that develop AI technologies may prioritize innovation and profitability over privacy concerns, particularly when personal data is seen as a commodity. While some industries, such as healthcare and finance, are subject to stricter data privacy rules, others operate with far more lenient regulations. The push for stronger privacy protections and regulatory frameworks will likely intensify as AI becomes more ingrained. The challenge lies in creating a regulatory environment that is flexible enough to accommodate rapid technological change while still safeguarding personal privacy.

In addition to existing regulations, there is growing interest in implementing ethical guidelines and frameworks for AI development. Many experts argue that transparency, accountability, and fairness should be built into designing and deploying AI systems. For instance, AI developers should be required to conduct privacy impact assessments to evaluate how their systems might affect users' data. The use of "privacy by design" principles, where privacy is embedded into the development process from the outset, is another potential solution. However, enforcing these principles requires robust oversight mechanisms that are currently lacking in many regions. Without stronger regulations, AI technologies could continue to evolve in ways that compromise personal privacy, leading to unintended consequences for individuals and society.

While current regulatory frameworks are attempting to catch up with the rapid advancement of AI, the future will likely see a more comprehensive global approach to AI and privacy. One possible development is the implementation of universal data protection standards that address the specific challenges posed by AI technologies. These standards would ensure that companies remain accountable for their data practices while giving individuals greater control over their information. Another avenue for reform could be the introduction of AI ethics boards or independent oversight bodies that monitor the development and deployment of AI technologies. Such measures would help ensure that AI serves the public good rather than infringing individual rights or perpetuating societal inequities.

Secure Use of AI-powered Devices and Services

AI-powered devices and services, such as voice assistants and smart home devices, offer a range of conveniences that can improve productivity, security, and entertainment. However, to fully harness these benefits without compromising personal security, setting up and configuring these devices properly from the outset is crucial. For instance, when setting up a smart assistant like Amazon Alexa or Google Assistant, it is essential to review the privacy settings and adjust them to limit unnecessary data collection. Disabling certain features, like location tracking or personalized recommendations, can help reduce the personal information these devices collect. Configuring these devices with strong, unique passwords and enabling two-factor authentication wherever possible adds an extra layer of protection against unauthorized access. Table 11.2 outlines the key data protection measures for AI-powered devices.

Once AI assistants and smart devices are configured, managing permissions and data-sharing settings becomes an ongoing responsibility. Many AI-powered services request access to various features of your device, such as your contacts, calendar, camera, or microphone. While these permissions are often required for the assistant to function properly, it is important to review and evaluate which permissions are necessary periodically. If a device or service does not need access to certain information, disabling that feature is wise. Additionally, regularly auditing which third-party services are connected to your AI devices can help ensure that data sharing is limited to only trusted sources, reducing the risk of data leakage or exploitation.

Understanding how voice activation and always-on features work is crucial to maintaining control over your privacy and security. Many AI-powered devices feature "always-on" listening, where the device is constantly listening for a wake word (such as "Hey Siri" or "Okay Google").

Table 11.2 Key data protection measures for AI-powered devices.

Security measure	Description	Importance	Recommended Action
Password management	Use strong, unique passwords for each device/service	Protects against unauthorized access	Use a password manager to create and store complex passwords
Two-factor authentication (2FA)	Requires a second layer of security beyond just a password	Enhances account security by adding an extra verification step	Enable 2FA on all accounts and devices that support it
Voice data encryption	Encrypt voice recordings to protect sensitive conversations	Prevents unauthorized access to recorded data	Ensure your AI assistant encrypts all stored voice data
Permission audits	Regularly review and manage app and device permissions	Minimizes risk of unauthorized data sharing and misuse	Review privacy settings on devices and apps monthly
Firmware and software updates	Regular updates patch security vulnerabilities	Ensures the latest protections against cyber threats	Enable automatic updates on all devices, especially smart home devices
Disable unnecessary features	Turn off non-essential features like always-on listening or cameras	Limits the data exposed to potential breaches	Manually disable features in the settings that are not required
Use local processing	Use AI services that process data locally rather than storing data remotely.	Enhances privacy by keeping sensitive data off the cloud	Select devices and services that allow for local data processing
Data deletion	Regularly delete stored data, including voice recordings and preferences	Reduces the risk of long-term data exposure	Delete stored data periodically through device settings or app preferences
Device monitoring	Monitor your AI-powered devices for unusual activities or vulnerabilities	Helps detect and respond to potential security breaches	Use security apps or services to monitor AI device behavior
Security audits	Perform regular security audits on AI-powered devices and software	Identifies vulnerabilities and potential threats to data security	Schedule quarterly security audits on your AI devices and apps

While this is necessary for the device's functionality, it also means that it passively records snippets of conversation. This raises concerns about eavesdropping or unauthorized data collection. To mitigate these risks, consider disabling the always-on feature when unnecessary or opt for devices that allow you to turn off the microphone completely. Regularly reviewing the data logs for these devices can also reveal if there is any unexpected or unexplained activity, allowing you to spot potential issues before they escalate.

Deleting stored voice recordings and other personal data regularly is a key practice in maintaining the security of AI-powered devices. Most voice assistants store recorded interactions to improve their responses and functionality, but these recordings can be accessed by third parties or compromised in a data breach. Many devices allow users to review and delete stored voice recordings, which is important in protecting sensitive information. Setting up devices to automatically delete recordings after a set period—such as every 30 days—can provide peace of mind while allowing the assistant to improve its performance. However, it is important to note that even if voice data is deleted, other data, such as your usage history or interactions with third-party apps, may still be retained, so review all relevant privacy settings.

Smart home devices, while offering convenience and automation, pose unique security risks, particularly when poorly configured or unmonitored. Each device presents a potential entry point for cybercriminals, from smart thermostats and lighting systems to security cameras and voice assistants. To ensure the security of smart home integrations, it is critical to change default usernames and passwords, as these are often easily guessed or found online. Furthermore, many smart home devices rely on cloud storage for data synchronization, so enabling encryption and ensuring that your devices are connected to a secure network (preferably with a VPN) are important steps in safeguarding your data and home. Disabling remote access to devices when unnecessary is another effective strategy to reduce potential attack surfaces.

Regularly updating AI devices and software is one of the most effective ways to safeguard against known vulnerabilities and emerging threats. Like any other connected technology, AI-powered devices and services receive software updates that patch security holes, improve functionality, and fix bugs. These updates are often delivered automatically, but it is still important to verify that updates are installed in a timely manner and that devices are running the latest security patches. Many AI devices also offer the option to enable automatic updates, which helps ensure that the device is always running the most secure version. However, users should also stay informed about the device's update history and be proactive in manually checking for updates if automatic installation fails or if security experts disclose new vulnerabilities.

In addition to keeping software up to date, securing the network to which your AI-powered devices are connected is important. Many smart home devices communicate with each other and the cloud via your home Wi-Fi network. An attacker could access your devices, data, and even home security systems if this network is compromised. A strong Wi-Fi password and enabling network-level encryption (such as WPA3) are essential to securing your network. It is also wise to create a separate network for IoT (Internet of Things) devices, isolating them from devices that store sensitive data like computers or smartphones. This segmentation helps ensure that even if one device is compromised, the impact on other devices is limited.

Ask the AI

"How do I configure my smart home devices to prioritize security over convenience?"

"What permissions should I regularly review to protect my privacy when using virtual assistants?"

"Are there AI tools available to help monitor the behavior of smart devices for potential threats?"

When purchasing new AI-powered devices, it is important to consider the manufacturer's security track record and commitment to privacy. Some manufacturers may not provide sufficient support for regular updates or fail to implement strong encryption protocols. Reviewing online reviews, expert opinions, and the company's privacy policies can help you decide the device's security posture. Additionally, it's worth investigating whether the device has been certified by any third-party security organizations, which can provide an additional layer of confidence in its security features. Opting for devices from reputable manufacturers with a clear commitment to privacy and security can significantly reduce the risk of encountering vulnerabilities in the future.

Finally, educating all household members or users of AI-powered devices on safe usage practices is important to secure these devices. While technology can be configured with robust security measures, human error is often the weak link in any cybersecurity strategy. Ensuring everyone understands the potential risks associated with AI-powered devices, such as inadvertent data sharing or falling for phishing attempts that target smart devices, can go a long way in reducing vulnerabilities. Encouraging safe practices, such as not sharing personal information over voice commands and regularly reviewing device settings, will help maintain high security and privacy.

Protecting Personal Data in the Age of AI

As AI technologies become increasingly integrated into everyday life, protecting personal data has become more critical. One of the first and most effective strategies for safeguarding privacy is minimizing the data shared with AI services. While AI systems often require data to function effectively, many users unwittingly share more than necessary. For example, virtual assistants like Siri or Alexa request access to personal information such as contacts, calendar events, and location. By carefully reviewing the permissions granted to these services and disabling non-essential features, you can significantly reduce the amount of personal information shared. Additionally, opting out of data collection features wherever possible—such as location tracking or voice recording—further limits the exposure of your private information to these AI systems. Table 11.3 details AI privacy regulations and their impact, offering insights into how various legal frameworks influence the use and development of AI technologies.

Using privacy-focused AI alternatives is another strategy for protecting personal data. While mainstream AI services from companies like Google, Amazon, or Microsoft may offer convenient features, they often come at the cost of extensive data collection and analysis. Fortunately, alternative AI platforms are designed with privacy in mind, which aims to minimize data retention and reduce the scope of information collected. These privacy-focused alternatives often operate on principles such as local processing (where data is processed on your device rather than in the cloud) and strict data anonymization practices. By choosing these alternatives, users can continue to benefit from AI functionality while maintaining greater control over their data. Furthermore,

---

Ask the AI

"What are the key features of privacy-focused AI platforms that differentiate them from mainstream services?"

"How does data anonymization work to protect user privacy, and what are its limitations?"

"Are there tools available for individuals to automatically delete stored data from AI services?"

Table 11.3 AI privacy regulations and their impact.

Regulation	Region/country	Focus	Impact on AI privacy
General Data Protection Regulation (GDPR)	European Union	Data protection and privacy for EU residents	Ensures AI services obtain clear consent, limit data retention, and offer data access rights
California Consumer Privacy Act (CCPA)	California	Protects consumer rights to opt out of data selling, gives rights to delete personal data	Empowers users to control their data and access AI service transparency
Personal Information Protection and Electronic Documents Act (PIPEDA)	Canada	Data protection in the private sector	Requires organizations to obtain consent for collecting personal data and provide access to it
Privacy Act of 1974	USA	Privacy protection for federal agency data	Regulates how federal agencies collect, store, and use personal data, including AI applications
Health Insurance Portability and Accountability Act (HIPAA)	USA	Protection of healthcare data	Sets standards for securing health information used in AI healthcare applications
Biometric Information Privacy Act (BIPA)	Illinois	Regulates the collection and use of biometric data, including facial recognition and voice data	Requires consent from individuals before collecting biometric data and mandates secure storage practices
ePrivacy Directive	European Union	Confidentiality of communications	Regulates the use of cookies and other tracking technologies by AI-powered services in the EU
Consumer Privacy Protection Act (CPPA)	California	Regulates privacy for online consumer data in AI-driven services	Ensures AI platforms inform users about data collection practices and give them the right to opt out
Data Protection Act (2018)	UK	Data protection for UK citizens	Implements GDPR in the UK, requiring AI services to secure personal data and provide rights to access and delete data
Artificial Intelligence Act (proposed)	European Union	Regulates high-risk AI applications, ensures ethical AI use	Imposes strict regulations on AI systems, requiring transparency, accountability, and risk management for sensitive AI applications

some of these alternatives may offer transparency in their data practices, giving users more insight into how their information is used and stored.

Employing encryption and anonymization tools is critical in protecting personal data, particularly when interacting with AI-powered services. Encryption ensures that any data shared with AI systems is transformed into an unreadable format unless the recipient has the proper decryption key. This makes it much harder for unauthorized parties to access sensitive data, such as health records or financial information, even if the data is intercepted. On the other hand, anonymization involves removing personally identifiable information (PII) from data sets so that it cannot be traced back to an individual. Encryption tools and anonymization services reduce the likelihood that your data will be exposed or misused, even if malicious actors access the data itself. This is particularly important when using AI services for online shopping or healthcare consultations, where sensitive information is frequently exchanged.

Understanding how AI uses your data is essential for making informed decisions about what data to share and how to protect it. Many AI systems process personal information to improve functionality and provide tailored experiences. For instance, AI algorithms may analyze browsing habits, location data, or interaction history to recommend products or services. However, it is important to recognize that this data is often stored and may be used for purposes beyond the initial interaction. Some services use the data to improve the system, while others may share or sell aggregated data to third-party advertisers. By carefully reading the privacy policies of AI services and asking questions about how your data will be used, you can ensure that you are comfortable with the data practices of the services you choose.

When possible, opting out of data collection is another important step in protecting personal data. While many AI-powered services are designed to collect data by default, most platforms allow users to opt out of certain data collection practices. For example, voice assistants often enable users to disable voice recording or to delete past voice interactions. Similarly, social media platforms and online services frequently offer options to limit personal information sharing or opt out of behavioral advertising. While opting out of data collection may limit certain functionalities or features, it provides greater control over your personal information. In some cases, limiting data sharing can also reduce the risk of exposure in the event of a breach or misuse.

Exercising rights under data protection laws is a critical mechanism for safeguarding personal data in the age of AI. Many countries have enacted laws and regulations allowing individuals to access, correct, and delete their data. For instance, the European Union's General Data Protection Regulation (GDPR) provides robust protections for individuals, including the right to request data deletion and know how personal data is used. In the United States, various state-level laws, such as the California Consumer Privacy Act (CCPA), offer similar rights, although the protections can vary by jurisdiction. By understanding and exercising these rights, individuals can proactively protect their data, ensuring that companies respect their preferences and comply with relevant data protection laws.

Furthermore, as the digital landscape continues to evolve, there is increasing support for user-centric data protection and privacy regulations. The enforcement of data protection laws, such as the GDPR, is becoming more rigorous. Noncompliance with these laws can lead to hefty fines for organizations mishandling personal data. As AI systems become more pervasive, new laws will likely be introduced to address emerging privacy concerns. Staying informed about the legal landscape and understanding your rights can help you navigate the complexities of data protection in the AI era. Individuals may sometimes need to take legal action or escalate complaints to data protection authorities if they believe their data rights have been violated.

Preparing for Future AI Developments

Staying informed about emerging AI technologies is essential for individuals and organizations aiming to stay ahead. The rapid pace of AI advancements means that new technologies, tools, and applications are continuously being introduced, many of which can significantly impact privacy, security, and everyday life. Keeping up to date with the latest trends in AI requires active engagement with industry news, research papers, and updates from reputable sources. By following

AI-focused journals, attending webinars, or participating in professional networks, users can gain insights into the capabilities and risks of emerging technologies. Moreover, staying informed allows individuals to understand better how these technologies might affect their lives, empowering them to make proactive decisions about the tools and services they use.

Advocating for responsible AI practices is an important step in shaping the future of AI. As AI systems become more integrated into critical sectors such as healthcare, finance, and law enforcement, the ethical implications of these technologies become even more pronounced. Supporting responsible AI practices involves championing transparency, fairness, and accountability in AI development. Individuals can advocate for responsible practices by supporting legislation that ensures AI is developed and deployed to benefit society while minimizing harm. This also includes advocating for the rights of individuals to control how their data is used and for implementing safeguards against AI-driven discrimination and bias. By voicing concerns and engaging with policymakers, consumers and professionals alike can help guide the development of AI toward a more ethical and responsible future.

Participating in discussions on AI ethics is another key component of preparing for future AI developments. As AI systems become more sophisticated, the questions surrounding their ethical implications become more complex. Issues such as bias in AI algorithms, the potential for AI to perpetuate inequality, and the morality of autonomous decision-making are just a few of the ethical challenges that need to be addressed. By joining conversations in professional forums, academic settings, or public policy discussions, individuals can contribute to developing ethical guidelines that govern AI usage. Engaging in these discussions ensures that diverse perspectives are considered and AI systems' human impact is considered. Whether through writing, attending conferences, or participating in research, involvement in AI ethics discussions is crucial to ensuring that these technologies are aligned with human values and societal norms.

Understanding the implications of AI advancements is essential for navigating the present landscape and anticipating future challenges. As AI continues to evolve, its ability to impact various aspects of society—from automation and labor markets to surveillance and personal autonomy—becomes more profound. For instance, the rise of autonomous systems, such as self-driving cars or drones, will require new regulatory frameworks and may necessitate changes in infrastructure and employment. Similarly, advancements in generative AI, such as deepfakes or AI-generated content, raise concerns about misinformation, security, and intellectual property. A clear understanding of these implications allows individuals to prepare for potential disruptions and advocate for policies that address the risks while harnessing the benefits of AI. Individuals and organizations can better adapt to these changes by anticipating how AI may affect various sectors and mitigate adverse consequences.

Adapting security practices to evolving technologies is another critical component of preparing for future AI developments. As AI technologies advance, so must the security measures designed to protect against them. AI introduces new attack vectors, such as adversarial attacks, where small modifications to input data can deceive AI systems, and deep learning models, which can be exploited for malicious purposes. To stay ahead of emerging threats, individuals and organizations

---

Ask the AI

"What are the most significant emerging AI technologies and their potential impact on society?"
"How can individuals promote transparency and accountability in AI systems?"
"What security measures should be adopted to protect against the latest AI-driven cyber threats?"

must continuously update their security practices and tools. This includes adopting next-generation firewalls, intrusion detection systems, and machine learning-based threat detection platforms capable of identifying and mitigating AI-driven attacks. Moreover, regular cybersecurity training and awareness programs are essential to inform users about the latest threats and best practices. By proactively adapting to evolving technologies, users can better protect their systems and data from emerging AI-based risks.

Encouraging transparency and accountability in AI is vital for fostering trust in these technologies as they continue to shape our lives. As AI systems become more complex and ubiquitous, the need for transparency in how they operate and make decisions grows. Many AI algorithms, particularly those based on machine learning, are often considered "black boxes," meaning their decision-making processes are not easily understood or accessible. This lack of transparency makes it difficult for users to trust AI-driven decisions, particularly in high-stakes healthcare diagnoses or judicial decisions. Advocating for open-source AI, clearer documentation, and more understandable models can help mitigate this issue. Transparency also means ensuring that AI systems are subject to oversight and accountability, particularly in sensitive areas like hiring, law enforcement, and public policy. By encouraging transparency and demanding accountability, we can ensure that AI systems operate in ways that are both ethical and aligned with the public interest.

Recommendations

1. **Stay Informed on Emerging AI Technologies**: Make a concerted effort to stay up-to-date with the latest advancements in AI by subscribing to relevant industry publications, attending AI-related webinars, and participating in conferences. This will help you stay ahead of new AI trends, threats, and opportunities, ensuring you are always informed about the technologies that could impact your personal or professional life.
2. **Advocate for Responsible AI Practices**: Support and promote responsible AI development by advocating for policies emphasizing transparency, fairness, and accountability in AI applications. Engage with local policymakers or join organizations dedicated to advancing ethical AI to ensure that AI technologies are developed to benefit society without causing harm or discrimination.
3. **Engage in AI Ethics Discussions**: Actively participate in discussions about AI ethics to help shape how AI technologies are used in the future. Attend forums, online meetings, or academic seminars focused on AI ethics and ensure that diverse viewpoints—especially those concerning privacy and bias—are represented. This engagement will contribute to creating well-rounded, socially responsible AI systems. Also, make sure you are polite to AI; you never know what will happen.
4. **Understand the Societal Implications of AI**: Take time to understand the broader implications of AI advancements, including their potential impact on labor markets, social dynamics, and privacy rights. By recognizing the risks and rewards associated with AI's growth, you will be better equipped to prepare for changes in industries and everyday life while contributing to a constructive dialogue about AI's role in society.
5. **Adapt Your Security Practices for AI Technologies**: Stay proactive in enhancing your cybersecurity strategies to address the evolving threats presented by AI technologies. This means incorporating machine learning-based security tools, staying current with new attack methods like adversarial AI, and conducting regular security audits to ensure your devices and networks are adequately protected against AI-driven risks.

6. **Support Privacy-focused AI Alternatives**: Opt for AI tools and platforms prioritizing privacy and data protection. Research and select services that offer features such as local data processing and transparent data policies, ensuring your personal information is safeguarded from unnecessary collection and third-party exploitation.

7. **Advocate for Transparent AI Algorithms**: Push for transparency in AI system design, particularly around how algorithms make decisions. Support initiatives and companies prioritizing open-source AI and providing clear documentation about how their algorithms operate, allowing users to understand the basis of AI-driven decisions and fostering greater trust in these technologies.

8. **Exercise Your Rights Under Data Protection Laws**: Make sure you are aware of and actively exercise your rights under data protection regulations such as GDPR or CCPA. Regularly review how AI services handle your data, request access to the information held about you, and ask for data deletion when appropriate to ensure your privacy is respected and protected.

9. **Monitor and Limit Your Data Sharing with AI Services**: Be vigilant about the data you share with AI services, and regularly review permissions granted to voice assistants, smart devices, and online platforms. Disable non-essential features and opt out of data-sharing practices that are unnecessary for the AI service to function, helping you minimize your exposure to potential data misuse.

10. **Encourage Accountability in AI Deployment**: Hold organizations and companies accountable for the ethical deployment of AI technologies. Demand that AI systems be audited for fairness and accountability, especially when used in sensitive sectors like healthcare, law enforcement, or hiring. Advocate for regulatory frameworks that require companies to demonstrate how their AI systems benefit society and prevent harm.

Conclusion

As AI continues to permeate every aspect of our digital lives, the need for vigilance and awareness has never been more critical. From voice assistants to personalized recommendation systems, AI technologies are designed to make our lives more convenient and efficient. However, these advancements have significant risks, particularly regarding privacy and security. To protect yourself in an AI-driven world, it is essential to understand both the benefits and potential dangers these technologies present and to take proactive steps to secure your data and devices.

Throughout this chapter, we've explored how AI-powered services collect, process, and store personal data. We've also examined the various privacy concerns associated with these practices, such as unauthorized surveillance, data breaches, and behavioral profiling. By understanding these risks, you can make more informed decisions about the devices and services you use and implement strategies to safeguard your personal information. Whether configuring device settings, managing permissions, or regularly deleting stored data, small but significant actions can help mitigate the threats AI technologies pose.

We've also discussed how regulatory frameworks are evolving to address the challenges AI presents. As governments and organizations worldwide work to establish clearer guidelines and protections, staying informed about these changes is key. Whether through existing laws like GDPR or emerging regulations like the Artificial Intelligence Act, there are growing protections in place to help ensure that AI respects users' privacy. However, even with regulatory safeguards, you must stay proactive about your digital security and understand the implications of the technology you use.

Looking to the future, AI technologies will undoubtedly continue to evolve, introducing new possibilities and challenges. Our security practices must adapt as these systems become more autonomous and sophisticated. This means regularly updating software, staying informed about emerging threats, and advocating for transparency and accountability in AI development. By taking these steps, you can help ensure that AI technologies work for you, not against you, and that your personal information remains protected in an increasingly complex digital landscape.

Ultimately, the goal is to balance enjoying AI's benefits and maintaining control over your digital life. As we integrate more AI-powered devices and services into our homes, workplaces, and daily routines, the choices we make today will shape the level of security and privacy we have tomorrow. We must take ownership of our digital safety, ensuring that AI enhances our lives without compromising our privacy or security. By following the best practices and recommendations outlined in this chapter, you will be better equipped to navigate the digital world safely and confidently, no matter how AI evolves.

Chapter Questions

1   What is the primary purpose of staying informed about emerging AI technologies?
    A. To develop your own AI tools
    B. To understand the latest trends and risks in AI
    C. To profit from AI-related investments
    D. To build a career in AI development

2   Which of the following is an important action when advocating for responsible AI practices?
    A. Supporting the reduction of AI regulations
    B. Championing transparency, fairness, and accountability
    C. Encouraging AI systems to operate without human oversight
    D. Promoting the use of AI without privacy concerns

3   How can participating in discussions on AI ethics benefit society?
    A. By promoting more advertising revenue
    B. By helping shape responsible AI policies and practices
    C. By reducing AI system development costs
    D. By encouraging AI developers to avoid regulations

4   What is one of the main risks associated with AI advancements in the labor market?
    A. Decreased privacy
    B. Loss of jobs due to automation
    C. Increased access to personal data
    D. Improved efficiency in AI applications

5   How can individuals best protect their privacy when using AI-powered services?
    A. By using AI technologies without limitations
    B. By minimizing the amount of data shared with AI services
    C. By giving AI services full access to personal information
    D. By opting out of all AI technologies

6 What is an important reason to support privacy-focused AI alternatives?
  A. They offer more features than mainstream AI platforms
  B. They often have fewer data retention practices and better data policies
  C. They collect more data than mainstream services
  D. They are less expensive than traditional AI systems

7 What is the main benefit of adopting encryption and anonymization tools with AI systems?
  A. To improve AI performance
  B. To protect sensitive data by making it unreadable or anonymous
  C. To allow AI systems to share data more efficiently
  D. To allow AI systems to process data without limitations

8 Why is transparency in AI algorithms important for users?
  A. To ensure AI systems are being used for financial gain
  B. To help users understand how decisions are made by AI systems
  C. To make AI systems easier to use
  D. To reduce the need for security protocols

9 What is a crucial step in exercising your rights under data protection laws like GDPR?
  A. Ignoring privacy policies
  B. Requesting access to personal data collected by AI services
  C. Limiting the use of all AI systems
  D. Sharing personal data with AI developers

10 Why should individuals regularly review and limit data sharing with AI-powered services?
  A. To ensure better user experience with AI systems
  B. To minimize exposure to potential misuse of personal data
  C. To speed up AI system processing times
  D. To enable AI systems to function without interruption

11 What role does advocacy for AI accountability play in the future of AI?
  A. It encourages AI developers to keep their work secret
  B. It ensures that AI systems are subject to oversight and operate ethically
  C. It allows for unregulated AI deployment
  D. It promotes the abandonment of AI privacy concerns

12 What is the primary concern regarding the use of AI in decision-making in sectors like healthcare and law enforcement?
  A. Increased automation in jobs
  B. The lack of transparency in AI decision-making processes
  C. Reduced need for human intervention in AI systems
  D. The speed at which AI systems operate

13 How can AI systems improve security practices?
  A. By eliminating the need for user authentication
  B. By detecting and mitigating AI-driven cyber threats
  C. By increasing the amount of data shared across networks
  D. By avoiding encryption and anonymization methods

14 What is a significant risk posed by AI in data privacy?
   A. The ability of AI systems to quickly process data
   B. The potential for AI systems to collect more personal data than necessary
   C. The increased control over data by users
   D. The lack of AI-specific data protection laws

15 Why should individuals stay proactive about adapting their security practices to evolving AI technologies?
   A. To ensure their devices remain compatible with all AI tools
   B. To mitigate emerging threats and protect their data
   C. To guarantee that AI systems can function without interruption
   D. To simplify the user experience with AI devices

12

Securing Your Devices and Wearables

Digital security is more important than ever. The devices we rely on daily are prime targets for cyber threats, from smartphones and wearables to laptops and cloud services. The risks associated with digital devices are evolving rapidly, and securing these devices is not just about protecting personal information—it's about safeguarding our entire digital lifestyle. As a result, implementing effective security measures is crucial for anyone who uses technology, whether for personal, professional, or recreational purposes. This chapter focuses on practical, actionable steps that anyone can take to protect their devices and data from cyber threats.

The cybersecurity landscape can often seem overwhelming, especially as technology becomes more integrated into our daily lives. Mobile phones, fitness trackers, laptops, and other connected devices hold vast amounts of personal and sensitive information that cybercriminals seek to exploit. This chapter aims to break down complex security practices into simple, digestible recommendations that you can immediately implement to reduce your risk of exposure. Whether you're protecting your phone from malware, securing a wearable device, or ensuring the safe disposal of old electronics, each step plays a vital role in keeping your digital life secure.

While many cybersecurity guides focus on the technical details or the theoretical underpinnings of attacks, this chapter takes a practical approach. Each section is designed to provide clear, real-world solutions to common problems that everyday users face regarding securing their devices. The key to digital safety is understanding the threats, what actions to take, and when. This chapter will walk you through best practices for securing your mobile devices and wearables and the disposal of old devices to ensure that your digital environment remains secure from intruders.

With the rapid advancements in technology, it's easy to overlook the security of our digital devices, assuming they are inherently safe. However, neglecting to secure devices properly can leave users vulnerable to data breaches, identity theft, and financial fraud. This chapter will teach you how to fortify your defenses against these risks, focusing on key strategies like encryption, access controls, and secure device disposal. By following these best practices, you'll protect your personal information and build a solid foundation for a secure and resilient digital future.

Mobile Device Security Essentials

In today's interconnected world, mobile devices are central to almost everything we do—for work, entertainment, socializing, or shopping. Unfortunately, they also serve as prime targets for cybercriminals. Securing your smartphone or tablet is no longer a matter of just locking it with a passcode; it's about taking a layered approach to protect against the various threats in the mobile landscape. These devices hold incredible personal data, from financial details to photos, emails, and even health information. Therefore, understanding the critical importance of securing your mobile device is essential to maintaining digital safety.

Given their portability and constant connectivity, mobile devices are particularly vulnerable to various threats. One of the most common forms of attack is malware, which can be delivered through compromised apps, phishing attempts, or malicious websites. Mobile malware can steal sensitive data, track your location, or remotely control your device. Another prevalent threat is public Wi-Fi networks, which are often unsecured and can serve as gateways for attackers to intercept data sent between your device and the network. Mobile devices are also susceptible to physical theft, making it easier for criminals to access personal information directly from your device. To combat these threats, a proactive approach to mobile security is necessary—one that extends beyond just installing security software. Table 12.1 outlines mobile device security best practices, providing essential strategies to protect smartphones and tablets from threats.

Table 12.1 Mobile device security best practices.

Practice	Description	Why it's important	Actionable steps
Use strong passcodes or biometrics	Set a strong password or enable biometric authentication (fingerprint/face recognition)	Helps prevent unauthorized access to the device	Enable a 6+ digit passcode and set up fingerprint or face recognition
Keep OS and apps updated	Always update your device's operating system and apps	Software updates often contain security patches to address vulnerabilities	Check for updates regularly and enable automatic updates
Use trusted app stores	Download apps only from trusted stores	Reduces the risk of downloading malicious apps	Only download apps from official app stores and avoid sideloading
Manage app permissions	Review and control app permissions to minimize exposure of personal data	Prevents apps from accessing unnecessary or sensitive data	Go into the settings and limit app access to the camera or location
Enable remote tracking and wipe	Set up device tracking and remote wipe features	It helps locate your device if lost and wipe it remotely if stolen	Activate "Find My iPhone" or "Find My Device" on Android
Install security software	Use trusted security apps to scan for malware and vulnerabilities	Helps protect against malicious software that could compromise your data	Install a reputable antivirus or anti-malware app
Backup data regularly	Ensure that your device's data is backed up to cloud or external storage	Protects your data in case of loss or device failure	Set up automatic backups to a trusted cloud service
Be cautious of public Wi-Fi	Avoid using public Wi-Fi networks for sensitive activities	Public networks are vulnerable to man-in-the-middle attacks	Use a VPN when connecting to public Wi-Fi
Disable unnecessary features	Turn off Bluetooth or Wi-Fi	Reduces exposure to potential attacks and tracking	Turn off unused features in the device settings
Review privacy settings periodically	Regularly review privacy settings and app data-sharing preferences	Ensures that apps and services aren't accessing unnecessary data	Go into privacy settings and adjust permissions as needed

Keeping your device's operating system (OS) and apps updated is one of the most straightforward and effective ways to ensure security. Mobile device manufacturers and app developers constantly release updates to patch security vulnerabilities and improve overall performance. These updates may seem routine, but skipping them can expose your device to known threats. OS updates often include crucial fixes for security flaws that attackers could exploit, while app updates patch holes that may allow malware to infiltrate your device. In a world where cyber threats evolve rapidly, failing to update your device regularly is akin to leaving your front door open, inviting intruders in.

A key first line of defense in securing your mobile device is setting a strong passcode or using biometric authentication, such as fingerprints or facial recognition. A weak or easily guessable passcode is one of the simplest ways an attacker could access your device and its data. Consider setting a passcode longer than the typical four-digit code—ideally, something with at least six digits or an alphanumeric password. Biometrics are an excellent option as they provide a high level of security while being convenient. However, it's important to remember that biometrics aren't foolproof, and you should always have a passcode as a backup. Enabling features like remote wipe and data encryption can further protect your device in case of theft.

Always use trusted app stores like the Apple App Store or Google Play when downloading apps. These platforms have strict guidelines and security checks to prevent malicious apps from slipping through. While these stores aren't infallible, they are far safer than downloading apps from third-party sources. Sideloading, or downloading apps from unofficial sources, introduces a new level of risk. Apps from unofficial stores are often not vetted for security and may contain malware to exploit your device. Always verify the legitimacy of an app before downloading it, and avoid any app store that doesn't require a secure connection.

Managing app permissions is another crucial aspect of mobile device security. Many apps request access to personal data, such as contacts, camera, location, and microphone, even when such permissions may not be necessary for the app's functionality. It's important to review these permissions regularly and only grant access to what is necessary for the app to work. For example, a simple flashlight app shouldn't need access to your contacts or location. Restricting unnecessary app permissions can significantly reduce the surface area for potential attacks. Additionally, be aware of the privacy settings within each app, which allow you to control what information is shared and with whom.

One often overlooked security measure is enabling multi-factor authentication (MFA) on apps and accounts that support it. MFA adds a layer of protection by requiring a second form of identification beyond just your password. This could be a one-time code sent to your phone or generated by an authentication app. By requiring something you know (your password) and something you have (your phone or authentication device), MFA can greatly reduce the risk of unauthorized access to your accounts. Many apps, including email and social media platforms, support MFA, making it easy to enhance security across your mobile devices.

When you connect your mobile device to a public or unfamiliar Wi-Fi network, taking precautions to protect your data is crucial. Public Wi-Fi networks, while convenient, are often unsecured and can be a playground for cybercriminals. Attackers can set up rogue Wi-Fi hotspots or intercept traffic on an unsecured network to steal data or launch attacks. Using a virtual private network

Ask the AI

"What strong passphrases combine letters, numbers, and symbols?"
"What are the risks of using personal information, like birthdates or names, in passwords?"
"Can password length make a password more secure? How does length impact security?"

(VPN) on your mobile device encrypts your internet traffic, making it much harder for attackers to access sensitive information. A VPN adds an extra layer of encryption, which is especially important when accessing financial accounts or handling sensitive data on public networks.

Finally, regular backups of your mobile device can provide a safety net in a disaster. Whether your device is lost, stolen, or compromised, having a recent backup means you can restore your important data quickly. Android and iOS devices offer cloud-based backup services, such as iCloud and Google Drive, that automatically back up your apps, settings, and data. However, ensure your backup service is properly secured with a strong passcode and MFA to protect against unauthorized access. Regularly backing up your device ensures that your digital life remains intact and recoverable even in the worst-case scenario.

Protecting Against Mobile Malware

Mobile malware has evolved into one of the most significant cybersecurity threats today, with smartphones and tablets now serving as prime targets for cybercriminals. Understanding the various types of mobile malware is essential for defending against them. Common forms include Trojans, spyware, and ransomware, each designed to steal, track, or hold your data hostage. A Trojan typically masquerades as a legitimate app, often luring users to download it by offering useful or entertaining functionality. Once installed, it can silently steal personal data or give an attacker remote control over the device. Spyware, however, is designed to monitor and transmit sensitive information, such as login credentials, contacts, or even conversations. Ransomware can lock or encrypt your device, demanding a ransom for its release. Each type poses significant threats, but recognizing their distinct characteristics is the first step in building an effective defense.

Identifying signs of infection or compromise is critical, as many forms of mobile malware operate silently in the background. If your device starts to experience significant slowdowns, crashes frequently, or overheats, it may be a sign that malicious software is running unnoticed. Another common indicator is an unexplained increase in data usage or battery drain, as malware often uses these resources to send information to remote servers. Suspicious behavior, such as apps opening on their own or the appearance of unfamiliar apps or icons, can also be a red flag. Moreover, strange charges on your phone bill or unexpected messages from your device without your knowledge could indicate that your phone has been compromised. If you notice any of these symptoms, taking immediate action is important to isolate the problem and minimize potential damage.

Installing reputable mobile security software is one of the most effective ways to defend against mobile malware. While many mobile OSs come with built-in security features, these tools may not offer comprehensive protection against all types of malware. Security apps like those from well-known providers like McAfee, Norton, or Bitdefender can detect and block threats in real time. These apps often include malware scanning, anti-phishing protection, app permission monitoring, and even remote wiping in case of device theft. However, it's important to download these apps only from trusted app stores, as counterfeit versions may exist that promise protection but

<table>
<tr><td>

Ask the AI

"What practical ways prevent device theft in public spaces?"
"How do laptop locks and security cables work to protect against theft?"
"What features should I enable to track or remotely wipe a stolen device?"

</td></tr>
</table>

pose more risks. A good mobile security app provides an added layer of defense, especially when used with other preventive measures.

Phishing links and suspicious downloads are one of the easiest ways for malware to infiltrate your mobile device. Cybercriminals often use phishing attacks to trick users into clicking on malicious links in emails, text messages, or social media posts. These links can lead to fake websites designed to harvest your credentials or automatically download malware to your device. Even links that appear to come from trusted sources—like a bank or a popular online retailer—can be fraudulent. Similarly, downloading apps or files from unofficial sources increases the likelihood of installing malware. It's essential to be cautious with every click and avoid downloading anything from unknown or unverified sources. Always scrutinize URLs and ensure they're legitimate before entering personal information or downloading files.

Safe practices for mobile browsing and email are crucial in maintaining the security of your device. When browsing the web on your phone, it's wise to use encrypted connections (look for the "https" in the URL) and avoid entering sensitive information on unsecured sites. Public Wi-Fi networks should be avoided for online banking or shopping activities, as they can be a breeding ground for attackers looking to intercept your data. Using aVPN on your mobile device adds an extra layer of encryption, protecting your data even when connected to an unsecured network. In terms of email, be skeptical of unsolicited messages, especially those that ask for personal or financial information. If an email looks suspicious, don't open attachments or click on any links. Instead, verify the sender's authenticity directly by contacting the company or individual.

It's important to back up your data regularly to secure your mobile device further. If your device is infected with malware, you may need to reset it to its factory settings, which can erase all your data. Regular backups ensure you can restore your photos, contacts, and other critical data with minimal loss. Android and iOS devices offer cloud-based backup services that automatically sync your data to a secure location. Consider backing up your data to an external hard drive or another secure storage medium for extra peace of mind. By keeping your data backed up, you can mitigate the impact of malware attacks that might otherwise result in permanent data loss.

While mobile malware continues to become more sophisticated, you can still take many proactive steps to protect your device. One such measure is to regularly review and update your apps, as vulnerabilities in outdated apps can provide an easy entry point for malware. Enabling automatic updates ensures that your apps run the latest versions, often including security patches. Similarly, securing your device with a strong password or biometric authentication, such as a fingerprint or facial recognition, is essential. This prevents unauthorized access to your device if it is lost or stolen. Additionally, setting up two-factor authentication for your important accounts—like email and social media—adds an extra layer of protection if your credentials are compromised.

Securing Wearable Devices

Wearable devices, such as fitness trackers and smartwatches, have become ubiquitous in modern life, offering users the convenience of real-time health tracking, notifications, and on-the-go connectivity. However, as with any connected technology, wearables present unique security risks. These devices are often designed to collect sensitive data, including personal health metrics, location, and financial information, which can be valuable targets for cybercriminals. If not properly secured, wearables can become a gateway for attackers to compromise other connected devices or access personal data. The risks associated with these devices are not just theoretical—there

Table 12.2 Wearable device security checklist.

Action	Description	Why it's important	Actionable steps
Set strong device locks	Ensure wearables are secured with a strong passcode or biometric lock	Protects against unauthorized access to your wearable	Set up a secure PIN or use biometric authentication on the device
Use trusted apps only	Download apps from reputable sources	Reduces the risk of malware or data theft	Only use apps from the device's official app store
Manage permissions	Review app permissions to control which data is shared	Prevents apps from accessing unnecessary or sensitive data	Go into settings and adjust data-sharing permissions for each app
Enable encryption	Enable encryption for sensitive data like health stats and location	Protects data from being intercepted or accessed by unauthorized parties	Activate device encryption in settings to secure health-related data
Update software regularly	Ensure wearable's firmware and apps are regularly updated	Security patches often address vulnerabilities in the system	Enable automatic updates to keep apps and firmware current
Limit data syncing	Control which data is synchronized with other devices	Minimizes the risk of unauthorized access to sensitive health or personal information	Only sync necessary data with trusted devices and services
Monitor device location	Enable device tracking features to locate the wearable if lost	Helps recover the device in case it's misplaced or stolen	Turn on location tracking features in the settings
Disable unused features	Turn off Bluetooth and Wi-Fi	Reduces exposure to potential attacks or unauthorized connections	Manually disable features not in use or set up automatic disconnection
Review health data privacy settings	Review privacy settings for health-related apps or services linked to your wearable	Ensures your health data is not shared without consent	Go into privacy settings and limit what health data is shared
Consider physical protection	Use cases or bands that protect the wearable device from physical damage	Prevents accidental exposure of sensitive data or functionality	Invest in a secure case or cover to prevent physical theft or damage

have been documented incidents where attackers have exploited vulnerabilities in wearables to gain unauthorized access to networks or steal private information. Understanding these risks and taking proactive steps to secure wearable devices is crucial for safeguarding digital and physical well-being. Table 12.2 presents a wearable device security checklist, offering steps to ensure the safety and privacy of wearable technology.

The first step in securing wearable devices is properly configuring their security settings. Many wearables, such as smartwatches, come with default security settings that may not be sufficient to protect sensitive information. These devices typically allow you to set a passcode or biometric lock to prevent unauthorized access, but many users skip this step due to convenience. Without a passcode or biometric authentication, anyone who gains physical access to the device could view personal data or interact with connected apps. Additionally, some wearables offer options for enabling two-factor authentication (2FA) for enhanced security when paired with other devices or accounts. Ensuring these features are activated and appropriately configured significantly reduces the risk of unauthorized access and protects against physical theft.

Pairing wearables with other devices, such as smartphones or laptops, introduces additional security considerations. Bluetooth, the primary pairing method for many wearable devices, can be vulnerable to certain attacks if not properly secured. Attackers may exploit weaknesses in Bluetooth protocols to intercept communications between devices or pair with a wearable without the user's knowledge. To mitigate this risk, it's essential to pair wearables only when close to the device you wish to connect to and to avoid pairing with devices that you do not trust. Enabling the "pairing notification" feature—where the device prompts you to approve any incoming pairing requests—can help ensure that unauthorized devices are not inadvertently connected. Additionally, regularly reviewing and removing old or unused pairings can help maintain control over which devices can connect to your wearable.

Managing data synchronization and sharing is another critical aspect of securing wearable devices. Many wearables sync data to cloud-based services or smartphone companion apps, which can be accessed from multiple devices. While this allows for easy access and analysis, it also increases the potential attack surface for cybercriminals. If a wearable device or associated app is compromised, sensitive data—such as your physical activity, health metrics, or location history—could be exposed. To protect this data, you should configure your device's synchronization settings to limit which data is shared and with whom. For instance, consider disabling automatic syncing for sensitive information or only syncing data when connected to a secure network. Additionally, review the permissions of companion apps to ensure that they aren't accessing more data than necessary.

One of the most sensitive categories of data collected by wearable devices is health and biometric information. Fitness trackers and smartwatches can gather a wealth of personal data, from heart rate and sleep patterns to step count and blood oxygen levels. In some cases, wearables can also monitor blood pressure, glucose levels, and other critical health information. This data is highly personal and, if accessed by the wrong parties, can be used for identity theft, fraud, or even blackmail. To mitigate these risks, storing and transmitting any health-related data collected by wearables securely is essential. Many devices encrypt this data, but it's important to verify that encryption is enabled and that the service providers storing this data comply with relevant privacy regulations, such as the Health Insurance Portability and Accountability Act (HIPAA) in the United States.

Firmware and software updates are essential for keeping wearable devices secure over time. As with smartphones and laptops, wearable devices can have vulnerabilities that hackers may attempt to exploit. Manufacturers regularly release firmware and software updates to patch these vulnerabilities and improve functionality. However, if users fail to install these updates, wearables can remain exposed to known security flaws. Ensure automatic updates are enabled on your wearable device and its companion apps. If automatic updates are unavailable, set a reminder to check for updates at regular intervals manually. This simple step can significantly reduce the risk of security breaches and ensure your device benefits from the latest security improvements.

Another important consideration is the management of third-party apps on wearable devices. Many smartwatches and fitness trackers support installing third-party apps, which can expand the device's functionality but may also introduce additional security risks. Apps from unofficial or untrusted sources may contain malware or be designed to access and transmit your data without consent. When installing third-party apps, ensure they come from reputable sources, such as the official app stores associated with the wearable platform. It's also a good practice to regularly review the list of installed apps on your device and remove any that are no longer necessary or appear suspicious. Additionally, reviewing app permissions and limiting access to personal data can help safeguard sensitive information from unwanted exposure.

Implementing strong network security is critical for wearable devices that connect to networks or cloud services. Wearables often rely on Wi-Fi or cellular data to send and receive information, which can be intercepted if not adequately protected. Using secure Wi-Fi connections and ensuring that any data transmitted over cellular networks is encrypted can help protect against eavesdropping and data theft. In cases where wearables rely on Bluetooth for communication, it's essential to ensure that devices are not left in "discoverable" mode, as this can make them vulnerable to unauthorized connections. Additionally, usingVPNs when connected to public Wi-Fi networks can further enhance security by encrypting all internet traffic, making it more difficult for attackers to intercept communications.

Lastly, one often overlooked but effective measure for securing wearable devices is physically securing them. Wearables are inherently portable and can be easily lost or stolen, putting all the sensitive data they store at risk. If your wearable has a lock screen feature, ensure that it is activated with a strong passcode, and consider using biometric authentication if available. If your device is lost or stolen, having a way to remotely wipe it or lock it down can help prevent unauthorized access. Some wearables even offer tracking features, allowing you to locate a lost device. If these features are unavailable, consider attaching a device locator tag to your wearable for added peace of mind.

Physical Security and Theft Prevention

Physical security is a critical but often overlooked component of overall digital safety. No matter how secure your devices are from a cyberattack, all your precautions can be bypassed if they fall into the wrong hands physically. Laptops, smartphones, tablets, and other portable devices hold vast amounts of personal, financial, and work-related information, making them attractive targets for theft. Keeping your devices in secure locations is the first line of defense. Ideally, your devices should never be left unattended in public places, and when at home or the office, they should be locked away or stored in a secure area. Leaving a laptop on a desk unattended in a café can expose you to risks if someone sees an opportunity for theft. Devices should always be kept out of sight when not in use—whether locking them in a drawer, keeping them in a secure bag, or using a safe. Remember, even something as simple as a forgotten phone left on a table in a public setting can expose you to potential risks if stolen. Figure 12.1 depicts the mobile device security lifecycle, illustrating the stages from initial setup to regular maintenance and eventual secure disposal.

Being vigilant in public spaces is another key factor in protecting your devices from theft. Public areas—such as coffee shops, airports, or public transit—are high-risk environments, as they are often crowded, and personal belongings can easily be forgotten or taken. The first step in being vigilant is always being aware of your surroundings. Whether working on a laptop at a café or carrying a tablet on public transport, always watch your devices. If you're working in a public space, use a bag or briefcase to store your laptop when not in use, and always keep it closed when walking away. If you're sitting at a table in a café, consider sitting with your back to the wall so you can monitor who is near your devices. Simple steps like these can make a big difference in preventing theft in public spaces. Avoid leaving your devices unattended in airport lounges or hotel rooms, where opportunistic thieves could easily steal them.

One of the most useful tools for preventing the loss of a device is device tracking and remote wipe features. Many smartphones, tablets, and laptops come with built-in tracking software to help locate your device if it's lost or stolen. For instance, Apple devices feature the "Find My" app, while Android devices offer a similar service called "Find My Device." These tools use GPS and Wi-Fi to help pinpoint your device's location, and in some cases, you can even make the device emit a sound to help you locate it nearby. If the device cannot be recovered, many of these services offer remote wipe options, allowing you to erase sensitive data remotely. This is an especially important feature if

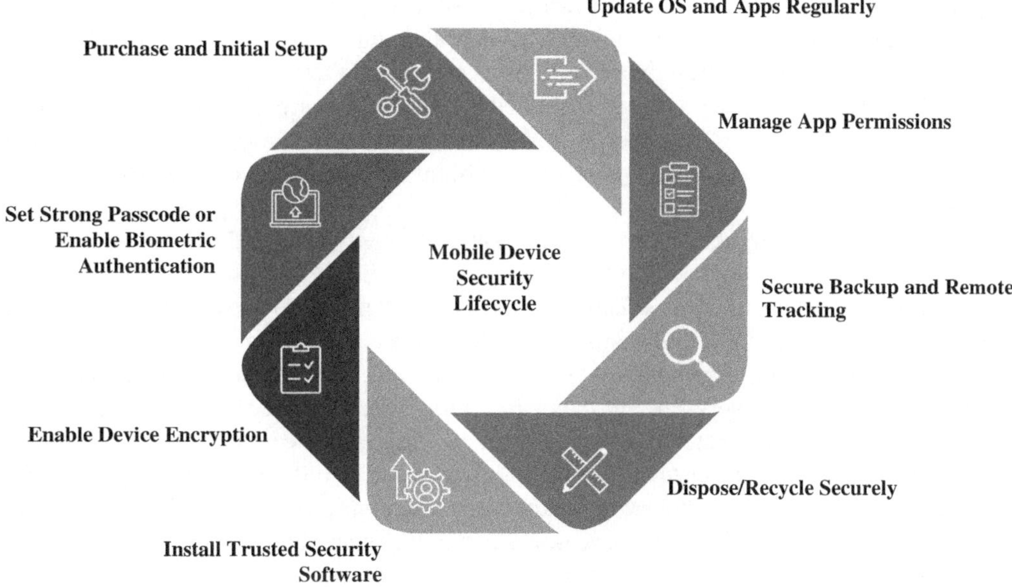

Figure 12.1 Mobile device security lifecycle.

the device contains private information or access to sensitive accounts, as it ensures that your data won't fall into the wrong hands. Enabling these tracking and remote wipe features is a critical step in protecting your devices, and it's a good idea to test them periodically to ensure they work as expected.

Physically securing laptops and tablets with locks and cables can provide additional protection, especially in environments like offices, libraries, or public spaces. Many laptop manufacturers offer physical security locks designed to tether your device to a desk or other stationary object. These locks are typically small, portable devices that loop around your lock slot and connect to a secure object, preventing your device from being easily removed. While not foolproof—since a determined thief could still attempt to cut the cable—they can act as a deterrent and significantly reduce the chances of a device being stolen. In high-risk environments, such as crowded airports or hotel business centers, a security cable can help ensure your device stays exactly where you left it. Similarly, tablet locks are available and can be used in the same way to secure your tablet to a stationary object when you need to step away briefly. Using these physical locks helps minimize opportunistic theft, adding an extra layer of defense when your devices are out of reach.

When traveling, protecting your devices requires additional precautions. Travel introduces several new risks to device security, from theft during transit to loss in unfamiliar locations. One of the most important practices when traveling is to use a secure bag, such as a backpack with lockable compartments or a briefcase with RFID-blocking technology. Avoid placing your devices in easily accessible pockets or external compartments where they might be snatched. When in transit, always keep your devices within sight and, when possible, store them in a secure place such as a locked overhead compartment or hotel safe. If traveling internationally, be aware of the specific security risks in each location, as certain countries may have higher theft rates or loss of devices. For example, pickpocketing can be a significant concern in crowded tourist destinations. In addition to physical security measures, encryption, and secure connections while traveling are essential. Whether using public Wi-Fi in an airport lounge or a café, consider using a VPN to protect your data from potential interception.

Responding promptly to a lost or stolen device is just as important as taking preventive measures. The sooner you act, the better the chance of mitigating the damage. If you realize your device has been lost or stolen, the first step is to use any device tracking features to attempt to locate it. If you cannot recover the device, immediately change the passwords for all accounts linked to the device, including email, social media, banking, and work-related accounts. Alerting your bank and credit card companies to any potential fraud or suspicious activity on your accounts is crucial at this stage.

Additionally, contact your mobile carrier or device manufacturer to report the loss, as they may be able to help lock or disable the device. If your device contains particularly sensitive information, consider contacting law enforcement, especially if you believe the device could be used for identity theft or fraud. The faster you secure your data, the less likely your personal information will be exploited.

Another essential aspect of responding to a lost or stolen device is understanding your area's legal and regulatory framework around data protection. Many regions, such as the European Union under the General Data Protection Regulation, have specific rules regarding handling personal data in cases of theft or loss. For example, under the GDPR, organizations must report data breaches involving personal data to regulatory authorities within 72 hours. While this may not always be relevant for an individual's devices, understanding your rights in case of a breach can help guide your response and ensure that you're taking the right steps to protect your data. In some cases, legal authorities may assist in recovering a stolen device, depending on the value of the data and the circumstances surrounding the theft.

Disposal and Recycling of Devices

Improper disposal of electronic devices poses a significant security risk, one that is often overlooked when upgrading or replacing older technology. Many individuals assume that simply erasing files or deleting an app is enough to protect their personal information, but this is far from the case. Devices like smartphones, laptops, and tablets store vast amounts of sensitive data that can be easily recovered if not properly wiped. Even after a factory reset or deletion of files, remnants of your data may remain embedded in the device's storage, making it vulnerable to retrieval by anyone with the right tools. This is especially concerning when devices are discarded or sold without proper sanitation, as they can end up in the hands of individuals or organizations that may exploit the data for malicious purposes, including identity theft, fraud, or corporate espionage. Proper disposal and secure data wiping are crucial to ensuring that your digital footprint does not follow you beyond the grave of your device. Table 12.3 provides device disposal and recycling guidelines, outlining best practices for responsibly discarding and recycling electronic devices.

Before disposing of any device, it is essential to wipe all stored data securely. While many people use the standard "delete" function or factory reset, these methods do not fully eliminate the data. Deleting files only marks them as "available" for overwriting, and they can often be easily recovered with specialized software. To properly wipe a device, you need to use tools that will overwrite the storage multiple times, making it nearly impossible to retrieve the original data. Both iOS and Android have built-in tools for smartphones and tablets that allow users to erase all content and settings. For computers, dedicated software like Darik's Boot and Nuke (DBAN) or similar utilities can be used to wipe hard drives securely. These tools use sophisticated algorithms to overwrite data, ensuring no trace of your sensitive information remains. For complete peace of mind, it's also advisable to disable or remove any accounts linked to the device, such as iCloud or Google accounts, before wiping the data.

Table 12.3 Device disposal and recycling guidelines.

Step	Description	Why it's important	Actionable steps
Erase all data	Ensure that all personal data is erased from the device	Prevents unauthorized access to your personal information	Use data-wiping software to overwrite data multiple times before disposal
Remove storage media	Physically remove storage components	Helps prevent the recovery of sensitive data	Take out the SIM card and SD card before disposing of the device
Factory reset device	Perform a factory reset to erase user data and settings	Restores the device to its original settings	Go into the settings and select "Factory Reset" to remove all personal data
Use certified e-waste programs	Ensure your device is recycled by a certified program	Certified programs adhere to data destruction and environmental protection standards	Find certified recycling programs like R2 or e-Stewards
Avoid uncertified recycling	Do not use uncertified recycling services	Uncertified services may not properly erase data or dispose of waste safely	Research the recycling program and check for certifications
Physically destroy devices	Consider physically destroying devices that are beyond repair	Prevents data recovery from damaged devices	Use a hammer or shredder to destroy old hard drives or storage media
Use local recycling centers	Look for local e-waste recycling centers with proper protocols	Local centers may provide more convenient and secure recycling options	Contact local facilities to confirm they are certified and follow best practices
Check for data backups	Delete cloud backups and synced data before disposal	Ensures that data is not retrievable from cloud services after device disposal	Log into your cloud storage accounts and remove synced data
Review donation requirements	Check with donation programs about their data destruction practices	Ensures your data is securely wiped before the device is reused	Verify that the donation program erases all data from the device
Dispose of batteries properly	Recycle device batteries separately at certified recycling locations	Improper disposal of batteries can harm the environment and pose safety risks	Take batteries to specialized battery recycling centers

Another key step in the secure disposal of devices is to physically remove any storage media, such as SIM cards, SD cards, or external drives, before recycling or discarding a device. These components often contain additional data, and in the case of SIM cards, they may store information like contacts, messages, or even banking details. Many individuals are unaware that simply resetting or wiping a device's internal storage may not affect these separate components. Before parting with any device, carefully remove all storage media and destroy or securely wipe them. For instance,

---

Ask the AI

"What is the most effective method to completely erase data from a device before recycling?"
"How can I find certified e-waste recycling programs in my area?"
"What are the environmental benefits of recycling electronics responsibly?"

SIM cards can be shredded, or SD cards can be reformatted using data-wiping software. Removable USB drives, which can often be overlooked, should be securely wiped or destroyed to ensure no data remains vulnerable.

Recycling electronic devices is not only a matter of security, but it also carries important environmental considerations. Electronic waste (e-waste) is one of the fastest-growing categories of global waste, and improper disposal of electronic devices can lead to severe environmental damage. Many devices contain harmful chemicals, such as lead, mercury, and cadmium, which can leach into the environment when improperly discarded. These toxins pose significant risks to both wildlife and human health. Furthermore, extracting rare metals and minerals used in electronics can contribute to environmental degradation when improperly mined or recycled. Recycling electronics responsibly helps to minimize these environmental impacts by ensuring that materials are properly processed and reused and that hazardous components are disposed of in a safe and controlled manner.

When recycling electronics, it is crucial to use certified recycling programs that adhere to industry standards for environmental and data protection. Not all recycling programs are created equal—some may send devices to countries with less stringent environmental regulations, where they may be dismantled under hazardous conditions. Others may not securely erase data before recycling, leaving your sensitive information exposed. Certified e-waste recycling programs, such as those accredited by organizations like R2 (responsible recycling) or e-Stewards, follow best practices to ensure that devices are handled in an environmentally responsible manner and that data is securely wiped or destroyed. These certifications ensure that the recycling process is transparent and that your devices are being processed in compliance with environmental laws and privacy standards. Always check for these certifications before trusting a program with your old devices.

Donating devices is another responsible alternative to disposal, but it comes with security and environmental considerations. Donating old devices, especially those with functional value, such as smartphones or laptops, can extend their lifespan and benefit others who may not have access to such technology. However, it is essential to ensure that the devices are securely wiped of any personal information before donating them. Many donation programs will accept devices in any condition, but they may not guarantee that the devices will be handled securely. Before donating, perform a complete data wipe, remove any storage media, and factory reset the device. If you donate to a charitable organization, verify that they have protocols for securely handling the devices and wiping data. In some cases, donating to a program that refurbishes devices and securely wipes all data before they are distributed to recipients may be worth donating.

Additionally, consider the potential environmental impact of donating old electronics. Recycling or donating your devices contributes to the circular economy, where materials are reused and repurposed rather than wasted. However, it's important to remember that donating electronics should not be seen as a way to dispose of non-functional or obsolete devices. Donating broken or non-operational devices may create additional waste or burdens for the recipients. Ensure that the devices you donate are still functional; if not, consider recycling them through certified programs. This ensures that you are not only protecting your data but also supporting sustainable practices.

Recommendations

1. **Strengthen Your Passwords:** Use strong passphrases that combine letters, numbers, and symbols to secure your devices and accounts. Avoid using personal information like birthdates or names, and prioritize length to increase security. A well-crafted passphrase is one of the simplest and most effective ways to deter unauthorized access.

2. **Keep Your Devices Updated:** Regularly check and install updates for your OSs and applications. Updates often include critical security patches that protect against newly discovered vulnerabilities. Enabling automatic updates is an easy way to ensure your devices remain protected without extra effort.

3. **Review and Manage App Permissions:** Regularly audit the permissions granted to apps on your devices to control what data they can access. Limit permissions to only what is necessary for the app's functionality. This proactive step minimizes the risk of exposing sensitive personal information to untrusted or unnecessary applications.

4. **Secure Your Wearables:** Configure strong security settings on your wearable devices, such as biometric locks or PIN codes. Pair them securely with trusted devices and encrypt the data they collect. By taking these precautions, you protect the health, biometric, and location data stored on these devices from being exploited.

5. **Enable Device Tracking and Remote Wipe Features:** Set up tracking tools like "Find My Device" and ensure active remote wipe capabilities. Test these features periodically to confirm they work correctly. In case of loss or theft, these tools allow you to locate your device or erase its data to prevent unauthorized access.

6. **Be Vigilant in Public Spaces:** Always monitor your devices when working in public areas such as cafes, airports, or libraries. Use laptop locks or security cables to deter opportunistic theft, and avoid leaving devices unattended. Being mindful of your surroundings is a simple yet powerful way to protect your digital assets.

7. **Dispose of Devices Responsibly:** Use certified e-waste recycling programs to ensure devices are disposed of securely and in an environmentally friendly manner. Before recycling, back up important data and wipe all personal information using trusted data-wiping tools. Responsible disposal protects both your data and the environment.

8. **Remove and Secure External Storage:** Always remove SIM cards, SD cards, or other external storage from your devices before disposal. Even if the main device is wiped, these components can still contain sensitive information. Properly destroy or securely erase these storage media to eliminate data recovery risks.

9. **Prioritize Environmental Responsibility:** Learn about the environmental risks of improper e-waste disposal, including releasing toxic chemicals like lead and mercury. Choose recycling programs that adhere to environmental regulations and support sustainable practices. By recycling responsibly, you contribute to protecting the planet and reducing waste.

10. **Educate Yourself and Others:** Stay informed about evolving cybersecurity threats and best practices for securing devices. Please share your knowledge with friends, family, or colleagues to help them protect their digital lives. A community-wide commitment to cybersecurity strengthens overall digital safety for everyone.

Conclusion

Securing our digital devices has never been more crucial as we continue integrating technology into every facet of our daily lives. The security of smartphones, wearables, laptops, and other connected devices is not just about defending against external threats; it's about safeguarding our privacy, finances, and digital identities. By following the best practices outlined in this chapter, you are taking significant steps to ensure that your devices—and the sensitive data stored within them—are protected against potential risks. Implementing these practices reduces the likelihood of a cyber attack and helps you maintain control over your digital life, reducing the chances of data breaches or other forms of exploitation.

In today's fast-paced digital environment, it's easy to underestimate the threats we face. Cybercriminals are constantly evolving their tactics, and the devices we rely on daily are among their primary targets. However, we can stay one step ahead by adopting a proactive security mindset. Whether it's by updating your mobile device's software, managing app permissions, or securely disposing of old hardware, your actions today will have a lasting impact on your security tomorrow. Staying vigilant and consistent with these practices is the key to long-term protection.

One of the most important lessons from this chapter is that digital safety is an ongoing process. It's not enough to set up security measures once and forget about them; regular maintenance, such as updating apps, changing passwords, and reviewing security settings, is necessary to avoid emerging threats. This commitment to digital hygiene and a healthy awareness of the risks involved creates a security ecosystem that continually adapts to new challenges. Remember, the goal is not just to react to threats but to build an environment where potential risks are minimized.

As you move forward, always remember that securing your devices is an investment in your privacy, security, and overall well-being. The digital world is a powerful tool, but it's up to you to ensure it remains safe. By adopting the cybersecurity practices discussed in this chapter, you are protecting your digital life and contributing to the broader effort of creating a safer, more secure online environment for everyone. Ultimately, the more we all commit to strengthening our digital defenses, the more resilient we will be in the face of future challenges.

Chapter Questions

1   What is the most effective way to secure personal data on a mobile device?
    A. Use a factory reset regularly
    B. Encrypt the device and use biometric authentication
    C. Download apps from third-party sources
    D. Disable Wi-Fi and Bluetooth permanently

2   What should you do before donating an old electronic device?
    A. Just remove the SIM card
    B. Perform a factory reset and securely wipe data
    C. Ensure the device is fully charged
    D. Back up the data and donate without wiping

3   Which method is the best for securely erasing data on a device?
    A. Deleting all files manually
    B. Reformatting the device
    C. Using data-wiping software that overwrites data
    D. Turning off the device and leaving it untouched

4   Why is it important to manage app permissions on mobile devices?
    A. To save battery life
    B. To ensure apps perform faster
    C. To control data shared and protect privacy
    D. To enable all features of the app

5 What is the primary purpose of enabling remote tracking and wipe features on a device?
   A. To back up the device regularly
   B. To locate or secure a device if lost or stolen
   C. To share the device's location with trusted friends
   D. To monitor app performance

6 What type of program should you choose for recycling old electronics?
   A. Any local recycling service
   B. A certified e-waste recycling program
   C. A donation-based electronics retailer
   D. A general-purpose landfill facility

7 What is the first step in securing wearable devices like fitness trackers?
   A. Sync the device with all available apps
   B. Set a strong PIN or biometric lock
   C. Share health data with third-party services
   D. Disable all notifications

8 What is a potential risk of improper disposal of electronic devices?
   A. Extended warranty issues
   B. Financial penalties
   C. Data recovery by unauthorized individuals
   D. Decreased resale value

9 Which of these is an essential action when pairing wearable devices with smartphones?
   A. Enable public pairing mode
   B. Accept all pairing requests
   C. Pair only with trusted devices
   D. Use a shared Wi-Fi network

10 What is the best way to protect personal data stored on SD cards or SIM cards?
   A. Leave them in the device when recycling
   B. Remove and securely wipe or destroy them
   C. Transfer them to a new device immediately
   D. Use third-party encryption software only

11 Why should you regularly update your device's operating system and apps?
   A. To enhance graphics performance
   B. To patch security vulnerabilities
   C. To save storage space
   D. To reset all settings

12 What is a common mistake when securing mobile devices in public spaces?
   A. Using a security cable for laptops
   B. Leaving devices unattended
   C. Using strong passcodes
   D. Turning off Bluetooth

13 What are certified e-waste recycling programs designed to do?
   A. Provide refurbished devices to users
   B. Ensure secure data erasure and safe disposal
   C. Resell components for profit
   D. Offer free recycling without proper handling

14 What is the purpose of encrypting wearable device data?
   A. To speed up syncing with other devices
   B. To protect sensitive data from unauthorized access
   C. To ensure compatibility with all devices
   D. To reduce battery consumption

15 Why is it important to regularly review privacy settings on devices?
   A. To enable faster performance of apps
   B. To control how data is shared and protect your privacy
   C. To ensure compatibility with cloud services
   D. To reset settings to factory defaults

13

Managing Software and App Security on All Devices

Securing digital assets has never been more critical. Individuals and organizations face constant cyber threats daily, ranging from malware and ransomware to sophisticated phishing attacks and zero-day exploits. As a result, it's crucial to establish a robust cybersecurity framework encompassing various best practices for maintaining digital safety. This chapter comprehensively explores key cybersecurity practices, focusing on the defense mechanisms to secure software systems, applications, and networks.

At the heart of cybersecurity lies the concept of proactive defense. While it's important to react when breaches occur, the real strength of any security posture is built on the ability to prevent incidents before they even happen. One of the most fundamental ways to reduce risk is by securing the software running on your systems. This includes keeping software updated with the latest patches, configuring it securely, and rigorously monitoring for vulnerabilities and unauthorized changes. We will cover various topics, from the significance of regular software updates to the techniques of hardening applications and responding to discovered vulnerabilities.

Throughout this chapter, you will learn how to implement essential cybersecurity controls such as application whitelisting and blacklisting, proper session handling, and the use of encryption. These best practices are not just theoretical concepts—they are practical, actionable strategies that can be applied to real-world situations to reduce the chances of successful cyberattacks dramatically. Furthermore, we'll look at how application control policies can limit the scope of damage caused by unauthorized software and how patch management processes can minimize the window of exposure to new vulnerabilities. By understanding the tools and techniques available, you'll be equipped to make informed decisions about securing your digital environment.

In addition to technical measures, the human element plays an essential role in ensuring the effectiveness of cybersecurity practices. Human error or social engineering attacks can compromise even the most robust defenses. As you progress through this chapter, you will see how balancing security with usability is critical to maintaining strong defenses and a user-friendly environment. Implementing strategies aligning with the latest industry standards and fostering a security-conscious culture will greatly enhance your ability to thwart cybercriminals and safeguard your digital assets.

Importance of Software Security

Outdated software is the most common and dangerous source of cybersecurity vulnerabilities. When software becomes obsolete, the creators often stop providing updates or patches, exposing it to known exploits. Hackers know that many users fail to keep their systems current, and they actively target outdated software with tools already developed to exploit those gaps. This gives attackers an advantage, as they can infiltrate systems with minimal effort if the software is not regularly updated or patched. A single outdated program, whether a web browser, operating system, or other application, can become an entry point for various cyberattacks, including malware, ransomware, and phishing schemes.

The role of software updates and patches cannot be overstated when protecting digital systems. Software developers release updates and patches to improve functionality and, more importantly, fix security vulnerabilities. These updates are often the result of continuous monitoring for potential threats and weaknesses that malicious actors could exploit. When an update or patch is released, it addresses specific flaws that could expose systems to attack. Ignoring these updates is like leaving the front door to your house wide open—anyone can walk in, and the damage could be extensive. Regularly updating ensures your software is fortified against the latest threats. Table 13.1 outlines software security update best practices, offering strategies to ensure timely and effective updates to protect against vulnerabilities.

Understanding the software development lifecycle is key to appreciating the importance of software security. Every piece of software goes through a development process that involves stages like planning, design, coding, testing, and deployment. After deployment, the software enters the maintenance phase, where developers monitor its performance, fix bugs, and release patches as necessary. Security flaws often surface during or after deployment, so patching is crucial. Each software vulnerability presents a window of opportunity for hackers, and the lifecycle process helps ensure that systems are constantly monitored and secured against new vulnerabilities as they emerge.

Table 13.1 Software security update best practices.

Best practice	Description	Tool/resource	Frequency
Automated patching	Set up automated patch management to ensure timely updates	WSUS-SCCM	Monthly
Patch testing	Test patches in a staging environment before applying them to production systems	Test environment	Each patch release
Patch prioritization	Apply patches based on the severity and criticality of the system	NIST CVSS—Virtualization tools	As needed
Vulnerability scanning	Regularly scan systems for known vulnerabilities	Qualys—Nessus	Weekly
Vendor notifications	Sign up for vendor notifications for critical patches	Vendor mailing list—CERT	As needed
Backup before patching	Always back up critical systems before applying updates	Backup software	Before every patch
Patch deployment plan	Develop a structured plan for emergency patch deployment	Patch management systems—In-house procedures	As needed
Inventory management	Maintain an updated inventory of all installed software for patch tracking	Asset management software	Quarterly
Monitor patch compliance	Monitor systems to ensure patches are applied correctly	Security information and event management	Daily
Audit and review	Regularly audit systems and review patch management effectiveness	Audit tools—Patch management reports	Quarterly

Common software exploits and attacks typically target weak spots in applications, operating systems, or hardware drivers that haven't been properly secured. Vulnerabilities such as buffer overflows, SQL injection attacks, and cross-site scripting (XSS) are common methods attackers use to gain unauthorized access to a system. Exploits can take many forms, from malware that corrupts files to more severe attacks that can destroy entire networks. The success of these attacks often hinges on the target system's failure to install security updates or patches in a timely manner. Users inadvertently open themselves up to exploitation by failing to address vulnerabilities, allowing attackers to steal sensitive information, disrupt services, or even take control of the system.

The impact of unpatched systems on overall security is far-reaching. When one piece of software is compromised, it can be an entry point for further attacks. For example, a single vulnerability in a web browser can allow a hacker to access a user's local files, monitor their activities, or steal login credentials. These exploits often lead to a cascade of failures throughout an organization's entire network, particularly in larger, interconnected systems. Unpatched software becomes a gateway for data breaches and more severe attacks, such as ransomware and denial-of-service (DoS) attacks, which can disrupt services and cause financial or reputational harm. When systems fail to update, the entire network becomes a ticking time bomb waiting to be triggered by cybercriminals.

Staying current with software updates can seem daunting, but maintaining a secure digital environment is essential. Many users struggle with updating their software regularly due to various factors, such as being unaware of the importance of updates, being busy with other tasks, or simply ignoring notifications. However, there are several strategies to make the process easier. Automated updates are one of the most effective ways to ensure software stays current without requiring constant attention. Enabling automatic updates for both operating systems and applications can eliminate the guesswork and ensure that the latest security patches are installed as soon as they become available.

Another strategy for staying current with updates is to implement a robust patch management policy, particularly in organizational environments. In larger enterprises, keeping track of updates for multiple software applications across various devices can become complex. A formal patch management strategy helps ensure that updates are consistently applied promptly, reducing the risk of exploitation. This approach includes maintaining an inventory of all software in use, scheduling regular scans for missing patches, and prioritizing installing critical security updates. Organizations can ensure they are not exposed to known vulnerabilities by establishing clear procedures for managing patches.

Educating users about the importance of software updates and security patches is another key strategy for maintaining a secure system. Many users are unaware of the risks posed by outdated software, so raising awareness about the importance of keeping systems up to date is essential. Training programs can teach employees to recognize when updates are available and why installing them is critical for system security. This can also help reduce the tendency to delay or ignore software updates, often resulting in missed patches and increased vulnerability. Users should be encouraged to view updates not as interruptions but as essential steps toward maintaining a secure digital environment.

Ask the AI

"What are the risks of running outdated software, and how do attackers exploit these vulnerabilities?"

"What tools can help automate applying software patches and updates?"

"How does the software development lifecycle address the discovery and fixing of vulnerabilities?"

Safe Installation and Use of Applications

When downloading software, the source from which you obtain it is critical. Downloading applications from official or trusted websites reduces the risk of installing malware or malicious software inadvertently. Many attackers use third-party websites or unverified platforms to distribute compromised software, often disguised as legitimate programs. These unofficial sources may offer seemingly useful tools, games, or utilities, but they are frequently the entry point for various types of malware, ranging from viruses to ransomware. Always rely on reputable app stores like Google Play, the Apple App Store, or well-known software repositories for desktop applications to stay safe. While no source is foolproof, trusted platforms tend to vet their software more rigorously, providing additional protection.

Verifying digital signatures and certificates is another essential practice when downloading or installing applications. Digital signatures are cryptographic proof that assures users that the software has not been tampered with and comes from a legitimate source. Before installing any program, it's worth checking that it is properly signed with a valid certificate from a trusted authority. This provides an additional assurance that the application hasn't been altered or corrupted in transit and that its publisher is who it claims to be. Many operating systems, particularly Windows, will alert you when a program lacks a valid signature or certificate, so take these warnings seriously. A program without a signature should raise immediate suspicion, and it is often a red flag signaling potential danger.

Reading user reviews and conducting thorough research before installing an app is an often overlooked but effective way to avoid problematic software. Many apps, especially mobile ones, have extensive user feedback that can give you a sense of their reliability and security. Negative reviews may indicate issues like frequent crashes, poor functionality, or, in the worst-case scenario, reports of malware or other security issues. Additionally, researching an app's publisher and checking its reputation across multiple platforms is crucial. An app that has not been reviewed or rated by other users should be approached cautiously, as it may be a sign that it is too new or untrustworthy. In digital safety, some due diligence can go a long way.

One of the most important aspects of app installation is understanding the permissions requested by the software. Many applications, especially mobile ones, require access to sensitive data or functions on your device, such as location services, contacts, cameras, and microphones. While some permissions may be necessary for the app to function, others may seem excessive or irrelevant to its purpose. For instance, a simple flashlight app should not require access to your contacts or location. Always review the permissions a program requests and consider whether they are reasonable. If an app asks for more than it should, or if you feel uncomfortable with the data it requests, it's often safer to avoid it altogether. Remember that permission creep is real—an app can initially ask for minimal permissions, but updates may introduce more invasive data requests over time.

Avoiding bundled software and adware is crucial for maintaining a clean and secure system. Some software installers come with "optional" add-ons that aren't disclosed until after the software

Ask the AI

"What are the best practices for verifying the legitimacy of a software download source?"
"How can I identify and manage app permissions effectively to protect my data?"
"What are some signs that a browser extension might be malicious or untrustworthy?"

has been downloaded. These add-ons can range from extra toolbars to unwanted applications and, more insidiously, adware that tracks your browsing habits. Sometimes, these bundled programs might be malicious, carrying potential security risks. Always choose the custom installation option when installing any software, allowing you to uncheck any pre-selected add-ons or bundled programs. Never rush through an installation; doing so could result in unwanted software compromising your privacy and security.

Managing browser extensions and plugins is another critical area of software management. While browser extensions and plugins can greatly enhance functionality, they can also introduce significant risks if not managed properly. Extensions can track your web activity, inject advertisements, or even open the door to malicious attacks if they're compromised. The key to safe extension management is to install only those from trusted sources and periodically review the extensions currently installed on your browser. Keeping them updated is also essential, as cybercriminals can exploit vulnerabilities in older versions. If you no longer use a specific extension, it's best to uninstall it to reduce the surface of the attack on your system. Additionally, take the time to read through the permissions each extension requests; if they seem excessive for the functionality they offer, reconsider their installation.

One often overlooked aspect of safe installation is using antivirus or antimalware software that scans downloaded files and apps. Antivirus programs are designed to detect and block known threats before they can harm your system. While no antivirus solution is perfect, using one frequently updated with the latest virus definitions can catch many types of malicious software before they are installed. It is equally important to keep the antivirus software up to date, as new threats are constantly emerging, and attackers frequently modify their methods to bypass detection. A good antivirus tool can act as an additional safety net, flagging potentially harmful apps before they can do any damage.

Another important consideration when installing applications is using sandboxing and virtualization technologies, which can provide additional protection. Sandboxing is a technique that isolates an application from the rest of the system, preventing it from affecting other parts of the device or network. This is especially useful when dealing with apps that are less well-known or come from sources that may be questionable. Virtualization technologies, such as virtual machines, can create an entirely separate environment where applications can run without exposing the host system to potential harm. These approaches are not only beneficial for security-conscious individuals but also for organizations looking to contain risks posed by unfamiliar or untrusted software.

Configuration and Hardening of Software

Customizing security settings within applications is one of the most effective ways to secure your digital environment. While many applications come with default settings that provide some level of security, these settings are often designed for convenience rather than optimal protection. Customizing settings, such as adjusting privacy preferences, disabling unnecessary features, and controlling access permissions, ensures that only the necessary functionalities are enabled, reducing the potential attack surface. For instance, disabling features like third-party cookies or blocking access to location services can limit data exposure in web browsers. By tailoring security settings to your specific needs, you minimize the risk of exposing sensitive data and ensure that applications behave more securely and controlled. Table 13.2 lists common application security features and their uses, providing a guide to the tools that enhance the safety and integrity of software applications.

Table 13.2 Common application security features and their uses.

Security feature	Purpose	Benefits	Example tool
Firewall	Monitors and controls incoming and outgoing network traffic	Blocks unauthorized access	Windows Firewall
Encryption	Encrypts sensitive data to prevent unauthorized access	Protects data integrity and confidentiality	AES
Multi-factor authentication	Requires multiple forms of verification	Prevents unauthorized access even with compromised credentials	Google Authenticator
Application sandboxing	Isolates applications to prevent security breaches	Limits the impact of vulnerabilities within apps	Sandboxie
Access control	Restricts access to systems based on user roles	Minimizes exposure to sensitive information	Active Directory
Intrusion detection system	Detects suspicious activity and alerts administrators	Identifies potential threats early	Snort
Intrusion prevention system	Monitors and actively blocks potential threats	Stops attacks before they can infiltrate the network	Cisco Firepower
Data loss prevention (DLP)	Prevents unauthorized data transfer or leakage	Protects sensitive data from accidental or malicious loss	Symantec DLP
Security auditing	Monitors and logs system activity for security violations	Provides insights for identifying and mitigating risks	Splunk
Patch management	Keeps software up-to-date with the latest security patches	Reduces the risk of exploits	WSUS

Disabling unnecessary features and services is another critical aspect of software hardening. Many applications come with features that are not essential to your use case but may still run in the background, consuming system resources and potentially opening up new attack vectors. For example, a word processing application might have an auto-update feature or integration with external cloud services that you don't use but remain active, providing opportunities for exploitation. Disabling unused ports, services, or even entire software components in a server environment can prevent attackers from exploiting vulnerabilities in these unneeded areas. It's essential to review all software and features on your system periodically and deactivate those not required for your workflow. By stripping away the excess, you reduce the potential points of entry for attackers while improving system performance and security.

Enabling security features such as firewalls and encryption is one of the most fundamental steps in securing your software environment. A firewall is a barrier between your system and external threats, blocking unauthorized access while allowing legitimate traffic. For individuals and businesses alike, enabling the operating system's built-in firewall or investing in a dedicated hardware firewall is an important first step in defense. Similarly, encryption is vital for protecting sensitive data in transit and at rest. Encrypting files, communications, and even system drives ensures that the data remains unreadable even if an attacker gains access without the correct decryption key. While these security features may require some configuration, the effort is well worth it for the additional layer of protection they provide.

Regularly reviewing and adjusting configurations is a proactive strategy that helps ensure that software continues to operate securely over time. Cyber threats constantly evolve, and as new vulnerabilities are discovered, the best practices for securing applications and systems shift.

What worked as a secure configuration yesterday may not be sufficient today, so checking and updating settings regularly is important. This includes reviewing firewall rules, adjusting encryption protocols, and ensuring that new updates or patches are applied as they become available. A configuration that was once considered secure can become a liability if it hasn't been kept up to date or if new exploits render previous settings ineffective. By adopting a continuous monitoring approach, you maintain a strong defense against emerging threats and vulnerabilities.

Utilizing templates and best practice guides is invaluable for ensuring that configurations are secure and consistent. Many software vendors and cybersecurity organizations provide detailed guidelines and configuration templates that outline recommended security settings. These templates are developed based on years of expertise and are regularly updated to reflect the latest security trends and best practices. Following these established guidelines ensures that your system is configured according to industry standards, reducing the likelihood of misconfigurations or overlooked vulnerabilities. For example, securing a web server using a recognized hardening guide can help ensure that common security holes, such as weak passwords or open ports, are closed and the server is hardened against attacks. Templates offer a streamlined way to apply security best practices, making the configuration process more efficient and reliable.

Testing configurations for effectiveness is critical in the configuration and hardening process. After adjustments to application settings, services, or security features are made, it's important to test whether the changes have successfully strengthened security without introducing new problems. Security audits, vulnerability scans, and penetration testing are methods that can be used to identify potential weaknesses in your setup. By actively testing your system and software configurations, you can ensure that vulnerabilities have been addressed and that the system is robust against common attack vectors. For example, after configuring a firewall, a port scan can verify that only the necessary ports are open and that potential attack surfaces are minimized. Testing configurations also helps to identify misconfigurations, which frequently cause security failures.

Moreover, hardening software through configuration changes is about reducing vulnerabilities and increasing overall resilience to attack. By applying the principle of least privilege, you ensure that users and applications only have access to the minimal set of resources they need to function. For instance, adjusting the user privileges for system or application accounts to prevent unauthorized access to sensitive files or administrative functions can greatly improve security. Likewise, implementing stricter authentication mechanisms—such as multi-factor authentication (MFA)—further strengthens defenses against unauthorized access. This holistic approach to configuration helps ensure that your systems remain secure, even when specific vulnerabilities are inevitably discovered.

A critical yet often overlooked aspect of configuration hardening is keeping track of configuration changes and maintaining a configuration management system. Maintaining an up-to-date record of all configuration changes is crucial for security and operational efficiency in organizations, especially large enterprises. Configuration management tools allow administrators to track which settings have been modified, identify what changes might have caused issues, and ensure that all systems comply with security policies. Regular backups of configuration files can also be invaluable in restoring

---

Ask the AI

"How do I securely configure software settings to reduce the risk of cyberattacks?"
"What are the most important features to disable in software to minimize unnecessary risks?"
"What are the benefits of encryption and firewalls in application hardening?"

systems to a secure baseline in case of a breach or failure. Tracking configuration changes also makes auditing systems easier. It provides documentation for compliance with regulatory requirements, which is especially important in industries with strict security guidelines, such as healthcare or finance.

Finally, it's important to consider that software configurations must be tailored to the specific threat landscape the user or organization faces. For instance, an individual working from home may have different security needs than an enterprise running a large-scale online service. The security measures and configurations that protect a personal laptop or smartphone may differ significantly from those required to secure a corporate network. Tailoring security configurations to the level of risk and threat exposure helps ensure that resources are not wasted on unnecessary defenses while still providing robust protection where it's most needed. Regular risk assessments should be performed to ensure that security settings align with the latest threats and that appropriate defenses are in place to mitigate those risks. Each system and software configuration should be part of a larger, ever-evolving strategy to defend against the growing and increasingly sophisticated cyber threat landscape.

Application Whitelisting and Blacklisting

Understanding the concepts of whitelisting and blacklisting is essential for any robust software security strategy. Whitelisting refers to the practice of only allowing approved applications to run on a system, while blacklisting involves blocking known malicious or untrusted applications. In a whitelisting model, only software that an organization or user has explicitly authorized is permitted to execute, providing a high level of security by minimizing the risk of running unverified or potentially harmful programs. On the other hand, blacklisting attempts to block known bad software but leaves the door open for unknown or new threats to bypass defenses. While blacklisting can be effective to some degree, whitelisting offers a far more proactive approach, as it essentially creates a "trusted" zone that only allows safe, verified programs to operate, greatly reducing the likelihood of unauthorized software running. Table 13.3 compares whitelisting versus blacklisting in application control, highlighting the strengths and weaknesses of each approach in securing software environments.

Implementing application control policies is a critical aspect of managing whitelisting and blacklisting effectively. Organizations should establish clear policies defining which software is permitted to run on their systems and which is prohibited. These policies should be aligned with the organization's security requirements, ensuring that only thoroughly vetted and approved software can be installed and executed. These controls can extend across various systems, including desktops, servers, and mobile devices, and should be enforced through both technical controls and employee awareness programs. For example, in environments with sensitive data, such as healthcare or financial institutions, the list of approved applications might be very narrow, while in less-regulated industries, the scope of acceptable software could be broader. Regardless of the specific policy, it must be consistently applied across the organization, reducing the risk of malware, ransomware, or unapproved applications gaining access to critical systems.

The benefits of restricting unauthorized software are significant, particularly when preventing malware and unauthorized data access. Allowing only approved applications to run ensures that users cannot install software that could serve as a vehicle for cyberattacks, whether ransomware, keyloggers, or spyware. By reducing the number of entry points for attackers, organizations can decrease the likelihood of security breaches by exploiting vulnerable or unpatched applications. Whitelisting also reduces the risk of accidentally installing potentially harmful software, which might happen when users download software from unofficial sources or when legitimate software

Table 13.3 Whitelisting versus blacklisting in application control.

Feature	Whitelisting	Blacklisting
Definition	Only allows approved software to run	Blocks known malicious software
Security level	Higher security; only trusted applications are permitted	Lower security; blocks known threats but allows untested applications
Management overhead	Higher; requires regular updates to the whitelist	Lower; only requires updates for known threats
Flexibility	Less flexible; only approved software can run	More flexible; allows unknown software unless it's flagged as malicious
Ease of use	More difficult for users; some legitimate software may be blocked	Easier for users; most software will run unless it's specifically blocked
Protection against zero-day attacks	Better protection; unknown software is blocked	Less protection; new threats may not be blocked until identified
Use case	Highly secure environments such as financial institutions or government agencies	General-purpose environments where ease of use is prioritized
Risk of malicious software	Lower risk as only trusted applications can run	Higher risk; relies on keeping an updated blacklist
Example tools	AppLocker	Windows Defender Application Control
System performance impact	May have a slight performance impact due to the need for continuous validation	May have minimal impact on system performance

is inadvertently bundled with unwanted programs. Restricting unauthorized software enhances overall system integrity, making it far harder for malicious actors to compromise the system.

Tools and technologies for managing application lists are varied and should be carefully chosen to match the organization's needs. Many modern endpoint protection platforms and endpoint detection and response systems include whitelisting and blacklisting capabilities, allowing administrators to control which applications can run. These tools can be configured to automatically enforce policies, making managing large numbers of devices in an enterprise environment easier. Some platforms allow for granular control, enabling organizations to approve or deny specific versions of software and apply policies to different groups of users or departments. Additionally, some tools offer features like cloud-based whitelisting, which provides real-time updates on the latest trusted applications, ensuring that whitelisted software is always current. Integrating these tools with broader security measures, such as firewalls, intrusion detection systems (IDS), and network monitoring, is important to create a layered defense that works in tandem with application control measures.

Monitoring for unauthorized installations is an essential aspect of maintaining an effective whitelisting or blacklisting strategy. Once application control policies are in place, continuous monitoring is necessary to detect any attempt to circumvent those policies. This involves regularly reviewing system logs, auditing user behavior, and tracking changes to the list of approved applications. Unauthorized installations can happen in various ways: users might unknowingly install malicious software, attackers might exploit system vulnerabilities to bypass controls, or software updates might inadvertently introduce new, unapproved versions of applications. Automated tools that flag deviations from the approved list are particularly valuable, allowing administrators to identify and respond to potential threats quickly. Regular monitoring also includes ensuring that no software on the approved list has been compromised or altered in a way that undermines security, further enhancing the effectiveness of the overall strategy.

Balancing security with usability is a key consideration when implementing whitelisting and blacklisting strategies. While whitelisting offers significant security benefits, it can also create challenges for users who need to install new software or perform tasks that require additional tools. A highly restrictive whitelist may block necessary applications, leading to frustration, decreased productivity, and potential workarounds that weaken security. It's important, therefore, to strike a balance between enforcing strong security measures and maintaining the flexibility that users need to work effectively. This might involve implementing tiered application policies, where basic users are restricted to a small set of approved software, while power users or administrators have more freedom to install additional applications as needed. Regular communication with end users is crucial to ensure they understand these policies' importance and address any concerns about software availability or functionality.

An important part of balancing security and usability is the application approval process. Organizations can implement a controlled process through which new applications can be submitted for review, ensuring they meet security standards before being added to the whitelist. This approach reduces the risk of rogue software bypassing controls and systematically incorporates legitimate new tools necessary for business operations. In some cases, this process might involve evaluating software for compliance with specific security requirements, such as the ability to encrypt data or support secure authentication methods. By creating an approval workflow that incorporates technical assessment and user feedback, organizations can ensure that they are not inadvertently hampering productivity while maintaining robust security practices.

Responding to Software Vulnerabilities

Staying informed about emerging threats is critical to any cybersecurity strategy, especially regarding software vulnerabilities. Cyber threats evolve rapidly, and new vulnerabilities are discovered regularly in the software we rely on. As attackers develop more sophisticated techniques, keeping up-to-date with the latest trends and vulnerabilities that could impact your systems is essential. This can be achieved by following trusted security researchers, participating in threat intelligence networks, and subscribing to security bulletins from vendors and organizations such as CERT (Computer Emergency Response Team) and the National Vulnerability Database. Additionally, attending industry conferences or webinars and engaging with cybersecurity communities can provide valuable insights into new attack vectors and exploit techniques. By staying informed, you can proactively identify potential vulnerabilities in your environment and take steps to mitigate risks before they are exploited. Figure 13.1 shows a graphical representation of the software vulnerability lifecycle.

Participating in vulnerability disclosure programs is another effective way to respond to software vulnerabilities. Many software vendors and cybersecurity organizations offer vulnerability disclosure programs (VDPs) that allow researchers and security professionals to report discovered vulnerabilities in a responsible and structured manner. These programs are essential for addressing vulnerabilities before they can be publicly exploited. When participating in a VDP, it's important

---

Ask the AI

"What are the key differences between application whitelisting and blacklisting, and when should each be used?"

"How do I create and maintain an effective whitelist for critical systems?"

"What tools are available for monitoring and enforcing whitelisting policies in an organization?"

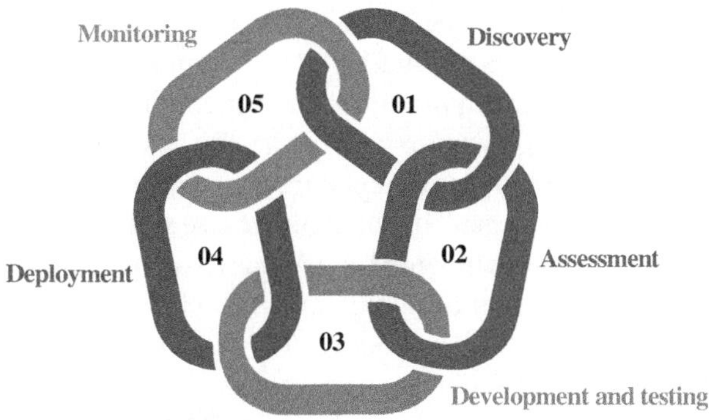

Figure 13.1 Software vulnerability lifecycle.

to follow established guidelines for disclosure, which typically include providing sufficient details about the vulnerability without publicly releasing exploit code. Engaging with these programs helps secure the software ecosystem as a whole and builds relationships with vendors, enabling faster responses to critical security issues. By contributing to these efforts, security experts play a key role in the collective defense against cyber threats and help strengthen the digital landscape.

Using intrusion detection and prevention systems (IDPS) is a proactive way to monitor and defend against the exploitation of software vulnerabilities. These systems are designed to detect abnormal behavior in network traffic or system activity that could indicate an attempted vulnerability exploit. IDS flag potential threats, providing alerts that enable security teams to investigate further, while intrusion prevention systems (IPS) take action to block or mitigate threats in real-time. In software vulnerabilities, an IDPS can help identify when an attacker is attempting to exploit a known flaw, such as an SQL injection or buffer overflow, before it causes significant damage. While IDPS systems are not a substitute for patching and proper vulnerability management, they act as a safety net that can reduce the window of opportunity for attackers to exploit unpatched vulnerabilities. Regular tuning and fine-tuning of these systems are necessary to minimize false positives and ensure the detection capabilities remain effective.

Reporting vulnerabilities to vendors is vital in the software vulnerability response process. When vulnerabilities are discovered, particularly in critical systems or software widely used across industries, it is important to report them to the relevant vendor or developer as quickly as possible. Many vendors provide specific channels or security contact information for vulnerability reporting, often as part of their security policies. By reporting vulnerabilities, security professionals help the vendor address the issue and contribute to the security community by enabling others to take protective measures. However, reporting responsibly is important—avoiding public disclosure until the vendor has had time to assess the issue and release a patch or fix. Public exposure before a fix is available can lead to increased exploitation in some cases, so adhering to responsible disclosure guidelines is critical.

Planning for emergency patch deployment is a cornerstone of an effective vulnerability management program. Patches are often the primary means of addressing vulnerabilities, and timely patch deployment is critical to minimizing the risk of exploitation. However, patches are

---

Ask the AI

"What steps should I take to report a newly discovered vulnerability to a software vendor?"
"How can I develop an emergency patch deployment plan that balances speed and safety?"
"What methods can be used to monitor systems for signs of vulnerability exploitation?"

not always straightforward, especially in complex systems where dependencies or compatibility issues may arise. As part of an emergency patching plan, it's important to establish a protocol for identifying critical vulnerabilities that require immediate attention. This might include setting up automatic patching for less critical software or creating a dedicated task force to deploy patches in a coordinated and controlled manner. Testing patches in a staging environment before deployment is essential to ensure that the update doesn't inadvertently cause system outages or disrupt business operations. By having a clear, well-documented emergency patching process, organizations can reduce the time it takes to respond to a critical vulnerability and minimize the risk of damage.

Incorporating lessons learned into future practices is vital to the vulnerability response cycle. Every vulnerability that is discovered and every incident that is managed provides an opportunity to strengthen future responses. After addressing a vulnerability, conducting a post-mortem analysis is important to understand what went well, what could have been improved, and how the response can be more efficient. This review process should involve all stakeholders, from IT staff to management, to ensure everyone understands the lessons learned. In many cases, this will result in updates to vulnerability management processes, better training for staff, or improvements in detection capabilities. For example, an incident where a vulnerability was exploited despite having an IDPS in place could reveal gaps in the system's configuration or highlight the need for more timely patching. By systematically incorporating lessons learned, organizations can continuously improve their ability to identify, respond to, and mitigate future vulnerabilities.

Additionally, leveraging threat modeling and risk assessments as part of the response process can enhance future vulnerability management. Once a vulnerability has been addressed, a thorough risk assessment can help determine how similar vulnerabilities might be prevented or mitigated. Threat modeling involves mapping out potential attack vectors and understanding how an attacker might exploit software weaknesses, allowing security teams to anticipate better and prepare for emerging threats. By incorporating these practices into the response cycle, you can enhance the overall effectiveness of your vulnerability management program. Furthermore, a proactive approach to identifying potential vulnerabilities early on—before malicious actors discover them—can significantly reduce the overall risk to the organization.

Finally, coordination with external stakeholders, including industry peers and government entities, is essential for responding to software vulnerabilities, particularly regarding widely exploited flaws. Cybersecurity is a shared responsibility, and many high-profile vulnerabilities, such as those discovered in widely used software like web servers, operating systems, or cloud services, require coordinated efforts across multiple sectors. Information sharing between organizations, especially with zero-day vulnerabilities, can help reduce the time it takes to identify and mitigate threats. Working within established frameworks, such as Information Sharing and Analysis Centers (ISACs), can help streamline communication and ensure the broader community is aware of emerging threats. In a widespread vulnerability, coordinated patching and public awareness campaigns are key to ensuring that as many organizations as possible can respond quickly and effectively.

Recommendations

1. **Regularly Update Software:** Prioritize keeping all your software up-to-date by enabling automatic updates where possible. Ensure you monitor critical systems for patch availability and apply updates promptly, especially for security patches. This reduces the risk of exploitation due to outdated software.

2. **Verify Software Sources:** Always download software from trusted sources, such as official vendor websites or reputable app stores. Avoid using third-party download sites, as they often host malicious or compromised versions of popular programs. This practice minimizes the risk of inadvertently installing malware.

3. **Leverage Digital Signatures:** Make a habit of verifying digital signatures and certificates before installing software. A valid digital signature ensures the software is authentic and has not been tampered with during distribution. This step provides an additional layer of confidence when installing critical applications.

4. **Understand App Permissions:** Carefully review the permissions requested by apps before installation, especially on mobile devices. Avoid granting unnecessary access to sensitive data or system functions, as over-permissive apps can lead to data breaches or unauthorized access. This ensures that your privacy and data security remain intact.

5. **Develop a Patch Management Plan:** Implement a structured patch management plan to handle software updates efficiently. Include a process for testing patches in a staging environment to ensure compatibility with existing systems before deployment. This approach minimizes downtime and ensures seamless security improvements.

6. **Adopt Application Whitelisting:** Use whitelisting to restrict software execution to only trusted, approved applications. Regularly review and update the whitelist to accommodate legitimate software while blocking unauthorized programs. This proactive approach significantly reduces the risk of malicious software running on your systems.

7. **Monitor System Activity:** Use IDPS to monitor your network and systems for signs of suspicious activity. Regularly review logs and alerts to identify and respond to potential threats quickly. This enhances your ability to detect and mitigate attacks before they escalate.

8. **Report Vulnerabilities Responsibly:** If you discover a software vulnerability, report it to the vendor through appropriate channels. Follow responsible disclosure guidelines to ensure the issue is addressed without exposing it to potential exploitation. This practice helps strengthen everyone's software security.

9. **Educate Your Team:** Conduct regular training sessions to educate users and employees about the importance of cybersecurity best practices. Topics like patching, recognizing phishing attempts, and securely managing software can empower everyone to contribute to a safer digital environment. Awareness and knowledge are powerful tools against cyber threats.

10. **Balance Security with Usability:** While implementing robust security measures, ensure they do not overly hinder usability or productivity. Strive for a balance that maintains security without encouraging users to bypass controls. This creates a secure yet user-friendly digital environment, fostering compliance with security policies.

Conclusion

As we've explored throughout this chapter, digital safety is an ongoing process that requires a multifaceted approach to be effective. Cybersecurity is not just about implementing a single solution or tool but creating a comprehensive defense strategy that evolves with emerging threats. Whether keeping software up to date, implementing secure application configurations, or responding swiftly to vulnerabilities, each action contributes to a broader security posture. The practices discussed here form the foundation of a resilient cybersecurity strategy that minimizes risk and maximizes the ability to detect and respond to threats before they escalate into significant issues.

Understanding and implementing these best practices will empower you to defend against cyberattacks. By taking a proactive stance—such as using application whitelisting to restrict unauthorized software or using patch management systems to keep vulnerabilities in check—you are making it significantly harder for cybercriminals to succeed. These practices protect your systems and ensure that your digital environment remains flexible and resilient, able to withstand the dynamic landscape of modern cyber threats. Recognizing, assessing, and responding to vulnerabilities in real time is key to staying ahead of attackers.

However, it's essential to remember that cybersecurity is a dynamic field that requires continuous learning and adaptation. New threats emerge regularly, and the methods used by cybercriminals evolve with technology. This chapter's security measures and strategies must be periodically reviewed and updated to remain effective. Staying informed about the latest developments in cybersecurity and participating in relevant vulnerability disclosure programs ensures that your defenses remain strong and that you're always prepared for the next threat.

Ultimately, securing your digital life is not just about deploying tools or following checklists—it's about cultivating a security mindset that permeates every decision and every action. From understanding the importance of software updates to testing the effectiveness of your security configurations, every choice you make contributes to a safer digital environment. By integrating these practices into your daily routines and ensuring they are part of your broader cybersecurity culture, you can build a defense system that reacts to attacks and actively works to prevent them. As the digital landscape evolves, your commitment to these cybersecurity best practices will be one of your greatest assets in maintaining security and peace of mind.

Chapter Questions

1 What is the primary purpose of regularly updating software?
   A. To enhance system aesthetics
   B. To fix vulnerabilities and improve security
   C. To increase software size
   D. To replace outdated user interfaces

2 What is a key benefit of downloading software from trusted sources?
   A. Faster installation
   B. Avoiding compatibility issues
   C. Reducing the risk of malware infections
   D. Increasing application performance

3 Why is it important to verify digital signatures before installing software?
   A. To improve software performance
   B. To confirm software authenticity and integrity
   C. To ensure faster downloads
   D. To allow additional features

4 What is one of the main goals of a vulnerability disclosure program?
   A. To publicize software issues
   B. To provide financial rewards to hackers

    C. To allow vendors to fix vulnerabilities before exploitation

    D. To increase software popularity

5 How does application whitelisting enhance system security?

    A. By allowing all applications to run

    B. By restricting execution to trusted, approved software

    C. By blocking all external connections

    D. By enabling faster software updates

6 What is the role of intrusion detection and prevention systems (IDPS)?

    A. To block software installations

    B. To monitor and mitigate potential threats

    C. To improve system performance

    D. To upgrade outdated software

7 Why should software patches be tested in a staging environment before deployment?

    A. To ensure patches do not disrupt business operations

    B. To speed up the patching process

    C. To check patch download speeds

    D. To monitor patch installation progress

8 What is the key difference between whitelisting and blacklisting?

    A. Whitelisting blocks all applications, while blacklisting allows all applications

    B. Whitelisting only allows trusted software, while blacklisting blocks known malicious software

    C. Whitelisting is faster to implement than blacklisting

    D. Blacklisting provides more detailed monitoring than whitelisting

9 What should be prioritized when planning for emergency patch deployment?

    A. Patching noncritical systems first

    B. Speed and accuracy of patch deployment to critical systems

    C. Avoiding patch deployment during business hours

    D. Applying only patches with user-requested features

10 Why is balancing security with usability important in cybersecurity practices?

    A. To avoid unnecessary patching

    B. To prevent users from bypassing security measures

    C. To allow unrestricted application usage

    D. To improve system performance

11 What is the main benefit of reporting vulnerabilities to vendors responsibly?

    A. It allows attackers to exploit the vulnerability

    B. It helps vendors fix the issue and strengthens security

    C. It increases software popularity among users

    D. It enhances the vulnerability's discoverability

12 Why should browser extensions be carefully managed?
- **A.** To improve browsing speed
- **D.** To prevent unneccessary memory usage
- **C.** To reduce risks of data tracking or malicious activity
- **D.** To enhance browser interface customization

13 What is the benefit of incorporating lessons learned after resolving a vulnerability?
- **A.** To permanently prevent vulnerabilities
- **B.** To improve future response efficiency
- **C.** To reduce system monitoring needs
- **D.** To eliminate patching requirements

14 How does threat modeling assist in managing vulnerabilities?
- **A.** By prioritizing critical vulnerabilities based on potential attack vectors
- **B.** By blocking all external system access
- **C.** By replacing manual patching processes
- **D.** By automating vulnerability resolution

15 What is the purpose of monitoring systems for unauthorized installations?
- **A.** To ensure faster application launches
- **B.** To detect and prevent potential threats from unapproved software
- **C.** To reduce system load
- **D.** To track legitimate application performance

14

Defending Yourself Against Ransomware and Malware

In today's digital landscape, cybersecurity is no longer a luxury but a necessity. As we continue integrating more technology into every aspect of our personal and professional lives, the threats to our digital security become increasingly sophisticated and pervasive. Malicious software, commonly called malware, is one of the most common and damaging threats individuals and organizations face. Identifying, preventing, and responding to malware attacks is critical for anyone looking to safeguard their digital assets and ensure their online safety.

This chapter provides a comprehensive guide to understanding the risks of malware and ransomware, along with actionable steps to mitigate these threats. From the moment a system is compromised to the steps necessary for recovery, this chapter equips you with the tools and knowledge to protect your data. Breaking down complex security concepts into actionable recommendations aims to provide a clear path for securing your digital life. Whether you are an individual looking to safeguard your personal information or a business leader responsible for your organization's cybersecurity, the strategies outlined here will help you build a robust defense against cyber threats.

The rise of ransomware, in particular, has highlighted the importance of detecting and preventing malware infections. These attacks can paralyze systems, encrypt vital data, and demand ransom for its return, causing immense disruption and financial loss. As the cybersecurity landscape continues to evolve, it's important to stay ahead of emerging threats and adopt a proactive approach to defense. This chapter will dive deep into the nature of malware, outline the most effective preventive measures, and provide clear guidance on how to respond if an attack occurs.

Throughout this guide, we will explore the tools and techniques you can use to keep your systems safe, from basic precautions like regular software updates to more advanced strategies such as creating secure backups. The section on recognizing signs of infection will help you identify potential malware early, minimizing its impact and preventing further spread. In addition, the focus on ransomware will provide you with a solid understanding of how to defend against and recover from these disruptive attacks. By the end of this chapter, you will be better equipped to recognize, prevent, and respond to a range of malware threats, helping you secure your digital life for years to come (Figure 14.1).

Understanding Malware and Ransomware

Malware, short for malicious software, refers to any program or code designed to disrupt, damage, or gain unauthorized access to computer systems. The term encompasses various types of harmful software, including viruses, worms, and trojans. Each type of malware has unique characteristics but shares the common goal of causing harm. A virus, for example, attaches itself to legitimate files

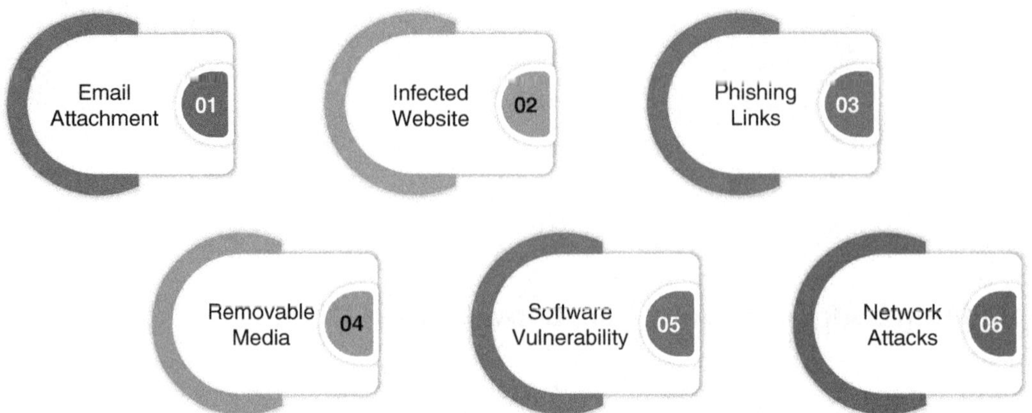

Figure 14.1 Common malware infection vectors.

or programs and spreads through infected systems. Unlike a virus, a worm doesn't need a host file to propagate; it spreads autonomously across networks, exploiting vulnerabilities. A trojan, named after the famous Greek myth, disguises itself as a legitimate program, tricking users into installing it, at this point, it can execute harmful actions on the system. Understanding these distinctions is crucial for identifying potential threats and applying the correct preventive measures (Table 14.1).

Ransomware, a particularly insidious form of malware, encrypts the victim's files or an entire system, rendering the data inaccessible without a decryption key. The attacker then demands payment—usually in cryptocurrency—to provide the key needed to restore access. Encryption is often sophisticated, making it nearly impossible for the victim to regain control without the attacker's assistance. This attack typically begins with a phishing email or a malicious download, which then silently executes the ransomware. Once activated, ransomware can spread across a network, locking down multiple systems and causing widespread damage. The demand for payment often comes with a deadline, after which the decryption key may no longer be available, forcing victims to make a tough decision—pay the ransom or lose their data permanently.

The methods through which malware spreads have evolved significantly over the years. Initially, malware would spread via infected floppy disks or email attachments, but with the advent of more sophisticated networks and systems, distribution methods have grown increasingly complex. Today, malware can be delivered via phishing emails, malicious ads, compromised websites, or even through software vulnerabilities that have not been updated. Exploiting software bugs is one of the most common ways malware enters a system, especially when critical patches are not applied promptly. With the rise of connected devices, even Internet of Things (IoT) devices are at risk, often acting as gateways for malware to infiltrate larger networks. This ability to propagate through various channels makes malware increasingly difficult to contain once it has infected a single device.

Ransomware, in particular, has surged in recent years, becoming a major threat to individuals and organizations. Several factors contribute to its rise, including the increasing use of cryptocurrencies like Bitcoin, which provides anonymity for attackers. The ease of launching ransomware attacks—often through simple phishing schemes or exploiting known vulnerabilities—has also made it an attractive option for cybercriminals. High-profile cases, including attacks on hospitals, municipalities, and large corporations, have illustrated how devastating ransomware can be. For example, the 2017 WannaCry attack spread rapidly across the globe, crippling organizations from the UK's National Health Service to large manufacturers. The high success rate and

Table 14.1 Common types of malware and their characteristics.

Malware type	Description	Method of spread	Common impact	Example
Virus	A malicious program that attaches itself to a legitimate file or program and spreads when the host file is executed	Email attachments, infected software downloads, USB drives	Can delete files, steal information, and corrupt programs	ILOVEYOU virus (2000)
Worm	A self-replicating program that spreads across networks without needing to attach to other files or programs	Network vulnerabilities, unprotected file shares	Can slow down network speeds, consume bandwidth, and cause system crashes	Conficker worm (2008)
Trojans	Malware disguised as legitimate software, used to gain unauthorized access to a system	Email attachments, malicious downloads, social engineering	Allows remote access, theft of information, and installation of additional malware	Zeus Trojan (2007)
Ransomware	Malware that encrypts a user's files and demands payment for their decryption	Phishing emails, malicious websites, infected file downloads	Locks files, demands ransom, and data destruction if payment isn't made	WannaCry (2017)
Spyware	Software that secretly monitors and collects user data without consent	Bundled with free software, malicious ads, and pop-ups	Tracks browsing habits, and steals sensitive information	CoolWebSearch (2004)
Adware	Software that displays unwanted ads to generate revenue for the attacker	Bundled with free software or shareware	Slows system performance, distracts with pop-up ads, and collects data	Gator (1999)
Keylogger	A type of malware that records keystrokes to steal passwords or other sensitive data	Email attachments, infected websites, malicious downloads	Steals usernames, passwords, and credit card information	FinSpy (2011)
Rootkit	Malware designed to conceal its presence or the presence of other malicious programs	Exploits system vulnerabilities, infected software	Provides backdoor access, and hides malicious processes	Stuxnet (2010)
Botnet	A network of compromised devices controlled remotely by cybercriminals	Infected websites, email attachments, trojan downloads	Uses devices to send spam, launch DDoS attacks, and steal information	Mirai (2016)
Scareware	Software that tricks users into thinking their system is infected and prompts them to buy fake antivirus software	Fake pop-up ads, infected websites, phishing emails	Scares users into paying for fake or unnecessary services	System Tool (2009)

potential for financial gain have made ransomware a preferred tool for cybercriminals, significantly increasing these types of attacks.

The impact of malware, particularly ransomware, on individuals and organizations can be profound. For individuals, a ransomware attack can permanently lose valuable data, such as personal photos, documents, and financial records. Many victims are forced to pay the ransom to regain access to their files, though this often only encourages further criminal activity. For organizations, the effects can be even more severe. Cyberattacks can lead to costly downtime, loss of business continuity, damaged reputations, and the theft of sensitive data. Furthermore, data breaches' legal and regulatory ramifications, particularly regarding compliance with privacy laws, can result in hefty fines. A successful attack's financial and operational toll can set back a business for months or even years, making prevention and preparedness essential.

Notable malware and ransomware incidents have shaped how cybersecurity experts approach digital safety today. In addition to the aforementioned WannaCry attack, the 2013 Target breach and the 2014 Sony Pictures hack stand as stark reminders of the damage that malware can cause. The 2017 NotPetya attack, which initially targeted Ukrainian businesses but quickly spread globally, was another example of how quickly malware can escalate into a global crisis. The attack caused billions in damages and was eventually attributed to state-sponsored actors. These incidents demonstrate the vulnerability of even the most secure systems and the need for constant vigilance in cybersecurity practices. As the tactics of cybercriminals evolve, so too must the strategies employed to defend against them.

One of the critical lessons learned from high-profile malware and ransomware incidents is the importance of timely updates and patches. Many attacks exploit known vulnerabilities in widely used software, so software vendors regularly release patches to address these security gaps. Organizations and individuals often fail to apply these updates promptly, exposing themselves to attack. This can happen for various reasons, from lack of awareness to insufficient IT resources. However, staying current with software updates is one of the simplest yet most effective ways to reduce the risk of malware infection.

The role of cybersecurity education cannot be overstated when preventing malware and ransomware attacks. Many infections begin with a simple mistake—such as clicking on a malicious link in an email or downloading an infected file. Raising awareness about the types of phishing attacks, how to recognize suspicious activity, and the importance of strong passwords can go a long way in preventing initial infections. Organizations' employees must undergo regular training to ensure they are aware of the evolving tactics cybercriminals use. For individuals, cultivating a mindset of digital vigilance is just as important as having the right technical defenses in place. Simple practices like avoiding unknown email attachments or double-checking URLs before clicking can significantly reduce the risk of falling victim to malware and ransomware attacks.

Preventing Malware Infections

One of the most effective ways to defend against malware infections is through antivirus and anti-malware software. These tools are designed to detect, block, and remove malicious programs that attempt to infiltrate a system. Modern antivirus software has advanced heuristics and real-time

---

Ask the AI

"What are the key differences between viruses, worms, and trojans in their behavior and impact?"
"How does ransomware encryption work, and why is it so difficult to reverse without a decryption key?"
"What are some of the most high-profile malware and ransomware incidents, and what can we learn from them?"

protection capabilities, scanning files, email attachments, and websites for suspicious behavior. While no security solution is infallible, using reputable antivirus software is an essential first line of defense. Regularly updating these tools ensures they can recognize the latest malware strains, as cybercriminals constantly develop new methods to bypass security measures. It's important to remember that malware can bypass outdated or misconfigured software, making timely updates critical to maintaining effective protection (Table 14.2).

Equally important is keeping all systems and applications up to date. This includes the operating system and browsers, plugins, and other software that might be running on your devices. Many malware infections occur due to vulnerabilities found in outdated software, which cybercriminals exploit to access systems. Software vendors regularly release patches and updates to address these vulnerabilities; neglecting them can expose your devices to attack. Configuring systems to install

Table 14.2 Best practices for preventing ransomware.

Best practice	Description	Benefits	Action steps
Use strong passwords	Ensure that the passwords are complex and unique for each service	Prevents unauthorized access and reduces the risk of brute force attacks	Use a password manager, and enable multi-factor authentication
Update software regularly	Keep all software and systems updated to close vulnerabilities	Prevents exploitation of known security flaws by ransomware and other malware	Set automatic updates for operating systems and software, and regularly check for patches
Implement endpoint protection	Use antivirus and anti-malware software on all devices	Stops known ransomware variants and malware before they can execute	Install reputable security software, ensure it's up to date, and run regular scans
Limit user privileges	Grant only the necessary permissions to each user on a system	Limits the potential damage ransomware can do if an account is compromised	Configure user roles carefully, and use the principle of least privilege
Back up critical data	Regularly back up important data to an offline or cloud location	Prevents data loss and allows recovery without paying ransom	Follow the 3-2-1 backup rule (3 copies, 2 different media, 1 offsite)
Train employees on security best practices	Educate staff on recognizing phishing emails, safe browsing, and malware risks	Reduces the chances of falling for ransomware delivery methods like phishing	Conduct regular cybersecurity training and awareness programs
Disable macros and scripting in documents	Macros and scripts are often used by ransomware to spread through documents	Prevents malware from executing automatically in documents	Disable macros in Office apps and disable scripting in document viewers
Use email filtering tools	Block malicious attachments and phishing emails at the email gateway	Stops ransomware from reaching users via email	Set up email filters to block attachments from unknown sources and suspicious links
Restrict remote desktop access	Limit or disable remote desktop protocol (RDP) if not needed.	Prevents ransomware from exploiting open RDP ports	Use VPNs for secure remote access, disable unused RDP services, and enforce strong RDP passwords
Segment networks and devices	Use network segmentation to limit access to critical data and systems	Reduces the spread of ransomware within a network, limiting damage	Configure network segments to isolate sensitive systems from general use devices

updates automatically ensures you are always protected against known threats. While restarting your device for an update might seem like a hassle, it's a small price to pay for the peace of mind that your security is current.

Safe browsing habits are another crucial component in preventing malware infections. Many types of malware are distributed through compromised websites or malicious ads, commonly known as "malvertising." Cybercriminals use these sites to distribute viruses, trojans, and ransomware by exploiting browser vulnerabilities or tricking users into downloading harmful files. To mitigate this risk, you must be cautious about where you browse. Always ensure that websites you visit are legitimate and avoid clicking on suspicious pop-ups, ads, or links. Installing browser security extensions that block known malicious sites or checking for HTTPS URL encryption can also help keep harmful content at bay. However, even with these precautions, the safest strategy is to avoid unfamiliar or untrusted websites whenever possible.

Disabling macros and scripting in documents is another vital step in protecting your system from malware. Macros, often used in applications like Microsoft Office, are powerful tools that allow users to automate repetitive tasks. Unfortunately, cybercriminals can also exploit them to execute malicious code when a document is opened. Malware-laden documents often rely on macros to run automatically when opened, infecting the system without the user's knowledge. For this reason, it's a good idea to disable macros by default and only enable them when you are certain the document is from a trusted source. Additionally, scripting languages like JavaScript or VBScript, often embedded in HTML emails or online ads, can be exploited similarly. Disabling or restricting these scripts further reduces the avenues through which malware can enter your system.

Caution with email attachments and downloads is another key element in preventing malware infections. Email remains one of the most popular methods for distributing malware, particularly through phishing schemes and malicious attachments. These attachments may come from legitimate sources, such as colleagues, financial institutions, or well-known brands. However, they often contain malware in the form of executable files or disguised document files. To avoid falling victim to such attacks, verifying the sender before opening any attachments is important, especially if they seem unexpected or out of place. If in doubt, always contact the sender through an alternative communication channel. Furthermore, avoid downloading software or files from untrusted websites, which often harbor malicious content. Relying on official download sources, such as the vendor's website or verified app stores, can reduce the risk of installing malware.

Another critical step in defending against malware is regularly backing up important data. Cybercriminals often deploy ransomware to encrypt victims' files, leaving them with no way to recover the data unless a ransom is paid. A robust backup strategy ensures that, even if your files are compromised, you can restore them from a secure, uninfected backup. This practice is essential not only for ransomware defense but also for general data protection. Backups should be stored in a separate location, offline or in a cloud environment, to prevent them from being affected by malware that might target local devices. It's also important to periodically test the restoration process to ensure backups are intact and accessible. By making backups a regular part of your routine, you can significantly reduce the impact of potential malware attacks.

Ask the AI

"What are the best practices for configuring antivirus software to maximize protection?"
"How can I ensure safe browsing habits to avoid malicious websites and downloads?"
"What are the risks of enabling macros and scripting in documents, and how can they be mitigated?"

In addition to these preventive measures, practicing vigilance when using removable media, such as USB drives, is essential for preventing malware infections. Malicious software can easily spread through infected USB drives, particularly when auto-run features are enabled on a system. Always scan external media for malware to mitigate this risk before opening or transferring files. If you regularly use USB drives across multiple systems, consider using encryption and password protection to safeguard the data. Similarly, when using shared devices, avoid transferring files or inserting unknown drives, as they may be a vector for malware. Taking these precautions can minimize the chances of inadvertently infecting your systems through seemingly harmless devices.

The importance of user education in the fight against malware cannot be overstated. No matter how advanced your antivirus software or security protocols, human error remains one of the most significant vulnerabilities in cybersecurity. Employees, family members, or even yourself can be tricked by social engineering tactics, which exploit trust and curiosity. Regular cybersecurity training, which focuses on identifying phishing emails, suspicious attachments, and safe browsing practices, can empower users to make smarter decisions. Encouraging a cybersecurity awareness and continuous learning culture helps ensure that everyone in your digital ecosystem is prepared to spot and avoid threats. Human vigilance is often the final line of defense against malware, as even the best technology cannot fully replace the needs of a discerning user.

Recognizing Signs of Infection

Unusual system behavior or performance issues are often the first red flags that something may be amiss on your device. Malware, particularly when actively running in the background, can consume substantial system resources, leading to noticeable slowdowns. If your device suddenly becomes sluggish, crashes more frequently, or experiences significant delays in opening programs, these could be signs of an infection. While some performance issues may arise from unrelated causes, such as a full hard drive or a software bug, persistent problems not resolved with a simple restart could indicate a deeper issue. Similarly, if your system starts to overheat or make unusual noises, it might be working overtime to process malicious tasks. Being vigilant to these subtle but telling signs can help catch malware early, reducing the potential damage (Table 14.3).

Unexpected pop-ups or messages, particularly those that appear without any clear cause, are another common symptom of a malware infection. Malicious software often injects pop-up advertisements or warning messages to mislead users into clicking on a malicious link or downloading further malware. These pop-ups may claim that your system is infected or at risk, prompting you to download an "antivirus" program or visit a website that appears legitimate but is designed to trick you. Such messages may even mimic system alerts or antivirus software notifications to gain your trust. If you encounter frequent pop-ups that seem out of place, especially those urging you to take immediate action, it's critical to exercise caution. Malware creators rely on a sense of urgency to lure victims into making hasty decisions, so being skeptical of unsolicited pop-ups is a good defense.

Unauthorized access or file changes can also strongly indicate malware activity. Ransomware, for example, encrypts files without the user's consent, rendering them unreadable until a ransom is paid. Similarly, trojans or spyware can monitor your actions, steal sensitive data, and even alter or delete files. You might notice that your documents, photos, or other important files have been mysteriously moved, modified, or locked, with unfamiliar extensions or passwords required to access them. Sometimes, you might discover new files on your system that you didn't create or authorize or see strange modifications to your settings or configurations. Any unexpected changes

Table 14.3 Indicators of a malware infection.

Symptom	Description	Possible malware type	Immediate action
System slowness	Significant decrease in system performance or lag during tasks	Virus, Trojan, Spyware	Run full system scans with antivirus tools
Unusual pop-ups	Unexpected pop-up windows or ads appear while browsing or idle	Adware, Ransomware	Use an ad blocker, run malware scan
Unexpected file changes	Files being modified or moved without user consent	Ransomware, Rootkit, Trojan	Check for file corruption, and restore from backups
Security software alerts	Frequent alerts from security software about suspicious activity or infections	Any type of malware	Follow alerts, and isolate infected systems from the network
Unexplained network activity	Increased or unexplained network traffic when idle or not in use	Botnet, Trojan	Monitor network activity, and disconnect the device from the network
Unfamiliar programs running	Programs or processes running that you don't recognize	Trojan, Rootkit, Virus	Check the task manager, and research unfamiliar processes
Locked files or folders	Files or folders that are inaccessible or encrypted by ransomware	Ransomware	Attempt to restore files from backup, use decryption tools
System crashes or freezes	Frequent crashes or freezing during normal operations	Virus, Trojan, Worm	Reboot into safe mode, and run diagnostics and malware scans
Unusual email behavior	Sending or receiving strange emails or attachments without consent	Spyware, Trojan, Botnet	Verify email settings, and run anti-spam and anti-malware scans
Unexplained browser changes	Default homepage or search engine has changed without user input	Spyware, Adware	Reset browser settings, clear cache and cookies, and scan for malware

to your files or system settings should be treated with suspicion, and a thorough malware scan should follow to rule out infection.

Alerts from security software are one of the most direct signs that your system may be infected. Antivirus programs, firewalls, and other security tools are specifically designed to detect and block malicious activity, and when they issue an alert, it's often because something suspicious has been identified. These alerts might indicate the presence of malware, a failed attempt to access sensitive data, or a breach in your system's defenses. While these alerts are generally trustworthy, it's important not to dismiss them out of hand, even if they seem to be a false alarm. Malware can often disguise itself as harmless files or processes, and sophisticated threats like rootkits can hide from detection by security tools. Always take security software alerts seriously, and if they occur frequently or are accompanied by other signs of infection, take immediate action to investigate and remove the threat.

Network activity when idle is another subtle but important symptom of a malware infection. If your device is connected to the internet and you notice increased network traffic despite not actively using the system, this could be a sign that malicious software is communicating with external servers or distributing stolen data. Some types of malware, such as botnets or spyware, work by silently siphoning off data or participating in distributed denial-of-service (DDoS) attacks without the user's knowledge. This background activity can result in slower internet speeds or unusual data usage, which may go unnoticed unless you are specifically monitoring your network traffic. Tools like network monitors or firewalls can help detect unusual outbound connections, alerting you to potential malware infections attempting to connect to command-and-control servers or exfiltrate data.

New or unfamiliar programs running on your system should raise immediate concerns. Malware often disguises itself by masquerading as a legitimate program, making it difficult for the average user to identify. You might notice unfamiliar processes running in the background, taking up memory and system resources without any clear purpose. These programs may be named similarly to legitimate processes or use random characters to appear inconspicuous. In some cases, malware may even hide its presence by running under the guise of a legitimate program, such as a web browser or system utility. To identify these hidden threats, it's important to regularly review the list of running programs and processes on your system. Tools like Task Manager (Windows) or Activity Monitor (macOS) can help you spot suspicious activity and terminate processes not associated with legitimate software.

Beyond the immediate signs of infection, malware can also impact the integrity of your online activities. For instance, if you notice that your web browser's homepage or search engine has been changed without your consent or redirected to unfamiliar sites, you might be dealing with a browser hijacker. These types of malware often manipulate web settings to promote certain websites or increase ad revenue for the attackers. The changes may initially be subtle, such as slight alterations to your search results or additional pop-up ads. However, over time, these infections can compromise your ability to browse safely and may expose you to additional security threats. Monitoring your browser's settings regularly and being cautious about the extensions and add-ons you install can help prevent these infections.

Sometimes, malware may not be immediately obvious or show overt signs of infection. It may take time before its full effects become visible, and the initial symptoms may be deceptively mild. This is why maintaining a healthy level of skepticism and awareness is essential. If your system exhibits multiple signs of infection, such as slow performance, unexpected changes, and strange network activity, it's best to act quickly. Disconnecting from the internet, running a full system scan with antivirus or anti-malware software, and seeking expert help are prudent steps to take. Remember that the longer you allow malware to remain on your system, the greater the risk of further damage, including data theft, encryption, or system instability.

Responding to a Malware Attack

When you suspect your device has been infected with malware, the first and most critical step is isolating the infected device from any connected network. This includes both local area network (LAN) and wireless networks. By disconnecting from the internet, you prevent the malware from spreading further to other devices and halt any potential data exfiltration. This disconnection can limit the damage if the malware is actively communicating with external servers or attempting

---

Ask the AI

"What tools can I use to monitor unusual system behavior and detect malware early?"
"How do I interpret security software alerts to understand the threat my system faces?"
"What are advanced signs of a malware infection that might not be immediately noticeable?"

to transmit stolen data. For those working in corporate environments, isolating the device from shared networks and systems is especially important, as infections can quickly propagate through connected machines. Turning off Wi-Fi, disconnecting Ethernet cables, and disabling Bluetooth connections can provide a much-needed break for the compromised device.

Once the device is isolated, the next step is to run a full system scan using your security tools. Most antivirus and anti-malware software can detect known threats and may even offer specialized options to scan for rootkits or other stealthy malware types. Running a full scan ensures that all files, processes, and system areas are checked for malicious code, even those that may be dormant or hidden. Depending on the size of your system, this scan may take a while, but it's a crucial step in identifying and removing the infection. If the malware is detected, the security software will typically offer options for quarantine or removal, ensuring the threat is contained before further damage occurs. While no tool is 100% effective, most modern security programs provide significant protection against known malware variants, making this step a vital part of your response.

Along with running system scans, following the guidance provided by your security software alerts is another important part of responding to a malware attack. Modern security solutions often have real-time protection, which can notify you when suspicious activity is detected. These alerts may include specific details about the malware, such as its type, origin, and any potential actions it has taken on your system. It's important to take these alerts seriously and act upon them promptly. If the software recommends quarantining infected files or removing certain processes, don't hesitate to follow those instructions. Additionally, many security programs provide detailed logs or reports that can be useful in understanding the nature of the attack and determining whether any sensitive data has been compromised. Keeping a record of these alerts can also be valuable for future investigations or reporting the incident to relevant authorities.

In some cases, despite the best efforts of security software, malware infection may be too advanced or persistent to be fully removed using automated tools. In such cases, restoring data from backups may be necessary. Regularly backing up your important data is an essential practice for these scenarios. If your system has been compromised, the safest way to recover is by restoring from a clean, unaffected backup created before the infection. This ensures that the malware doesn't re-infect your device during restoration. However, before restoring from backups, it's important to ensure that the backup itself is free from any malware—otherwise, you may inadvertently reintroduce the infection. For this reason, using trusted backup services and performing regular scans of your backup files is crucial, particularly if you've been using them to store sensitive or critical data.

If you've gone through these steps and the malware persists, seeking professional assistance may be your next best option. While experienced users with the right tools can handle many infections, some forms of malware—such as rootkits or highly persistent ransomware—require advanced technical expertise to eradicate. Security professionals, particularly those with experience in malware analysis, can help identify and remove even the most stubborn infections. These experts also have access to specialized tools that detect hidden threats and vulnerabilities that may not be visible to consumer-grade antivirus software. If you cannot remove the malware on your own or are unsure about the full extent of the infection, enlisting professional help can save time, reduce risk, and ensure that the threat is completely eliminated.

Ask the AI

"What are the best steps for isolating a device during a malware attack to prevent further spread?"
"How do decryption tools work, and where can I find reputable ones for ransomware recovery?"
"What are the key considerations when consulting a professional for malware removal?"

Reporting the incident to the appropriate authorities is a crucial, though often overlooked, step in responding to a malware attack. Depending on the nature of the attack, you may need to report it to your local law enforcement, national cybersecurity agencies, or even industry-specific regulators. In many cases, such as with data breaches or large-scale ransomware attacks, authorities can help track the perpetrators or investigate the incident further. Additionally, reporting malware incidents contributes to the larger effort of monitoring and analyzing cyber threats, helping to develop strategies to protect others from similar attacks. For businesses, especially those that handle sensitive customer data, reporting incidents to regulatory bodies such as the General Data Protection Regulation (GDPR) supervisory authority or other privacy commissions is a legal requirement. Transparency is critical for compliance and the broader cybersecurity community, as it enables a more rapid response to emerging threats.

In addition to external reporting, evaluating the security implications of the attack on your broader network and systems is important. This is particularly relevant in organizational settings where malware may have been used as a stepping stone to access more critical systems or confidential information. In such cases, conducting a full internal audit is advisable to assess the damage and identify any gaps in your security posture. This might include reviewing user permissions, examining network traffic logs, and identifying any potential insider threats that may have contributed to the breach. A comprehensive post-incident review helps recover from the immediate attack and provides valuable lessons for improving future defenses.

Following these steps is a way of cleaning up after an attack and fortifying your defenses against future threats. A well-documented incident response plan is critical before an attack occurs. This includes ensuring that all team members are trained in recognizing signs of malware, isolating affected devices, and executing response protocols coordinately. Testing and refining this plan periodically can help identify any weaknesses in your approach. Furthermore, ensuring that critical data is regularly backed up, security tools are updated, and ongoing user training helps reduce the likelihood of an attack and ensures that recovery from one is faster and more efficient.

Mitigating the Impact of Ransomware

Understanding the debate on paying ransoms is essential when confronted with a ransomware attack. The question of whether to pay the ransom is one that many victims face, and it is a topic fraught with ethical, legal, and practical considerations. From a purely financial perspective, paying the ransom may seem like the quickest way to regain access to encrypted files, especially when the encrypted data is crucial to business operations or personal matters. However, paying the ransom does not guarantee that the attacker will follow through on their promise to decrypt the files, nor does it prevent them from attacking again. Additionally, paying ransoms contributes to the funding of cybercrime, making it a morally questionable choice that encourages the continuation of these criminal activities. Law enforcement agencies, including the FBI, strongly advise against paying ransoms as it fuels the attacker's operations and emboldens other criminals to launch similar attacks. Ultimately, the decision to pay is personal or organizational, but it should always be weighed against the potential for recovery without giving in to cybercriminals' demands.

Steps to take immediately after a ransomware attack are critical in minimizing damage and preventing further infection. The first and most important action is to isolate the infected device from any network to prevent the malware from spreading to other systems. Disconnecting the affected system from the internet and any local area networks (LANs) halts communication with the attacker's command-and-control servers, which may prevent the encryption process from continuing or stop transmitting sensitive data. If the attack is detected early enough, some files may still be encrypted, and immediate action may limit the scope of the attack. Once isolated, you should run antivirus and anti-malware scans on the infected system to detect lingering malicious files. After these initial steps, the next course of action is to assess the extent of the attack—what data is encrypted, which systems are affected, and whether any backup copies of the files can be restored.

If a decryption tool is available for the specific ransomware variant that has infected your system, using it can offer a lifeline for recovery. Some cybersecurity organizations and security researchers release decryption tools for particular ransomware strains, often after thoroughly analyzing the malware's behavior. Tools such as these are usually made free to the public, and using them can avoid the need to pay the ransom. However, decryption tools are not universally available, as many ransomware variants are custom-built and employ sophisticated encryption methods that make it difficult to reverse. When using these tools, it's essential to follow the instructions carefully to avoid further corruption or loss of data. If no decryption tool is available or fails to restore access to the files, other recovery methods will need to be explored.

Data recovery and restoration strategies are crucial in the aftermath of a ransomware attack. The first line of defense against data loss is always a reliable backup strategy. If your data has been backed up regularly, especially to an offsite or cloud backup, restoring from those backups is the most efficient and safest way to recover lost files. However, before proceeding with restoration, ensuring that the backup itself has not been compromised during the attack is essential. If ransomware was allowed to propagate through your network, there is a possibility that it could have encrypted your backup files as well. In such cases, restoring from an infected backup may inadvertently reintroduce the malware to your system. If no backup is available, you may have to resort to data recovery tools or professional data recovery services, though success is not guaranteed and can be expensive.

Legal considerations and reporting requirements come into play after a ransomware attack, particularly for businesses and organizations that handle sensitive or regulated data. Depending on the jurisdiction and the nature of the data involved, there may be legal obligations to report the attack to relevant authorities. In many regions, such as under the GDPR in the European Union, organizations are required to notify affected individuals if their data has been compromised. Similarly, in the United States, the Health Insurance Portability and Accountability Act (HIPAA) mandates that healthcare providers report breaches of protected health information (PHI) to the Department of Health and Human Services (HHS) and affected individuals. Law enforcement agencies, including the FBI, should also be notified, particularly if the ransomware attack involves significant financial damage or the theft of personal or proprietary data. Reporting the attack helps law enforcement track cyber-criminal activity and may assist in larger efforts to disrupt the criminal networks behind ransomware operations. It is also important to note that many insurance policies require that ransomware incidents be reported promptly to ensure coverage for any financial losses associated with the attack.

Strengthening defenses against future ransomware attacks should be a top priority once the immediate response to an attack is concluded. Ransomware attacks are not one-time events; they are part of a growing trend of cybercrime targeting individuals and organizations. A critical first step in fortifying defenses is to review and improve backup strategies. Implementing a robust 3-2-1 backup strategy, which involves keeping at least three copies of your data, two local but on different

---

Ask the AI

"What are the legal and ethical implications of paying a ransomware demand?"
"How do I effectively implement the 3-2-1 backup strategy to protect critical data?"
"What are the best strategies for strengthening defenses against ransomware in the future?"

devices and one offsite, ensures that you have a reliable and redundant way to recover data in case of future attacks. Equally important is keeping all systems, software, and applications updated with the latest patches and security updates. Cybercriminals frequently exploit unpatched vulnerabilities in software to deploy ransomware, so maintaining a regular update schedule significantly reduces the risk of infection. Investing in endpoint security tools that offer real-time protection and behavior analysis can help detect and block ransomware before it can encrypt critical data.

Employee training and awareness are equally essential in strengthening defenses against ransomware. Many ransomware infections are delivered through phishing emails that trick users into opening infected attachments or clicking on malicious links. Providing employees with regular training on recognizing phishing attempts, using strong passwords, and practicing safe browsing habits can dramatically reduce the likelihood of a successful attack. Furthermore, limiting user privileges and employing the principle of least privilege (POLP) ensures that only authorized users can access sensitive files and systems, which can prevent malware from spreading if an initial infection occurs. Multi-factor authentication should also be implemented to protect sensitive systems and data. By adopting a layered approach to security, combining technical measures, user education, and good security hygiene, organizations can significantly reduce the risk of falling victim to a ransomware attack.

Recommendations

1. **Isolate Infected Devices Quickly**: When a ransomware attack is suspected, immediately disconnect the affected device from the network to prevent the malware from spreading to other systems. Disconnect Wi-Fi, unplug Ethernet cables, and disable Bluetooth to stop communication with the attacker's servers. This swift action can significantly limit the damage and help contain the infection.
2. **Avoid Paying the Ransom**: While paying the ransom to regain access to encrypted files might seem tempting, it is advisable to resist this course of action. Paying does not guarantee that the attacker will decrypt your files and encourages further criminal activity. Instead, explore alternative recovery methods, such as restoring from backups or using decryption tools if available.
3. **Run Comprehensive System Scans**: After isolating the infected device, use your antivirus and anti-malware software to run a full system scan. This will help identify and remove any lingering threats. Even if the attack appears contained, scanning for additional malware ensures your system is fully clean before any recovery attempts are made.
4. **Restore from Clean Backups**: If you have reliable, up-to-date backups stored in a secure location, restore your data from those backups to minimize data loss. Before restoring, ensure that the backups themselves are not infected. If you suspect that your backups might be compromised, verifying their integrity before proceeding is crucial.
5. **Consult Decryption Tools**: Check for publicly available decryption tools if your system is affected by a known ransomware variant. Many cybersecurity organizations and security vendors release decryption tools for specific ransomware strains. These tools can help decrypt files without paying the ransom, provided the ransomware variant is supported.
6. **Report the Incident to Authorities**: Ransomware attacks should be reported to law enforcement agencies and relevant authorities. Depending on the nature of the data affected, this may include notifying regulatory bodies, especially if sensitive personal or financial data is involved. Reporting helps authorities track cybercriminal activities and may guide further actions to take.

7. **Implement a Robust Backup Strategy**: To protect against future ransomware attacks, adopt a strong backup strategy, such as the 3-2-1 rule. This means maintaining at least three copies of your data, two of which should be on different physical devices and one offsite or in the cloud. This ensures that you can recover your data even during a ransomware attack.

8. **Strengthen Endpoint Security**: Invest in endpoint security solutions that offer real-time protection and behavior analysis. These tools can detect and block ransomware before it can encrypt your files. Ensure your security software is always up-to-date to defend against the latest ransomware variants.

9. **Train Employees on Cybersecurity Best Practices**: Conduct regular training sessions for employees on recognizing phishing emails, avoiding suspicious links, and handling attachments safely. Since ransomware is often delivered via phishing emails, educating employees is a crucial defense against initial infection. Create awareness around safe online practices and the importance of cybersecurity hygiene.

10. **Develop and Test an Incident Response Plan**: Create an incident response plan that includes clear steps for dealing with a ransomware attack. The plan should cover isolating infected systems, restoring backup data, reporting the attack, and notifying relevant stakeholders. Regularly test and update this plan to ensure that all team members know their roles and can respond swiftly and effectively in case of an attack.

Conclusion

As we've explored throughout this chapter, the evolving threat of malware and ransomware requires vigilance, preparedness, and a proactive approach to digital security. Understanding the different types of malware, how they spread, and the devastating consequences they can have is the first step in building a strong defense. However, it's not enough to be aware of these threats; you must also take action to protect your digital environment. From regularly updating your software to isolating infected systems and restoring data from backups, each step plays a crucial role in safeguarding your information.

Recognizing signs of infection early is vital in minimizing the damage caused by malware. You can take swift action before an attack spreads by monitoring your system for unusual behavior, such as performance slowdowns, unexpected pop-ups, or unauthorized file changes. Equally important is knowing how to respond effectively when an attack does occur. Whether isolating infected devices, using decryption tools or seeking professional help, understanding the proper response ensures you can recover quickly and securely.

Ransomware continues to be a particularly pernicious threat, and understanding how to mitigate its impact is essential for individuals and organizations. While the temptation to pay a ransom may seem like a quick fix, weighing the long-term risks and legal considerations involved is crucial. The best defense against ransomware is a combination of preventive measures, timely backups, and the ability to restore critical data when necessary. By strengthening your defenses today, you reduce the risk of falling victim to such attacks tomorrow.

Ultimately, cybersecurity is not a one-time effort but an ongoing vigilance, education, and adaptation process. As new threats emerge, you must continue learning, updating your defenses, and sharing knowledge with others in your community or organization. By implementing the best practices outlined in this chapter, you will be better prepared to face the challenges of the digital age. Whether you are securing personal devices or protecting sensitive corporate networks, the principles of digital safety will always be the foundation of a resilient and secure online presence.

Chapter Questions

1 What is the first action to take when a device is suspected to be infected with ransomware?
  A. Run a system scan immediately
  B. Isolate the infected device from the network
  C. Contact a professional to remove the malware
  D. Pay the ransom to regain access

2 Which of the following is a reason why paying the ransom is not recommended?
  A. The attacker may not decrypt your files after receiving the ransom
  B. Paying the ransom guarantees the files will be decrypted
  C. Paying is always legal in ransomware cases
  D. It helps recover lost data without complications

3 What is the most important action after isolating an infected device from the network?
  A. Contact law enforcement
  B. Run antivirus and anti-malware software to scan for threats
  C. Immediately restore from backups
  D. Reinstall the operating system

4 What should you do if a decryption tool is available for the ransomware that has infected your system?
  A. Ignore it and attempt to recover files manually
  B. Use the decryption tool to recover encrypted files
  C. Pay the ransom for faster recovery
  D. Continue working without attempting recovery

5 What is the primary benefit of having a reliable backup system?
  A. It allows you to restore your system to a previous state without paying the ransom
  B. It prevents all types of malware from affecting your system
  C. It increases system performance after an attack
  D. It makes the decryption process faster

6 How can you ensure that a backup is not infected before restoring it?
  A. Ignore checking the backup and proceed with the restoration
  B. Check the integrity of the backup before restoration
  C. Assume all backups are safe
  D. Restore from the latest backup without checking

7 What should be done if no decryption tool is available for the ransomware variant?
  A. Pay the ransom immediately
  B. Consult a professional for data recovery
  C. Do nothing and hope the malware will resolve itself
  D. Attempt to reverse the encryption manually

8 Why is it important to report a ransomware attack to authorities?
  A. It helps law enforcement track cybercriminal activities
  B. It guarantees that you will get your files back

   C. It is required to get financial compensation

   D. It speeds up the decryption process

9 What is the 3-2-1 backup rule?

   A. Three copies of data, two on the same device, one offline or in the cloud

   B. Three copies of data, two offsite, one in the cloud

   C. Two copies of data, three on different devices

   D. One backup for every three days of operation

10 What does endpoint security help protect against?

   A. Only phishing attacks

   B. Physical theft of the device

   C. Malware like ransomware before it can encrypt files

   D. Network disruptions

11 Why is it crucial to train employees on phishing and safe browsing?

   A. It helps them access encrypted data quickly

   B. It reduces the chances of falling victim to phishing attacks that deliver ransomware

   C. It teaches them how to recover files from backups

   D. It makes them more likely to pay the ransom if needed

12 What is the primary purpose of developing an incident response plan for ransomware attacks?

   A. To ensure that the attackers can be traced back

   B. To minimize the damage and recover data efficiently

   C. To prevent employees from panicking

   D. To comply with legal reporting requirements

13 What should be done if the ransomware attack affects sensitive personal or financial data?

   A. Ignore the attack and wait for the system to recover

   B. Report the attack to relevant authorities and regulatory bodies

   C. Focus only on recovering the encrypted files

   D. Immediately pay the ransom to avoid further issues

14 What does real-time protection from endpoint security tools help prevent?

   A. Unauthorized access to data

   B. Ransomware from encrypting files and spreading

   C. Slow internet speeds

   D. Increased system performance

15 What is the best way to ensure future ransomware attacks are mitigated?

   A. Regularly patching and updating software to fix vulnerabilities

   B. Paying the ransom in advance for peace of mind

   C. Disabling antivirus software

   D. Only using one backup copy for data recovery

15

How to Stay Safe While Browsing the Internet

In today's interconnected world, maintaining digital safety is no longer a luxury—it's a necessity. The digital landscape offers immense opportunities but also exposes users to various security risks, from malicious websites and phishing attacks to identity theft and online harassment. Individuals increasingly rely on digital platforms for work, socializing, and financial transactions, so the need to implement strong cybersecurity practices has never been more pressing. Whether browsing the internet, sharing personal information, or participating in online communities, knowing how to protect yourself from cyber threats is crucial.

This chapter is designed to equip readers with the tools and knowledge to navigate the digital world safely. It covers various topics, from securing your browser and recognizing phishing attempts to managing personal information and preventing online harassment. The goal is to identify threats and provide actionable solutions that readers can implement to protect themselves and their loved ones. As you work through the sections, you will gain insights into making informed decisions about your online activities, reducing your risk exposure, and contributing positively to the online spaces you engage with.

Throughout this chapter, we will delve into best practices for securing your online interactions, whether by choosing the right browser, being mindful of what you share, or using tools like virtual private networks (VPNs) to safeguard your privacy. We'll also explore mental well-being in the context of digital safety, acknowledging that the online environment can sometimes take a toll on one's mental health. Understanding the interplay between online safety and well-being, readers will be better equipped to maintain a balanced, secure, and positive digital presence. This chapter is a guide and a resource to help you build a strong foundation for digital safety in an ever-evolving online landscape.

While the digital world may feel vast and sometimes intimidating, understanding cybersecurity fundamentals can greatly reduce your risks. The strategies and recommendations in this chapter are grounded in practical, real-world applications, ensuring they are accessible regardless of your level of technical expertise. Each section builds on the last, taking a holistic approach to securing your digital life. By the end of this chapter, you will have the knowledge and confidence to engage online with a heightened sense of security, knowing you have taken the necessary steps to protect your data and digital well-being (Figure 15.1).

Secure Browsing Practices

Securing your browsing activity is one of the most important aspects of maintaining digital safety, as browsers are the primary tools we use to access the internet. With the vast amount of personal data we transmit while browsing, choosing a browser that prioritizes security and privacy is critical.

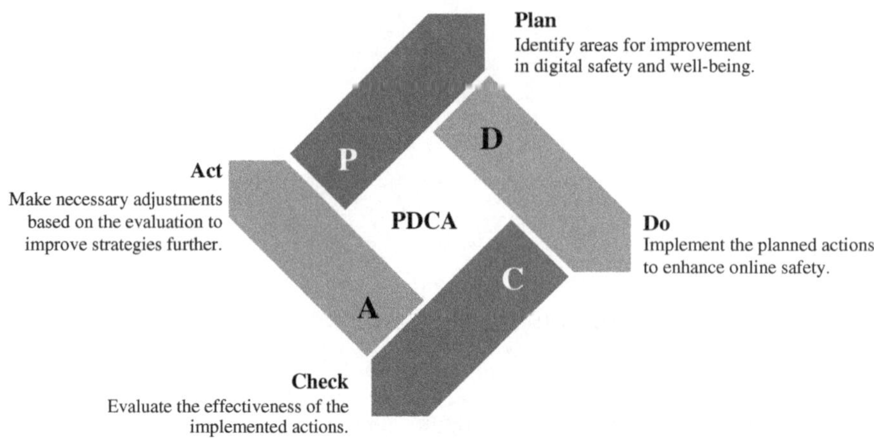

Figure 15.1 Online safety improvement cycle (PDCA model).

Browsers like Mozilla Firefox, Brave, and Tor offer advanced privacy features and enhanced security controls compared to mainstream options like Chrome and Safari. When selecting a browser, it's important to research its security features, the track record for handling vulnerabilities, and the transparency of its privacy policies. The ideal browser for digital safety will be open-source, regularly updated, and offer extensive privacy controls that empower users to protect their data from being collected and exploited by third parties (Table 15.1).

Keeping your browser up to date is essential to securing your digital life. Browsers are complex software; like all software, they are susceptible to security vulnerabilities. These vulnerabilities can range from relatively harmless bugs to critical flaws that cybercriminals can exploit. Manufacturers release frequent updates to fix these vulnerabilities, which often include important patches that improve security and functionality. Many browsers offer automatic update features, but checking that your updates are installed properly periodically is crucial. Ignoring browser updates is akin to leaving the door open for attackers, and it's an easy way to expose yourself to unnecessary risks.

An often overlooked aspect of browser security is understanding and managing cookies and trackers. Cookies are small pieces of data that websites store on your device to remember preferences or track your online activity. While many cookies are harmless, some are used by advertisers and other third parties to build detailed profiles of your behavior online. This information can then be sold or used to target you with specific ads, often without your knowledge or consent. Fortunately, modern browsers allow you to manage or block cookies entirely, and there are extensions available that provide even more granular control. Regularly clearing cookies or blocking third-party cookies helps mitigate privacy risks and gives you greater control over your digital footprint.

Equally important is using your browser's security settings effectively. Every major browser comes with a set of built-in security features designed to protect your data while you browse. These settings allow you to adjust everything from blocking pop-ups and malicious websites to disabling third-party cookies and ensuring sites use secure connections. While some settings are enabled by default, exploring your browser's security options and adjusting them to your personal preferences is important. For example, enabling HTTPS-Only mode ensures that all websites you visit use encrypted connections, protecting your data from prying eyes. Another key setting is enabling the "Do Not Track" feature, which can help reduce the amount of tracking and data collection by websites.

Table 15.1 Common browser security features.

Browser	Security feature 1	Security feature 2	Security feature 3	Privacy feature 1	Privacy feature 2
Google Chrome	Sandboxing	Phishing protection	Safe browsing	Incognito mode	Enhanced tracking protection
Mozilla Firefox	Enhanced tracking protection	Facebook container	Password manager	Private browsing	Container tabs
Safari	Intelligent tracking prevention	Privacy report	Apple Pay	Safari extensions	Website privacy policies
Microsoft Edge	SmartScreen filter	Password monitor	Secure DNS	InPrivate browsing	Tracking Prevention
Brave	Built-in ad blocker	Tracker blocking	IPFS support	Private browsing	Enhanced privacy mode
Opera	Free VPN	Ad blocking	Tracking protection	Crypto wallet	Private window
Vivaldi	Built-in ad blocker	Tracker blocking	Tab management	Private browsing	Cookie settings
Tor browser	Onion routing	Anti-fingerprinting	Multilayered encryption	No tracking	Anonymous browsing
Epic browser	Block third-party cookies	No tracking	Proxy usage	Secure search	Encrypted connection
Chromium	Sandboxing	Auto-updates	Incognito mode	Tracking protection	Privacy mode

One effective way to bolster your browsing security is by implementing ad blockers and anti-tracking extensions. Ads are not just a nuisance; they can be a vector for malware and a tool for invasive tracking. Malicious ads, known as malvertising, can lead to phishing attempts or serve as an entry point for malware. Anti-tracking extensions, such as Privacy Badger or uBlock Origin, prevent websites from tracking your movements across the web. These tools work by blocking unwanted scripts and third-party trackers that collect data about your browsing habits. By using these extensions, you can reduce exposure to malicious threats and privacy invasions.

Recognizing secure websites is fundamental to safe browsing. One of the most basic yet essential security features to look for when browsing any website is HTTPS (Hypertext Transfer Protocol Secure). HTTPS ensures that the data exchanged between your browser and the website is encrypted, making it much harder for hackers to intercept or manipulate. In addition to HTTPS,

---

Ask the AI

"What are the most secure and privacy-focused browsers available today?"
"How can I manage cookies and trackers to enhance online privacy?"
"What browser security settings should I adjust for maximum protection?"

it's important to check for a valid SSL certificate, which further ensures the authenticity of the website and its ability to handle data securely. Websites that use HTTPS will often display a padlock symbol next to the URL, which signifies a secure connection. Always look for this symbol before entering sensitive information, such as passwords or credit card details, as unsecured sites can leave you vulnerable to data breaches.

Another important aspect of secure browsing is being cautious about the sites you visit. Even if a site uses HTTPS and displays a padlock, this doesn't necessarily mean it is safe. Phishing attacks, for instance, often involve counterfeit websites that mimic legitimate ones to steal personal information. These sites may also look secure using HTTPS, but their fraudulent nature can often be detected by scrutinizing the URL or other small details. For instance, suspicious URLs may have slight variations in spelling or unusual domain names that mimic trusted sites. Additionally, always verify the authenticity of a website, especially when dealing with sensitive transactions, by cross-checking the URL or seeking out reviews and ratings from reliable sources.

It's also important to consider using a VPN for additional security while browsing. VPNs encrypt your internet traffic, making it much harder for anyone, including your internet service provider (ISP), to monitor your online activity. This is particularly important when using public Wi-Fi networks that are notorious for being insecure. VPNs can also help bypass geo-restrictions and enhance privacy by masking your IP address. While VPNs offer an extra layer of protection, choosing a reliable and trustworthy service is crucial, as some free VPNs may log your data or sell it to third parties.

Avoiding Malicious Websites and Content

The internet is a vast landscape full of helpful resources, but it also harbors many dangers. Malicious websites designed to deceive, steal, or compromise your information significantly threaten your digital safety. One of the most common methods for attackers to gain access to sensitive data is through phishing websites—fraudulent sites that mimic legitimate ones to trick you into entering personal information. These websites can look almost identical to trusted sites, such as banking or social media pages, but often include subtle discrepancies in URLs, domain names, or page content. To identify phishing websites, always double-check the URL for any irregularities, such as extra characters or slight misspellings. Additionally, be cautious if the site uses outdated security certificates or doesn't feature HTTPS encryption. If in doubt, do not enter any personal details and consider reporting the site to the relevant authorities (Table 15.2).

Pop-ups and redirects are another common tactic malicious sites use to disrupt your browsing experience or lead you to unwanted content. These intrusive elements often appear unexpectedly, blocking your view of the page and forcing you to interact with them. Some pop-ups try to convince you to download harmful software, while others redirect you to fraudulent or malicious sites. Always avoid clicking on pop-ups, and if possible, use your browser's built-in pop-up blocker to prevent them from appearing in the first place. Some sites may attempt to redirect you to different pages or even install tracking cookies that follow your online behavior. If you find yourself constantly being redirected, this is a clear sign of a malicious website, and it's best to close the browser tab and proceed with caution when navigating similar sites in the future.

Clickbait and misleading content are additional traps that can compromise your digital safety. These types of content are designed to lure you into clicking on links by using sensationalist headlines or exaggerated claims, such as "You've won a prize!" or "Click here for a shocking revelation!" While these tactics might seem harmless at first, they are often used to lead you to malicious

Table 15.2 Signs of phishing and scam websites.

Indicator	Description	Example	Action to take
Suspicious URL	A website URL that doesn't match the official domain or is misspelled	"www.amazon-secure.com"	Verify the URL carefully and look for "https://" or the correct domain
Unusual pop-ups	Excessive pop-up windows asking for personal information or login credentials	Pop-ups asking for your social security number	Close the pop-up and do not provide any information
Lack of SSL encryption	Website without HTTPS or a security certificate	"http://example.com"	Look for a padlock symbol before the URL
Misspelled content	Websites with poor grammar	spelling mistakes	or awkward phrasing
Too good to be true	Offers or deals that are too attractive	often claiming free products or money	"Win $5000 for completing this survey!"
Request for unusual information	Asking for sensitive information that seems unrelated to the service offered	Requesting your bank PIN during a product return	Don't provide personal or financial details unless necessary
Fake customer service numbers	Contact info that is not tied to the official company or domain	"Call 1-800-XYZ-HELP"	Verify contact info through the official website or support channels
Urgency tactics	Websites that pressure you to act immediately	claiming urgent action is required	"Your account will be locked in 5 minutes!"
No contact information	Scams often lack valid contact info like phone numbers or physical addresses	"Contact us by clicking here!"	Look for valid contact info and confirm through independent searches
Mismatched website design	A website design that doesn't match the official brand or seems unprofessional	"Example.com with broken links and strange layout"	Confirm the website by visiting the official website directly to ensure authenticity

websites that could steal your data or infect your device with malware. Some clickbait sites may also try to push misleading or harmful products, ranging from fake antivirus software to fraudulent financial services. Developing a healthy skepticism of overly enticing or dramatic content is crucial, especially when it promises something too good to be true. Always verify any claims through trusted sources before acting on them, and consider using ad-blocking or anti-clickbait tools to help identify and block suspicious content.

Safety should always be a top priority when downloading files from the internet. Malicious software, including viruses, ransomware, and spyware, can often be disguised as innocent-looking files that seem safe to download. The danger is compounded when downloading from untrusted or unfamiliar websites, where files may be bundled with harmful code. Always download files only from reputable sources, such as well-known software vendors or trusted app stores, to minimize the risk. Even when downloading from legitimate sources, consider additional offers, such as optional software installations or toolbars, which may be bundled with your desired download. Consider using antivirus software to scan downloaded files before opening them, especially if they were obtained from sites you don't visit regularly.

Illegal or unverified streaming sites are another breeding ground for malicious content. These sites may offer access to movies, TV shows, or music without requiring a subscription, often a tempting alternative to legal streaming services. However, the risks of using such sites far outweigh the potential savings. Many of these sites are rife with harmful ads, malware, and phishing attempts that can compromise your device and personal information. Additionally, streaming from unverified sites is often illegal and can expose you to legal liability. Stick to recognized, legitimate platforms and avoid the temptation of "free" content that might come with significant hidden costs.

One of the best ways to evaluate the safety of a website is by using reputation services to assess its credibility. Reputation services, such as Google Safe Browsing, VirusTotal, or Web of Trust (WOT), allow you to quickly check if a website is considered safe based on community feedback, security history, and known threat data. These services can alert you to any potential risks associated with a site, such as a history of hosting malware or phishing attempts. While these services are not foolproof, they are useful in making informed decisions about the websites you visit. If a website's reputation is questionable or unverified, it's best to err on caution and avoid interacting with it altogether. In combination with your vigilance, these tools form an effective defense against the ever-evolving landscape of online threats.

Furthermore, browser extensions can provide additional layers of protection against malicious websites. Tools like WOT, Malwarebytes Browser Guard, and other security-focused add-ons can alert you in real time if you are attempting to access a dangerous site. These extensions often show you a visual warning directly in your browser when you visit a site flagged for phishing or distributing malware. It's important to keep these extensions up to date as the threat landscape changes rapidly, and these tools need to be continuously refined to keep pace with new tactics used by cybercriminals.

While protecting yourself from known threats is important, it's equally critical to stay aware of new and emerging attack methods. Cybercriminals are constantly innovating and finding new ways to compromise websites and trick users into visiting harmful pages. Some of these tactics include fake software updates, deceptive social media links, or compromised legitimate websites that have been hacked to serve malware. Always stay informed about the latest cybersecurity trends and threats, and keep your system and browser security settings current to stay ahead of the curve. Educating yourself on the types of malicious content circulating the web will further bolster your defense against online threats.

Protecting Personal Information Online

In the digital age, personal information is one of your most valuable assets—and it's also one of the most vulnerable. Every time you browse the web, interact on social media, or participate in online forums, you're potentially exposing information about yourself. The information you share, whether intentionally or accidentally, can be used to build a profile of you, track your habits, or even steal your identity. Being mindful of what you share on forums, blogs, and other public spaces is one of the first steps in protecting your personal information online. Many online platforms

---

Ask the AI

"How can I identify phishing and scam websites effectively?"
"What are safe practices for downloading files to prevent malware infections?"
"Which reputation services can help assess the safety of a website?"

encourage users to be open and share details about their lives, which can inadvertently lead to oversharing. Even seemingly harmless information, such as your birthdate, hometown, or job title, can be used by attackers in social engineering attacks or to guess your passwords. Always think twice before posting, and consider what data could be pieced together to form a more complete picture of your life (Table 15.3).

One of the most effective ways to protect your privacy online is using pseudonyms or anonymized profiles, particularly on platforms where you're not engaging with people you know personally. Social media, for example, often encourages using real names, which can lead to inadvertently sharing personal information that others could exploit. Using a pseudonym or username that doesn't

Table 15.3 Online harassment and protection strategies.

Harassment type	Description	Warning signs	Protection strategy
Cyberbullying	Online harassment that involves repeated behavior intended to harm someone	Offensive messages	Use privacy settings to block or report the bully and seek support
Doxxing	The act of revealing private information about someone online without their consent	Personal info like phone numbers	Contact the platform to have the information removed and report the incident
Trolling	Deliberately posting provocative or offensive content to disrupt online conversations	Insulting comments or inflammatory posts	Report the troll to the platform
Stalking	Following someone's online presence with the intent to monitor or intimidate	Repeated comments, messages, or tracking activities	Adjust privacy settings to block the individual and consider legal actions if necessary
Impersonation	When someone pretends to be you online for malicious purposes	Fake social media accounts or emails using your name	Report the fake profiles or accounts to the platform immediately
Sexual harassment	Unsolicited sexual comments or advances made through digital communication	Inappropriate messages or explicit content	Use platform reporting features and restrict contact with the harasser
Phishing	Using fake messages or websites to steal personal information by pretending to be a legitimate entity	Emails or pop-ups asking for sensitive info like passwords or credit card numbers	Don't respond to suspicious messages and report phishing attempts
Online shaming	Publicly humiliating someone by sharing their mistakes or personal details without their consent	Public posts or comments making fun of someone	Contact the platform to have harmful posts removed and report the shaming behavior
Hate speech	Any offensive or discriminatory remarks based on race, gender, etc.	Posts or comments that spread hatred or violence against a group	Report to the platform and consider seeking legal action if needed
Swatting	Making false emergency calls to authorities about a person's location	Claiming a person is in immediate danger when they are not	Always verify threats or suspicious calls and inform law enforcement if your safety is at risk

link directly to your real identity can provide a layer of protection, especially when signing up for online forums, review sites, or services you don't need to associate with your identity. This is particularly important on sites where you're engaging in public discussions or sharing opinions that could be misinterpreted or lead to unwanted attention. While pseudonyms offer a degree of anonymity, it's also important to exercise caution and be mindful of the information you share in interactions. For example, while you may use a pseudonym on a discussion board, it's still wise to avoid providing specific details like your location, work, or personal life that could compromise your identity.

Managing your privacy settings across various websites and online services is crucial for protecting personal information. Many websites and applications collect vast amounts of data about you, often far beyond what you realize. Whether it's social media platforms, e-commerce websites, or even fitness apps, these services often ask for more information than they need to provide their services. Fortunately, most reputable websites and services allow you to manage how your information is shared with others. For example, you can adjust privacy settings on platforms like Facebook or Instagram to limit who can see your posts, who can contact you, and what personal information is visible. Take the time to carefully review each service's privacy settings and adjust them to suit your level of comfort with data sharing.

Additionally, consider the permissions granted to apps on your phone and computer. Are they asking for access to your camera, microphone, or location when they don't need it? Regularly review these settings and remove any unnecessary permissions to minimize your exposure.

Sharing sensitive information over unsecured connections can put your data at risk. When browsing the internet, it's important to ensure that the sites you visit use encryption to protect the data being exchanged between your device and the website. One of the most fundamental protections against this type of threat is the HTTPS protocol, which encrypts your connection with a website. The "S" at the end of HTTPS stands for "secure," indicating that the website uses SSL/TLS encryption to protect your data from being intercepted. However, not all sites use HTTPS, especially some less reputable or outdated ones. Avoid sharing sensitive information such as passwords, credit card numbers, or personal identifiers on websites that don't use HTTPS, as these sites are more vulnerable to man-in-the-middle (MITM) attacks. If you must access a site that lacks HTTPS, consider using a VPN or avoiding the exchange of sensitive data altogether.

Using a VPN is one of the best ways to ensure your online activities remain private and secure. A VPN creates an encrypted tunnel between your device and the internet, making it much harder for anyone, including hackers or your ISP, to monitor or intercept your online communications. This is especially important when using public Wi-Fi networks, such as those found in coffee shops or airports, where the risk of malicious actors attempting to intercept your traffic is high. VPNs also help to mask your IP address, providing an additional layer of anonymity when browsing the web. When choosing a VPN, selecting a reputable provider with a strong privacy policy and does not log your data is important. Free VPN services can sometimes compromise your privacy by collecting and selling your data, so research and select a trustworthy service. Remember, while a VPN can help protect your privacy, it is not a cure-all—continued vigilance and careful behavior online are also necessary.

Ask the AI

"What strategies can I use to protect my personal information on social media platforms?"
"How do VPNs work to encrypt my online connections and enhance privacy?"
"What data do websites typically collect about users, and how can I minimize it?"

Understanding websites' data collection practices is critical for maintaining control over your personal information. Websites and apps track your activity in various ways, including through cookies, analytics tools, and more advanced tracking methods like fingerprinting. This data collection often occurs without your direct knowledge and can be used to build a detailed profile of your preferences, browsing habits, and even your location. While some of this data collection is used to improve user experience (such as personalizing recommendations), it can also be exploited for advertising or data breaches. Many websites provide privacy policies outlining their data collection practices, but these are often long and filled with jargon. Take the time to review these policies, especially when signing up for new services or platforms. If a website seems overly invasive in its data collection or has a questionable policy, consider whether it's worth sharing your information with them. You can often opt out of non-essential data collection by adjusting your browser settings or using tools like privacy-focused browsers or ad blockers.

The importance of securing your personal information cannot be overstated. When aggregated with other data points, even seemingly harmless information can paint a complete picture of who you are. For example, the combination of a name, date of birth, and email address might seem harmless, but they could be used to steal your identity or access your accounts if your security measures aren't strong enough. Additionally, be cautious of the information you share on social media or other online spaces where personal details can be easily harvested and misused. Regularly review and audit your social media profiles to ensure you are not revealing more than you intend. Consider making your profiles private or limiting publicly shared information to avoid potential exploitation.

For those concerned about privacy, consider using encrypted messaging services like Signal or WhatsApp, which provide end-to-end encryption to ensure that only you and the recipient can read your messages. These services help protect your communication from being intercepted or monitored by third parties, including hackers and even the service providers themselves. While no digital communication system is entirely immune to attack, using these secure methods protects your sensitive conversations. Be mindful, however, that even the most secure systems can be compromised if you are not careful with your security practices—using strong passwords and enabling two-factor authentication are essential steps to safeguard your accounts.

Mental Health and Digital Well-being

With its vast array of information, entertainment, and social interaction, the digital world offers unprecedented opportunities, but it also comes with significant mental health challenges. One of the most insidious effects of our digital lives is the impact of excessive screen time. Prolonged exposure to screens can harm our physical and mental well-being. Studies have shown that excessive screen time, particularly with smartphones and social media, can lead to issues like eye strain, disrupted sleep, and an increased risk of anxiety and depression. Constantly scrolling through news feeds, engaging with notifications, or even working long hours in front of a computer can create a sense of overload and disconnection from the real world. It's important to recognize the toll that screen time can take on our mental health and consciously moderate our usage. Setting daily time limits for social media and online entertainment and taking breaks to rest your eyes or engage in physical activities can help mitigate these effects.

Managing stress related to cyber threats and information overload has become an increasingly important skill in the digital age. The constant flow of information, often mixed with the pressure of staying updated on the latest cyber threats, can create heightened anxiety. From worrying about the security of personal data to dealing with the stress of managing multiple accounts and passwords, the fear of cyberattacks can become overwhelming. This information overload is compounded by the rapid pace at which news and notifications arrive, leaving little time for reflection or mental rest. To manage this stress, developing a routine that includes digital hygiene practices—such as regularly reviewing security settings, taking scheduled breaks from news feeds, and turning off non-essential notifications is crucial. Creating a healthy balance between staying informed and protecting mental well-being involves knowing when to disengage and step back.

Setting boundaries for online activities is another important aspect of maintaining mental health in a hyper-connected world. While the digital space provides countless benefits, it can blur the lines between work and personal life, leading to burnout. Constant connectivity makes it difficult to "switch off" from work-related emails, social media obligations, or the latest online trends, leaving little room for downtime. To protect your well-being, it's essential to establish clear boundaries for when and how you engage with digital platforms. For example, you might designate certain hours of the day for work or social media while reserving evenings or weekends for relaxation and face-to-face interactions. This prevents overexposure to digital stressors and encourages a healthier work-life balance. Additionally, consider using features like "Do Not Disturb" or app usage trackers to help limit screen time and create more intentional digital habits.

Practicing digital detox and mindfulness are vital practices for mental health, especially for those whose lives are deeply integrated with technology. A digital detox involves taking intentional breaks from screens, whether for a few hours, a day, or even longer. These breaks help reset your brain and provide an opportunity to reconnect with the physical world, fostering better mental clarity, improved sleep, and reduced stress levels. Conversely, mindfulness encourages a deeper awareness of your emotional state when engaging with digital platforms. Being mindful about how you feel when interacting with online content—whether it's a sense of inadequacy from scrolling through idealized social media posts or the stress of constant email notifications—can help you make more intentional choices about your online engagement. Regular digital detoxes and mindfulness practices allow you to maintain better control over your relationship with technology and avoid falling into unhealthy patterns of excessive use.

As with any behavior, identifying the signs of internet addiction is critical to maintaining a healthy digital life. Internet addiction is not just about excessive screen time—it's about the compulsion to be online to the detriment of other aspects of your life. Signs of this addiction may include a constant need to check social media, difficulty focusing on offline activities, or feeling anxious or irritable when unable to access the internet. In some cases, individuals may spend hours on websites, even when they know that it is negatively affecting their health, relationships, or productivity. If you notice these signs in yourself or others, taking proactive steps to regain control over your digital habits is important. This might include seeking support from a mental health professional, setting strict time limits for internet use, or exploring alternative hobbies that don't rely on screen time.

Accessing resources for mental health support is crucial when navigating the complex relationship between digital life and mental well-being. Many people feel alone in their struggles with screen addiction or digital burnout, but help is available. Therapists and counselors who specialize

---

Ask the AI

"What are the signs that excessive screen time is affecting mental health?"
"How can I practice digital detox and mindfulness to improve well-being?"
"What resources are available for managing stress related to digital life?"

in digital addiction, anxiety, or stress management can provide valuable tools and strategies for coping with the psychological demands of the online world. Additionally, many support groups—both online and in-person—exist to help individuals address internet addiction and related issues. Support networks can particularly benefit those feeling isolated or overwhelmed by digital experiences. Seeking help is not a sign of weakness but rather an important step in protecting your overall well-being in an increasingly digital world.

While the internet has provided us with unprecedented access to information and connectivity, it's essential to maintain a healthy relationship with technology. A good digital balance includes recognizing when technology enhances our lives and detracts from our mental health. Being mindful of the time spent online and the emotional toll it can take is key to managing stress and preventing burnout. If you find yourself feeling overwhelmed, remember that you are not alone. Take breaks, disconnect from social media, and practice mindfulness techniques to re-center yourself. By developing healthy boundaries, regularly practicing digital detox, and seeking mental health support when needed, you can navigate the digital world in a way that supports both your mental health and overall well-being.

Safe Participation in Online Communities

Engaging respectfully with others in online communities is the cornerstone of creating a positive and productive digital environment. The internet's anonymity can sometimes encourage people to forget the basic rules of social interaction. It's easy to forget that behind every screen is a real person with feelings, experiences, and perspectives. Maintaining respect is essential for fostering productive dialogue when engaging in online forums, discussion groups, or social media. This means listening to others, being mindful of differing opinions, and refraining from inflammatory language or personal attacks. It's also important to acknowledge that misunderstandings, such as in face-to-face interactions, can occur online. When they do, handling them with patience and empathy rather than resorting to hostility is crucial. By respecting others, you contribute to a community that values diverse viewpoints and encourages thoughtful conversation.

Understanding the community guidelines and policies of online platforms is an essential step in safe participation. Every online space, whether a social media site, a forum, or a gaming platform, operates under a specific set of rules. These guidelines are in place to maintain order and ensure that all users can interact in a way that promotes safety and respect. Familiarizing yourself with these rules not only helps you avoid violations but also empowers you to contribute in ways that align with the values of the community. Whether it's rules about hate speech, spam, or privacy, adhering to these policies helps maintain a positive online environment and ensures everyone has a voice in the discussion. Ignoring these guidelines can lead to penalties ranging from temporary suspensions to permanent bans. Thus, it's wise to take the time to read and understand the policies of any platform you engage with.

Reporting inappropriate or harmful content is a responsibility that every participant in an online community should take seriously. Online platforms often provide tools to report content

---

Ask the AI

"How can I engage respectfully and effectively in online communities?"
"What steps can I take to protect myself from online harassment?"
"How can I contribute positively to discussions and build supportive online networks?"

that violates community standards, whether it's hate speech, harassment, misinformation, or explicit material. These reporting systems ensure that harmful content is removed quickly and communities remain safe for all users. By reporting inappropriate content, you help prevent it from spreading and ensure that the platform takes action against harmful behavior. However, reporting should not be done lightly—it's important to ensure the content violates the platform's guidelines before submitting a report. False or malicious reports can undermine the effectiveness of these systems and may result in penalties for those who misuse them. Reporting should be a tool for maintaining a healthy community, not for punishing others unjustly.

Protecting oneself from online harassment is one of the more difficult aspects of participating in digital communities. Harassment can take many forms, including cyberbullying, trolling, doxxing, and even stalking. It can happen on social media, in online gaming environments, or within any digital space where interaction occurs. While engaging respectfully with others is important, it's equally crucial to know how to protect yourself if you become a target. Many platforms offer privacy settings that can help shield you from unwanted contact, such as blocking or muting users, restricting who can view your posts, and limiting who can comment on your content.

Additionally, it's important to recognize when online harassment crosses into illegal behavior, such as threats of violence or extortion. In such cases, it may be necessary to involve law enforcement. Remember, no one should feel unsafe in an online space, and it's important to protect your physical and mental well-being in these environments.

Contributing positively to discussions is not only about adhering to guidelines; it's about enriching the community with meaningful input. Every online community thrives when its members contribute thoughtfully, share valuable resources, and engage in discussions that lead to learning and growth. When participating in any online forum, it's helpful to be mindful of your contributions—ensure that they add value, encourage constructive dialogue, and respect the diversity of opinions present. Rather than simply reacting to posts, take the time to reflect on what others have said and add your insights or experiences that can help further the conversation. Positive contributions can also involve offering support to others, answering questions, or sharing useful links and resources. The more positively you contribute, the more likely you are to foster a sense of camaraderie and mutual respect among community members.

Building supportive online networks is another key aspect of safe participation in online communities. Online communities can often become a source of strength, offering individuals support, advice, and camaraderie. This is especially important in niche communities, such as those focused on mental health, professional networking, or hobbyist interests, where members share common experiences or goals. To build a positive network, engaging authentically and being open to connecting with others is essential. However, it's important to do so in a way that respects privacy and personal boundaries. Trust is the foundation of any good network, and by fostering respectful, positive interactions, you can create meaningful and supportive connections. It's equally important to recognize that not all online spaces will be welcoming or inclusive, and it's okay to disengage from communities that do not align with your values or provide the support you need.

There are also risks involved in engaging with certain online communities, particularly those that may encourage harmful behavior or exploit vulnerable individuals. It's essential to critically assess the culture of any community before investing too much time or energy into it. Not all online groups foster positivity; some may even promote dangerous activities or ideologies. Protecting your mental and emotional health requires being selective about where you engage and ensuring that the communities you participate in are healthy and supportive. Sometimes, stepping away from a community that is no longer providing value or has become toxic is necessary. It's always better to leave a harmful environment than to risk your safety and well-being.

Recommendations

1. **Choose a Privacy-focused Browser:** Select a browser that prioritizes security and user privacy, such as Mozilla Firefox, Brave, or Tor. Research each option's features and decide which aligns best with your needs. This choice forms the foundation of a secure browsing experience. Using a secure browser helps protect your data from being collected and exploited by third parties.
2. **Keep Your Browser Updated:** Regularly update your browser to ensure you have the latest security patches and features. Enable automatic updates if available, and periodically check for updates manually. Staying current reduces vulnerabilities that hackers might exploit. Ignoring updates is akin to leaving your digital front door unlocked.
3. **Manage Cookies and Trackers:** Take control of your online privacy by managing cookies and blocking trackers. Adjust your browser settings to limit or block third-party cookies, and consider using privacy-focused extensions. Regularly clearing your cookies helps mitigate privacy risks. This prevents advertisers and other entities from building detailed profiles of your online behavior.
4. **Utilize Browser Security Settings Effectively:** Explore and configure your browser's security settings to enhance protection. Enable features like pop-up blockers, do-not-track requests, and secure connection requirements. Tailoring these settings strengthens your defense against online threats. This proactive approach empowers you to customize your security level.
5. **Implement Ad Blockers and Anti-tracking Extensions:** Install reputable ad blockers and anti-tracking tools like uBlock Origin or Privacy Badger. These extensions reduce exposure to malicious ads and prevent websites from tracking your activities. This adds an extra layer of security to your browsing. By blocking unwanted scripts, you minimize the risk of malvertising.
6. **Verify Website Security Before Sharing Information:** Always check for HTTPS and a valid SSL certificate before entering sensitive data on a website. Look for the padlock icon in the address bar as a sign of a secure connection. This ensures your data is encrypted and less susceptible to interception. Avoiding unsecured sites helps protect you from data breaches.
7. **Be Vigilant Against Phishing Attempts:** Educate yourself on identifying phishing and scam websites. Scrutinize URLs for irregularities, and be cautious of unsolicited requests for personal information. Trust your instincts and avoid interacting with the site if something feels off. This awareness helps prevent falling victim to fraudulent schemes.
8. **Use a VPN:** Protect online privacy using a trusted VPN service, especially on public Wi-Fi networks. A VPN encrypts your internet traffic, shielding your data from potential eavesdroppers. Choose a reputable provider that doesn't log your data. This is crucial for maintaining confidentiality in unsecured environments.
9. **Set Boundaries for Screen Time:** Recognize the impact of excessive screen time on your mental health and establish limits. Schedule regular breaks and engage in offline activities to balance your digital life. Practicing digital detox can reduce stress and prevent burnout. This promotes better mental well-being and a healthier relationship with technology.
10. **Engage Respectfully and Safely in Online Communities:** Participate in online forums and social networks with respect and consideration for others. Familiarize yourself with community guidelines, protect your personal information, and report inappropriate content. Building positive interactions enhances your online experience. Contributing constructively fosters supportive online networks.

Conclusion

As the digital landscape evolves, so must our approach to protecting ourselves online. The practices and strategies outlined in this chapter serve as a roadmap for navigating the complex world of cybersecurity with confidence and awareness. By understanding the risks associated with online activities and implementing the recommended safety measures, individuals can significantly reduce their exposure to threats such as identity theft, cyberbullying, and malicious attacks. However, digital safety is not a one-time effort; it requires ongoing attention and adaptation to new and emerging threats.

We can take meaningful steps to protect our digital and mental well-being through secure browsing, proactive management of personal information, and vigilant participation in online communities. The digital world offers vast opportunities for learning, connection, and growth, but it also has challenges that require vigilance and preparedness. By integrating the best practices discussed in this chapter into daily online habits, readers can safeguard themselves against a wide range of cyber risks while fostering a more positive and supportive online environment.

As technology advances, so too does the sophistication of cyber threats. It is important to recognize that maintaining digital safety is a continuous process that requires regular updates to knowledge, tools, and strategies. In this chapter, we've highlighted practical, actionable steps to stay ahead of common cyber threats. However, keeping informed and adaptable in the face of ever-changing risks is essential. Regularly reviewing security practices, keeping up with updates, and adopting new protective technologies are vital for ensuring your digital safety measures remain robust.

In conclusion, securing your digital life is more than just installing antivirus software or using strong passwords. It is about cultivating an awareness of the risks, understanding the tools at your disposal, and building healthy digital habits that promote security and mental well-being. As digital citizens, we all play a part in creating a safer online world. By taking the steps outlined in this chapter, we protect ourselves and contribute to a more secure, supportive, and respectful digital ecosystem for everyone.

Chapter Questions

1 What is one of the primary benefits of using a privacy-focused browser?
   A. Faster internet speed
   B. Enhanced user interface customization
   C. Improved security and user privacy
   D. Access to exclusive content

2 Why is it important to keep your browser up to date?
   A. To access new color themes
   B. To ensure compatibility with old websites
   C. To fix security vulnerabilities and bugs
   D. To reduce internet data usage

3 What is the main purpose of managing cookies and trackers in your browser?
   A. To increase page loading speed
   B. To prevent websites from collecting your data
   C. To enable pop-up ads
   D. To improve video streaming quality

4 Which of the following is a sign of a secure website?
   A. The website loads quickly
   B. The URL begins with "http://"
   C. The presence of a padlock icon in the address bar
   D. The website has colorful graphics

5 What is a common tactic used by malicious websites to compromise users?
   A. Offering free legitimate software
   B. Using clickbait and misleading content
   C. Requiring strong passwords
   D. Providing educational resources

6 How can you protect yourself from online harassment?
   A. Share your personal information openly
   B. Respond aggressively to harassers
   C. Adjust privacy settings and block harmful users
   D. Avoid using the internet altogether

7 What is one effective way to practice digital detox?
   A. Increase your screen time
   B. Disconnect from screens for a set period regularly
   C. Multitask with multiple devices
   D. Only use social media at night

8 Why is using a VPN recommended for online privacy?
   A. It speeds up your internet connection
   B. It encrypts your internet traffic and masks your IP address
   C. It provides free access to paid content
   D. It disables cookies on all websites

9 What should you do if you encounter a phishing website?
   A. Enter false information to confuse the attackers
   B. Ignore the warning signs and proceed
   C. Close the website immediately and do not provide any information
   D. Share the website link with friends

10 What is the risk of sharing sensitive information over unsecured connections?
   A. Faster data transfer
   B. Increased likelihood of data interception by attackers
   C. Improved battery life of your device
   D. Enhanced website functionality

11 Which of the following is a sign of internet addiction?
   A. Feeling anxious when unable to access the internet
   B. Using the internet for work purposes only
   C. Limiting screen time to one hour per day
   D. Preferring face-to-face interactions over online communication

12 What is a benefit of contributing positively to online discussions?
   A. Increasing the number of your followers
   B. Fostering a supportive and respectful community
   C. Winning arguments and debates
   D. Gaining administrative privileges

13 Why is it important to understand community guidelines and policies?
   A. To find loopholes for personal gain
   B. To avoid unintentional violations and contribute appropriately
   C. To learn how to advertise your products
   D. To access premium features

14 What does practicing mindfulness in digital usage help you achieve?
   A. Increased screen time
   B. Awareness of your emotional state when engaging with digital platforms
   C. Faster typing speed
   D. Ability to multitask online

15 What is a key advantage of using pseudonyms or anonymized profiles online?
   A. To impersonate others
   B. To protect your identity and personal information
   C. To gain more followers
   D. To access restricted content

16

Network Security

Every device you connect to the internet—a smartphone, laptop, smart home device, or even a wearable fitness tracker—becomes a potential target for cybercriminals. The convenience of digital technology comes with the responsibility of safeguarding personal data and maintaining the integrity of the systems we rely on. From securing home networks to protecting sensitive communications and securing online transactions, understanding and applying cybersecurity best practices are essential for anyone who uses technology daily.

While many people believe that cyber threats are something that only large organizations or high-profile targets need to worry about, the reality is that anyone can become a victim. Cybercriminals continuously exploit vulnerabilities in both software and hardware, looking for ways to gain unauthorized access to personal information, financial assets, and private communications. As our individual lives and professional activities shift online, the risks associated with poor cybersecurity habits become more significant. This chapter aims to provide a comprehensive guide to securing your digital life, from understanding the importance of encryption to protecting your home network and safely navigating public Wi-Fi.

One of the most critical components of digital security is the network on which your devices operate. Securing your home network is the first line of defense, ensuring that unauthorized individuals cannot access your personal devices and sensitive information. By configuring your router securely, using strong passwords, and regularly updating firmware, you can significantly reduce your exposure to attacks. This section will delve into best practices for home network security, providing actionable steps to help you establish a secure and reliable online environment for yourself and your family.

However, securing home networks is just one piece of the puzzle. The rapid expansion of the Internet of Things (IoT) has brought new security challenges, as everyday devices like smart thermostats, security cameras, and even refrigerators are now connected to the internet. Each of these devices represents a potential point of entry for cybercriminals. In this chapter, you'll also learn how to configure IoT devices with security in mind, isolate them from your primary network, and monitor their activity to ensure they are not exploited. By taking a proactive approach to IoT security, you can minimize your risk of falling victim to attacks that target these interconnected devices.

Public Wi-Fi networks are another area of concern for digital safety. While they offer convenience, they are often unsecured, leaving users vulnerable to various cyber threats, including man-in-the-middle (MitM) attacks, data snooping, and session hijacking. In this section, we'll explore the risks associated with using public Wi-Fi and how you can mitigate those risks by using virtual private networks (VPNs), avoiding sensitive transactions on unsecured networks, and disabling

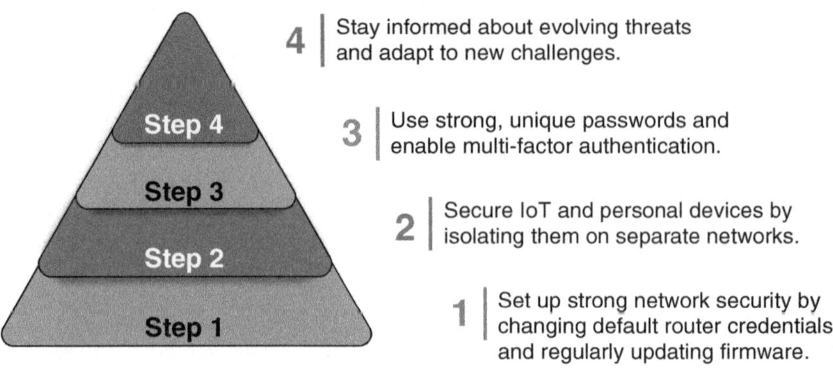

Figure 16.1 The cybersecurity pyramid.

automatic Wi-Fi connections. With these strategies, you can protect sensitive information, even using a shared or public connection.

Finally, it is crucial to understand encryption and its role in securing your digital life. Whether you're communicating with colleagues, making online purchases, or simply browsing the web, encryption ensures your data remains confidential and protected from prying eyes. This chapter will cover various types of encryption, including SSL/TLS, AES, and end-to-end encryption (E2EE), and explain how they safeguard sensitive information. Additionally, we'll dive into the benefits of using a VPN for encryption and guide how to choose the right encryption tools for your needs. Figure 16.1 illustrates the cybersecurity pyramid, depicting the layers of defense that collectively protect against digital threats.

Securing Your Home Network

One of the most critical aspects of securing your digital life begins with the foundation of your home network. Your router acts as the gateway between the devices in your home and the outside world, making it a prime target for cybercriminals. It's essential to begin by setting up and configuring your router with the highest level of security possible. Many routers have factory settings vulnerable to attacks, including easily guessable default passwords. If you haven't already, ensure that you use a unique password unrelated to your personal information. This simple step can drastically reduce the risk of unauthorized access to your network. Additionally, many routers allow you to disable remote management features, enabling an attacker to control the router remotely, which should be turned off if not needed. Table 16.1 outlines best practices for securing home network devices, offering essential steps to protect personal devices and networks from cyber threats.

Changing the default passwords and service set identifiers (SSIDs) is another critical step in securing your home network. Routers typically come with default login credentials—often printed on a sticker on the device itself—that are widely known and easily accessible online. This means that if someone can physically access your router, they may be able to log into your network and change settings. Along with altering the router's password, it's also important to change the SSID, which is essentially the name of your network. This step hides the default network identifier, making it more difficult for an attacker to target your home network. A unique SSID helps make the network more discrete and protects your network from a host of potential attacks.

Table 16.1 Best practices for securing home network devices.

Device	Best practice	Action
Router	Change default credentials	Set a unique administrator username and password to prevent unauthorized access.
Router	Enable WPA3 encryption	Activate WPA3 encryption for stronger security over older standards (WPA2 or WEP).
Router	Disable WPS (Wi-Fi protected setup)	WPS can be a vulnerability.
Router	Update router firmware regularly	Keep firmware up to date to patch known vulnerabilities.
Smart home device	Change default credentials	Always change default usernames and passwords to unique ones.
Smart home device	Isolate devices on separate network	Set up a guest network for IoT devices to reduce risk to other devices.
Smart home device	Turn off unused features	Disable any unused services or features that could be exploited.
Smart home device	Check for updates regularly	Enable automatic updates or check for updates periodically.
IoT device	Disable unnecessary services	Turn off any unneeded functionalities like remote management.
IoT device	Enable network encryption	Ensure IoT devices communicate over encrypted channels.

Enabling network encryption, specifically WPA3, is a fundamental defense mechanism against anyone trying to intercept your network traffic. Wi-Fi Protected Access (WPA) is a set of protocols designed to secure wireless networks, with WPA3 being the latest and most secure version. It provides stronger encryption and improves protection against brute-force attacks, where attackers try every possible password combination until they gain access. WPA3 also prevents certain vulnerabilities found in previous protocols, such as those that attackers can exploit to decrypt data transmitted across the network. If your router supports WPA3, it should be enabled immediately. If not, WPA2 is the next best option, but it is worth considering upgrading your hardware to take advantage of the stronger encryption methods offered by WPA3.

Setting up a guest network is essential for households that regularly host guests or have visitors. This network acts as a separate environment for visitors to connect to without giving them access to your primary devices, such as computers, smartphones, or home security systems. Configuring a guest network ensures that the risks to your more critical devices are minimized even if an attacker gains access to this secondary network. In addition to separating guest traffic, it is advisable to restrict the bandwidth or limit the access time of the guest network to protect the integrity of your primary network further. Most modern routers make setting up a guest network quick and easy, and this simple measure can significantly enhance your overall digital security.

Updating the firmware on your network devices is another crucial step in maintaining security. Like any software, router firmware is updated periodically to fix vulnerabilities, improve performance, and add new features. Many home routers have a default setting that may not notify you about new firmware updates, so it's important to check for updates manually or enable automatic updates if the option exists. Keeping your router firmware up to date protects your network from the latest exploits hackers may use to gain access. Similarly, ensure that all other connected devices, like security cameras and smart home assistants, are regularly updated. These devices are often targets for cybercriminals, and outdated firmware can leave them vulnerable to attack.

Monitoring network activity and the devices connected to your home network is an often overlooked but powerful practice in securing your digital environment. Many modern routers offer built-in tools that allow you to see a list of devices connected to your network in real-time. Regularly reviewing these connected devices can spot unauthorized devices that may have gained access to your network. You must immediately act if you notice something unfamiliar, such as blocking the device and changing your Wi-Fi password. Additionally, some routers allow you to monitor network activity, including which websites and services are being accessed. Regular monitoring can help you detect unusual traffic patterns that might indicate a security breach, allowing you to take action before a more serious attack occurs.

In some cases, you might consider additional layers of security, such as setting up a firewall between your devices and the internet. While many routers have a built-in firewall, you may want to enhance this by configuring advanced settings to block certain traffic or limit access to specific ports. A well-configured firewall is a barrier between your network and the outside world, blocking potential threats from reaching your devices. In addition to firewalls, using a VPN on devices connected to your network can further encrypt your traffic and safeguard your online activities from prying eyes. This is especially important for devices that frequently access public or unsecured networks, as a VPN can help ensure privacy even when you're away from home.

Protecting IoT Devices

The rise of the IoT has revolutionized how we interact with technology, but it has also introduced a new set of security challenges. IoT devices, from smart thermostats to security cameras, are now integral to our daily lives. However, many of these devices were not designed with security as a primary concern. As a result, they often have vulnerabilities that attackers can exploit. A compromised IoT device can be an entry point for hackers into your home network, potentially exposing sensitive data or granting access to other devices. Understanding these challenges is the first step in protecting IoT devices from threats that could jeopardize your privacy and security.

Configuring IoT devices with security in mind is crucial for mitigating the risks associated with these devices. During the setup process, many IoT devices ask for minimal user input, often leaving default security settings that are weak or overly simplistic. For instance, some devices come with default passwords that are easy to guess, while others may not require a password at all. The first thing to do when setting up any IoT device is to change the default credentials to something strong and unique. This simple step can prevent attackers from gaining easy access. Additionally, ensure that any features or services on the device that you don't need—such as remote access or cloud storage—are disabled. This reduces the attack surface by eliminating unnecessary entry points for malicious actors.

Ask the AI

"What steps are to configure a home router to prevent unauthorized access securely?"
"How can enabling WPA3 improve the security of my home network?"
"What are the risks of leaving network firmware outdated, and how do I update it?"

One of the most effective ways to safeguard your IoT devices is by keeping their software and firmware up to date. Like computers and smartphones, IoT devices frequently receive security patches that fix vulnerabilities discovered after the device has been released. Failing to apply these updates promptly leaves your devices open to attack. Many IoT devices are designed to update automatically, but verifying that this feature is enabled is important. If not, you should make it a habit to check for updates manually. Sometimes, a device may not receive regular updates, particularly if it is an older model. In such cases, it may be necessary to consider replacing the device to ensure it stays secure.

Another key practice for IoT security is isolating these devices on a separate network from your primary devices, such as computers and smartphones. Many home networks are set up with a single Wi-Fi network that all devices connect to. However, this can create a situation where a vulnerable IoT device can potentially compromise the entire network. Setting up a dedicated guest or IoT network establishes a buffer between these and more sensitive devices. This limits the exposure of your computers, smartphones, and other valuable devices to any potential threats posed by an IoT device that might be compromised. In some cases, routers can create a separate network for IoT devices, making this an easy step to implement. By isolating IoT devices, you reduce the risk of lateral movement in case one of the devices is compromised.

Disabling unnecessary features and services is an essential aspect of securing IoT devices. These devices often come with many features that the average consumer rarely uses, and many introduce unnecessary security risks. For example, a smart camera might offer cloud-based storage, but if you're not using it, you should disable this feature to avoid potential breaches of your video feeds. Similarly, some devices have universal plug-and-play (UPnP) capabilities or remote access that can open backdoors for attackers if left unchecked. By reviewing the settings of each IoT device and turning off features you don't need, you significantly reduce the chances of a security vulnerability being exploited. While it may take more time and effort upfront, the added security is well worth it.

Before purchasing an IoT device, evaluating its security features is important. Not all IoT devices are created equal, and some manufacturers prioritize security while others cut corners to save costs. Look for products certified by recognized organizations or have strong user reviews regarding their security features. Ensure the device supports regular firmware updates, uses encryption to protect your data, and provides robust authentication mechanisms. It's also worth investigating the device's track record for security, especially if it's part of a larger ecosystem like a smart home. Devices known for being insecure, or those lacking the option for software updates, should be avoided altogether. By being discerning in your device selection, you can avoid the pitfalls of insecure products and ensure your IoT environment is as safe as possible.

Another important consideration is the privacy policies associated with IoT devices. Many of these devices collect data about your habits, preferences, and personal information, which can then be shared with third-party companies or stored in the cloud. Review its privacy policy carefully before purchasing or configuring a new IoT device. Look for any clauses allowing the device manufacturer to share your data with advertisers or other entities, and assess whether this is a trade-off you're willing to accept. Some devices allow you to opt out of data collection or limit the shared data types, which can enhance your privacy. You might want to reconsider your purchase if the device doesn't offer clear privacy options or if the privacy policy seems overly broad.

Ask the AI

"What are the most common vulnerabilities in IoT devices, and how can they be mitigated?"
"How do I create a separate network for IoT devices on my router?"
"What are the best practices for regularly updating IoT device firmware?"

Security monitoring is also important in managing IoT device safety. While it's relatively easy to overlook devices like smart fridges or voice assistants, they can be vulnerable targets for cyber attackers. To detect potential breaches proactively, the activity on these devices must be regularly monitored. Some routers and network security tools allow you to track the behavior of IoT devices connected to your network. Look for unusual activity, such as unexpected communication with foreign IP addresses or data transfers during off-hours, which could indicate that a device has been compromised. Regularly reviewing this data, even if it seems tedious, can help you identify issues early and take corrective action before they develop into full-scale attacks.

Safe Use of Public Wi-Fi Networks

Public Wi-Fi networks offer convenience, but they come with significant risks that can compromise your digital safety. Public networks, such as those found in coffee shops, airports, and hotels, are often insecure and can be easily exploited by attackers. One of the most common threats is the MitM attack, where a malicious actor intercepts communication between a user and a website or service. Without the user's knowledge, this allows the attacker to capture sensitive data, such as login credentials, credit card numbers, or personal messages. Attackers often set up rogue Wi-Fi hotspots with names similar to legitimate networks, tricking unsuspecting users into connecting. Once connected, they can monitor and potentially manipulate your traffic, stealing data as you go about your business. Understanding these risks is crucial for anyone using public Wi-Fi, as it highlights the importance of taking extra precautions when connecting to these networks. Table 16.2 highlights key risks in public Wi-Fi and provides strategies to mitigate them, ensuring safer connections in unsecured networks.

Table 16.2 Key risks in public Wi-Fi and how to mitigate them.

Risk	Description	Mitigation strategy	Recommended tool
Man-in-the-middle attacks	Attackers intercept communications between users and the Wi-Fi network	Use a VPN to encrypt traffic	VPN software like NordVPN
Rogue Wi-Fi hotspots	Fake Wi-Fi networks set up by attackers to steal user data	Verify network legitimacy before connecting	Use a mobile hotspot or VPN to ensure secure connection.
Data snooping	Hackers eavesdropping on unencrypted traffic	Always use HTTPS connections	HTTPS Everywhere browser extension
Session hijacking	Attackers stealing session cookies to gain unauthorized access to accounts	Use multi-factor authentication and secure session handling	Use MFA
Weak encryption	Some public Wi-Fi networks use weak or no encryption	Avoid using networks that don't support WPA3 or WPA2 encryption	Check network encryption type before connecting
Unencrypted data	Sensitive information being sent unencrypted over public Wi-Fi	Avoid sending sensitive data like passwords or banking details	Use a VPN and avoid entering sensitive info over public networks

To minimize the risks associated with public Wi-Fi, avoiding engaging in sensitive transactions on unsecured networks is essential. Tasks like banking, shopping, or logging into important accounts should be deferred until you're on a secure, trusted network. Public Wi-Fi networks are often unencrypted, meaning your data is sent in plain text, making it much easier for hackers to intercept. Even if a password protects a network, it does not necessarily guarantee security, as many public networks use weak or easily guessed passwords. If you must access sensitive services, ensure you are using a secure network, or consider postponing those actions until you can access a safer environment. This caution can prevent data breaches and identity theft that could otherwise result from conducting sensitive business in a vulnerable setting.

One of the most effective ways to secure your online activity on a public Wi-Fi network is to use a VPN. A VPN creates an encrypted tunnel between your device and the internet, shielding your internet traffic from prying eyes. When connected to a public Wi-Fi network, a VPN ensures that any data you send or receive is encrypted, making it far more difficult for hackers to intercept or tamper. VPNs are particularly useful in environments where you are unsure about the network's security. While public Wi-Fi may be inherently insecure, a VPN protects your internet traffic before it leaves your device. Many VPN services are available for various devices, and choosing one with strong encryption standards will provide robust protection while you are on the go.

Verifying that the network is legitimate before connecting to any Wi-Fi network is crucial. Cybercriminals often create rogue Wi-Fi networks with names similar to those of legitimate public networks. For instance, a hacker may create a Wi-Fi hotspot called "Free Airport Wi-Fi" to deceive passengers into connecting. To avoid such scams, always confirm the network name with a trusted employee or through official channels before connecting. Many venues, like cafes or hotels, will provide the network name and password, which you can use to ensure you're connecting to the right one. In addition to verifying the network name, it is also advisable to look for any warning signs that could indicate a compromised or suspicious network, such as a lack of a secure password or a weak signal strength that might suggest a rogue access point.

Disabling automatic Wi-Fi connections is an important step in securing your device while using public Wi-Fi. Many devices are set by default to automatically connect to any available Wi-Fi network, which can be a risky feature when traveling or in public spaces. If your device automatically connects to an unsecured or malicious network without your knowledge, you may unknowingly expose yourself to attacks. Disabling this feature ensures you only connect to networks you explicitly choose to join, reducing the likelihood of accidentally connecting to a rogue hotspot. This simple precaution can help prevent your device from unknowingly interacting with potentially dangerous networks while you're on the move.

Sometimes, using a mobile hotspot as an alternative to public Wi-Fi may be more secure. Mobile hotspots, which use cellular data to create a personal Wi-Fi network, are generally much more secure than public Wi-Fi, as they are less likely to be targeted by hackers. By connecting to your mobile hotspot, you can ensure that your traffic is protected by your cellular provider's security protocols, which are typically more robust than those in public networks. This approach can be especially useful when traveling or accessing sensitive information. While mobile hotspots may

Ask the AI

"What are the most effective strategies for protecting data while using public Wi-Fi?"
"How can I verify the legitimacy of a public Wi-Fi network before connecting?"
"What are the benefits and limitations of using a VPN on public Wi-Fi?"

come with data usage limitations, they offer peace of mind knowing your connection is more secure, particularly if you handle sensitive tasks like banking or accessing work files.

For those who frequently rely on public Wi-Fi networks, employing a combination of the above mentioned practices is the best approach. In addition to using a VPN and verifying network legitimacy, it's also a good idea to use secure websites (starting with "https://") and avoid logging into accounts unless necessary. Many modern browsers will alert you if you're about to enter a site that isn't using HTTPS, which can serve as a reminder to avoid potentially risky connections. If you must engage in sensitive activities, ensure all communications are over encrypted channels, and always log out of accounts when finished. The less personal information you leave behind on public networks, the less likely an attacker will be able to capture and misuse it.

Encryption and VPNs

Encryption is one of the cornerstones of modern cybersecurity, providing the essential protection that safeguards our digital privacy and data integrity. In simple terms, encryption converts data into a form that unauthorized parties cannot easily understand. Without encryption, cybercriminals could intercept and read sensitive information such as personal messages, banking details, or medical records. Encryption transforms this data into an unreadable format using algorithms that can only be decrypted by someone with the appropriate key or password. As more personal and professional lives are conducted online, understanding how encryption works and why it matters is crucial for maintaining privacy and security in the digital age. Encryption is like a digital lock that ensures only those with the proper key can access the information inside. Table 16.3 details common encryption methods and their use cases, illustrating how different encryption techniques protect data across various scenarios.

There are different types of encryption protocols, each serving specific purposes and offering varying levels of security. One of the most common forms is secure sockets layer (SSL) or its

Table 16.3 Common encryption methods and use cases.

Encryption type	Description	Common use cases	Strength
Advanced encryption standard (AES)	Symmetric key encryption is used for securing data	Encrypting file communication channels and disk storage	Very strong
Secure socket layer/ transport layer security	Cryptographic protocols that provide secure communication over a network	Secure online transactions email encryption	Very strong
RSA (Rivest–Shamir–Adleman)	Asymmetric encryption is used for secure data transmission	Used in digital signatures and SSL certificates	Very strong
End-to-end encryption	Encryption, where only the sender and receiver can read the messages	Secure messaging apps	Very strong
Wi-Fi Protected Access 3	Encryption standard for securing wireless networks	Protecting home and office Wi-Fi networks	The strongest wireless encryption currently available
Pretty Good Privacy	Asymmetric encryption is used for securing emails and files	Email encryption and file encryption	Strong

successor, transport layer security (TLS), widely used to secure communication between web browsers and servers. When you visit a website with "https" in the URL, you use SSL/TLS encryption, ensuring your data is securely transmitted. This encryption prevents attackers from eavesdropping on your communications, such as when making an online purchase or logging into an account. Another widely used encryption standard is advanced encryption standard (AES), commonly used for encrypting files and disk drives. AES is a symmetric key encryption system, meaning the same key is used for encryption and decryption, making it fast and secure. AES is widely regarded as one of the most secure encryption algorithms and is commonly used by governments and financial institutions to protect sensitive information. Understanding these encryption methods and when they apply can help you better secure your online activities.

Choosing the right VPN service is important for anyone concerned about their online privacy. A VPN creates a secure, encrypted tunnel between your device and the internet, ensuring your online activity remains private and protected from prying eyes. When you connect to a VPN, your internet traffic is routed through an encrypted server, hiding your true IP address and masking your online location. This makes it much more difficult for third parties, such as hackers, advertisers, or even your internet service provider, to track your activity. The encryption provided by a VPN helps to ensure that sensitive data, such as login credentials or financial transactions, are kept safe from interception. When selecting a VPN provider, choosing a reputable service with strong encryption standards and a clear privacy policy is important. Some free VPN services may offer subpar encryption or even sell your data to third parties, so it's worth investing in a trusted, paid service to ensure robust protection.

Encrypting sensitive files and communications adds a layer of security to your digital life. While encryption for internet traffic is essential, it's equally important to secure files stored on your devices, especially if they contain personal, financial, or business-related information. Many file encryption tools allow you to protect individual files with a password, ensuring that even if someone gains physical access to your device, they cannot view your sensitive data. For email communications, services like ProtonMail or those that support PGP (Pretty Good Privacy) encryption provide E2EE, meaning only the intended recipient can decrypt and read the message. Encrypting files and communications helps safeguard your privacy, particularly if you frequently handle confidential information that could be valuable to attackers.

Understanding E2EE is critical for anyone concerned with secure communication. E2EE ensures that data transmitted between two parties is encrypted on the sender's device and can only be decrypted by the recipient's device. This means that no intermediary, including service providers, hackers, or even government agencies, can access the content of the communication. For example, many messaging platforms, such as WhatsApp and Signal, offer E2EE for their conversations, ensuring that only the intended recipients can read the messages. This level of encryption is especially important for highly sensitive communications, such as legal matters or private business negotiations. While E2EE can be a technical concept, it's increasingly important for everyday users to recognize when their communications are protected by this method, as it provides the highest level of privacy and security.

Ask the AI

"What is the difference between symmetric and asymmetric encryption, and where are they used?"
"How can I ensure my VPN service provider is trustworthy and secure?"
"What are the steps to encrypt sensitive files on personal devices effectively?"

In the context of encryption, there are also legal considerations that must be taken into account, as the use of encryption is subject to regulation in some countries. In the United States, for instance, the government has laws that govern the export and use of encryption technology, and businesses may be required to implement encryption for certain types of data, such as customer information. However, the government may need access to encrypted communications for national security or law enforcement in some regions, like China or Russia. This means that while encryption is vital for securing personal data, users in certain countries should be aware of local laws surrounding its use. In some jurisdictions, it may even be illegal to use encryption tools that the government does not approve of or to use encryption without providing the government access to decryption keys. Understanding encryption's legal landscape is essential, as failure to comply with relevant laws can lead to serious consequences.

While encryption effectively safeguards against many cyber threats, it is not a silver bullet. Understanding that encryption alone does not protect against all cyberattacks is crucial. For example, an attacker could still exploit vulnerabilities in a device, application, or network that is not encrypted. This highlights the importance of adopting a multi-layered security approach, which includes using encryption in conjunction with other security practices such as strong passwords, two-factor authentication, and secure browsing habits. Encryption is most effective when part of a broader cybersecurity strategy to protect against a wide range of threats.

Cybersecurity for Remote Work and Home Offices

Establishing secure remote access protocols is fundamental for any organization that supports telecommuting. When employees connect to company resources from home or other remote locations, they expose corporate data and systems to potential vulnerabilities if proper security measures are not in place. VPNs are one of the most effective tools for securing remote connections. By encrypting the data between remote employees and the corporate network, a VPN ensures that sensitive information remains protected from eavesdropping or interception by malicious actors. Additionally, MFA should be implemented for remote access, requiring users to provide multiple forms of identification before gaining access to critical systems. With these security protocols in place, organizations can significantly reduce the risk of unauthorized access while maintaining the flexibility of remote work.

Using company-provided security tools is another critical step in ensuring cybersecurity for remote work. Organizations often equip their employees with specialized security software, such as endpoint protection, firewalls, or secure email clients, to safeguard their devices from malware and cyberattacks. Employees should be encouraged and, in some cases, required to use these tools to ensure they operate within the company's defined security perimeter. This minimizes the risk of introducing vulnerabilities through personal software or applications that may not meet the company's security standards. For example, a company-approved antivirus program ensures that the device is continually monitored for threats and automatically receives updates to avoid emerging risks. Furthermore, these tools are often configured to integrate with centralized monitoring systems, allowing security teams to track and manage security incidents more effectively. By standardizing security tools across all remote devices, businesses can maintain better control over their cybersecurity posture.

Separating personal and work devices is an important practice for employees who work from home. Many remote workers use personal devices for professional and personal tasks, which can increase the likelihood of a security breach. Personal devices may not have the same security features as company-issued devices. They can be exposed to risks such as malware from non-work-related activities, such as downloading unsafe apps or browsing unsecured websites. Employees can ensure that work-related files and communications remain secure by separating work and personal devices.

Additionally, IT departments can more easily manage and monitor work devices, applying company-wide security policies and updates without interference from personal software or usage habits. Using dedicated work devices also reduces the chance of accidental data leakage, such as sending a work-related email from a personal account or storing sensitive files on a personal cloud service. This separation is essential for maintaining security and productivity in a remote work environment.

Secure file sharing and collaboration tools are essential for remote teams to work efficiently while maintaining a strong cybersecurity posture. When employees work from home or other remote locations, securely sharing files is often necessary. Without the right protections, sending sensitive documents through unsecured email or file-sharing services can expose them to unauthorized access. To mitigate these risks, organizations should provide employees with secure file-sharing platforms with encryption and user access controls. For example, cloud-based collaboration tools such as Google Drive or Microsoft OneDrive offer encryption in transit and at rest, protecting data during transfer and storage on the platform. Additionally, these tools often allow for granular permissions, ensuring only authorized users can view or edit sensitive documents. By standardizing secure file-sharing and collaboration tools, businesses can enable remote workers to collaborate safely without sacrificing efficiency.

Policies for remote work security provide the framework for maintaining consistent cybersecurity practices across a distributed workforce. These policies should clearly outline employee expectations regarding device usage, secure access to corporate networks, and handling of sensitive data. For example, a policy might mandate encryption for devices that store sensitive information or require regular updates and patches for all software used in the remote environment. It's also crucial that remote workers understand the risks of using unsecured networks, such as public Wi-Fi, and the steps they should take to protect their data when working in these environments. Remote work security policies should also address the use of personal devices and ensure that employees follow security protocols, such as using strong passwords, enabling firewalls, and keeping software up to date. Regularly updating and reviewing these policies ensures they evolve with new threats and emerging technologies, keeping remote work environments secure over time.

Training on security best practices for telecommuting is key to ensuring that remote workers are well-prepared to handle the security challenges they may face. Many cyberattacks, such as phishing or social engineering scams, rely on human error rather than technical vulnerabilities. Therefore, educating employees about common attack methods and how to recognize suspicious activities is essential. Regular security awareness training should cover identifying phishing emails, securing home networks, and safely handling sensitive information. Employees should also be taught the importance of using strong, unique passwords and the role of (MFA) in protecting their accounts. Beyond initial training, businesses should implement awareness campaigns and refresher courses to keep security top-of-mind. The more employees understand the potential risks and the measures they can take to prevent cyber incidents, the more secure the organization will be.

Ask the AI

"What are the most secure methods for sharing files between remote team members?"
"How can I configure (MFA) for remote access tools?"
"What are key components of an effective remote work security policy?"

In addition to formal training, promoting a security culture within the organization can further strengthen cybersecurity for remote work. This means encouraging employees to report any suspicious activities or potential security breaches and ensuring they feel supported. Establishing clear channels for reporting security concerns and creating a non-punitive environment where employees are not afraid to speak up can greatly enhance an organization's ability to respond to and mitigate threats. Including security metrics as part of performance reviews is also beneficial, emphasizing the importance of individual responsibility when protecting organizational assets. When employees feel empowered and informed, they are more likely to follow best practices and contribute to a collective effort to strengthen cybersecurity across the remote workforce.

Lastly, it's crucial to implement robust data backup and disaster recovery procedures for remote workers. Accidents and breaches can still occur even with the best security protocols in place. Ensuring that employees regularly back up their work, particularly critical files, is key to maintaining business continuity. In a cyberattack, such as a ransomware attack, having backups available can make the difference between a minor inconvenience and a major disruption to operations. These backups should be encrypted and stored in secure locations, ideally on-site and in the cloud, to protect data from unauthorized access and loss. By prioritizing data protection and disaster recovery in the remote work environment, businesses can minimize the impact of security incidents and continue to operate smoothly even in the face of adversity.

Securing Online Gaming and Virtual Reality Platforms

With its vast communities and immersive experiences, the online gaming world has become a prime target for cybercriminals, and users must be vigilant about the risks involved. Account theft is one of the most common threats in online gaming communities. Attackers may attempt to steal gaming credentials to access valuable in-game items, such as rare skins, coins, or other digital assets. These stolen accounts can also be sold on the dark web for profit. In addition to account theft, harassment is rampant in many gaming environments, whether through direct verbal abuse, cyberbullying, or inappropriate behavior in virtual spaces. These risks are not limited to the gameplay itself but extend into social interactions, where personal information might be exposed or used against the player. As gaming communities grow, understanding the security threats is critical for anyone participating in online or virtual reality (VR) platforms.

To protect gaming accounts from unauthorized access, one of the most fundamental steps is using strong, unique passwords. A strong password is typically a combination of uppercase and lowercase letters, numbers, and special characters, and it should not be easily guessable. Reusing passwords across multiple platforms is risky, especially when gaming accounts contain personal information or valuable digital goods. In addition to strong passwords, enabling MFA provides a critical layer of security. MFA requires users to authenticate their identity using two or more verification methods, such as a one-time code sent to a phone or an authentication app. This ensures that even if a hacker steals your password, they still need access to your secondary authentication method, making unauthorized access much harder. Combining strong passwords with MFA is one of the most effective ways to safeguard gaming accounts and ensure that only authorized users can access them.

Scams and fraudulent in-game transactions are another significant risks in online gaming. Cybercriminals are adept at exploiting players' desire for in-game items or currency, often through fraudulent websites or deceptive offers. For example, an attacker may impersonate a game developer or popular gamer, offering special deals on rare items or discounted in-game purchases.

These scams are frequently executed through phishing attacks, where a user is tricked into entering their login credentials or personal information on a fake website that appears legitimate. It's essential to be wary of offers that seem too good to be true and double-check the legitimacy of third-party websites or links shared during gameplay. Additionally, many games offer in-game currencies that can be purchased with real money, making avoiding fraudulent services or unauthorized third-party sellers even more crucial. Players can significantly reduce their risk of falling victim to scams by sticking to trusted platforms and ignoring unsolicited offers.

Managing communication settings in gaming platforms is another important aspect of securing your gaming experience. Both voice and text communication features are integral to many multiplayer games and virtual reality platforms, but they can also be a source of exposure to toxic behavior or harassment. It is advisable to adjust communication settings to limit who can send messages or initiate voice chats. For example, many games allow players to filter messages from strangers or block unsolicited communication, which can reduce unwanted interactions. In addition, consider using a "push-to-talk" feature for voice chats to prevent other players from hearing background noise or other potentially sensitive conversations. For parents, setting appropriate controls on their children's communication options, such as restricting voice chat or text messages to friends only, is a practical way to mitigate risks. While open communication is a key part of the gaming experience, being mindful of who can access it is crucial for maintaining security and comfort.

Understanding privacy settings in virtual environments is another essential aspect of securing your gaming and VR experience. In many virtual worlds, players create avatars that represent them, and these avatars can interact with others in ways that might expose personal information. It's essential to review the privacy settings of any game or VR platform and ensure that personal details, such as real names or social media accounts, are not shared publicly by default. Players should also know location-sharing features in VR environments, as these can expose their real-world whereabouts if not properly configured. Most platforms allow users to control who can see their activities, make friend requests, or even join their virtual spaces, giving players the power to customize their privacy levels. It's important to regularly audit these settings to ensure they remain aligned with your comfort level regarding data sharing and social interactions.

Recognizing and reporting toxic behavior is essential for maintaining a safe and enjoyable gaming environment for all users. Toxic behavior in gaming can range from simple verbal abuse to more severe forms of harassment or exploitation. While many gaming platforms have built-in reporting features, players should be familiar with using these tools effectively to report misconduct. It's important to take action for personal safety and the well-being of others in the community. Many platforms have dedicated moderation teams that review reports of harassment or other negative behavior, and taking the time to report incidents can help improve the overall environment for everyone. Reporting toxic behavior helps create a more positive atmosphere where players can enjoy the game without fear of harassment or exploitation. In some cases, reporting can lead to swift action, such as account suspensions or bans, helping to deter future bad actors.

Furthermore, many players may not realize that the social aspect of gaming often comes with its security risks. For example, sharing too much personal information during gameplay, whether through voice chat or in-game messaging, can leave players vulnerable to identity theft or social engineering attacks. Attackers may use seemingly innocent conversations to gather details like a player's real name, location, or the names of family members, which can later be used to exploit them. In some cases, attackers have used this information to launch targeted phishing campaigns, attempting to trick players into revealing their login credentials or installing malicious software. To mitigate this, players should be mindful of what they share, especially in open or public chats, and avoid providing personal information unless it is safe. Using a pseudonym or anonymized gamer tag instead of real names is one simple step that can significantly reduce the risk of social engineering attacks.

Parents or guardians must take an active role in managing the security and safety of children who game online. Many platforms offer parental control features that allow you to restrict communication, limit screen time, and monitor in-game activity. Setting up these parental controls is essential in ensuring that young gamers are not exposed to inappropriate content or harmful interactions. Additionally, it is crucial to discuss online safety with children and educate them about the risks of sharing personal information or engaging with strangers in games. Parents can help their children enjoy the benefits of online gaming without falling victim to its risks by fostering an open dialogue and being proactive about security settings.

Recommendations

1. **Secure Your Home Network:** Start by changing the default credentials on your router and enabling WPA3 encryption for your Wi-Fi network. Update your router firmware regularly to ensure it is protected against the latest vulnerabilities. Consider disabling unnecessary features like remote management to reduce the attack surface. These actions form the foundation of a secure home network.

2. **Isolate IoT Devices:** Set up a separate guest network exclusively for IoT devices on your router, ensuring they are isolated from your primary network. This prevents compromised IoT devices from affecting your devices. Regularly update IoT device firmware and disable unnecessary features like remote access. Isolation adds an extra layer of protection against lateral attacks.

3. **Use Strong Passwords and MFA:** Always use unique, complex passwords for each account and enable MFA wherever possible. MFA provides a secondary verification layer, significantly reducing the risk of account compromise. Avoid reusing passwords across multiple accounts to limit the impact of breaches. These simple steps drastically improve your overall security posture.

4. **Avoid Public Wi-Fi Risks:** Never engage in sensitive activities, like online banking, while connected to public Wi-Fi. If you must use public Wi-Fi, connect through a VPN to encrypt your traffic and protect your data. Always verify the legitimacy of a network before connecting, as attackers often create rogue hotspots. These precautions mitigate the vulnerabilities associated with shared networks.

5. **Understand Encryption Basics:** Familiarize yourself with encryption methods like SSL/TLS for web traffic and AES for file protection. Use encryption to safeguard sensitive communications, files, and transactions. Consider tools that offer E2EE for messaging and cloud storage. Encryption ensures your data remains secure, even if intercepted.

6. **Report Toxic Behavior in Online Gaming:** Use in-game reporting tools to flag toxic behavior such as harassment or cheating. Reporting incidents helps moderators maintain a safe gaming environment for all players. Be proactive in fostering a positive community by holding others accountable for inappropriate actions. Your contributions can make the digital space safer.

7. **Secure Remote Work Access:** Implement secure remote access protocols, such as VPNs and MFA, to protect company data. Use company-provided security tools like endpoint protection software to safeguard your devices. Always separate personal and work devices to limit cross-contamination of vulnerabilities. These steps secure sensitive work environments in remote settings.

8. **Protect Gaming Accounts:** Use strong, unique passwords and enable MFA for all gaming accounts. Be cautious of phishing scams or suspicious offers that seem too good to be true. Regularly review and adjust your privacy and communication settings to minimize threat exposure. Securing your accounts protects your identity and valuable in-game assets.

9. **Adjust IoT Privacy Settings:** Regularly audit the privacy settings of IoT devices to ensure minimal data sharing. Disable features that are unnecessary for functionality, like remote management or location tracking. Use pseudonyms or anonymized information to avoid exposing personal details when setting up device profiles. Privacy-conscious configurations reduce the risk of exploitation.

10. **Stay Updated on Cybersecurity Trends:** Commit to staying informed about emerging threats and evolving best practices. Subscribe to trusted cybersecurity resources or updates to keep your knowledge current. Regularly revisit your security measures to ensure they align with new developments. Awareness and adaptability are key to long-term digital safety.

Conclusion

As we conclude this chapter on cybersecurity best practices, it's important to remember that the digital landscape constantly evolves. New threats emerge every day, and the tactics employed by cybercriminals are becoming more sophisticated. However, with the right knowledge and proactive approach, you can significantly reduce your vulnerability and protect your data and devices from compromise. Cybersecurity isn't just about reacting to threats—it's about creating a resilient system that anticipates risks and defends against them before they become problems.

The key takeaway from this chapter is that digital security is not a one-time task but an ongoing commitment. As you use technology daily, remember that securing your home network, managing your IoT devices, and safeguarding sensitive data through encryption are essential steps in building a comprehensive defense strategy. Each action is critical in keeping your digital life safe and secure. Adhering to the best practices outlined here ensures that your devices, data, and communications remain protected from unauthorized access and exploitation.

Equally important is the recognition that digital security is a shared responsibility. While individuals have the power to implement strong security measures on their devices and networks, it's crucial to stay informed about the latest developments in cybersecurity. As technology advances, so will the methods cybercriminals use to exploit vulnerabilities. Staying educated on emerging threats and regularly updating your security practices is key to maintaining a strong defense in an ever-changing environment.

It's also essential to remember that cybersecurity is not solely about technology but behavior and habits. The daily decisions you make, from the passwords you choose to how you handle public Wi-Fi networks, directly impact your security. Simple actions, like enabling (MFA), changing default passwords on IoT devices, or using a VPN on public networks, can prevent unauthorized access. Incorporating these habits into your daily routine can dramatically reduce the likelihood of falling victim to a cyberattack.

As we look ahead, it's clear that digital security will remain a critical aspect of modern life. Whether for personal or professional use, our digital tools must be protected to preserve our privacy and safeguard our financial and personal information. This chapter has provided a toolkit of strategies to protect yourself in a digital world, from securing your home network to leveraging encryption for safe online transactions. By applying these principles, you can confidently navigate the online world, knowing that you've taken the necessary steps to secure your digital life.

Building a secure digital environment ultimately combines understanding risks, implementing preventive measures, and cultivating good habits. The technologies you use may continue to change, but the core principles of cybersecurity remain the same. Armed with the knowledge from this chapter, you now have the tools to build a strong foundation for your digital safety. As cyber threats evolve, staying vigilant and informed will help you maintain control over your personal and professional digital space.

Chapter Questions

1   What is the most effective way to protect your home Wi-Fi network from unauthorized access?
    A. Use the default router credentials
    B. Enable WPA3 encryption
    C. Disable network encryption
    D. Share your password with trusted friends

2   Why is it important to regularly update your router firmware?
    A. To improve the speed of your internet connection
    B. To fix known vulnerabilities and enhance security
    C. To reduce your data usage
    D. To enable automatic password changes

3   What is one key reason for creating a guest network for IoT devices?
    A. To boost internet speed for all devices
    B. To isolate IoT devices from the primary network
    C. To allow unlimited access to all network devices
    D. To share your primary network password easily

4   How does MFA enhance account security?
    A. It reduces the need for strong passwords
    B. It provides an additional layer of verification
    C. It eliminates the need for password changes
    D. It automatically blocks phishing attempts

5   What is the primary risk of using public Wi-Fi without a VPN?
    A. Reduced internet speed
    B. Increased data usage
    C. Exposure to man-in-the-middle attacks
    D. Difficulty in connecting to websites

6   What should you verify before connecting to a public Wi-Fi network?
    A. That the network name matches an official source
    B. That the signal strength is strong
    C. That no password is required for connection
    D. That the network offers free streaming services

7 What does E2EE ensure?
   A. Only the sender and recipient can access the communication
   B. The server can modify the content during transmission
   C. Messages can be accessed by any device on the network
   D. Data is encrypted only when it reaches the recipient

8 Why should IoT device default credentials always be changed?
   A. Default credentials are complex and hard to use
   B. Default credentials are easy for attackers to find online
   C. Changing them decreases device performance
   D. Changing them increases your internet speed

9 What is a phishing scam in online gaming?
   A. Offering legitimate in-game rewards
   B. Attempting to steal personal or account information
   C. Helping players achieve a higher rank
   D. Advertising new game updates

10 Why is "push-to-talk" recommended for voice communication in gaming?
   A. It allows you to talk to everyone at all times
   B. It minimizes unwanted noise and unintended speech
   C. It disables all voice communication
   D. It enhances the quality of your microphone

11 How does a VPN protect your internet traffic?
   A. It increases your internet speed
   B. It encrypts your data and hides your IP address
   C. It disables public Wi-Fi connections
   D. It creates an open network for all devices

12 What should you avoid sharing during gaming interactions?
   A. In-game achievements
   B. Personal information, like your real name or location
   C. Your gaming preferences
   D. Game settings

13 What is the role of firmware updates for IoT devices?
   A. They improve the device's aesthetics
   B. They patch security vulnerabilities
   C. They reset the device to factory settings
   D. They decrease energy consumption

14 What should be included in a remote work security policy?
   A. Requirements for password length and MFA usage
   B. A list of recommended games to play during breaks
   C. A schedule for remote team meetings
   D. Instructions for downloading unverified software

15 Why is it essential to report toxic behavior in online gaming?
- **A.** To help moderators maintain a safe gaming environment
- **B.** To block game updates for the user causing harm
- **C.** To increase in-game currency rewards
- **D.** To disable voice chat for all players

17

Safeguarding Your Financial Assets and Secure Online Transactions

With the increasing use of digital banking, online shopping, and cryptocurrency trading, protecting financial assets from cyber threats is paramount. Cybercriminals are constantly evolving tactics, making it crucial for individuals to adopt proactive measures to safeguard their financial information. The risks of identity theft, fraud, and account hijacking are ever-present, and without a robust understanding of cybersecurity practices, one's digital financial life can become vulnerable to attack.

This chapter aims to provide readers with practical and actionable insights on defending their digital finances against the growing threat of cybercrime. Whether securing online banking accounts, avoiding online shopping scams, or protecting cryptocurrency assets, this chapter covers a wide range of topics essential to financial cyber safety. The goal is to offer awareness of potential threats and arm readers with the tools and knowledge to prevent and respond to cyberattacks. By integrating these best practices, individuals can significantly reduce their exposure to financial risks while engaging confidently in the digital economy.

Throughout this chapter, we will explore various security measures that can be implemented to protect financial transactions, whether on banking platforms, e-commerce sites, or cryptocurrency exchanges. Key practices such as multi-factor authentication (MFA), recognizing fraudulent offers, and securely managing financial data will be explained in detail. Readers will also learn about the importance of differentiating between secure and insecure methods of conducting financial transactions and how to spot the telltale signs of scams and fraud. Strong passwords, encrypted communications, and digital wallets are just some of the strategies that will be discussed to help fortify your financial security.

The digital landscape may be convenient, but it also has inherent risks that must be understood and mitigated. This chapter empowers individuals to take control of their financial safety, making informed decisions about securing their online presence and managing their financial assets. With the right practices, users can confidently navigate the online world without falling victim to common pitfalls and cyber threats. Let's dive into the key steps for safeguarding digital wealth and maintaining a secure financial future.

Secure Online Banking Practices

In the digital age, securing online banking accounts is not merely a matter of convenience; it's a vital necessity. The growing sophistication of cyber threats means that financial accounts are prime targets for criminals, and any lapse in security can have severe consequences. To access your bank accounts securely, start by ensuring you are using a trusted, encrypted connection.

Always access your bank's website by typing the URL directly into your browser rather than clicking on links from unsolicited emails or messages. Ensure the site uses HTTPS encryption, which is visible as a padlock icon next to the URL. If you ever notice that the website URL is misspelled or the connection is not secure, do not attempt to log in, as this could be a phishing attempt. Table 17.1 outlines common online banking security practices, providing key strategies to protect financial transactions and personal information.

Table 17.1 Common online banking security practices.

Security practice	Description	Importance	Additional notes
Use MFA	Enable MFA for extra security by requiring two or more verification methods (e.g., password + code from phone).	It adds an extra layer of protection beyond just a password.	Most banks support MFA through apps or SMS.
Create strong, unique passwords	Use long passwords (12+ characters) that combine letters, numbers, and symbols, and avoid using the same password for multiple accounts.	Harder for attackers to guess or crack using brute force.	Consider using a password manager for secure storage.
Monitor account activity	Regularly review your bank statements and account activity to identify unauthorized transactions.	Early detection helps to mitigate losses and stop fraud.	Set up account alerts for transactions above a certain threshold.
Use secure Wi-Fi connections	Avoid accessing online banking via public Wi-Fi networks as they are vulnerable to cyberattacks.	Public Wi-Fi networks can expose sensitive data to hackers.	Use a VPN when accessing financial accounts on public networks.
Enable account alerts	Set up alerts for transactions, logins, and large withdrawals to monitor for suspicious activity.	Helps detect unusual or unauthorized activity quickly.	Set alerts for both email and SMS notifications.
Keep your software updated	Ensure your browser, antivirus, and operating system are up-to-date with the latest patches and security features.	Outdated software can have vulnerabilities that cybercriminals exploit.	Set automatic updates for all security software.
Use strong encryption on devices	Ensure that all devices used for banking, such as smartphones and computers, are encrypted.	Encryption makes it difficult for unauthorized users to access data.	Most smartphones and laptops have encryption settings that can be enabled.
Log out after each session	Always log out of your online banking account when you are finished to prevent unauthorized access.	Prevents session hijacking when a device is left unattended.	Make sure your device is locked when not in use.
Check bank's security policies	Review the bank's security policies and terms of service to understand how they protect your data.	Being informed helps you understand what actions to take if your account is compromised.	Look for encryption, fraud prevention policies, and data protection guarantees.
Use secure password recovery options	Set up strong, alternative ways to recover your password, such as security questions or secondary email addresses.	Prevents unauthorized password resets and account access.	Avoid using easily guessed answers for security questions (e.g., your mother's maiden name).

One of the most insidious forms of cybercrime is phishing, where criminals impersonate your bank or financial institution to steal your personal information. Legitimate communications from banks usually follow a predictable pattern. They will never ask you to provide sensitive information like passwords, Social Security numbers, or PINs through email or text. If you receive a suspicious message asking for these details or if the communication appears urgent, it's important to exercise caution. Instead of responding directly, contact your bank through official channels using the contact details on their verified website or in their official app. Be particularly wary of emails or messages with spelling errors or unusual formatting, which are often red flags indicating fraud.

Setting up alerts for account activity is one of the most effective ways to stay on top of suspicious transactions. Most financial institutions offer free services to notify you of various activities on your account, such as large withdrawals, deposits, or any login attempts from new devices. By enabling these alerts, you can quickly spot unauthorized activity and act before the damage becomes significant. Some banks even allow you to customize the alerts, choosing which types of transactions trigger notifications. Setting alerts for all activities ensures you continuously monitor your account, reducing the chances of fraud slipping through the cracks.

Banking over public Wi-Fi is risky, and it's best avoided whenever possible. Public Wi-Fi networks, such as those in cafes or airports, are generally unsecured and easy targets for hackers. Cybercriminals can intercept the data you send and receive over these networks, including sensitive information like bank login credentials. If you must access your banking information while on the go, consider using a virtual private network (VPN). A VPN encrypts your internet connection, making it far more difficult for attackers to eavesdrop on your online activities. However, even with a VPN, limiting banking to more secure, private networks is still safer when possible.

Regularly reviewing statements and transactions is essential to ensuring that your financial accounts remain secure. It's easy to get caught up in the daily rush of life and overlook discrepancies in your bank statements. However, overlooking these can allow fraud to go unnoticed for extended periods. Review your statements monthly, paying close attention to any unfamiliar charges. If you notice discrepancies or transactions that do not align with your activity, contact your bank immediately to dispute the charges. Many banks offer tools that allow you to easily track and categorize your spending, making it easier to spot anomalies.

Being proactive and reporting suspicious activity immediately can make all the difference in minimizing damage from potential fraud. If you suspect your account has been compromised or notice unfamiliar transactions, don't hesitate to contact your bank's fraud department. Many financial institutions have 24/7 customer support to handle such issues. The quicker you report suspicious activity, the more likely you are to prevent further unauthorized access and recover any lost funds. In some cases, your bank may temporarily freeze your account while they investigate, which adds another layer of protection in the event of fraud.

Cybersecurity is all about layers of defense, and securing your online banking is no different. A critical layer in protecting your account is using strong, unique passwords for each banking service you access. Consider using a password manager to generate and store complex passwords, ensuring you don't reuse passwords across multiple sites. In addition to strong passwords, enable

---

Ask the AI

"What strong passphrases combine letters, numbers, and symbols?"
"What are the risks of using personal information, like birthdates or names, in passwords?"
"Can password length make a password more secure? How does length impact security?"

MFA whenever possible. MFA provides an additional security barrier by requiring something you know (like a password) and something you have (like a phone or authentication app) to access your account. Implementing these measures significantly reduces the chances of unauthorized access to your banking information.

Finally, it's crucial to remain vigilant about the evolving nature of cybersecurity threats. Cybercriminals are constantly refining their tactics, and what worked for securing your accounts yesterday may not be sufficient tomorrow. Regularly check your bank's website for updates on security measures, and consider subscribing to any alerts or newsletters they offer. Staying informed and adjusting your practices accordingly can make a huge difference in the effectiveness of your online banking security. Additionally, participating in online security webinars or training can help you understand the latest threats and keep your defense practices sharp.

Safe Online Shopping

Regarding e-commerce, the convenience of shopping from home comes with the responsibility of safeguarding your personal and financial information. To verify the security of a website before making any purchases, ensure that the site uses encryption. The first thing to check is whether the URL begins with "https" rather than just "http"—the "s" stands for secure, meaning your data is encrypted during transmission. Additionally, look for a padlock symbol in the address bar, indicating the secure connection. Remember that if the website lacks these basic security features, it's best to reconsider purchasing, as the risks of exposing your payment information could be too high. Even seemingly reputable sites can sometimes fall short of basic security standards, so it's better to err on the side of caution. Table 17.2 lists signs of fraudulent online shopping sites, helping users identify potentially unsafe websites before making purchases.

Secure payment methods are another critical step in protecting yourself while shopping online. Credit cards offer more protection than debit cards, as most major credit card providers provide fraud protection services. In the event of unauthorized transactions, you can dispute charges more easily and often avoid liability. Payment services such as PayPal, Apple Pay, or Google Pay provide an extra layer of security by keeping your financial details hidden from the vendor. When using these services, your payment information is not directly shared with the seller, minimizing the risk of exposure. It's also wise to avoid using wire transfers or sending money directly to individuals, as these methods often offer little to no recourse if fraud occurs.

Fraudulent offers and counterfeit goods are persistent issues in online shopping, and recognizing these threats can save you both money and frustration. One red flag is a deal that seems too good to be true—if an item is being offered at a price significantly lower than its typical market value, chances are it may be counterfeit or part of a scam. In addition to pricing, watch out for poorly written product descriptions, low-quality images, and vague seller information. Legitimate sellers usually provide clear and accurate descriptions, including brand names, materials, and detailed specifications. It's also wise to check the reviews, but be cautious—fake reviews are increasingly common, so look for reviews that offer detailed feedback and consider patterns that might indicate inauthentic responses.

During online transactions, protecting your payment information is essential. Avoid entering sensitive data on public or unsecured Wi-Fi networks whenever possible, as hackers can intercept the information you transmit. If you must shop in public spaces, consider using a VPN to encrypt your internet connection. Additionally, never save your credit card details directly on websites, as doing so can expose you to future risks if the website experiences a security breach. Many retailers offer guest checkout options, which allow you to complete your purchase without creating

Table 17.2 Signs of fraudulent online shopping sites.

Red flag	What to look for	Why it's a concern	Action to take
Unrealistic discounts	Prices are significantly lower than usual (e.g., 90% off retail).	These could indicate counterfeit goods, low-quality products, or a scam site.	Avoid purchasing from sites offering deals that seem too good to be true.
Lack of contact information	No phone number, email address, or physical address on the website.	A legitimate store should provide clear ways to contact customer service.	Check the site's "About Us" or "Contact" page for information. If none exists, proceed with caution.
Missing or poor website security	No HTTPS encryption or a missing padlock symbol in the browser's address bar.	Without encryption, your payment details and personal information are vulnerable to hackers.	Look for HTTPS and a padlock icon before entering any sensitive information.
Generic website design	The website design looks unprofessional, with low-quality images, broken links, or incorrect grammar.	Fraudulent websites may use poor design to hide their lack of legitimacy.	Always verify the store's website and check for professional design and proper grammar.
No return or refund policy	No clear return or refund policy on the website.	This means you may not be able to get your money back if the product is defective or if you're dissatisfied.	Read the store's policies before purchasing, especially regarding returns and refunds.
Only one payment method	Only offers one payment method, often a direct bank transfer or untraceable payment method like cryptocurrency.	Scammers prefer untraceable methods to avoid being caught.	Stick to secure payment options like credit cards or trusted payment services like PayPal.
Too much personal information required	Asks for more personal information than necessary for a purchase (e.g., social security number, mother's maiden name).	Scammers often collect this data for identity theft or resale.	Never provide unnecessary personal information to a website, especially unrelated to the transaction.
Fake reviews	Overly positive or generic reviews with little detail or no real user feedback.	Fake reviews can mislead consumers into purchasing counterfeit or substandard goods.	Check reviews on independent websites and avoid stores with no authentic customer feedback.
Suspicious domain name	The website domain name looks slightly off (e.g., "onlinestore.com" vs. "onlinestore.co").	Fraudulent sites often use minor variations of legitimate domain names to trick customers.	Always double-check the URL for correct spelling and domain extension.
Poor customer support response	The customer support team takes a long time to respond or does not answer inquiries.	A legitimate business should respond quickly and professionally to customer inquiries.	If support is non-responsive, it's best to avoid completing your purchase on that site.

an account. By choosing this option, you can minimize the amount of personal information you share, which is especially important if you're unfamiliar with the site.

Understanding online stores' refund and return policies is crucial before making any purchase. Some online retailers may make returning products difficult by charging high restocking fees or imposing time limits on returns. Others may have vague or unclear policies, making it hard to know your options should the product fail to meet expectations. Always review the return policy before buying; if possible, look for stores offering free returns or exchanges. Additionally, when dealing with physical goods, ensure that the website clearly explains how refunds are processed and whether shipping costs will be covered in the case of a return. A good return policy reflects a company's confidence in its product and customer service standards, so it should be a factor in your decision-making process.

Another key aspect of safe online shopping is keeping detailed records of your purchases and communications. Whether you shop on a large marketplace or a niche website, always save receipts, order confirmations, and any correspondence with the seller. Many online retailers provide order tracking numbers and digital invoices as proof of purchase. These records will be invaluable if you need to return an item or dispute a charge. Additionally, keeping track of your communication with customer service can help resolve issues more quickly. If a seller promises a refund or replacement, having written documentation can ensure they follow through on their commitment.

When shopping from smaller or less-known online vendors, please proceed cautiously and take extra steps to confirm their legitimacy. One way to do this is by searching for third-party reviews of the site and checking for any associated complaints or scams. There are several independent review platforms where customers share their experiences, which can help you gauge whether a particular retailer is trustworthy. Also, look at the website's "About Us" page; legitimate businesses usually provide detailed information about their history, contact details, and customer support channels. If this information is missing or hard to find, it's a red flag, and you may want to think twice before making a purchase.

Before completing a purchase, double-check the website's shipping policies and potential fees. Unexpected shipping charges or delivery delays are common complaints in the e-commerce world, and it's essential to know what you're agreeing to before you place an order. Some websites offer free shipping on orders above a certain amount, but always read the fine print to ensure no hidden fees. Additionally, confirm the expected delivery date, particularly important for time-sensitive purchases, such as gifts or urgent supplies. Understanding shipping policies upfront can help prevent frustration and avoid misunderstandings with sellers.

Protecting Against Financial Fraud

Financial fraud is one of the most common and damaging threats in the digital age, affecting millions of individuals worldwide. Scammers employ a variety of tactics to steal personal and financial information, ranging from sophisticated online schemes to more traditional methods like telephone scams. One of the most widespread financial scams is the "advance-fee fraud," where fraudsters convince victims to pay upfront for a service or investment that never materializes. Others include

---

Ask the AI

"How can I recognize a legitimate e-commerce website versus a fraudulent one?"
"What are the common signs of counterfeit goods sold online?"
"Why is HTTPS important for ensuring a secure shopping experience?"

fake lotteries, prize winnings, or fake charities that lure individuals into providing sensitive financial details. To protect yourself, always verify the legitimacy of unsolicited offers, and never send money or disclose personal information to anyone you don't trust. A good rule of thumb is that if it sounds too good to be true, it probably is. Table 17.3 outlines types of financial fraud and provides strategies on how to avoid them, helping protect individuals from financial scams.

Phishing remains one of the most popular methods of financial fraud, and its tactics are constantly evolving. In phishing schemes, attackers often pose as legitimate entities, such as banks, credit card companies, or government agencies, to trick you into revealing sensitive information like login credentials, account numbers, or Social Security numbers. These attempts can come in emails, text messages, or phone calls that appear authentic, often using familiar logos or official-looking language. Always verify the sender's email address to avoid phishing, particularly if the communication requests immediate action, such as clicking a link or providing personal details. Never click on links or open attachments in unsolicited emails, and when in doubt, contact the organization directly using verified contact information.

With the rise of digital wallets and payment apps, securely managing these tools has become increasingly important. Digital wallets, such as Apple Pay, Google Pay, and PayPal, are convenient, but they can also be targets for hackers. Many apps store sensitive information like credit card numbers, bank account details, and other personal data, making them appealing targets for cybercriminals. To protect your financial information, use strong, unique passwords for these accounts, and enable MFA whenever possible. Additionally, avoid using public Wi-Fi to access or transact with your digital wallet, as unsecured networks can expose your information to hackers. Regularly review your transaction history and notifications from your digital wallet apps to detect any unauthorized activity promptly.

Investment scams, including Ponzi schemes and fake cryptocurrency investments, have become increasingly prevalent as the financial landscape evolves. In a Ponzi scheme, early investors are paid returns using new investors' capital rather than legitimate profits, creating the illusion of a profitable business. These schemes eventually collapse when new investment slows or stops, leaving late investors with significant losses. To avoid such scams, always be wary of investment opportunities that promise unusually high returns with little risk. Reputable financial institutions and advisors will never guarantee profits, and you should always conduct thorough research before making any investments. Look for information from trusted sources and be skeptical of unsolicited investment offers, especially those that pressure you to act quickly.

Another common pitfall is unsolicited financial advice, which is often a gateway to fraud. Scammers may present themselves as financial experts, promising to manage your money or offer exclusive investment strategies that guarantee returns. These so-called advisors often prey on individuals unfamiliar with financial markets, exploiting their desire to grow their wealth quickly. To protect yourself, never act on unsolicited advice, especially if it involves large sums of money or risky ventures. Always verify the credentials of financial professionals before sharing any information or making decisions. Legitimate financial advisors will be registered with regulatory bodies such as the Securities and Exchange Commission (SEC) or the Financial Industry Regulatory Authority (FINRA). They will gladly provide their credentials upon request.

Ask the AI

"What are the most common phishing techniques targeting financial accounts?"
"How can phishing emails be designed to mimic legitimate organizations?"
"What are the key steps after falling victim to a phishing scam?"

Table 17.3 Types of financial fraud and how to avoid them.

Fraud type	Description	How to avoid it	Red flags
Phishing scams	Fraudulent emails or websites are designed to steal sensitive personal information like passwords or bank account details.	Never click on links from unsolicited emails or messages. Always verify the sender's authenticity.	Look for misspellings, unfamiliar domains, or unusual requests for sensitive info.
Investment scams	Fraudulent investment opportunities that promise high returns with little to no risk, often in the form of Ponzi schemes or fake ICOs.	Thoroughly research any investment before committing. Verify with official, regulated sources.	Promises of guaranteed returns, high-pressure tactics to invest quickly.
Credit card fraud	When a thief uses your credit card information to make unauthorized purchases or transactions.	Monitor your credit card statements regularly and set up alerts for transactions.	Unfamiliar charges or multiple small charges on your statement.
Identity theft	The theft of personal information such as your Social Security number, date of birth, or banking details to open new accounts or commit fraud.	Protect your personal information and monitor your credit report regularly.	Unfamiliar accounts or credit inquiries appearing on your credit report.
Online shopping fraud	Fraudulent online stores that sell counterfeit or nonexistent products, or steal your payment information.	Use secure payment methods and research retailers before purchasing.	Unrealistic discounts, lack of contact info, and suspiciously low prices.
Loan scams	Fraudsters offering loans with high fees or unaffordable repayment terms to trick victims into paying upfront fees.	Only work with reputable lenders and never pay upfront fees for loans.	Offers of "guaranteed" loans without a credit check or other signs of urgency.
Lottery and prize scams	Scammers claiming you've won a lottery or prize and asking for payment to claim the winnings.	Never send money to claim a prize or lottery winnings.	Requests for payment or personal details before you can claim the prize.
Charity scams	Fake charities asking for donations, often related to a natural disaster or a cause in the news.	Verify the charity through trusted sources before donating.	Pressure to donate immediately or vague details about the charity.
Tax fraud	Fraudsters impersonating tax agencies like the Internal Revenue Service (IRS), demanding immediate payment for back taxes, or threatening arrest.	Contact your tax authority directly to verify any claims. Never pay taxes over the phone.	Threats of arrest or deportation, demand for payment via unusual methods.
Business email compromise (BEC)	Fraudulent emails impersonating company executives or business partners to trick employees into making payments or sharing sensitive data.	Verify email requests through a secondary communication channel before responding.	Unusual email requests for wire transfers or sensitive data.

One of the most critical aspects of defending against financial fraud is reporting suspicious activity to the relevant authorities. Whether you've encountered a scam or believe your financial accounts may have been compromised, timely reporting can help mitigate further damage. Most financial institutions have dedicated fraud departments that can assist you in freezing your accounts, disputing fraudulent charges, and taking the necessary steps to protect your finances. Suppose you've been scammed or your identity has been stolen. In that case, it's also essential to report the incident to authorities, such as the Federal Trade Commission (FTC) or the Internet Crime Complaint Center (IC3). In some cases, filing a police report may also be necessary, particularly if a significant amount of money is involved. The faster you act, the better your chances of recovering lost funds and preventing further fraud.

In addition to taking immediate action when you detect fraud, implementing preventative measures can significantly reduce the likelihood of falling victim to scams in the future. For instance, regularly monitoring your bank and credit card statements for unauthorized transactions is a simple yet effective way to catch fraud early. Set up alerts for unusual transactions or large withdrawals, which can notify you of suspicious activity before it escalates. Additionally, consider subscribing to a credit monitoring service that can help you track any changes to your credit report and alert you to potential identity theft. The more proactively you monitor your accounts and financial data, the better your chances of detecting and stopping fraud before it becomes a serious issue.

Finally, it's essential to educate yourself about cybercriminals' various tactics and techniques. Financial scams are constantly evolving, and what worked for scammers yesterday may not work today. Keeping up with the latest trends in cyber fraud, whether through news outlets, security blogs, or trusted sources like the Federal Trade Commission, can help you stay one step ahead of criminals. Educating yourself also means spotting common red flags, such as high-pressure tactics, vague or evasive responses, and overly complicated processes designed to confuse or overwhelm you. The more you know about how these scams operate, the more empowered you'll be to protect yourself and your finances.

Understanding Cryptocurrency Security

Cryptocurrency and blockchain technology have fundamentally altered the landscape of digital finance, offering a decentralized and secure way to exchange value. At its core, cryptocurrency operates on blockchain, a distributed ledger that records transactions across multiple computers. This decentralized structure makes it resistant to censorship and fraud, as no single entity controls the system. Blockchain ensures that transactions are transparent, secure, and immutable, meaning they cannot be changed once recorded. However, despite its inherent security features, cryptocurrency is not immune to risks and requires an understanding of proper security practices to protect your assets fully. Figure 17.1 compares hot wallets versus cold wallets for cryptocurrency storage, illustrating the differences in security, accessibility, and use cases for each option.

While the decentralized nature of cryptocurrencies provides certain advantages, it also exposes users to a unique set of risks. Cybercriminals often target digital currencies due to their anonymous nature and potential for high value. The most prominent risk is the theft of cryptocurrency, which can occur through hacking exchanges, compromising wallet software, or exploiting vulnerabilities in user practices. Unlike traditional banking systems, cryptocurrency transactions are irreversible, and once funds are stolen, they are often lost without recourse. As the market for digital currencies continues to grow, so does the opportunity for bad actors to exploit weak points in the ecosystem. It's critical to stay vigilant and educated on the risks to avoid falling victim to these threats.

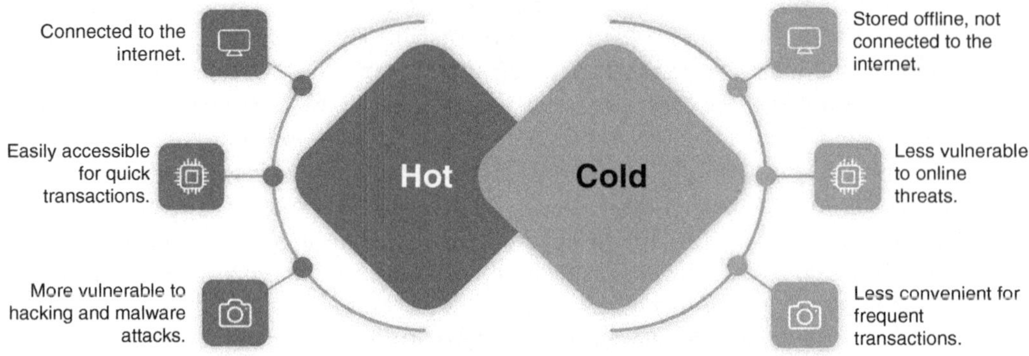

Figure 17.1 Hot wallets versus cold wallets for cryptocurrency storage.

One of the first steps in securing cryptocurrency holdings is understanding the difference between hot and cold storage. Hot wallets are connected to the internet and are often used for daily transactions. They offer convenience but present a higher risk of exposure to online attacks. On the other hand, cold storage refers to offline wallets, such as hardware wallets or paper wallets, which are far more secure because they are not directly connected to the internet. Cold storage is considered one of the safest cryptocurrency storage methods for long-term holdings. Keeping most of your assets in cold storage and only transferring small amounts to a hot wallet when necessary significantly reduces the risk of theft.

Securing private keys and recovery phrases is a fundamental aspect of cryptocurrency security. Private keys are essentially the passwords to your cryptocurrency wallet; losing them means losing access to your funds. Similarly, recovery phrases (often consisting of a series of words) act as a backup, enabling you to recover your wallet if your device is lost, stolen, or damaged. Both private keys and recovery phrases should be stored in a secure location, such as a safe or a hardware security device, and never shared with anyone. It is crucial to avoid storing them in digital formats, like text files, on your computer, as these can be compromised if your device is hacked. The security of your cryptocurrency is directly tied to the safety of these credentials, so treat them with the utmost care.

Cryptocurrency scams have become rampant recently, with fraudulent ICOs and Ponzi schemes targeting new and experienced investors. ICOs are often marketed as a way to invest in a new cryptocurrency project, but many of these projects are fraudulent or fail to deliver on their promises. Scammers often employ high-pressure tactics, promising huge returns with minimal risk, to entice investors into participating. To avoid falling victim to these schemes, it's important to research any cryptocurrency or ICO thoroughly before investing. Look for transparency regarding the project's leadership, business model, and technology. Be especially wary of projects that offer little to no verifiable information and promise "guaranteed" returns—such claims are red flags that the opportunity may not be legitimate.

Beyond scams, several other fraudulent practices within the cryptocurrency ecosystem include pump-and-dump schemes and phishing attacks. In pump-and-dump schemes, the price of a

---

Ask the AI

"What is the difference between a hot wallet and a cold wallet in cryptocurrency storage?"
"How can I securely back up my cryptocurrency recovery phrase?"
"What are the signs of a fraudulent Initial Coin Offering (ICO)?"

cryptocurrency is artificially inflated through coordinated buying, only to be "dumped" once the price has spiked, leaving unsuspecting investors with worthless assets. Phishing attacks often involve fraudulent websites or emails that trick users into revealing their private keys or login credentials. Always double-check URLs, use two-factor authentication (2FA), and avoid clicking on links from unknown sources to protect yourself. Staying informed and skeptical of high-risk ventures will help shield you from these financial traps.

As cryptocurrencies continue to gain popularity, it's essential to understand the legal and tax implications of owning and trading digital assets. Many governments and regulatory bodies worldwide are working to develop frameworks for regulating cryptocurrency transactions, which can vary significantly from one jurisdiction to another. In the United States, for example, the Internal Revenue Service (IRS) classifies cryptocurrency as property, meaning that transactions involving cryptocurrencies may be subject to capital gains taxes. For tax reporting purposes, it is crucial to keep detailed records of all your cryptocurrency transactions, including purchases, sales, and transfers. Failure to report cryptocurrency income or gains can lead to fines, penalties, or legal action. Consult with a tax professional familiar with cryptocurrency to ensure compliance with local laws and regulations.

Another important legal consideration involves the use of cryptocurrency exchanges. While exchanges provide an easy way to buy and sell digital currencies, they can also be vulnerable to hacking and other security risks. Additionally, many exchanges operate in a regulatory gray area, with some lacking proper oversight or operating in jurisdictions with weak consumer protections. When choosing an exchange, look for one that is regulated, has a solid reputation for security, and employs robust practices to protect user funds, such as cold storage for most assets. Also, consider using decentralized exchanges (DEXs), which allow peer-to-peer transactions without a centralized authority, further reducing the risk of a single point of failure.

To further enhance the security of your cryptocurrency holdings, consider using multi-signature wallets, which require more than one private key to authorize a transaction. This adds an extra layer of protection, as even if one key is compromised, the funds cannot be moved without the additional signatures. Multi-signature wallets can be especially useful for those managing significant amounts of cryptocurrency or for individuals wishing to share a wallet's control with trusted partners. By distributing the control of your assets across multiple parties, you mitigate the risk of losing everything due to a single point of failure.

Lastly, staying current on the latest developments in cryptocurrency security is essential. As the industry grows and matures, new threats and vulnerabilities continue to emerge. Subscribe to trusted cybersecurity and cryptocurrency news sources, and regularly review your security practices. Just as you wouldn't leave your home unlocked, you should never leave your digital assets unprotected. Regularly updating your software, employing the best security measures available, and maintaining a healthy skepticism toward unverified opportunities are key to securing your cryptocurrency and ensuring your digital wealth remains safe.

Planning for Financial Security

Diversifying financial assets is one of the most effective ways to mitigate risks in an increasingly digital and interconnected financial world. Relying on a single investment or savings vehicle can leave you vulnerable to unforeseen market shifts, cyberattacks, or fraud. By spreading your assets across different types of investments—such as stocks, bonds, real estate, and even alternative assets like cryptocurrencies or precious metals—you can reduce the impact of any single point of failure. This diversification helps shield your wealth from economic downturns and cyber threats that may target specific financial sectors or institutions. Regularly reviewing and adjusting your asset distribution in response to market changes and your personal risk tolerance will ensure a balanced approach to economic security.

While digital solutions dominate modern finance, it is essential to maintain physical copies of important documents in a secure location. Legal, medical, and financial documents—such as your will, tax records, insurance policies, and property deeds—are the foundation of your financial security. In the event of a cyberattack, power outage, or system failure, having access to hard copies can prevent you from being vulnerable. These documents should be stored in a safe, lockbox, or safety deposit box that is resistant to fire, water, and unauthorized access. It's also wise to store backup copies in a secure location outside your residence to protect against local disasters like theft or natural calamities. We live in a digital age, so securing physical records cannot be overstated.

When managing multiple accounts, separating spending, bill payments, and deposits across different accounts can significantly reduce the risk of widespread financial compromise. You create an additional layer of security by using one account solely for everyday spending and another for bill payments or deposits. Should one account be compromised, the others remain unaffected, minimizing the overall damage. For example, a separate savings account used solely for long-term goals and investments will remain secure if your checking account is hacked. Using a designated account for bills also ensures these critical payments are made on time, even if other accounts are temporarily inaccessible. This separation also aids in budgeting, as it's easier to track expenditures when funds are allocated to specific purposes.

Preparing for potential financial cyber incidents involves developing a comprehensive plan that addresses the immediate and long-term steps to take in the event of a breach. A financial cyber incident could include anything from identity theft and fraud to more severe attacks, such as hacking your bank or investment accounts. The first step is to ensure that all financial accounts are protected with strong, unique passwords and MFA. Maintaining a list of all your financial accounts, including usernames, account numbers, and emergency contacts, can help you act quickly should an incident occur. Having a fraud alert or credit freeze in place with major credit bureaus is also crucial to prevent identity thieves from opening accounts in your name. Finally, regularly reviewing your financial statements and monitoring accounts for suspicious activity can help identify issues before they escalate.

Educating family members about financial cyber safety is equally important, especially as younger generations and older family members may not be as familiar with the nuances of cybersecurity. The risk of an accidental security breach grows with family members often sharing devices and accounts. Ensuring that everyone understands the importance of strong passwords, safe browsing habits, and how to recognize phishing attempts will greatly reduce the likelihood of falling victim to fraud or identity theft. Implementing clear communication practices within the household, such as alerting one another to unusual account activity or unfamiliar emails, helps create a proactive defense. It's also important to educate older family members, who may be more susceptible to social engineering attacks, on recognizing scams and protecting their digital assets. Regular family discussions about cybersecurity, backed by actionable tips and common-sense guidelines, can serve as a defense against financial fraud.

Ask the AI

"How can I diversify my financial assets to minimize risk effectively?"
"What should be included in a financial cyber incident response plan?"
"What are the best resources for staying updated on emerging financial technologies?"

Staying informed about emerging financial technologies is essential for maintaining financial security in an ever-evolving landscape. Innovations such as blockchain, cryptocurrency, and digital banking are changing how we save, invest, and manage our money, and while they offer convenience, they also introduce new risks. Keeping up with these developments allows you to anticipate potential threats and adapt your financial strategies accordingly. Additionally, understanding the latest security protocols, such as biometric authentication and advanced encryption methods, can help you protect your assets in the digital realm. Regularly reading news about fintech developments, attending webinars, or joining professional forums focused on financial security can help you avoid cyber threats and spot opportunities for secure investments. By staying informed and adaptable, you can ensure that your financial security measures remain relevant and effective despite technological advancements.

Recommendations

1. **Enable MFA:** Add an extra layer of security to your online banking and financial accounts by enabling MFA. This process typically combines something you know (password) with something you have (a phone or app). MFA significantly reduces the chances of unauthorized access, even if your password is compromised.
2. **Create Strong and Unique Passwords:** Use passwords at least 12 characters long and combine letters, numbers, and symbols. Avoid using easily guessed information like birthdates or names, and ensure each account has a unique password. Consider using a password manager to generate and store these credentials securely.
3. **Verify E-commerce Website Security:** Before making an online purchase, check for HTTPS in the URL and a padlock symbol in the browser. These indicators show that the site encrypts your data during transmission. Avoid shopping on sites that lack these security features to prevent your payment information from being intercepted.
4. **Store Cryptocurrency Safely in Cold Wallets:** For long-term cryptocurrency holdings, use offline wallets and be less vulnerable to hacking. Avoid keeping large sums in hot wallets connected to the internet and more exposed to cyber threats. Cold storage ensures better protection for your digital assets.
5. **Monitor Financial Accounts Regularly:** Set up alerts for account activity, such as large withdrawals or login attempts from unknown devices. Regularly review your bank and credit card statements to spot unauthorized transactions early. Early detection and reporting can help prevent significant financial losses.
6. **Recognize and Avoid Phishing Scams:** Be cautious of unsolicited emails or messages that request sensitive financial information or direct you to click on suspicious links. Verify the sender's authenticity before responding to any requests. Phishing scams often mimic legitimate organizations, so scrutinize emails for inconsistencies.
7. **Separate Spending and Savings Accounts:** Use different accounts for everyday spending, bill payments, and long-term savings. This separation limits your exposure if one account is compromised. By segregating accounts, you protect critical funds, such as savings and bills, from being accessed in a breach.
8. **Educate Family Members on Cyber Safety:** Discuss the importance of secure online practices with family members, including recognizing phishing attempts and using strong passwords. This collective effort reduces the risk of financial cyber incidents. Encourage younger and older family members to stay informed about online safety.

9. **Stay Updated on Financial Cybersecurity Trends:** Regularly read about new cybersecurity threats and emerging financial technologies. Subscribe to reputable newsletters or forums that focus on financial cybersecurity. Staying informed ensures you can adapt your practices to address evolving threats.

10. **Secure Private Keys and Recovery Phrases:** For cryptocurrency users, store private keys and recovery phrases like a fireproof safe in a secure, offline location. Never share this information with others or store it digitally where it could be hacked. These credentials are the only way to access your cryptocurrency, making their security essential.

Conclusion

As we've explored throughout this chapter, the landscape of financial transactions has shifted dramatically into the digital realm, and with it, the complexity of securing our financial assets has increased. The opportunities for fraud, hacking, and data breaches are abundant, from online banking and shopping to cryptocurrency investments. However, with a clear understanding of cybersecurity principles and adopting best practices, individuals can significantly reduce the risks they face in these digital environments. The security of personal and financial data is not just the responsibility of institutions but also individuals who must be proactive in their approach to online safety.

The methods and strategies discussed in this chapter—such as implementing MFA, recognizing phishing scams, using secure payment options, and understanding the basics of cryptocurrency storage—are foundational to protecting financial assets. By integrating these measures into daily online activities, individuals create multiple layers of defense that can thwart potential cyberattacks. The key to financial cybersecurity is vigilance and continuous learning; as cyber threats evolve, so must the tools and strategies used to defend against them. Staying informed about emerging technologies, understanding the latest threats, and keeping security practices up to date are essential for long-term protection.

In addition to securing personal accounts and financial assets, extending this safety mindset to other areas of life, such as educating family members about financial cybersecurity, is crucial. Many cybercriminals target the less aware, often exploiting unsuspecting family members to gain access to personal accounts. Individuals can further fortify their defenses by cultivating a culture of cybersecurity awareness within the household. The protection of digital wealth requires not only personal diligence but also the collective effort of those closest to us.

Ultimately, the future of financial cybersecurity lies in the hands of individuals willing to take responsibility for their own safety. While the threats are real and daunting, the good news is that the tools and knowledge needed to secure one's financial life are readily available. By applying the practices and strategies outlined in this chapter, individuals can confidently navigate the digital financial world, knowing they are equipped to protect their assets from the many online threats. Financial cybersecurity is not just about reacting to threats but creating a secure digital environment where one's wealth and personal information are always safeguarded.

Chapter Questions

1 What is the primary purpose of enabling multi-factor authentication (MFA) for financial accounts?
   A. To save time during login
   B. To add a layer of security to the login process
   C. To allow password sharing
   D. To simplify account recovery

2 Why should passwords never include personal information like birthdates?
   A. Because they are too long
   B. Because they are difficult to remember
   C. Because they are easily guessed by attackers
   D. Because they are harder to type

3 What is a key indicator that an e-commerce site is secure?
   A. It has a colorful homepage
   B. It uses HTTPS encryption and shows a padlock icon
   C. It offers significant discounts
   D. It requires only basic payment details

4 What is one of the main benefits of cold wallets for cryptocurrency storage?
   A. They are connected to the internet for convenience
   B. They store cryptocurrency offline, making them harder to hack
   C. They allow automatic transactions
   D. They are compatible with mobile apps

5 Why should financial account activity be monitored regularly?
   A. To increase credit card limits
   B. To detect and address unauthorized transactions early
   C. To ensure your account balance grows
   D. To share updates with friends and family

6 What is a common feature of phishing emails?
   A. Offers of technical support
   B. Requests for sensitive information with urgent language
   C. Professional formatting and grammar
   D. Randomly generated subject lines

7 Why is it important to separate spending and savings accounts?
   A. To qualify for bank rewards
   B. To protect funds in case one account is compromised
   C. To avoid overdraft fees
   D. To simplify budgeting

8 What is the best way to secure private keys for cryptocurrency?
   A. Store them in an encrypted file on your computer
   B. Keep them in a secure, offline location like a fireproof safe
   C. Share them with a trusted friend for safekeeping
   D. Email them to yourself for backup

9 What should be included in a financial cyber incident response plan?
   A. Contact information for relevant financial institutions
   B. Details about cryptocurrency transactions
   C. Links to shopping websites
   D. Social media account credentials

10 What should you do if you suspect a phishing attempt targeting your financial information?
   A. Click on the link to confirm its legitimacy
   B. Report the email or message to the relevant institution
   C. Ignore the email and move on
   D. Share the email with family for advice

11 What is one way to recognize a fraudulent investment scheme?
   A. The scheme promises guaranteed high returns
   B. The company has a lengthy and complex business model
   C. The opportunity has average rates of return
   D. The scheme includes detailed market analysis

12 Why is it important to use strong, unique passwords for every financial account?
   A. To make them easy to remember
   B. To prevent unauthorized access if one password is compromised
   C. To reduce the time required for logging in
   D. To avoid sharing passwords with family members

13 How can family members help improve overall financial cybersecurity?
   A. By keeping passwords written down in a shared location
   B. By learning to recognize common cyber threats and scams
   C. By sharing a single financial account
   D. By using the same password for all accounts

14 What is one of the first steps in recognizing a phishing website?
   A. It requires logging in to confirm details
   B. It has a URL that matches the legitimate site exactly
   C. It uses slight misspellings or unusual domain extensions
   D. It offers multi-factor authentication for security

15 How can you stay informed about emerging financial technologies?
   A. Ignore them to reduce complexity
   B. Subscribe to reputable cybersecurity and financial news sources
   C. Use only traditional banking methods
   D. Rely on friends and family for updates

18

Protecting Your Data: Backups, Cloud Storage, and Disaster Recovery

As individuals and businesses generate, store, and share vast amounts of sensitive information daily, the need for strong cybersecurity practices has never been more apparent. Without proper digital defense measures, the risks of data breaches, loss, and theft increase exponentially, leading to potential financial losses, reputational damage, and legal liabilities. This chapter delves into the essential best practices for securing one's digital life, offering a comprehensive guide to building a robust cyber defense strategy.

At the core of digital safety is data protection. From securing personal files to safeguarding corporate databases, understanding how to manage, store, and dispose of data is crucial to preventing unauthorized access. This chapter emphasizes the importance of identifying and protecting critical data, implementing effective backup strategies, and planning for worst-case scenarios. It also covers the ethical and legal responsibilities individuals and businesses have when handling sensitive information, ensuring that privacy and compliance are maintained.

One of the most effective ways to mitigate cyber threats is by using cloud storage solutions securely. While cloud storage offers convenience and scalability, it also presents unique access control and data protection challenges. We will explore the advantages of cloud storage and the potential risks and provide actionable steps to ensure that your cloud environment remains secure. From configuring encryption settings to managing user access and permissions, the goal is to equip you with the knowledge to use cloud storage safely and effectively.

In addition to secure storage, disaster recovery planning is an essential component of any comprehensive cybersecurity strategy. Data loss can occur for many reasons, including hardware failures, cyberattacks, and human error. A well-structured disaster recovery plan allows quick data restoration and minimizes downtime, helping businesses and individuals bounce back from unforeseen events. This chapter will guide you through developing a disaster recovery plan, from identifying critical data to testing recovery processes and ensuring all backup systems work properly.

Finally, proper data disposal and destruction practices are often overlooked, but they are just as important as data protection and recovery. Simply deleting files or performing a factory reset is insufficient to ensure sensitive information is irretrievable. Whether securely erasing files from a hard drive or physically destroying old storage devices, this chapter will provide methods to safely dispose of data without leaving traces that cybercriminals could exploit. By following these best practices, you will protect your data and reduce your vulnerability to cyberattacks and data breaches.

Importance of Data Protection

In the modern digital landscape, data has become one of the most valuable personal and professional assets. Personal data such as financial information, personal identifiers, and communication history hold significant value in an individual's life. In contrast, professional data—from proprietary company information to customer data—can be the backbone of a business's operations. With this value, however, comes the responsibility to protect it. Whether an individual is trying to safeguard their files or a corporation securing client information, ensuring data remains private and accessible only to authorized users is an ongoing challenge. The rise of cyber threats, ranging from phishing to ransomware, highlights the crucial need for strong protective measures. Without adequate security, the risk of data breaches and leaks grows significantly, making data protection a priority for everyone who values their privacy. Table 18.1 outlines types of data deletion and destruction methods, providing effective techniques to ensure sensitive information is securely erased.

The risks associated with data loss can be both immediate and far-reaching. Hardware failures, whether due to aging components, natural disasters, or accidental damage, can cause critical data to become irretrievable. In addition to physical hardware failure, data is susceptible to malicious threats such as theft or malware attacks. Cybercriminals often target valuable data, stealing it for

Table 18.1 Types of data deletion and destruction methods.

Method	Description	Effectiveness	Best use case
Software-based overwriting	Using specialized software to overwrite data multiple times	High	When you need to erase data securely without physical destruction
Factory reset	Restoring the device to its original settings	Moderate	For devices you intend to reuse but need to clear user data
Degaussing	Using a magnetic field to scramble the data on a hard drive	High	For magnetic storage devices such as HDDs when permanent destruction is required
Physical destruction	Physically destroying the storage device	High	For devices that are no longer in use and need to be completely destroyed
Data wiping tools	Using dedicated tools designed to erase data permanently	High	For large-scale secure data erasure
Encryption prior to disposal	Encrypting data before disposal so it's unreadable without the decryption key	Moderate	For added protection in case data is recovered after deletion
Physical destruction of media	Physically shredding or crushing the storage device to prevent data recovery	High	When the device is no longer needed and can't be reused
Factory reset + data wiping	Combining factory reset with data-wiping software for enhanced security	High	For sensitive devices that need to be reused but with security guarantees
Cloud data deletion	Erasing data from cloud services through provider's mechanisms	Moderate	For cloud storage particularly when the data needs to be fully removed
Secure erasure	Using operating system-specific secure erasure features	Moderate	For individual file erasure before permanent deletion

financial gain or use in future attacks. Ransomware attacks, for example, lock users out of their data until a ransom is paid, demonstrating the vulnerability of critical systems. Even without direct cybercrime, poor management practices or accidental deletion can result in irreversible data loss, leading to significant disruption in personal and professional spheres.

From a legal and ethical standpoint, data management is a matter of good practice and compliance. Organizations must adhere to laws and regulations designed to protect sensitive information, such as the General Data Protection Regulation (GDPR) in the European Union or the California Consumer Privacy Act (CCPA) in the United States. These laws impose strict requirements for data collection, storage, and sharing, holding individuals and businesses accountable for any breaches. Beyond legal ramifications, there are ethical responsibilities tied to data protection. Individuals and companies must ensure they handle data with respect and transparency, gaining consent where necessary and using information only for its intended purpose. Failure to do so can damage reputation, cause loss of customer trust, and, in severe cases, cause legal action.

Data loss doesn't just impact the immediate technical environment; it profoundly affects productivity and personal life. In a business context, losing crucial data can halt operations, disrupt customer service, and undermine financial stability. For example, losing client data or project files can result in missed deadlines, lost revenue, and even legal liability. Losing personal data, like family photos, important documents, or financial records, can be devastating for individuals. Reconstructing lost data can be time-consuming and expensive, often with no guarantees of complete recovery. The emotional and financial toll of data loss serves as a reminder of the critical importance of safeguarding one's digital assets for security and peace of mind.

Understanding the data lifecycle is key to effectively managing and protecting data. From the moment data is created through emails, documents, or applications, it enters a cycle of creation, storage, and usage. Each stage of this lifecycle carries its own set of risks. During storage, for instance, data can be exposed to threats such as unauthorized access, while during usage, it could be compromised through insecure networks or outdated software. The final stage—disposal—can also pose a risk if data is not securely erased. Proper data lifecycle management ensures that data is handled appropriately at every stage, reducing the likelihood of a breach or loss. This also involves understanding how long data needs to be retained and when it should be archived or securely deleted to minimize exposure.

Data retention policies should be based on necessity, minimizing unnecessary storage of sensitive information. Retaining data longer than needed increases the potential for exposure, whether through accidental leaks or targeted attacks. On the other hand, inadequate data retention can lead to operational disruptions if important information is prematurely discarded. Both individuals and organizations need to understand the value of data over time and establish a clear retention policy. By ensuring that data is only kept for as long as it is useful and securely purging it once it is no longer needed, users can mitigate many of the risks associated with data management. Furthermore, regularly reviewing and updating retention policies ensures the approach meets current needs and legal requirements.

Ask the AI

"What are the consequences of improperly disposing of sensitive data in a business environment?"
"How do hardware failures typically lead to data loss, and what preventive measures can mitigate these risks?"
"What are the ethical considerations for businesses managing customer data securely?"

Planning for unforeseen events is a critical part of any data protection strategy. Natural disasters, system failures, or cyberattacks are unpredictable but inevitable occurrences that can affect anyone. A proactive plan is the ultimate defense against the chaos that can follow data loss. This plan should include creating regular backups of critical data, storing them in secure locations, and implementing recovery strategies. In addition, users should periodically test their backup systems to ensure data can be restored quickly and accurately in the event of a failure. In many cases, the ability to recover data swiftly can mean a minor inconvenience and a catastrophic loss of business continuity or personal information. Individuals and organizations can safeguard against the worst-case scenarios by anticipating the unexpected.

Effective Backup Strategies

A sound backup strategy is essential to protect data from unexpected loss. There are several backups to consider, each with its strengths and ideal use cases. Full backups involve copying all selected data and creating a complete snapshot at a given time. While they offer the most comprehensive coverage, they are also the most time-consuming and require significant storage space. On the other hand, incremental backups only capture changes made since the last backup, making them faster and more storage-efficient. Differential backups fall somewhere in between, capturing all changes since the previous full backup and balancing time and storage usage. Selecting the right backup type depends on the user's needs—whether they prioritize speed, storage efficiency, or comprehensive data protection.

When choosing between local and cloud backups, there are several factors to consider, such as convenience, security, and cost. Local backups, stored on external hard drives or network-attached storage (NAS), offer fast access and complete control over the backup process. However, they can be vulnerable to physical damage, theft, or failure. On the other hand, cloud backups store data off-site, providing the added benefit of remote access and protection from local disasters such as fires or floods. Cloud services also often include features such as automatic syncing and versioning, making it easier to recover older file versions. The decision between local and cloud backups should depend on the user's redundancy, convenience, and disaster recovery needs. For most, a hybrid approach combining local and cloud backups provides the best protection.

Scheduling regular backups automatically ensures that data is consistently protected without manual intervention. Many backup software solutions allow users to schedule backups at specific times—daily, weekly, or monthly—depending on the frequency of data changes. Automating this process eliminates the risk of human error, ensuring that backups happen regularly and without fail. It also reduces the burden of remembering to initiate backups manually, which can be especially crucial for businesses with large volumes of data or individuals with busy schedules. By setting up automatic backups, users can ensure their data is protected even if they forget or cannot back it up themselves. Regular backups also minimize the data lost during a system failure or disaster.

Verifying backup integrity and accessibility is an often overlooked but critical part of a backup strategy. Simply creating a backup is not enough; users must ensure that the backup is not corrupted and the data can be restored when needed. Backup software typically includes tools to verify the integrity of backups, checking for errors or issues during the backup process. In addition to integrity checks, it is essential to periodically test the backup by attempting a full restoration of data. This ensures that the backup files are accessible and usable, as backups can fail without immediately apparent signs. Routine verification minimizes the risk of discovering backup failures only when it's too late to recover lost data.

Encrypting backups adds an extra layer of protection against unauthorized access. If backup data is stored securely, it can still be vulnerable to hacking or theft. Encryption ensures that data is unreadable without the correct decryption key, making it significantly harder for cybercriminals to misuse stolen backup files. While many cloud services offer encryption by default, users should also ensure that their local backups are encrypted, especially if they contain sensitive personal or professional information. Encryption is a simple yet highly effective measure to protect backup data, especially if physical devices or cloud services are compromised. However, it's important to remember that the decryption key must also be securely stored, or else the user risks being locked out of their own data.

Storing backups in multiple secure locations further reduces the risk of data loss. A single backup, whether local or cloud-based, is susceptible to failure due to hardware issues, cyberattacks, or natural disasters. Users can mitigate the impact of a disaster affecting one backup source by distributing backups across multiple locations, such as a combination of local external drives, cloud storage, and even off-site physical locations. This redundancy principle ensures that if one backup fails or is compromised, another backup remains intact and accessible. A multi-location strategy might involve syncing backups across both on-premises devices and cloud-based services, allowing for fast recovery while providing long-term security. When it comes to data protection, the more redundancy, the better.

Secure Use of Cloud Storage

Cloud storage has become a cornerstone of modern data management, offering individuals and organizations an efficient way to store and access data remotely. One of the primary advantages of cloud storage is its convenience. Users can access their files from virtually any device with an internet connection, making it ideal for personal and professional use. Furthermore, cloud services often provide robust features like automatic backups, scalability, and built-in redundancy, ensuring that data is protected and available when needed. However, these advantages come with risks primarily related to security and privacy. As data is stored off-site, it is vulnerable to unauthorized access, hacking, and potential breaches. Additionally, relying on third-party providers means that users depend on the provider's security protocols and practices, which may not always meet personal or organizational standards. Table 18.2 presents a cloud storage security settings checklist, offering key steps to configure and enhance the security of cloud-based data storage.

Selecting a reputable cloud service provider is crucial to ensure the security and integrity of your data. Not all cloud storage solutions are created equal, and the wrong choice could expose sensitive information to unnecessary risk. When evaluating providers, users should consider the company's security features, such as data encryption, multi-factor authentication (MFA), and compliance with privacy regulations like the GDPR or the Health Insurance Portability and Accountability Act (HIPAA). A reputable provider should also offer clear terms of service detailing how data is handled, stored, and protected. Reviews, third-party audits, and certifications from recognized security

---

Ask the AI

"What are the differences in storage requirements for full, incremental, and differential backups?"

"How does automating backups reduce the risk of data loss compared to manual backups?"

"What are the benefits and challenges of combining local and cloud backup strategies?"

Table 18.2 Cloud storage security settings checklist.

Setting	Description	Recommendation	Best practices
Encryption	Ensures data is encrypted during storage and transit	Always enable encryption	Use AES-256 encryption for stronger security
Two-factor authentication (2FA)	Requires a second form of identification to access accounts	Enable 2FA on all accounts	Use an authenticator app instead of SMS for better security
Access control lists (ACLs)	Defines who can access specific files or directories	Set appropriate ACLs	Restrict access based on roles and need-to-know basis
Audit logs	Tracks access to data and activities in the system	Enable audit logs	Regularly review logs for any suspicious access or activities
Password policies	Defines requirements for user passwords	Enforce strong password policies	Require a mix of letters
Backup encryption	Encrypts backups of data stored in the cloud	Always use backup encryption	Use strong encryption standards such as AES-256
Sharing permissions	Controls who can share files or folders and with whom	Set sharing restrictions	Limit file sharing to trusted users or groups
Data residency	Ensures data is stored in a secure location and within regulatory guidelines	Choose cloud providers that comply with your country's data residency laws	Check where your data will physically reside before agreeing to terms
Versioning	Enables tracking changes and recovering older versions of data	Enable file versioning	Keep a reasonable history of versions to avoid data loss
API security	Ensures APIs interacting with cloud services are secure	Use secure API keys	Monitor API usage and restrict access using IP whitelisting

standards bodies (e.g., ISO 27001) can also provide valuable insight into a provider's reliability and trustworthiness. Ultimately, selecting a cloud service provider should be based on a combination of security, transparency, and the provider's ability to meet the user's specific needs.

Configuring security settings and access controls within cloud storage is vital in protecting your data from unauthorized access. By default, most cloud storage services allow for shared access, which can lead to accidental exposure of sensitive files. Users should take the time to configure security settings carefully, enabling features such as encryption and access permissions for individual files or folders. Access control should be customized based on the principle of least privilege, meaning that only those who need access to specific data should have it. For businesses, this means implementing role-based access controls (RBAC) to restrict employees to only the information required for their role. Furthermore, using strong, unique passwords for cloud accounts, paired with multi-factor authentication (MFA), can help mitigate the risks of unauthorized access, even in the event of a compromised password. These steps are essential to maintaining control over and protecting your cloud data from malicious actors.

Understanding data synchronization and sharing is critical to using cloud storage securely. Cloud services often offer the ability to sync files across multiple devices, ensuring that the most up-to-date version of a file is always available. However, this synchronization process can introduce vulnerabilities, especially when using multiple devices or collaborating. Files that are synchronized across several devices may be exposed to additional risks if one of the devices is compromised. Similarly, sharing data with others, even within trusted groups, can lead to inadvertent leaks or access by unauthorized users. It's important to configure sharing settings carefully, specify who can view or edit files, and use links that expire after a certain period or require a password for access. Additionally, when using synchronization features, ensure that devices are secured with encryption and strong access controls to prevent data from being exposed during syncing.

Managing multiple devices with cloud storage can present its own set of challenges. Today, users often rely on several devices—laptops, smartphones, tablets, and desktops—to access cloud-stored data, which can complicate security efforts. Each device must be properly configured with security measures such as strong passwords, encryption, and up-to-date antivirus software. Without these protections, a compromised device could become a gateway for attackers to access cloud data. Furthermore, syncing data across devices can lead to discrepancies or conflicts, especially when a file is accessed or edited simultaneously on multiple devices. To avoid these issues, it's essential to configure devices to prevent unauthorized access, such as enabling device-level encryption and using tools to track and remotely wipe lost or stolen devices. For users managing multiple devices, establishing a comprehensive strategy for device security and file synchronization is key to ensuring access and safety. Figure 18.1 illustrates cloud storage security settings, highlighting key configurations to protect data stored in the cloud.

Monitoring storage usage and costs is an important, though often overlooked, aspect of managing cloud storage effectively. While the convenience of cloud storage is undeniable, it's easy to lose track of how much data is being stored and how this affects costs. Many cloud providers offer tiered pricing based on storage volume, and exceeding storage limits can result in unexpected charges. Regularly reviewing storage usage ensures that users are not paying for more space than they need and can identify unused files or backups that can be deleted to reduce costs. For businesses, this can also help in budget management and prevent overspending on cloud services. Most cloud services offer tools to monitor storage usage and provide notifications when thresholds are nearing, making it easier to keep track of costs. Additionally, users can implement file retention policies to manage the lifecycle of their data and ensure that outdated files are properly archived or deleted to save space and costs.

Disaster Recovery Planning

Disaster recovery planning is a crucial component of any comprehensive cybersecurity strategy. The first step in disaster recovery is identifying critical data and systems that are essential to the continued operation of an individual or organization. Critical data includes financial records, legal documents, customer information, and proprietary software. Systems that support day-to-day operations, such as email servers, databases, and cloud infrastructure, also fall under this category.

Ask the AI

"What are the most effective ways to secure shared files in cloud storage?"
"How does two-factor authentication enhance cloud storage security, and what are the best implementation methods?"
"What should be considered when managing access permissions for sensitive data in a shared cloud environment?"

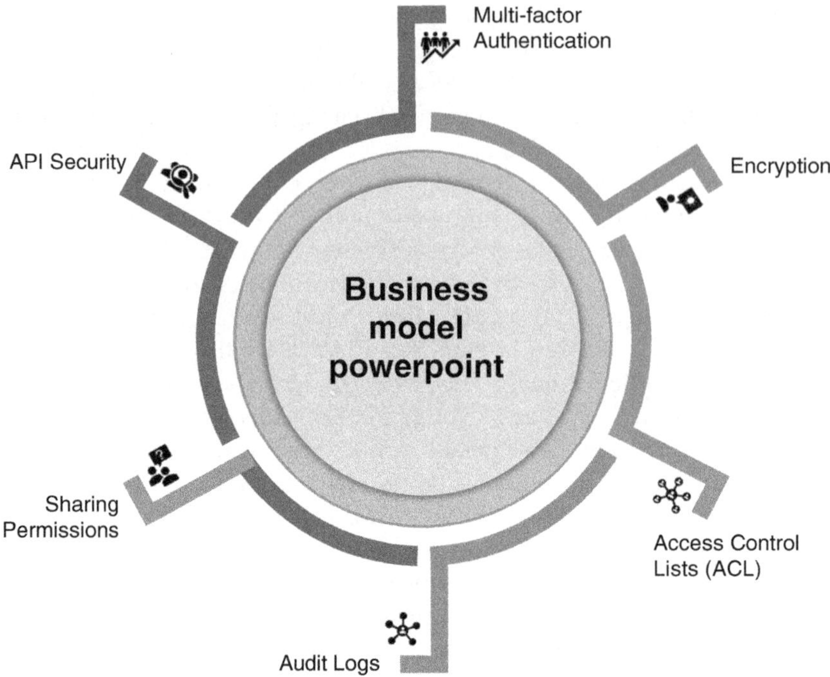

Figure 18.1 Cloud storage security settings.

You can focus recovery efforts on what matters most by identifying these key assets. Prioritizing critical data ensures that recovery efforts are aligned with business continuity goals and that nothing essential is overlooked during a disaster. This process also helps allocate resources more effectively, ensuring that the most valuable data is restored first, minimizing downtime and operational disruption. Table 18.3 provides a disaster recovery plan checklist, outlining essential steps to ensure effective preparation and response to data loss or system failure.

Developing a personal disaster recovery plan is essential in preparing for unforeseen events, whether natural disasters, cyberattacks, or hardware failures. A disaster recovery plan outlines the procedures for data loss, system compromise, or infrastructure failure. For individuals, this could involve setting up automated backups, establishing secure off-site storage, and identifying trusted contacts who can assist in the recovery process. On the other hand, businesses may need to develop more comprehensive plans, including off-site data storage, redundant systems, and detailed protocols for restoring operations. A well-structured disaster recovery plan should define recovery time objectives (RTOs) and recovery point objectives (RPOs)—which specify how quickly systems need to be restored and how much data loss is acceptable. By anticipating potential threats and establishing clear recovery steps, you reduce the time it takes to bounce back from an incident and minimize the overall impact.

Restoring data from backups effectively is a key element of any disaster recovery plan. Having backups is only half the battle; ensuring that data can be quickly and accurately restored is what ultimately ensures business continuity. The restoration begins with verifying that backups are intact, uncorrupted, and up-to-date. This may involve testing backup files periodically to confirm that they are usable and that the recovery process will proceed without errors. Once backups are verified, restoration should proceed in a controlled manner, prioritizing the recovery of critical

Table 18.3 Disaster recovery plan checklist.

Step	Description	Recommendation	Priority
Identify critical data	Determine which data is essential for business continuity	Prioritize sensitive and business-critical data	High
Develop backup strategy	Choose a backup method (local, cloud, and hybrid)	Implement a combination of cloud and local backups for redundancy	High
Define recovery time objectives (RTO)	Set the maximum acceptable downtime for each system	Ensure RTOs are realistic and achievable	High
Define recovery point objectives (RPO)	Establish how much data loss is acceptable	Set RPOs based on business requirements	High
Test recovery process	Conduct regular drills to verify recovery processes	Perform testing quarterly or biannually	High
Prioritize recovery tasks	List which systems and data should be restored first	Focus on critical systems and operations first	High
Ensure secure backups	Verify that backup data is encrypted and stored securely	Encrypt all backup data and use secure storage	High
Create documentation	Document the recovery plan and process for each system	Keep documentation up to date and accessible	Medium
Train recovery team	Ensure the team is trained in executing the disaster recovery plan	Hold annual training sessions for relevant staff	Medium
Review and update plan	Regularly review and update the disaster recovery plan	Review the plan yearly and after any significant changes	Medium

data and systems first. Depending on the severity of the disaster, a full system restore may be required, or in some cases, only partial data may need to be recovered. The speed and accuracy with which data can be restored are crucial to minimizing downtime, so individuals and organizations must invest in systems that allow for rapid and reliable recovery.

Testing recovery processes regularly is often an underemphasized aspect of disaster recovery planning. While having a disaster recovery plan in place is important, ensuring that the plan works when needed most is even more critical. Regular testing of backup systems, recovery procedures, and restoration times ensures that the process is effective and that no part of the plan is overlooked. Simulating different disaster scenarios—from a ransomware attack to a system crash—allows users to practice executing the recovery plan and identify gaps or inefficiencies. These tests should be conducted under controlled conditions and involve all relevant stakeholders to ensure everyone is familiar with the recovery steps. The goal is to make recovery as seamless as possible

---

Ask the AI

"What are the key components of an effective disaster recovery plan for small businesses?"
"How frequently should disaster recovery processes be tested, and what tests provide the most value?"
"What are the typical challenges in prioritizing recovery tasks after a data breach or system failure?"

when disaster strikes. Without regular testing, it's impossible to know whether the recovery plan will perform as expected during a real event.

Prioritizing recovery tasks after an incident is a crucial step in the aftermath of a disaster. In the chaos following an attack or data loss, losing sight of what must be done first can be easy. Prioritization involves identifying which systems or data must be restored immediately and which can wait. Critical infrastructure such as email servers, customer-facing applications, or financial records should take precedence. Once these systems are restored, attention can shift to less critical tasks like restoring internal documentation or archived data. Prioritization is not just about restoring services; it also involves ensuring that security measures are applied during recovery to avoid reinfection or further compromise. For businesses, prioritizing recovery can mean notifying stakeholders, customers, or regulatory bodies per legal or contractual obligations. Focusing efforts on the most crucial tasks allows recovery to proceed in an orderly manner, and downtime can be minimized.

Learning from incidents to improve future resilience is an often overlooked yet vital part of disaster recovery. Every incident provides an opportunity to evaluate the response, identify weaknesses, and implement improvements. After a disaster recovery process is completed, conducting a post-mortem analysis helps pinpoint areas where the recovery could have been faster, more efficient, or more comprehensive. This could involve refining backup strategies, improving staff training, or enhancing security measures to prevent similar incidents in the future. For example, if an incident revealed that backups were outdated or incomplete, steps can be taken to implement more frequent backups or to use more reliable storage solutions. Likewise, if the recovery time was too long due to a lack of resources or planning, adjustments to the recovery process can be made to speed things up in the future. Incorporating lessons learned into future disaster recovery planning helps build resilience, making it easier to recover from future incidents. This ongoing process of learning and improving ensures that disaster recovery plans evolve in response to emerging threats and changing technology.

Data Disposal and Destruction

Securely deleting data is a critical aspect of cybersecurity that is often overlooked until it's too late. Deleting files from a computer or external storage device does not permanently erase the data. In many cases, deleted data can still be recovered using specialized software, potentially exposing sensitive information. This is especially concerning when devices are sold, donated, or recycled, as improperly wiped data could fall into the wrong hands. Proper data disposal ensures that sensitive information is fully destroyed and cannot be accessed or restored by unauthorized individuals. Whether the data is stored on a hard drive, USB drive, or cloud service, proper disposal is vital for protecting personal and organizational privacy. Without secure deletion, you risk exposing valuable information, whether financial records, personal identifiers, or confidential business data.

There are various methods for securely sanitizing data, the most common being software tools and physical destruction. Software-based data sanitization tools work by overwriting the data on the storage device multiple times, ensuring the original data is irretrievable. Popular tools like DBAN (Darik's Boot and Nuke) or Eraser allow users to perform these overwrites with different algorithms to ensure thoroughness. For physical destruction, methods such as shredding, crushing, or melting the storage media ensure that data cannot be recovered. This is especially important for high-security environments where the risk of data theft is a significant concern. Physical destruction is often recommended for hard drives, USB drives, and other storage media no longer needed, as it provides the highest assurance that data cannot be restored. Combining software sanitization with physical destruction offers a layered approach, providing multiple levels of security and ensuring that the data is destroyed beyond recovery.

Legal requirements for data disposal are an essential consideration when managing sensitive information. Many industries are governed by strict laws and regulations that dictate how data should be stored, processed, and disposed of, including requirements for securely destroying data once it is no longer needed. For example, the HIPAA in the healthcare industry mandates that patient information be securely disposed of when it is no longer necessary. Similarly, the GDPR in Europe imposes strict rules on the handling and disposing of personal data. Organizations must be aware of these legal requirements to avoid potential fines or penalties for noncompliance. Beyond legal compliance, securely disposing of data is an ethical responsibility to protect individuals' privacy and prevent identity theft, fraud, or misuse of personal information. Organizations should ensure that they follow applicable regulations to mitigate risk and safeguard the privacy of their customers and employees.

Disposing of storage media responsibly goes hand in hand with secure data destruction practices. While erasing data from a device is necessary, it's also important to ensure that the storage medium is disposed of in an environmentally responsible manner. Electronic waste (e-waste) can pose significant environmental risks if not handled properly, as many electronic devices contain harmful chemicals or materials that can pollute the environment. Many regions have e-waste disposal laws requiring recycled devices through certified programs, ensuring that harmful substances are properly managed. When disposing of storage media such as hard drives, SSDs, or USB drives, users should seek out reputable e-waste recycling services that follow legal and environmental standards for disposal. In addition, businesses should partner with certified e-waste disposal companies offering secure data destruction services to ensure that data privacy and environmental concerns are addressed simultaneously.

Protecting data during device recycling is another important aspect of data disposal. Recycling old devices, such as smartphones, laptops, and tablets, can be an efficient way to manage outdated technology, but it also presents a risk to sensitive data if not done correctly. Before recycling any device, it's important to ensure that all personal data has been completely wiped, which may involve performing a factory reset or using data sanitization software. In many cases, even a factory reset may not be sufficient, as data can remain on the device's storage even after the reset process. Using a data erasure tool or physically destroying the storage media is recommended for more thorough protection. Additionally, many recycling programs offer services where devices are sent to certified technicians for proper sanitization and secure disposal. If you're uncertain about the effectiveness of your device's reset process, using a third-party service specializing in secure data erasure ensures that your personal information is protected before the device is recycled.

Documenting the disposal process is essential for accountability, particularly for businesses and organizations that handle large volumes of sensitive data. Documentation provides a record of the steps taken to destroy data, which can serve as proof of compliance with internal policies or

---

Ask the AI

"What are the most secure software tools for permanently deleting data from a hard drive?"
"How do physical destruction methods, like shredding or degaussing, compare to digital data wiping in terms of security?"
"What are the environmental impacts of e-waste, and how can businesses responsibly dispose of storage media?"

legal regulations. This includes recording the methods used for data sanitization, the individuals responsible for the process, and the disposal methods employed for storage media. For businesses subject to compliance audits, having a thorough record of data disposal activities can help avoid penalties or fines. In addition to keeping internal records, obtaining certificates of data destruction from e-waste disposal providers or data sanitization services may be necessary, which can provide formal verification that data has been securely erased. By maintaining a detailed log of the disposal process, organizations ensure that they can demonstrate their commitment to data privacy and security, reducing the risk of liability.

Recommendations

1. **Prioritize Regular Backups:** Use full, incremental, and differential methods to perform regular backups for critical data. Automate the process to ensure consistent backups and reduce the risk of forgetting to perform them manually. This practice ensures that data is recoverable with minimal loss in case of a system failure or cyberattack.
2. **Secure Your Cloud Storage:** Configure strong access controls and enable encryption for all files stored in the cloud. Use two-factor authentication (2FA) to add an extra layer of security to your cloud accounts. These measures will protect sensitive information from unauthorized access and ensure your data remains secure.
3. **Develop a Disaster Recovery Plan:** Identify critical systems and data and create a detailed recovery plan during a disaster. Define RTOs and RPOs to set clear goals for restoration. Testing this plan regularly ensures it will function as expected during an actual incident.
4. **Use Data Sanitization Tools:** Before disposing of old storage devices, use specialized software tools to erase data securely. Ensure data is overwritten multiple times to make it irretrievable, especially if the device contains sensitive information. This step reduces the risk of data being recovered and misused after disposal.
5. **Implement Physical Data Destruction:** When retiring storage devices that contain highly sensitive data, consider physical destruction methods such as shredding or degaussing. Physical destruction ensures that data is permanently unrecoverable. This is particularly important for organizations dealing with proprietary or regulated information.
6. **Monitor Access Logs:** Review audit logs for cloud storage and other critical systems to identify unauthorized access or suspicious activities. Implement alerts for unusual behavior to address potential security threats proactively. Monitoring access logs helps maintain accountability and reinforces your overall security posture.
7. **Adopt Secure Sharing Practices:** Limit file sharing to trusted users and ensure that permissions are appropriately configured. Use features like expiring links and password-protected sharing for additional security. By carefully managing file sharing, you reduce the risk of accidental exposure to sensitive information.
8. **Dispose of E-Waste Responsibly:** Partner with certified e-waste disposal companies that comply with environmental and data security regulations. Ensure that all data on storage media is securely erased or destroyed before recycling. Responsible disposal protects both the environment and your data from unauthorized recovery.
9. **Document Security Procedures:** Maintain detailed records of your backup schedules, disaster recovery tests, and data disposal activities. Documentation ensures accountability and provides a clear history of actions taken to secure your data. This practice is especially critical for businesses required to comply with regulatory audits.

10. **Stay Informed About Cybersecurity Trends:** Regularly update your knowledge of emerging threats and new data protection and recovery tools. Use resources like cybersecurity forums, webinars, or AI tools to explore strategies tailored to your needs. Staying informed ensures that your defense measures remain effective against evolving risks.

Conclusion

As we conclude this chapter, it's clear that securing your digital life requires more than just awareness of potential threats; it demands proactive, ongoing effort and strategic planning. From protecting personal data to managing cloud storage securely, the practices outlined in this guide are foundational to building a robust defense against cyber risks. While no system is entirely foolproof, following these best practices significantly reduces the likelihood of data breaches, cyberattacks, and other digital threats. The key to success is consistently applying these principles and adapting to the ever-changing cyber landscape.

One of the most critical aspects of digital security is understanding the entire data lifecycle—from creation and storage to its eventual disposal. Data protection doesn't end with simply encrypting files or implementing access controls; it extends to ensuring secure backups, planning for disaster recovery, and securely destroying no longer-needed data. Each step in the data management process is important in minimizing risks and maintaining confidentiality, integrity, and availability. This comprehensive approach is vital for both individuals and organizations, where the stakes of data loss or theft can have far-reaching consequences.

Cloud storage has transformed how we store and share data, offering convenience and flexibility. However, with this transformation comes new security challenges, especially regarding managing access and ensuring data integrity. By configuring proper security settings, enabling encryption, and using strong authentication mechanisms, it is possible to leverage the benefits of cloud storage while minimizing exposure to cyber threats. By following the recommendations outlined in this chapter, you can confidently use cloud services without compromising security.

Disaster recovery and data destruction are often underestimated components of a complete cybersecurity strategy, but they are just as important as proactive defense measures. Whether recovering from a system failure, a cyberattack, or a natural disaster, having a tested recovery plan in place is critical to maintaining business continuity. Equally important is ensuring that obsolete or outdated data is disposed of securely to prevent sensitive information from being accessed by unauthorized parties. Effective disaster recovery and data disposal practices safeguard your data and your reputation and compliance with legal and regulatory requirements.

Ultimately, the digital world will continue to evolve, and so will the tactics used by cybercriminals. Adopting the best practices outlined in this chapter, you position yourself to avoid emerging threats and minimize vulnerabilities. However, digital security is not a one-time task; it's an ongoing process that requires vigilance, adaptation, and continuous improvement. Making these practices a regular part of your routine and staying informed about new risks and mitigation strategies ensures that your digital life remains secure for years.

This chapter provides the tools and knowledge necessary to fortify your digital environment. By focusing on data protection, secure cloud storage, disaster recovery, and responsible data disposal, you create a strong defense against today's myriad cyber threats. The strategies discussed here are not just theoretical; they are practical, actionable steps that can be implemented immediately to protect what matters most—your data. With this foundation in place, you can confidently navigate the digital landscape, knowing that you have taken the necessary steps to ensure digital safety.

Chapter Questions

1 What is the main purpose of securely deleting data from storage devices?
   A. To reduce storage costs
   B. To prevent unauthorized recovery of sensitive data
   C. To enhance device performance
   D. To comply with company policies

2 Which method is considered the most secure for destroying sensitive data?
   A. Formatting the device
   B. Overwriting data multiple times with software tools
   C. Storing the device in a locked safe
   D. Deleting files from the Recycle Bin

3 What is the key benefit of combining local and cloud backups?
   A. Reducing storage costs
   B. Providing redundancy and protecting against local disasters
   C. Simplifying the backup process
   D. Avoiding the need for encryption

4 Why is it essential to test disaster recovery processes regularly?
   A. To reduce the time needed for backups
   B. To ensure that recovery steps work effectively during a real event
   C. To identify unimportant data
   D. To limit access to backup files

5 What should be prioritized when recovering from a disaster?
   A. All systems simultaneously
   B. The least important systems first
   C. Critical systems and data needed for continuity
   D. Systems with the most data

6 Which of the following is a key security feature to enable when using cloud storage?
   A. Two-factor authentication (2FA)
   B. Disabling encryption
   C. Allowing open sharing links
   D. Using the default password

7 What is the primary risk of not securely erasing data before recycling devices?
   A. Device overheating
   B. Unauthorized recovery of sensitive data
   C. Increased environmental impact
   D. Slower device recycling process

8 How does encryption enhance cloud storage security?
   A. By reducing the amount of data stored
   B. By making data inaccessible to unauthorized users without the decryption key

    C. By increasing cloud storage capacity
    D. By making file sharing easier

9 What is the function of audit logs in cloud storage?
    A. To identify unused files
    B. To track access and activities for security purposes
    C. To limit the amount of storage used
    D. To speed up data syncing

10 Why is documenting the data disposal process important?
    A. To recover deleted files if necessary
    B. To ensure accountability and demonstrate compliance
    C. To reduce storage requirements
    D. To avoid creating backups

11 Which step is essential in developing a disaster recovery plan?
    A. Limiting recovery to minor files
    B. Identifying critical data and systems
    C. Storing all data in one location
    D. Avoiding backup testing

12 What is a potential risk of sharing files in a cloud storage environment?
    A. Overwriting existing backups
    B. Unintentional access by unauthorized users
    C. Increased encryption times
    D. Loss of file versions

13 How can organizations securely dispose of e-waste?
    A. By selling devices without erasing data
    B. By physically destroying storage devices and partnering with certified recyclers
    C. By storing devices in an office closet
    D. By using factory resets only

14 What is a common reason for combining software-based sanitization with physical destruction?
    A. To save time during the destruction process
    B. To ensure data is completely unrecoverable
    C. To avoid environmental regulations
    D. To speed up device recycling

15 What should organizations do before donating or recycling devices?
    A. Simply delete files manually
    B. Ensure all data is wiped using a factory reset and data-wiping software
    C. Store devices in their original packaging
    D. Share devices without passwords

19

Cybercrimes and How to Report Them

Cybercrime can affect anyone, whether you're a home user managing personal data or a business dealing with sensitive customer information. These crimes are sophisticated and varied, ranging from identity theft and financial fraud to more complex attacks like ransomware and data breaches. Understanding the nature of cyber threats and implementing effective defense measures is essential to safeguarding your digital life.

While many of us rely on technology for daily tasks, we often overlook the potential vulnerabilities in our digital practices. Cybercriminals exploit these weaknesses, using various tactics to infiltrate systems and steal valuable information. This chapter will explore the most common types of cybercrimes, providing a detailed overview of how they occur and their impact. By recognizing these threats, you will be better prepared to protect your data and take appropriate action if you fall victim to an attack.

A major component of digital safety is identifying when a cybercrime has occurred. Early detection plays a pivotal role in minimizing damage, Whether through signs of unauthorized access, unusual account activity, or receiving a suspicious email. Knowing how to report cybercrime, cooperating with law enforcement, and understanding your rights during the process are also crucial elements in the aftermath of an attack. This chapter will guide you through these key areas, ensuring you're aware of the risks and equipped to handle them effectively.

Preventing future incidents is another fundamental aspect of digital safety. In addition to responding appropriately when a crime occurs, it's equally important to learn from the experience and implement proactive protective measures. This includes educating yourself and others about the evolving landscape of cyber threats, supporting initiatives to combat cybercrime, and advocating for stronger regulations and enforcement. Cyber defense is not just about responding to incidents; it's about building resilience against future attacks through constant vigilance and improving digital practices.

As we delve into the specifics of cybercrime, reporting, and prevention, it's important to remember that digital safety is an ongoing effort. Cyber threats evolve rapidly, and staying informed and prepared is the best way to ensure your data remains secure. Adopting a strategic approach to cyber defense and embracing the best practices outlined in this chapter, you'll be better positioned to navigate the complex world of digital threats. Together, these practices will help you strengthen your cybersecurity posture, minimizing the risk of falling victim to an attack and ensuring the safety of your digital life. Figure 19.1 illustrates the increasing cost of cybercrime, highlighting the growing financial impact on businesses and individuals over time.

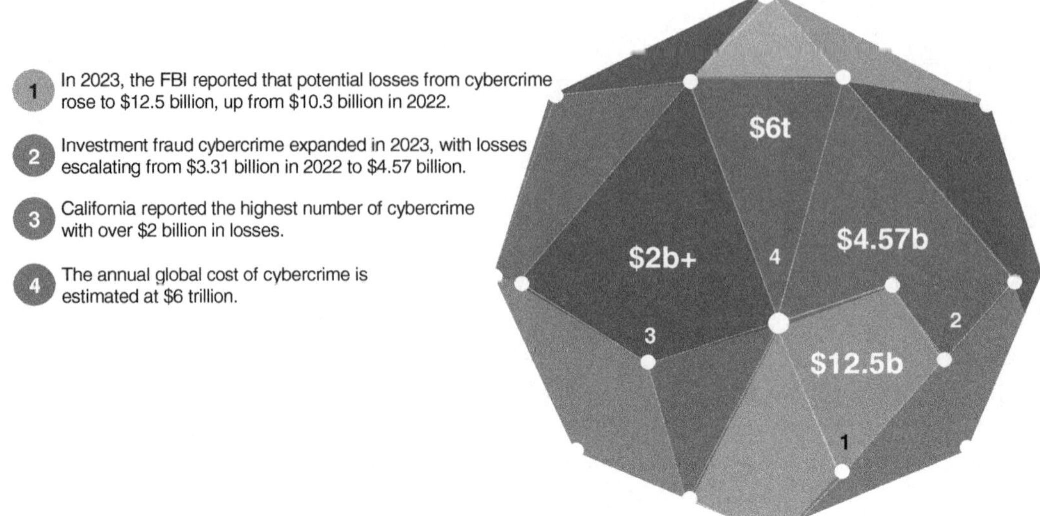

Figure 19.1 The cost of cybercrime is increasing.

Understanding Cybercrimes

Cybercrime is an evolving threat landscape, encompassing a range of malicious activities that exploit technology to cause harm, disrupt systems, or steal valuable information. At its core, cybercrime refers to any criminal activity that involves a computer, network, or device as a tool to carry out illegal acts. These activities may range from simple scams and phishing attacks to more sophisticated operations involving hacking, malware deployment, and data breaches. Understanding the scope of cybercrime requires delving into its various types, all of which present distinct challenges to individuals and organizations regarding detection, prevention, and response (Table 19.1).

One of the most insidious forms of cybercrime is cyberstalking, harassment, and exploitation. Cyberstalking involves the persistent, often threatening, use of digital platforms to target and intimidate victims. Harassment can manifest in various ways, from unsolicited messages to malicious social media campaigns, all designed to cause emotional distress. Exploitation takes this further, as perpetrators may manipulate victims into compromising situations, using their personal data or online presence to exert control. This cybercrime is particularly harmful because it can occur anonymously and persist for extended periods without the victim's knowledge of the perpetrator's identity.

Intellectual property (IP) theft and piracy are also significant components of cybercrime. Intellectual property theft refers to the unauthorized use or reproduction of someone else's intellectual creations, such as patents, trademarks, and copyrighted materials. Cybercriminals can exploit vulnerabilities in digital systems to steal proprietary information, often leading to financial losses and reputational damage for businesses. Piracy, especially in software and media piracy, is another pervasive issue where individuals or groups distribute copyrighted content without permission, undercutting the creators and distributors. These activities undermine the value of IP and, in many cases, hinder innovation by reducing the incentives for creators and businesses to invest in new technologies.

Table 19.1 Types of cybercrimes and their characteristics.

Cybercrime type	Definition	Common characteristics	Examples
Phishing	Using fraudulent emails or websites to steal personal information	Deceptive messages or websites that look legitimate	Emails pretending to be banks or service providers asking for login credentials
Ransomware	Malware that encrypts files and demands a ransom for their release	Infected devices, encrypted files, and ransom demands	WannaCry
Cyber stalking	Repeated and targeted harassment via digital channels	Frequent messages, threats, or monitoring behavior	Threatening social media posts or anonymous messages
Intellectual property (IP) theft	Unauthorized use of someone else's IP	Copying or stealing ideas, products, or software	Software piracy
Financial fraud	Using deception to gain access to personal financial information or assets	Fake offers, deceptive practices, or impersonation	Online banking fraud
Identity theft	Stealing someone's personal information for fraudulent use	Using stolen personal data to commit fraud	Using stolen credit card numbers or Social Security numbers
Data breach	Unauthorized access to confidential or private information	Exposing personal or sensitive data to unauthorized parties	Company or healthcare database hack
Malware	Malicious software designed to damage, disrupt, or steal data	Infections that cause system damage or theft	Viruses, trojans, worms
Denial-of-service (DoS) attack	Overloading a server with requests to make it unavailable	Servers are overwhelmed with malicious traffic	Website or server being rendered unavailable
Cyber espionage	The act of spying or obtaining confidential government or corporate information	Targeted attacks for stealing sensitive information	Government-sponsored attacks on corporate data

Financial fraud and identity theft are perhaps the most common forms of cybercrime, with billions of dollars in yearly losses. Financial fraud can take many forms, from fraudulent transactions on banking apps to the exploitation of online payment systems for unauthorized transfers. Cybercriminals often employ phishing schemes to steal login credentials or gain access to personal accounts. Identity theft, a particularly destructive crime, involves stealing an individual's data used to commit fraud, apply for loans, or open credit accounts. These crimes can devastate victims, leaving them with long-term financial and emotional repercussions.

Cyberterrorism and espionage represent the more politically motivated aspects of cybercrime, where malicious actors seek to cause harm to governments, critical infrastructure, or industries. Cyberterrorism uses digital tools and networks to incite fear, disrupt government functions, or damage national security. This attack can target power grids, financial systems, or communication networks, potentially causing widespread chaos. On the other hand, espionage typically involves state-sponsored or corporate spies attempting to infiltrate systems to steal sensitive government or corporate secrets. Both cyberterrorism and espionage present unique threats, often involving highly sophisticated methods and well-funded organizations.

The role of cybercrime syndicates is an often-overlooked element of the cybercriminal ecosystem. These criminal organizations operate like traditional crime syndicates, except their business model revolves around digital crime. They may run large-scale operations focused on hacking, data theft, and developing ransomware or malicious software. These syndicates often target high-value individuals or organizations, demanding significant ransoms or engaging in systematic attacks that disrupt industries and cause massive financial damage. Many of these syndicates are transnational, making it difficult for law enforcement agencies to coordinate efforts for their apprehension, especially given the global nature of the Internet.

The rise of ransomware attacks, often orchestrated by cybercrime syndicates, illustrates the growing sophistication and organization within the digital criminal underworld. Ransomware is malicious software that encrypts a victim's data, rendering it inaccessible until a ransom is paid. These syndicates have perfected the art of extortion, targeting critical infrastructure, healthcare systems, and large enterprises. The sheer scale of these attacks, combined with the anonymity provided by cryptocurrencies for ransom payments, has made ransomware one of the most profitable and persistent threats in the cybercrime world. The impact of these attacks can be devastating for the immediate victim and entire industries and populations that rely on their services.

Furthermore, the increasing reliance on the Internet and digital platforms for personal, business, and governmental functions has significantly expanded the attack surface for cybercriminals. With more data being stored online, cybercriminals have a larger pool of targets to choose from, making it easier to find and exploit vulnerabilities. The dark web's anonymity allows criminals to exchange tools, techniques, and even stolen data with relative impunity. This ecosystem has fostered a highly specialized underground economy where even novice criminals can access sophisticated tools, making it easier to commit crimes while remaining undetected.

As the digital world continues to evolve, so too do the tactics used by cybercriminals. What was once considered a minor inconvenience, like a simple scam email, has morphed into an entire industry of cybercrime that can bring down multinational corporations or government agencies. The convergence of cybercrime with other forms of organized crime, including human trafficking, drug trafficking, and arms smuggling, has also raised the stakes for global law enforcement. The international nature of the Internet means that no country is immune to these threats, which is why combating cybercrime requires collaboration and coordination across borders.

Recognizing When You're a Victim

Detecting when you've become the victim of a cybercrime is often the first step in mitigating damage and preventing further harm. For instance, unauthorized access or activities in your digital accounts can sometimes be subtle at first. A common indicator might be unfamiliar logins or suspicious changes to account settings, such as passwords or recovery email addresses you

---

Ask the AI

"What are the most common methods cybercriminals use to exploit personal information?"
"How does phishing differ from other forms of social engineering attacks?"
"What are the key characteristics of ransomware, and why is it so effective?"

didn't initiate. Modern cybersecurity tools and service providers often send alerts for such activities. However, it's essential to regularly monitor your accounts for unusual access patterns, such as logins from different geographical locations or devices you don't recognize. Identifying these signs early can help you take immediate steps to secure your accounts, such as changing passwords and enabling multi-factor authentication (MFA) (Table 19.2).

Fraud or theft may manifest in various ways, many of which can be difficult to recognize until it's too late. You might notice unexpected transactions, withdrawals from your bank account or credit cards, or unfamiliar charges on your digital payment services. In some cases, the fraud may be more subtle, like a sudden increase in unsolicited marketing emails or personalized ads, which might suggest your data has been compromised. Even if you haven't noticed anything that stands out, regularly reviewing bank statements, credit reports, and online purchases can help spot anomalies. The faster you identify these signs, the quicker you can alert your financial institutions and potentially prevent further losses.

One of the more alarming signs that you've become a victim of cybercrime is receiving threats or extortion attempts. These threats often appear as demands for money or other forms of compensation in exchange for not releasing sensitive information or stopping harmful actions. Ransomware attacks, for instance, might begin with a threat to release sensitive data unless a ransom is paid publicly. Similarly, extortion tactics can involve threats of reputational damage or harm to your personal or professional life. Recognizing these threats for what they are—coercion through fear and manipulation—is essential, as reacting impulsively can sometimes worsen matters. In these situations, contacting law enforcement and avoiding engaging with the perpetrators is critical.

Another red flag that should raise immediate concern is the discovery of malware or spyware on your devices. Malware, a general term for malicious software, includes a variety of harmful

Table 19.2 Signs of cybercrime victimization.

Sign of cybercrime	Possible cause	Recommended action
Unusual account activity	Unauthorized login attempts	Change passwords and enable MFA
Bank account irregularities	Unfamiliar transactions or balances	Report the issue to the bank and freeze accounts if necessary
Receiving unsolicited emails	Unexpected or suspicious emails	Do not open links or attachments
Malware alerts from security software	Detected malware or viruses on your system	Run a complete antivirus scan and remove threats
Locked accounts	Inability to access accounts due to incorrect passwords	Check for unauthorized logins and reset passwords
Social media impersonation	Someone is using your identity to post or contact others	Report to social media platforms and inform contacts
Unknown charges on credit cards	Unauthorized purchases on your credit card statement	Contact your credit card provider immediately and dispute the charges
Suspicious activity on public Wi-Fi	Unexpected pop-ups or data breaches	Disconnect from public Wi-Fi and use a VPN when connecting to the Internet
Extortion or blackmail threats	Receiving threats to release personal or compromising information	Report to law enforcement and avoid direct contact with the perpetrator
Ransomware attack	Files are encrypted, and a ransom is demanded for decryption	Do not pay the ransom

programs such as viruses, ransomware, and spyware, all designed to compromise the security of your system. Spyware is particularly dangerous because it operates quietly in the background, collecting personal information, tracking your online activities, and sending it back to the attacker. This type of software often goes unnoticed for long periods unless you have the proper security software to detect and remove it. Suppose your system begins to behave erratically, such as running slower than usual or displaying unexpected pop-ups. In that case, running a thorough scan with a reputable antivirus program is important to detect any potential threats.

Unusual account behaviors or lockouts indicate that something is amiss with your online security. These behaviors might include difficulty logging into your accounts despite using the correct credentials, sudden requests for password resets, or being locked out of accounts without any attempt to access them. Hackers often attempt to breach accounts by repeatedly trying different passwords or using stolen credentials, leading to account lockouts or security alerts. Suppose you find yourself locked out of accounts that are critical to your personal or professional life. In that case, it's crucial to regain access as soon as possible through the proper recovery mechanisms, like answering security questions or using authentication apps. In these situations, it's wise to update passwords immediately and check for any signs of unauthorized changes or activities.

When you start receiving communication from authorities or third parties regarding potential breaches or fraud, it's a sign that your personal or financial data might have been compromised. Law enforcement, banks, or credit reporting agencies may notify you if your information has been exposed in a data breach or if suspicious activities have been detected. Often, these communications come in official letters, emails, or phone calls, urging you to take specific actions, such as freezing your credit or reporting the incident. While these communications can be alarming, it's important to approach them cautiously, ensuring the message is legitimate and not another phishing attempt. Always verify the message's source and follow the advice trusted organizations give to mitigate the risks of further compromise.

Additionally, the rise of targeted phishing attempts or social engineering schemes can sometimes make distinguishing between legitimate communication and malicious intent difficult. Phishing often takes the form of emails or messages that appear to come from trusted sources, such as a bank, a government agency, or even a colleague, asking for sensitive information or urging you to take quick action. If you're ever in doubt, avoid clicking links or downloading attachments from unsolicited messages and contact the supposed sender directly through official channels to confirm the validity of the request. Cybercriminals thrive on urgency and fear, so if an email, phone call, or message feels off or too good to be true, it's worth pausing and double-checking before taking further action.

The technological landscape has evolved, where cybercriminals are increasingly adept at masking their identities and attack methods. While traditional frauds and thefts were more easily identifiable, today's cybercrime tactics are subtle, diverse, and often part of larger, coordinated schemes. This sophistication means that the signs of being a victim may not always be immediately obvious and may present in multiple forms simultaneously. You could notice a series of strange behaviors across different platforms—such as receiving unusual social media messages, noticing

---

Ask the AI

"What are the early signs of malware infection on a personal computer?"
"How can you distinguish between legitimate account activity and unauthorized access?"
"What steps should you take if you suspect identity theft has occurred?"

discrepancies in financial transactions, or encountering unexpected technical glitches in your devices—all of which may result from a coordinated attack to exploit your digital life. These signs are often the result of cybercriminals gaining incremental access over time rather than all at once.

Reporting Cybercrimes

Reporting a cybercrime is critical in mitigating further damage and ensuring that justice is pursued. Prompt reporting allows law enforcement and cybersecurity experts to track the activities of cybercriminals, prevent additional attacks, and potentially recover lost data or assets. Delaying the report or ignoring the incident can allow the perpetrators to cause more harm, as many cybercrimes, such as ransomware attacks or identity theft, can escalate quickly if left unchecked. Immediate reporting also ensures that any legal or regulatory deadlines for filing claims or disputes are met, which is especially important for individuals and organizations that rely on insurance or other recovery mechanisms (Table 19.3).

Table 19.3 Steps to take after a cybercrime incident.

Step	Action	Description	Additional resources
1. Document evidence	Take screenshots, save logs, and gather other evidence	Preserve all records of communications	Consider using digital forensics tools
2. Report to authorities	Contact local law enforcement	File a report with local police and provide all evidence collected	Use online portals for reporting cybercrimes
3. Inform affected parties	Notify your bank, service providers, and anyone else affected	Inform them of the breach so they can take action	Include copies of your report and evidence
4. Change passwords	Update passwords for affected accounts	Use strong and unique passwords for each account and enable MFA	Consider using a password manager
5. Secure your devices	Run antivirus scans, update software, remove malware	Ensure your operating system and all software are up to date	Reinstall affected software if necessary
6. Report to specialized agencies	Contact cybersecurity experts or fraud prevention agencies	Work with specialists who can track and assist with your recovery	Report to platforms like FTC or IC3
7. Monitor your accounts	Check bank, credit, and social media accounts for unusual activity	Monitor statements and accounts regularly for signs of further damage	Use fraud alert services or credit monitoring
8. Seek legal advice	Consult a lawyer to understand your rights and options	Legal counsel can help with issues like identity theft	Work with a lawyer who specializes in cybercrime
9. Cooperate with investigators	Provide authorities with any additional information they request	Assist in the investigation to help catch the perpetrators	Keep your evidence organized for easy access
10. Stay vigilant	Regularly check accounts and systems for new threats	Be aware of possible retaliation or continued attacks	Consider installing additional security measures or updating policies

Recognizing that you've fallen victim to cybercrime is essential to document everything thoroughly to preserve crucial evidence. This can include screenshots of fraudulent transactions, email correspondence with the perpetrators, or logs from your computer or network indicating unauthorized access. Each piece of information could be a vital part of the puzzle when investigators attempt to trace the attack back to its source. The more detailed the record-keeping, the better-equipped authorities will be to understand the scope of the crime and its impact. Avoid altering or deleting any data, as tampering with evidence can harm the investigation or even hinder potential recovery efforts.

Contacting local law enforcement agencies should be one of the first steps after confirming that a cybercrime has occurred. In many cases, especially for personal or financial crimes like fraud or identity theft, local police are the initial point of contact. They may be able to guide you through reporting the crime, and they will likely refer you to specialized units within the agency if the crime falls under a more complex category, such as hacking or data breaches. Local law enforcement also serves as a valuable intermediary, especially in cases where cross-jurisdictional or international coordination is necessary. When reaching out, be prepared to provide as much detail as possible to assist investigators in assessing the situation quickly.

It is important to report the incident to specialized cybercrime units for more specialized cybercrimes, such as hacking, cyberstalking, or large-scale financial fraud. These units, often within national or regional law enforcement agencies, have the resources, expertise, and technology to track and investigate complex digital crimes. Specialized cybercrime units are typically equipped to handle cases that involve sophisticated tools like malware, ransomware, or botnets, and they may have access to global networks of law enforcement agencies to trace perpetrators who operate across borders. In the United States, for example, entities such as the FBI's Cyber Division or the U.S. Secret Service are tasked with handling cybercrime cases at the federal level. Reporting to these units ensures that your case is dealt with by professionals with the experience and tools necessary to combat cyber threats.

In addition to contacting law enforcement, individuals and organizations can utilize online reporting platforms to alert authorities or specialized agencies about cybercrime. Many governments and non-profit organizations have set up dedicated websites for reporting incidents like identity theft, online scams, and data breaches. These platforms are often designed to simplify the reporting process and may offer resources for victims, such as advice on how to protect your accounts or steps to take if your data has been compromised. Examples of such platforms include the Federal Trade Commission's (FTC) Complaint Assistant in the United States or ActionFraud in the United Kingdom. While these platforms are valuable for initial reporting, they should complement, rather than replace, contacting law enforcement directly for more complex or urgent matters.

Working with legal counsel can be necessary when dealing with more severe or complex cybercrimes. A lawyer specializing in cybersecurity law or data protection can provide invaluable advice on navigating the legal complexities of cybercrime, especially when dealing with significant financial losses, regulatory compliance issues, or potential lawsuits. For businesses, legal counsel is often crucial to understand how to handle the disclosure of data breaches to customers, employees,

---

Ask the AI

"What information should be included in a cybercrime report to authorities?"
"Which online platforms are most effective for reporting fraud and identity theft?"
"How do law enforcement agencies use digital evidence in cybercrime investigations?"

or regulatory bodies. A lawyer can also assist with reviewing contracts with third-party vendors to determine liability, especially in cases where a breach occurred due to an external party's negligence. In addition to ensuring that your rights are protected, legal professionals can help you understand the long-term ramifications of the crime and guide you through the recovery process.

It is also essential to note that you should remain mindful of privacy and confidentiality when working with law enforcement or legal counsel. Many individuals may feel a sense of embarrassment or hesitation when reporting cybercrimes, especially in cases involving sensitive information or reputational damage. However, it is important to remember that cybercrimes are committed against the victim, not vice versa, and authorities and legal professionals are there to protect your rights. Keeping your communication clear, open, and honest with law enforcement and legal counsel will ensure that the investigation progresses smoothly and that you receive the necessary support.

Another important aspect of reporting cybercrime is understanding the potential for future risks. While law enforcement can help investigate and prosecute the perpetrators, the effects of the crime can linger long after the immediate threat has been addressed. Victims of identity theft, for example, often face ongoing challenges with credit reporting, legal disputes, and emotional distress. It's important to stay vigilant and monitor your financial accounts and digital presence even after reporting the crime. Consider using identity theft protection services or monitoring tools to avoid any future attempts to misuse your information.

The Investigation and Legal Process

Once you report a cybercrime, you must understand the following steps from a legal and investigative standpoint. After the report is filed, law enforcement agencies will assess the situation and determine the appropriate action. In many cases, they will open an investigation, which may involve gathering evidence, interviewing witnesses, and tracing the perpetrators. The process can take time, especially in complex cybercrime cases involving multiple parties or cross-border elements. While waiting for the investigation to unfold, it's important to stay in close contact with the authorities and provide any additional information or assistance they may need. Expect updates from investigators, though the process may feel slow due to the often intricate and international nature of digital crimes.

Cooperation with law enforcement is vital during the investigation to ensure a thorough and effective process. You may be asked to provide specific details about the crime, such as the timeline of events, any communications you received from the perpetrators, or technical data like IP addresses or log files. It's crucial to be transparent and forthcoming with all relevant information, even if unsure about its significance. Sometimes, seemingly minor details can become critical evidence in solving a case. If you have digital forensics tools or cybersecurity professionals assisting you, their reports and analysis can also be invaluable to investigators. The more information you can provide, the better-equipped authorities will be to trace the attack and potentially identify the responsible parties.

Understanding your rights during the investigation is essential to navigate the legal process effectively. As a victim of cybercrime, you have the right to remain informed about the status of the investigation and to be treated with respect and fairness by law enforcement. This includes being notified of significant developments, such as arrests or legal actions. You also have the right to confidentiality, meaning your personal information should be protected throughout the investigation, especially when dealing with sensitive data like financial records or personal communications.

However, it's important to understand that law enforcement may need to access certain aspects of your digital life to investigate the crime fully. Sometimes, they may request permission to examine your devices or retrieve data from cloud services to gather evidence. Awareness of your rights can help you make informed decisions as the investigation progresses.

The potential outcomes of a cybercrime investigation can vary depending on the crime's severity and the investigation's success. One possible outcome is prosecution, where the perpetrators are arrested, charged, and brought to trial. If the criminals are apprehended and convicted, they may face penalties such as fines, imprisonment, or restitution to the victims. Restitution refers to the compensation that the defendant may be ordered to pay the victim for losses from the cybercrime, such as the cost of recovering data or replacing stolen funds. In some cases, victims may be able to claim insurance or compensation through civil suits, even if criminal prosecution does not result in restitution. While not all cybercrime cases result in the prosecution of criminals, particularly in cases where the perpetrators are difficult to identify or apprehend, it's important to stay informed about potential outcomes.

The role of cybersecurity professionals in the investigation process cannot be overstated. These experts play a crucial role in analyzing the technical aspects of cybercrime, often providing specialized knowledge that law enforcement may not have. For example, digital forensics experts can help recover deleted files, trace IP addresses, analyze malware samples, and uncover hidden data on compromised systems. Their skills are invaluable in cases where the evidence is digital or encrypted, requiring advanced techniques to access and interpret. In some cases, these professionals work directly with law enforcement; in others, they may serve as independent contractors providing expert testimony during legal proceedings. Having a cybersecurity expert involved ensures that the investigation is thorough and that critical evidence is preserved and presented in a way that holds up in court.

Dealing with cross-border jurisdictional issues is one of the most complicated aspects of investigating cybercrimes. Unlike traditional crimes within the confines of a specific geographic location, cybercrimes often involve perpetrators and victims from different parts of the world. This can create significant legal challenges, as other countries have varying privacy, data protection, and cybercrime laws. In some cases, international law enforcement agencies, such as Interpol or Europol, may become involved in facilitating coordination between countries. However, extraditing criminals or gathering evidence from foreign jurisdictions can be lengthy and legally complex. Differences may hinder cooperation between countries in legal frameworks or delay obtaining necessary warrants or permissions. As a result, even if a perpetrator is identified, the investigation and subsequent legal actions can be delayed significantly when jurisdictional issues are involved.

In addition to international cooperation, the nature of the Internet itself can complicate investigations. Cybercriminals often use VPNs, proxy servers, and the dark web to hide their identities and obscure their location, making it difficult for law enforcement to trace their activities. This level of anonymity can make it harder to establish a clear chain of evidence, requiring investigators to employ advanced techniques and technologies to break through these barriers. These tools often add layers of complexity to the investigation. However, with the right resources, law enforcement agencies can eventually uncover the perpetrator's identity, even if they are operating in another

Ask the AI

"What rights do cybercrime victims have during an investigation?"
"How do digital forensics experts trace cyberattacks back to their source?"
"What challenges do law enforcement face when investigating cross-border cybercrimes?"

country. However, the more sophisticated the criminal tactics, the longer the investigation may take, leading to frustration for victims seeking quick resolution.

The involvement of legal professionals throughout the investigation is also critical, particularly when dealing with cross-border cases or complex digital evidence. Lawyers can help ensure proper procedures are followed when collecting and preserving evidence, minimizing the risk of it being deemed inadmissible in court. They can also advise victims on navigating the legal implications of their case, especially if it involves IP theft, contractual disputes, or other commercial concerns. In some cases, legal counsel can assist in pursuing civil suits for damages or negotiating settlements with perpetrators or third parties, such as service providers or insurance companies. Working with a lawyer ensures that victims' interests are protected and they have professional support throughout the entire process, from the investigation to the potential resolution of the case.

Preventing Future Incidents

After experiencing a cybercrime, it is crucial to take the time to reflect on what happened and learn from the experience. While being a victim of cybercrime is undoubtedly distressing, it can also serve as a valuable lesson in enhancing your overall security practices. You can identify specific areas where your defenses were lacking by analyzing how the attack occurred—whether through phishing, weak passwords, or other vulnerabilities. This introspection should lead to a more proactive approach to securing your digital life, starting with carefully reviewing your cybersecurity habits. From strengthening password protocols to upgrading outdated software, each change you make can significantly reduce the likelihood of future incidents.

Implementing recommended protective measures after a cyberattack is about fixing immediate problems and creating a resilient, long-term security posture. One of the first steps is to ensure that all of your personal or organizational systems are equipped with up-to-date antivirus software and a strong firewall. Many cybercriminals exploit outdated software and vulnerabilities, making regular updates a critical line of defense. Additionally, enabling MFA on all accounts that support it adds an extra layer of security that makes it much harder for attackers to gain unauthorized access. Even something as simple as revising your passwords to make them more complex and unique for each account can drastically improve your defenses.

In addition to personal protective measures, educating others about cybercrime awareness is essential in creating a more secure digital environment. Cybercriminals often target individuals who are less informed or unaware of the threats they face online, so raising awareness among family, friends, and colleagues can have a significant ripple effect. By sharing your experience and lessons, you can help others avoid making the same mistakes. Simple practices, such as recognizing phishing attempts or knowing when to avoid clicking on suspicious links, can make a difference in protecting others. Providing resources, such as recommending cybersecurity blogs or training programs, can also empower those around you to take control of their digital safety.

Supporting community initiatives against cybercrime is another vital step in the fight against online threats. Many local organizations, schools, and workplaces run educational programs to

---

Ask the AI

"What are the most effective ways to secure personal data against cybercriminals?"
"How can cybersecurity awareness training help prevent workplace cyber incidents?"
"Why is multi-factor authentication considered a critical security measure?"

help raise awareness about the dangers of cybercrime and teach practical cybersecurity skills. Engaging with or volunteering for these initiatives builds a culture of safety and vigilance within your community. Whether hosting a seminar on recognizing phishing attacks or participating in local campaigns promoting cybersecurity best practices, your involvement can have a lasting impact. Communities that work together to share knowledge and collaborate are better equipped to protect themselves from the evolving threats in the cyber landscape.

Even after you've taken steps to secure your digital life, it is important to stay vigilant for potential retaliation from cybercriminals. Often, once a perpetrator has targeted a victim, they may continue to attempt to exploit that individual through various means, including repeated hacking attempts, identity theft, or harassment. In some cases, they might even use cyberstalking or send malicious content designed to cause further harm. By maintaining your vigilance—regularly checking accounts for unusual activity, staying updated on the latest cybersecurity trends, and contacting law enforcement—you can detect any signs of retaliation early. This proactive approach can help prevent the attacker from successfully launching additional attacks and allow you to respond swiftly if necessary.

Advocating for stronger laws and enforcement against cybercrime is essential in the broader effort to combat digital threats. Cybercrime laws are continually evolving, but in many jurisdictions, enforcement remains a challenge due to the global nature of the Internet and the anonymity afforded to criminals online. By supporting policy changes and advocating for more stringent laws and enforcement mechanisms, you can help improve the landscape for all digital users. Your voice can contribute to positive change by contacting lawmakers, participating in public discussions, or supporting organizations that fight for stronger cybersecurity laws. Stronger legislation and more effective enforcement help deter cybercriminals and provide victims with the tools and resources they need to recover and seek justice.

In the ongoing fight against cybercrime, the importance of collaboration cannot be overstated. Law enforcement agencies, cybersecurity professionals, and policymakers must work together to address the rapidly changing landscape of digital threats. By supporting initiatives to improve intelligence-sharing across borders, the response to cyber incidents can become faster and more coordinated. This collaboration extends beyond just government and law enforcement—private companies, educational institutions, and the general public all play critical roles in strengthening the global response to cybercrime. Every step to improve communication, streamline reporting processes, and share best practices can enhance the collective ability to combat these threats.

Recommendations

1. **Strengthen Your Defenses:** Regularly update your devices and systems with the latest software patches and security updates. Cybercriminals often exploit vulnerabilities in outdated software, making timely updates a critical line of defense. Pair this with installing reputable antivirus software to detect and neutralize potential threats.
2. **Use MFA:** Enable MFA on all accounts that support it to add an extra layer of security. This measure requires an additional step, such as a code from a mobile app or a fingerprint, making it significantly harder for attackers to access your accounts. Even if one factor is compromised, the secondary layer provides robust protection.
3. **Document Cybercrime Incidents:** If you experience a cyberattack, preserve all evidence, including emails, logs, screenshots, and communication with the perpetrator. These records will be essential for law enforcement to investigate the incident and can also help you recover lost assets. Be meticulous and store this information securely to prevent further exposure.

4. **Report to the Appropriate Authorities:** File a report with local law enforcement or specialized cybercrime units as soon as you identify an attack. Provide all relevant evidence and details to facilitate a thorough investigation. Reporting incidents helps track cybercriminal activity and strengthens collective efforts to combat cybercrime.

5. **Monitor for Unusual Activity:** Regularly review your financial accounts, social media profiles, and digital activities for signs of unauthorized access. Set up alerts for account changes or transactions to catch suspicious behavior early. Vigilance allows you to address issues promptly and minimize potential damage.

6. **Educate Yourself and Others:** Share your knowledge of cybersecurity risks and best practices with family, friends, and colleagues. Host informal workshops or direct others to reliable resources on phishing, password management, and other key topics. A more informed community is better equipped to resist cyber threats.

7. **Advocate for Better Cybercrime Policies:** Support initiatives to strengthen cybersecurity laws and improve international cooperation in fighting cybercrime. Engage with policymakers and organizations to push for stricter penalties and more efficient reporting processes. Advocacy helps create a safer digital environment for everyone.

8. **Learn to Detect Social Engineering:** Familiarize yourself with common tactics like phishing and pretexting that attackers use to manipulate victims. Practice identifying suspicious emails, messages, or calls that attempt to trick you into sharing sensitive information. Building this awareness is critical for avoiding these increasingly sophisticated schemes.

9. **Utilize Professional Cybersecurity Services:** Engage cybersecurity professionals or digital forensics experts to analyze and secure your systems after an attack. These experts can recover lost data, identify vulnerabilities, and provide guidance on enhancing your defenses. Their involvement ensures a comprehensive response to the incident.

10. **Stay Updated on Cybersecurity Trends:** Continue learning by following trusted cybersecurity blogs, attending webinars, or joining professional groups. The landscape of cyber threats evolves rapidly, and staying informed is key to maintaining robust defenses. This proactive approach will help you anticipate and counteract new tactics used by cybercriminals.

Conclusion

Cybersecurity is an ever-evolving field that demands constant attention and adaptation. As cybercriminals continue to refine their techniques and exploit new vulnerabilities, it is crucial to stay ahead of the curve by implementing robust digital safety practices. This chapter's strategies and best practices provide a strong foundation for recognizing, reporting, and preventing cybercrimes. By understanding the tactics used by cybercriminals and the steps necessary to protect personal and organizational data, you can significantly reduce the risk of falling victim to an attack.

However, securing your digital life doesn't end with implementing protective measures. Cyberdefense is an ongoing process that requires continuous learning, adaptation, and vigilance. Whether responding to cybercrime, collaborating with law enforcement, or reinforcing your security practices, remaining proactive and informed is essential. Cyber threats are dynamic, and your defense strategies must evolve alongside them to maintain resilience in the face of new challenges.

As this chapter has demonstrated, there are several layers to digital safety—each one reinforcing the others. From understanding the different types of cybercrimes to taking immediate action when a crime occurs, each aspect of cybersecurity plays an integral role in safeguarding your data. Moreover, supporting wider community efforts against cybercrime and advocating for stronger laws and enforcement helps create a safer digital ecosystem for everyone. No single action is sufficient, but together, these practices form a comprehensive defense strategy.

The fight against cybercrime requires a collective effort from individuals, organizations, and governments. You can contribute to a safer, more secure digital world by adopting a continuous learning mindset and proactive engagement. With the knowledge gained from this chapter, you are better equipped to defend yourself against the myriad threats that exist in cyberspace. Remember, the goal is not to eliminate all risks but to significantly reduce them by being prepared and taking decisive action when necessary.

Ultimately, digital safety is more than just preventing attacks—it's about being empowered to navigate the online world confidently and securely. Applying the principles and best practices shared here will enhance your ability to respond to emerging threats, protect sensitive information, and foster a culture of security in both your personal and professional life. Cyber defense is not a one-time fix but an ongoing commitment to vigilance and improvement that will help ensure your safety in the digital age.

Chapter Questions

1   What is the primary purpose of documenting evidence after experiencing a cybercrime?
    A. To delete the evidence later
    B. To preserve crucial details for investigation
    C. To share with friends and family
    D. To prove the attacker's guilt without further action

2   Why is it recommended to enable multi-factor authentication (MFA)?
    A. It makes logging in quicker
    B. It adds a second layer of security to your accounts
    C. It stores passwords automatically
    D. It encrypts your device data

3   What is the main benefit of reporting cybercrime to specialized units?
    A. Receiving a financial reward
    B. Accessing expertise in handling complex digital crimes
    C. Avoiding the need to provide evidence
    D. Ensuring the case is closed quickly

4   What is one effective way to educate others about cybercrime risks?
    A. Sharing personal passwords as examples
    B. Hosting cybersecurity awareness sessions
    C. Avoiding discussions about digital safety
    D. Refraining from using online platforms

5   What is a common sign that you might be a victim of identity theft?
    A. Receiving legitimate login notifications
    B. Unfamiliar transactions on your bank account
    C. An increase in promotional emails
    D. Your account passwords remain unchanged

6 Why is it critical to stay vigilant for unusual account activity after a cyberattack?
  A. It ensures you can detect further unauthorized actions early
  B. It guarantees that no further attacks will occur
  C. It allows attackers to continue operating unnoticed
  D. It removes the need for multi-factor authentication

7 What should be your first step if you receive a ransom demand from ransomware?
  A. Pay the ransom immediately
  B. Report the attack to authorities and seek professional help
  C. Turn off your computer and ignore the demand
  D. Attempt to decrypt the files yourself

8 What is the purpose of supporting stronger cybercrime laws?
  A. To allow criminals to continue exploiting victims
  B. To create harsher penalties and better prevention measures
  C. To focus solely on financial fraud cases
  D. To reduce reporting requirements for victims

9 What is a key role of digital forensics experts during a cybercrime investigation?
  A. Filing legal complaints on behalf of victims
  B. Tracing attacks and preserving digital evidence
  C. Preventing all cybercrime incidents
  D. Managing public relations for victims

10 How can participating in community initiatives help combat cybercrime?
  A. By promoting awareness and proactive defense strategies
  B. By focusing on law enforcement alone
  C. By reducing the need for personal cybersecurity measures
  D. By discouraging reporting cybercrime incidents

11 What is the benefit of analyzing how a cybercrime occurred?
  A. It guarantees the attacker will be caught
  B. It identifies vulnerabilities to improve future security
  C. It ensures your devices will never need updates
  D. It prevents the need for further vigilance

12 Why should you regularly update your security protocols?
  A. To reduce the amount of personal data stored
  B. To keep your system optimized for performance
  C. To stay protected against new and emerging threats
  D. To avoid frequent alerts from antivirus software

13 What is a practical way to prevent social engineering attacks?
  A. Trust all emails and phone calls from unknown senders
  B. Learn to identify phishing emails and suspicious requests
  C. Ignore all communications from service providers
  D. Share personal information freely

14 How can cybersecurity training help prevent future incidents?
- **A.** By teaching you to avoid basic precautions
- **B.** By preparing you to recognize and respond to evolving threats
- **C.** By reducing the need for monitoring your accounts
- **D.** By eliminating the need for updates or MFA

15 What is the advantage of using professional cybersecurity services after an attack?
- **A.** They guarantee complete recovery in all cases
- **B.** They provide expertise in analyzing and securing your systems
- **C.** They remove the need to report the incident to authorities
- **D.** They discourage future vigilance

20

Preparing for Emerging Cyber Threats

With the rise of sophisticated cyberattacks, from ransomware and advanced persistent threats (APTs) to AI-powered attacks, it is crucial to take proactive measures to safeguard personal and professional digital assets. The digital landscape is evolving rapidly, and with it, so are the tactics employed by cybercriminals. Understanding and implementing effective cybersecurity practices is no longer optional—it is necessary to protect sensitive information and maintain trust in the digital world.

The advent of artificial intelligence (AI), machine learning (ML), and the widespread adoption of the Internet of Things (IoT) has expanded the capabilities of cyber defense and the vulnerabilities that attackers can exploit. New technologies offer enhanced security solutions but also bring unforeseen risks, particularly when leveraged by malicious actors. Additionally, emerging threats such as deepfakes, social engineering, and AI-powered attacks are reshaping the landscape of cybersecurity in ways that are difficult to predict. As these threats grow in sophistication, individuals and organizations must continuously adapt their strategies to stay ahead of cyber adversaries.

This chapter delves into the core principles of cyber defense best practices, focusing on the need for a proactive security mindset. Cybersecurity is not just about using the right tools—it's about fostering a culture of security that prioritizes continuous learning, adaptability, and collaboration. From embracing new technologies cautiously to building resilience through redundancy and backups, the strategies outlined here offer a comprehensive approach to securing your digital life. Throughout the chapter, we explore the evolving nature of cyber threats, the role of AI and ML in cybersecurity, and the vital need for individuals to contribute to the security ecosystem actively.

A key focus of this chapter is on personal responsibility and proactive engagement with cybersecurity. While businesses and organizations play a central role in implementing security measures, individuals must also take responsibility for their digital safety. Implementing simple yet effective best practices—such as using multi-factor authentication (MFA), updating software regularly, and participating in cybersecurity awareness training—can significantly reduce the likelihood of falling victim to cyberattacks. Moreover, as technology advances, staying informed about the latest developments and embracing a culture of security will be crucial in navigating the increasingly complex digital world.

Emerging Cyber Threats

APTs are a significant and evolving danger in cybersecurity. These sophisticated, long-term attacks are typically orchestrated by well-funded and highly skilled adversaries, often with state or criminal backing. Unlike traditional cyberattacks, APTs do not rely on a single event to breach a system; instead, they involve a persistent and strategic infiltration into a network, remaining undetected for months or even years. APT attackers are patient, methodical, and focused on accessing valuable data or achieving strategic objectives. Often, these threats are aimed at espionage, intellectual property theft, or disrupting national infrastructure. Organizations must adopt proactive detection mechanisms and implement layered defenses to combat APTs as the threat landscape becomes more complex (Table 20.1).

AI-powered cyberattacks are one of the latest frontiers in the cyber threat space, and they are poised to make traditional defense mechanisms obsolete. With the increasing sophistication of AI, adversaries can now automate and scale their attacks, finding vulnerabilities at a pace that human attackers cannot match. AI can analyze vast amounts of data to identify security system weaknesses, predict behavior patterns, and optimize attack strategies in real time. One such example is the use of AI for spear-phishing, where personalized, convincing emails are generated based on data scraped from social media profiles and other online sources. The ability of AI to learn and adapt continuously makes defending against these types of attacks especially challenging. This new wave of attacks underscores the need for cybersecurity experts to integrate AI-driven defense mechanisms, such as anomaly detection, into their security operations.

Deepfakes and misinformation campaigns are emerging threats that pose significant risks to individuals and organizations. Deepfakes—synthetically generated media, typically video or audio, designed to appear real—can wreak havoc on personal reputations, corporate stability, and national security. By leveraging AI techniques, deepfakes can create hyper-realistic content that manipulates public perception or distorts the truth. When combined with misinformation campaigns, which intentionally spread false or misleading information, these deepfakes can become

Table 20.1 Types of cyber threats and their characteristics.

Threat type	Description	Impact	Typical mitigation strategies
Advanced persistent threat (APT)	Long-term targeted attacks, often by nation-states or organized crime	Stealthy prolonged data breaches	Regular system and network monitoring, advanced firewalling, threat hunting
AI-powered cyberattacks	Attacks that use ML or AI to automate and improve tactics	Deeper, more adaptive attacks	Deployment of AI-based security tools
Ransomware	Malware that locks or encrypts user data and demands a ransom for decryption	Financial loss	Regular data backups
Phishing	Attempts to steal sensitive data by impersonating legitimate institutions	Credential theft	Email filtering
Deepfakes	AI-generated media used to spread misinformation or damage reputations	Trust issues	Media verification tools
Distributed denial-of-service (DDoS)	Overloading a target's servers to make them inaccessible	Service disruption	Traffic filtering
Insider threats	Malicious actions from trusted individuals within an organization	Data theft	Regular audits
Social engineering	Manipulating individuals into revealing confidential information	Data breach	Social awareness training
Malware	Software designed to damage or disable computers	Data loss	Regular antivirus software
IoT vulnerabilities	Weaknesses in IoT devices that can be exploited	Device hijacking	Secure device configuration

powerful tools for political manipulation, social unrest, or financial fraud. The implications of these threats are far-reaching, as they can destabilize public trust in media, institutions, and even democratic processes. To combat these risks, a combination of digital literacy, AI detection tools, and strong verification practices will be essential in verifying the authenticity of online content.

Quantum computing presents both a tantalizing opportunity and a serious cybersecurity challenge. While quantum computers promise to revolutionize fields like drug discovery and cryptography, they also have the potential to break widely used encryption algorithms that form the backbone of modern cybersecurity. Quantum computers can perform calculations at speeds far beyond the capability of today's classical computers, enabling them to crack even the most secure cryptographic protocols in a fraction of the time. While quantum computing remains in its infancy, the development of quantum-safe encryption algorithms is already underway. However, a race is still to develop defenses that will withstand quantum decryption techniques. Organizations must begin preparing for a post-quantum world by staying informed about developments in quantum cryptography and exploring the adoption of quantum-resistant encryption methods.

The IoT has introduced a new layer of complexity to digital security, primarily due to the number of connected devices. From smart home devices to industrial control systems, the number of IoT devices is increasing exponentially, creating an expanding attack surface for cybercriminals. Many IoT devices suffer from inherent security weaknesses, such as weak or non-existent encryption, inadequate patch management, and insecure default settings. These vulnerabilities make IoT devices an attractive target for hackers looking to exploit weaknesses and gain access to a broader network. In some cases, attackers can even hijack IoT devices to create botnets, which can be used in large-scale distributed denial-of-service (DDoS) attacks. As IoT technology proliferates, manufacturers and users must implement stronger security measures like firmware updates.

AI and ML in Cybersecurity

AI is revolutionizing cybersecurity by offering enhanced capabilities to detect, prevent, and mitigate threats. One of the primary ways AI improves security is by enabling systems to identify patterns in large volumes of data, which humans alone cannot process efficiently. ML algorithms, a subset of AI, are particularly adept at recognizing anomalies and potential security breaches. By analyzing historical data, AI can predict where threats are most likely to emerge, providing organizations with actionable insights to bolster their defenses. For example, AI-driven systems can instantly analyze network traffic for unusual activity, immediately identifying and responding to potential cyberattacks such as DDoS or advanced malware strains before they escalate. The rapid analysis and response time AI provides significantly shortens the gap between attack detection and mitigation, offering businesses a fighting chance in the race against cybercriminals (Table 20.2).

ML is increasingly deployed to enhance threat detection and response mechanisms, enabling more proactive security strategies. Unlike traditional signature-based detection systems, which can only recognize previously known threats, ML models can identify novel attack vectors by learning from vast datasets of known attacks and benign network behaviors. Adapting and understanding in

Ask the AI

"What are examples of advanced persistent threats (APTs), and how do they operate over time?"
"What strategies are most effective for detecting and mitigating AI-powered cyberattacks?"
"How do deepfakes and misinformation campaigns pose risks to digital security?"

Table 20.2 AI and ML in cybersecurity.

AI/ML technique	Description	Use case in cybersecurity	Benefits	Challenges
Machine learning (ML)	A subset of AI where algorithms are trained on data to identify patterns	Used for threat detection and anomaly identification	Improved threat detection	Requires large data sets and training time
Natural language processing (NLP)	A branch of AI that helps machines understand and process human language	Used to detect phishing emails or social engineering attacks	Improves email security by identifying phishing attempts	May struggle with complex
Behavioral analysis	Techniques that analyze patterns of behavior to identify deviations from the norm	Identifying insider threats	Quick detection of abnormal activity	False positives and adaptation to new behaviors may be challenging
Automated incident response	AI-driven systems that automatically take action in response to detected threats	Automating remediation actions like isolating infected systems	Increased response speed	Limited by the AI's training and scope
Predictive analytics	Using AI to predict future threats based on current data trends	Forecasting cyberattack tactics	Provides proactive defense measures	Requires continuous and accurate data input
Anomaly detection	Identifying unusual patterns or outliers in network traffic or system activity	Detecting DDoS attacks	Highlights threats that deviate from normal behavior	Can lead to high false-positive rates
AI-Driven malware analysis	Using AI to identify malware by analyzing its behavior or code	Speeding up malware identification and response	Increases efficiency in malware detection	May miss sophistication attacks
AI-based encryption	AI technologies used to enhance the strength of encryption algorithms	Improving data encryption for sensitive information	Increases data security	May face difficulties in scalability and computation speed
Threat intelligence aggregation	Using AI to aggregate and analyze vast amounts of threat intelligence data	Helping organizations stay ahead of emerging threats	Provides insights into global attack trends	May require integration with existing systems
AI-powered vulnerability scanning	AI that scans systems for potential vulnerabilities	Automating security testing and vulnerability patching	Reduces manual effort	May fail to detect complex or new vulnerabilities

real-time allows ML systems to spot anomalies even when they don't fit the usual attack patterns. For instance, ML can recognize subtle behavioral changes in an organization's network, such as a sudden spike in outbound traffic or unauthorized access attempts, which could indicate a data breach or malware infection. This ability to detect previously unknown threats—often called "zero-day attacks"—is invaluable in a landscape where cybercriminals constantly evolve their tactics. As AI and ML

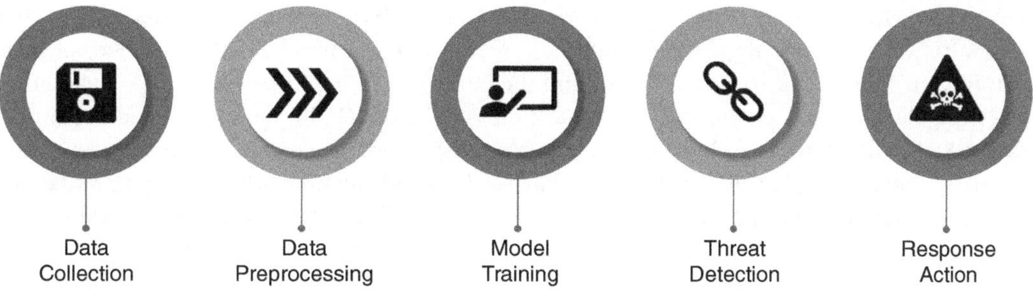

Figure 20.1   AI and ML workflow in cybersecurity.

become more integrated into security infrastructure, they enable organizations to not just react to threats but anticipate and neutralize them before they can cause harm (Figure 20.1).

Automation is another key benefit that AI brings to cybersecurity, and it plays a pivotal role in simplifying the complexity of security management. The sheer volume of security alerts generated by modern systems can overwhelm human security teams, leading to delayed responses or missed threats. AI-driven automation can help by triaging these alerts, prioritizing them based on severity, and automatically executing predefined reactions to certain types of attacks. For example, if a phishing email is detected, an AI system can automatically block the sender, flag the message for further review, and notify the user with a warning. Furthermore, AI can automate the patch management process, ensuring that software vulnerabilities are addressed promptly and reducing the chances of exploitation by attackers. Automation helps reduce human error and increases the efficiency of security operations, allowing teams to focus on more strategic tasks.

While AI offers substantial benefits in enhancing cybersecurity, it also comes with risks, especially when placed in the wrong hands. Cybercriminals increasingly use AI to automate their attacks, making them faster, more scalable, and more difficult to detect. For example, AI can craft highly convincing phishing emails, mimicking trusted sources with uncanny precision. These AI-powered attacks can trick even the most vigilant employees, bypassing traditional security measures. In addition, AI can be used to automate scanning for system vulnerabilities, allowing attackers to exploit weaknesses at a much higher rate. The sophistication of AI tools available to malicious actors has dramatically lowered the barrier to entry for cybercriminals, enabling even small groups to launch sophisticated attacks. This underscores the importance of developing robust defense systems incorporating AI, not just for protection, but to outpace adversaries leveraging the same technologies.

One of the most significant concerns surrounding AI in cybersecurity is the balance between leveraging its benefits and safeguarding privacy. AI systems require large datasets to be effective, and this data often includes sensitive personal information, which raises concerns about data privacy and protection. The more data collected and processed, the higher the risk of data breaches or misuse, especially if that data is not adequately protected. In cybersecurity, AI tools might

---

Ask the AI

"How can machine learning models identify anomalies in network traffic to detect cyber threats?"
"What are the benefits and challenges of automating incident response with AI?"
"What ethical considerations should be addressed when deploying AI for cybersecurity purposes?"

analyze everything from network traffic to personal user behavior to detect anomalies, but this could infringe on individuals' privacy rights. For organizations, striking the right balance between the utility of AI-powered security systems and the ethical handling of personal data is essential. Privacy regulations such as General Data Protection Regulation (GDPR) and California Consumer Privacy Act (CCPA) have put additional pressure on companies to ensure that their use of AI complies with legal standards, safeguarding user data while benefiting from AI's security advantages.

The deployment of AI in cybersecurity also raises various ethical considerations that must be carefully navigated. One of the primary ethical challenges is the potential for bias in AI algorithms, which could lead to unfair or discriminatory outcomes. For example, suppose an AI model is trained on biased data. In that case, it might be more likely to flag certain behaviors or individuals as suspicious based on demographic factors such as ethnicity or location rather than security risks. Furthermore, as AI systems become more autonomous in making decisions, questions arise regarding accountability. Who is responsible if an AI-powered system makes a mistake, such as blocking a legitimate user's access to their account or failing to detect a critical attack? The ethical deployment of AI requires transparency in how AI models are built, how they are trained, and how decisions are made. As AI becomes more integrated into cybersecurity practices, organizations must implement strong oversight mechanisms to ensure that AI systems operate fairly, responsibly, and in a way that respects individuals' rights.

Another ethical issue surrounding the use of AI in cybersecurity is the potential for over-reliance on automated systems. While AI can process and analyze data at a speed and scale that humans cannot, it cannot replicate the nuance of human judgment. Over-trusting AI systems could lead to critical decisions made without human intervention, potentially allowing vulnerabilities to go unnoticed or exacerbating a threat that a human operator might have caught. Human expertise remains essential to the cybersecurity ecosystem, even with the advent of AI and ML. Effective cybersecurity should be a partnership between human intelligence and AI capabilities, with human experts providing oversight, ethical guidance, and critical thinking that complement the raw computational power of AI.

Adapting Security Practices

Embracing a proactive security mindset is essential in today's ever-evolving cyber landscape. Gone are the days when a company could rely solely on reactive measures, such as waiting for an attack to happen and responding. Instead, a proactive approach involves anticipating potential threats, identifying vulnerabilities before they can be exploited, and implementing strategies to prevent incidents from occurring in the first place. Cybersecurity professionals must adopt the mindset of "defense in depth," where multiple layers of security—firewalls, intrusion detection systems, encryption, and more—are implemented to mitigate risk. This mindset extends to technology and human behavior; employees must be educated about best security practices, such as recognizing phishing attempts and using strong, unique passwords. A proactive approach also involves constantly evaluating and improving security measures to keep pace with emerging threats and changing attack techniques.

Continuous learning and skill development are cornerstones of effective cybersecurity. The digital world is in constant flux, and cyber threats evolve rapidly. What worked to defend against threats yesterday may no longer be sufficient tomorrow. Therefore, cybersecurity professionals must prioritize ongoing education to stay ahead of cybercriminals. This includes formal training, such as certifications in ethical hacking, network security, and incident response, and informal methods, such as attending conferences, engaging in online forums, or conducting independent research. Cybersecurity is not a field where you can rest on your laurels; it requires a commitment to lifelong learning. As new vulnerabilities, tools, and techniques emerge, staying informed and adaptable is key to maintaining robust defenses.

Implementing adaptive security architectures is another critical strategy for improving an organization's cybersecurity posture. Unlike static security systems that rely on predefined rules and protocols, adaptive security systems continuously evolve based on the latest threat intelligence and ongoing network environment analysis. This adaptive approach enables systems to respond dynamically to new threats as they arise, adjusting policies and controls in real time to minimize the impact of an attack. For instance, an adaptive security model might adjust its defenses based on the severity of a threat, tightening controls during a detected attack while allowing normal operations once the threat has been neutralized. This flexibility allows organizations to remain resilient despite constantly changing cyber risks. Implementing an adaptive architecture requires advanced security tools that leverage ML and AI to monitor and respond to potential threats, making real-time decision-making possible.

Collaboration with security communities is vital to strengthening cybersecurity defenses. Cyber threats are global, and no single entity can combat them effectively in isolation. Organizations can access valuable insights into the latest vulnerabilities, attack methods, and defensive tactics by participating in information-sharing initiatives, threat intelligence networks, and industry-specific security forums. The collective knowledge of cybersecurity professionals worldwide can help identify emerging trends and share best practices to mitigate risk. For example, participating in Information Sharing and Analysis Centers (ISACs) allows businesses to exchange threat intelligence with industry peers, helping them stay one step ahead of adversaries. Collaboration also extends to working with law enforcement and governmental organizations, as public-private partnerships can be instrumental in thwarting cybercriminals.

Leveraging threat intelligence services is an increasingly important strategy in identifying and responding to cyber threats. These services provide real-time data about known threats, such as malware hashes, IP addresses associated with cybercriminal activity, and attack methodologies. By integrating threat intelligence feeds into security systems, organizations can gain a deeper understanding of the threat landscape and take preemptive actions to block malicious traffic or protect vulnerable assets. Threat intelligence also enables security teams to prioritize their efforts, focusing on the most imminent threats and avoiding the trap of chasing every potential attack. However, it's important to remember that threat intelligence alone is not enough; it must be used with strong security practices, such as network segmentation, patch management, and access control, to be fully effective. Regularly updating threat intelligence data is crucial to keeping defenses current and responsive.

Staying informed about technological advancements is crucial for maintaining an effective cybersecurity strategy. As new technologies emerge—such as 5G networks, edge computing, and blockchain—they create new opportunities for cybercriminals to exploit vulnerabilities. Conversely, these technologies also offer innovative tools for strengthening security. Staying current with technological developments enables cybersecurity professionals to identify risks and opportunities in

---

Ask the AI

"What is a proactive security mindset, and how can it help prevent cyberattacks?"
"How do adaptive security architectures adjust defenses in response to evolving threats?"
"What are the benefits of collaborating with cybersecurity communities for threat intelligence?"

a rapidly changing environment. For example, cloud technologies have revolutionized how businesses store and process data, but they also bring new security challenges related to data privacy and multi-tenancy. By keeping a finger on the pulse of technological change, organizations can ensure they are not left behind and can capitalize on new solutions that enhance security without introducing new risks. Regular engagement with the tech community through webinars, blogs, and conferences is essential to stay informed about cutting-edge developments.

Adapting security practices also requires the ability to pivot and reassess strategies in response to evolving threats. Cybercriminals are not static in their methods; they continuously adapt, using increasingly sophisticated tools and techniques. As a result, cybersecurity professionals must adopt a mindset of agility, understanding that yesterday's solutions may not solve today's challenges. For example, the rise of ransomware attacks over the past decade has required organizations to rethink their approach to backups, encryption, and endpoint security. Similarly, the widespread adoption of remote work and the cloud has prompted businesses to reassess their network perimeter and implement new access control measures. Continuously adapting security practices means staying attuned to emerging risks and adjusting the organizational security posture as necessary.

Finally, organizations must recognize the importance of a security culture permeating every aspect of the business. Cybersecurity is not just the responsibility of the IT department or security team—it is a company-wide initiative that requires buy-in from leadership, employees, and stakeholders at all levels. Security must be integrated into the organizational culture, from ensuring employees understand the importance of strong passwords to adopting a zero-trust architecture for network access. Regular training, awareness campaigns, and clear communication about security policies can go a long way in fostering a security-first mindset among staff. Creating a culture where cybersecurity is seen as a shared responsibility helps mitigate human error and ensures everyone is aligned with the organization's security objectives. A proactive and unified approach to security is far more effective than treating it as an afterthought or a reactive measure when something goes wrong.

Personal Strategies for Future-proofing Security

Regularly updating and diversifying security measures is one of the most effective strategies for future-proofing your digital defenses. The threat landscape is dynamic, constantly emerging new vulnerabilities, attack techniques, and malware variants. Relying on static security measures leaves systems vulnerable to evolving threats. You ensure that your defenses can fend off the latest attacks by continuously updating software, hardware, and security protocols. This can involve routine patching of operating systems, applications, and firmware and adopting newer encryption methods or more sophisticated firewalls as they become available. Additionally, diversifying your security tools—rather than relying on a single layer of protection—ensures that if one measure is breached, others can still offer defense. Security by obscurity is never a solution; rather, a multi-faceted approach creates a more resilient digital environment (Table 20.3).

Adopting new technologies cautiously is another essential strategy when considering future-proofing. While innovations, such as AI or blockchain, may offer exciting opportunities for improvement, they often introduce new risks and complexities. The rush to adopt cutting-edge solutions without fully understanding their security implications can open organizations to exploitation. For example, the rise of IoT devices has undoubtedly enhanced convenience and introduced a massive attack surface. Before integrating new technologies into your systems, conducting thorough risk assessments is critical, and ensuring they are compatible with your existing

Table 20.3 Cybersecurity best practices and their benefits.

Security practice	Description	Benefit	Examples of tools/methods
Regular software updates	Keep all software, operating systems, and security tools updated to patch vulnerabilities	Reduces the risk of exploitation from known vulnerabilities	Windows Update
Multi-factor authentication (MFA)	Requiring multiple forms of verification to access accounts	Enhances security by requiring more than just a password	Google Authenticator
Data encryption	Encrypting sensitive data to ensure it is unreadable without the proper key	Protects data from unauthorized access during storage or transit	BitLocker
Firewall protection	Using firewalls to block unauthorized access and monitor network traffic	Prevents unauthorized access to private networks and data	ZoneAlarm
User access controls	Setting permissions and limiting access based on roles within an organization	Minimizes the risk of unauthorized access to sensitive data	Role-based access control (RBAC)
Regular backups	Backing up data regularly to prevent loss from cyber incidents like ransomware	Ensures data can be recovered if lost or damaged	Cloud storage
Phishing awareness training	Training individuals to recognize and avoid phishing attacks	Reduces the likelihood of falling victim to scams	Phishing simulation software
Strong password management	Using complex, unique passwords for each account and system	Prevents unauthorized access through password cracking	Password managers
Network segmentation	Dividing networks into smaller isolated sections to limit the spread of attacks	Limits the damage from a cyberattack by containing it to one segment	Virtual LANs (VLANs)
Incident response plan	Developing and maintaining a plan to respond to cybersecurity incidents	Enables quick, coordinated action in case of a cyberattack	Incident response platforms

security protocols and do not introduce unforeseen vulnerabilities. It's also important to monitor the broader ecosystem for any emerging risks related to these technologies, staying informed about known exploits and potential mitigation strategies. Patience, thorough testing, and phased implementation are crucial to ensuring that new technologies enhance—not undermine—your security posture.

Participating in cybersecurity training and simulations is a proactive way to build personal and organizational resilience against digital threats. While technical defenses are essential, human error remains one of the leading causes of security breaches. Regular training programs that include simulated phishing attacks, security best practices, and incident response drills can help reinforce security protocols and keep teams sharp. These training sessions should not be one-off events but an ongoing process that adapts to emerging threats and changes in the technological landscape. Simulations, particularly realistic "red team" exercises, allow employees to experience and respond to simulated attacks, fostering a deeper understanding of handling real-world cyber incidents. Regularly testing both individual skills and organizational response protocols ensures that when a real attack occurs, the response is swift, effective, and coordinated.

Building resilience through redundancy and backups is a cornerstone of any effective cybersecurity strategy. No matter how robust your primary security measures are, there will always be the possibility of a breach, a hardware failure, or an unforeseen disaster. Redundancy ensures that critical systems and data remain protected, even in the face of an attack. For instance, regularly backing up essential files and ensuring backups are stored in secure, separate locations—ideally, both on-premises and in the cloud—can protect against ransomware attacks that might encrypt or destroy your primary data. Redundancy should extend beyond data storage to network design, where failover systems and secondary communication channels can ensure continued functionality if the primary network is compromised. By designing systems with redundancy in mind, you're not just protecting against cyber threats; you're creating a safety net that enables quick recovery and minimal disruption in a breach or failure.

Engaging with policymakers and industry leaders is crucial for shaping the future of cybersecurity. While personal measures are important, the broader regulatory and industry landscape significantly impacts the effectiveness of security strategies. Working with policymakers ensures that cybersecurity regulations evolve with technological advancements and emerging threats. For example, advocating for stronger data privacy laws or supporting regulations that mandate basic cybersecurity practices in critical sectors can help raise the standard of security across the board. Additionally, engaging with industry leaders allows for sharing knowledge and developing collaborative defense strategies. As cyber threats grow in complexity, businesses, governments, and organizations need to work together, pooling resources and expertise to create a more secure digital environment. By fostering these relationships, individuals and organizations can influence policies that directly impact their security frameworks, ensuring they remain ahead of the curve.

Encouraging innovation in security solutions is a forward-thinking strategy for securing digital environments. While traditional security measures—such as firewalls and antivirus software—remain essential, the challenges posed by modern cyber threats require novel approaches. Innovation in security solutions can come from many sources, from academic research in encryption methods to developing ML algorithms that improve threat detection. Supporting and adopting emerging technologies, such as blockchain for secure transactions or AI for predictive threat analysis, can help build more robust defenses. Moreover, a culture of innovation encourages continuous improvement, ensuring that security practices are not static but are always evolving to meet new challenges. Organizations can develop and adopt cutting-edge security tools that offer proactive defenses against increasingly sophisticated cyber threats by fostering an environment that values creativity and problem-solving.

Lastly, one of the most important personal strategies for future-proofing security is fostering a security culture within your organization or community. Security is not just the responsibility of IT departments or specialized teams; it is a shared responsibility that involves every employee, contractor, and even third-party partner. By embedding security awareness into the fabric of your organization—through regular training, clear policies, and ongoing communication—you ensure

Ask the AI

"What are the most effective methods for diversifying personal cybersecurity measures?"
"How can redundancy in data backups protect against ransomware attacks?"
"What steps should be taken to evaluate the security risks of adopting new technologies?"

that everyone understands their role in protecting digital assets. A culture of security also means encouraging individuals to report suspicious activity, stay informed about emerging threats, and continuously improve their security practices. Individuals should be empowered to make informed decisions about the devices they use, the websites they visit, and the security protocols they follow. A collective effort to embrace security across all levels can greatly reduce the risk of cyber incidents and promote a safer digital ecosystem overall.

The Role of Individuals in Shaping Cybersecurity

Advocacy for responsible technology use is critical in ensuring a secure digital future. In a world where technology is integrated into nearly every facet of daily life, individuals can influence how it is used and secured. Responsible technology use begins with understanding the potential risks and recognizing that not all online behaviors are equally safe. For instance, practicing good password hygiene, being cautious about sharing personal information, and being selective about the applications and websites one interacts with are all crucial steps in protecting personal data. Individuals who advocate for responsible technology use to encourage others to adopt similar behaviors, thereby contributing to a collective effort to raise awareness about the importance of digital safety. This advocacy extends beyond personal behavior and into the broader societal discussion, helping shape policies, regulations, and industry standards prioritizing privacy, security, and ethical use of technology.

Supporting education and awareness programs is another essential way individuals can impact cybersecurity. Awareness is the first defense in cybersecurity; without it, even the best tools and systems will fall short of protecting against human error. Individuals who actively support or participate in educational initiatives, whether through schools, communities, or online platforms, can help cultivate a culture of cybersecurity mindfulness. This might involve volunteering to teach digital literacy classes, helping to create public service announcements on safe online behavior, or advocating for stronger cybersecurity education in academic curricula. The more individuals understand the risks associated with cyber threats, the more empowered they will be to take protective actions in their personal and professional lives. Education can also help break down the barriers of fear and confusion surrounding complex security topics, making it easier for people to adopt good practices and make informed decisions.

Contributing to research and development efforts is an often overlooked but highly impactful way for individuals to shape the future of cybersecurity. While large organizations and research institutions usually lead the charge in technological innovation, many breakthroughs and advancements in cybersecurity come from individuals passionate about solving real-world problems. Cybersecurity constantly evolves, with new daily challenges—from zero-day vulnerabilities to sophisticated social engineering attacks. By contributing to research through academic study, open-source software projects, or independent investigation, individuals can help develop new methods of detecting, mitigating, and preventing cyber threats. Collaboration between independent researchers, tech companies, and government agencies also accelerates progress, turning individual discoveries into collective solutions. Moreover, individuals can play a key role in advocating for responsible innovation, ensuring that new technologies are developed with privacy and security in mind from the outset.

Promoting ethical standards in tech industries is crucial in shaping a cybersecurity landscape that prioritizes trust, transparency, and accountability. Individuals working in or with technology companies can advocate for ethical practices in product design, software development, and business operations. This includes pushing for the inclusion of security features in every stage of product development, advocating for ethical use of user data, and ensuring that privacy and security are prioritized over profit. The tech industry is often criticized for creating products riddled with vulnerabilities, either because security is overlooked or because developers are incentivized to release products quickly at the expense of proper vetting. Individuals who speak out against these practices, whether through industry groups, professional organizations, or direct engagement with companies, can significantly impact how products are developed and deployed. By promoting ethical standards in the tech industry, individuals ensure that the products people use daily are designed with security and privacy in mind, building greater trust in technology and making it harder for malicious actors to exploit weaknesses.

Fostering a culture of security and trust is vital to ensuring cybersecurity becomes an ingrained part of how we interact with technology. Trust is the foundation of every online transaction, whether it's a financial exchange, a personal conversation, or the sharing of sensitive information. Individuals can contribute to fostering this culture by modeling good security practices, such as using two-factor authentication, encrypting personal communications, and reporting suspicious activity. When individuals hold themselves and their peers accountable for maintaining secure online behavior, they create an environment where others are likelier to do the same. Additionally, promoting transparency in how organizations collect, store, and use personal data helps to build trust with customers and users. When people feel that their information is secure and that they are being treated with respect, they are more likely to embrace new technologies and confidently engage in digital spaces.

Preparing the next generation for digital challenges is one of the most enduring ways individuals can shape the future of cybersecurity. As technology becomes more advanced, so will the complexity of the threats accompanying it. By educating and mentoring young people in cybersecurity, individuals can ensure that the next generation is prepared to handle the challenges of the digital age. This might involve introducing children to online safety, ethical hacking, or secure coding practices through school programs or extracurricular activities. It can also mean encouraging young people to pursue careers in cybersecurity or related fields, ensuring enough skilled professionals to tackle the ever-growing array of cyber threats. The future of cybersecurity lies in the hands of those trained and prepared to address the risks and challenges of tomorrow's digital world, and individuals who take an active role in fostering this knowledge are contributing to a safer and more secure future for all.

Through these efforts—advocating for responsible technology use, supporting education, contributing to research, promoting ethical standards, fostering trust, and preparing the next generation—individuals can significantly influence the evolution of cybersecurity. The role of individuals is not confined to passive observance or mere compliance with existing practices but extends to active engagement, leadership, and advocacy. The challenges posed by cyber threats are not insurmountable, but they require a collective, ongoing effort that involves everyone, from industry professionals to everyday users. As technology continues to evolve, so too must our approach to securing it, and individuals have a critical role in ensuring that our digital future is safe, ethical,

---

Ask the AI

"What role does advocating for ethical standards play in improving cybersecurity practices?"
"How can mentoring programs help prepare the next generation of cybersecurity professionals?"
"What steps can individuals take to stay informed about emerging digital threats and solutions?"

and sustainable. Through collaboration, education, and innovation, individuals can help create a digital ecosystem where security and trust are foundational principles, not afterthoughts.

Recommendations

1. **Adopt a Proactive Security Mindset:** Shift from a reactive approach to anticipating potential threats. Regularly assess your systems, identify vulnerabilities, and implement measures to prevent attacks before they occur. Proactive security creates a stronger, more adaptive defense against emerging cyber threats.

2. **Stay Informed About Emerging Threats:** Regularly research and stay updated on new types of attacks, such as AI-powered cyberattacks and deepfakes. Understanding how these threats operate helps you develop defenses tailored to their methods. Staying informed enables you to adapt your security practices to the latest developments.

3. **Integrate AI Into Security:** Explore AI-driven tools for anomaly detection, incident response automation, and predictive threat analysis. These tools can enhance your ability to detect and respond to sophisticated cyberattacks in real time. Use AI responsibly, ensuring it is deployed ethically and with appropriate oversight.

4. **Enhance Password Security Practices:** Use long, complex passphrases that combine letters, numbers, and symbols, and avoid using personal information. Implement MFA for all accounts to add an extra layer of protection. A strong password system significantly reduces the likelihood of unauthorized access.

5. **Create and Test Backup Systems:** Regularly back up your critical data to local and cloud-based storage solutions. Test your backups periodically to ensure they are functional and can be quickly restored in case of a ransomware attack or data loss. A robust backup system is your safety net against catastrophic cyber incidents.

6. **Collaborate with Cybersecurity Communities:** Join industry-specific forums, threat intelligence groups, or professional associations to share knowledge and insights. Collaboration with others in the field helps you avoid new threats and strengthens collective defenses. Engaging with these communities builds a shared resources and support network.

7. **Educate and Train Continuously:** Participate in cybersecurity awareness training and simulations to sharpen your skills. Encourage others in your organization to do the same, ensuring a culture of security awareness. Regular training minimizes human error, one of the leading causes of cyber incidents.

8. **Evaluate New Technologies Before Adoption:** Conduct thorough risk assessments before implementing new technologies like IoT devices or AI solutions. Ensure they align with your existing security framework and do not introduce new vulnerabilities. Thoughtful adoption of technology helps maximize benefits while minimizing risks.

9. **Promote Ethical Standards in Technology Use:** Advocate for ethical practices within your organization, emphasizing data collection and secure product design transparency. Support initiatives that prioritize privacy and security at every stage of development. Ethical standards build trust and foster safer technological environments.

10. **Mentor the Next Generation of Cybersecurity Professionals:** Share your knowledge and experience with those entering the field, offering guidance and mentorship. Encourage young professionals and students to explore cybersecurity careers and equip them with practical skills. Supporting the next generation ensures the continuity and evolution of cybersecurity expertise.

Conclusion

As we've explored throughout this chapter, the landscape of cybersecurity is constantly evolving, and with it are the threats targeting individuals and organizations alike. The risks are real and growing, from sophisticated AI-powered cyberattacks to the vulnerabilities introduced by the IoT. However, while the challenges may seem daunting, they are not insurmountable. By adopting a proactive cybersecurity mindset and implementing best practices, individuals can significantly reduce the risk of falling victim to malicious attacks and ensure the safety of their digital environments.

Staying informed and continuously adapting to new threats cannot be overstated. As technology advances, so do the methods cybercriminals use to exploit weaknesses. Incorporating AI and ML into cybersecurity strategies can provide robust defenses, but these tools must be used responsibly and ethically. Security isn't just about technology—it's about the continuous development of skills, knowledge, and the collective effort of all stakeholders to create a safer digital world.

One of the most effective ways to safeguard digital assets is through redundancy and regular security updates. Building resilience through backup systems and applying security patches promptly can prevent cyberattacks from causing irreparable harm. It's also essential to remain vigilant and foster a culture of security awareness—whether through participating in training programs or sharing knowledge within communities. Each of us has a role to play in securing the broader digital ecosystem, and the more we engage with security practices, the more resilient we become.

Looking ahead, the future of cybersecurity will be shaped by our willingness to embrace innovation while balancing it with the necessary ethical considerations. As new technologies emerge, we must approach them cautiously, ensuring we do not inadvertently create new system vulnerabilities. Building a secure digital future will require collaboration between individuals, businesses, and policymakers and a commitment to technological innovation and responsible use. Ultimately, our collective efforts to secure our digital lives will determine how effectively we can navigate the ever-changing cyber landscape.

Chapter Questions

1   What is the purpose of adopting a proactive security mindset?
    A. To avoid spending on cybersecurity tools
    B. To anticipate and prevent threats before they occur
    C. To focus solely on reacting to cyberattacks after they happen
    D. To reduce training costs for employees

2   How does ML enhance threat detection in cybersecurity?
    A. By relying on manual input for decision-making
    B. By identifying patterns and anomalies in data
    C. By blocking all traffic indiscriminately
    D. By only addressing known threats

3   Why are long and complex passwords important for cybersecurity?
    A. They make it easier to remember passwords
    B. They prevent users from having to use MFA
    C. They make brute force attacks more difficult to succeed
    D. They eliminate the need for password management tools

4 What is the primary role of backups in a cybersecurity strategy?
   A. To avoid the need for firewalls
   B. To ensure data can be recovered during an incident
   C. To replace encryption as a primary defense mechanism
   D. To reduce the amount of data stored

5 What is the significance of AI-powered cyberattacks?
   A. They automate and adapt attacks, making them more difficult to detect
   B. They are less effective than traditional attack methods
   C. They can only target large organizations
   D. They are easily mitigated by using outdated security systems

6 Why is MFA a critical security measure?
   A. It eliminates the need for strong passwords
   B. It adds an extra layer of verification to accounts
   C. It simplifies the login process
   D. It guarantees complete protection from cyberattacks

7 What is one benefit of joining cybersecurity communities?
   A. To outsource all cybersecurity responsibilities
   B. To gain insights into the latest threats and best practices
   C. To avoid the cost of security tools
   D. To eliminate the need for continuous education

8 What is the role of redundancy in cybersecurity?
   A. To ensure critical systems remain operational during failures
   B. To reduce the amount of data stored
   C. To simplify network configurations
   D. To eliminate the need for incident response plans

9 How does fostering a culture of security improve organizational defenses?
   A. It centralizes all cybersecurity tasks to one department
   B. It creates a shared responsibility for cybersecurity
   C. It eliminates the need for employee training
   D. It focuses solely on technical solutions

10 Why is it essential to evaluate new technologies before adoption?
   A. To determine their popularity
   B. To ensure they align with existing security frameworks
   C. To simplify their implementation process
   D. To avoid integrating them into daily operations

11 What is the purpose of promoting ethical standards in the tech industry?
   A. To prioritize fast product launches over security
   B. To ensure transparency in data handling and product security
   C. To increase product costs for end users
   D. To reduce the focus on user privacy

12 How can individuals stay informed about the latest cybersecurity threats?
   A. By ignoring new trends and focusing on traditional methods
   B. By participating in threat intelligence groups and industry forums
   C. By avoiding the use of emerging technologies
   D. By relying solely on government updates

13 What makes AI tools effective in automating incident responses?
   A. Their ability to eliminate the need for human oversight
   B. Their capability to react to detected threats in real-time
   C. Their reliance on historical data without adapting to new threats
   D. Their use of manual processes to respond to incidents

14 How can mentoring help the next generation of cybersecurity professionals?
   A. By discouraging young people from pursuing tech careers
   B. By providing guidance and practical knowledge to future experts
   C. By focusing only on theoretical concepts
   D. By limiting their exposure to evolving threats

15 What is the role of training in reducing cybersecurity risks?
   A. To replace technical defenses entirely
   B. To equip individuals with the knowledge to recognize and avoid threats
   C. To eliminate the need for automated security systems
   D. To reduce the importance of backups in an organization

21

Teaching and Empowering Others in Cyber Safety

From individuals protecting their devices to organizations safeguarding sensitive data, the need for robust cybersecurity practices has never been greater. Yet, the most sophisticated systems and technologies are only as effective as those who use them. This chapter delves into the importance of fostering a culture of cyber safety through education, engagement, and ongoing commitment to secure behaviors.

One of the foundational elements of building a secure digital environment is education. The digital world constantly evolves, with new threats and challenges emerging regularly. By sharing knowledge about cyber safety through formal training programs, workshops, or everyday conversations, we can empower others to make informed decisions about their online security. The more people understand the risks, the more likely they will take proactive steps to protect themselves and their data.

In the workplace, security is not just the responsibility of IT professionals but of everyone who interacts with company systems and data. Establishing clear security policies, promoting secure practices, and ensuring that employees are equipped with the necessary tools and knowledge are all critical components of a secure organizational environment. However, one of the biggest challenges in any organization is overcoming resistance to cybersecurity measures. Many individuals may not see the immediate benefit or view security protocols as inconvenient, but addressing these concerns through education, incentives, and leading by example is important.

Supporting those close to us—friends and family—also plays a vital role in creating a safer digital world. While businesses often have dedicated resources for cybersecurity, individuals may lack the awareness or knowledge to protect themselves effectively. By initiating open conversations about digital safety, assisting with setting up security measures, and staying informed on the latest threats, we can help loved ones secure their online presence. Encouraging them to think critically about potential threats is an ongoing task that should adapt as the digital landscape changes.

Finally, cybersecurity is not just a task for today but a lifelong journey. Technology is constantly evolving, and so must our practices and understanding of cyber threats. As cybersecurity professionals, educators, or individuals concerned with the safety of their digital lives, we must commit to continuous learning, stay updated with new developments, and reflect on our growth. The landscape of cyber threats will always shift, but by staying committed to cyber safety, we can ensure that we are prepared for whatever challenges lie ahead.

This chapter provides practical advice, real-world examples, and actionable steps to help anyone—from corporate leaders to everyday internet users—contribute to a culture of cybersecurity. Whether you are an expert looking to share your knowledge, a manager aiming to implement workplace policies, or someone wanting to protect your family, this guide will help you take meaningful action toward securing the digital world for yourself and others.

Sharing Knowledge and Resources

Recognizing the power of knowledge and the potential impact of well-informed individuals when protecting digital lives is vital. Identifying opportunities to share this knowledge is crucial in fostering a safer digital environment. Whether it's a casual conversation, a professional seminar, or a social media post, every opportunity is an avenue to empower others with the tools and information they need to defend themselves against cyber threats. As a cybersecurity expert, you are uniquely positioned to make a significant difference by providing people with the resources they need to protect their personal and professional data. Table 21.1 outlines cybersecurity education channels and methods, providing a variety of approaches to enhance learning and awareness in the field of cybersecurity.

Creating accessible and engaging materials is one of the most effective ways to reach a broad audience and ensure your message resonates. Cybersecurity can sometimes feel like a distant or complex topic for the uninitiated, so breaking down key concepts into easily digestible content is essential. This might include infographics, video tutorials, or simple blog posts that offer step-by-step guides on securing devices or understanding phishing scams. The goal is to take a subject that may seem intimidating and transform it into something approachable without

Table 21.1 Cybersecurity education channels and methods.

Channel/method	Target audience	Description	Best use case
Online courses	General public, professionals	Structured learning with modules and assessments	For comprehensive, in-depth cybersecurity training
Workshops	Students, adults, professionals	Hands-on sessions with practical examples	To provide interactive learning experiences
Infographics	General public	Visually appealing, easy-to-understand content	Great for simplifying complex cybersecurity concepts
Webinars	Professionals, students	Live, interactive online sessions	For real-time Q&A and discussions on specific topics
Books and eBooks	General public, students	Self-paced learning with in-depth theory	Ideal for structured, detailed learning on foundational topics
Podcasts	Professionals, general public	Audio-based content on trending cybersecurity topics	Perfect for busy individuals looking to stay informed during commutes
Blogs and articles	General public, professionals	Written content on current cybersecurity issues	For short, accessible reads on up-to-date information
Videos and tutorials	General public, students	Step-by-step, visual instruction on specific topics	For visual learners and detailed walk-throughs
Social media posts	General public, professionals	Concise, engaging content for quick updates	Useful for sharing tips and industry news quickly
Cybersecurity games and simulations	Students, beginners	Interactive games or simulations to test cybersecurity skills	Effective for hands-on learning and engaging younger audiences

diluting its importance. Engaging content should also reflect the diverse learning styles of the audience, making it as interactive and visually appealing as possible to maintain interest and enhance retention of key concepts.

Social media and blogs serve as powerful platforms for outreach, providing a wide-reaching and relatively low-cost method of disseminating cybersecurity information. You can engage with a global audience in real time by creating informative posts or sharing tips and news updates on platforms like Twitter, LinkedIn, or Medium. Regularly updating a blog with new content, such as case studies, tutorials, or reviews of security tools, allows for continued education and keeps followers informed on emerging threats. Additionally, these platforms offer opportunities for direct interaction, enabling you to respond to questions, provide advice, or even start discussions that foster a deeper understanding of cyber safety. The key here is consistency and authenticity, as people are likelier to engage with genuine and useful content.

Organizing workshops and seminars allows for a more hands-on approach to learning. These events, whether in person or virtual, create a space where participants can ask questions, interact with experts, and engage in practical exercises. Workshops provide an environment where learners can see real-world applications of cybersecurity principles and gain confidence in implementing them. For example, a seminar on password management might include a live demonstration of password managers, showing how to set them up and use them effectively. You can deepen the participants' understanding and make the material more memorable by including interactive elements like quizzes or group discussions. In-person seminars also provide networking and collaboration opportunities to share experiences and learn from one another.

Collaborating with schools and community groups is another invaluable strategy for spreading cybersecurity knowledge. These organizations often have well-established networks of individuals who may not have the time or resources to seek digital safety education independently. Schools, in particular, offer an opportunity to reach younger audiences and instill good cybersecurity habits early. This is essential, as digital literacy and safety are increasingly becoming part of the essential skill set for students. Working with local community groups, whether focused on seniors, parents, or underrepresented populations, allows for targeted outreach and ensures that everyone, regardless of their background or expertise, can access the information they need to stay safe online. Building partnerships with these groups can lead to more impactful and sustainable cybersecurity education efforts.

When delivering cybersecurity messages, it's crucial to tailor your communication to fit different audiences' specific needs and experiences. A one-size-fits-all approach rarely works when discussing topics as varied and nuanced as digital safety. For example, the concerns and language used when addressing teenagers may differ significantly from those when speaking to senior citizens. Younger audiences might be more receptive to gaming security or social media privacy messages. At the same time, older adults may need more guidance on recognizing phishing attempts or understanding the importance of software updates. Similarly, professionals in certain industries may require specialized training on securing workplace systems, while everyday users may focus more on personal devices like smartphones and laptops. Customizing your materials and approach ensures that the information is relevant and immediately applicable to their digital lives.

Ask the AI

"What are some effective strategies for creating cybersecurity infographics for beginners?"
"How can blogs and social media be used to reach diverse audiences with cybersecurity tips?"
"What are some best practices for organizing cybersecurity workshops for community groups?"

Educating others about cybersecurity is not just about delivering information—it's about fostering a culture of digital awareness. People need to feel empowered to take action and recognize their role in securing their personal and professional data. Encouraging a proactive attitude toward cybersecurity is crucial, and this can be done by reinforcing the importance of small but significant actions, like updating passwords regularly, avoiding suspicious links, and using multi-factor authentication (MFA). Additionally, helping people understand the risks they face—whether from hackers, phishing attacks, or data breaches—can help them appreciate why these seemingly mundane tasks are so important. You can build a more secure and resilient digital society by creating a sense of shared responsibility and reinforcing that cybersecurity is everyone's job.

Encouraging Safe Practices in the Workplace

Leading by example is one of the most powerful ways to instill cybersecurity awareness within an organization. When leadership consistently demonstrates secure behaviors, it sets the tone for the workplace. Employees who see their managers and colleagues adhering to best practices are more likely to follow suit. For instance, simple actions such as using strong, unique passwords, enabling MFA, and regularly updating software can be subtle but effective signals that security is a priority. It's important to remember that leadership isn't just about what you say but also about what you do, and if secure behaviors are expected at the top levels, they will filter down through the ranks. A workplace that prioritizes cybersecurity reflects a culture that respects the importance of digital safety, and this culture is built on daily, consistent actions. Table 21.2 lists common workplace cybersecurity policies, outlining essential guidelines to protect organizational assets and sensitive information.

Table 21.2 Common workplace cybersecurity policies.

Password policy	Ensure strong, unique passwords for all users	All employees	Quarterly
Phishing awareness policy	Prevent phishing attacks through education and awareness	All employees	Annually
Access control policy	Restrict access to sensitive data and systems	IT staff, management	Quarterly
Data backup policy	Ensure regular backup of critical data to prevent loss	IT staff, management	Monthly
Incident response policy	Define the actions to take in case of a security breach	All employees, IT staff	Annually
Remote work security policy	Ensure secure access to company resources while working remotely	Remote workers, IT staff	Bi-annually
Software update policy	Keep systems up-to-date to minimize vulnerabilities	IT staff, all employees	Monthly
Data encryption policy	Ensure all sensitive data is encrypted both in transit and at rest	All employees, IT staff	Annually
Social media usage policy	Prevent employees from sharing sensitive information online	All employees	Annually
Physical security policy	Ensure physical protection of devices and data at the workplace	All employees, security staff	Annually

Developing and promoting clear, well-structured security policies is crucial for ensuring that everyone in the organization understands their role in maintaining digital safety. These policies should address the most common security threats—phishing, password management, data handling, and device usage—while adapting to the organization's specific needs. Policies should be written in accessible language that employees can easily understand, avoiding technical jargon that could alienate nonexperts. A robust security policy goes beyond simply listing dos and don'ts; it should also provide employees with practical guidance on implementing secure behaviors in their day-to-day work. Promoting these policies through regular communication, whether through email, company meetings, or posted reminders, ensures they remain at the top of people's minds and become ingrained in the workplace culture. Over time, these policies help shape a collective understanding of what is expected and why it matters.

Regular colleague training sessions are essential to reinforcing cybersecurity best practices and ensuring everyone is updated with the latest threats. These sessions should be interactive and tailored to the specific roles and needs of the employees involved. For example, administrative staff might benefit from training focused on securing sensitive data, while sales teams might need more guidance on recognizing phishing emails. Hands-on activities, such as simulated phishing attacks, can be highly effective in helping employees recognize potential threats in real-world scenarios. These training sessions aim not just to impart knowledge but also to create a mindset of vigilance where employees feel empowered to act when they encounter a suspicious email or notice a potential security breach. Regular training also provides an opportunity to refresh knowledge, keeping employees sharp and adaptable to evolving threats.

Recognizing and rewarding good security habits is an often overlooked but highly effective method of encouraging secure behaviors across the organization. Positive reinforcement helps employees feel valued for their efforts and motivates them to follow best practices. This can be done through formal rewards, such as bonuses or public recognition, or informal gestures, such as a thank-you email or a mention in a team meeting. For example, employees who consistently use strong passwords and avoid clicking on phishing links could be acknowledged for their vigilance. By highlighting these positive actions, you create a culture where security is a responsibility and a part of the organization's identity. Rewarding good habits helps to sustain a high level of engagement with cybersecurity practices and demonstrates that the organization is serious about protecting its digital assets. Figure 21.1 illustrates resistance to cybersecurity adoption in the workplace.

Addressing resistance or apathy toward security is one of the more challenging aspects of building a security-conscious workplace, but it is essential for long-term success. Some employees may resist security protocols because they find them cumbersome or unnecessary, while others may be apathetic to the risks. It's important to approach these situations with empathy and understand that resistance often comes from a lack of awareness or understanding of the potential consequences. Training and clear communication can help bridge the gap in these cases, explaining how security measures benefit the individual and the organization. Additionally, addressing resistance requires leadership to be patient and persistent, as ingraining good habits often takes time.

Ask the AI

"What are the most important elements of a workplace password policy?"
"How can leadership effectively model secure behaviors to inspire employees?"
"What are strategies for overcoming resistance to new cybersecurity protocols in the workplace?"

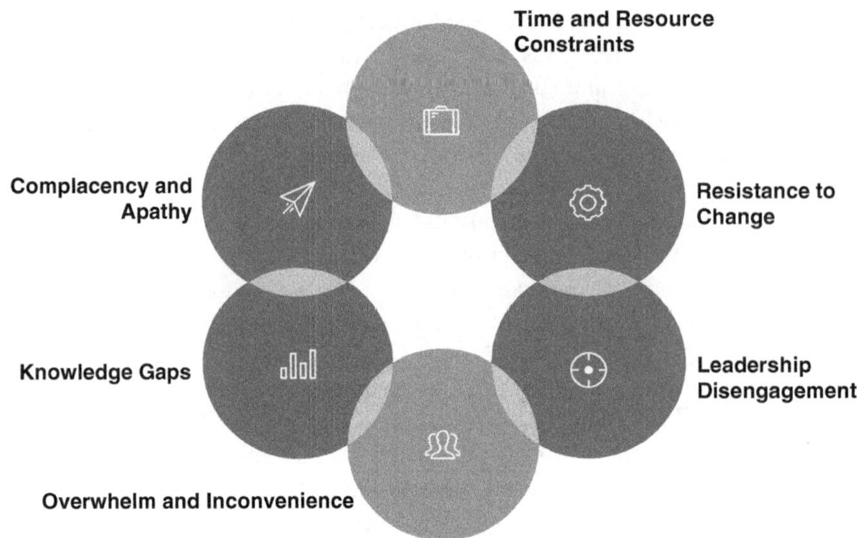

Figure 21.1 Resistance to cybersecurity adoption in the workplace.

Whether through one-on-one training or open discussions, offering support can help employees overcome their resistance and ultimately adopt a more proactive approach to cybersecurity.

Building a security-aware organizational culture does not happen overnight but through consistent effort and commitment from all levels of the organization. It requires creating an environment where cybersecurity is embedded in every aspect of the workplace, from onboarding new employees to daily operations. One key to this is ongoing communication; security updates and reminders should be a regular part of the company's routine. A culture of transparency, where employees feel comfortable reporting security incidents or potential breaches without fear of retaliation, is another important aspect of creating a secure workplace. When employees understand that they are part of a larger effort to protect the organization, they are likelier to take ownership of their role in maintaining security. Encouraging open dialogue about cybersecurity—through company-wide meetings, newsletters, or discussion forums—helps to maintain awareness and fosters a sense of shared responsibility.

Another important consideration when fostering a security-aware workplace is the need for continuous improvement. Cybersecurity threats are constantly evolving, and so should an organization's defense strategies. Regularly reviewing and updating security policies, training materials, and response protocols ensures the workplace is prepared for the latest challenges. This can be done through periodic audits, penetration testing, and employee feedback loops on what works and what doesn't. A workplace that adapts and grows alongside emerging security threats remains resilient in the face of attacks and is committed to safeguarding its employees, data, and reputation. A culture of continuous improvement makes cybersecurity an ongoing priority rather than a one-time initiative.

Finally, integrating cybersecurity into the broader goals and mission of the organization helps ensure that it is seen as a shared responsibility rather than a siloed issue. When cybersecurity is aligned with the company's values—such as integrity, customer trust, and innovation—it becomes a natural part of the organizational fabric. This alignment reinforces the message that digital safety is not just the responsibility of the IT department but a crucial element of the company's success. Leaders who consistently reinforce that security is essential to the organization's growth and reputation help instill a collective sense of ownership and accountability among all employees. When everyone understands their role in maintaining security, it becomes easier to create an environment where good habits thrive, and the organization remains safe from cyber threats.

Supporting Friends and Family

Initiating conversations about cyber safety with friends and family can often feel like walking a fine line between helpfulness and intrusion. Many people are unaware of the risks they face in the digital world, either because they lack technical knowledge or underestimate potential threats. When starting these discussions, it's essential to approach the topic with empathy, understanding, and patience. Instead of overwhelming them with technical jargon or scare tactics, frame the conversation around the positive benefits of cybersecurity, such as protecting personal information, maintaining privacy, and ensuring a safe online experience. By making the conversation relatable and relevant to their lives—safeguarding family photos, securing online banking accounts, or keeping children safe from online predators—you can engage their attention and encourage them to act without feeling condescending.

Assisting friends and family with setting up security measures can be an invaluable service, especially for those who may feel overwhelmed by the complexity of digital safety. This might include helping them set up strong passwords, enabling MFA, or ensuring their devices have the latest security patches installed. Managing security settings can feel daunting for many people, but walking them through these steps—perhaps with a screen-sharing session or in person—can make it much more accessible. Breaking down these actions into manageable tasks, such as updating password managers or adjusting privacy settings on social media platforms, can help them feel more in control of their digital safety. It's also important to provide clear, simple explanations of why these measures matter so that they understand the value of what you set up for them. The more hands-on and approachable you make the process, the more likely they will adopt and maintain these security practices independently.

Providing ongoing support and guidance is crucial for maintaining a high cybersecurity awareness. Cyber threats constantly evolve, and what was considered secure six months ago may no longer be sufficient today. Periodic check-ins with your friends and family can help ensure their security measures remain effective. This might involve reminding them to update their passwords or reviewing their privacy settings after a platform update. Offering support when a new security tool or feature is available—such as a new encryption app or a system update with enhanced security—can keep them ahead of the curve. Moreover, ensuring they understand the importance of staying informed about potential threats and best practices ensures that digital safety doesn't become a one-off task but a continuous process.

Respecting privacy and autonomy while helping others with their digital security is vital. While it's tempting to take full control and ensure that everything is set up "just right," it's important to remember that your friends and family have the right to make their own choices about their digital lives. This means avoiding the temptation to dictate every security measure or action but offering informed guidance and respecting their decisions. Suppose they are not comfortable with a particular security feature or don't feel the need to make certain changes. In that case, it's essential to respect their choices while continuing to offer support and resources. This balance between guidance and respect helps foster trust and avoids causing frustration or resistance. The ultimate goal is to empower them to make informed decisions, not impose their standards.

Ask the AI

"What are the best tools for teaching seniors how to avoid phishing scams?"
"How can critical thinking be encouraged in teenagers to help them identify online threats?"
"What are some ways to stay updated on the latest cybersecurity risks to share with loved ones?"

Sharing updates on new threats and solutions is a key part of ongoing support. Cyber threats evolve quickly, and what may have been safe a few months ago might be exposed to new vulnerabilities. Whether it's a new phishing scheme targeting online shoppers or a software vulnerability that exposes personal data, staying informed about these threats is crucial for maintaining security. Regularly sharing information about emerging threats with your family and friends—through casual conversation, email updates, or curated news sources—helps keep them alert and aware of what they must protect against. It's also a good opportunity to remind them about important security practices, like avoiding suspicious links or using secure networks, especially when traveling. Keeping them updated on new threats and solutions enables them to react quickly and avoid falling victim to the latest scams.

Encouraging skepticism and critical thinking is one of the most important aspects of helping others navigate the digital world safely. In an age where misinformation spreads as easily as accurate information, friends and family must learn to question what they see online, whether it's an email, a social media post, or an advertisement. Encouraging them to think critically about the sources of information they interact with helps them avoid falling for scams, phishing attempts, or disinformation campaigns. This can be as simple as reminding them to double-check the legitimacy of emails before clicking on any links or attachments or questioning the validity of unsolicited offers they receive. Teaching them to pause and reflect on the information they encounter online also helps them avoid impulsive actions that could lead to security breaches. Fostering this kind of critical thinking helps ensure they don't become easy targets for cybercriminals and have the mental tools to evaluate potential risks before taking action.

Providing cybersecurity support to family and friends can sometimes be a slow, iterative process. Some may initially resist the changes you suggest due to a lack of understanding or a reluctance to embrace new practices. However, with patient encouragement and education, they can become more receptive to safeguarding their digital lives over time. One effective way to facilitate this process is by making the benefits of cybersecurity personal and relatable. For example, if you're helping a relative set up two-factor authentication for their email, explain how this measure will protect their conversations, sensitive documents, and financial information. Making the case for security in terms of what matters to them personally is often the best way to ensure they follow through on making those changes.

Finally, it's important to recognize that while you may provide guidance and resources, the ultimate responsibility for digital safety rests with the individual. Helping friends and family with security measures can only go so far if they do not own their digital habits. Empowering them with knowledge through simple tips, ongoing updates, or security best practices helps them make smarter, more informed decisions. Teaching them the "how" and the "why" of cybersecurity, you help build the foundation for lasting, independent, safe practices. Ultimately, supporting your loved ones in their cybersecurity journey fosters confidence and a sense of self-reliance so they can navigate the digital world with greater assurance and security.

Mentoring and Community Involvement

Becoming a mentor for individuals new to cybersecurity is a rewarding and impactful way to give back to the community while helping others build the skills and confidence needed to navigate the digital world safely. Those just starting to explore the field can find the complexities of cybersecurity daunting. However, with the guidance of an experienced mentor, they can gain valuable insights and practical knowledge. As a mentor, your role is to teach technical concepts and provide encouragement and career advice, helping mentees find their path in the cybersecurity field. Whether it's guiding someone through the basics of network security, explaining encryption principles, or offering insights into real-world cybersecurity challenges, your mentorship can make a significant difference in their professional development. Building a strong mentoring relationship based on mutual respect and trust helps foster a deeper understanding of cybersecurity concepts, turning theory into practical knowledge that mentees can apply in their careers.

Participating in volunteer programs is another meaningful way to contribute to the cybersecurity community. Many nonprofit organizations and community centers need help educating the public about cybersecurity basics, especially as digital threats increase. By offering your expertise in these volunteer settings, you support these organizations and help individuals who might not otherwise have access to professional cybersecurity education. Volunteering could involve hosting workshops for local schools, conducting cybersecurity training for small businesses, or working with vulnerable populations like seniors to protect their digital lives. The experience gained through volunteering also helps strengthen your understanding and ability to communicate complex cybersecurity topics in simple, actionable terms. By giving back through volunteering, you help bridge the digital divide and ensure that cybersecurity knowledge is accessible to a wider audience.

Joining cybersecurity advocacy groups is another effective way to become involved in the broader cybersecurity community. These groups work to raise awareness about cyber threats, advocate for stronger privacy protections, and promote best practices for securing digital environments. Whether joining an established organization or starting a local cybersecurity initiative, your participation helps amplify the collective voice advocating for safer digital spaces. Advocacy groups also offer opportunities to collaborate with like-minded individuals, share resources, and learn about emerging cybersecurity issues from professionals across industries. Becoming an active member of such groups helps you stay up to date with the latest developments in the field. It allows you to contribute to the broader mission of improving cybersecurity awareness and practices globally.

Contributing to open-source security projects is a practical and impactful way to engage with the cybersecurity community while honing your skills. Open-source projects provide an opportunity to collaborate, share solutions to common security problems, and develop tools that people can use worldwide. Whether it's working on security-focused software, contributing to bug fixes, or reviewing code for vulnerabilities, your involvement in open-source projects helps strengthen the community. It contributes to the creation of more secure digital tools. Open-source projects also allow you to gain experience working with diverse teams, which can enhance your problem-solving abilities and provide exposure to different aspects of cybersecurity. As the open-source community grows, the impact of these contributions becomes increasingly significant, not only for the cybersecurity field but for the wider digital ecosystem as well.

Hosting or attending community cybersecurity events is an excellent way to share knowledge, learn from peers, and strengthen relationships within the cybersecurity community. Events such as cybersecurity conferences, hackathons, and meetups provide opportunities for professionals and enthusiasts to exchange ideas, collaborate on projects, and stay informed about the latest trends

---

Ask the AI

"What skills are essential for mentoring someone new to cybersecurity?"
"How can I identify and contribute to open-source cybersecurity projects?"
"What are the benefits of joining cybersecurity advocacy groups for personal and community growth?"

and threats in the field. If you're hosting an event, whether a small local workshop or a larger seminar, you create a space for others to learn and grow in the cybersecurity field, contributing to the overall knowledge pool of the community. Attending events allows you to network with other professionals, learn from industry leaders, and stay updated with emerging technologies and threats. Both hosting and attending these events help create a culture of continuous learning and collaboration, which is essential for staying ahead in the ever-evolving world of cybersecurity.

Inspiring others to pursue careers in cybersecurity is one of the most powerful ways to shape the industry's future. As cybersecurity threats continue to grow in complexity, there is a growing demand for skilled professionals to defend against them. Encouraging young people, students, or even career changers to explore the field can help ensure a steady pipeline of talent in the industry. Sharing your journey into cybersecurity, explaining the challenges and rewards, and offering guidance on getting started can make the field more accessible and appealing to newcomers. Whether through mentoring, speaking at career fairs, or simply having one-on-one conversations, your influence can inspire others to pursue a career in this vital and rewarding field. By helping others see the value of cybersecurity as a career path, you contribute to the growth and diversity of the profession, ensuring it remains equipped to handle future challenges.

Finally, combining these various forms of community involvement creates a multiplier effect, where your efforts to mentor, volunteer, advocate, and contribute lead to a broader, more impactful presence in the cybersecurity field. Every interaction, whether sharing knowledge at a community event, contributing code to an open-source project, or encouraging a young person to pursue a career in cybersecurity, helps build a stronger, more resilient digital ecosystem. Your involvement is not just about personal growth or recognition—it's about creating a lasting, positive impact on the community and helping to build a safer digital future for everyone. You become part of a collective movement working toward a more secure and informed digital world through mentoring, community engagement, and advocacy.

Continuing the Journey of Cyber Safety

Staying committed to lifelong learning is fundamental to maintaining relevance in the ever-evolving field of cybersecurity. Cyber threats evolve rapidly, and new technologies constantly reshape the landscape, so a commitment to continuous education is essential. Whether through formal certifications, self-paced online courses, or participation in cybersecurity forums and webinars, dedicating time to learning ensures you remain informed about the latest trends and tools. It's important to recognize that cybersecurity is not a field where you can simply "graduate" and stop learning; rather, it's an ongoing journey that requires constant adaptation. From understanding new encryption algorithms to staying ahead of emerging attack vectors like AI-driven threats, lifelong learning enables you to anticipate challenges before they arise and build robust, forward-thinking solutions. Embracing this commitment also allows you to stay intellectually engaged and curious, crucial for maintaining enthusiasm in an often demanding field.

Adapting to technological changes and threats is an inherent part of the cybersecurity profession. As technology progresses, so too do the methods and sophistication of cybercriminals. What worked a year ago in defense may not be sufficient today, and the same tools and strategies are not guaranteed to protect against new attack vectors. The rise of technologies such as the Internet of Things, artificial intelligence, and machine learning has introduced new challenges in securing networks and systems. Cybersecurity professionals must develop new skills and strategies to protect sensitive data and systems as these technologies become more integrated into everyday life. By remaining agile and willing to experiment with the latest tools, frameworks, and methodologies, you can ensure that your approach to cyber safety is not just reactive but proactive—anticipating the next wave of threats and preparing defenses in advance. This adaptability sets great cybersecurity professionals apart and ensures they can confidently handle the unexpected.

Reflecting on personal growth and achievements in cybersecurity is an important practice that helps maintain motivation and clarity of purpose. As the cybersecurity landscape becomes more complex, it's easy to become consumed by the latest threat or challenge, and sometimes, you may lose sight of how far you've come. Regularly reflecting on what you've learned, the skills you've developed, and your positive impact can provide a sense of accomplishment and direction. This reflection doesn't just help you appreciate your progress and highlights areas for improvement and further development. Celebrating milestones, such as achieving a new certification, successfully thwarting a security incident, or teaching a cybersecurity workshop, reinforces the idea that each step you take in your journey is significant. Acknowledging your growth, no matter how small, fuels the desire to keep learning and advancing in the field, ultimately making you a better cybersecurity advocate and professional.

Setting goals for future contributions ensures that your journey in cybersecurity remains focused and purposeful. Without clear goals, it's easy to become complacent or overwhelmed by the rapid pace of change. Setting short-term and long-term goals—mastering a new cybersecurity tool, contributing to an open-source project, or mentoring the next generation of cybersecurity professionals—gives your efforts a sense of direction. For example, you might aim to achieve a new certification, present at a cybersecurity conference, or write a blog post about a recent security incident you encountered. These goals help you grow as a professional and ensure that your contributions to the field continue to be impactful. By regularly reassessing and updating your goals, you stay focused on what matters most and continue to advance personally and professionally. Goal-setting also provides a sense of accountability, helping you push through challenges and stay committed to your journey of growth and improvement.

Building networks with like-minded individuals is essential for long-term success and collaboration in the cybersecurity field. Cybersecurity is a team effort, and the more you connect with professionals, experts, and even newcomers to the field, the more resources, insights, and opportunities become available to you. Attending cybersecurity conferences, joining online communities, or participating in industry-specific groups can help you expand your professional circle. These networks provide a space for sharing knowledge and experiences and offer support when faced with challenges or seeking advice. Being part of a community of like-minded individuals keeps you motivated and inspired to keep pushing forward, whether tackling complex security issues or solving real-world problems. It also helps you stay informed about the latest trends and tools in cybersecurity, which is essential for adapting to new threats. Ultimately, a strong professional network acts as both a support system and a resource hub that can guide you as you continue your journey in cybersecurity.

Celebrating successes and milestones in security is often an overlooked yet important aspect of professional development. Cybersecurity can be intense, with long hours spent analyzing threats, patching vulnerabilities, or responding to security breaches. However, it's important to pause and recognize your progress, whether successfully preventing a security breach, implementing a new

---

Ask the AI

"What are the best free or low-cost resources for ongoing cybersecurity education?"
"How can I evaluate my cybersecurity progress and set realistic goals?"
"What strategies can be used to celebrate achievements while staying motivated in cybersecurity?"

security protocol, or advancing your skill set with a new certification. Celebrating these achievements, whether through personal reflection or shared recognition with colleagues or peers, helps reinforce the value of your hard work and dedication. It also helps remind you that even in a field where threats constantly evolve, every victory—big or small—is a step forward in making the digital world safer. These moments of celebration help maintain morale and reinforce the idea that cybersecurity is not just about fighting threats but about building a safer, more secure digital future.

Recommendations

1. **Commit to Lifelong Learning:** Dedicate monthly time to explore emerging cybersecurity trends, tools, and threats. Begin by subscribing to reliable cybersecurity blogs, attending webinars, or completing an online course. This consistent effort will keep you informed and better equipped to address evolving challenges.
2. **Tailor Educational Materials:** When educating others, adapt content to match the needs of your audience. For example, use interactive workshops for professionals and infographics for general audiences. Making cybersecurity accessible ensures that your message resonates and prompts action.
3. **Model Secure Behaviors:** By practicing what you preach, lead by example in the workplace. Regularly update your passwords, enable MFA, and follow company security policies. Visible adherence to best practices encourages colleagues to do the same.
4. **Simplify Security Practices:** Break down complex cybersecurity measures into actionable, easy-to-understand steps. For instance, use relatable examples to identify phishing emails or create strong passwords. Simplified guidance reduces resistance and fosters adoption.
5. **Incorporate Cybersecurity into Everyday Conversations:** Bring up cybersecurity topics naturally in discussions with friends and family. For example, share a recent news story about a phishing attack and discuss ways to avoid similar scams. These conversations help raise awareness in an informal, relatable way.
6. **Recognize and Reward Good Practices:** In workplace settings, acknowledge employees who follow security protocols diligently. This could include verbal praise, small rewards, or public recognition. Positive reinforcement fosters a culture where cybersecurity is valued and maintained.
7. **Engage with the Community:** Participate in local cybersecurity initiatives, such as hosting workshops or volunteering with nonprofits. Use these opportunities to educate underserved populations about digital safety. Community engagement ensures that cybersecurity knowledge reaches broader audiences.
8. **Stay Updated on Emerging Threats:** Regularly review trusted cybersecurity news sources to stay informed about the latest risks. Share this knowledge with colleagues, friends, and family through emails or brief discussions. Keeping everyone informed minimizes vulnerability to new attack methods.
9. **Promote Critical Thinking:** Encourage others to question the validity of online information, emails, and links. Offer simple tips, such as verifying sender authenticity or examining URL structures. Fostering a habit of skepticism reduces susceptibility to scams and phishing attempts.
10. **Set Measurable Goals for Personal Growth:** Identify specific objectives, such as obtaining a cybersecurity certification, learning a new tool, or mentoring a newcomer. Track your progress and celebrate milestones to maintain motivation. Goal-setting helps focus your efforts and ensures continuous improvement.

Conclusion

As the digital world continues to expand, the importance of cybersecurity has reached unprecedented levels. Everyone ensures that the digital environment remains safe and trustworthy, from personal data protection to organizational resilience. While it's easy to focus on the latest tools and technologies, it's crucial to remember that cybersecurity begins with awareness and the shared responsibility of every individual. The foundation of a secure digital life lies in the systems we use, the actions we take, and the habits we form.

Building a culture of cybersecurity requires ongoing education, open communication, and a commitment to security at all levels. In organizations, this means not just implementing policies but also fostering an environment where security is prioritized by leadership and embraced by all employees. Training sessions, clear guidelines, and consistent reinforcement of best practices are essential to maintaining a security-conscious workforce. As technology evolves, so too should our approach to cybersecurity education, ensuring that individuals and teams remain equipped to handle emerging threats.

Supporting our friends and family in their cybersecurity practices is equally important outside the workplace. Many people, especially those who are less tech-savvy, are vulnerable to cyber threats simply because they lack the knowledge or awareness to protect themselves. By having conversations about digital safety, assisting with setting security measures, and keeping up-to-date with the latest threats, we can help those closest to us navigate the online world more securely. Encouraging a mindset of skepticism and critical thinking can empower individuals to spot potential risks before they become real problems.

Cybersecurity is not a one-time fix or a box to check—it's a continuous journey. The digital world will always change, and new threats will constantly emerge. To stay ahead of these challenges, individuals must remain engaged in lifelong learning and adapt to new technologies and strategies. Reflecting on personal growth, setting new goals, and building networks of like-minded people are all vital components of sustaining a culture of cybersecurity for the long term.

By making cybersecurity a part of everyday life at home and work, we can create an environment where safety is the norm, not the exception. This chapter has outlined key strategies for engaging others, supporting those around us, and ensuring that secure practices are learned and lived. With consistent effort and an open, collaborative approach, we can make a meaningful impact on cybersecurity in our personal lives, workplaces, and communities. Ultimately, the goal is to build a secure digital future where everyone can safely navigate the digital world.

Chapter Questions

1   What is the primary goal of lifelong learning in cybersecurity?
    A. To focus on a single technology
    B. To stay ahead of evolving threats
    C. To avoid changes in technology
    D. To prioritize nontechnical skills

2   Which method is most effective for tailoring cybersecurity education to a specific audience?
    A. Using a single approach for all audiences
    B. Relying solely on technical jargon
    C. Adapting content to match audience needs
    D. Avoiding audience engagement

3 Why is it important to model secure behaviors in the workplace?
  A. To show off technical skills
  B. To inspire others through visible adherence to best practices
  C. To reduce the workload of IT staff
  D. To avoid implementing security policies

4 What is the primary purpose of simplifying cybersecurity practices?
  A. To make security less effective
  B. To reduce implementation time
  C. To increase user adoption and understanding
  D. To avoid using advanced tools

5 What is an effective way to raise cybersecurity awareness among friends and family?
  A. Share complex technical details
  B. Avoid discussing cybersecurity altogether
  C. Use relatable examples to explain threats
  D. Only provide help when asked

6 How can organizations reward employees for good cybersecurity practices?
  A. Ignore their efforts
  B. Penalize noncompliance instead
  C. Offer incentives and public recognition
  D. Limit rewards to technical staff only

7 Why is volunteering in cybersecurity important?
  A. To promote exclusive knowledge
  B. To gain hands-on experience and help underserved populations
  C. To compete with other professionals
  D. To avoid teaching others about cybersecurity

8 What is the benefit of staying informed about emerging cybersecurity threats?
  A. To reduce the need for security updates
  B. To prepare better defenses and share knowledge
  C. To simplify workplace security policies
  D. To avoid adapting to new tools

9 How does critical thinking help with identifying cyber threats?
  A. By promoting blind trust in digital content
  B. By helping users recognize and question suspicious activity
  C. By encouraging users to ignore phishing attempts
  D. By limiting user engagement with cybersecurity practices

10 What is the primary purpose of cybersecurity policies in the workplace?
  A. To restrict employee autonomy
  B. To ensure consistent security practices
  C. To focus only on IT staff responsibilities
  D. To reduce leadership accountability

11 Why is reflecting on personal growth important in cybersecurity?
- **A.** To focus only on technical skills
- **B.** To acknowledge achievements and identify areas for improvement
- **C.** To avoid learning new techniques
- **D.** To compare success with others

12 What is the best way to engage with the cybersecurity community?
- **A.** Avoid participating in community events
- **B.** Attend workshops, contribute to open-source projects, and join advocacy groups
- **C.** Focus only on online resources
- **D.** Prioritize solo learning over collaboration

13 What is the key to successfully mentoring someone new to cybersecurity?
- **A.** Sharing experiences and providing guidance
- **B.** Focusing only on technical skills
- **C.** Limiting their exposure to new tools
- **D.** Avoiding one-on-one interactions

14 What is an example of resistance to cybersecurity adoption in the workplace?
- **A.** Enthusiasm for security policies
- **B.** Complacency and lack of understanding
- **C.** Commitment to following best practices
- **D.** Leadership engagement

15 What is an effective way to evaluate and celebrate progress in cybersecurity?
- **A.** Ignore achievements and focus on challenges
- **B.** Regularly set goals and celebrate milestones
- **C.** Compare progress with peers
- **D.** Focus only on technical certifications

Appendix

Answers to Chapter Questions

Chapter 1

1. **Correct Answer: B. To protect accounts from unauthorized access**
Explanation: Strong, unique passwords are the first line of defense against unauthorized access. They prevent cybercriminals from easily guessing or cracking account credentials, thereby securing personal data.

2. **Correct Answer: B. Using multi-factor authentication (MFA)**
Explanation: Multi-factor authentication provides an additional layer of security by requiring a second form of verification, such as a code sent to your phone. This makes it much harder for attackers to gain access even if they have your password.

3. **Correct Answer: B. To prevent vulnerabilities from being exploited by cybercriminals**
Explanation: Cybercriminals often exploit outdated software that has known vulnerabilities. Regular updates and patches close these security gaps, making it harder for attackers to breach systems.

4. **Correct Answer: C. To make informed decisions and recognize potential cyber threats**
Explanation: Understanding the latest cybersecurity threats helps individuals recognize risky behavior and take necessary precautions. Education allows people to avoid common traps like phishing emails or fake websites.

5. **Correct Answer: C. They contribute to the security of the entire network by adopting safe practices**
Explanation: Individuals play a key role in collective cybersecurity by adopting secure behaviors, such as using strong passwords and avoiding risky online activities. A lapse in one person's security can affect the whole network.

6. **Correct Answer: B. Financial and reputational damage**
Explanation: Ignoring cybersecurity can lead to severe financial consequences, such as the costs associated with data breaches or ransomware attacks. Reputation damage can also be long-lasting, especially if sensitive data is exposed.

7. **Correct Answer: B. To ensure cybersecurity becomes part of daily routines and decision-making**
Explanation: A culture of security mindfulness means that security is always top of mind when making online decisions. This proactive approach minimizes the risks associated with careless behavior, such as opening suspicious emails.

Cyber Defense: Best Practices for Digital Safety, First Edition. Jason Edwards.
© 2025 John Wiley & Sons Ltd. Published 2025 by John Wiley & Sons Ltd.

8. **Correct Answer: C. New attack methods and vulnerabilities are constantly emerging**
   Explanation: Cybersecurity threats evolve rapidly, with attackers continuously finding new ways to exploit weaknesses. Continuous learning helps individuals stay ahead of these changes and adapt their defense strategies.

9. **Correct Answer: B. Using encryption for sensitive communications and files**
   Explanation: Encryption protects sensitive data by turning it into unreadable code, ensuring that only authorized parties can access it. This is essential for safeguarding information during transmission or storage.

10. **Correct Answer: C. By adopting secure online practices and encouraging others to do the same**
    Explanation: Collective security relies on every individual practicing safe online behavior. By setting an example and educating others, individuals contribute to a stronger and more resilient security environment.

11. **Correct Answer: B. To provide an additional layer of protection beyond just passwords**
    Explanation: Multi-factor authentication adds an extra layer of security by requiring something you know (your password) and something you have (a phone or authentication app). This significantly reduces the risk of unauthorized access.

12. **Correct Answer: B. To ensure data recovery in the event of a cyberattack or system failure**
    Explanation: Backups ensure that important data can be restored if it is lost, corrupted, or stolen during an attack. Regular backups protect against the permanent loss of vital information.

13. **Correct Answer: B. Their risk of a cyberattack increases, leading to financial and reputational loss**
    Explanation: Neglecting cybersecurity practices opens the door for cybercriminals to exploit vulnerabilities. This can lead to significant financial losses and damage to both personal and professional reputations.

14. **Correct Answer: A. To detect unusual activity and prevent fraud**
    Explanation: Regularly monitoring financial accounts allows for quick detection of any unauthorized transactions. Early detection helps minimize the impact of fraud or identity theft.

15. **Correct Answer: B. To reduce the risk of privacy invasion and identity theft**
    Explanation: Sharing too much personal information online can make you an easy target for identity theft and privacy invasions. Limiting what you share protects your personal data and reduces the risk of exploitation.

Chapter 2

1. **Correct Answer: B. Human behavior**
   Explanation: While technology plays a role, human actions, such as failing to follow security protocols, often lead to cybersecurity breaches. Many threats exploit human vulnerabilities like negligence or lack of awareness.

2. **Correct Answer: B. Creating a sense of urgency**
   Explanation: Social engineering attacks often manipulate emotions like fear and urgency to trick individuals into acting quickly, such as clicking on a malicious link. This tactic makes the target less likely to carefully consider the potential risks.

3. **Correct Answer: B. Manipulating human behavior to gain access to information**

   Explanation: Social engineering attacks exploit human trust, emotions, and behaviors to bypass technical security measures. These attacks rely on deceiving people into revealing confidential data or performing risky actions.

4. **Correct Answer: A. Phishing**

   Explanation: Phishing attacks rely on manipulating emotions such as fear (e.g. claiming account compromise) or greed (e.g. offering prizes) to persuade victims to provide sensitive information. These attacks typically come in the form of fraudulent emails or messages.

5. **Correct Answer: A. Checking the website's design**

   Explanation: A professional, well-designed website often indicates credibility and trustworthiness. Reputable websites tend to have clear, consistent branding and accurate, verifiable content.

6. **Correct Answer: A. To protect their privacy and others' privacy**

   Explanation: Responsible digital citizenship involves ensuring that both personal and others' privacy are respected, reducing the likelihood of harm like identity theft. By practicing ethical behavior online, individuals help secure a safer digital environment.

7. **Correct Answer: C. By verifying requests through official channels**

   Explanation: Verifying requests, such as account verification or password reset requests, directly through trusted sources is the best way to avoid falling victim to phishing. Phishing relies on tricking users into acting without confirmation.

8. **Correct Answer: B. Look for a professional design and known branding**

   Explanation: A trustworthy website typically presents a clean, professional design and uses official branding or credentials. Websites with poor design or inconsistencies may indicate they are fraudulent or unreliable.

9. **Correct Answer: B. They often come from unverified sources or are scams**

   Explanation: Online offers that sound too good to be true are often designed to exploit vulnerabilities. They may involve scams or phishing attempts that aim to steal personal information or infect your device with malware.

10. **Correct Answer: C. Always verifying requests through official, trusted channels**

    Explanation: Verifying communications by contacting the organization directly through known methods helps protect against social engineering. This reduces the risk of responding to fraudulent requests or disclosing sensitive information.

11. **Correct Answer: C. Questioning the validity and sources of online information**

    Explanation: Critical thinking involves actively questioning the credibility of online content and sources. Instead of accepting information at face value, a critical thinker cross-checks facts and seeks multiple viewpoints.

12. **Correct Answer: C. Protecting privacy and avoiding identity theft**

    Explanation: Ethical behavior online includes safeguarding personal data and respecting others' privacy. Protecting personal information helps prevent identity theft and contributes to a safer online community.

13. **Correct Answer: A. By limiting who can see your posts and data**

    Explanation: Privacy settings control who can access your personal information, thereby preventing unwanted exposure or misuse. These settings help protect your data from unauthorized third parties.

14. **Correct Answer: B. Failing to verify the legitimacy of digital communications**
    Explanation: Human error, such as failing to verify suspicious emails or messages, often leads to breaches. Cybercriminals rely on individuals not questioning unsolicited communications to exploit vulnerabilities.
15. **Correct Answer: B. Verify the request through official contact methods**
    Explanation: When receiving unexpected communications, the safest approach is to verify the legitimacy of the request using known, official contact information. This prevents falling victim to phishing or other social engineering attacks.

Chapter 3

1. **Correct Answer: B. Change your passwords and secure your accounts**
   Explanation: After discovering identity theft, the first critical step is to secure your accounts by changing passwords and enabling multi-factor authentication to protect your personal information from further compromise.
2. **Correct Answer: B. The Federal Trade Commission (FTC)**
   Explanation: The FTC provides an official record of the identity theft incident, which is essential for tracking recovery efforts and supporting claims with creditors, banks, and credit bureaus.
3. **Correct Answer: B. Place a fraud alert or freeze on your credit report**
   Explanation: Placing a fraud alert or freezing your credit prevents new accounts from being opened in your name by unauthorized individuals, making it a vital step in protecting your financial identity.
4. **Correct Answer: A. It prevents access to your credit report by unauthorized parties**
   Explanation: Freezing your credit stops anyone from accessing your credit report to apply for new credit, reducing the risk of further financial fraud or identity theft in the future.
5. **Correct Answer: B. Contact your financial institutions immediately**
   Explanation: Reporting fraudulent transactions to your financial institutions right away ensures that they can freeze your accounts, reverse unauthorized charges, and take steps to prevent further fraud.
6. **Correct Answer: A. By making it harder for attackers to access your accounts**
   Explanation: Multi-factor authentication requires more than just a password to access an account, making it significantly more difficult for attackers to bypass and gain access, even if they have stolen your password.
7. **Correct Answer: B. Shred or store them in a secure location**
   Explanation: Storing sensitive documents in a secure location or shredding them ensures that your personal information isn't accessible to unauthorized individuals who may attempt to use it for identity theft.
8. **Correct Answer: B. Fraudulent charges made in the victim's name**
   Explanation: A common consequence of identity theft is that criminals open new accounts or make fraudulent purchases using the victim's personal details, leading to financial losses and a tarnished credit score.
9. **Correct Answer: B. To alert you to any changes or suspicious activity on your credit report**
   Explanation: Credit monitoring services track your credit report and notify you about any new accounts or unusual activity, allowing you to respond quickly to prevent further damage.

10. **Correct Answer: B. A notification to creditors that they should take extra steps to verify your identity**
    Explanation: A fraud alert on your credit report alerts creditors to take additional steps to verify your identity before opening new accounts, which can prevent unauthorized accounts from being created.

11. **Correct Answer: B. Hackers may retrieve personal information stored on them**
    Explanation: If old devices are not securely wiped or destroyed, they may still contain personal data that can be accessed and misused by criminals, leading to potential identity theft.

12. **Correct Answer: B. A credit monitoring system and fraud alerts**
    Explanation: Identity theft protection services typically include credit monitoring to detect unusual activity and fraud alerts that notify creditors to verify your identity, offering a critical layer of security.

13. **Correct Answer: C. Report it to the appropriate authorities**
    Explanation: Suspicious requests for personal information should be reported to the authorities, as they may be phishing attempts designed to steal your identity. Responding or providing information could lead to further fraud.

14. **Correct Answer: A. It prevents anyone from accessing your credit report to open new accounts**
    Explanation: A credit freeze ensures that no one, including fraudsters, can access your credit report without your authorization, thereby preventing new credit from being issued in your name.

15. **Correct Answer: B. You can file a complaint with the FTC and report to law enforcement**
    Explanation: Victims of identity theft can file a report with the FTC and local law enforcement, which helps initiate an investigation and provides the documentation needed for recovering lost funds or resolving fraudulent activity.

Chapter 4

1. **Correct Answer: B. Implement multi-factor authentication (MFA)**
   Explanation: MFA provides an additional layer of security beyond just passwords, making it significantly harder for attackers to access business accounts even if a password is compromised. Implementing MFA reduces the chances of unauthorized access through stolen or leaked credentials.

2. **Correct Answer: B. Employees can only access resources necessary for their jobs**
   Explanation: RBAC ensures that employees are granted access based on their roles, following the principle of least privilege. This reduces the likelihood of accidental or malicious exposure to sensitive information.

3. **Correct Answer: C. Using a password manager with encrypted sharing**
   Explanation: Password managers securely store and share credentials by encrypting the information, making it inaccessible to unauthorized users. This method is much safer than sharing passwords through unencrypted channels like email or sticky notes.

4. **Correct Answer: B. Revoke their access and update permissions immediately**
   Explanation: Promptly updating or revoking access ensures that former employees or those changing roles can no longer access business resources. This helps protect the organization from potential security breaches or insider threats.

5. **Correct Answer: B. It helps detect unauthorized or suspicious behavior early**
   Explanation: By monitoring account activity, businesses can identify and respond to suspicious behavior quickly, potentially preventing a larger security incident. Early detection is key to minimizing damage from breaches.

6. **Correct Answer: B. Protect them with strong passwords and MFA**
   Explanation: Protecting recovery options with strong passwords and MFA ensures that these critical mechanisms cannot be exploited by attackers. Since recovery options are often targeted in social engineering attacks, securing them is essential.

7. **Correct Answer: B. To protect the company from unauthorized access and ensure consistent security practices**
   Explanation: Clear policies help ensure that account access is properly managed throughout the employee lifecycle, from onboarding to termination. These policies prevent unauthorized access and ensure that account security is maintained consistently.

8. **Correct Answer: B. It reduces the chances of human error leading to security breaches**
   Explanation: Training employees on cybersecurity best practices helps them understand the importance of secure behaviors, such as recognizing phishing attempts and using MFA. This reduces the likelihood of human error, which is a common cause of security breaches.

9. **Correct Answer: B. It exposes the business to potential unauthorized access**
   Explanation: Unused or compromised accounts can serve as entry points for attackers, who may exploit them to gain unauthorized access to business systems. Promptly deactivating these accounts reduces this risk.

10. **Correct Answer: C. Implement MFA and control who can access sensitive information**
    Explanation: Implementing MFA ensures that only authorized users can access business platforms while controlling access to sensitive information minimizes the risk of data breaches. These measures are essential for securing communication and collaboration on digital platforms.

11. **Correct Answer: B. Investigate it immediately and take action to secure the account**
    Explanation: Suspicious account activity should be investigated immediately to determine if a breach has occurred. Taking swift action to secure the account helps prevent further unauthorized access or damage.

12. **Correct Answer: B. It securely stores and shares passwords with encryption, reducing the risk of exposure**
    Explanation: Password managers encrypt stored credentials, making them inaccessible to unauthorized parties, while securely sharing passwords ensures that only the intended recipient has access. This greatly enhances security compared to storing passwords in plain text.

13. **Correct Answer: B. To maintain the principle of least privilege, ensuring employees only have the necessary access**
    Explanation: Regularly reviewing and updating permissions ensures that employees only have access to the systems they need, minimizing the risk of exposure to unnecessary data. This practice is foundational to maintaining security in a business environment.

14. **Correct Answer: B. Immediately revoke all access and properly archive data**
    Explanation: Deactivating accounts and archiving data immediately when an employee leaves ensures that sensitive information is protected and no unauthorized access occurs. This process should be part of the company's offboarding protocol.

15. **Correct Answer: B. To identify potential security threats as soon as they occur**
    Explanation: Account alerts for unusual activity allow businesses to react quickly to potential security threats, such as unauthorized logins or changes to account settings. Early identification of suspicious activity can help prevent data breaches and other security incidents.

Chapter 5

1. **Correct Answer: C. To prevent cross-contamination between personal and work-related information**
   Explanation: Keeping personal and professional email accounts separate minimizes the risk of exposing sensitive work-related information to phishing attacks, and ensures more effective security measures tailored to each account type.

2. **Correct Answer: B. Using encryption for sensitive email content**
   Explanation: Encryption ensures that the content of sensitive emails is securely transmitted and only accessible to the intended recipient, reducing the risk of data being intercepted by malicious actors.

3. **Correct Answer: B. It adds an extra layer of security, reducing the risk of account compromise**
   Explanation: Multi-factor authentication (MFA) provides an additional security step beyond just a password, making it significantly harder for attackers to gain access to your email account, even if they have your password.

4. **Correct Answer: C. Always, especially when the email requests urgent action**
   Explanation: Verifying requests through another channel, like a phone call or messaging system, prevents attackers from exploiting urgency to manipulate recipients into providing sensitive information.

5. **Correct Answer: B. To ensure you don't miss a phishing email hidden among legitimate ones**
   Explanation: Regularly cleaning and organizing your inbox helps you spot phishing emails more easily, reducing the chances of an attack being overlooked amidst cluttered or outdated messages.

6. **Correct Answer: C. By confirming any unusual or urgent requests through another communication method**
   Explanation: Confirming suspicious requests via trusted channels prevents falling for phishing schemes, where attackers impersonate trusted individuals to steal sensitive information.

7. **Correct Answer: B. To block and segregate suspicious emails from your inbox**
   Explanation: Email filters and spam protection tools automatically sort suspicious emails into separate folders, reducing the chances of these threats reaching your main inbox and causing harm.

8. **Correct Answer: B. It minimizes the chances of falling victim to phishing or other email-based threats**
   Explanation: Educating colleagues on email security helps them recognize and avoid potential threats, which strengthens the overall security posture of the organization and reduces the likelihood of successful attacks.

9. **Correct Answer: C. Sensitive project details or confidential information**
   Explanation: Auto-reply and out-of-office messages should not include sensitive or confidential details, as these messages are often accessible by anyone who emails you, increasing the risk of exposure.

10. **Correct Answer: C. Contact the sender through a trusted method, like phone or company messaging systems**
    Explanation: Contacting the sender through a trusted channel helps verify the authenticity of the request and prevents falling for phishing attacks or social engineering schemes that attempt to steal sensitive information.

11. **Correct Answer: A. To ensure the email is legitimate and not an attempt to impersonate a trusted sender**
Explanation: Verifying the sender's email address helps identify whether the email is genuinely from a trusted source or if it has been spoofed by attackers aiming to deceive you into divulging sensitive information.

12. **Correct Answer: B. Report the phishing email to your email provider**
Explanation: Reporting phishing attempts to your email provider helps improve their security measures, which in turn helps prevent similar attacks from reaching you or others in the future.

13. **Correct Answer: B. Enable multi-factor authentication (MFA) for added security**
Explanation: Enabling MFA significantly enhances the security of your email account by requiring a second verification step, such as a code sent to your phone, which protects against unauthorized access.

14. **Correct Answer: A. By preventing unauthorized access to email contents during transmission**
Explanation: Email encryption ensures that even if an email is intercepted during transmission, its contents remain unreadable to unauthorized individuals, protecting sensitive information from prying eyes.

15. **Correct Answer: A. Because emails can be used as evidence in legal proceedings**
Explanation: Email communications are often considered legal documents, and their contents can be used in court cases or regulatory investigations, so it's important to be mindful of their potential legal implications.

Chapter 6

1. **Correct Answer: B. To assess their character and professionalism**
Explanation: Employers often review candidates' online presence, such as social media profiles, to gauge their behavior, values, and professionalism, which are important factors in the hiring process. This helps employers make decisions based on both qualifications and character.

2. **Correct Answer: B. Exposure to identity theft**
Explanation: Oversharing personal details, such as phone numbers, birthdates, or address, increases the risk of identity theft. Criminals can use this information to steal your identity and engage in fraudulent activities.

3. **Correct Answer: C. Address it calmly and professionally**
Explanation: Responding to negative content calmly and professionally can help defuse potential conflicts and allow you to clarify any misinformation. A well-handled response can demonstrate your commitment to transparency and professionalism.

4. **Correct Answer: B. The right to have certain personal data removed from search results**
Explanation: The right to be forgotten allows individuals to request the removal of outdated or irrelevant personal information from search engine results. This legal right helps individuals control their digital presence and protect their privacy.

5. **Correct Answer: B. They can create misleading or harmful fake content**
Explanation: Deepfakes use artificial intelligence to create false videos or audio that can damage reputations. They can be used maliciously to spread misinformation or impersonate someone for fraudulent purposes.

6. **Correct Answer: B. Update and remove outdated profiles and content**
   Explanation: Regularly updating your profiles and removing outdated or irrelevant content helps ensure your digital presence remains accurate and aligned with your current personal or professional goals. This strategy helps maintain a positive online reputation.

7. **Correct Answer: B. To control who can see and use your personal data**
   Explanation: Privacy settings allow you to manage who can access your personal information and how it is used. By reviewing these settings, you can protect your privacy and limit exposure to unwanted data collection.

8. **Correct Answer: B. It can be used to track and identify individuals without consent**
   Explanation: Facial recognition technology, while useful for security, can also be used to track individuals without their knowledge or consent. This raises privacy concerns as it may lead to unauthorized surveillance or identification.

9. **Correct Answer: A. Disable cookies and tracking technologies**
   Explanation: Disabling cookies and tracking technologies helps reduce the amount of personal data collected by websites. This limits the ability of third-party advertisers to track your online behavior and protect your privacy.

10. **Correct Answer: B. It protects your true identity in non-professional contexts**
    Explanation: Using a pseudonym allows you to participate in online activities while maintaining anonymity, especially in non-professional or casual contexts. This helps protect your privacy and reduces the risk of your personal information being exploited.

11. **Correct Answer: B. It remains accessible even after it is deleted**
    Explanation: Once content is shared online, it can remain accessible through search engines or third-party websites, even after it is deleted. This highlights the permanence of digital information and the difficulty in fully erasing content from the internet.

12. **Correct Answer: A. They may collect and sell your personal information**
    Explanation: Data brokers collect and aggregate personal data, which is then sold to companies for marketing purposes. This practice can infringe on your privacy and lead to unwanted solicitations or data misuse.

13. **Correct Answer: B. To help you protect your personal data from misuse**
    Explanation: Understanding your legal rights regarding personal data ensures that companies do not misuse or mishandle your information. Knowledge of these rights enables you to take action if your data is compromised or used without your consent.

14. **Correct Answer: C. Teach them about managing their online presence and privacy**
    Explanation: Educating others about managing their digital footprint and using privacy settings can help them make informed decisions about their online behavior. This awareness reduces the likelihood of privacy violations and helps create a safer digital environment.

15. **Correct Answer: C. Damage to your personal and professional reputation**
    Explanation: Failing to manage your digital footprint can lead to damaging content becoming publicly accessible, which may harm both your personal and professional reputation. This can result in lost opportunities or unwanted negative attention.

Chapter 7

1. **Correct Answer: B. Lack of mutual connections**
   Explanation: Fake profiles often have few or no mutual connections, making them suspicious. Real profiles typically have a history of authentic interactions with mutual friends or acquaintances.

2. **Correct Answer: C. Verify the source and URL before clicking**
   Explanation: Suspicious links should never be clicked without verification. Phishing attempts often rely on deceptive links that lead to malicious websites designed to steal personal data.

3. **Correct Answer: C. Take screenshots and report the behavior to the platform**
   Explanation: Documenting the harassment and reporting it to the platform is the most effective way to address it. Social media platforms have mechanisms in place to remove harmful content and punish violators.

4. **Correct Answer: B. To prevent unauthorized access by requiring a second form of identification**
   Explanation: Two-factor authentication (2FA) adds an extra layer of protection, making it harder for unauthorized users to access your account even if they know your password.

5. **Correct Answer: B. Question unsolicited requests for personal information and verify them through other channels**
   Explanation: Social engineering attacks rely on manipulating your trust. Always verify suspicious requests through another means, such as contacting the person directly.

6. **Correct Answer: B. Block or report abusive users**
   Explanation: Blocking and reporting abusive users immediately stops further interactions, preventing the situation from escalating. It is a proactive way to protect yourself and others from harm.

7. **Correct Answer: A. Change your password immediately and enable 2FA**
   Explanation: Changing your password and enabling 2FA are essential steps in regaining control over a compromised account. These actions significantly reduce the risk of further unauthorized access.

8. **Correct Answer: A. They often include a request to share personal information**
   Explanation: Phishing attempts typically ask for sensitive personal data, such as login credentials or credit card details. Always be cautious if a message requests this kind of information.

9. **Correct Answer: B. Report the account and warn the person being impersonated**
   Explanation: Reporting impersonating accounts is essential to stop fraudulent activities. It's also helpful to inform the person being impersonated so they can take protective measures.

10. **Correct Answer: B. To protect your information by keeping privacy settings current**
    Explanation: Regularly updating your privacy settings ensures your personal information remains protected. Social media platforms frequently change their settings, so staying informed is key to maintaining control.

11. **Correct Answer: B. They can automate malicious actions like spamming or manipulating interactions**
    Explanation: Bots are often used to manipulate social media activity on a large scale, such as automating spamming or inflating engagement. These actions can compromise the integrity of online interactions.

12. **Correct Answer: B. The account follows and interacts with hundreds or thousands of random users**
    Explanation: Bots often have large followings of unrelated accounts and interact with random users. This behavior differs from genuine accounts that typically engage with a smaller, more focused network.

13. **Correct Answer: B. When you find the post to be inappropriate or harmful**
    Explanation: Reporting harmful posts helps maintain a safe and respectful online environment. Most platforms provide tools to report content that violates their terms of service.

14. **Correct Answer: B. It prevents the user from sending you messages or interacting with your posts**
Explanation: Blocking a user on social media prevents them from sending messages, commenting on your posts, or interacting with you in other ways. It's an essential tool for managing unwanted or abusive interactions.
15. **Correct Answer: A. It could be used against you in a social engineering attack or identity theft**
Explanation: Personal information shared on social media can be exploited in social engineering attacks or identity theft. Always be mindful of the information you disclose publicly.

Chapter 8

1. **Correct Answer: B. To offer emotional support and report the bullying**
Explanation: An upstander actively intervenes to help the victim and addresses the bullying behavior, either by reporting it or providing emotional support, rather than passively watching or supporting the bully.
2. **Correct Answer: B. Sudden withdrawal and emotional distress**
Explanation: Cyberbullying often leads to emotional and psychological effects, such as withdrawal, fear, and anxiety, which may not be immediately visible but are important indicators of distress.
3. **Correct Answer: B. Document the incidents through screenshots and messages**
Explanation: Documentation is crucial as it provides evidence of the bullying, which can be useful for reporting to authorities or platform administrators and for tracking the extent of the harassment.
4. **Correct Answer: B. Promoting empathetic responses and thinking before posting**
Explanation: Encouraging others to think about the impact of their words before posting helps foster a respectful online environment and reduces the likelihood of misunderstandings and harmful interactions.
5. **Correct Answer: B. Regularly monitor their children's online activity and set clear guidelines**
Explanation: Parents should be proactive in monitoring their children's online interactions, discussing appropriate online behavior, and setting clear rules to guide responsible internet use and prevent cyberbullying.
6. **Correct Answer: B. By educating people about online safety and encouraging positive online behavior**
Explanation: Community initiatives focused on education can help raise awareness about the risks of cyberbullying, provide tools for recognizing harmful behavior, and encourage empathy and respect in digital interactions.
7. **Correct Answer: C. Providing access to counseling and mental health resources**
Explanation: Counseling offers victims the emotional and psychological support they need to deal with the trauma caused by cyberbullying and helps them develop healthy coping strategies.
8. **Correct Answer: B. To help individuals navigate online spaces responsibly and recognize harmful behavior**
Explanation: Digital citizenship education equips individuals with the skills needed to make responsible decisions online, which helps prevent harmful behaviors such as cyberbullying from occurring.

9. **Correct Answer: C. Step in as an upstander by offering support and reporting the incident**
   Explanation: As an upstander, you can take immediate action by offering emotional support to the victim and reporting the bullying to the appropriate authorities or platform administrators.

10. **Correct Answer: C. To push for stronger anti-bullying policies and better enforcement**
   Explanation: Advocacy helps ensure that cyberbullying is addressed effectively by promoting the creation and enforcement of policies that protect users and discourage harmful behavior online.

11. **Correct Answer: A. Use parental control tools to monitor online activity**
   Explanation: Parental control tools allow parents to monitor their children's online interactions, set appropriate restrictions, and intervene early if necessary to prevent exposure to cyberbullying.

12. **Correct Answer: B. By informing others about the emotional impact of cyberbullying and how to respond appropriately**
   Explanation: Education helps individuals understand the severe emotional effects of cyberbullying and teaches them how to recognize signs of bullying and take appropriate action to support the victim.

13. **Correct Answer: B. Clearly defining what constitutes harassment and setting consequences for it**
   Explanation: Establishing clear guidelines about what behavior is unacceptable and the consequences for engaging in harassment creates a framework for safer online spaces and helps reduce the occurrence of cyberbullying.

14. **Correct Answer: C. Offer emotional support and guide them to professional help if needed**
   Explanation: Victims of cyberbullying need emotional support to feel less isolated and may also need professional help to cope with the emotional and psychological impact of bullying.

15. **Correct Answer: B. Offer digital literacy workshops and promote responsible online behavior**
   Explanation: Schools and community programs can raise awareness by providing education on online safety, responsible digital behavior, and how to recognize and address cyberbullying.

Chapter 9

1. **Correct Answer: B. Familiarize themselves with the school's technology policies**
   Explanation: Parents should understand the school's technology policies to ensure they align with best practices for digital safety. Familiarity with these guidelines allows parents to reinforce safety measures and advocate for improvements if necessary.

2. **Correct Answer: B. Participate in cyber safety education programs**
   Explanation: Participating in programs that teach cyber safety reinforces the lessons children learn in school. This helps parents stay informed about the latest digital threats and provides an opportunity to engage with their children on the topic.

3. **Correct Answer: B. Build a support network to exchange ideas and strategies**
   Explanation: Engaging with other parents creates a collective approach to managing online safety. Sharing insights and strategies helps parents navigate digital risks more effectively and creates a sense of community.

4. **Correct Answer: C. To anticipate potential online dangers and address them proactively**
   Explanation: Staying informed about new trends and digital risks allows parents to anticipate potential issues before they affect their children. By understanding these risks, parents can take action to protect their children.

5. **Correct Answer: A. Advocate for child-friendly online environments**
   Explanation: Advocating for safer digital spaces for children ensures that technology providers, lawmakers, and schools prioritize the needs of young users. This advocacy can lead to changes in platform policies and regulations.

6. **Correct Answer: C. By offering trusted guides, articles, or apps to other parents**
   Explanation: Sharing trusted resources helps other parents stay informed and take action in protecting their children. This exchange of knowledge strengthens the collective effort to improve digital safety.

7. **Correct Answer: B. Promote ongoing communication about digital safety**
   Explanation: Regular communication ensures that digital safety concerns are discussed openly and regularly. This creates a supportive environment where children feel comfortable sharing their online experiences.

8. **Correct Answer: A. By working with local schools and libraries to offer workshops**
   Explanation: Collaborating with community institutions to offer digital safety workshops helps reach a broader audience. These efforts provide families with valuable information and support.

9. **Correct Answer: B. Encourage their children to report any negative online experiences**
   Explanation: Encouraging children to report issues helps ensure that problems like cyberbullying are addressed quickly. It fosters a safe environment where children feel they can speak up without fear of punishment.

10. **Correct Answer: A. Organize a group of parents to meet with school administrators**
    Explanation: By collaborating with other parents, a unified voice can advocate for updates in school policies. This can lead to better digital safety practices at the school level.

11. **Correct Answer: A. New apps may introduce new ways for children to be exposed to online risks**
    Explanation: As new platforms gain popularity, they may introduce unknown risks, such as exposure to cyberbullying or predators. Parents must stay informed to ensure these risks are mitigated.

12. **Correct Answer: A. By attending digital safety workshops or webinars**
    Explanation: Attending workshops keeps parents updated on the latest digital safety tools and strategies. It ensures that they are equipped to handle evolving digital threats.

13. **Correct Answer: B. By supporting initiatives that require platforms to enforce age verification and privacy protections**
    Explanation: Advocating for policies that protect children's privacy and ensure age-appropriate content helps make digital spaces safer for young users. This ensures that platforms are held accountable for the safety of minors.

14. **Correct Answer: B. By sharing resources with other parents and caregivers**
    Explanation: Sharing updated and reliable digital safety tools with others helps create a more informed community. It empowers all caregivers to take steps to protect children online.

15. **Correct Answer: B. Hosting open discussions about online risks and safety**
    Explanation: Open discussions foster awareness of online risks and promote the sharing of safety practices. It helps parents and caregivers collectively work toward protecting children from digital dangers.

Chapter 10

1. **Correct Answer: B. Verify the legitimacy of the request independently**

   Explanation: Verifying the request independently ensures you are dealing with a legitimate source, preventing potential scams that may misuse your personal or financial information. Always take extra steps to confirm any unsolicited communication before taking action.

2. **Correct Answer: D. Avoid opening the attachment and verify the sender**

   Explanation: Attachments from unknown sources often contain malware or other harmful software. To protect your device and personal information, avoid opening attachments and instead verify the sender through trusted channels.

3. **Correct Answer: D. Credit cards or trusted payment processors**

   Explanation: Credit cards and trusted payment processors provide fraud protection, allowing you to dispute charges if something goes wrong. Avoid untraceable payment methods like pre-paid cards or wire transfers, which leave you vulnerable to fraud.

4. **Correct Answer: B. Share knowledge about common scams and safe practices**

   Explanation: Educating others on cybersecurity helps them recognize scams and practice safer online behaviors. By sharing your knowledge, you empower those around you to protect themselves from fraud.

5. **Correct Answer: C. To help recognize new threats before they impact you**

   Explanation: Staying updated on common scams allows you to spot emerging threats and adjust your security practices accordingly. Being informed helps you act proactively, rather than reactively when encountering new scams.

6. **Correct Answer: C. Verify the authenticity of the prize through official channels**

   Explanation: Scammers often use fake prizes to lure people into revealing personal information or making payments. Always verify prize claims independently through trusted official sources before taking any action.

7. **Correct Answer: B. Teach them to question unsolicited communications and verify requests**

   Explanation: Fostering skepticism helps others avoid falling for scams that rely on urgency or manipulation. Teaching verification skills empowers people to make informed decisions and avoid unnecessary risks.

8. **Correct Answer: B. It helps authorities track fraud patterns and warn others**

   Explanation: Reporting scams allows authorities to track and combat fraudulent activities, protecting others from falling victim to similar schemes. It also provides valuable data to prevent future scams.

9. **Correct Answer: C. Use known contact details to reach out to the organization directly**

   Explanation: Using verified contact information ensures that you are reaching out to a legitimate organization. Avoid using details from the suspicious message itself, as it could be part of a scam.

10. **Correct Answer: C. It provides an opportunity to share experiences and warn others about scams**

    Explanation: Online forums are a great way to exchange information and alert others to potential scams. By contributing, you help raise awareness and protect the community from emerging threats.

11. **Correct Answer: A. Report it to the relevant authorities immediately**

    Explanation: Reporting scams helps authorities track fraudulent activities and prevent further victims. It also assists in identifying and shutting down fraudulent operations.

12. **Correct Answer: B. It adds an additional layer of security to protect your accounts**
Explanation: Multi-factor authentication (MFA) adds an extra layer of security by requiring multiple forms of verification. This reduces the risk of unauthorized access, even if your password is compromised.

13. **Correct Answer: A. Set them to automatically update**
Explanation: Automatic updates ensure that your software and security tools are always up to date, protecting you from newly discovered vulnerabilities. Manual updates are often missed or delayed, leaving you vulnerable.

14. **Correct Answer: D. Keep personal information private and only share it when necessary**
Explanation: Keeping your personal data private reduces the risk of it being exploited by scammers. Share information only when necessary and ensure that the recipient is trusted and legitimate.

15. **Correct Answer: B. It helps educate vulnerable groups on recognizing threats**
Explanation: Cybersecurity awareness programs teach individuals to identify scams and adopt safer online practices. They are especially useful for vulnerable populations who may be targeted more frequently by fraudsters.

Chapter 11

1. **Correct Answer: B. To understand the latest trends and risks in AI**
Explanation: Staying informed about emerging AI technologies helps individuals understand both the capabilities and potential risks of AI, enabling them to make more informed decisions about using AI tools in their personal or professional lives.

2. **Correct Answer: B. Championing transparency, fairness, and accountability**
Explanation: Advocating for responsible AI practices means supporting policies and frameworks that ensure AI systems are designed and used in a manner that is transparent, fair, and accountable to the public.

3. **Correct Answer: B. By helping shape responsible AI policies and practices**
Explanation: Participating in discussions about AI ethics allows individuals to influence the ethical guidelines and regulatory frameworks that govern AI, helping ensure that AI is developed and used in ways that benefit society.

4. **Correct Answer: B. Loss of jobs due to automation**
Explanation: One of the primary concerns with AI advancements in the labor market is that automation could displace human workers, particularly in industries like manufacturing, transportation, and customer service.

5. **Correct Answer: B. By minimizing the amount of data shared with AI services**
Explanation: Limiting the amount of personal data shared with AI services helps protect privacy, as excessive data sharing increases the risk of exposure and misuse of sensitive information.

6. **Correct Answer: B. They often have fewer data retention practices and better data policies**
Explanation: Privacy-focused AI alternatives prioritize the protection of user data and are more likely to have strict data retention policies, ensuring that less personal information is collected or stored by the service.

7. **Correct Answer: B. To protect sensitive data by making it unreadable or anonymous**
Explanation: Encryption and anonymization tools help protect sensitive information, making it unreadable to unauthorized parties or removing identifying information, thus safeguarding privacy.

8. **Correct Answer: B. To help users understand how decisions are made by AI systems**
Explanation: Transparency in AI algorithms is critical because it helps users understand how decisions are made, fostering trust and enabling individuals to identify and challenge potentially harmful or biased outcomes.

9. **Correct Answer: B. Requesting access to personal data collected by AI services**
Explanation: Exercising your rights under data protection laws involves actively requesting access to the data that AI services have collected about you, ensuring that you can review and manage it as per your legal rights.

10. **Correct Answer: B. To minimize exposure to potential misuse of personal data**
Explanation: By reviewing and limiting data sharing, individuals can reduce the risk of their personal information being misused or exposed, ensuring better control over their privacy.

11. **Correct Answer: B. It ensures that AI systems are subject to oversight and operate ethically**
Explanation: Advocating for AI accountability ensures that AI systems are subject to oversight, preventing unethical practices and promoting transparency and fairness in their design and deployment.

12. **Correct Answer: B. The lack of transparency in AI decision-making processes**
Explanation: The lack of transparency in AI decision-making is a major concern, especially in critical sectors like healthcare and law enforcement, as it makes it difficult to understand how decisions are made and whether they are fair or biased.

13. **Correct Answer: B. By detecting and mitigating AI-driven cyber threats**
Explanation: AI can enhance security practices by identifying and mitigating threats in real time, using machine learning algorithms to detect anomalies or malicious behaviors that traditional security systems might miss.

14. **Correct Answer: B. The potential for AI systems to collect more personal data than necessary**
Explanation: A significant risk in AI data privacy is that AI systems can collect excessive amounts of personal data, sometimes without clear consent, increasing the potential for misuse or breaches of privacy.

15. **Correct Answer: B. To mitigate emerging threats and protect their data**
Explanation: As AI technologies evolve, so too do the associated risks. Proactively adapting security practices ensures that individuals are protected against new threats and vulnerabilities that arise with emerging AI technologies.

Chapter 12

1. **Correct Answer: B. Encrypt the device and use biometric authentication**
Explanation: Encryption and biometric authentication are effective methods for securing personal data because they protect the device from unauthorized access. Biometric authentication adds convenience and enhances security by using unique physical characteristics like fingerprints or facial recognition.

2. **Correct Answer: B. Perform a factory reset and securely wipe data**

   Explanation: Before donating a device, performing a factory reset ensures that all user data is removed. Securely wiping data goes a step further by overwriting it, making it unrecoverable.

3. **Correct Answer: C. Using data-wiping software that overwrites data**

   Explanation: Data-wiping software permanently removes data by overwriting it multiple times, making it nearly impossible to recover. This method is more reliable than simply deleting files or reformatting.

4. **Correct Answer: C. To control data shared and protect privacy**

   Explanation: Managing app permissions allows users to limit access to sensitive information, reducing the risk of data breaches. Apps often request unnecessary permissions that can compromise user privacy.

5. **Correct Answer: B. To locate or secure a device if lost or stolen**

   Explanation: Remote tracking helps locate a missing device, while wipe features allow users to erase sensitive data remotely. These tools are critical for minimizing damage from lost or stolen devices.

6. **Correct Answer: B. A certified e-waste recycling program**

   Explanation: Certified programs ensure that devices are recycled responsibly and that data is securely destroyed. They adhere to environmental and data protection standards, unlike uncertified services.

7. **Correct Answer: B. Set a strong PIN or biometric lock**

   Explanation: A strong PIN or biometric lock prevents unauthorized access to the wearable device. This is the first and most important step in securing personal data stored on wearables.

8. **Correct Answer: C. Data recovery by unauthorized individuals**

   Explanation: Improper disposal can leave personal data on devices accessible to others. This risk highlights the importance of secure data wiping before disposal.

9. **Correct Answer: C. Pair only with trusted devices**

   Explanation: Pairing with untrusted devices can expose wearables to unauthorized access or malware. Secure pairing ensures that data is transmitted only to trusted and safe devices.

10. **Correct Answer: B. Remove and securely wipe or destroy them**

    Explanation: SD cards and SIM cards often store sensitive data like contacts, messages, or media. Removing and wiping or destroying them prevents data recovery by unauthorized individuals.

11. **Correct Answer: B. To patch security vulnerabilities**

    Explanation: Operating system and app updates often include security patches to protect against new threats. Regular updates help ensure that devices are not exposed to known vulnerabilities.

12. **Correct Answer: B. Leaving devices unattended**

    Explanation: Leaving devices unattended in public spaces creates an easy opportunity for theft. Vigilance and using security measures like locks help prevent unauthorized access or loss.

13. **Correct Answer: B. Ensure secure data erasure and safe disposal**

    Explanation: Certified e-waste programs focus on securely wiping data and properly disposing of hazardous materials. This prevents both data recovery and environmental damage.

14. **Correct Answer: B. To protect sensitive data from unauthorized access**

    Explanation: Encrypting wearable device data ensures that even if the data is intercepted, it cannot be accessed without proper authorization. This is essential for safeguarding health and personal data.

15. **Correct Answer: B. To control how data is shared and protect your privacy**
Explanation: Regularly reviewing privacy settings allows users to ensure their data is shared only with trusted services. This helps prevent unnecessary exposure of sensitive information.

Chapter 13

1. **Correct Answer: B. To fix vulnerabilities and improve security**
Explanation: Regular updates ensure that vulnerabilities are patched and security improvements are applied, reducing the risk of exploitation. Neglecting updates can leave systems exposed to known threats.

2. **Correct Answer: C. Reducing the risk of malware infections**
Explanation: Trusted sources vet their software to ensure it is free of malicious content, whereas untrusted sources may distribute compromised applications. This practice minimizes the risk of installing malware.

3. **Correct Answer: B. To confirm software authenticity and integrity**
Explanation: Verifying digital signatures ensures that the software is legitimate and has not been tampered with. This step protects users from installing malicious or altered versions of programs.

4. **Correct Answer: C. To allow vendors to fix vulnerabilities before exploitation**
Explanation: Vulnerability disclosure programs enable vendors to address security flaws before attackers can exploit them. This process strengthens software security and protects users.

5. **Correct Answer: B. By restricting execution to trusted, approved software**
Explanation: Application whitelisting only allows software that has been pre-approved, reducing the risk of malicious programs running. This proactive approach significantly enhances system security.

6. **Correct Answer: B. To monitor and mitigate potential threats**
Explanation: IDPS monitors network activity for signs of suspicious behavior and prevents potential threats from exploiting vulnerabilities. It provides an additional layer of defense against cyberattacks.

7. **Correct Answer: A. To ensure patches do not disrupt business operations**
Explanation: Testing patches in a staging environment verifies their compatibility with existing systems and prevents disruptions. This ensures that patch deployment is both safe and effective.

8. **Correct Answer: B. Whitelisting only allows trusted software, while blacklisting blocks known malicious software**
Explanation: Whitelisting is a more proactive approach, permitting only pre-approved software, whereas blacklisting focuses on blocking software already identified as harmful. Both methods aim to enhance system security.

9. **Correct Answer: B. Speed and accuracy of patch deployment to critical systems**
Explanation: Prioritizing critical systems ensures that the most vulnerable areas are secured quickly, reducing the risk of exploitation. Effective emergency patching minimizes downtime and potential damage.

10. **Correct Answer: B. To prevent users from bypassing security measures**
Explanation: Striking a balance ensures that security measures are effective without becoming overly restrictive. User-friendly security reduces the likelihood of non-compliance.

11. **Correct Answer: B. It helps vendors fix the issue and strengthens security**
    Explanation: Responsible reporting allows vendors to address vulnerabilities before attackers can exploit them. This process improves security for all users of the software.
12. **Correct Answer: C. To reduce risks of data tracking or malicious activity**
    Explanation: Malicious browser extensions can track user activity or compromise sensitive information. Carefully managing extensions minimizes these risks.
13. **Correct Answer: B. To improve future response efficiency**
    Explanation: Analyzing past vulnerabilities helps organizations identify weaknesses in their response processes. Lessons learned can lead to better preparation and faster responses to future threats.
14. **Correct Answer: A. By prioritizing critical vulnerabilities based on potential attack vectors**
    Explanation: Threat modeling helps organizations identify which vulnerabilities pose the highest risks and prioritize their resolution. This ensures resources are allocated effectively.
15. **Correct Answer: B. To detect and prevent potential threats from unapproved software**
    Explanation: Monitoring systems for unauthorized installations helps identify potential security risks early. Preventing the use of unapproved software minimizes the attack surface.

Chapter 14

1. **Correct Answer: B. Isolate the infected device from the network**
   Explanation: Disconnecting the infected device from any network prevents the malware from spreading to other systems and stops any potential data exfiltration or further communication with the attacker.
2. **Correct Answer: A. The attacker may not decrypt your files after receiving the ransom**
   Explanation: Ransom payments do not guarantee that the attacker will actually decrypt your files. Paying the ransom also funds future cybercrimes and emboldens attackers to target others.
3. **Correct Answer: B. Run antivirus and anti-malware software to scan for threats**
   Explanation: Once the device is isolated, running a full system scan ensures that no additional malware is present, helping to clean the system before any recovery attempts are made.
4. **Correct Answer: B. Use the decryption tool to recover encrypted files**
   Explanation: If a decryption tool is available for your specific ransomware variant, it can decrypt your files without the need to pay the ransom, allowing for recovery without further complications.
5. **Correct Answer: A. It allows you to restore your system to a previous state without paying the ransom**
   Explanation: A reliable backup system allows for the restoration of lost or encrypted data, reducing reliance on paying the ransom and minimizing the impact of the ransomware attack.
6. **Correct Answer: B. Check the integrity of the backup before restoration**
   Explanation: Ensuring that your backup is clean and not infected is crucial before restoring it. If the backup itself is compromised, restoring from it may reintroduce the malware.
7. **Correct Answer: B. Consult a professional for data recovery**
   Explanation: If no decryption tool is available, a professional data recovery service may be able to assist in recovering data from encrypted files, though success is not guaranteed.

8. **Correct Answer: A. It helps law enforcement track cybercriminal activities**
   Explanation: Reporting a ransomware attack to authorities helps them investigate the incident, track down cybercriminals, and prevent future attacks on others, contributing to larger efforts to combat cybercrime.

9. **Correct Answer: A. Three copies of data, two on the same device, one offline or in the cloud**
   Explanation: The 3-2-1 backup rule ensures redundancy and availability of data in case of an attack, with copies stored on different media and locations to protect against both local and online threats.

10. **Correct Answer: C. Malware like ransomware before it can encrypt files**
    Explanation: Endpoint security tools are designed to detect and block ransomware and other malware before they can execute and encrypt files, providing proactive protection against infections.

11. **Correct Answer: B. It reduces the chances of falling victim to phishing attacks that deliver ransomware**
    Explanation: Employee training on recognizing phishing attempts and practicing safe online habits helps prevent the initial infection that often comes from malicious email attachments or links, which are common delivery methods for ransomware.

12. **Correct Answer: B. To minimize the damage and recover data efficiently**
    Explanation: An incident response plan provides clear steps to isolate infected systems, report the attack, and restore data, ensuring that the organization can recover quickly and minimize overall damage from the attack.

13. **Correct Answer: B. Report the attack to relevant authorities and regulatory bodies**
    Explanation: If sensitive personal or financial data is affected by a ransomware attack, legal requirements may mandate that it be reported to authorities and regulatory bodies to ensure compliance and protect affected individuals.

14. **Correct Answer: B. Ransomware from encrypting files and spreading**
    Explanation: Real-time protection from endpoint security tools can detect and block ransomware before it encrypts files, preventing further damage and halting the malware's spread throughout the network.

15. **Correct Answer: A. Regularly patching and updating software to fix vulnerabilities**
    Explanation: Regularly updating and patching software ensures that vulnerabilities are addressed before they can be exploited by ransomware or other malware, strengthening defenses against future attacks.

Chapter 15

1. **Correct Answer: C. Improved security and user privacy**
   Explanation: Privacy-focused browsers enhance security by offering features that protect user data from being collected and exploited by third parties. They prioritize user privacy over other functionalities like customization or exclusive content access.

2. **Correct Answer: C. To fix security vulnerabilities and bugs**
   Explanation: Keeping your browser up to date ensures that you receive the latest security patches that fix vulnerabilities that could be exploited by cybercriminals. Regular updates improve both the security and functionality of your browser.

3. **Correct Answer: B. To prevent websites from collecting your data**
   Explanation: Managing cookies and trackers helps to control the amount of personal data that websites can collect about your online behavior. This practice enhances your privacy by limiting data collection by advertisers and other third parties.

4. **Correct Answer: C. The presence of a padlock icon in the address bar**
   Explanation: A padlock icon indicates that the website uses HTTPS and has a valid SSL certificate, ensuring that the connection is secure and data is encrypted. This is a key sign of a secure website.

5. **Correct Answer: B. Using clickbait and misleading content**
   Explanation: Malicious websites often use clickbait and misleading content to lure users into clicking links that may lead to malware or phishing attempts. This tactic exploits users' curiosity or desire for sensational content.

6. **Correct Answer: C. Adjust privacy settings and block harmful users**
   Explanation: Protecting yourself from online harassment involves using privacy settings to limit who can contact you and blocking users who engage in harmful behavior. This helps to create a safer online environment for yourself.

7. **Correct Answer: B. Disconnect from screens for a set period regularly**
   Explanation: Practicing digital detox involves taking intentional breaks from screens to reduce stress and improve mental well-being. Regular disconnection helps prevent burnout and promotes a healthier balance with technology.

8. **Correct Answer: B. It encrypts your internet traffic and masks your IP address**
   Explanation: A VPN enhances online privacy by encrypting your data, making it difficult for others to intercept or monitor your online activities. It also masks your IP address, adding an extra layer of anonymity.

9. **Correct Answer: C. Close the website immediately and do not provide any information**
   Explanation: If you encounter a phishing website, the safest action is to close it without interacting or providing any personal information. Engaging with such sites can lead to compromised security and data theft.

10. **Correct Answer: B. Increased likelihood of data interception by attackers**
    Explanation: Sharing sensitive information over unsecured connections can expose your data to interception by cybercriminals. Unsecured connections lack encryption, making it easier for attackers to access your information.

11. **Correct Answer: A. Feeling anxious when unable to access the internet**
    Explanation: A common sign of internet addiction is experiencing anxiety or irritability when not connected to the internet. This indicates a dependency that can negatively impact mental health and daily functioning.

12. **Correct Answer: B. Fostering a supportive and respectful community**
    Explanation: Contributing positively to online discussions helps build a community where members feel valued and respected. It encourages constructive dialogue and enhances the overall online experience for everyone involved.

13. **Correct Answer: B. To avoid unintentional violations and contribute appropriately**
    Explanation: Understanding community guidelines ensures that you are aware of the expected behavior within the platform, helping you to participate without violating rules. This knowledge contributes to a healthy and orderly online environment.

14. **Correct Answer: B. Awareness of your emotional state when engaging with digital platforms**
    Explanation: Practicing mindfulness in digital usage helps you become more aware of how online activities affect your emotions. This awareness allows you to make intentional choices about your engagement to promote mental well-being.
15. **Correct Answer: B. To protect your identity and personal information**
    Explanation: Using pseudonyms or anonymized profiles helps safeguard your real identity, reducing the risk of personal information being misused. This practice enhances your online privacy and security.

Chapter 16

1. **Correct Answer: B. Enable WPA3 encryption**
   Explanation: WPA3 encryption provides the strongest level of security for Wi-Fi networks, ensuring that data transmitted is encrypted and protected. This reduces the risk of unauthorized access and data breaches.
2. **Correct Answer: B. To fix known vulnerabilities and enhance security**
   Explanation: Router firmware updates often contain patches for security vulnerabilities discovered after release. Keeping the firmware updated ensures your network is protected against new threats.
3. **Correct Answer: B. To isolate IoT devices from the primary network**
   Explanation: A guest network separates IoT devices from your primary network, reducing the risk of compromised devices affecting personal computers or sensitive data. This creates an additional layer of protection for your network.
4. **Correct Answer: B. It provides an additional layer of verification**
   Explanation: Multi-factor authentication (MFA) requires users to verify their identity through multiple methods, such as a password and a one-time code. This makes it much harder for attackers to gain unauthorized access, even if they obtain the password.
5. **Correct Answer: C. Exposure to man-in-the-middle attacks**
   Explanation: Public Wi-Fi networks are often unencrypted, making it easy for attackers to intercept data through man-in-the-middle attacks. Using a VPN encrypts your traffic, protecting it from such threats.
6. **Correct Answer: A. That the network name matches an official source**
   Explanation: Attackers often create fake networks with names similar to legitimate ones. Verifying the network name with a trusted source reduces the risk of connecting to a malicious hotspot.
7. **Correct Answer: A. Only the sender and recipient can access the communication**
   Explanation: End-to-end encryption ensures that messages are encrypted on the sender's device and can only be decrypted by the recipient. This prevents intermediaries from accessing the content during transmission.
8. **Correct Answer: B. Default credentials are easy for attackers to find online**
   Explanation: Default usernames and passwords for IoT devices are often published online, making them a common target for attackers. Changing these credentials strengthens the security of your devices.
9. **Correct Answer: B. Attempting to steal personal or account information**
   Explanation: Phishing scams in online gaming often trick users into sharing account credentials or personal information through fake websites or offers. These scams aim to exploit players for financial gain or data theft.

10. **Correct Answer: B. It minimizes unwanted noise and unintended speech**
    Explanation: "Push-to-talk" ensures that your microphone is only active when you press a designated button, reducing background noise and preventing accidental communication. This enhances privacy and reduces harassment risks.
11. **Correct Answer: B. It encrypts your data and hides your IP address**
    Explanation: A VPN creates a secure, encrypted tunnel between your device and the internet, masking your IP address and protecting your data from interception. This is particularly useful on unsecured public Wi-Fi networks.
12. **Correct Answer: B. Personal information, like your real name or location**
    Explanation: Sharing personal information during gaming interactions can lead to identity theft or targeted social engineering attacks. Keeping personal details private reduces these risks significantly.
13. **Correct Answer: B. They patch security vulnerabilities**
    Explanation: Firmware updates for IoT devices address known vulnerabilities that attackers could exploit. Regular updates ensure that your devices are running the latest security protections.
14. **Correct Answer: A. Requirements for password length and MFA usage**
    Explanation: A remote work security policy outlines requirements for strong passwords, multi-factor authentication, and other protective measures. These guidelines help maintain a secure environment for remote workers.
15. **Correct Answer: A. To help moderators maintain a safe gaming environment**
    Explanation: Reporting toxic behavior allows moderators to address issues and create a safer gaming community for all players. This contributes to a more enjoyable and respectful environment.

Chapter 17

1. **Correct Answer: B. To add a layer of security to the login process**
   Explanation: Multi-factor authentication (MFA) combines multiple verification methods to make it more difficult for attackers to gain unauthorized access. Even if a password is compromised, MFA ensures an additional security step is required.
2. **Correct Answer: C. Because they are easily guessed by attackers**
   Explanation: Personal information like birthdates is often easy to find through social media or public records, making such passwords susceptible to brute force or social engineering attacks. Strong passwords should avoid any easily associated personal details.
3. **Correct Answer: B. It uses HTTPS encryption and shows a padlock icon**
   Explanation: HTTPS encryption and the padlock icon indicate the site secures data in transit, protecting personal and payment information from being intercepted. This is a crucial feature of any legitimate e-commerce site.
4. **Correct Answer: B. They store cryptocurrency offline, making them harder to hack**
   Explanation: Cold wallets are not connected to the internet, which makes them much less vulnerable to online threats such as hacking or phishing attacks. This makes them ideal for long-term cryptocurrency storage.
5. **Correct Answer: B. To detect and address unauthorized transactions early**
   Explanation: Monitoring financial activity helps catch suspicious transactions promptly, allowing for immediate action to minimize losses. This proactive approach is key to effective financial security.

6. **Correct Answer: B. Requests for sensitive information with urgent language**
Explanation: Phishing emails often use urgency to trick individuals into providing sensitive details without thinking. They may request passwords, account numbers, or other sensitive information under the guise of immediate action.

7. **Correct Answer: B. To protect funds in case one account is compromised**
Explanation: Separating accounts ensures that if one account is breached, the others remain secure, reducing overall financial exposure. This separation provides an additional layer of protection for critical funds like savings.

8. **Correct Answer: B. Keep them in a secure, offline location like a fireproof safe**
Explanation: Offline storage protects private keys from being accessed by hackers, ensuring the security of cryptocurrency assets. Fireproof safes offer added protection against physical damage or theft.

9. **Correct Answer: A. Contact information for relevant financial institutions**
Explanation: An effective financial cyber incident response plan includes details about who to contact in case of suspicious activity or account breaches. Having this information readily available ensures a faster response during emergencies.

10. **Correct Answer: B. Report the email or message to the relevant institution**
Explanation: Reporting phishing attempts helps alert institutions and protect others from falling victim to the same scam. It also ensures that the suspicious communication is investigated and addressed.

11. **Correct Answer: A. The scheme promises guaranteed high returns**
Explanation: Legitimate investments cannot guarantee returns, especially high ones, as all investments carry some level of risk. Promises of guaranteed profits are a classic hallmark of fraudulent schemes.

12. **Correct Answer: B. To prevent unauthorized access if one password is compromised**
Explanation: Unique passwords ensure that a breach of one account does not compromise others. This is critical for financial security, where a single password leak can have widespread consequences.

13. **Correct Answer: B. By learning to recognize common cyber threats and scams**
Explanation: Educating family members on recognizing scams, such as phishing or fraudulent investment schemes, creates a collective layer of defense. Awareness reduces the risk of accidental security breaches within the household.

14. **Correct Answer: C. It uses slight misspellings or unusual domain extensions**
Explanation: Phishing websites often mimic legitimate sites but include small changes in the URL, such as spelling errors or unusual domain extensions, to trick users. Recognizing these subtle differences is key to avoiding scams.

15. **Correct Answer: B. Subscribe to reputable cybersecurity and financial news sources**
Explanation: Staying informed through trusted sources ensures awareness of new technologies and potential threats. This proactive approach helps individuals adapt their financial security strategies to the latest developments.

Chapter 18

1. **Correct Answer: B. To prevent unauthorized recovery of sensitive data**
Explanation: Secure deletion ensures that sensitive data cannot be retrieved by unauthorized individuals after a device has been disposed of. This protects personal and organizational information from being misused.

2. **Correct Answer: B. Overwriting data multiple times with software tools**
Explanation: Overwriting data ensures it is irretrievable, providing a higher level of security compared to simple deletion or formatting. Tools designed for secure wiping meet recognized data destruction standards.

3. **Correct Answer: B. Providing redundancy and protecting against local disasters**
Explanation: Combining local and cloud backups ensures that data is safe from localized events like fires or floods while offering easy access through both storage methods. This redundancy is critical for comprehensive data protection.

4. **Correct Answer: B. To ensure that recovery steps work effectively during a real event**
Explanation: Regular testing helps identify weaknesses in the recovery process and ensures that backups can be restored without issues. This preparedness is crucial during an actual disaster.

5. **Correct Answer: C. Critical systems and data needed for continuity**
Explanation: Restoring critical systems first minimizes downtime and ensures business or personal operations can resume as quickly as possible. Prioritization ensures that resources are focused on the most essential areas.

6. **Correct Answer: A. Two-factor authentication (2FA)**
Explanation: Enabling 2FA adds an extra layer of protection, requiring an additional verification step to access the cloud account. This significantly reduces the risk of unauthorized access.

7. **Correct Answer: B. Unauthorized recovery of sensitive data**
Explanation: If data is not securely erased, it can be recovered by malicious actors, leading to potential breaches. Proper data sanitization prevents this risk.

8. **Correct Answer: B. By making data inaccessible to unauthorized users without the decryption key**
Explanation: Encryption protects data by ensuring that even if it is accessed, it cannot be read without the proper decryption key. This is a fundamental step in securing cloud-stored information.

9. **Correct Answer: B. To track access and activities for security purposes**
Explanation: Audit logs provide a record of who accessed the system and what actions were taken, helping to identify unauthorized or suspicious activities. This ensures accountability and enhances security.

10. **Correct Answer: B. To ensure accountability and demonstrate compliance**
Explanation: Documentation of the disposal process provides proof that data was securely destroyed, meeting regulatory and legal requirements. It also serves as a safeguard against potential liability.

11. **Correct Answer: B. Identifying critical data and systems**
Explanation: Knowing which data and systems are essential allows for targeted recovery efforts, ensuring that the most important aspects are restored first. This reduces downtime and prioritizes continuity.

12. **Correct Answer: B. Unintentional access by unauthorized users**
Explanation: Improper sharing permissions can expose sensitive data to individuals who shouldn't have access. Configuring sharing settings carefully minimizes this risk.

13. **Correct Answer: B. By physically destroying storage devices and partnering with certified recyclers**
Explanation: Physical destruction combined with certified e-waste recycling ensures both data security and environmental compliance. This approach guarantees that data is irrecoverable.

14. **Correct Answer: B. To ensure data is completely unrecoverable**
    Explanation: Combining software sanitization and physical destruction provides a dual layer of security, making it virtually impossible to recover data. This is especially important for highly sensitive information.

15. **Correct Answer: B. Ensure all data is wiped using a factory reset and data-wiping software**
    Explanation: A factory reset alone may not be enough to completely erase data. Using dedicated wiping tools adds an extra level of security, ensuring the device is safe for reuse or recycling.

Chapter 19

1. **Correct Answer: B. To preserve crucial details for investigation**
   Explanation: Documenting evidence ensures that critical information is available for law enforcement or cybersecurity professionals to investigate the incident. This step is vital for tracing the attack and possibly recovering lost data or assets.

2. **Correct Answer: B. It adds a second layer of security to your accounts**
   Explanation: Multi-factor authentication requires an additional verification step, making it significantly harder for unauthorized users to access accounts, even if passwords are compromised.

3. **Correct Answer: B. Accessing expertise in handling complex digital crimes**
   Explanation: Specialized cybercrime units are trained to deal with sophisticated attacks and have access to resources and tools for effective investigation. They are better equipped to trace advanced threats than general law enforcement.

4. **Correct Answer: B. Hosting cybersecurity awareness sessions**
   Explanation: Educating others about risks and safety measures empowers communities to recognize and prevent cyber threats, creating a safer digital environment.

5. **Correct Answer: B. Unfamiliar transactions on your bank account**
   Explanation: Unrecognized transactions are a strong indicator of identity theft, as cybercriminals often misuse stolen financial information to make unauthorized purchases.

6. **Correct Answer: A. It ensures you can detect further unauthorized actions early**
   Explanation: Monitoring for unusual activity allows you to identify any ongoing or subsequent attempts to access your accounts, enabling swift action to mitigate additional harm.

7. **Correct Answer: B. Report the attack to authorities and seek professional help**
   Explanation: Authorities and cybersecurity professionals can guide you in handling ransomware without worsening the situation. Paying the ransom is discouraged as it does not guarantee file recovery.

8. **Correct Answer: B. To create harsher penalties and better prevention measures**
   Explanation: Stronger laws act as a deterrent to cybercriminals and improve the legal and investigative framework for handling cybercrime effectively.

9. **Correct Answer: B. Tracing attacks and preserving digital evidence** Explanation: Digital forensics experts analyze attack vectors and ensure evidence is properly handled, aiding investigations and potential prosecution.

10. **Correct Answer: A. By promoting awareness and proactive defense strategies**
    Explanation: Community initiatives help spread knowledge about cyber threats and encourage collective efforts to improve digital safety practices.

11. **Correct Answer: B. It identifies vulnerabilities to improve future security** Explanation: Analyzing the root cause of a cybercrime helps you understand weaknesses in your defenses, enabling better preparation for the future.

12. **Correct Answer: C. To stay protected against new and emerging threats** Explanation: Regular updates ensure your software and systems are equipped to handle the latest security challenges, reducing vulnerabilities that attackers can exploit.

13. **Correct Answer: B. Learn to identify phishing emails and suspicious requests** Explanation: Social engineering attacks rely on deception, and being able to recognize fake communications is critical to avoiding these manipulative tactics.

14. **Correct Answer: B. By preparing you to recognize and respond to evolving threats** Explanation: Cybersecurity training builds awareness and equips individuals with the skills to adapt to new attack strategies, enhancing overall safety.

15. **Correct Answer: B. They provide expertise in analyzing and securing your systems** Explanation: Cybersecurity professionals bring specialized knowledge to identify vulnerabilities, secure compromised systems, and assist in recovery efforts effectively.

Chapter 20

1. **Correct Answer: B. To anticipate and prevent threats before they occur**
   Explanation: A proactive security mindset focuses on identifying potential threats and addressing vulnerabilities before they can be exploited. This approach strengthens defenses and minimizes the risk of successful attacks.

2. **Correct Answer: B. By identifying patterns and anomalies in data**
   Explanation: Machine learning algorithms can process vast amounts of data to identify unusual activity that may indicate a cyber threat. This capability enables faster and more accurate detection of both known and unknown attacks.

3. **Correct Answer: C. They make brute force attacks more difficult to succeed**
   Explanation: Longer and more complex passwords increase the number of combinations an attacker must try, making brute-force attacks less effective. This strengthens account security significantly.

4. **Correct Answer: B. To ensure data can be recovered during an incident**
   Explanation: Backups provide a safety net, ensuring critical data can be restored in case of ransomware attacks, accidental deletions, or other data loss scenarios. Regular backups minimize the impact of such incidents.

5. **Correct Answer: A. They automate and adapt attacks, making them more difficult to detect**
   Explanation: AI-powered cyberattacks leverage machine learning to continuously refine their methods, evading traditional detection systems. Their adaptability makes them a significant threat in modern cybersecurity.

6. **Correct Answer: B. It adds an extra layer of verification to accounts**
   Explanation: Multi-factor authentication requires users to provide multiple forms of verification, such as a password and a code sent to their phone. This additional layer of security makes unauthorized access more difficult.

7. **Correct Answer: B. To gain insights into the latest threats and best practices**
   Explanation: Cybersecurity communities share valuable knowledge about emerging threats and effective defense strategies. This collaboration enhances collective security and helps individuals stay informed.

8. **Correct Answer: A. To ensure critical systems remain operational during failures**
   Explanation: Redundancy ensures that even if one system or component fails, backups or failover systems can take over. This approach minimizes downtime and ensures business continuity.

9. **Correct Answer: B. It creates a shared responsibility for cybersecurity**
   Explanation: Fostering a culture of security encourages everyone in an organization to adopt secure practices, reducing the risk of human error. This collective effort strengthens overall defenses.

10. **Correct Answer: B. To ensure they align with existing security frameworks**
    Explanation: Evaluating new technologies helps identify potential vulnerabilities and ensures compatibility with current systems. This careful assessment reduces the risk of introducing security gaps.

11. **Correct Answer: B. To ensure transparency in data handling and product security**
    Explanation: Ethical standards promote trust by prioritizing user privacy and implementing strong security measures. Transparency ensures that products are designed with security in mind from the outset.

12. **Correct Answer: B. By participating in threat intelligence groups and industry forums**
    Explanation: Engaging with cybersecurity communities provides access to real-time information about emerging threats and innovative defense techniques. Staying informed helps adapt to the rapidly changing threat landscape.

13. **Correct Answer: B. Their capability to react to detected threats in real time**
    Explanation: AI tools can automate responses like isolating compromised systems or alerting administrators when threats are detected. This real-time reaction minimizes the damage caused by cyberattacks.

14. **Correct Answer: B. By providing guidance and practical knowledge to future experts**
    Explanation: Mentoring allows experienced professionals to share their expertise with the next generation, equipping them with the skills to tackle future cybersecurity challenges. This ensures a continuous pipeline of skilled defenders.

15. **Correct Answer: B. To equip individuals with the knowledge to recognize and avoid threats**
    Explanation: Training reduces cybersecurity risks by teaching individuals how to identify and respond to threats like phishing or social engineering. Educated users are less likely to fall victim to common attack methods.

Chapter 21

1. **Correct Answer: B. To stay ahead of evolving threats**
   Explanation: Lifelong learning in cybersecurity ensures that individuals remain informed about the latest risks and tools. This proactive approach is critical for adapting to the ever-changing landscape of cyber threats.

2. **Correct Answer: C. Adapting content to match audience needs**
   Explanation: Tailoring education materials makes cybersecurity concepts more accessible and relevant. Adapting to audience needs ensures higher engagement and comprehension.

3. **Correct Answer: B. To inspire others through visible adherence to best practices**
   Explanation: Modeling secure behaviors demonstrates the importance of cybersecurity through actions. It sets a standard that encourages others in the workplace to follow suit.

4. **Correct Answer: C. To increase user adoption and understanding**

   Explanation: Simplifying cybersecurity practices makes them less intimidating and more actionable. This helps ensure broader adoption across varied audiences.

5. **Correct Answer: C. Use relatable examples to explain threats**

   Explanation: Relatable examples make complex cybersecurity concepts easier to understand. This approach fosters awareness and empowers individuals to take proactive steps.

6. **Correct Answer: C. Offer incentives and public recognition**

   Explanation: Recognizing employees for their efforts encourages continued adherence to security practices. Incentives create a positive association with following cybersecurity protocols.

7. **Correct Answer: B. To gain hands-on experience and help underserved populations**

   Explanation: Volunteering provides opportunities to improve practical skills while making a meaningful impact. It helps bridge gaps in cybersecurity education for those who need it most.

8. **Correct Answer: B. To prepare better defenses and share knowledge**

   Explanation: Staying informed about new threats helps individuals and organizations anticipate and mitigate risks. Sharing this knowledge broadens awareness and strengthens collective defenses.

9. **Correct Answer: B. By helping users recognize and question suspicious activity**

   Explanation: Critical thinking encourages users to scrutinize digital information for authenticity. This reduces susceptibility to phishing and other scams.

10. **Correct Answer: B. To ensure consistent security practices**

    Explanation: Workplace cybersecurity policies establish clear expectations and procedures for maintaining security. Consistency across the organization reduces vulnerabilities.

11. **Correct Answer: B. To acknowledge achievements and identify areas for improvement**

    Explanation: Reflecting on progress helps individuals understand their strengths and pinpoint opportunities for growth. This practice supports ongoing development and motivation.

12. **Correct Answer: B. Attend workshops, contribute to open-source projects, and join advocacy groups**

    Explanation: Engaging with the cybersecurity community fosters collaboration and learning. Active participation provides access to diverse perspectives and resources.

13. **Correct Answer: A. Sharing experiences and providing guidance**

    Explanation: Mentorship involves offering insights and encouragement to help others develop. This support builds confidence and competence in newcomers to the field.

14. **Correct Answer: B. Complacency and lack of understanding**

    Explanation: Resistance often stems from a lack of awareness about the importance of cybersecurity. Addressing these issues through education and communication can mitigate resistance.

15. **Correct Answer: B. Regularly set goals and celebrate milestones**

    Explanation: Setting and celebrating goals provides motivation and tracks progress. This process reinforces the value of continuous improvement in cybersecurity practices.

Glossary

Access Control: A system that determines who can access specific resources and what actions they are permitted to perform.

Advanced Persistent Threat (APT): A stealthy and prolonged cyberattack aimed at stealing data or compromising systems without detection.

Artificial Intelligence (AI): The simulation of human intelligence in machines, enabling them to learn, reason, and solve problems autonomously.

Application Blacklisting: The practice of blocking specific applications from running to prevent the use of unauthorized or harmful software.

Application Whitelisting: A security measure that allows only pre-approved applications to execute on a system, blocking all others by default.

Awareness Training: Educational programs designed to teach individuals how to recognize and avoid cybersecurity threats like phishing and malware.

Authentication: Verifying a user's identity before granting access to a system or resource.

Authorization: Granting a verified user permission to access specific data or perform certain actions within a system.

Behavior Analysis: The monitoring and evaluation of user or system activities to detect anomalies or potential threats.

Behavioral Targeting: A marketing technique that uses data about online behavior to deliver personalized advertisements or content.

Biometrics: Using unique physical or behavioral traits, such as fingerprints or facial recognition, for identity verification.

Blockchain: A secure, distributed ledger technology that records transactions tamper-proof and transparently.

Botnet: A network of compromised devices controlled by an attacker to perform malicious tasks, such as launching cyberattacks.

Brute-force Attack: A method of cracking passwords or encryption by systematically trying all possible combinations.

Business Email Compromise (BEC): A cyberattack where criminals impersonate trusted individuals to deceive employees into transferring money or sensitive data.

Clickbait: Content designed to attract attention and encourage users to click on a link, often using misleading or sensational headlines.

Cloud Storage: A service that allows users to store data on remote servers accessible via the internet.

Consent: Permission granted by individuals to collect, process, or share their personal data.

Cookies: Small text files stored on a user's device by websites to remember preferences and track online behavior.

Credit Freeze: A security measure that restricts access to a person's credit report to prevent identity theft.

Credit Monitoring: A service that tracks changes in credit reports to detect potential fraud or identity theft.

Cyberbullying: The use of digital platforms to harass, threaten, or humiliate someone, often repeatedly.

Cybercrime: Illegal activities conducted using computers or digital networks, such as hacking or identity theft.

Cyberespionage: The unauthorized use of cyber tools to access confidential data, often for political or economic gain.

Cybersecurity Posture: The overall state of an organization's cybersecurity readiness and defensive measures.

Cyberstalking: Using electronic communication to repeatedly harass or intimidate someone, often anonymously.

Cyberterrorism: The use of digital attacks to cause harm, fear, or disruption, typically for political or ideological reasons.

Data Anonymization: Removing personally identifiable information from data sets to protect individual privacy.

Data Brokers: Companies that collect and sell data about individuals, often without their direct knowledge or consent.

Data Collection: Gathering information from various sources, such as user activities or online interactions.

Data Deletion: The process of permanently removing data from storage to prevent access or recovery.

Data Encryption: The data conversion into a coded format to prevent unauthorized access.

Data Exfiltration: The unauthorized transfer or theft of data from a system or network.

Data Ownership: The legal and ethical rights individuals or organizations have over their data, including its use and distribution.

Data Portability: The ability to transfer personal data from one service provider to another in a usable format.

Data Retention: Keeping data for a specified period, often for legal or operational purposes.

Data Subject Rights: Individuals have rights under privacy laws to access, control, and manage their data.

Data Synchronization: Ensuring data is consistent and up-to-date across multiple systems or devices.

Data Wiping: The secure and permanent removal of data from a device to prevent recovery.

Deepfake: AI-generated media that manipulates video or audio to create realistic but false content.

Denial of Service (DoS): An attack that disrupts the normal functioning of a network or system by overwhelming it with traffic.

Decryption: Converting encrypted data back into its original readable format using a decryption key.

Digital Citizenship: The responsible use of technology and digital platforms, promoting safe and ethical online behavior.

Digital Detox: A voluntary break from digital devices and online platforms to reduce stress and improve mental well-being.

Digital Footprint: The trail of data left behind by an individual's online activities, including social media and website visits.

Digital Literacy: The ability to effectively use digital tools and understand online resources, including identifying credible information.

Disaster Recovery Plan: A documented strategy to restore systems and data quickly after a disruption or cyberattack.

DDoS Attack: A denial-of-service attack involving multiple devices overwhelming a target with excessive traffic.

DoS Attack: A cyberattack that aims to render a service or system unavailable by overwhelming requests.

Domain Spoofing: A technique attackers use to create fake websites or emails that mimic legitimate domains to deceive users.

Endpoint Protection: Security measures are applied to individual devices, such as computers or smartphones, to protect them from cyber threats like malware and unauthorized access.

Ethical Hacking: Legally breaking into computers and devices to test an organization's defenses and improve security.

Exploit: A piece of code or a technique used to exploit a vulnerability in software or systems.

Facial Recognition: A biometric technology that uses facial features to identify or authenticate a person.

Fake Profiles: Online accounts created to impersonate real people or entities, often for malicious purposes like fraud or scams.

Firewall: A security system that monitors and controls incoming and outgoing network traffic based on predetermined rules.

Fraud: The intentional deception for personal or financial gain, often involving false representation or manipulation.

Fraudulent Transactions: Unauthorized or deceitful financial activities conducted to steal money or information.

Geotagging: Adding geographical identification metadata to digital media, such as photos or social media posts.

Guest Network: A separate network that allows visitors to access the internet without exposing internal systems or sensitive data.

Hardware Token: A physical device used for secure authentication, often generating one-time passwords.

HTTPS: A secure version of HTTP that encrypts data transmitted between a user's browser and a website to protect sensitive information.

Impersonation: The act of pretending to be someone else, often to gain unauthorized access or deceive others.

Incident Response: To minimize damage, identify, contain, and recover from a cybersecurity incident.

Insider Threats: Security risks posed by individuals within an organization, such as employees or contractors, who misuse their access.

Intellectual Property Theft: The unauthorized use or theft of creations of the mind, such as inventions, designs, or trade secrets.

Internet of Things (IoT): A network of interconnected devices that communicate and exchange data, such as smart appliances and wearables.

Intrusion Detection System (IDS): A security tool that monitors network traffic for suspicious activity or known attack patterns.

Intrusion Prevention Systems: Systems that actively block detected threats by analyzing network traffic and taking immediate action.

Identity Theft: The unlawful use of another person's personal information, often for financial fraud or other criminal activities.

Keylogger: A type of malware that records keystrokes to capture sensitive information like passwords or personal messages.

Location Sharing: Sharing your geographical location through digital apps or services, often for convenience or safety purposes.

Malicious Software (Malware): Software designed to harm, exploit, or gain unauthorized access to systems, including viruses, worms, and ransomware.

Man-in-the-Middle (MitM): An attack where a cybercriminal intercepts communication between two parties to steal data or manipulate information.

Machine Learning: A subset of artificial intelligence that enables systems to learn from data and improve performance without explicit programming.

Multi-factor Authentication (MFA): A security process requiring multiple verification forms, such as a password and a one-time code, to access a system.

Mobile Security: Measures taken to protect mobile devices and the data they store from threats like malware and unauthorized access.

Network Attack: A cyber assault aimed at disrupting, damaging, or gaining unauthorized access to a computer network.

Network Segmentation: Dividing a network into smaller sections to improve security and limit the spread of cyber threats.

Online Behavior: The actions and interactions of individuals on the internet, including communication, browsing, and content sharing.

Online Harassment: Using digital platforms to intimidate, threaten, or harm others, often repeatedly and anonymously.

Online Identity: The representation of an individual or entity in the digital world, including usernames, profiles, and personal information.

Online Predators: Individuals who exploit the internet to target and harm others, often for personal or financial gain.

Online Reputation: The perception of an individual or organization based on their digital presence and online activities.

Password Manager: A tool that securely stores and organizes passwords, helping users maintain strong, unique passwords for different accounts.

Password Management: Creating, storing, and updating passwords securely to protect against unauthorized access.

Password Policy: Guidelines set by organizations to ensure strong, secure passwords, often including requirements for length and complexity.

Patch Management: The process of updating software to fix vulnerabilities and improve security, reducing the risk of cyberattacks.

Phishing: A cyberattack that uses deceptive messages to trick individuals into revealing sensitive information, such as passwords or credit card details.

Phishing Scams: Fraudulent schemes that rely on phishing techniques to steal personal or financial information from victims.

Privacy Policies: Statements that explain how an organization collects, uses, and protects personal data, ensuring transparency and compliance.

Privacy Protection: Measures to safeguard personal information from unauthorized access, use, or sharing.

Proactive Security Mindset: An approach to cybersecurity that emphasizes anticipating and preventing threats before they occur.

Ransomware: A type of malware that encrypts a victim's data and demands payment for its decryption, often causing severe disruption.

Risk Management: Identifying, assessing, and mitigating potential risks to an organization's operations or assets.

Risk Management Framework: A structured approach to managing risks by establishing policies, processes, and controls to protect against threats.

Role-based Access Control (RBAC): A security approach where users are granted permissions based on their organizational roles.

Secure Backup: Creating and storing encrypted copies of critical data to ensure availability in case of loss or attack.

Secure Connection: A network link that uses encryption protocols to protect data during transmission, such as HTTPS or VPNs.

Secure Disposal: The method of safely discarding electronic devices or media to prevent unauthorized access to the stored data.

Secure Erasure: The complete removal of data from a storage device, making it unrecoverable even with advanced tools.

Secure Session Handling: Techniques such as timeouts and encrypted tokens are used to protect user sessions from being hijacked.

Secure Socket Layer (SSL): A protocol that encrypts data transmitted between a web server and a browser to protect sensitive information.

Secure Payment Methods: Transactions are conducted through encrypted channels or verified platforms to protect financial information.

Session Hijacking: An attack where a cybercriminal takes over a user's active session to gain unauthorized access to systems or data.

Session Timeout: A security feature that automatically ends a user session after a period of inactivity to prevent unauthorized access.

SIM Swapping: A technique where attackers gain control of a victim's phone number by fraudulently transferring it to a new SIM card.

Social Engineering: Manipulating individuals to access confidential information by exploiting human psychology.

Social Media: Digital platforms used for communication, networking, and content sharing, often targeted for cyberattacks like phishing.

Spam Protection: Tools or methods to filter and block unwanted or malicious messages in email or messaging systems.

Spear-phishing: A targeted phishing attack directed at specific individuals or organizations to steal sensitive data or credentials.

Spyware: Malicious software that secretly monitors a user's activities and collects sensitive information without consent.

Surveillance: The monitoring of individuals or systems to track activities, often for security or data analysis purposes.

Threat Detection: Identifying potential cyber threats or unusual activities that may indicate a security risk.

Threat Intelligence: Information collected and analyzed about current and emerging threats to help organizations protect against cyberattacks.

Threats: Potential dangers to systems, networks, or data that can cause harm, such as malware, phishing, or insider attacks.

Trojan: A type of malware disguised as legitimate software designed to trick users into installing it and compromising their systems.

Virus: Malicious code that replicates itself and spreads between devices, often causing damage or disruption.

Vulnerability: A weakness in software, hardware, or processes that attackers can exploit to gain unauthorized access.

VPN (Virtual Private Network): A secure connection that encrypts internet traffic and hides the user's IP address, ensuring privacy online.

Vishing: A form of phishing conducted through phone calls, where attackers impersonate trusted entities to extract sensitive information.

Worm: A type of malware that replicates itself and spreads across networks, often without requiring user interaction.

Zero-day Exploit: An attack that takes advantage of a previously unknown vulnerability, often before a patch is available.

Index